Psychosocial Treatment of Schizophrenia

Other volumes in the series:

Volume 1: The Neurology of Schizophrenia
(Editors: H.A. Nasrallah and D.R. Weinberger)

Volume 2: Neurochemistry and Neuropharmacology of Schizophrenia
(Editors: F.A. Henn and L.E. DeLisi)

Volume 3: Nosology, Epidemiology and Genetics of Schizophrenia
(Editors: M.T. Tsuang and J.C. Simpson)

Handbook of Schizophrenia

Edited by H.A. NASRALLAH

VOLUME 4

Psychosocial Treatment of Schizophrenia

Editors:

Marvin I. HERZ

Department of Psychiatry, State University of New York, Buffalo, NY, USA

Samuel J. KEITH

Division of Clinical Research, National Institute of Health, Rockville, MD, USA

John P. DOCHERTY

Nashua Brookside Hospital, Nashua, NH, USA

1990

ELSEVIER

Amsterdam – New York – Oxford

ISBN 0 444 81250 4
ISBN SERIES 0 444 90437 9

Library of Congress Cataloging-in-Publication Data

Psychosocial treatment of schizophrenia / editors, M.I. Herz, S.J. Keith, J.P. Docherty.
p. cm. -- (Handbook of schizophrenia ; v. 4)
Includes bibliographical references.
ISBN 0-444-81250-4 (U.S.)
1. Schizophrenia--Treatment. 2. Schizophrenia--Social aspects.
I. Herz, M. I. II. Keith, Samuel J. III. Docherty, John P., 1944–
IV. Series.
[DNLM: 1. Schizophrenia--therapy. 2. Social Environment. WM 203 H2358 1986 v. 4]
RC514.P71896 1990
616.89'8--dc20
DNLM/DLC 90-3097
for Library of Congress CIP

Published by:
Elsevier Science Publishers B.V. (Biomedical Division)
P.O. Box 1527
1000 BM Amsterdam
The Netherlands

Sole distributors for the USA and Canada:
Elsevier Science Publishing Co. Inc.
655 Avenue of the Americas
New York, NY 10010
U.S.A.

Printed in The Netherlands

Contributors

C.M. ANDERSON
Western Psychiatric Institute and Clinic, University of Pittsburgh School of Medicine, 3811 O'Hara Street, Pittsburgh, PA 15213, U.S.A.

C.C. BEELS
Department of Psychiatry, Columbia University College of Physicians and Surgeons, New York, NY 10032, U.S.A.

H.D. BRENNER
Psychiatric Clinic, University of Bern, Sidlerstrasse 5, 3012 Bern, Switzerland

R.D. BUDSON
Department of Psychiatry, Harvard Medical School, McLean Hospital, 115 Mill Street, Belmont, MA 02178, U.S.A.

R.J. DIAMOND
Clinical Sciences Center, Department of Psychiatry, University of Wisconsin Medical School, 600 Highland Avenue, Madison, WI 53792, U.S.A.

J.P. DOCHERTY
Nashua Brookside Hospital, 11 Northwest Boulevard, Nashua, NH 03063, U.S.A.

T.A. ECKMAN
Clinical Research Center for Schizophrenia and Psychiatric Rehabilitation at UCLA School of Medicine, Brentwood VA Medical Center and Camarillo State Hospital, Wilshire and Sawtelle Boulevards, Los Angeles, CA 90073, U.S.A.

R.M. FACTOR
Clinical Sciences Center, Department of Psychiatry, University of Wisconsin Medical School, 600 Highland Avenue, Madison, WI 53792, U.S.A.

I.R.H. FALLOON
Buckingham Mental Health Service, 22 High Street, Buckingham, MK18 1NU, U.K.

A. FRANK
McLean Hospital, 115 Mill Street, Belmont, MA 02178, U.S.A.

S.M. GOLDFINGER
Harvard Medical School, Massachusetts Mental Health Center, 74 Fenwood Road, Boston, MA 02115, U.S.A.

M.J. GOLDSTEIN
Department of Psychology, University of California, Los Angeles, 1283 Franz Hall, Los Angeles, CA 90024-1563, U.S.A.

J.G. GUNDERSON
McLean Hospital, 115 Mill Street, Belmont, MA 02178, U.S.A.

H.M. HAFEZ
Nashua Brookside Hospital, 11 Northwest Boulevard, Nashua, NH 03063, U.S.A.

M.I. HERZ
Department of Psychiatry, State University of New York at Buffalo, 462 Grider Street, Buffalo, NY 14215, U.S.A.

G.E. HOGARTY
Western Psychiatric Institute and Clinic, University of Pittsburgh School of Medicine, 3811 O'Hara Street, Pittsburgh, PA 15213, U.S.A.

H.M. KATZ
McLean Hospital, 115 Mill Street, Belmont, MA 02178, U.S.A.

S.J. KEITH
Division of Clinical Research, National Institute of Mental Health, 5600 Fishers Lane, Room 10C-06, Parklawn Building, Rockville, MD 20857 U.S.A.

N. KIENZLE
Psychiatric Clinic, University of Bern, Sidlerstrasse 5, 3012 Bern, Switzerland

R.P. LIBERMAN
Clinical Research Center for Schizophrenia and Psychiatric Rehabilitation at UCLA School of Medicine, Brentwood VA Medical Center and Camarillo State Hospital, Wilshire and Sawtelle Boulevards, Los Angeles, CA 90073, U.S.A.

U. MALM
Psychiatric Department Centrum, Göteborgs Sjukvård, Lillhagen Hospital, Box 3005, 442 03 Hisings Backa, Sweden

W.R. MCFARLANE
Biosocial Treatment Research Division, Department of Psychiatry, College of Physicians and Surgeons, Columbia University *and* New York State Psychiatric Institute, New York, NY 10032, U.S.A.

R. MOREINES
Fair Oaks Hospital, 19 Prospect Street, Summit, NJ 07901, U.S.A.

M.A. MOSTERT
Department of Psychiatry, State University of New York at Buffalo, School of Medicine and Biomedical Sciences, Faculty of Health Sciences, Erie County Medical Center, 462 Grider Street, Buffalo, NY 14215, U.S.A.

D.J. REISS
Western Psychiatric Institute and Clinic, University of Pittsburgh School of Medicine, 3811 O'Hara Street, Pittsburgh, PA 15213, U.S.A.

V. RODER
Psychiatric Clinic, University of Bern, Sidlerstrasse 5, 3012 Bern, Switzerland

N.R. SCHOOLER
Department of Psychiatry, Western Psychiatric Institute and Clinic, University of Pittsburgh, 3811 O'Hara Street, Pittsburgh, PA 15213, U.S.A.

S.G. SIRIS
Hillside Hospital Division of the Long Island Jewish Medical Center, Glen Oaks, NY, U.S.A.

A.E. SLABY
Fair Oaks Hospital, 19 Prospect Street, Summit, NJ 07901, U.S.A.

L.I. STEIN
Department of Psychiatry, Clinical Sciences Center, University of Wisconsin Medical School, 600 Highland Avenue, Madison, WI 53792, U.S.A.

P. VINE
HIV Center, Research Foundation for Mental Hygiene, Inc., New York Psychiatric Institute Division, New York, NY, U.S.A.
Mailing address: 168 Warburton Avenue, Hastings-on-Hudson, NY 10706, U.S.A.

Contents

Introduction

There has been a growing trend in psychiatry to emphasize pharmacological approaches in the treatment of schizophrenia with relatively less interest in psychosocial treatment approaches. This may in part be due to reports of negative results of studies of psychoanalytic therapy and in addition the growing belief that the disorder has some biological basis. It should be clear, however, that the course of schizophrenia is strongly influenced by psychosocial factors and that contemporary pharmacotherapy only addresses one aspect of serious life disturbances associated with this disorder. This is also true of many medical disorders such as diabetes mellitus and rheumatoid arthritis. While antipsychotic medication is beneficial in helping to prevent relapse in schizophrenia and decreasing the severity of positive and negative symptoms during acute phases, it is probably not helpful in reducing negative symptoms during phases of remission where, in fact, antipsychotic medication may worsen negative symptoms and has little direct impact on social or vocational rehabilitation.

In order to develop realistic treatment planning for schizophrenic patients, it is important to know the natural course and outcome of this disorder, which usually begins in late adolescence or early adult life. In recent years, a number of investigators have reported the results of long-term outcome studies (1 – 6). A few of these will be summarized.

Manfred Bleuler reported on the study of 208 schizophrenic patients whom he had personally treated and whose cases he had followed until their death or for at least 22 years. He also studied detailed case reports of other groups of schizophrenic patients who had been hospitalized. All patients included in his statistics had gone through at least one severe psychotic phase in their lives, and all had been hospitalized. All were diagnosed by several psychiatrists as schizophrenic; borderline psychotic patients were not included. He emphasized that course should not be considered a diagnostic criteria. Bleuler found that after a duration of five years, the psychosis did not progress any further; rather, it tended to get better. Improvements after five years were frequent in patients whose illness was characterized by acute psychotic episodes, while they were rare in those whose psychosis followed a more chronic course, steadily and progressively worsening. He observed that many improved schizophrenic patients remain underactive after a psychotic episode. They lack personal initiative, and have somewhat apathetic, colorless personalities, the so-called deficit symptoms of schizophrenia.

Qualifications for full recovery included a lack of psychotic symptoms, a normal social integration and the ability to work. According to Bleuler, at least 25% of all schizophrenic patients recover entirely after the initial episode. On the other hand, he found that about 10% of schizophrenic patients remain permanently hospitalized as severely psychotic individuals, while a middle group of 50 – 75% of the patients alternate between acute psychotic phases and phases of improvement or recovery. Acute relapses become rarer for this middle group only at an advanced age. Bleuler believes that the average course of schizophrenic psychosis has changed in this century, with chronicity becoming less frequent while the number of patients characterized by a phasic course with frequent hospitalizations has increased. Of course, this could have been caused largely by a change in psychiatric practice: the deinstitutionalization of schizophrenic patients, rather than by a fundamental change in the illness per se.

Ciompi conducted a follow-up study of former patients of the Psychiatric University Hospital of Lausanne, born between 1873 and 1897 and hospitalized from the beginning of this century until 1962, who lived in a catchment area of about 500,000 inhabitants today. High mortality during the follow-up period and other factors introduced a slight favorable statistical bias in the course of the illness. The follow-up sample consisted of 289 patients who were examined in their homes by a psychiatrist using a semi-structured interview of about two hours' duration. Additional information was systematically collected from various sources, including hospital files, family members, etc. Average duration between the first admission and follow-up examination was 36.9 years, with 50% of the cases having had over 40 years elapse. Results were as follows: regarding course of the illness, an acute onset combined with a phasic course and a favorable outcome was exhibited by 25% of the sample and was the most frequent type. Only 10% of this sample had just one psychotic episode and one hospitalization, compared to 25% of Bleuler's sample. Six percent of the cohort had the most unfavorable course with a severe end state. Global outcome of schizophrenia, measured by symptomatology at the end states, was found to be favorable in 49% of cases. Of these, 27% achieved complete remission and 22% had minor residual symptomatology. Forty-two percent had unfavorable outcomes of an intermediate or severe degree, and nine percent had uncertain outcomes. Social outcome was reported as follows: 40% of patients lived with their families or by themselves, 20% were in community institutions and the rest were in hospitals. Although the mean age at follow-up was 74 years, more than half were still working, about two-thirds employed part-time and one-third full-time. On a global scale of social adaptation, only one-third were rated good or fair, whereas two-thirds were rated as having intermediate or bad social adaptation. Thus, the main negative residual of the illness was not persistent schizophrenic symptoms, but impaired social functioning.

The German psychiatrist Huber studied a sample of schizophrenic patients who had never been previously hospitalized and who were admitted to the university psychiatry clinic in Bonn between 1945 and 1959. They were systematically followed up between 1967 and 1973. Well-defined Bleulerian and Schneiderian criteria were used in diagnosis. Out of an original sample of 758 individuals, 502 could be followed up. The average duration of follow-up was 22.4 years. Patients were usually interviewed in their home environments. Eighty-five percent of them lived at home. Twenty-two percent of the patients were in a state of complete remission, but 40% of the patients, while having no schizophrenic symptoms, were considered to be in a residual deficit state. They suffered from such symptoms as cognitive disturbances, physical and mental exhaustion, disturbance of general well-being and efficiency, loss of drive, energy and endurance, exaggerated impressionability, reduced threshold tolerance to non-specific stress, sleep disturbance, hypersensitivity to noise and weather, decrease in initiative, tendency to sub-depressive moods, loss of liveliness and directness, increased need for sleep and reduced capacity for adaptation. The remaining 35% were categorized as characteristic outcome types of schizophrenia with residual psychotic symptoms. Huber states that the overall pattern of findings is similar to previous long-term studies from Zurich and Heidelberg. He concludes that schizophrenia does not seem to be a disease of slow progressive duration. Even in the second and third decades of illness, there is still potential for full or partial recovery. Approximately 56% of patients were fully employed; of these, one-third were employed below and two-thirds at their previous occupational level. Patients seemed to maintain better stability after the age of 50.

In summary, studies of the course and outcome of schizophrenia have found that there is no such thing as a specific course or outcome of this disorder. The majority of patients have a course characterized by phases of acute exacerbations and phases of full or partial recovery. Regarding outcome, almost 50% of patients have favorable end states with little or no evidence of schizophrenic symptomatology. The major disability throughout the course of this disorder is impairment in social and vocational role functioning. Only slightly more than 10% of patients continue to remain grossly psychotic and non-functional throughout the course of the illness. It should be noted that none of these studies used DSM-III-R criteria, which require six months of illness, and therefore, patients who would be considered schizophreniform were included. Furthermore, it is likely that more severe cases were lost to follow-up.

Much of the impairment in social and vocational functioning in schizophrenic patients is related to deficit symptomatology, difficulties in information processing, inability to screen out relevant from irrelevant stimuli and problems in affect control and regulation. While antipsychotic medication is usually a necessary component of treatment, it is not sufficient. If we are to improve role functioning and coping skills in these patients, psychosocial treatment interventions are clearly necessary.

We have chosen contributors who are leading experts in particular aspects of the psychosocial treatment of schizophrenia. Most have conducted controlled research studies in their specific areas of expertise, often testing the effectiveness of psychosocial treatment strategies that they themselves developed. Our aim was to provide information about a broad spectrum of treatment approaches, especially emphasizing data about efficacy. We have not attempted to synthesize or integrate the various contributors' points of view with each other, although we have tried to reduce duplication.

MARVIN I. HERZ
SAMUEL J. KEITH
JOHN P. DOCHERTY

REFERENCES

1. Bleuler ME (1978) The long term course of schizophrenic psychoses. In: Wynne L, Cromwell RL, Mattysse S (Eds.), *The Nature of Schizophrenia.* Wiley, New York.
2. Ciompi L (1980) The natural history of schizophrenia in the long term. *Br. J. Psychiatry, 136,* 413.
3. Huber G, Gross G, Schuttler R, Linz M (1980) Longitudinal studies of schizophrenic patients. *Schizophr. Bull., 6,* 592.
4. Harding CM, Brooks GW, Ashikaga T, Strauss JS, Breier A (1987) The Vermont longitudinal study of persons with severe mental illness, II: long-term outcome of subjects who retrospectively met DSM-III criteria for schizophrenia. *Am. J. Psychiatry, 144,* 727.
5. Engelhardt DM, Rosen B, Feldman J, Engelhardt JA, Cohen P (1982) A 15-year followup of 646 schizophrenic outpatients. *Schizophr. Bull., 8,* 493.
6. Tsuang MT, Woolson RF, Fleming JA (1979) Long-term outcome of major psychoses, I. Schizophrenia and affective disorders compared with psychiatrically symptom-free surgical conditions. *Arch. Gen. Psychiatry, 39,* 1295.

CHAPTER 1

Psychosocial factors relating to etiology and course of schizophrenia

MICHAEL J. GOLDSTEIN

Psychosocial issues is a term referring to psychological attributes of individuals or their social environment that play a contributory role in the onset, course, or treatment of a schizophrenic disorder. Most contemporary researchers investigate psychosocial variables within the context of a vulnerability-stress model (1) in which behavioral markers of personal vulnerability are studied within the context of environmental stressors, both intra- and extrafamilial.

While the vulnerability-stress model is intuitively appealing, to be useful it requires greater specification of potential vulnerability markers and stressor conditions likely to relate to the onset and course of schizophrenia. Similarly, with regard to issues of treatment, a more articulated statement of the model would be valuable in guiding the development of effective psychosocial or multimodal interventions. Fig. 1 presents one model developed by Nuechterlein and Liberman (2), designed to specify the variables likely to relate to the onset and course of schizophrenia. Note that the scheme proposed is an iterative one in which similar variables, hypothesized to be present in the premorbid phase of development, are also relevant factors after an episode of the disorder has occurred. The scheme in Fig. 1 also distinguishes between factors which increase the *risk* for the onset of relapse of the disorder and those deemed *protective* against these events.

There is some question as to the conceptual independence of risk and protective factors, as it has been noted that frequently one is simply the inverse of the other. Ideally, a protective factor should be identified by its ability to modify the outcome for an individual previously identified as being at risk for a disorder. At present, there are no clear biological or behavioral markers of the risk for schizophrenia applicable to individuals that permit a clear analysis of modification of life course by protective factors. However, there are some suggestions from the high risk studies summarized below that research of this sort will be possible in the near future.

In this review, I shall first examine the nature of the evidence for personal vulnerability markers for schizophrenia. Following this, I shall examine the evidence regarding stressors which may interact with these personal vulnerability factors to increase the probability of an initial episode of a schizophrenic disorder. In the remaining sections of the paper, I shall evaluate the role of vulnerability and stress factors in determining the *course* of schizophrenia and the implications of these findings for intervention programs.

Handbook of Schizophrenia, Volume 4: Psychosocial Treatment of Schizophrenia.
M.I. Herz, S.J. Keith and J.P. Docherty, editors.

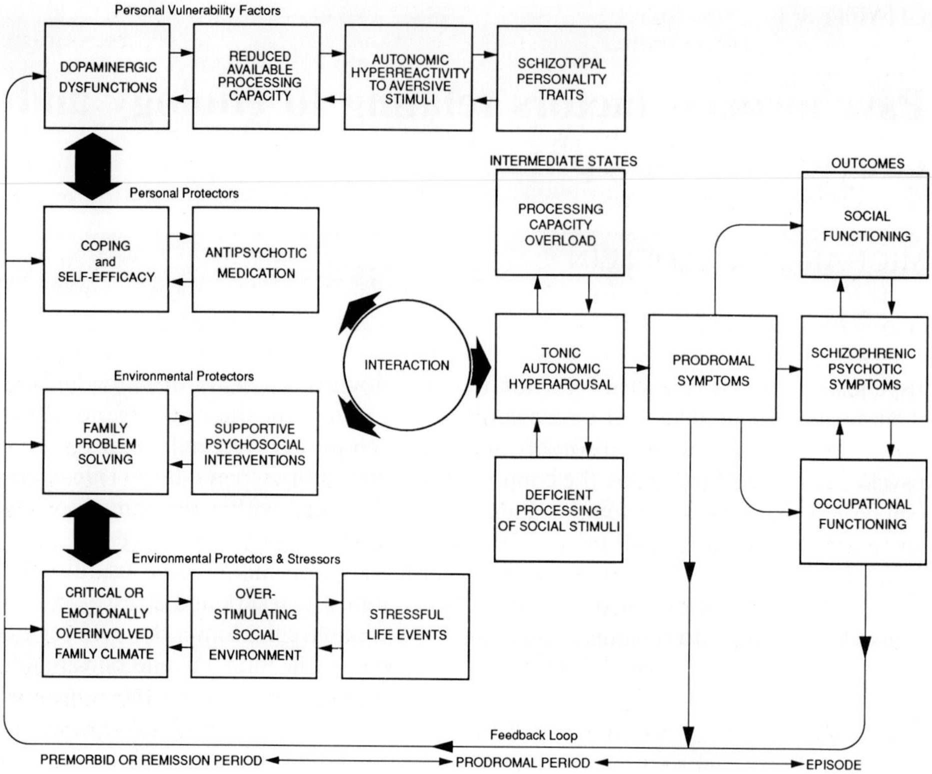

FIG. 1 *A schematic articulation of the vulnerability-stress model which specifies the complex interactions among hypothetical personal vulnerability and stressor conditions involved in the onset and course of schizophrenia. For both vulnerability and stress conditions, factors potentially protective of their impact are suggested as well. (From Nuechterlein (2)).*

INDIVIDUAL VULNERABILITY MARKERS

Most of the evidence regarding early behavioral signs of vulnerability to schizophrenia has come from what have been termed high risk studies, in which samples of individuals hypothesized to be at greater than the population risk for schizophrenia are studied prospectively from a developmental period that antedates the onset of schizophrenia or its prodromal phases. Most high risk projects have examined children considered to be at risk by virtue of having a biological parent with schizophrenia. Compared to a risk of 1 – 2% in the general population, children with one schizophrenic parent have a lifetime risk of 12%, while children with two schizophrenic parents have the exceptionally high risk of 35 – 46% (3). Most studies have, in fact, studied children with only one parent with the disorder.

While this type of high risk research strategy has much to recommend it, it does possess one major limitation, namely that 85 – 90% of schizophrenic persons do not have schizophrenic parents, so that it is unclear how readily vulnerability markers derived from these high risk samples can be generalized to samples which lack this family history. It is possible that the behavioral attributes found to be predictive of schizophrenia only have value as vulnerability indices in the context of parental schizophrenia. Thus, it will ultimately be necessary to test the value of these vulnerability markers in samples without parents with schizophrenia to determine whether they can be utilized in large-scale screening or preventive intervention trials.

It should also be recognized that not all offspring of schizophrenic parents will manifest vulnerability to the disorder; only 10 – 16% will in fact do so (based on family genetic studies). Thus, high risk studies are designed to answer three important questions: (a) Are there behavioral indicators which can discriminate between offspring of schizophrenics who are likely to develop the disorder and those who are not? (b) Are these discriminating attributes unique to schizophrenia, or are they merely non-specific signs of maladaption indicative of a vulnerability to psychiatric disorder in general? (c) Are these attributes observed in the children of psychiatrically unaffected parents, and do they have any prognostic significance in this context? I shall attempt to review the evidence from the high risk studies completed to date to determine the answers currently available to these questions.

It is important to recognize that analogous questions are applicable to the identification of stressor conditions likely to increase the risk for schizophrenia in vulnerable persons, namely: Do these stressor conditions have a specific connection to schizophrenia, or are they non-specific stressors likely to increase the risk for psychiatric disorder in general? Are they generalizable to samples where parental schizophrenia was not present?

THE SEARCH FOR VULNERABILITY MARKERS

The various high risk studies have started with samples of offspring of different ages, some beginning at birth or even before, others in early childhood, while still others begin in late childhood or early adolescence. This review will attempt to collate the findings from various studies and to provide a hypothetical picture of the developmental processes associated with adult-onset schizophrenia. Obviously, there are numerous hazards in sketching a picture of life span development from a series of longitudinal studies, each of which covers a limited portion of the pre-onset developmental period. Fortunately, there are some studies that have covered a substantial period, from infancy to early adulthood, which permit the verification of trends observed in shorter-term studies.

To provide a developmental perspective of potential vulnerability markers for schizophrenia, I consider separately the results of studies for four age periods: (a) conception to infancy; (b) early childhood; (c) middle childhood; and (d) adolescence. The potential vulnerability markers fall into three broad categories: (i) *neurointegrative functioning,* a general term which refers to neuromotor, attentional, autonomic nervous system reactivity, and cognitive processes; (ii) *social behavior;* and (iii) *early symptoms of maladjustment.*

Each finding discussed is either based on statistically significant differences found between offspring of schizophrenics as a group, and offspring of normal parents or of psychiatrically disturbed parents with disorders other than schizophrenia, or reflects some variable associated with a subsequent schizophrenic breakdown in a subsample of offspring of schizophrenics. Because, as indicated above, only subgroups of high-risk children are expected to develop schizophrenia, the latter type of finding is more informative. It should be noted that different high risk studies have used different kinds of comparison groups. Generally, when high-risk subjects were compared with children of parents with other forms of psychiatric disorder, the differences were less pronounced than when they were compared with children of normal controls. This section of this report is based on a previous review of the high risk literature by Asarnow and Goldstein (4).

Conception to infancy

Much of the data on the general status and neurointegrative functioning of the infant are contradictory. Walker and Emory (5) conclude that the bulk of the evidence on fetal and neonatal death, and birth weight of surviving infants, indicates no significant differences between children of schizophrenics and controls. The exception is the finding of McNeil et al. (6) that children of schizophrenics were small for their gestational age relative to the offspring of controls, but no different in length, head circumference or shoulder circumference. This may relate to reports from other studies of children of schizophrenics of erratic growth and deviations in musculoskeletal development (7, 8). As Walker and Emory (5) point out, being small for gestational age may reflect intrauterine growth retardation, which, when extreme, has been linked to later learning and attentional problems.

Three studies (7, 9–13) have identified subgroups of infant children of schizophrenic mothers who showed deviant development and which were the subgroup most likely to develop schizophrenia or related disorders in adulthood. However, the type of deviant development identified was not consistent across studies. Fish's deviant sample showed pandysmaturation or periods when gross motor, visual motor, and physical development were transiently disorganized. Pre-schizophrenic and pre-schizotypal infants in the Danish sample (12) were described as passive, unenergetic and having short attention spans, while Marcus et al. (10) described 13 infants of schizophrenic mothers who showed poor motor and sensorimotor performance during their first year. While these findings are intriguing, as they suggest the emergence of signs of vulnerability to schizophrenia in infancy, they must be interpreted with caution, as there is little evidence that these patterns are consistent across studies or that they are specific markers for subsequent schizophrenia.

It has frequently been hypothesized that certain patterns of social behavior in infancy might serve as vulnerability markers for schizophrenia. A number of high risk studies have investigated this issue, and according to a recent review of these studies (4), infants of schizophrenic mothers were found to have more difficult temperaments, show lower threshold to stimulation, be more inhibited, apathetic or withdrawn, less responsive to verbal commands, and be less spontaneous and initiating. Recent findings (14) indicate that offspring of psychotic parents are less likely to show a fear of strangers during the first year of life. One-year-old infants of schizophrenics, but not infants of mothers with other psychotic conditions, were also found to show significantly increased rates of anxious attachment as defined by Ainsworth and Wittig's (15) classification system. This finding should be viewed with caution however, as Sameroff et al. (16) did not find deviant attachment patterns in infants of schizophrenic mothers.

Early childhood (ages 2 – 4)

Two studies support observations of neurointegrative problems in early childhood. Sameroff et al. (16) found lower reactivity in 2½-year-old children of schizophrenics than in controls, and Hanson et al. (1976) reported poorer gross and fine motor performance in children of schizophrenics compared to children of non schizophrenic psychiatric controls.

With regard to signs of deviance in social behavior in early childhood, Sameroff et al. (16) found more parental reports of depression in children of schizophrenics than in children of healthy controls. Goodman (17) found that children of schizophrenic mothers were more likely to receive diagnoses of developmental disorders than were children of depressed or well mothers. Hanson et al. (18) reported that children of schizophrenics were more often described as schizoid (i.e., emotionally flat, withdrawn, distractable, passive, irritable, and negativistic). These studies also suggest that the children with the most disturbed mothers tend to be subjected to a negative family environment lacking warmth, and low expectations for child achievement (16, 19).

Middle childhood (ages 5 – 12)

Reports of the various high risk studies that have assessed neuropsychological functioning during this age period have consistently indicated some impairment in some high-risk children (20, 7, 10, 11, 21, 22). Impaired fine motor coordination is the only sign reported by all investigators (20). Several studies also report delays in motor development similar to those reported in infancy and early childhood. Marcus et al. (10, 11) in their follow-up of the Israeli high risk study, showed that 5 of 6 children who later showed 'schizophrenia spectrum psychoses' had shown earlier difficulties in neuropsychological functioning.

In the analyses of attention and information processing tasks (AIP) in children of schizophrenics in middle childhood, 3 of 5 studies (for reviews see refs. 20 and 23) found some impairment in children of schizophrenics. With one exception (24), studies have found that children of schizophrenics tend to show cognitive impairment on more complex tasks that assess impairment under stimulus overload conditions (20, 25 – 27).

Furthermore, when subgroups of children of schizophrenics that manifest these AIP deficits in middle childhood are followed up into late adolescence, these children, in contrast to non-impaired offspring of schizophrenics, are more likely to require some form of psychiatric treatment (25). However, while the sensitivity and composite index of multiple measures of AIP in middle childhood for predicting later psychopathology was excellent, the specificity was only moderate.

Consistently with the data from earlier age periods, data from middle childhood indicate that a subset of children of schizophrenics shows disturbed social functioning relative to children of normal controls (26, 28 – 30). However, in these studies, impaired social role functioning in the child relates to the severity of parental psychopathology in general rather than to the existence of parental schizophrenia per se, as children of severely disturbed affective disorder parents show comparable social dysfunction to offspring of severely disturbed schizophrenics.

While psychological disturbance has been observed in children of schizophrenics, it does not typically reach the level found in children referred for clinical levels of psychopathology (26, 30). Despite previous theories that emphasize social withdrawal as a vulnerability marker for schizophrenia, no specific pattern of disturbance in social relations has been identified across studies. As with many samples of clinically disturbed children, some children of schizophrenia have been negatively evaluated, variously by their peers and teachers, as aggressive, disruptive, low in social and cognitive competence, emotionally flat, withdrawn, distractable, passive, irritable, negativistic, hyperactive, emotionally labile and immature (9, 18, 26, 21, 30 – 33).

Adolescence

Several studies point to the continued existence of neurointegrative problems of children of schizophrenics studied as adolescents. Marcuse et al. (34) found deficits in motor coordination, balance and sensory perceptual signs in adolescent children of schizophrenics. When the subjects from the Erlenmeyer-Kimling project (35) were re-evaluated as teenagers, it was found that comparable patterns to those observed earlier were found on AIP measures. Furthermore, the middle childhood AIP measures were strongly related to adolescent clinical status.

Early reports from the Danish high risk study (36) indicated that when tested in adolescence, offspring of schizophrenics, who subsequently developed schizophrenia, showed unusual patterns of autonomic nervous system reactivity to a series of loud tones, particularly in skin conductance reactivity and recovery pattern. However, recent studies (see ref. 37 for a review) have not supported these findings to date.

Studies that have included or started with adolescent samples have, without exception, shown some evidence of social dysfunction in offspring of schizophrenics. Similarly to the findings in middle childhood, many of the deviant social patterns are also found in other clinical and other high-risk populations.

In the Danish high risk project (12), teacher's reports of poor affective control (child easily upset, affect persists when excited, disturbs class by unusual behavior, presents disciplinary problems) and difficulty in making friends, were found to discriminate between those offspring of schizophrenics who developed schizophrenia in early adulthood and those with healthier outcomes. Poor affective control at school was correlated with later ratings of formal cognitive disturbance, whereas difficulty in making friends was related to poor emotional rapport. These findings suggest that poor affective control and poor interpersonal relationships may comprise two discrete dimensions of pre-psychotic social behavior, each of which is predictive of a different component of a schizophrenic disorder.

SUMMARY OF STUDIES ON PRE-ONSET VULNERABILITY MARKERS

(a) Children of schizophrenic parents show a number of early signs and dysfunctions that discriminate them from their peers. Typically, however, only a subsample of the offspring shows these signs and dysfunctions, and it appears that it is these offspring who are at greater risk for the disorder.
(b) Some signs of neurointegrative and social dysfunction appear in infancy studies, but the patterns become clearer and more pronounced in middle childhood and adolescence.
(c) Most signs of neurointegrative and social deficits do not appear to be specific to the offspring of schizophrenics or unique predictors of subsequent schizophrenia. However, there are suggestions that certain types of deficits in AIP may be associated with a specific risk for schizophrenia.
(d) There is little evidence as yet that these measures of neurointegrative and social deficits can serve as vulnerability markers in children whose parents have not manifested a schizophrenic disorder. Their value as screening devices in a general population sample remains to be demonstrated.

STRESS FACTORS RELATED TO THE ONSET OF SCHIZOPHRENIA

As indicated previously in this chapter, the second part of the vulnerability-stress model outlined schematically in Fig. 1 attempts to specify the nature of stressful life events which interact with indices of personal vulnerability. We can see in Fig. 1 that heavy emphasis is placed on the family environment as a source of chronic stress. The attempt to identify patterns of family relationships that may play a contributory role in the development of schizophrenia goes back to the mid-1950s, when clinical investigators, working with families with adult schizophrenic offspring, hypothesized that unique patterns of family organization and relationships existed in the families of schizophrenics. These investigators (38 – 40) further speculated that these patterns antedated the onset of the disorder and continued to support the schizophrenic condition in the affected family member. Unfortunately, the data on which these theories were based did not justify such sweeping conclusions, and the family therapy models which emerged from them did not appear effective in curing schizophrenia (41). Moreover, their implementation, despite the therapist's adherence to a neutral family system model, had the unfortunate side-effect of alienating the relatives of the schizophrenic patient and increasing their sense of guilt about causing the disorder (42).

At present there is a resurgence of interest in the study of family relationships as they relate to schizophrenia. In the period from the early 1950s to the late 1960s, research on the family proliferated (for reviews see refs. 43 – 46). However, the late 1960s to the late 1970s represents a kind of Dark Ages in research on intrafamilial relationships related to schizophrenia. Publication in this area diminished markedly, and enthusiasm for what could be learned from direct observation waned. In order to appreciate the current state of family research related to the major mental disorders, it is helpful to contrast the assumptions and methods of the 1950s and 1960s with those of the present.

The earlier studies summarized in the reviews cited above were cross-sectional, involving families in which mental disorder was present in some member, usually a young adult, often for a considerable period before the research was carried out. These earlier studies assumed that direct observation contrasting families with and without a mental disorder could provide clues to the psychological precursors of that disorder. They were further guided by an ambitious family system theoretical organization which assumed: (a) that disturbances in family relationships were a prominent but not exclusive cause of mental disorders in general, and (b) that each mental disorder resulted from distinctive patterns of family dynamics.

The major barrier to testing these assumptions was that families were studied long after a major mental disorder in a member had affected the family system. The cross-sectional family interaction data collected obviously reflected a complex amalgam of family processes, some of which may indeed have antedated the onset of the disorders while others represented diverse forms of accommodation by family members to the presence of disorder. The great difficulties in replicating findings across studies (see refs. 45 – 47) characteristic of this earlier period were due in part to the fact that each sample varied in the pattern of pre- and post-onset family adaptations. Other factors that limited replicability were wide variations from sample to sample in the criteria used to diagnose mental disorder, the methods for eliciting interactional data, and the coding systems used to reduce the data to quantifiable units. Gradually, researchers recognized that cross-sectional studies carried out after a mental disorder had been present for some time were limited in their ability to reveal etiological processes.

The decline in family research in the late 1960s was not due entirely to the above issue. During this same period, convincing evidence appeared of strong genetic predisposition to schizophrenia. These findings, combined with powerful evidence of the efficacy of pharmacotherapy for these disorders, challenged the underlying paradigm of the previous family studies, in which intrafamilial transactions were proposed as the predominant etiological agents and family therapy as a potent intervention.

Current investigators recognize that a more complex etiological model is needed to guide research. Most studies in the last ten years have been guided by the previously described vulnerability-stress model (1, 48). According to this model, a predisposition to a disorder such as schizophrenia is inherited, and forms the basis for various indexes of vulnerability to the disorder. This vulnerability is modified by life events, particularly those in family life, which in turn modifies the likelihood of expression of the disorder later on. The stress-vulnerability model is also applicable to the post-onset stage of psychiatric disorder, as vulnerability to future episodes of the disorder is modified by recurrent life events within and outside the family.

The implications of the vulnerability-stress model for family interaction research are profound. This model implies that researchers must investigate the *interaction* between intrafamilial relationships and indexes of vulnerability to a particular psychiatric disorder. Ideally, researchers should have available one or more established vulnerability markers that can be investigated in the context of different family environments, some of which may be provocative of, and others protective against, the expression of a disorder.

Nevertheless, the recognition of the vulnerability-stress model has stimulated a new sense of purpose and vigor among family researchers during the last ten years. They realized that tests of this model from a family perspective required longitudinal prospective designs in which family relationships are observed prior to the onset of a disorder, in either its prodromal or active forms, followed by careful evaluations of targeted offspring over subsequent years as they pass through the risk period for the disorder. Studies using this 'high risk' paradigm have re-invigorated the field of family research.

We noted above that earlier cross-section studies could not separate pre-onset from post-onset patterns of family dynamics. Studies now make a clear distinction between two models regarding family factors as they relate to the major mental disorders: the etiological model and the maintenance model. Research on the etiological model involves longitudinal prospective studies in which intrafamilial relationships are studied well before the initial onset of a psychiatric disorder.

The maintenance model refers to family relationships that are observed later in the course of a disorder once an initial episode has occurred. Research on the maintenance model also involves longitudinal prospective studies, but these are typically initiated at the time of an index episode, and follow through a period of remission to determine whether and how family relationships affect the likelihood of reappearance of the acute symptoms of the disorder. It should be noted that research on family factors associated with the maintenance of psychiatric disorder need not assume that these relationships are continuous with those which had bearing on the onset. One can assume, as some investigators have done (49), that family factors related to the maintenance of disorder contain no information concerning determinants of the initial onset.

Current thinking in developmental psychopathology reflects a more sophisticated view of the complex transactions (16) between parent and child as they impact upon one another sequentially from birth onward. It is now recognized that children have unique, biologically based individuality that has a powerful effect on the type of parenting behavior elicited by the child, as well as determining the influence of variations in parent behavior on the child at various stages of development. The transactional model is a complex one and demands sophisticated research strategies to uncover factors associated with healthy or psychopathological development. It also does not lend itself to simplistic formulations in which one generation can be indicted for producing the ills of the next.

ETIOLOGICALLY BASED STUDIES

Despite the emotionality generated by attempts to isolate stressful patterns of family relationships which may interact with individual vulnerability to a schizophrenic disorder, the fact is that there is a very limited body of empirical evidence to support this position. The best evidence requires longitudinal prospective studies, in which intrafamilial transactional processes are observed long before the onset of the disorder. Ideally, such studies should also include some indices of vulnerability to the disorder so that interactions between vulnerability and stressors can be evaluated.

Studies of family factors also require a clear specification of the family processes believed to be stressful for the vulnerable offspring. Two types of variable have been suggested to be particularly stressful for the vulnerable person, namely disordered communication among family members, termed communication deviance (CD) by Wynne et al. (50), and a negative affective climate in the family, termed high expressed emotion (high EE) (51) or, as indexed in direct interaction, negative affective style (AS) (52).

These variables, primarily measured in parents, were utilized in a longitudinal prospective study carried out by Goldstein and associates (52–55), in which a sample of 64 families of mild to moderately disturbed adolescents were studied for the 15 years subsequent to their assessment at an outpatient psychological clinic. A key part of this assessment was the intensive study of parental communication style, affective attitudes and interactive behavior, as well as information about the form of the adolescent behavioral disturbance. The parental data were coded blindly for CD (high, intermediate, or low), EE (high or low) and AS (benign, intermediate or negative), then related to subsequent psychiatric assessments carried out on the former teenagers (and their siblings, where relevant) at 5- and 15-year follow-ups. Data on the psychiatric status of 54 of 65 cases were available for analysis.

Goldstein (54, 55) reported that the incidence of schizophrenia and related disorders (schizotypal, paranoid, schizoid personality disorders) was highest in families originally classified as high in communication deviance (CD) 15 years earlier. In fact, there were no cases of schizophrenia in the low-CD cases, and only one case was diagnosed in the extended schizophrenia spectrum (as schizoid personality). Furthermore, the addition of measures of affective climate (high EE or negative AS) sharpened the ability to identify cases likely to manifest schizophrenia spectrum disorders in the follow-up period.

Although these family measures did identify family units at high risk for offspring schizophrenia or related disorders, there was also a notable number of offspring with diagnoses of borderline personality disorder in the high-CD cohort, raising the question of whether the high-CD, high EE, negative AS aggregation of family attributes has any *specific* linkage to schizophrenia spectrum disorders, or whether it measures high-stress family units linked to severe offspring psychopathology in general. A recent study by Miklowitz (56) that contrasted parents of schizophrenics and parents of manic patients, in which equal levels of CD were found in the two groups, argues against the specificity of high CD for schizophrenia.

Unfortunately, the Goldstein study did not find interactions between attributes of the offspring (form of adolescent behavioral difficulties) and parent attributes. This limited the ability of this study to test interactions between individual vulnerability factor and family stress. The study also lacked the kind of vulnerability markers (i.e., AIP deficits) found promising in the other high risk studies, so that precise tests of the interacton of these processes with family stress factors were not feasible.

One attempt to test the vulnerability-stress hypothesis is in the Goldstein et al. study (55) which involved estimates of the presence or absence of a family history of psychosis. This index of a positive or negative family history did not relate to the CD level of the family, indicating that this was not redundant information. However, as shown in Table 1, the combination of a considerable genetic load for psychosis and high CD greatly increased the risk that the offspring would manifest a disorder in the extended schizophrenia spectrum.

The findings of the Goldstein study (54, 55) indicate that there is a correlation between certain family stress factors and the subsequent probability of schizophrenia or related disorders in the offspring. The study does not, however, provide a test or a causal link between the two, as it began relatively late in the offspring's life, by which time complex transactions between child and parent attributes may have shaped the observed patterns. This study merely indicates two things, namely that further investigations of these markers of family stress may be profitable in samples studied much earlier in life in order to evaluate their epigenesis, and secondly that these measures may be useful in prevention-oriented research in identifying family units with moderately disturbed teenagers who may be at higher than average risk for schizophrenia or schizophrenia-spectrum disorders.

The second study which bears on this issue is that of Tienari et al. (57) in Finland. This study does consider the vulnerability to schizophrenia by contrasting the psychiatric status of adopted-away offspring of schizophrenic mothers with adopted-away offspring of non-psychiatric cases. The cases were drawn from a nationwide sample of schizophrenic women and matched controls, all of whom gave away offspring for adoption to a non-relative.

TABLE 1 *Rate of broad- and narrow-spectrum disorder in high communication deviance families as a function of family history of mental illness*

	Broad spectrum outcomes		Narrow spectrum outcomes	
	N	%	N	%
Positive family history (N = 7)	6	86	5	71
Negative family history (N = 5)	1	20	1	20

While this study is still underway, as of April 1985 (58) a total of 247 adoptive families (112 index and 135 controls) has been studied. This study attempts to investigate both genetic and environmental factors in the development of schizophrenia, as it assesses the incidence of schizophrenia in offspring as a function of the quality of the rearing environment. Ratings of the interactional patterns in the family are based upon: (a) a joint interview with the whole family; (b) a joint interview with the parents only; (c) a family interaction task based on the conjoint Rorschach procedure; and (d) ratings on the Interpersonal Perception Methods (59). In addition, the adoptive parents receive an individual interview, Rorschach test, and portions of the Wechsler Adult Intelligence Test (60).

To date, these various measures of family relationships have been reduced to categorical ratings, ranging from healthy to severely disturbed. While ratings of measures used in the Goldstein study cited above (54, 55) (CD, EE, AS) are available from the data collected in the Tienari et al. study (51) they have not been completed as yet.

The data reported so far (58) strongly support the role of genetic factors in schizophrenia, since, of the 10 psychotic offspring in the sample, 8 were found in the adopted-away offspring of schizophrenic mothers (7.14%), while the population base rate was found in the control families (2/135 = 1.48%).

However, the data support a vulnerability-stress model as well, since all the schizophrenic cases in the 92 families rated thus far occurred in families rated as disturbed (see Table 1). In fact, the adopted-away offspring of schizophrenics with rearing environments rated as 'healthy' have rates of schizophrenia at or below the general population rate.

These data also weaken the argument against a purely environmental etiology of schizophrenia, as similar patterns of family disturbance did not relate to a notable incidence of schizophrenia in the adopted-away offspring of non-psychiatric biological parents.

Although the study designs and data bases are quite different, both the Goldstein et al. (52 – 55) and Tienari et al. (57) studies are quite congruent in supporting the vulnerability-stress model outlined previously in this chapter.

While the data from the Tienari project are intriguing, their limitations must be recognized. The study is not a prospective one, at least in its original conception,

TABLE 2 *The rate of psychosis observed in adopted-away offspring of schizophrenic mothers as a function of rearing family environment*

Offspring diagnosis	Adoptive family rearing environment Healthy N = 49	 Seriously disturbed N = 43
Psychotic*	0%	16.3%
Borderline psychotic	0%	20.9%

Taken from Tienari et al. 1985 (57).
* 5 diagnosed schizophrenic, 2 paranoid psychosis.

and it is entirely possible that disturbed family relationships evolved concurrently with or after the emergence of pscychiatric disorder in an offspring. In order to answer this criticism, this study is being continued as a high risk project in which the unaffected offspring of index and control parents will be studied prospectively to determine if ratings of the rearing environment antedate the emergence of schizophrenia and related disorders.

Summary of stress factors as precursors of schizophrenia

As indicated above, only two studies relate to the question of whether one type of stress, disturbed family relationships, interacts with individual vulnerability to increase the risk for the onset of schizophrenia. Each of these studies has considerable limitations, yet the congruence between them suggests that it may be premature to reject the hypothesis that family stress may be a significant component in the epigenesis of schizophrenia. More research is needed on the role of these family factors much earlier in life in order to understand the complex transactions among the emerging signs of individual vulnerability and caretaker-child interaction.

Studies of this topic are limited by the absence of a reliable marker of the genetic predisposition to schizophrenia. The current risk markers are largely statistical in nature, as they indicate the risk within a particular family line, but not which individuals are at risk. Thus, at present, it is difficult to map the transactions between stress and vulnerability markers with precision.

MAINTENANCE STUDIES

A similar vulnerability-stress model has been utilized in research on the course of schizophrenia once the disorder develops. Returning once again to Fig. 1, we can see that the personal vulnerability factors outlined are related to: (a) brain biochemistry (dopaminergic dysfunction); (b) AIP dysfunction (reduced available processing capacity); (c) autonomic nervous system hyperactivity; and (d) certain personality traits (schizotypal personality, in particular).

Since evidence regarding most of these topics is covered in other reviews in this Handbook, I will focus on what are termed environmental potentiators and stressors. Once again, most of the research in recent years has been directed towards one of these stressor conditions, a critical or emotionally involved family climate, termed high expressed emotion (high EE) in the early British studies (49). While we focus on this one form of stress, it should be recognized that, as indicated in Fig. 1, other, non-familial factors (stressful life events, for example) have been suggested to be major risk factors for a poor course (relapse or impaired social role functioning). However, recent research on the latter topics has been negligible and indicative of weak relationships to the course of the disorder.

It should be recognized that while most research has focused on the affective climate in the family, many schizophrenic patients are either estranged from or in minimal contact with their families, and therefore their clinical course cannot be explained by family stress factors. It is also essential to recognize that the best predictor of risk for relapse or poor clinical course is non-compliance with anti-psychotic medication, and that all studies on psychosocial stress factors must be considered within the context of medication compliance.

Research on expressed emotion

The concept of expressed emotion evolved from a series of studies carried out at the MRC Social Psychiatry Unit in London over the last 30 years, designed to understand why some discharged schizophrenic patients could cope in the community and others could not. An excellent description of the evolution of this research can be found in the work of Brown (61) and of Leff and Vaughn (49).

This research, that began before the widespread application of anti-psychotic medication, started with the observation, not since replicated, that patients who returned to family homes relapsed more frequently than patients who went to other living arrangements (62). This led to an investigation of attributes of the family environment which might potentiate relapse in an already vulnerable person who had suffered a recent schizophrenic episode. Observation of families resulted in the notion that high levels of tension and emotion characterized those family units with the most relapse-prone patients, originally termed 'emotional involvement' (61, p. 19). This research was facilitated by the development of an interview procedure by Rutter and Brown (63), termed the Camberwell Family Interview (CFI). This interview looks at the 3-month period prior to the onset of an episode of schizophrenia and focuses upon various types of events in families (quarrels, how often household tasks were done, amount of face-to-face contact, etc.), as well as the psychiatric history, irritability and clinical symptoms of the patient-relative in that same 3-month period. The main aim of the interviewing procedure is to stimulate respondents to express themselves in ways that reflect their inner feelings. The whole interview is rated on a series of scales (warmth, hostility, emotional overinvolvement), and frequency counts are made on the number of critical comments and positive remarks made about the patient.

In the original study (64) it was found that 76% of patients returning to homes rating high on criticism and/or emotional overinvolvement relapsed, while only 28% of those returning to homes with low emotional involvement did so. Note that by contemporary standards, high and low involvement are now called high and low EE.

Since this original study, a number of replications have been carried out (64, 51, 66 – 69), all of which have confirmed the original trends. However, three reports exist in the literature which show non-replication (70 – 73). The Hogarty publication (70) is particularly important in pointing out that most of the replications have found that high EE status is predictive predominantly for *male* schizophrenic patients.

The 1976 Vaughn and Leff paper (51) indicated that high EE status interacted with the patient's level of compliance with anti-psychotic medication and the amount of face-to-face contact. However, recent studies have not supported these findings and have shown instead that medication and family EE status are independent and *additive* predictors of clinical course (66, 67, 69), and that the contact effect has not been replicated.

The greatest controversy in this research has to do with the interpretation of these findings and their implications regarding the direction of effects. In both the 1962 and 1972 studies of Brown et al. (64, 65), relationships were found between ratings of patient 'behavioral disturbance' in the 3-month pre-hospitalization period and relapse. However, when this patient attribute was entered into a prediction equation with EE status, it failed to add anything to the prediction from EE status. The 1976 Vaughn and Leff study (51) found that ratings of the severity of psychopathology at discharge were unrelated to EE status, a finding subsequently confirmed by Miklowitz et al. (74) in the United States.

It might be expected that the patient's premorbid history would relate to the EE attitudes of relatives as those relatives who have been faced with a socially ineffective child or spouse (a poor premorbid patient), might be more critical and/or emotionally overinvolved after a schizophrenic breakdown, as this is experienced as yet another sign of dysfunctional adaptation in the patient. Miklowitz et al. (74) failed to find such a relationship for relatives defined as high-EE on the basis of the criticism criterion, but did find that relatives rated as high-EE on the basis of emotional overinvolvement had schizophrenic offspring with a poor premorbid history.

Along a similar line of investigating, a possible link between the EE status of relatives and the history of the patient's illness, MacMillan et al. (69) report that an association between pre-admission duration of illness (the time between the reported initial signs of the first episode of schizophrenia and first lifetime hospital admission for the disorder) and EE status, a longer history being associated with a greater probability of high-EE attitudes. These authors further conclude from logistic regression analyses that EE was not a significant predictor of relapse when duration of illness was also entered as a predictor.

Statistical removal of the duration of untreated illness from the predictor equation does not eliminate the significance of EE attitude for the future course of the patient's disorder. It is one thing to clarify the origins of contemporary attitudes or behaviors (high or low EE status) but quite another to assume that contemporary attitudes are irrelevant determinants of the behavior of others. It is also interesting to note that a recent report by Nuechterlein et al. (68) of preliminary data from a comparable sample of recent onset, predominantly first admission schizophrenic patients, failed to replicate the association between EE status of relatives and duration of illness. Also, a re-analysis of the data for first life time admission cases in the Nuechterlein study (75) revealed that the relationship of EE to duration in the study of MacMillan et al. (69) was an artifact of differential exposure by relatives to the early stages of their relative's disorder.

The relationship between relatives' EE status and relapse in schizophrenic patients does not clarify the nature of mediating mechanism between family attitude and patient response. A number of studies have attempted to address this problem by observing actual interactional patterns among patients and relatives. Three studies (76 – 78) have indicated that high-EE relatives do, in fact, express more negative affect (coded by the affective style coding system) (52) in experimentally induced interactional sessions. Furthermore, the types of negative affective message parallel the subtypes of high-EE attitudes, since relatives classified as high-EE on criticism express more criticism, but those rated as high-EE on emotional overinvolvement do not, but instead are more intrusive.

A critical issue in EE research is whether these family attitudes are state-dependent or are consistent across time, independently of the patient's clinical state. In a recent study, Miklowitz et al. (79) estimated EE in the conventional way by administering the CFI during the patient's hospitalization. A brief measure of EE, the five-minute speech sample (FMSS) (80) was used as a probe for the stability of EE 5 – 6 weeks after the patients had been discharged and had returned home. These investigators found that over half of the original high-EE relatives were low-EE after remission, while few if any low-EE relatives had changed. They further found that the most negative interaction patterns were found in the families rated as consistently high-EE, while those where relatives shifted from high to low EE were not discriminable from those with consistently low-EE relatives. These results suggest that it is valuable to obtain estimates of EE over time, to separate those relatives whose high-EE attitudes are largely state-dependent from those who maintain this attitude consistently from acute episode to remission phases of the disorder.

A number of studies have found that these verbal interchanges are paralleled by increasing psychophysiological arousal and reactivity in the patient (81, 82) and, in one study with disturbed teenagers thought to be at risk for schizophrenia, in both parents and offspring (76). These data suggest that a negative affective climate in the family may enhance the likelihood of relapse by raising the level of arousal in the patient beyond the limits of his vulnerable post-psychotic coping mechanisms.

That the affective climate of the family may be causally related to relapse have been investigated within the framework of the aftercare intervention study of Falloon et al. (83), which contrasted a behavioral family management program with a comparable individual, patient-focused program, where all patients received regular maintenance anti-psychotic medication. The direct interaction task used in the study of Miklowitz et al. (74) was repeated twice by Falloon et al., once before entry into the study and once after 3 months of intensive treatment (83). The parental data was coded by the affective style system on both occasions. Pre-post comparisons (84, 85) indicated that not only did the family management program produce on average a greater reduction of negative affect in the family than the individual patient-focused intervention, but also that those families where this reduction occurred were least likely to experience a relapse in their young adult schizophrenic offspring by the 9-month follow-up point.

Similar findings were recently reported by Hogarty et al. (86) using the original CFI method of EE assessment before and after one year of either family management, social skills training for the patient, a combination of the two, or regular maintenance drug therapy. All families in these studies were originally selected as being high-EE. The rate of change from high to low EE status was greatest in the family treatment groups (family alone or family and social skills) and lowest in the drug-only condition. However, regardless of the assigned treatment condition, when relatives did shift to a low EE status, the patient relapse rate was 0%, whereas when this did not occur, the rate averaged 40%.

While studies carried out to date suggest that relatives' affective attitudes towards a recently discharged schizophrenic patient may play some role in the subsequent course of the patient's disorder, there are still a number of unanswered questions in this area. First, while there is little evidence that high-EE attitudes are simply reactions to variations in the clinical state of the patient, many of the direct interaction studies have not carefully examined the more subtle aspects of how patients relate to their family members. Given that EE is measured when family members are going through a major crisis involving either the hospitalization or rehospitalization of a spouse or child, there may be attributes of the crisis or its history, as suggested by MacMillan et al. (69), that can help us understand variations in these responses to the patient's disorder. It is very likely that high-EE attitudes and negative affective behaviors towards patient-relatives have complex origins, as suggested by Leff and Vaughn (49), and that investigators should go beyond the convenient high-low EE typology in order to understand not only the natural history of a schizophrenic disorder, but also the natural history of relatives' varying efforts to cope with the many difficult demands of a close relative with schizophrenia residing in or near their home. Two recent studies (87, 88) have attempted a more sophisticated look at this issue by examining the behavior of patients towards relatives defined as either high- or low-EE. These studies have found that the pattern of negative escalation observed in high-EE families reflects complex reciprocal transactions between patients and relatives, and cannot be accounted for by a simple linear model in which the affective tone of interactions is determined solely by the relative's behavior. This literature will ultimately profit from a reinterpretation of the data within the framework of a vulnerability-stress model applied to the *relatives* of schizophrenics as well.

Family intervention studies

The burden experienced by relatives of schizophrenics who are frequently required to care for their patient-relative after discharge following a relatively brief hospitalization, has generated considerable interest in the development of family intervention programs designed to reduce stress on all family members and thereby reduce the risk of patient relapse. Unquestionably, the development of these programs and the controlled clinical trials that were carried out have gained considerable impetus from the EE research, since these studies specified family attributes that were likely targets for effective modification. However, the programs which have been tested so far cannot be seen as strictly derived from the EE model, as they frequently involve a complex set of interventions that include information, support, communication training and instruction in the development of new coping skills for all family members (89). However, as noted above, one consequence of these programs has been the reduction in the negative affective messages in the family.

Despite wide variations in format and theoretical model (in one study, by Leff et al. (91), only relatives were involved in groups), the four controlled clinical trials carried out to date (90, 91, 83, 86) found outcomes remarkably consistent with one another in revealing a substantial reduction in relapse rate for the family-based intervention in comparison either to regular drug treatment, or, in the study of

Falloon et al. (83), with drug plus individual therapy. A noteworthy finding in the study of Hogarty et al. was that the combination of family management, individual social skills training for the patient and regular drug treatment produced the lowest rate of relapse (0%) at one year after discharge. This finding is particularly important, as previous research on individually based treatments for schizophrenia have not produced encouraging results, and this is the first positive evidence on this score. All these family intervention programs are superimposed on regular maintenance anti-psychotic drug treatment, and appear to add something of significance to the protection provided by drug treatment.

There are several unresolved issues regarding these family programs, namely: (a) How much of the efficacy is due to the provision of information and support, and how much to the specific behavioral alterations targeted by the model of treatment? (b) Do these programs actually prevent relapse, or merely delay its occurrence? (c) How, and in what ways, do these family programs, designed to reduce family stress, interact with different pharmacological strategies for maintenance treatment? If the vulnerability-stress model is an accurate one for accounting for risk of relapse, then factors that reduce stress should permit variations in the protection required against vulnerability in the patient. This suggests that variations in dose (so-called low-dose strategies) or pattern of medication (targeted or intermittent medication) would be more likely to be effective when the stress level is lowered. This is the basic design of the NIMH Health Treatment Strategies in Schizophrenia Cooperative Agreement Program (92); the results of that study will shed considerable light on this question.

Summary of stress factors associated with the course of schizophrenia

Various studies have supported the view that a negative affective climate in the family is predictive of relapse in a patient-relative in the short term. The origins of these family attitudes are quite complex, and warrant careful investigation to determine whether they antedate the onset of the disorder, are reactive to or provoked by attributes of the patient-relative's premorbid and post-morbid social and clinical behavior, and how they relate to coping mechanisms used by relatives to handle the very real difficulties of having a remitted schizophrenic person at home.

The controlled clinical trials contrasting family intervention and drug therapy programs with regular maintenance drug treatment only, have produced clear and consistent evidence of the added effectiveness of a family management program. However, the evidence regarding duration of these effects beyond 9 months to one year after discharge have not been consistent. Further research in this area should involve studies of other modalities of psychological treatment (as in the social skills training module of Hogarty et al. (86)) that could be added to or extend beyond the typical period of family management studies to date, in order to develop a comprehensive rehabilitation program for schizophrenic patients. A successful family management program may merely stabilize the patient at a level of clinical and social functioning that permits the introduction of patient-focused, psychosocial rehabilitation programs designed to go beyond relapse prevention. New and innovative models of patient-focused psychosocial rehabilitation programs are urgently needed to extend and amplify the family-based programs tested to date.

ACKNOWLEDGEMENTS

The preparation of this chapter was greatly facilitated by a contract from NIMH (MH08744) and a grant from the John D. and Catherine T. MacArthur Foundation for the Network on Risk and Protective Factors in the Major Mental Disorders. The author is also greatly indebted to Joan Asarnow, Ph.D., for her analyses of high risk research literature.

REFERENCES

1. Zubin J, Spring BJ (1977) Vulnerability: a new view of schizophrenia. *J. Abnorm. Psychol., 86,* 103.
2. Nuechterlein K (1987) Vulnerability models for schizophrenia: state of the art. In: Hafner H, Gattaz WF, Janzarik W (Eds), *Search for the Causes of Schizophrenia,* pp. 296 – 316. Springer-Verlag, Heidelberg.
3. Erlenmeyer-Kimling E (1968) Studies on the offspring of two schizophrenic parents. *J. Psychiatr. Res., 6,* 65.
4. Asarnow J, Goldstein MJ (1986) Schizophrenia during adolescence: a developmental perspective on risk research. *Clin. Psychol. Rev., 6,* 211.
5. Walker E, Emory E (1983) Infants at risk for psychopathology: offspring of schizophrenic parents. *Child Dev., 54,* 1269.
6. McNeil TF, Kaij L, Malmquist-Larsson A, Nasland B, Persoon-Blennow I, McNeil N, Blennow G (1983) Development of a longitudinal study of children at high risk. *Acta Psychiatr. Scand., 68,* 234.
7. Fish B (1984) Characteristics and sequelae of the neurointegrative disorder in infants at risk for schizophrenia: 1952 – 82. In: Watt N, Anthony EJ, Wynne L, Rolf J (Eds), *Children at Risk for Schizophrenia: A Longitudinal Perspective,* pp, 423 – 439. Cambridge University Press, New York.
8. Ragins N, Schacter J, Elmer E, Preisman R, Bowes A, Harway V (1975) Infants and children at risk for schizophrenia. *J. Am. Acad. Child Psychiatry, 14,* 150.
9. Fish B (1987) Infant predictors of the longitudinal course of schizophrenic development. *Schizophr. Bull., 13,* 395.
10. Marcus J, Hans S, Lewow E, Wilkinson L, Burack C (1985) Neurological findings in the offspring of schizophrenics: childhood assessment and 5-year follow-up. *Schizophr. Bull., 11,* 85.
11. Marcus J, Hans SL, Nagler S, Auerbach JG, Mirsky AF, Aubrey A (1987) Review of the NIMH Israeli kibbutz-city study and the Jerusalem infant development study. *Schizophr. Bull., 13,* 425.
12. Parnas J, Schulsinger F, Schulsinger H, Mednick S, Teasdale T (1982) Behavioral precursors of schizophrenia spectrum. *Arch. Gen. Psychiatry, 39,* 658.
13. Parnas J, Schulsinger F, Teasdale TW, Schulsinger H, Feldman PM, Mednick SA (1982) Perinatal complications and clinical outcome within the schizophrenia spectrum. *Br. J. Psychiatry, 140,* 416.
14. Nasland R, Persson-Belnnow I, McNeil T, Kaij L, Malmquist-Larsson A (1984) Offspring of women with nonorganic psychosis: fear of stranger during the first year of life. *Acta Psychiatr. Scand., 69,* 435.
15. Ainsworth MD, Wittig BA (1969) Attachment and exploratory behavior of 1-year-olds in a strange situation. In: Foss BM (Ed), *Determinants of Infant Behavior, IV,* pp.

111 – 136. Methuen, London.
16. Sameroff AJ, Barocas R, Seifer R (1984) The early development of children born to mentally ill women. In Watt NF. Anthony EJ, Wynne LC, Rolf JE (Eds), *Children at Risk for Schizophrenia: a Longitudinal Perspective,* pp. 482 – 514. Cambridge University Press, New York.
17. Goodman SH (1987) Emory University Project on children with disturbed parents. *Schizophr. Bull., 13,* 411.
18. Hanson D, Gottesman I, Heston L (1976) Some possible childhood indicators of adult schizophrenia inferred from children of schizophrenics. *Br. J. Psychiatry, 129,* 142.
19. Baldwin AL, Cole RE, Baldwin CP (1982) *Monogr. Soc. Res. Child Dev., 47,* 72.
20. Erlenmeyer-Kimling L, Cornblatt BA, Golden R (1983) Early indicators of vulnerability to schizophrenia in children at high genetic risk. In: Guze SB, Earls FJ, Barrett JE (Eds), *Childhood Psychopathology and Development,* pp. 247 – 261. Raven Press, New York.
21. Reider RO, Nichols PL (1979) The offspring of schizophrenics, III. *Arch. Gen. Psychiatry, 36,* 665.
22. Orvaschel H, Mednick S, Schulsinger F, Rock D (1979) The children of psychiatrically disturbed parents. *Arch. Gen. Psychiatry, 36,* 691.
23. Asarnow R (1983) Schizophrenia. In: Tarter R (Ed), *The Child at Psychiatric Risk,* pp. 150 – 194. Oxford University Press, New York.
24. Harvey P, Weintraub S, Neale J (1985) Span of apprehension deficits in children vulnerable to psychopathology: a failure to replicate. *J. Abnorm. Psychol., 94,* 410.
25. Cornblatt BA, Erlenmeyer-Kimling L (1985) Global attentional deviances as a marker of risk for schizophrenia: specificity and predictive validity. *J. Abnorm. Psychol. 94,* 470.
26. Nuechterlein K (1983) Signal detection in vigilance tasks and behavioral attributes among offspring of schizophrenic mothers and among hyperactive children. *J. Abnorm. Psychol., 92,* 4.
27. Rutschmann J, Cornblatt B, Erlenmeyer-Kimling L (1977) Sustained attention in children at risk for schizophrenia: report on a continuous performance test. *Arch. Gen. Psychiatry, 34,* 571.
28. Wynne LC (1984) The University of Rochester Child and Family Study: overview of research plan. In: Watt NF, Anthony EJ, Wynne LC, Rolf JE (Eds), *Children at Risk for Schizophrenia: a Longitudinal Perspective,* pp. 335 – 347. Cambridge University Press, New York.
29. Wynne LC, Cole RE, Perkins P (1987) University of Rochester Child and Family Study: risk research in progress. *Schizophr. Bull., 13,* 463.
30. Rolf JE (1972) The social and academic competence of children vulnerable to schizophrenia and other behavior pathologies. *J. Abnorm. Psychol., 80,* 225.
31. Fisher L, Harder D, Kokes R, Schwartzman P (1982) School functioning of children at risk for behavioral pathology. *Monogr. Soc. Res. Child. Dev., 47,* 12.
32. Watt NF (1978) Patterns of childhood social development in adult schizophrenics. *Arch. Gen. Psych., 35,* 160.
33. Weintraub S, Neale J (1984) The Stony Brook high-risk project. In: Watt NF, Anthony EJ, Wynne LC, Rolf JE (Eds), *Children at Risk for Schizophrenia: a Longitudinal Perspective,* pp. 243 – 263. Cambridge University Press, New York.
34. Marcuse Y, Cornblatt B (1986) Children at high risk for schizophrenia: predictions from infancy to childhood functioning. In: Erlenmeyer-Kimling L, Miller N (Eds), *Life Span Research on the Prediction of Psychopathology,* pp. 81 – 100. Lawrence Earlbaum and Associates, New Jersey.
35. Erlenmeyer-Kimling L, Cornblatt B (1987) The New York high-risk project: a follow-up report. *Schizophr. Bull., 13,* 451.

36. Mednick SA, Schulsinger F (1968) Some premorbid characteristics related to breakdown in children with schizophrenic mothers. In: Rosenthal D, Kety SS, *The Transmission of Schizophrenia,* pp. 267 – 291. Pergamon Press, New York.
37. Dawson ME, Nuechterlein KH (1984) Psychophysiological dysfunctions in the developmental course of schizophrenic disorders. *Schizophr. Bull., 10,* 204.
38. Lidz T, Cornelison AR, Fleck S, Terry D (1957) The intrafamilial environment of schizophrenic patients, II. Marital schism and marital skew. *Am. J. Psychiatry, 114,* 241.
39. Bowen M (1960) A family concept of schizophrenia. In: Jackson DD (Ed), *The Etiology of Schizophrenia,* pp. 346 – 372. Basic Books, New York.
40. Bateson B, Jackson D, Haley J, Weakland J (1956) Toward a theory of schizophrenia. *Behav. Sci., 1,* 252.
41. Massie HN, Beels CC (1972) The outcome and family treatment of schizophrenia. *Schizophr. Bull. 6,* 24.
42. Hatfield AB (1983) In: McFarlane WR (Ed), *Family Therapy in Schizophrenia,* pp. 41 – 65. Guilford Press, New York.
43. Riskin J, Faunce E (1972) An evaluative review of family interaction research. *Fam. Process, 11,* 365.
44. Goldstein MJ, Rodnick EH (1975) The family's contribution to the etiology of schizophrenia. *Schizophr. Bull. 14,* 48.
45. Jacob T (1975) Family interaction in disturbed and normal families: a methodological and substantive review. *Psychol. Bull., 82,* 33.
46. Liem J (1980) Family studies of schizophrenia: an update commentary. *Schizophr. Bull., 6,* 429.
47. Helmerson P (1983) Family Interaction and Communication in Psychopathology: An Evaluation of Recent Perspectives. Academic Press, London.
48. Rosenthal D (1970) Genetic Theory and Abnormal Behavior. McGraw-Hill, New York.
49. Leff J, Vaughn C (1985) Expressed Emotion in Families. Guilford Press, New York.
50. Wynne LC, Singer MT, Bartko JJ, Toohey ML (1977) Schizophrenics and their families: research on parental communication. In: Tanner JM (Ed), *Developments in Psychiatric Research,* pp. 254 – 286. Hodder & Stoughton, London.
51. Vaughn CE, Leff JP (1976) The influence of family and social factors on the course of psychiatric illness: a comparison of schizophrenic and depressed neurotic patients. *Br. J. Psychiatry, 129,* 125.
52. Doane JA, West KL, Goldstein MJ, Rodnick EH, Jones JE (1981) Parental communication deviance and affective style: predictors of subsequent schizophrenia spectrum disorders in vulnerable adolescents. *Arch. Gen. Psychiatry, 38,* 679.
53. Goldstein MJ, Judd LL, Rodnick EH, Alkire AA (1968) A method for the study of social influence and coping patterns in the families of disturbed adolescents. *J. Nerv. Ment. Dis., 147,* 233.
54. Goldstein MJ (1985) Family factors that antedate the onset of schizophrenia and related disorders: the results of a fifteen-year prospective longitudinal study. *Acta Psychiatr. Scand., 71,* 7.
55. Goldstein MJ (1987) The UCLA high risk project. *Schizophr. Bull., 13,* 505.
56. Miklowitz DJ, Goldstein MJ, Nuechterlein KH, Snyder KS, Mintz J (1988) Family factors and the course of bipolar affective disorder. *Arch. Gen. Psychiatry, 45,* 225.
57. Tienari P, Sorri A, Naarala M, Lahti I, Pohjola J, Bostrom C, Wahlberg K (1983) The Finnish adoptive and family study: adopted-away offspring of schizophrenic mothers. In: Stierlin H, Wynne LC, Wirsching M (Eds), *Psychosocial Intervention in Schizophrenia,* pp. 21 – 34. Springer-Verlag, Berlin.
58. Tienari P, Sorri A, Lahti I, Naarala M, Wahlberg K-E, Moring J, Pohjola J, Wynne LC

(1987) Genetic and psychosocial factors in schizophrenia: the Finnish adoptive family study. *Schizophr. Bull., 13,* 477.
59. Laing RD, Philipson H, Lee AE (1966) Interpersonal Perception: a Theory and a Method of Research. Tavistock Publications, London.
60. Wechsler D (1981) Manual for the Wechsler Adult Intelligence Scale. Psychological Corporation, New York.
61. Brown GW (1985) The discovery of expressed emotion: induction or deduction? In: Leff J, Vaughn C (Eds), *Expressed Emotion in Families,* pp. 7–25. Guilford Press, New York.
62. Brown GW (1959) Experiences of discharged chronic schizophrenic mental hospital patients in various types of living group. *Millbank Meml. Fund Q., 37,* 105.
63. Rutter M, Brown GW (1966) The reliability and validity of measures of family life and relationships in families containing a psychiatric patient. *Soc. Psychiatry, 1,* 38.
64. Brown GW, Monck EM, Carstairs GM, Wing JK (1962) Influence of family life on the course of schizophrenic illness. *Br. J. Prev. Soc. Med., 16,* 55.
65. Brown GW, Birley JLT, Wing JK (1972) Influence on the course of schizophrenic disorders: a replication. *Br. J. Psychiatry, 121,* 241.
66. Vaughn CE, Snyder KS, Jones S, Freeman WB, Falloon IRH (1984) Family factors in schizophrenic relapse: replication in California of the British research on expressed emotion. *Arch. Gen. Psychiatry, 41,* 1169.
67. Jenkins JH, Karno M, de la Selva A, Santana F, Telles C, Lopez S, Mintz J (1986) Expressed emotion, maintenance pharmacotherapy, and schizophrenic relapse among Mexican-Americans. *Psychopharmacol. Bull., 22,* 621.
68. Nuechterlein KH, Snyder KS, Dawson ME, Rappe S, Gitlin M, Fogelson D (1986) Expressed emotion, and fixed-dose fluphenazine decanoate maintenance, and relapse in recent-onset schizophrenia. *Psychopharmacol. Bull., 22,* 633.
69. MacMillan JF, Gold A, Crow TJ, Johnson AL, Johnstone EC (1986) Expressed emotion and relapse. *Br. J. Psychiatry, 148,* 133.
70. Hogarty GE (1985) Expressed emotion and schizophrenic relapse: implications from the Pittsburgh study. In: Alpert M (Ed), *Controversies in Schizophrenia,* pp. 354–365. Guilford Press, New York.
71. Dulz B, Hand I (1986) Short-term relapse in young schizophrenics: can it be predicted and affected by family (CFI), patient and treatment variables? An experimental study. In: Goldstein MJ, Hand I, Hahlweg K (Eds), *Treatment of Schizophrenia: Family Assessment and Intervention,* pp. 59–75. Springer-Verlag, Berlin.
72. McCreadie RG, Phillips K (1988) The Nithsdale schizophrenia survey, VII. Does relatives' high expressed emotion predict relapse? *Br. J. Psychiatry, 152,* 477.
73. Parker G, Johnston P, Hayward L (1988) Parental expressed emotion as a predictor of schizophrenic relapse. *Arch. Gen. Psychiatry, 45*, 806–813.
74. Miklowitz DJ, Goldstein MJ, Falloon IRH (1983) Premorbid and symptomatic characteristics of schizophrenia from families with high and low levels of expressed emotion. *J. Abnorm. Psychol., 92,* 359.
75. Mintz LI, Nuechterlein KH, Goldstein MJ, Mintz J (1989) The initial onset of schizophrenia and family expressed emotion: some methodological considerations. *Br. J. Psychiatry, 154,* 212–217.
76. Valone K, Norton JP, Goldstein MJ, Doane JA (1983) Parental expressed emotion and affective style in an adolescent sample at risk for schizophrenia spectrum disorders. *J. Abnorm. Psychol., 92,* 399.
77. Miklowitz DJ, Goldstein MJ, Falloon IRH, Doane JA (1984) Interactional correlates of expressed emotion in the families of schizophrenics. *Br. J. Psychiatry, 144,* 482.

78. Strachan AM, Leff JP, Goldstein MJ, Doane JA, Burtt C (1986) Emotional attitudes and direct communication in the families of schizophrenics. *Br. J. Psychiatry, 149,* 279.
79. Miklowitz DJ, Goldstein MJ, Doane JA, Nuechterlein KH, Strachan AM, Snyder KS, Magana A (1989) Is expressed emotion an index of transactional process? I: relative's affective style. *Fam. Process, 28,* 153.
80. Magana AB, Goldstein MJ, Karno M, Miklowitz DJ, Jenkins J, Falloon IRH (1986) a brief method for assessing expressed emotion in relatives of psychiatric patients. *Psychiatry Res., 17,* 203.
81. Tarrier N, Vaughn C, Lader MH, Leff JP (1979) Bodily reactions to people and events in schizophrenia. *Arch. Gen. Psychiatry, 36,* 311.
82. Sturgeon D, Kuipers L, Berkowitz R, Turpin G, Leff J (1981) Psychophysiological responses of schizophrenic patients to high and low expressed emotion relatives. *Br. J. Psychiatry, 138,* 40.
83. Falloon IRH, Boyd JL, McGill CW, Razani J, Moss HG, Gilderman A (1982) Family management in the prevention of exacerbations of schizophrenia: a controlled study. *New Engl. J. Med., 306,* 1437.
84. Doane JA, Falloon IRH, Goldstein MJ, Mintz J (1985) Parental affective style and the treatment of schizophrenia: predicting the course of illness and social functioning. *Arch. Gen. Psychiatry, 42,* 34.
85. Doane JA, Goldstein MJ, Miklowitz DJ, Falloon IRH (1986) The impact of individual and family treatment on the affective climate of families of schizophrenics. *Br. J. Psychiatry, 148,* 279.
86. Hogarty GE, Anderson CM, Reiss DJ, Kornblith SJ, Greenwald DP, Javna CD, Madonia MJ (1986) Family psychoeducation, social skills training, and maintenance chemotherapy in the aftercare treatment of schizophrenia. *Arch. Gen. Psychiatry, 43,* 633.
87. Hahlweg K, Goldstein MJ, Nuechterlein KH, Magana AB, Mintz J (1989) Expressed emotion and patient-relative interaction in families of recent onset-schizophrenics. *J. Consult. Clin. Psychol, 57,* 11.
88. Strachan AM, Feingold D, Goldstein MJ, Miklowitz DJ, Nuechterlein KH (1989) Does expressed emotion index a Transactional Process? II. Patient's coping style. *Fam. Process, 28,* 169.
89. Goldstein MJ (1981) New Developments in Interventions with Families of Schizophrenics. Jossey-Bass, San Francisco.
90. Goldstein MJ, Rodnick EH, Evans JR, May PRA, Steinberg M (1978) Drug and family therapy in the aftercare of acute schizophrenics. *Arch. Gen. Psychiatry, 35,* 1169.
91. Leff JP, Kuipers L, Berkowitz R, Eberlein-Vries R, Sturgeon D (1982) A controlled clinical trial of social intervention in the families of schizophrenic patients. *Br. J. Psychiatry, 141,* 121.
92. Schooler NR, Keith SJ (1983) Treatment Strategies in Schizophrenia Study Protocol. National Institute of Mental Health, Rockville, MD.

CHAPTER 2

Early intervention in schizophrenia

MARVIN I. HERZ

INTRODUCTION

While symptoms typical of schizophrenia have been recognized for many years, long-term studies of the course and outcome of schizophrenia have been carried out only recently. In 1978, Manfred Bleuler (1) reported on a study of 208 schizophrenic patients whom he had personally treated for at least 22 years. He stated that at least 25% of all schizophrenic patients recover completely after the initial episode, while about 10% remain permanently hospitalized with severe psychosis. The majority of patients (50 – 75%) alternate between acute psychotic phases and phases of improvement or recovery.

Ciompi (2) conducted a long-term outcome study of schizophrenia in Switzerland; the average duration between first admission and follow-up examination was 36.9 years. He found that 25% of the sample had had an acute onset combined with a phasic course and favorable outcome. In terms of the global outcome of schizophrenic symptoms, 27% of the sample achieved complete remission and 22% had minor residual symptomatology. A study by Huber et al. (3) had similar results.

The basic conclusion of these studies is that for most patients, schizophrenia is an illness characterized by exacerbations and remissions. The most common outcome after an acute psychotic episode is a nonpsychotic deficit state characterized by apathy, blunted affect, low energy levels, social withdrawal, and increased vulnerability to stress.

In contrast to most chronic medical illnesses, such as diabetes, where there has been a great deal of investigation of early warning signs of dyscontrol, it is not until recently that there has been a systematic study of the course of schizophrenia, emphasizing the early signs of relapse and the decompensation process itself. In the case of diabetes, it would be unheard of for physicians not to know the natural course of the illness, or not to alert patients and family members about early danger signals of dyscontrol in order to prevent the development of serious complications. It may be that psychiatry did not address the question of the process of relapse and early intervention to prevent relapse in schizophrenia because in the past most patients were housed in custodial institutions with little attention paid to fluctuations in the course of the illness. Today, since most schizophrenic patients live in the community, they are more visible when they relapse, especially if they require rehospitalization because of aggressive or disruptive behavior.

Handbook of Schizophrenia, Volume 4: Psychosocial Treatment of Schizophrenia.
M.I. Herz, S.J. Keith and J.P. Docherty, editors.

The majority of schizophrenic patients who live in the community are in homeostatic balance with the environment. Patients may be asymptomatic, manifest non-psychotic symptoms such as tension, anxiety or insomnia, they may have deficit symptoms of schizophrenia, or they may have positive symptoms such as delusions, hallucinations or thought disorder. Zubin and Spring (4) and Liberman (5) postulate a vulnerability model of schizophrenia. They believe that schizophrenic individuals are more vulnerable to life stresses than normal individuals. Thus, if we are to treat schizophrenic patients successfully, we must be able to: (a) avoid or decrease psychosocial, cultural, or biological stressors which may precipitate relapse, and (b) utilize therapeutic interventions with the patient to increase coping skills or strengthen the social support system so that the patient's vulnerability to stress will be decreased. Antipsychotic medication presumably decreases the patient's vulnerability to stress. A combined approach of decreasing stress and strengthening the patient's ability to cope should decrease the likelihood of psychotic relapse. This chapter will present data about the relapse process with special emphasis on early signs of decompensation, and then discuss a treatment strategy which is intended to abort the development of severe relapse through early intervention when patients begin to exhibit prodromal signs of relapse. It is postulated that the use of this strategy will decrease morbidity in patients and decrease the likelihood and necessity of re-hospitalization.

THE PROCESS OF RELAPSE

A search of the literature conducted in the mid-1970s disclosed that there were no large-scale systematic studies of the relapse process. Docherty and associates (6) reviewed the literature on stages of onset of schizophrenic psychosis and concluded that despite its obvious importance, there was very little hard data available on the decompensation process. Most studies had been carried out by gifted clinicians whose usual approach was a detailed case study in which information was gathered retrospectively from patients and family members. Donlon and Blacker (7), using a different approach, interviewed schizophrenic patients who were being withdrawn from medication and were beginning to relapse. However, their observations did not involve systematic ratings, and their data was reported anecdotally. In their review, Docherty and associates (6) said that despite the different methods used to study the question, there was a concordance of descriptions of identifiable premonitory signs, as well as of a regular and sequential unfolding of psychological states before psychotic breakdown. They differentiated five stages in schizophrenic decompensation, of which the first two were nonpsychotic:

(a) The first stage is *over-extension.* The person begins to experience a sense of being overwhelmed, an increasing mental effort is required. Symptomatically, the period is characterized by persistent anxiety, irritability, parapraxes, decreasing performance efficiency and distractability. From the description, it appears that the individual in this stage is experiencing a stress and reacting to it.

(b) The second stage is *restricted consciousness.* During this phase, boredom, apathy and listlessness are typically present. There is social withdrawal and decreased move-

ment. Obsessional and phobic symptoms appear or worsen, and somatization frequently appears. This stage appears to be a defense against loss of control with an attempt to limit external stimulation and a reinforcement of neurotic defenses.
(c) The third stage, *disinhibition,* is the first psychotic stage with a breakdown of neurotic defenses. During this phase, relatively unmodulated impulses are expressed. It may bear a close resemblance to hypomania, with sexual promiscuity, rage attacks, and unrestricted spending. Disassociative phenomena and ideas of reference may appear, and previously repressed material begins to appear in consciousness.
(d) The fourth stage is *psychotic disorganization,* with three distinct subphases: destructuring of the external world with an increased perceptual and cognitive disorganization; destructuring of the self with the person losing his sense of self-identity (severe anxiety and the effects of panic and horror are often present, along with hallucinatory phenomena); total fragmentation, in which the person experiences complete loss of self-control and phenomena such as catatonia appear.
(e) The fifth stage is *psychotic resolution.* This period is marked by decreased anxiety and increased organization, although it is on a psychotic level. The forms this resolution takes typically involve the development of an organizing delusional system (paranoid type) or the massive denial of all unpleasant affects and responsibility (hebephrenic type). In our own study, which will be described below, patients were unable to distinguish between the two distinct nonpsychotic prodromal stages. They did, however, report symptoms which occur in both the first and second stages of Docherty's formulation.

Systematic study of the prodromal phase of relapse

Since the literature was largely anecdotal, Herz and Melville decided to study systematically a large sample of patients from two locations (8). In Atlanta (Group A), 99 outpatients and 80 family informants at two community mental health centers were interviewed. Later, in an attempt to obtain data closer to the time of relapse, Group B was added, consisting of 46 hospitalized patients in Buffalo who had recently experienced a psychotic episode.

All patients were diagnosed as schizophrenic according to DSM-II and had no secondary diagnosis. The outpatients were being maintained on antipsychotic medication at the time of interview. Most patients had been hospitalized at least two or three times. At the time of the study, outpatients were considered to be functioning at a stable level and inpatients had recompensated sufficiently to cooperate with the research interviewer.

Demographic information was collected from both groups. Group A was primarily suburban or rural and white; 67% were women and 33% were men. Their average age was 38 years and their mean level of education was 9.8 years. The level of employment was low, only 15% working full or part-time. Thirty-three percent were married, 21% were divorced or separated, 6% were widowed, and 40% had never been married. Approximately 73% had been hospitalized three or more times.

Group B was largely urban. Of the 46 patients, 70% were women and 30% were men; 68% were white, 28% black, and 4% Puerto Rican. Their average age was 38 years and average level of education was 9.2 years. The rate of employment was somewhat higher than that in Group A: 26% were employed, 67.5% were unemployed, and for 6.5% data were unavailable. Most patients were unmarried: 23.9% were married, 30.4% were divorced or separated, 6.5% widowed, 37% had never been married, and for 2.2% data were unavailable. Information on patient's living arrangements was collected only from Group B. Only 17% lived alone, 70% lived with either a spouse, child or parents, and 9% lived in a supervised facility; for 4% information was unavailable. More than half of the patients in Group B were involuntary hospital admissions.

A structured inverview with a few open-ended questions was constructed, based on items contained in the Psychiatric Status Schedule (9), Research Diagnostic Criteria (10), and on clinical experience. The Early Signs Questionnaire, modified in Buffalo on the basis of experience gained during the Atlanta study, contains 52 items describing symptoms and feelings and other questions relevant to the period of relapse. An interview normally lasted between 30 and 45 minutes.

Each patient was interviewed individually by a research member of the staff, after indicating willingness to answer questions about his or her illness. The patient was informed that the information obtained would be included in the patient's chart and used in treatment planning. The same interview was conducted with available relatives. In Buffalo the family sample was very small because of difficulties in arranging appointments; therefore, these data are not included, and family data are reported for the Atlanta group only.

Results

In response to the question, 'Could you tell that there were any changes in your thoughts, feelings, or behaviors that might have led you to believe you were becoming sick and might have to go to the hospital?', approximately 70% of patients in both groups noticed changes and 30% did not. Families were much more likely to notice changes in the patients (92.6%) than were the patients themselves. In about 66% of the cases, the patient and the family informant agreed that there were recognizable early signs of decompensation, indicating a high level of concordance.

The time interval between the beginning of symptoms and the need for hospitalization is extremely important if medication and crisis intervention techniques are to be used to help prevent full relapse. According to the results of the interviews (Table 1), only 7 – 8% of patients and 11% of family members stated that the time period was less than 1 day. Approximately 15% of Group B patients and 8% of Group A patients and their families noticed a prodromal period of only one to three days. However, most of the patients and family members said that the interval was more than a week – 52% of Group B families, 48% of Group A patients, and 68% of Group A families. Thus, for most patients, relapse is not abrupt and sudden, and it is possible to institute effective crisis treatment to prevent full relapse.

When asked, 'What did you do about these changes when you realized that they might become serious?' almost 50% of patients responded that they sought professional help and 60% of the relatives said that they arranged for professional help

TABLE 1 *Time between perception of symptoms and hospitalization in schizophrenic patients*

			Atlanta Group			
	Buffalo Group (N = 46)		Patients (N = 99)		Families (N = 80)	
Time	N	%	N	%	N	%
< 1 day	3	6.5	8	8.1	9	11.2
1 – 3 days	7	15.2	8	8.1	6	7.5
4 days-1 week	4	8.7	14	14.1	7	8.8
1 – 2 weeks	1	2.2	8	8.1	16	20.0
2 – 4 weeks	9	19.6	16	16.2	3	3.7
> 1 month	14	30.4	23	23.2	35	43.8
Unknown	8	17.4	22	22.2	4	5.0

From: *American Journal of Psychiatry, 137* (1980) 801 – 805, July 1980 (Herz, Melville). Copyright 1980, the American Psychiatric Association. Reprinted by permission.

for the patient. Approximately 33% of Group B patients and 26% of Group A patients reported that they did nothing.

Since antipsychotic medication is especially effective in treating acute symptoms, it is disconcerting that less than 4% of all patients and family members said that patients took more medication when they realized that symptoms were becoming serious. Approximately 24% of Group A patients and 33% of Group B patients claimed that no medication had been prescribed for them, but it is possible that some of them chose simply to ignore their prescriptions. Only 26% of Group B patients and 50% of Group A patients stated that they were taking medication as prescribed. The primary reason given by patients for not taking medication as prescribed was that it did not help (Group A, N = 12, 12%; Group B, N = 6, 13%). The next most commonly mentioned reason was that it had unpleasant side effects (Group A, N = 2, 2%; Group B, N = 6, 13%). If withdrawal of medication does not lead to increased symptomatology for most stabilized patients, they might conclude that the medication was not helping and therefore was not necessary. In fact, there are reports of an increased energy level and sense of well-being when medication is terminated (11). For some patients this may be due to an amelioration of an unrecognized extrapyramidal side effect, akinesia.

What were the symptoms that either appeared or worsened in the prodromal period before full relapse and hospitalization? The Atlanta patients were outpatients in a relatively stable condition and the Buffalo patients had recently been hospitalized and were recovering from an acute episode. In spite of these and other differences between the two groups, the rank-order correlation of symptoms that appeared or worsened before hospitalization between the Buffalo and Atlanta patients was 0.85 ($P \leq 0.001$) (Table 2). Becoming tense and nervous was the symptom reported by most patients in both groups. Generally, the symptoms most frequently mentioned

TABLE 2 *Symptoms that appeared or worsened before hospitalization in schizophrenic patients*[a]

	Buffalo group (N = 46)		Atlanta group Patients (N = 99)		Atlanta group Families (N = 80)	
Symptom	Rank	%	Rank	%	Rank	%
Tense and nervous	1	80.4	1	70.7	1	83.3
Eating less	2	71.7	10	49.5	17	52.5
Trouble concentrating	3	69.6	5	56.6	3	76.3
Trouble sleeping	4	67.4	3	61.6	7	68.8
Enjoy things less	5	65.2	8	52.5	8	67.5
Restlessness	6	63.0	4	58.6	2	78.8
Can't remember things	6	63.0	14	46.5	10	60.0
Depression	8	60.9	2	63.6	3	76.3
Preoccupied with one or two things	9	59.6	12	48.5	9	65.0
Seeing friends less	9	59.6	7	54.5	18	50.0
Am being laughed at, talked about	9	59.6	9	51.5	14	53.8
Loss of interest in things	12	56.5	5	56.5	6	73.8
More religious thinking	13	54.3	10	49.5	19	47.5
Feeling bad for no reason	13	54.3	19	40.4	22	37.5
Feeling too excited	15	52.2	25	30.3	14	53.8
Hear voices, see things	16	50.0	17	42.4	10	60.0
Feeling worthless	17	48.8	15	44.5	12	56.3
Talking in nonsensical way	18	45.6	13	47.5	3	76.3
Believe someone else is controlling	18	45.6	18	41.4	21	38.8
Bad dreams	18	45.6	21	38.4	23	33.8
Too aggressive (pushy)	18	45.6	24	32.3	20	40.0
Feeling angry at little things	22	41.3	22	33.3	14	53.8
Not caring about way I look	22	41.3	19	40.4	12	56.3
Having trouble with spouse, mate	24	30.4	26	29.3	29	20.0
Thoughts of hurting, killing self	24	30.4	22	33.3	26	31.3
Frequent aches, pains	26	28.3	27	28.3	23	33.8
Fear of 'going crazy'	26	28.3	15	44.5	23	33.8
Thoughts of hurting, killing others	28	23.9	29	10.1	27	27.5
Drinking more, using drugs	29	21.7	28	20.2	28	25.0

[a] Spearman rank-order correlation for Buffalo patients and Atlanta patients = 0.85, and for Atlanta patients and families = 0.78 ($P < 0.001$).

From: *American Journal of Psychiatry, 137* (1980) 801 – 805, (Herz, Melville).

by patients and family members were symptoms of dysphoria that nonpsychotic individuals experience under stress, such as tension and anxiety, eating less, having trouble concentrating, having trouble sleeping, depression and seeing friends less. Among the first ten most commonly noted early psychotic symptoms were feelings of being laughed at or talked about, which are ideas of reference.

The rank-order correlation of frequency of symptoms reported by Atlanta patients and their relatives was also very high ($R = 0.78$, $P \leq 0.001$). Some relatives who are sensitive to the patient might notice dysphoric signs before the patient did, although insensitive relatives who are not in touch with the patient's feelings or behavior might tend not to notice early symptoms, and rate more severe psychopathology high. The only psychotic symptom for which there seemed to be a large degree of disagreement was talking in a nonsensical way, which was ranked third by families and 13th by patients. Relatives ranked hearing voices and seeing things 10th and patients ranked it 17th. These differences could also be related to patient's denial of psychotic symptoms.

When patients were asked, 'What were the *first* changes in thoughts, feelings, or behavior that might have led you to believe that you were becoming sick and might have to go to the hospital?', there was little agreement. Among the symptoms mentioned were tension, anxiety, nervousness, insomnia, and depression. Hearing voices was mentioned by five Group B patients and eight Group A patients as the first change noticed.

When asked whether the pattern of development of symptoms was similar for each episode, 50% of the patients answered 'yes' and 50% answered 'no'. Whether or not individual patients have the same sequential pattern of symptoms each time they relapse is of great importance to the psychiatrist who plans the treatment strategy.

Only Buffalo patients were asked, 'Can you tell me which symptoms are present when you are feeling well?' Sixty percent stated that they had feelings of loneliness. This seems high considering that many of these patients lived with a relative. A large number of nonpsychotic dysphoric symptoms, such as tension and nervousness, feeling sad or blue, and worrying were reported by 48% of patients. A smaller number of psychotic symptoms, such as thought broadcasting (reported by 30%) and hearing voices (reported by 26%), were indicated as being present during a state of presumed stability. Astrachan and associates (12) reported similar findings after interviewing schizophrenic patients 2–3 years after hospital discharge.

Subsequent studies of early relapse

McCandless-Glimcher et al. (13) interviewed 62 outpatients with chronic schizophrenia and schizoaffective disorder and found that their patients reported a very similar pattern of early symptoms of relapse to those reported in the Herz and Melville study (8). The most frequently reported symptoms included nervousness, tenseness, trouble sleeping, greater than usual fatigue, depression, difficulty in thinking or concentrating, less active than usual, unable to get going, irritability, difficulty doing work, avoiding activities with others and moodiness. Further down the list were psychotic symptoms of hearing voices when no one was present (37%), people talking or laughing about you (33%), getting special messages from the newspaper or TV (31%). Thus there was great overlap in the results of these two studies with regard to nonpsychotic symptomatology. In the Herz and Melville study, the earliest psychotic symptoms were those of being laughed at or talked about (60%), and delusions and hallucinations (approximately 50%). The frequency of non-psychotic symptoms (e.g., tension and nervousness) ranged up to 80%.

Subsequent prospective studies have verified the occurrence of prodromal symptoms and the beneficial effects of early clinical intervention when these symptoms appear. Carpenter et al. (14) conducted a controlled study comparing patients who were openly off medication using a targeted approach (medication given when signs of relapse appear) with patients on maintenance medication. In a report derived from this study, Heinrichs and Carpenter (15) describe prodromal symptoms gathered in medicated and unmedicated patients during early decompensation. Clinicians and psychiatric residents were asked to record each occasion when they judged a decompensation to have begun, and the changes in signs and symptoms that they used to recognize the beginning of illness or exacerbation.

Forty-seven episodes of decompensation resulted in 213 recorded symptoms with a mean of 4.5 symptoms per episode. There were 32 different symptom dimensions represented. There were five symptoms that occurred in more than 25% of the episodes, seven in more than 20% and 16 in more than 10%. Most episodes were effectively managed on an outpatient basis with prompt pharmacological intervention. Hospitalization was required for only three of the 47 patients in the study. According to the authors,

> 'The prodromal symptoms were a mixture of psychotic and nonpsychotic manifestations. A major role for affectivity in the early phase of schizophrenic psychosis is clear. Three of the ten most common symptoms were dysphoric states. There is extensive similarity between these symptoms and those reported by Herz and Melville in their retrospective study. Seven of the ten most common symptoms in our study were among the ten most common in at least one of the three samples reported in the Herz and Melville study. All symptoms were reported at a much higher rate in that study, probably reflecting the use of a systemic interview and the fact that the entire prodromal phase was considered not just the time until initial recognition of impending relapse.'

The Heinrichs and Carpenter group used and open-ended and unstructured request to the treating clinicians to report whatever changes they used in identifying an impending relapse. The most frequently reported symptoms were hallucinations (53%), suspiciousness (43%), changes in sleep (43%) and anxiety (38%). It should be noted that in the Herz and Melville study, delusions and hallucinations had occurred in approximately 50% of cases, but that nonpsychotic dysphoric symptoms were reported at a much higher frequency. The explanation of the difference offered by Heinrichs and Carpenter seems a reasonable one.

Herz et al. (16) conducted a large-scale study comparing intermittent medication (given only at early stages of relapse) with maintenance medication in stable schizophrenic outpatients. This was a controlled double-blind study. By the end of the first year of the study, results showed that of the 101 patients who entered this study, 61 had had at least one episode (22 on the active regimen and 39 on the placebo). There were a total of 91 prodromal episodes for patients who had been in the study for one year. Only 13 episodes (14%) resulted in hospitalization, indicating that early intervention to prevent relapse is effective.

If we compare the results of all these studies and include another study of intermittent versus maintenance medication, that by Hirsch et al. (17) in England, the following early symptoms of relapse appear most frequently: tension and nervousness, trouble in sleeping, depression, trouble in concentrating, impaired social relations, enjoying things less, hallucinations, suspiciousness, and delusions. It is important to recognize that these early symptoms are a combination of nonspecific dysphoric symptoms and symptoms of schizophrenia which would be considered exacerbations of illness. In the author's experience, there is not a great deal of thought disorganization, disruptive behavior, or patients being out of control during the early phase of relapse for the majority of episodes, thus enabling the therapist to utilize an early intervention strategy. One should remember that ratings for psychotic symptoms such as hallucinations can range in severity from mild to marked. Mild might indicate, for example, that they are not disturbing to the patient or are infrequent in occurrence. A rating of marked might be used when the patient is terribly troubled by the accusations of the voices and their relentlessness. It should be emphasized that, based on our experience and other reports in the literature, the relapse process is not an all-or-none phenomena. It is a process which takes place over time with increasing severity of symptomatology if left untreated.

In the Herz et al. (16) study, patients who had the longest and most severe episodes and who were most likely to be re-hospitalized tended to be markedly paranoid, with suspiciousness and delusions occurring early in the episode. As a result, these patients became uncooperative, refused medication, refused to see the therapist, and their symptoms increased in severity without treatment. Heinrichs et al. (18) report that patients who lack insight, that is, who fail to recognize that they are becoming sicker, are more likely to have severe episodes and relapses. Severe relapses and re-hospitalizations are also more likely to occur when patients and families wait too long before requesting therapeutic intervention, or when onset of psychotic symptomatology is rapid, often precipitated by illicit drugs or alcohol. As reported in the Herz and Melville (8) study of the prodromal period, family members generally recognize early symptomatology of relapse more frequently than do patients. In utilizing an early intervention strategy, it is important to have a collaborator, whether it be a family member, a case manager, or a manager of a single room occupancy hotel. Any individual who sees the patient at least a few times a week and who is ready to collaborate in the treatment process can be of great benefit.

To illustrate various clinical pictures characterizing prodromal episodes, the following case vignettes from the Herz et al. double-blind intermittent drug study (16) are presented:

Vignette 1. A nonpsychotic prodromal episode in a patient with no baseline psychotic symptoms

Eric Z, a 33-year-old white male, diagnosed as a Chronic Paranoid Schizophrenic, had been hospitalized twice. The episode leading to the second hospitalization began with withdrawn behavior, which increased over a period of six months. He was unable to function in his job as an electrician, and stopped going to work. The patient complained of gastrointestinal symptoms and was brought to the hospital emergency room where he was seen by a psychiatrist. During the interview, he admitted to a belief that his food was being poisoned, causing the stomach pains. He also said that he had great difficulty falling asleep during the previous week. Eric told his parents that he feared that something would happen to them and he paced anxiously in his room. He believed that he was Jesus Christ and was willing to be sacrificed to save the world. The patient expressed a fear that people were after him because he was someone special. He felt that he could begin World War III by pressing a button. After hospital discharge, he was stabilized over a period of six months and entered the study.

His baseline behavior was that of a quiet, pleasant, cooperative man who was compliant with medication and attendance at weekly group sessions. His affect was flat; he was socially isolated with no meaningful social relationships. His only social activities revolved around a supportive family which lived next door. At times, he had been able to obtain gainful employment as an electrician.

Eric had one episode during the study. He presented for a scheduled individual session following his absence from a group meeting and reported sleep difficulties, only three to four hours of sleep a night over the course of four nights. He said he felt depressed and admitted to remaining in bed for long periods of time, although he was not sleeping. He also reported increased irritability and diminished desire to engage in usual family social activities. He had recently quit a good job as an electrician because he felt unable to handle the pressure. The therapist thought that this was a minor episode which could be treated with lorazepam 1 mg at bedtime. However, about a week later, his mother called the therapist to report that Eric was becoming increasingly withdrawn, irritable, and remained in bed almost all day and that he was unresponsive to her phone calls. The therapist attempted to reach Eric by phone, but he refused to speak to her. Finally, four days later, he agreed to attend a session. He appeared somewhat unkempt, admitted to increased social isolation, tension and nervousness, increasing irritability, poor appetite and a marked decrease in his prior level of functioning. He was not able to attend to his usual household tasks and remained in bed almost all the time. Haloperidol 8 mg a day was initiated, twice his baseline dose. Two weeks later he began to stabilize and returned to baseline within three weeks.

Comment This patient had a gradual deterioration in functioning following his feeling of failure in a job. Introduction of a minor tranquilizer and supportive psychotherapy did not arrest the deterioration. Therefore, antipsychotic medication was started with favorable results within a few weeks.

Vignette 2. A patient with baseline psychotic symptoms with exacerbation of schizophrenic symptoms

William T. is a 30-year-old white male with a diagnosis of Chronic Undifferentiated Schizophrenia. He had been hospitalized three times prior to entry into the study. During the last episode, he had been brought to the hospital by ambulance after the family had found him lying in bed staring at the ceiling and unresponsive to verbal stimuli. The mother reported that he had had difficulty falling asleep for the previous two months, decreased appetite and increasingly withdrawn behavior, and that sometimes his speech was difficult to understand. His baseline auditory hallucinations had increased in intensity and duration, and the patient felt that Satan was controlling his mind and giving him thoughts to kill someone. He also believed that other people could read his mind.

After hospital discharge, he was stabilized over a period of six months before entering the study, but he continued to have occasional non-threatening auditory hallucinations. In treatment he formed a positive relationship with the therapist although he was somewhat dependent. As part of his treatment, he entered a vocational rehabilitation program and a sheltered workshop.

The episode occurred after five months in the study. The patient's mother reported increasingly withdrawn behavior over a period of 3 to 4 days, suspiciousness, and the patient's fear that the devil was controlling him. His baseline auditory hallucinations increased, and became negative in nature: 'I hear voices telling me that I am no good and they are laughing at me'. Active medication was initiated, trifluoroperazine 20 mg/day, twice his double-blind medication dose. William was seen every other day and required an increase in medication to 25 mg/day in the first week. As the symptoms improved and he stabilized, the medication was reduced to baseline over a five-week period. It is possible that a life event contributed to this episode. The patient had an increase in his workload in the vocational rehabilitation program, and his supervisors started to put pressure on him to increase his speed and productivity.

Comment In the case of a patient who has baseline delusions and hallucinations, it has been our experience that there is an immediate increase in these psychotic symptoms when a new episode starts to develop.

Vignette 3. Nonpsychotic episodes resolved without introduction of antipsychotic medication

Patricia G. is a 27-year-old white female who was chronically anxious and received benzodiazepines in addition to her study medication for most of the two years in the study. Her diagnosis was Schizoaffective Depressed.

Her first hospitalization had occurred at age 25, when she was brought into the Mental Health Emergency Room in an actively psychotic state. She described hearing the voice of her brother-in-law telling her to get rid of her family members one by one, and claimed that the television and radio were saying bad things about her. The mother reported that the patient had been depressed and withdrawn for 9 months prior to this hospitalization. The symptoms seemed to follow the loss of her job as a secretary. The boss had hired his daughter in her place. Patricia stopped seeing all friends, remained in her room most the time, was irritable and lost approximately twenty pounds. After this hospitalization, she was readmitted about a month later because of increased auditory hallucinations. She believed that God was talking to her. She also expressed a fear that a girl was trying to hurt her but could give no further explanation than this. After hospital discharge, she was stabilized over a period of 5 months.

When she entered the study, here baseline behavior was that of a quiet, soft-spoken young woman who seemed helpless and dependent. She dressed rather seductively and was superficial in conversation. She denied hallucinations or delusions but was preoccupied somatically. Chronically anxious, with occasional anorexia and sleep difficulties, she had no friends and was extremely dependent on her family. Patricia developed a very dependent relationship with her therapist and responded well to a supportive therapeutic approach.

A preprodromal episode (an episode not requiring immediate introduction of antipsychotic medication according to the study protocol) was declared following the patient's being terminated from a vocational training program. She requested a therapy session and presented with complaints of increased anxiety and restlessness. She was unable to sit still. There was a decrease in sleep, from 8 to 5 hours per night, and a decrease in appetite. After supportive therapy sessions for one week, the symptoms disappeared. The patient had a similar experience when her mother went out of town for a week. She complained of continuous anxiety for two days with nausea and a decrease in appetite as well as sleep difficulties. Her hygiene was poor and she expressed a fear that the therapist might abandon her. During both episodes, she was given lorazepam 1 mg t.i.d. in addition to supportive counseling. These symptoms also lasted only one week.

Comment Both of these episodes of symptom elevation resolved without the introduction of major tranquilizers in a schizophrenic patient. This underscores the importance of the therapist being able to relate to the patient, knowing the patient's typical reaction to stress and understanding the patient's underlying personality. This individual was a chronically anxious, dependent, somewhat hysterical individual, who was subject to mini-episodes which were not precursors of the relapse process.

Vignette 4. Patient with early symptoms of hostility and paranoia

Dorothy R. is a 53-year-old white female with a diagnosis of Chronic Paranoid Schizophrenia. She had three hospitalizations prior to entry into the study. Symptomatology leading up to the last hospitalization was as follows: auditory hallucinations that had become increasingly negative and hostile in the course of the previous three months. The patient believed that the voices she heard were those of 'aliens or little people such as ET', invisible neighbors who had recently moved into the apartment next door, who were telling her that she was bad and shouldn't be allowed in the neighborhood. According to her daughter, Dorothy scoured her apartment with huge quantities of antiseptics to get rid of germs left by the neighbors. Just prior to her admission, she called the police saying the neighbors were sick and needed help, and she physically attacked her daughter, causing some scratches and contusions. Dorothy was hospitalized for three weeks, and followed while she stabilized for the next six months before entering the study. According to her daughters, the patient at baseline was a somewhat withdrawn irritable individual who, for the past six years, often had feelings of paranoia, and who would talk to herself occasionally.

Shortly after her entry into the study, the patient became anxious following a family argument, and over preparations for a bridal shower she was giving for one of her daughters. The daughter contacted the therapist, describing Dorothy as increasingly hostile and argumentative, and talking to herself more than usual. She was unable to convince the patient to see the therapist, and when the latter initiated a call to Dorothy, the patient angrily hung up, accusing both the therapist and the doctor of not caring about her. Since she refused all contact with the study staff, the family was encouraged to bring Dorothy to the Emergency Room.

Three weeks after entry into the study, the patient was hospitalized. She reported receiving messages from the Virgin Mary, and the ability to communicate directly with ET. She also admitted that she had stopped taking her study medications two weeks before.

The patient recompensated after eight days in the hospital. Her study medications were switched to an equivalent dose of fluphenazine decanoate, and she resumed study participation and the double-blind study medications within eight weeks. Dorothy completed the remaining two years in the study without any further problems.

Comment This case demonstrates the problem with compliance in a patient who becomes hostile, paranoid and negativistic very early in an episode. Such patients typically have full-blown psychotic episodes, even when prodromal symptoms are recognized, because they refuse treatment.

Vignette 5. Prodromal episode followed by a psychotic episode induced by substance abuse

Constance S., diagnosed as Chronic Undifferentiated Schizophrenic, is a 31-year-old black female, with a history of two psychiatric hospitalizations. The first occurred following the birth of her son. She became increasingly withdrawn for a period of several weeks, experienced decreased appetite, decreased sleep, and paranoid delusions ('Someone is tapping the telephone and trying to track me down'). Her auditory hallucinations included voices which threatened her with physical harm.

During the study, a prodromal episode began when the patient began to experience dysphoric symptoms such as feeling very tense and sad, loss of appetite and insomnia. She was tearful in a therapy session and described mounting tension with her stepfather. 'He tells other people that I am crazy and that I have been sick.' She denied any psychotic symptoms. She continued to have counseling sessions and was put on lorazepam 1 mg b.i.d. About a month later, she broke up with her boyfriend.

After a week, her therapist made a home visit, and found the patient depressed with decreased appetite and increased restlessness. The parents asked Constance to move out of the house, stating that she was too difficult to live with. The patient agreed to look for an appartment within two weeks. She seemed to be improving and stated that she had resumed her relationship with her boyfriend. Her symptomatology had returned to baseline. However, about one week later, the patient presented for a scheduled session in an acute psychotic state with paranoid delusions that people wanted to hurt her and gross thought disorganization. She said that she felt that she was a dog or a cat and that people were watching her on the street and would try to harm her. Inappropriately silly, she laughed frequently throughout the session. She was religiously preoccupied and stated that she was receiving biblical messages from the television and radio. She admitted to cocaine use for several days before this episode occurred. Antipsychotic medication was initiated and continued until the symptoms abated three weeks later.

Comment Cocaine and other illicit street drugs can rapidly precipitate florid acute psychotic symptomatology in vulnerable schizophrenic patients without the prior appearance of nonpsychotic dysphoric symptoms.

Stress and relapse

As stated previously, it is postulated that schizophrenic individuals are more vulnerable to life stressors than are normal individuals (4, 5). Various events, both pleasant (having a birthday party, or being promoted in a job), and unpleasant (the illness or death of a close relative or a demotion in a job), have been identified as stressful. All individuals have to cope with such stresses during their lifetimes, but patients with schizophrenia seem to have more difficulty in handling them. In an investigation of the frequency of occurrence of certain life events during the few weeks immediately preceding the onset of acute relapse in schizophrenia, Brown and Birley (19) found a marked increase in such events in schizophrenic patients compared to control groups. The association between the events and relapse did not diminish, even after the authors excluded events that could have been the result rather than the cause of a recrudescence of symptoms. In a retrospective study (8), most patients questioned weeks or months after a relapse were not able to identify particular events that contributed to the recurrence of acute symptoms. However, the great majority of patients interviewed during a prodromal phase were able to identify specific events which occurred before the onset of the episode. When the number of life events reported prior to an episode of illness was compared with the number reported at routine cross-sectional evaluations conducted every six months over a two-year period, there were significantly more life events which occurred prior to prodromal episodes (16). When patients begin to show signs of early relapse, clinicians should carefully question the patient and family members about possible precipitants. Once a precipitant is identified, the clinician can usually provide more effective crisis therapy, since he knows more about the patient's current life situation.

Other types of stressors that have been identified as being related to relapse include family factors and pressures from therapists. Family stress is discussed in other chapters of this volume. Hogarty and Goldberg (20) found that overly ambitious therapists might hasten or precipitate relapse. They found that symptomatic schizophrenic patients who were not on medication were more likely to relapse if they had Major Role Therapy (a type of social casework) compared to non-medicated patients who had no psychosocial treatment. They postulated that the patient-therapist interaction was a stressful one and patients were particularly vulnerable when not protected by antipsychotic medication. Similarly, a study by Linn et al. (21) of day hospital programs demonstrated that patients had less favorable outcomes in day hospitals which had high patient turnover rates and a good deal of individual and group therapy as compared to those programs which had lower turnover rates and an emphasis on vocational therapies. In the Linn study, the investigators believed that day hospitals with less favorable outcomes were those which unintentionally caused more stress on the patients. Therapists must be particularly sensitive to a patient's strengths and weaknesses and be neither too demanding nor too pessimistic in expectations for improved functioning. Both overstimulation and understimulation are harmful for schizophrenic patients.

Clinical issues

Creer and Wing (22) in England conducted a survey of 80 relatives of schizophrenic patients which revealed that virtually none of the relatives had received any sensible advice about the nature of the condition, about how to supervise medication, about the likely outcome of treatment or about how best to respond to disturbed or disturbing behavior. They found this to be in sharp contrast with management of chronic physical illnesses. Usually, when a family member has a chronic physical disability such as paraplegia or renal failure, management is worked out in detail and patients and relatives are taught to predict and prevent many problems and know what to do in time of crisis. Since the publication of their paper in 1974, there has been an improvement in therapeutic approaches to patients and families.

The basic principle used in treating a patient and family should be that treatment is a collaborative effort. When a psychiatrist evaluates a newly referred schizophrenic patient, he should ask the patient what he knows about his own prodromal symptoms, and whether there is a specific pattern that occurs prior to relapse. Do episodes occur at special times of the year, such as birthdays or the anniversary of the death of a loved one? Are they usually in response to specific life events such as beginning school or school examinations? What is the frequency of such episodes, and what does the patient do when these symptoms appear? The same questions should be asked of family members regarding the patient's prior episodes. Then, the therapist whould educate both patients and families about the typical prodromal symptoms and should record on the patient's chart any particular idiosyncratic symptoms of relapse reported by the patient or family members. For example, a patient's family might say that he stays in his room when an episode is beginning, or that she puts on too much cosmetic makeup when the episode is starting to manifest itself. These particular idiosyncratic clues can be very helpful. Patients and family members should be able to notify a therapeutic team as soon as early symptoms appear.

In the intermittent drug study (16) patients are seen weekly in groups to facilitate monitoring of their clinical status, and families are invited to attend monthly family groups. At the beginning of each group session, patients fill out a brief questionnaire about any changes in their symptomatology or role functioning during the previous week. This has been found to be helpful, because some patients do not actively participate verbally in the group, but they do report increased symptoms on the questionnaire. If necessary, after the session, the therapist can meet with the patient individually to discuss the problems. The groups are basically supportive in nature and attempt to provide a social network for these isolated individuals. They are non-threatening, non-demanding, and often focus on particular everyday problems. A sharing of feelings and information is encouraged. In order to increase a sense of comfort and involvement, coffee and cake are served, and each week a particular patient is designated to bring the cake. At times, there is role playing and modeling using a social skills training approach. The groups provide a cost effective way of monitoring patients on a weekly basis, and many patients benefit from the psychosocial treatment.

Coping strategies

A major therapeutic goal is to help patients develop more effective coping mechanisms to deal with the onset of early symptoms of relapse. In a study by McCandless-Glimcher et al. (13), patients were questioned about their ways of coping with the onset of prodromal symptoms. Those who recognized that they were getting worse reported changes in their behaviors which were then categorized into three groups by the investigators. The first group consisted of behaviors related to self-treatment, such as self-medicating, engaging in some diversionary activity or attempting to ignore the symptoms. The second group of behaviors involved seeking assistance from a mental health professional or mental health agency, and the third group consisted of behaviors involving both self-treatment and seeking assistance.

In the author's experience, it is often helpful for patients to become aware of life events that are stressful to them and then to be helped to cope more effectively with these stressful events. A structured life events questionnaire is useful when a patient develops prodromal symptoms, especially when he says that nothing has happened recently which could have upset him. When asked about specific categories of life events, patients often recall something that has happened which they did not associate with the onset of symptoms. A patient might say, 'well, this happened but it did not upset me'. As is well known, many schizophrenic patients use the psychological defense mechanism of denial to a great extent, not only denial of illness but also denial of any unpleasant emotional impact of a stressful life event. Patients need to be made aware that certain life situations may be too stressful for them and that one effective way of handling them might be partial withdrawal. As a matter of fact, at the beginning of a prodromal episode, many patients automatically use protective withdrawal, which in itself may be therapeutic because it can act to reduce excessive stimulation on the patient at a time when he is most vulnerable. Of course, withdrawal in the extreme becomes pathological and needs to be dealt with in treatment. Patients should be taught that taking more medication is usually helpful when prodromal symptoms appear because it can help to maintain their stability. Some patients have the insight, judgment and intelligence to regulate their own medication. In a study conducted by Thurm and Haefner (23), besides asking for help, patients also reported some intrapsychic coping mechanisms when prodromal symptoms or early schizophrenic symptoms occurred. These mechanisms were mainly reality testing and distancing from psychotic thoughts and experiences by rational control and internal dialogue. When experiencing the idea of reference that car license plates had suddenly assumed a personal significance, one female patient told herself that it was logically impossible, that the plates had never meant anything to her before and that she must have misinterpreted them. Other strategies concerned conscious efforts not to be influenced by hallucinatory voices but to ignore them or to argue with them.

As part of ongoing treatment when patients are not in episodes, their coping defenses can be strengthened to include the development of an observing ego, enabling patients to distance themselves emotionally from psychotic experiences. One can utilize an educational approach with patients who have a history of experiencing referential ideas early in episodes, such as the patient mentioned above. A second example, a patient who attached special significance to another woman in her office wearing red when she was wearing a red dress, was taught that this was a warning signal of an impending episode. She learned that such phenomena were symptoms of her illness and occurred when she was starting to develop early signs of relapse. It was emphasized that when she recognized these symptoms she should notify her psychiatrist. In addition, there was an attempt to find out whether there was any relationship to some recent stressful life event which she was not dealing with effectively, leading to the appearance of early psychotic symptomatology. If patients can learn to connect the development of prodromal symptomatology with real life events, they can start to learn how to deal with these events in a more effective manner, rather than totally focusing on the symptoms as if they were the source of their emotional disturbance. As stated above, many schizophrenic patients have the capacity to deny the emotional impact of a particular life stressor, whether it be a relationship with another person, a problem in the family, or an event, and because of this denial, it is often difficult to deal therapeutically with the actual stressor causing them difficulty. For example, a patient who was living at home with his parents reported that his father started to yell at him because he hadn't worked in two years and accused him of being lazy, not doing anything around the house and not looking for a job. When asked for his response, the patient said, 'It didn't bother me at all; I felt perfectly fine. He has a right to expect me to work'. For the following three nights he had trouble sleeping, was very tense and anxious, and began to have feelings that people were looking at him and talking about him. A competent therapist would provide reassurance and support and increase medication to control the developing symptomotology and later when the patient was stabilized, help him to deal with his feelings about his father's criticism more directly. The therapeutic task during a prodromal episode is to contain it through increased medication, support, and reassurance. Depending on the circumstances and the patient's ego strengths, examination of the impact and meaning of stressful life events may be touched upon as the episode is resolving or after it has been resolved. The primary goal of treatment during an episode is to help the patient recover and return to baseline. As therapy continues, stressful experiences can be reviewed while the patient is in a stable state, hopefully enabling the patient to be more effective when such events occur in the future.

Of course, this clinical example illustrates the importance of working with all families of schizophrenic patients, not only because their interactions might be stressful for the patient but also because families bear a great deal of burden living with a schizophrenic patient, and they need support, education, and guidance in coping with this difficult situation. In the intermittent drug study, families are involved in the treatment process from the very beginning. Psychoeducation and support are provided and after several individual meetings, family members are invited to attend multi-family groups where they can share their experiences with others. Family members have been found to be very helpful in the collaborative process of managing the patient, both in calling attention to early prodromal symptoms and during the prodromal episodes themselves.

Families have participated enthusiastically in the optional family groups. We believe that their regular attendance is due to the satisfaction they derive from the educational, social, and supportive aspects of the meetings. Families have a positive sense that they are collaborators with the clinical staff in managing problems relating to the patient's illness. Many patients and family members have stated spontaneously that gaining information about the illness, especially about prodromal symptoms and knowing that they can turn to us for help when they recognize the beginning of an episode has dispelled a feeling of powerlessness and helplessness. Prior to this program, they felt that the course of the patient's illness was out of their control. In other words, they were unable to predict decompensation in the patient, or to do very much about it. Now they do have a positive feeling that they can affect the course of the illness and help prevent relapse and re-hospitalization. For them, the locus of control has shiften from an external one to an internal locus of control which gives them some sense of mastery.

Crisis strategies

Whenever a patient or family members report prodromal symptoms or exacerbations of illness, it is incumbent upon the therapist to see the patient and family as soon as possible, to evaluate the clinical status of the patient, and institute treatment. Therapeutic techniques include reassurance, support, reality testing, functioning as an auxiliary ego to help the patient attempt to deal effectively with his symptomatology, and reinforcing positive defenses and coping skills in the patient. Family members should receive support, reassurance and, if possible, some understanding of the situation. Antipsychotic medication should be increased according to the clinical needs of the patient. Patients should be seen frequently and if necessary, home visits should be made, especially if patients become uncooperative. Such patients' episodes often progress into full relapse unless vigorous attempts to engage them in treatment, including the use of antipsychotic medication, are attempted. Families can often be of great assistance in helping to enlist the cooperation of non-insightful, paranoid patients who refuse treatment.

Conclusion

More research is needed to refine and improve our techniques of early recognition of relapse and treatment strategies to prevent full relapse. However, much is already known. The principles of treatment which have been discussed in this chapter, emphasizing active collaboration of clinicians with patients and their families, psychoeducational approaches and rapid intervention during incipient stages of relapse, should be very effective. This should lead to a lessening of the severe morbidity associated with acute psychotic episodes, including the likelihood of hospitalizaton, thereby reducing the pain and suffering experienced by both patients and family members.

ACKNOWLEDGEMENTS

The author wishes to express his thanks for the editorial assistance of Jacqueline Simon, and the vignettes by Patricia Smith and Eileen Trigoboff.

REFERENCES

1. Bleuler ME (1978) The long-term course of schizophrenic psychoses. In: Wynne L, Cromwell RL, Matthysse S (Eds), *The Nature of Schizophrenia,* pp. 631–651. Wiley, New York.
2. Ciompi L (1980) The natural history of schizophrenia in the long run. *Br. J. Psychiatry, 136,* 413.
3. Huber G, Gross G, Schuttler R, Linz M (1980) Longitudinal studies of schizophrenic patients. *Schizophr. Bull., 6,* 592.
4. Zubin J, Spring B (1977) A new view of schizophrenia. *J. Abnorm. Psychol., 86,* 103.
5. Liberman RP (1982) Social factors in schizophrenia. In: Grinspoon L (Ed), *Psychiatry 1982: Annual Review.* American Psychiatric Press, Washington, DC.
6. Docherty JP, van Kammen DP, Siris SG, Marder SR (1978) Stages of schizophrenic psychosis. *Am. J. Psychiatry, 135,* 420.
7. Donlon PT, Blacker KH (1975) Clinical recognition of early schizophrenic decompensation. *Dis. Nerv. Syst., 36,* 323.
8. Herz MI, Melville C (1980) Relapse in schizophrenia. *Am. J. Psychiatry, 137,* 801.
9. Spitzer RL, Endicott J, Cohen MS (1968) *Psychiatric Status Schedule.* Evaluation Unit, Biometrics Research. New York State Department of Mental Hygiene, New York.
10. Spitzer RL, Endicott J, Robins E (1975) *Research Diagnostic Criteria,* 2nd ed. New York State Psychiatric Institute, New York.
11. Hogarty GE, Goldberg C, Collaborative Study Group (1973) Drugs and sociotherapy in aftercare of schizophrenia patients. *Arch. Gen. Psychiatry, 28,* 54.
12. Astrachan BM, Brauer L, Harrow M, Schwartz C (1974) Systematic outcome in schizophrenia. *Arch. Gen. Psychiatry, 31,* 155.
13. McCandless-Glimcher L, McKnight S, Hamera E, Smith BL, Peterson KA, Plumblee

AA (1986) Use of symptoms by schizophrenics to monitor and regulate their illness. *Hosp. Community Psychiatry, 37,* 929.
14. Carpenter WT, Heinrichs DW (1983) Early intervention, time-limited, targeted pharmacology of schizophrenia. *Schizophr. Bull., 9,* 533.
15. Heinrichs DW, Carpenter Jr. WT (1985) Prospective study of prodromal symptoms in schizophrenic relapse. *Am. J. Psychiatry, 142,* 371.
16. Herz MI, Glazer W, Mostert M, Sheard M, Finn J (1988) Intermittent medication in schizophrenia: one year results (Symposium on long-term treatment issues in schizophrenia). *Proceedings of the American Psychiatric Association Annual Meeting,* Montreal, Quebec, Canada. American Psychiatric Association, Washington, DC.
17. Jolley AG, Hirsch SR (1989) Brief intermittent neuroleptic prophylaxis for stable schizophrenic outpatients. *Schizophr. Res., 2,* 508.
18. Heinrichs DW, Cohen BP, Carpenter WT (1985) Early insight and the management of schizophrenic decompensation. *J. Nerv. Ment. Dis., 173,* 133.
19. Brown GW, Birley JLT, Wing JK (1972) Influence of family life on the course of schizophrenic disorders: a replication. *Br. J. Psychiatry, 121,* 241.
20. Hogarty GE, Goldberg SC, Schooler NR, Collaborative Study Group (1974) Drugs and sociotherapy in the aftercare of schizophrenic patients, III. Adjustment of non-relapsed patients. *Arch. Gen. Psychiatry, 31,* 609.
21. Linn M, Caffey EM, Klett CJ, Hogarty GE, Lamb HR (1979) Day treatment and psychotropic drugs in the aftercare of schizophrenic patients. *Arch. Gen. Psychiatry, 36,* 1055.
22. Creer C, Wing JK (1974) *Schizophrenia at Home.* National Schizophrenia Fellowship, London.
23. Thurm I, Haefner H (1987) Perceived vulnerability, relapse risk and coping in schizophrenia. *Eur. Arch. Psychiatry Neurol. Sci., 237,* 46.

CHAPTER 3

Role of medication in psychosocial treatment

NINA R. SCHOOLER AND SAMUEL J. KEITH

Beliefs regarding the relationship of medication to psychosocial treatments in schizophrenia have guided the design of research regarding these two broad treatment modalities virtually since the introduction of neuroleptic medications into the treatment armamentarium over a generation ago. As a result, the data available regarding their relationship is limited, since very little research has been conducted that allows for the examination of additive or interactive effects of the two treatment modalities.

Perhaps the most common current belief, one often tacitly accepted by pharmaceutical advertisements, is that medication makes patients more receptive to psychotherapeutic efforts. According to this model, medication, essential for the control of symptoms, enables patients to participate in psychotherapy. At one time, formal psychotherapy was seen as an essential element in the treatment of schizophrenia. In the landmark study by Grinspoon and colleagues (1) conducted between 1961 and 1968, it was considered unethical to 'withhold' psychotherapy from patients. Therefore, all patients received psychotherapy throughout the two-year study treatment period. Antipsychotic medication was experimentally introduced periodically during that time. In contrast, Cole (2) commenting on the investigation by May and colleagues (3) noted that the conclusive results of that study regarding the efficacy of antipsychotic medication made it unlikely that future research would include experimental groups that did not receive medication. More recently, as described in Chapter 4 of this volume, Stanton and Gunderson's (4, 11) study comparing two forms of individual psychotherapy involved expectation of medication prescription for a considerable length of time 'probably well into the post-hospitalization phase of treatment' (4, p. 534) and the review of medication prescription by a senior consultant. In point of fact, the same J.O. Cole whom we cited above was the senior consultant for this study. Extent of use of medication was taken as a measure of psychotherapy effectiveness.

Optimally, a model of the role of medication and psychosocial treatment in schizophrenia needs to accommodate a number of dimensions in addition to medication and psychosocial treatment: diagnosis, e.g., schizophrenia vs. schizophreniform; symptomatology, e.g., negative vs. positive symptoms; stage of treatment, e.g., acute vs. chronic or maintenance; specific medication, e.g., neuroleptic, antidepressant, lithium; specific psychosocial treatment, e.g., individual psychotherapy, behavioral treatment, family treatment. Clearly, adequate

Handbook of Schizophrenia, Volume 4: Psychosocial Treatment of Schizophrenia.
M.I. Herz, S.J. Keith and J.P. Docherty, editors.

data are not available to complete such a complex matrix; we cannot even assess the role of antipsychotic medications in the simplest tabulation that arrays the classes of psychosocial treatments discussed in the chapters of this volume. Furthermore, in order to assess the independent effects of medication and psychosocial treatments, study designs must include comparison treatments for both modalities, and such designs have rarely been implemented. In part, this is because of the expectations in the field regarding appropriate treatments for study, but also because such studies are difficult to design and to carry out.

Our goal in this chapter is to integrate the evidence regarding the role of medication in psychosocial treatments based on research and clinical reports. In the remainder of this chapter we will do the following: (a) briefly review data regarding the efficacy of antipsychotic medication in the treatment of schizophrenia at various stages of the disorder; (b) examine the evidence regarding the role of medication in the context of specific psychosocial treatments; individual treatment or psychotherapy, family treatment, behavioral therapies and group therapy. We will conclude by offering a model for the relationship of antipsychotic medication *vis-a-vis* psychosocial treatments of schizophrenia, and suggest some strategies for testing that model.

EFFICACY OF ANTIPSYCHOTIC MEDICATION IN THE TREATMENT OF SCHIZOPHRENIA

Numerous reviews during the past quarter century have examined the efficacy of antipsychotic medication in the treatment of schizophrenia. The following points are generally accepted:

(a) Currently marketed antipsychotic drugs, despite substantial variability of chemical structure, are distinguishable in terms of side-effects but not of efficacy.
(b) Antipsychotic medication is effective in reducing acute symptoms of schizophrenia in the majority of patients, including so-called negative symptoms seen in the context of florid psychotic symptoms.
(c) Medications also serve to prevent relapse and symptom exacerbation in remitted patients, although there are patients for whom medication may not be needed continuously.
(d) The dosage requirements for relapse prevention may be substantially lower than that needed for treatment of acute symptomatology.
(e) Non-compliance with medication can contribute to relapse, but relapse occurs even in the presence of guaranteed compliance through the use of injectable medication.
(f) Higher dosages of medication do not provide increased benefit, but do carry additional side-effect burdens. Recent evidence suggests that dosage reduction from currently accepted standards can be achieved without harm in both acute and maintenance treatment.

EFFICACY OF ANTIPSYCHOTIC MEDICATIONS IN RELATION TO PSYCHOSOCIAL TREATMENTS

As we have suggested above, little of the available research literature provides conclusive information regarding the role of medication in relationship to specific psychosocial treatments. The most desirable research design to provide such information is presented in Table 1. As can be seen from this table, four groups are required: a group that receives the psychosocial treatment of interest alone (cell 2); a group that receives the medication treatment alone (cell 3); a group that receives both the psychosocial and medication treatments (cell 1); and a group that receives neither (cell 4). Such a design allows the evaluation of the following hypotheses:

(a) The experimental medication treatment is better (or worse) than the control medication treatment, regardless of which psychosocial treatment patients receive. In analysis of variance terms this is a main effect of medication – cells 1 and 3 are compared with cells 2 and 4.

(b) The experimental psychosocial treatment is better (or worse) than the control psychosocial treatment, regardless of which medication treatment patients receive. This is a main effect of psychosocial treatment – cells 1 and 2 are compared to cells 3 and 4.

(c) The effects of the psychosocial treatment depend on which of the medication treatments a patient receives. There are a number of possible forms that such an interaction can take. For example, the experimental psychosocial treatment may be better than the control but only if patients also receive the experimental medication treatment. Cell 1 is better than cell 3, but there is no difference between cells 2 and 4.

(d) The effects of the medication depend on which of the psychosocial treatments a patient receives. The statistical test for this interaction is the same as for hypotheses framed in terms of the psychosocial treatment, but the focus and interpretation are different. For example, the experimental medication treatment may only be better than the control if patients receive the experimental psychosocial treatment. Cell 1 is better than cell 2, but there is no difference between cells 3 and 4.

Incomplete designs can obviously only test some of the kinds of hypotheses outlined. A common incomplete design is one in which all subjects receive standardized medication and an experimental psychosocial treatment is compared to 'no treatment' or to an established psychosocial regimen. The only hypothesis that such

TABLE 1 *Study design for evaluation of medication and psychosocial treatment*

Psychosocial Treatment	Medication Treatment	
	Experimental	Control
Experimental	1	2
Control	3	4

a design can test is that the psychosocial treatment combined with medication is better than the medication alone. Most importantly for the topic under review in this chapter, such designs may not be very informative about the role of medication in psychosocial treatment. Since medication is held constant, the ability to detect a relationship of medication to the psychosocial treatment is eliminated. More informative incomplete designs, at least with respect to the role of medication in psychosocial treatment, are those that compare psychosocial treatments in which medication is allowed to vary so that medication use can be assessed as an outcome.

In the rest of this section we will review studies that address the role of medication in psychosocial treatment. In identifying studies for consideration, we have relied heavily on prior reviews, in particular our own (5 – 8). However, in this review we emphasize studies that meet the following criteria:

(a) Patients are diagnosed as schizophrenic, or schizophrenic patient subgroups can be distinguished.
(b) One of the psychosocial treatments that we are concerned with (individual treatment or psychotherapy; behavioral therapy; family treatment; group therapy) is identified and described.
(c) Treatment with antipsychotic medication is described beyond statements that patients were treated as needed or that all patients were receiving medication.
(d) There are experimental treatment conditions that allow: (i) comparison of psychosocial treatments with medication use standardized or evaluated; (ii) comparison between psychosocial and medication treatments; or (iii) comparison of the additive and interactive effects of medication and psychosocial treatment because both medication and psychosocial treatments are experimentally controlled.
(e) Assignment to treatment is random.

Individual treatment: psychotherapy

In Table 2 we have listed studies that provide data regarding the relationship of medication to individual treatment. Although not the focus of this chapter, it should be clear that the term psychotherapy encompasses a very broad range of treatment approaches. Three of the studies (9, 3, 10) include groups that received medication alone and psychotherapy alone. The May study (3) also included a group that received the same psychotherapy and medication; Karon and VandenBos (9) included a group receiving psychotherapy and medication, but the psychotherapy was different from that provided to the group that did not receive medication. The Stanton and Gunderson (4, 11) study did not include groups receiving either medication or psychotherapy alone, but compared two forms of psychotherapy in patients, all of whom received medication. Rogers and his colleagues (10) compared a group receiving usual hospital care (including medication) with one that received psychotherapy and for whom receipt of medication represented a protocol violation, but no details regarding drug treatment are provided. Grinspoon, Ewalt and Shader (1) compared a group that received psychotherapy and medication to one that received psychotherapy alone. Of all these studies, only the one by Grinspoon, Ewalt and Shader employed placebos for medication.

TABLE 2 *Studies of individual treatment in relation to medication*

Study (1st Author)	Date	Medication (Dosage)	Design	Setting	N	Duration
May	1969	Trifluoperazine	5 Groups	Inpatient	228	Variable
			Ther alone			
			Milieu, ECT			
		(max. 4 – 120 mg/day)	Ther + med			
		(max. 10 – 120 mg/day)	Med alone			
Grinspoon	1972	Thioridazine	2 Groups	Inpatient	20	2 years
		(300 – 1000 mg/day)	Ther + med			
			Ther alone			
Hogarty	1974	Chlorpromazine	4 Groups	Outpatient	374	2 years
		(270 ± 145 mg/day)	MRT + med			
			MRT + Pbo			
		(270 ± 145 mg/day)	Med alone			
			Pbo alone			
Hogarty	1979	Fluphenazine	4 Groups	Outpatient	105	2 years
		(10.8 mg/day)	MRT + oral			
			Oral alone			
		(depot 39.1 mg/ 2 weeks	MRT + depot			
			Depot alone			
Karon	1981	Chlorpromazine	3 Groups	In and out	33	20 months
		(equivalents)	Ther alone			
		(150 – 600 mg/day)	Ther + med			
		(100 – 1400 mg/day)	Med/hosp			
Stanton	1984	Antipsychotics	2 Groups	In and out	95	2 years
		Rcd 264 days	EIO			
		Rcd 264 days	RAS			

The studies of individual treatment listed in Table 2 by Hogarty and his colleagues (12 – 14) are not strictly speaking individual psychotherapy, but fit that rubric better than the other categories of psychosocial treatment under review. Major Role Therapy (MRT), so named by the investigators, is an individually focused interpersonal intervention that targets role performance and personal adjustment. Medication in the 1974 study was placebo-controlled. Furthermore, these studies and the May study are the only ones in this group that incorporate the full design capable of evaluating both additive and interactive effects of medication and individual treatment.

Integrating the results of these studies is a formidable task. As can be seen from Table 2, the studies vary greatly in design and in the attention provided to issues of medication. The most recent, by Stanton and Gunderson (4, 11), is disappointing in the limited amount of information regarding medication (11). The only information provided is the number of days patients received antipsychotic medication and lithium in the first and second years. There is no information regarding dosage. The only difference reported is that patients receiving reality-adaptive, supportive (RAS) therapy received lithium significantly more of the time (34% in the second year) than patients who received exploratory, insight-oriented (EIO) therapy (12% of the time). Patients received antipsychotic medication more than 70% of the time in the first year and almost 60% of the time in the second year, but there were no differences between the groups. Lithium was used far more sparingly.

The data from the May study (3) support the conclusion that the groups that received medication were significantly 'better' than those not receiving medication; the psychotherapy groups were not better than those not receiving psychotherapy (the medication alone and milieu groups). The only reported interaction indicated that, among patients who received psychotherapy, costs were reduced during the first year if they also received medication, suggesting a positive role for medication. In terms of the question being addressed here, it appears that medication did provide some advantage to delivery of psychotherapy, i.e., the enabling model can be supported as far as cost is concerned. But since there was no therapeutic advantage to psychotherapy, this is a very limited statement.

The Hogarty studies (12 – 14) support an interaction between medication and individual treatment that is time-dependent. In the 1974 study, medication was significantly more effective than placebo in forestalling relapse, but there were no general effects of the individual therapy on relapse either overall or differentially between medication and placebo. However, there was an interaction, suggesting that medication had an enabling effect on the response to MRT. Among patients who did not relapse before 18 months of treatment (clearly a selected group) those treated with medication in addition to MRT showed better adjustment than those treated with MRT and placebo. Indeed, patients treated with MRT and placebo fared less well in terms of psychopathology and adjustment than placebo-treated patients who received minimal attention. In the 1979 study, which utilized a similar individual treatment in the context of guaranteed injectable or oral medication, there was a trend indicating that patients who received individual treatment were less likely to relapse in the second year if they also received guaranteed injectable medication, a further example of the possible enabling effect of medication on psychological treatment.

The design of the Grinspoon studies allows for a direct evaluation of the hypothesis that medication is either enabling or hindering in psychotherapy. In the two studies reported, patients all received psychotherapy: for two years in the case of the chronic population; for eight weeks in the case of the acutely ill patients. Patients were randomly assigned to medication or placebo groups. Among the chronically ill patients there was significantly greater improvement among the medication-treated group; among the acutely ill patients, significantly greater improvement was seen among patients treated with thioridazine than placebo, but not between haloperidol and placebo. In both these studies, there are virtually no patients who were removed from the placebo groups early (in contrast to other antipsychotic medication-placebo studies), and the authors suggest that this is a function of the psychotherapy. Since there is no control group for psychotherapy, this point remains speculative.

The Karon study apparently presents a quite different picture from the studies described above. First, it should be noted that this study emphasizes the importance of therapist training, and the investigators evaluate outcome separately, within condition for supervisors and trainees. If we ignore this distinction and simply focus on the three treatment groups, hospital treatment with medication, analytic psychotherapy alone and ego-analytic therapy with adjunctive medication, a picture more consistent with other studies emerges. As shown in Table 3, when we ignore therapist experience, it appears that for number of days hospitalized, the mean values consistently favor the group that received psychotherapy and medications. For the Clinical Status Interview (CSI), scores cannot be compared over time but only at a given evaluation because they 'have an arbitrary zero point' (9, p. 423). At six months the medication and psychotherapy group is best, at 12 months there are no apparent differences among the groups, and at 20 months the psychotherapy alone group has the best scores. On balance, it appears that the differences among the groups in this study provide support for our conclusion that the role of medication in individual treatment is to facilitate such treatment.

Family treatment

Table 4 presents studies that include data that allow the examination of family treatment in relation to medication in schizophrenia. As can be seen from this table, this has been an active area of research during the last decade and provides some of the most definitive data available with respect to the relationship of medication to psychosocial treatments. One of the studies includes controls for both modalities and allows analysis of both additive and interactive effects (15); in one study medication was kept relatively constant and compliance with medication was used as a control (16), so that the additive effects of family treatment could be assessed; one study excluded non-medication-compliant patients from analysis (17, 18); and in one study medication prescription was independent of the delivery of

TABLE 3 *Karon and VandenBos study hospitalization and clinical status interview (CSI)*[a]

Assessment	Treatment group					
	Hospital/medication		Therapy alone		Therapy/medication	
	Days hosp.	CSI	Days hosp.	CSI	Days hosp.	CSI
6 months	60	0.93	79	0.80	34	1.03
12 months	93	0.92	124	1.08	39	1.06
20 months	114	0.89	126	1.22	43	0.94

[a] Although these numbers are calculated precisely from data in Karon and VandenBos (9), since standard deviations are not included, significance testing was not possible.

TABLE 4 *Studies of family treatment in relation to medication*

Study (1st Author)	Date	Medication (Dosage)	Design	Setting	N	Duration (follow-up)
Goldstein	1978	Fpz enanthate	4 Groups	Outpatient	104	6 weeks (6 months)
		(6.25 mg/2 wks)	FT + low dose			
		(25 mg/2 wks)	FT + mod. dose			
		(6.25 mg/2 wks)	Low dose alone			
		(25 mg/2 wks)	Mod. dose alone			
Leff	1982 1985	All on antipsych.	2 Groups	Outpatient	24	9 months (2 years)
		21 Long acting,	Fam. social intervention			
		3 Oral	Routine care			
Falloon	1985	Optimal medication	2 Groups	Outpatient	36	9 months (2 years)
		(mean 245 mg CPZeq)	Family manag.			
		(mean 338 mg CPZeq)	Ind. case manag.			
Hogarty	1986	Fpz decanoate	4 Groups	Outpatient	103	1 year
		Standard dose	Family treatm.			
		Standard dose	Social skills			
		Standard dose	FT + SS			
		Standard dose	Medication alone			

psychosocial treatment, so that use of medication could be treated as a dependent variable (19).

The study by Goldstein and his colleagues (15) is the only one to date to examine a possible interaction of medication and family treatment. Goldstein and his colleagues compared moderate to low-dose fluphenazine enanthate and brief six-week family-oriented crisis intervention or no psychosocial treatment in a 2 × 2 factorial design that represents the full design shown in Table 1. The group receiving moderate dose and family treatment experienced no relapses during the six-week treatment exposure, whereas each of the other three groups experienced some. The low-dose group that did not receive family treatment had the highest relapse rate (24%). Thus, in the acutely ill young schizophrenic patients studied, the results indicated an additive effect of medication and family treatment. Examination of data regarding symptoms supports the picture of medication and family therapy working together in an additive fashion. For example, scores on several factors of the Brief Psychiatric Rating Scale (BPRS) were significantly reduced after six weeks in patients who received therapy as compared to those who did not, but there were no significant interactions with medication. Examination of scores for withdrawal suggests that the difference in favor of therapy was greater when patients received a moderate rather than a low dosage of medication. Finally, examination of data from a six-month follow-up supports the same conclusion. There were no relapses among the patients who had received both the moderate dose and family therapy, and the group with the highest relapse rate (48%) had received the low dose and no family therapy. By six months, however, there is an interactive effect for symptoms, so that the positive effect of therapy on withdrawal is only significant in the moderate dose group.

The study by Hogarty and his colleagues (16) compared family treatment, individual social skills training (SST), the combination of the two psychosocial treatments, and a group that received medication alone. Patients in all groups were maintained on a 'standard' dose of medication, preferably fluphenazine decanoate. Among medication compliant patients approximately 65% were actually maintained on the decanoate, including 82% of the group that received medication only. Results indicate additive effects for the psychosocial treatments beyond the effect of medication. The effect is clearest when the assessment is restricted to the sample of 90 patients defined as 'treatment takers' but a similar pattern, significant for family therapy but not for SST is seen even when only medication compliant patients are included. Forty percent of patients receiving medication alone relapsed in the first year, as did 20% of those receiving either of the psychosocial treatments alone and *none* of those who received both SST and family therapy. The effect of the psychosocial treatments is additive, and in this study, as in the one reported by Goldstein, the positive effect of family treatment cannot be accounted for simply as an enhancement of compliance, since the decreased rate of relapse with family therapy is seen even when analyses are restricted to patients who were medication-compliant.

Falloon and his colleagues (19, 20) compared home-based behavioral family therapy with clinic-based individual, supportive psychotherapy. All patients received 'optimal' dosages of antipsychotic medication prescribed by physicians who were independent (and blind) to the psychosocial treatment assignment (21). Since medication was not experimentally controlled, both compliance with medication and drug dosage were examined as outcome variables. Compliance ratings were not different in the family and individually treated groups. Drug dosage tended to be lower in the family treated group; 245 mg of chlorpromazine or its equivalent per day compared to 338 mg/day for the individually treated cases averaged over the nine months of treatment. The investigators tested for differences in linear trends over time between dosage in the two groups and found a difference that approached significance $P = 0.07$ (21, 20). However, inspection of the data presented in Fig. 1 shows that the family treated group maintained relatively steady dose (means during the nine months varied between 200 and 300 mg per day). In contrast, although the individually treated patients were receiving comparable doses at the start of

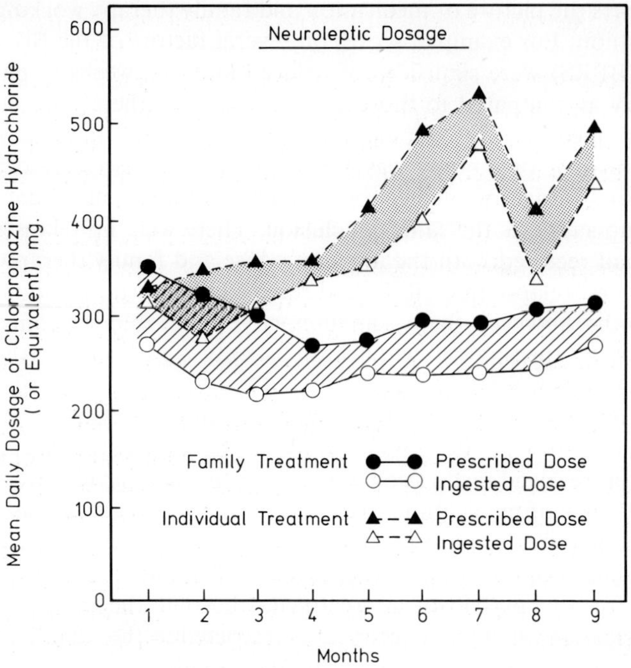

FIG. 1 *Mean daily dosages of prescribed and ingested neuroleptic drugs expressed as chlorpromazine equivalents (20).*

treatment (250 mg per day), dosage in that group increased between the fourth and seventh months to a peak of 500 mg per day and then decreased to a final mean at nine months of 400 mg per day. Thus, a comparison that examined *non-linear* trends might have shown a significant difference favoring the family treated group. In any event, the direction of the difference in dosage between the family and individual groups suggests that family treatment (the more effective psychosocial treatment) is associated with *reduction* of medication rather than increase. This may appear to be different from the additive effects we have described in both the Goldstein and the Hogarty (15, 16) studies. In this treatment model, when medication is allowed to fluctuate, the less effective psychosocial treatment is associated with increased medication use over time. It should be noted that the doses used by the pharmacotherapists in this study were generally in the low range. Based on their recent review of the literature, Davis and Andriukaitis (22) have concluded that doses less than 300 mg/day chlorpromazine equivalence are not effective either in treatment of acute psychosis or in maintenance treatment and that additional medication beyond 1000 mg/day does not add any further therapeutic benefit. Thus, according to their criteria, medication in the family treated group was, on average, below the threshold for therapeutic effect. It appears that family treatment more than offset the low dose of medication. The family treated group had a more favorable outcome than the individual therapy patients, despite the fact that the former group was below the therapeutic range, suggesting a synergistic effect of the family treatment employed.

The final study in this group was conducted by Leff and his colleagues (17, 18). By design, all patients were maintained on fluphenazine decanoate in order to insure medication compliance (21 of 24 patients were so treated) because the study goal was, as in the work by Hogarty and his colleagues (16), to study the additive effects of family treatment. Patients were then randomly assigned to receive a family oriented package of social interventions or 'routine' clinical care. The social intervention lasted for nine months. Patients were followed and evaluated for a total of two years. By the end of two years, three patients in the control group and two from the experimental group had discontinued medication – a non-compliance rate of 21%. Medication discontinuation in the group receiving the social intervention occurred only after the nine months of treatment; two of the three cases in the control group discontinued medication during the first nine months. The initial report of the nine month assessment (17) had stated that *all* patients in both groups were medication-compliant. The investigators report that comparison of the compliant samples revealed only two differences between experimental and control groups. The social intervention sample was older and had experienced more unemployment before study entry. Moreover, neither of these two characteristics was related to relapse at the two-year follow-up. Because the goal of the study was to examine the additive effects of social intervention, only medication-compliant patients were included in analysis of the two-year follow-up. This was not done for the nine month comparison (17). In Table 5, we have re-analyzed the data from the study presenting the relapse rates for the full sample and for medication-compliant patients only, both at 9 months and at two years. Although we agree with the merits of a design that explicitly tests an additive model, the *post hoc* exclusion of cases assigned to groups without also presenting results based on the full samples does not seem correct to us. As can be seen from Table 5, if all cases are considered, the difference in relapse rate between the groups is no longer significant at two years. Further, it should be noted that one-tailed significance tests were used by the investigators. Our re-analysis also presents significance levels based on one-tailed tests. If more conservative two-tailed significance levels had been used, the only difference in relapse rate to reach the customary 0.05 probability level would have been that among

TABLE 5 *Relapse and medication compliance (17, 18)*

Group	All patients		Medication-compliant	
	9 months N (% rel)	2 years N (% rel)	9 months N (% rel)	2 years N (% rel)
Social intervention	12 (8)	12 (33)	12 (8)	10 (20)
Control	12 (50)	12 (75)	10 (50)	9 (78)
Fisher's exact test				
P value one-tail	0.032	0.09	0.041	0.017

medication-compliant patients at two years.

On balance, the studies of family treatment also support an additive model of the relationship of psychosocial treatment to medication. The data of Falloon et al. (20, 21) are in some ways the strongest, because those results suggest that family treatment can substitute for medication – not only does family treatment improve outcome, it does so with less medication.

Behavioral and social skills training (SST)

The four relevant studies in this area that we have identified are presented in Table 6. Although this is an extremely active area of research, very little of this work is both specific to patients with a diagnosis of schizophrenia and provides data regarding medication administration. Even recent literature is satisfied with statements regarding medication such as: 'psychiatric staff administered neuroleptic medication to all patients in accord with current clinical practice' (23). The conclusions that we are able to draw regarding the relationship of medication to the effectiveness of such treatment approaches will, we hope, encourage investigators either to incorporate experimental control of medication in their studies of social skill acquisition or to investigate the influence of such training on medication use.

The first study presented in Table 6, that by Hersen and colleagues (24), utilized a multiple baseline design with a single case. Phenothiazine treatment and standard ward treatment (including participation in a token economy, group and occupational therapy) were provided. Despite these interventions, seven weeks after admission the patient's clinical condition was described as poor but stable. An individualized intensive social skills program was designed and implemented over a five-week period in which three skills (eye contact, decreasing response latency and making requests) were introduced sequentially. Outcome was assessed by measuring

TABLE 6 *Studies of social skills training (SST) in relation to medication*

Study (1st Author)	Date	Medication (Dosage)	Design	Setting	N	Duration
Hersen	1975	Chlorpromazine, Trifluoperazine	Single Case	Inpatient	1	5 weeks
Paul	1977	Psychotropics 10.7% rcvd 17.9% rcvd 100% rcvd	3 Wards SST Milieu Hosp. control	Inpatient	84	4.5 years
Wallace	1985	Neuroleptics ($\bar{x}$ 350 mg)	2 Groups SST Holistic	Inpatient	28	9 weeks
Hogarty[a]	1986	Fluphenazine	4 Groups	Outpatient	103	1 year

[a] See Table 4

these three parameters, overall assertiveness in training sessions, and initiations of conversation in ongoing group therapy. The outcome data presented for the specific skills in which training was given are less convincing than the data for initiation of conversation in group therapy and outcome during the subsequent follow-up period. For example, although training for requests was not introduced until the fourth week, the number of requests increased during the preceding weeks of training. In the 22-week follow-up period which included discharge on maintenance phenothiazine medication and placement in a job training program, the patient maintained interpersonal gains, improvement in appearance and personal hygiene and was asymptomatic. The authors comment that the patient became 'fond' of the female role model and seemed motivated to please her. Thus, although the authors state that the study supports the advantage of the combination of medication and training, they do not test the assumption that medication was a sine qua non for the progress made.

The study by Paul and Lentz (25) represents perhaps the most ambitious, detailed and extensive study conducted to date of a social reinforcement program. As described elsewhere in this volume, extremely chronic (mean current hospitalization over 14 years) schizophrenic patients were randomly assigned to remain in a State Hospital or to be transferred to either a 'social learning' or 'milieu therapy' ward at a regional mental health center. At the time of randomization, 92% of patients were receiving psychotropic medication. A medication withdrawal study was carried out on the two experimental wards (26). Patients in each ward were either maintained on medication or received placebo. During the first four weeks following withdrawal, bizarre behavior improved significantly more in the placebo group than in the group that remained on medication in both wards. However, by the end of the 17-week withdrawal study, there were no differences between the drug and placebo groups. As stated in an earlier review by one of us,

> 'The data support the conclusion that withdrawal of medication in very chronic non neuroleptic responsive patients does not lead to an increase in psychopathology. . . . the differences . . . suggest at least transient superiority and no indication of greater pathology for the placebo group.' (7, p. 1162).

It must be noted that the study was carried out in wards with newly initiated psychosocial treatment programs.

The comparison of the social learning, milieu therapy and hospital control wards continued for an additional four years. During this time, medication was not controlled but was allowed to vary. The prescribing attitudes of physicians in the two experimental wards was influenced by the results of the withdrawal study just described. Table 7 presents information regarding the use of medication on the two experimental wards as well as for the hospital control ward. Information for the hospital comparison is only available for baseline and after the four and a half years of the study. As can be seen from Table 7, medication use in the experimental wards varied over time, but after the baseline evaluation was never higher than 50%. As described by Paul and Lentz (25), the increase at 18 months was associated with a restriction on the use of 'time out' as a behavior control method. Use of medication

TABLE 7 *Medication use in Paul and Lentz study (25)*

Group	Assessment							
	Baseline		6 months	18 months	36 months	42 months	48 months	56 months
	n	% rcvd	% rcvd	% rcvd	% rcvd	% rcvd	% rcvd	% rcvd
Social learning	28	89.3	89.3	< 50	< 25	25	14	11
Milieu therapy	28	96.4	<50	< 25	< 29	21	18	18
Hospital control	28	89.3	–	–	–	–	–	100

did not differ between the two experimental programs. At several assessment points, receipt of medication was correlated with time asleep during the day for patients on both wards, possibly due to side-effects. There were no significant relationships between receipt of medication and level of functioning in any of the groups at any time during the course of the study. It should be noted that outcome in the social learning ward was significantly better than in the milieu program, particularly in reduction or elimination of extreme bizarre behavior. However, the investigators document clearly that the efficacy of the program depended heavily on tight control of all environmental contingencies. For example, the reduction in allowable 'time out' during the third year from two days to two hours resulted in both a decline in the effectiveness of both treatment approaches and an increase in use of medication described above. Medication per se was not the relevant variable.

Wallace and Liberman (27) also compared two treatment approaches that differed on a number of parameters, the major one being an emphasis on SST or holistic health therapy. The ward on which the study was conducted was designed to provide a 'consistent behavior therapy milieu'. In contrast to the Paul and Lentz study (25), patients were young, newly hospitalized and in relative remission from florid psychotic symptoms. The study involved a nine-week treatment program and a two-year community follow-up. Optimal doses of neuroleptic medication were prescribed by psychiatrists who were apparently blind to psychosocial treatment assignment. Mean dosage was approximately 350 mg per day and did not differ between the two treatment groups. There were no significant differences between the groups in measures of psychopathology, relapse or re-hospitalization. The investigators attribute this to the influence of similar doses of medication given to both groups and limited power due to small sample size (14 patients in each group.)

The final study in this group by Hogarty and his colleagues (16) has already been described in the section on family treatment. As noted, this study examined relapse rates for all patients assigned to treatment as well as for the subgroup of patients who were medication-compliant. When all patients are included, SST significantly reduces relapse rates in an additive fashion – 20% when administered alone, 0% when administered in combination with family treatment, compared to 41% in medication-treated controls. When comparison is limited to medication-compliant patients, the effect of SST is at the trend level (17%, $P < 0.09$). As described above, the effect of family treatment in this study was still significant when analysis was limited to medication-compliant patients.

As we suggested at the beginning of this section, there are few studies that provide data to assess the contribution of medication to the efficacy of SST. In the Hogarty study, restriction of the comparison to medication-compliant patients only reduced the SST group from 20 to 18 patients – one of the non-compliant patients relapsed and one did not. Should the absence of a significant effect among compliant patients only be interpreted to mean that SST exerts its effect by influencing compliance? We think not. Based on the extremely limited data presented here, we would conclude that SST is apparently effective in medication-responsive patients who are receiving medication. It does not appear that SST can be used to reduce the need for medication in these patients, as is suggested by the data from the Falloon study of family treatment. For patients clearly non-responsive to medication (25), SST is more effective than routine hospital treatment, despite the fact that less medication is administered.

Group psychotherapy

Table 8 presents five studies of group psychotherapy (GT) in which data are available to assess either additive or interactive effects of this treatment in relation to medication. As we shall indicate, the only study that provides data regarding interactive effects with medication is the earliest study by Gorham and Pokorny (28). The other studies allow examination of additive effects only or, in the study by Malm (29), the examination of medication use as a dependent variable.

Gorham and his colleagues (28) studied newly hospitalized patients who received thioridazine alone, GT alone and both treatments in combination. Patients who could not complete the full 12-week treatment period were replaced, so the magnitude of the effects reported is probably underestimated. Dosage of thioridazine was increased to 400 mg/day within the first two weeks of treatment and then could be adjusted between 300 and 500 mg/day for the remaining 10 weeks

TABLE 8 *Studies of group therapy (GT) in relation to medication*

Study (1st Author)	Date	Medication (Dosage)	Design	Setting	N	Duration (follow-up)
Gorham	1964	Thioridazine (300 – 500 mg/day)	3 Groups Medication alone GT alone GT + med	Inpatient	150	12 weeks
Borowski	1969	Chlorpromazine (300 – 600 mg/day)	2 Groups med alone med + GT	Not stated	80	2 months
O'Brien	1972	Phenothiazines	2 Groups med + GT med + ind ther	Outpatient	100	24 months
Claghorn	1974	Antipsychotics Thiothixene (15 – 30 mg/day) Chlorpromazine (150 – 300 mg/day)	4 Groups thio alone thio + GT Cpz alone Cpz + GT	Outpatient	49	6 months
Malm	1982	Fpz decanoate (18 mg/2 wks) (19 mg/2 wks) (13 mg/2 wks) (12 mg/2 wks)	2 Groups GT 1st yr Cont. 1st yr GT 2nd yr Cont. 2nd yr	In and out-patient	68	1 year (2 years)

of treatment. No further information regarding dosage is given. The general model of effects was that medication alone or in combination with GT was significantly better than GT alone in reducing symptoms associated with schizophrenia. This was true for global measures and for 10 of 16 items of the BPRS. For two symptoms, anxiety and motor retardation, there was an interactive effect, such that more improvement was seen with the combination treatment than with either treatment alone. With the exception of these two symptoms, conclusions from this study are that GT does not potentiate medication (thioridazine) for acutely ill patients.

Borowski and his colleagues (30) compared 40 patients who received chlorpromazine alone with an equal number who received chlorpromazine and GT. They concluded that the patients who received GT in addition to chlorpromazine alone had a more favorable outcome. However, in our re-analysis of the data (Table 9) we found no statistically significant difference in improvement between the two groups. Two further measures – number of weeks until delusions disappeared, and return of insight, were also examined by the authors. Delusions disappeared in 58% of the patients who received GT (median time to disappearance 7.7 weeks) compared to 35% of the patients in the medication only groups (median time to disappearance greater than 10 weeks). Reanalysis of these data using survival analysis indicated that time to disappearance of delusions was significantly shorter in the group that received GT (P = 0.008). Return of insight did not differ (46%) in the two groups. Thus, on balance, only a limited additive effect of GT was demonstrated in this study.

O'Brien and his colleagues (31) compared GT and individual therapy in newly discharged, chronic outpatients. All patients in both groups began the study on 'therapeutic' doses of phenothiazine drugs. There were no differences in drug prescription or reported medication use between the GT and individual therapy. Patients who received GT were more likely to remain in treatment for the first 12 months, more likely to be discharged after 24 months and to have improved significantly in psychopathology (BPRS) and Social Effectiveness at the end of 24 months. The authors note that drugs and side-effects were frequent topics for group discussion and that medication could have been a mediating factor in treatment outcome despite the fact that there were no differences in either prescribed or reported drug use. This study does suggest that there are positive effects of GT beyond the effects of medication.

As shown in Table 8, Claghorn and his colleagues (32) randomly assigned 49 outpatients to receive antipsychotic medication only (thiothixene or chlorpromazine) or the same medications and GT. Thus, there were four treatment groups in the study.

TABLE 9 *Improvement in Borowski and Tolwinski study (30)*[a]

Treatment	Improvement mean (SD)
Drug therapy	1.4 (0.87)
Drug + GT	1.7 (1.02)

[a] Improvement scoring. None = 0; marked = 3; t = 1.42; P = 0.16.

In terms of evaluating the effects of medication in relation to GT, this study was able to detect only additive effects. As indexed by the BPRS, there was significant change over time on all measures of psychopathology, but there were no differences in psychopathology among the four groups after six months of treatment. The analysis did not examine the possibility of interaction effects between the two treatment modalities. However, inspection of the mean scores after treatment reveals that they are at a uniformly low level, so that statistical discrimination among them would have been unlikely.

In addition, the authors compared patients who received GT with those who did not on measures from the Interpersonal Test Battery. Reported differences suggest that after six months patients who have received GT perceive themselves as less dominant and affiliative and others as more dominant and affiliative. These psychological changes appear to reflect improved accuracy of social perception, but they are not necessarily psychological improvements. In terms of the efficacy of GT, this study does not demonstrate clinically significant improvement beyond that provided by medication.

As shown in Table 8, Malm (29) randomly assigned patients either to depot fluphenazine and a standard three-month social skills training program or to an experimental program in which a year of communication-oriented GT was added to the standard package. As shown in Table 8, there were no differences between the two groups in the amount of medication received, although medication dosage was reduced in both groups during the second year, which was a follow-up period. Thus, any effects of GT can be interpreted as additive to medication. The experimental group showed significantly greater improvement in measures of emotional communication, anhedonia, free time activities, and 'entry into the social field'. When patients were further divided into more and less psychotic, the more psychotic patient who received GT had more days out of the hospital than the control group; among the less psychotic, the rate of remission was higher in the GT patients. However, there were no overall differences in course of illness between the two treatment groups. Assessment of outcome after a follow-up period for GT, during which patients were reliably maintained on medication, allowed determination of the persistence of effects. We conclude that additive effects of GT have been shown in this study for several measures that are not generally influenced by medication in long-term treatment.

Research on group therapy, although extensive (reviewed in Chapter 10 of this volume), has not often been the subject of studies from which inferences can be drawn regarding medication. Perhaps this is because group psychotherapy has been considered as 'best performer in a supportive role'. In our review, we have only identified one study (28) that allowed the examination of the effects of GT alone and therefore the possibility of detecting an interactive effect. In that study, medication alone and medication in combination with GT were equally better than GT alone, providing no evidence for an interactive or synergistic effect of the combination. All the other studies permitted the examination only of additive effects. In this context, both the Borowski and Malm (30, 29) studies suggest specific but limited benefits of adding GT to medication.

DISCUSSION

As we indicated at the outset of this chapter, a comprehensive model of the relationship of medication and psychosocial treatments for schizophrenia needs to specify a number of dimensions beyond treatment. Although we have indicated our general endorsement of this truism, in our detailed review of specific studies we have paid little attention to these factors beyond specifying whether studies were conducted with inpatients or outpatients. Partly, this is because many of the studies do not provide the information needed to make these evaluations. Also, in most of the areas under review, there is little comparability among studies. Thus, it is not possible to determine whether apparently similar or dissimilar findings are a function of diagnostic differences, patient chronicity, age, sex or a number of other factors beyond treatment that can influence course and outcome.

Although we cannot pursue each of these factors in detail, we shall use gender as an example of a factor that can influence outcome differentially depending on treatment.

When gender is reported (in many of the studies we reviewed it is not), and when analyses of outcome allow its influence to be assessed, gender differences in treatment effects appear. This is true for studies of medication (33), psychosocial treatment (34) and, most importantly, for studies of the interaction of medication and psychosocial treatments. Both the Goldstein (15) and Hogarty (12, 13) studies reported differences in treatment outcome for men and women. The Malm study (29) included both men and women, and although 63% of the patients were men, no analyses of outcome examined gender differences. Paul and Lentz (25) had equal numbers of men and women in each of their treatment groups. They reported that women were more likely to improve and to be discharged from their milieu ward compared to the hospital ward, but provided no information regarding gender and drug dosage. Gorham and Pokorny (28) worked exclusively with male patients in the VA system.

Assessment of diagnosis and the consistency of diagnosis is another issue that must be addressed. Over the time spanned by the studies reviewed here, clinical practice has changed markedly, both replacing and influencing the diagnostic systems in use. The assessment of diagnosis now generally goes beyond reporting that found in clinical charts and the diagnostic specificity has changed as well. The *Diagnostic and Statistical Manual* of the American Psychiatric Association has gone from 134 pages in 1968 to 494 larger pages in 1980, to 568 pages in 1987. The criteria for a diagnosis of schizophrenia and related disorders have also changed. It is not clear that studies conducted in the 1960s and those conducted in the 1980s include similar patients and are comparable.

The importance of the assessment of the relationship of medication and specific psychological treatments is obvious. Medication is not administered in a therapeutic vacuum. As we have described above, specific psychosocial treatments are effective beyond the insurance of medication compliance. Data supporting this are provided both by studies in which medication compliance was controlled (15) or specifically addressed (16, 18), and studies that examined medication use or drug plasma levels and found no differences between groups (e.g., 29, 27). However, we also have evidence that under some conditions specific psychosocial treatments may have disadvantages. Examples include insight-oriented GT (35, 32) and individual treatment in the absence of medication (14).

Perhaps the easiest way to obtain further information regarding the role of medication in psychosocial treatments is to examine studies of psychosocial treatments already completed that have data available regarding medication that have not been analyzed. The data from the Falloon study presented in Fig. 1 represent perhaps the clearest example of the kinds of information that lurk within other data banks ready to enhance our understanding of the influence of medication on psychosocial treatment effects. We have provided examples of such re-analyses in this paper when necessary data could be extracted from the published materials.

The second method is to conduct formal studies that are capable of examining both additive and interactive effects of medication and specific psychosocial treatments. The National Institute of Mental Health is conducting such a study under our direction in collaboration with investigators at five hospitals (36). The study design is presented in Table 10. The medication component compares standard antopsychotic drug maintenance treatment with two strategies for dosage reduction that are hypothesized to reduce the risk of developing tardive dyskinesia. One group (standard dosage) receives fluphenazine decanoate in dosages between 12.5 and 50 mg bi-weekly. A second group (continuous low dose) receives between 2.5 and 10 mg bi-weekly. The third group (targeted) receives the injection vehicle only. Patients in all groups are administered open label fluphenazine at the first signs of impending relapse. Treatment continues for two years.

Patients and their families also participate in one of two treatment approaches designed to reduce stress, improve social functioning and buffer the increased risk of relapse incurred by medication reduction. The design of these treatments grows out of the studies reviewed above in the section on family treatment. Family members in both treatment groups participate in an initial workshop designed to provide education about the illness, stress and its management, communication, and

TABLE 10 *Treatment strategies in schizophrenia study design*

Family treatment	Medication (i.m. fluphenazine decanoate dosage/2 weeks)		
	Standard (12.5 – 50 mg)	Low (2.5 – 10 mg)	Targeted vehicle only
Applied			
Supportive			

problem-solving skills modeled after the Survival Skills Workshop developed by Anderson, Reiss and Hogarty (37). Patients and families also attend monthly family group meetings. These elements represent Supportive Family Management. In addition, patients and families in the second treatment group, Applied Family Management, participate in individual family sessions conducted in the home, modeled after the behavioral family therapy developed by Falloon and his colleagues.

This study represents a significant advance in research on treatment efficacy for schizophrenia because it builds directly on the findings of a series of pharmacologic studies of dosage reduction as well as studies of the efficacy of specific family treatments. Dosage reduction paradigms represent a strategy for the investigation of the relationship of other specific psychosocial treatments to medication that should be increasingly employed in future research. In addition to allowing the study of the interaction of medication and psychosocial treatments, there are some reasons to expect that reduced dosage of antipsychotic medication can facilitate the effectiveness of some psychosocial treatments (20, 38; and S.R. Marder and R.P. Liberman, personal communication).

In summary, this volume reviews the richness of psychosocial treatment approaches to schizophrenia. What we have attempted to do in this chapter is to set these into the context of medication use. We have identified few studies in which medication hindered the application of psychosocial treatment, although there is some evidence that high dosage of antipsychotic drugs may not be helpful. As can be seen from the tables, most studies in which positive additive effects were seen have employed low to moderate dosages and there have been no direct studies of high dosage in relation to psychosocial treatments. In general, we find that compatibility, rather than competition, represents the appropriate model for integration of these two broad treatment modalities.

REFERENCES

1. Grinspoon L, Ewalt JR, Shader R (1972) *Schizophrenia: pharmacotherapy and psychotherapy,* Williams and Wilkins, Baltimore, MD.
2. Cole JO (1968) A unique study which may never be repeated. In: May PRA (Ed), *Treatment of Schizophrenia,* pp. 309–340. Science House, New York.
3. May PRA (1968) *Treatment of Schizophrenia.* Science House, New York.
4. Stanton AH, Gunderson JG, Knapp PH, Frank AF, Vanicelli ML, Schnitzer R, Rosenthal R (1984) Effects of psychotherapy in schizophrenia, I. Design and implementation of a controlled study. *Schizophr. Bull. 10,* 520.
5. Keith SJ, Matthews SM (1982) Group, family, and milieu therapies and psychosocial rehabilitation in the treatment of schizophrenic disorders. In: Grinspoon L (Ed), *Psychiatry, 1982: Annual Review.* American Psychiatric Press, Washington, DC.
6. Mosher LR, Keith SJ (1980) Psychosocial treatment: individual, group, family, and community support approaches. *Schizophr. Bull., 6,* 10.
7. Schooler NR (1978) Antipsychotic drugs and psychological treatment in schizophrenia. In: Lipton MA, DiMascio A, Killam KF (Eds), *Psychopharmacology: A Generation of Progress,* p. 1155. Raven Press, New York.
8. Schooler NR, Hogarty GE (1987) Medication and psychosocial strategies in the treat-

ment of schizophrenia. In: Meltzer HY (Ed), *The Third Generation of Progress,* pp. 1111 – 1119. Raven Press, New York.

9. Karon BP, VandenBos GR (1981) *Psychotherapy of Schizophrenia.* Aronson, New York.
10. Rogers CR (1967) *The Therapeutic Relationship and Its Impact.* University of Wisconsin Press, Madison, WI.
11. Gunderson JG, Frank AF, Katz HM, Vannicelli JL, Frosch JP, Knapp PH (1984) Effects of psychotherapy in schizophrenia, II. Comparative outcome of two forms of treatment. *Schizophr. Bull., 10,* 564.
12. Hogarty GE, Goldberg SC, Schooler NR, Ulrich RF, Collaborative Study Group (1974) Drug and sociotherapy in the aftercare of schizophrenic patients, II. Two-year relapse rates. *Arch. Gen. Psychiatry, 31,* 603.
13. Hogarty GE, Schooler NR, Ulrich RF, Mussare F, Ferro P, Herron E (1979) Depot fluphenazine and social therapy in the aftercare of schizophrenic patients: relapse analyses of a two-year controlled trial. *Arch. Gen. Psychiatry, 36,* 1283.
14. Hogarty GE, Goldberg SC, Schooler NR, Collaborative Study Group (1974) Drug and sociotherapy in the aftercare of schizophrenic patients, III. Adjustments of nonrelapsed patients. *Arch. Gen. Psychiatry, 31,* 609.
15. Goldstein MJ, Rodnick EH, Evans JR, May PRA, Steinberg MR (1978) Drug and family therapy in the aftercare of acute schizophrenics. *Arch. Gen. Psychiatry, 35,* 1169.
16. Hogarty GE, Anderson CM, Reiss DJ, Kornblith SJ, Greenwald DP, Javna CD, Madonia MJ, Environmental/Personal Indicators in the Course of Schizophrenia Research Group (1986) Family psychoeducation, social skills training, and maintenance chemotherapy in the aftercare treatment of schizophrenia. *Arch. Gen. Psychiatry, 43,* 633.
17. Leff J, Kuipers L, Berkowitz R, Eberlein-Vries R, Sturgeon D (1982) A controlled trial of social intervention in the families of schizophrenic patients. *Br. J. Psychiatry, 141,* 121.
18. Leff J, Kuipers L, Berkowitz R, Sturgeon D (1985) A controlled trial of social intervention in the families of schizophrenic patients: Two year follow-up. *Br. J. Psychiatry, 146,* 594.
19. Falloon IRH, Boyd JL, McGill CW, Razani J, Moss HB, Gilderman AM (1982) Family management in the prevention of exacerbations of schizophrenia. *New Engl. J. Med., 306,* 1437.
20. Falloon IRH, Boyd JL, McGill CW, Williamson M, Razani J, Moss HB, Gilderman AM, Simpson GM (1985) Family management in the prevention of morbidity of schizophrenia. *Arch. Gen. Psychiatry, 42,* 887.
21. Moss HB, Mcdonald N, Falloon IRH, Simpson GM (1985) Biological factors affecting the outcome of schizophrenia. In: Falloon IRH, et al. (Eds), *Family Management of Schizophrenia,* pp. 124 – 136. Johns Hopkins University Press, Baltimore, MD.
22. Davis JM, Andriukaitis S (1986) The natural course of schizophrenia and effective maintenance drug treatment. *J. Clin. Psychopharmacol., 6,* 2S.
23. Bellack AS, Turner SM, Hersen M, Luber RF (1984) An examination of the efficacy of social skills training for chronic schizophrenic patients. *Hosp. Community Psychiatry, 35,* 1023.
24. Hersen M, Turner SM, Edelstein BA, Pinkston SG (1975) Effects of phenothiazines and social skills training in a withdrawn schizophrenic. *J. Clin. Psychol., 31,* 588.
25. Paul GL, Lentz RJ (1977) *Psychosocial Treatments of Chronic Mental Patients.* Harvard University Press, Cambridge, MA.
26. Paul GL, Tobias LT, Holly BL (1972) Maintenance psychotropic drugs in the presence

of active treatment programs: A 'triple blind' withdrawal study with long term mental patients. *Arch. Gen. Psychiatry, 27,* 106.

27. Wallace CJ, Liberman RP (1985) Social skills training for patients with schizophrenia: a controlled clinical trial. *Psychiatry Res., 15,* 239.
28. Gorham DR, Pokorny AD (1964) Effects of a phenothiazine and/or group psychotherapy with schizophrenics. *Dis. Nerv. Syst. 25,* 77.
29. Malm U (1982) The influence of group therapy on schizophrenia. *Acta Psychiatr. Scand. (Suppl.) 297,* 1.
30. Borowski T, Tolwinski T (1969) Treatment of paranoid schizophrenics with chlorpromazine and group therapy. *Dis. Nerv. Syst., 30,* 201.
31. O'Brien CP, Hamm KB, Ray BA, Pierce JF, Luborsky L, Mintz J (1972) Group vs. individual psychotherapy with schizophrenics. *Arch. Gen. Psychiatry, 17,* 474.
32. Claghorn JL, Johnstone EE, Cook TH, Itschner L (1974) Group therapy and maintenance treatment of schizophrenics. *Arch. Gen. Psychiatry, 31,* 361.
33. Goldberg SC, Schooler NR, Davidson EM, and Kayce M (1966) Sex and race differences in response to drug treatment among schizophrenics. *Psychopharmacologia, 9,* 31.
34. Haas GL, Glick ID, Clarkin JF, Spencer JH, Lewis AB, Peyser J, DeMane N, Good-Ellis M, Harris E, Lestelle V (1988) Inpatient family intervention: a randomized clinical trial. *Arch. Gen. Psychiatry, 45,* 217.
35. Kanas N, Rogers M, Kreth E, Patterson OTR, Campbell R (1980) The effectiveness of group psychotherapy during the first three weeks of hospitalization. *J. Nerv. Ment. Dis., 168,* 487.
36. Schooler NR, Keith SJ (1983) *Treatment Strategies in Schizophrenia Study Protocol.* National Institute of Mental Health, Rockville, MD.
37. Anderson CM, Reiss DJ, Hogarty GE (1986) *Schizophrenia and the Family.* Guilford Press, New York.
38. Kreisman D, Blumenthal R, Borenstein M, Woerner M, Kane J, Rifkin A, Reardon G (1988) Family attitudes and patient social adjustment in a longitudinal study of outpatient schizophrenics receiving low-dose neuroleptics: the family's view. *Psychiatry, 51,* 3.

CHAPTER 4

Individual psychodynamically oriented psychotherapy for schizophrenic patients

HOWARD M. KATZ AND JOHN G. GUNDERSON

INTRODUCTION

Individual psychotherapy for schizophrenic patients has been a source of controversy and interest from the time it was first introduced as a treatment. The intensity of debate about psychotherapy for this group of patients stems in part from the paradox of attempting to heal through the means of a relationship those people whose abilities to form and use relationships are most impaired. Between 1945 and 1965, when psychoanalytic investigators were focusing increasingly on early development and more severe psychopathology, there was an expansion of academic interest, clinical practice and institutional support for both the practice and the study of psychotherapy with schizophrenic patients. Since then, however, support for psychodynamic psychotherapy has decreased. Persistent questions about the efficacy of psychotherapy for schizophrenic patients and positive developments in psychopharmacology as well as other domains of psychosocial treatment call for a reappraisal of the role of individual psychotherapy. In this chapter, we first present a historical review summarizing developments in the clinical and research literature, and then we turn attention to current perspectives and controversies in clinical practice, examining, in particular, the degree to which current systematic research has bearing on clinically relevant questions.

HISTORICAL PERSPECTIVE

The development of modern psychodynamic psychotherapy

Psychodynamic psychotherapy for schizophrenic patients evolved first out of psychoanalysis, but over the years psychodynamic approaches have also embraced concepts derived from other bodies of thought about human relationships and the mind. A psychoanalytic approach to schizophrenic patients developed slowly at first, primarily due to the impact of Freud's theoretically based reservations. Freud's studies of the autobiographical account of Shreber (1), and his further considerations of narcissism (2) led him to the conclusion that the schizophrenic could not benefit from psychoanalysis, because narcissistic attachment of libido would prohibit the development of a transference neurosis. While Freud himself had little

Handbook of Schizophrenia, Volume 4: Psychosocial Treatment of Schizophrenia.
M.I. Herz, S.J. Keith and J.P. Docherty, editors.

contact with schizophrenics, a number of his followers worked more extensively with psychotic patients and believed that they could be helped by psychoanalytically based treatment.

Among the few early proponents of psychoanalytic work with schizophrenics were Tausk (3) and Federn (4), both of whom contributed to the concept of ego boundaries. Federn believed that the schizophrenic could form a transference to the therapist, and he discouraged interpretation of the negative transference with these patients. He felt that the therapist must support the patient's deficient ego, and thereby help the patient to rely less on primary process thinking.

Melanie Klein's (5) work with children led her to formulate theoretical constructs of primitive defenses which gave rise to the child's developing mental structure and object relations. A number of her followers, including Segal (6), Fairbairn (7), and Rosenfeld (8), applied Klein's formulations to work with patients with severe psychopathology, including schizophrenics. Primitive defenses such as splitting, fragmentation, projection, and introjection, which were emphasized by Klein, remain prominent in modern conceptualizations of the dynamics of schizophrenia.

Marguerite Sechehaye (9) sought to understand and respond symbolically to her patient's primitive needs and fears, calling her approach 'symbolic realization'. Rosen's 'direct analysis' (10) was likewise an intensive treatment (8 to 16-hour sessions at times) aimed at directly engaging the patient on the most primitive level, in his case more by direct and early 'id' interpretation than by symbolic reenactment. These dramatic approaches and the enthusiastic reports of their effectiveness generated considerable excitement and strongly influenced the field. Many therapists believed in the need for intensity in the therapeutic interaction and for some form of entry into the primitive world of the patient, even if they did not practice this in so dramatic a fashion as Sechehaye or Rosen.

While consideration of more primitive defenses and the primary process remained an undercurrent in the development of psychotherapy, attention was also given to the role of schizophrenics' logical and understandable, albeit maladaptive, responses to ordinary life events. This focus was most prominent in the United States, where Adolf Meyer's (11) emphasis on environmental influences on psychopathology led to a more optimistic view of both the general prognosis for schizophrenic patients and the more specific benefit of psychotherapy. In a climate strongly influenced by Meyer, especially in the Baltimore-Washington area, Harry Stack Sullivan's (12, 13) inspirational efforts to see schizophrenia as a human process and to develop an interpersonal theory of schizophrenia flourished.

A substantial number of therapists combined Sullivan's emphasis on interpersonal relations with psychoanalytic formulations of the unconscious to elaborate a theory and technique for working with schizophrenics. Frieda Fromm-Reichmann (14, 15) did much to expand and define the modern psychoanalytic psychotherapy of schizophrenia. Her approach was similar to psychoanalysis in using frequent sessions, emphasizing the transference and countertransference, and paying attention to unconscious processes and symptoms as a reformulation of old, frustrating interpersonal relationships. Fromm-Reichmann articulated important shifts from classic psychoanalytic technique, however; shifts which she thought were necessary for work with psychotic patients. She recommended against free association and the use of the couch, and sought to actively provide structure for the patient's thinking process and containment of anxiety. Regression was seen as unavoidable, but to be limited if possible. While she saw psychotic manifestations as meaningful, the focus was not so much on the content of psychotic thinking and behavior as on the conditions giving rise to the symptoms.

Sullivan and Fromm-Reichmann had a pronounced influence on the theory and practice of psychotherapy with schizophrenic patients. Their work was further extended by the contributions of many of their students, including Arieti (16), who has studied schizophrenic thinking and defined therapeutic approaches which focus on the thought disorder, Will (17), who has eloquently articulated the problems of attachment encountered in intensive work with schizophrenics, and Searles (18), who has contributed detailed and extensive investigations of the transference-countertransference constellations encountered in work with schizophrenic patients.

John Whitehorn (19), a student of Meyer's, encouraged active personal participation with schizophrenics and stressed the value of appraising the patient's personality as a whole, including its strengths. Semrad was influenced by Whitehorn's point of view (20) and integrated it with psychoanalytic theories of motivation. Semrad subsequently elaborated his view of treatment as helping the patient acknowledge, bear, and put into perspective his feelings and painful experiences (21, 22). His teaching in the Boston area had major influence (23).

Interest in psychotherapy with more disturbed patients intensified through the 1950s and 1960s, and was closely related to new work in ego psychology and object relations theory, and a fuller understanding of the impact of pre-oedipal development on adult psychopathology. In the last twenty years, interest in individual psychotherapy with schizophrenic patients has been sustained, though a series of empirical studies has raised questions about the value of psychotherapy for this population.

Empirical studies

During the 1950s, several developments in our understanding of schizophrenia helped to lay the groundwork for later empirical studies. Greater realization of the impact of the patient's social environment on his illness led to increasingly sophisticated milieu treatments, community programs, and rehabilitation approaches. On another front, researchers were beginning to delineate the neurobiological underpinnings of schizophrenia, and great strides were made in the development of neuroleptic drug treatment which could be evaluated according to the clinical investigative methods used regularly in other areas of medicine. These factors led to assertion by some that milieu and drug treatments were more appropriate for schizophrenia than was psychotherapy. Some investigators perceived a need for more systematic empirical scrutiny of psychotherapy. Five major studies completed in the 1960s addressed the issue (see Table 1). They have been reviewed extensively elsewhere (24 – 29) and will be described here briefly. The findings of the more recent Boston Psychotherapy Study (30, 31) will be described more extensively.

Studies conducted from 1960 – 1970

Fairweather and his colleagues (32) conducted the first significant controlled study of psychotherapy with schizophrenic patients. The authors compared treatment outcomes of four groups of patients, one of which received individual psychotherapy by moderately experienced therapists for three to five hours per week. While there was some evidence that the individual psychotherapy group did better than the control group, their improvement was not appreciably better than that of the groups receiving active group and milieu treatments. Limitations in the size and diagnostic definition of the sample, lack of systematic pharmacotherapy, and uncharacterized psychotherapy, all limit the interpretability of the study.

In the Massachusetts Mental Health Center Study (33), chronic patients were treated twice weekly by experienced therapists. Those psychotherapy patients who received neuroleptic medication had better outcomes than those who did not. When the study patients receiving psychotherapy were compared to a similar group of patients who remained on a ward which emphasized drug treatment and which did not offer psychotherapy, no significant advantages were found for the psychotherapy group. Conclusions about the value of psychotherapy from this study were limited because of the chronicity of the sample, non-random assignment of the comparison group, and differences between the milieus on which the treatments were given.

Rogers and his coworkers (34) studied hospitalized chronic patients who were treated with Rogers' client-centered psychotherapy and followed for two years. Those who received psychotherapy showed modest advantages over those who did not after 18 months, in terms of recidivism in the year following discharge. The inexperience of the therapists, chronicity of the patients, failure to control pharmacotherapy, and limited engagement of most patients in the therapy have all been cited as limiting the conclusions from the study.

Karon and his collaborators (35 – 37) used both experienced and inexperienced therapists to provide psychoanalytical oriented psychotherapy to a sample of largely black inner city chronic schizophrenic patients. After 1 year, and again after 20 months of treatment, the study showed significant advantages for groups treated with psychotherapy. The findings also showed that more experienced therapists had better results than those with less experience. However, because the non-psychotherapy group was treated in a markedly different milieu, and medication usage was uncontrolled, the findings are considerably weakened.

The most influential and best controlled study was done by May (38). In this study, hospitalized non-chronic patients received milieu treatment to which psychotherapy was added for one group, pharmacotherapy for another, and combined psychotherapy and pharmacotherapy for a third comparison group. A fourth group received milieu treatment plus electroconvulsive therapy (ECT). The psychotherapy added little to the milieu treatment, whether or not patients also received medication, although the psychotherapy plus medication group showed slightly greater improvement on expressions of anger and on insight than the other groups. Despite improvements in design over other studies, May's study has been criticized for its use of inexperienced therapists over a relatively short time (6 months) and for its failure to investigate areas of change that might be more specifically related to psychotherapy, such as psychological and interpersonal functioning.

Although interpretations of these early studies were confounded by the limitations of the designs and methodologies, two conclusions can be drawn: (a) treatment by a dynamically informed psychotherapist provides no assurance of additional improvement for schizophrenic patients; and (b) the improvements attributable to psychotherapy are rarely obvious and hardly dramatic. Nevertheless, these conclusions had limited impact on the practitioners who advocated and provided intensive psychotherapy for schizophrenic patients. Thoughtful proponents argued that these studies failed to use therapists who were sufficiently skilled, to follow patients for long enough periods of time to detect the gradual change which occurs in psychotherapy, to use patients for whom good results could be expected, and to use outcome measures sensitive to the kinds of changes psychotherapy can bring about. Moreover, advocates still found the series of unusual successes that had been documented in individual cases convincing. Reports by therapists such as Fromm-Reichmann, Sechehaye, Arieti, Will, Benedetti, Wexler, Schulz and others suggested that intensive psychotherapeutic interventions had brought about dramatic resolutions in schizophrenic psychopathology. However, these reports were easily criticized as uncontrolled exceptions which were subject to bias.

The problems in the interpretation of the controlled research studies and in generalizing from clinical case reports provided the background for the conduct of more definitive research into the effects of psychotherapy with schizophrenic patients. Even those who were most skeptical about the value of such therapy recognized the hazards of bringing premature closure to the first treatment which laid claim to affecting the core aspects of schizophrenic psychopathology.

The Boston Psychotherapy Study

The Boston Psychotherapy Study (30, 31) attempted to provide a more rigorous test of whether dynamically based psychotherapy added appreciably to the benefits of the usual supportive treatment of schizophrenic patients. Exploratory, insight-oriented (EIO) psychotherapy, provided by experienced, motivated therapists two to three times each week was compared to reality-adaptive, supportive (RAS) therapy which was also provided by experienced and motivated clinicians on a less intensive schedule, meeting once a week or once every two weeks. As highlighted in Table 1, this study offered clear advantages over its predecessors in terms of assessing areas of outcome appropriate to psychodynamic therapy, having experienced therapists who were motivated, having balanced and informed pharmacotherapy for both groups, meeting explicit and strict diagnostic criteria, and involving a significant duration of therapy.

The design excluded the very chronic and the very acute subgroups of schizophrenic patients. Despite changes in diagnostic standards between 1972 when the design was formulated and 1984 when the study was completed, all patients met research criteria for schizophrenia and most fulfilled the narrow DSM-III criteria. Because it was expected that the putative advantages of EIO therapy would emerge only after a minimum duration of treatment, all study subjects were required to be

TABLE 1 *Comparative designs of psychotherapy of schizophrenia studies*[a]

	Fairweather et al. (1960)	Rogers et al. (1967)	May (1968)	Karon (1969 – 70)	Grinspoon et al. (1972)	Boston (1984)
Patient Number index cases	20	16	44[c]	12	10[b]	23[c]
Chronicity	Mixed	High	Medium	Medium	High	Medium
Therapist experience	High and Low	Low	Low	High and Low	High	High
Therapy duration (months)	6	2 – 36	6	12	24	24
Frequency (h per week)	2 – 4	2	2	1 – 5	2	2
Contrast condition	+	+	+ + +	0	0	+ +
Dynamically oriented outcome assessments	0	+	+	+	0	+ + +
Process assessment	0	+	0	0	0	+ +

[a] See Feinsilver and Gunderson (24); Stanton et al., (30).
[b] The patients receiving psychotherapy with drugs were compared to patients receiving drugs without psychotherapy in another milieu.
[c] Refers to psychotherapy patients for whom drug therapy was known to be similar to a comparison group and thus psychotherapy's effects could be isolated.

in their assigned treatment for six months. Ninety-five patients formed the study sample. Fifty-one of these remained in their assigned treatment (28 RAS and 23 EIO) for the two-year study period.

All patients were initially hospitalized and, in addition to their randomly assigned form of psychotherapy, they received active milieu treatment, pharmacotherapy, and the usual range of aftercare services such as halfway houses and day care. Each group of therapists averaged ten years' prior experience. RAS therapists were mainly psychopharmacologists who emphasized the biological underpinnings of schizophrenia and who focused in treatment on adherence to the medication regimen and management of practical issues of daily life. In contrast, EIO therapists were mainly psychoanalysts, believed schizophrenia had developmental determinants, and focused treatment on exploration of interpersonal relationships and the influence of past experience on the present (39). EIO therapists were generally more composed, less action-oriented, and more likely to see problems as internal than the RAS therapists.

Outcome was assessed with an array of measures which included extensive evaluation of often neglected areas of intrapsychic features, ego function, interpersonal relations, and cognition. The study also gave greater attention than its predecessors to the study of the therapy itself. Process measures obtained from patient reports, therapist reports, and tape recordings were directed at providing a portrait of what actually occurred in treatment.

The findings of the study include information on attrition of the patient population which, in turn, influences the interpretation of other outcome assessments. Of 162 patients originally beginning in the assigned treatment, 95 (59%) stayed in the assigned treatment for six months, long enough to become study patients included in the outcome assessments. Patients left treatment most often because of resistance of their own or of their families to the specific form of treatment offered (40). The patients who remained in RAS were systematically different from those who remained in EIO. Patients who had positive symptoms of schizophrenia (such as manifest cognitive and behavioral disturbance) and were relatively optimistic about their prospects for recovery proved more likely to experience favorably, and to remain in, adaptive supportive (RAS) therapy. By contrast, the patients who proved more likely to be positively involved and to remain in insight-oriented (EIO) therapy had more negative symptoms such as social isolation, apathy and emotional blunting. They were more pessimistic regarding their futures. These findings contrast with the usual assumptions about which patients are most suited for intensive psychodynamic psychotherapy, which are discussed more fully in the section on clinical perspectives.

The outcome results of the Boston Psychotherapy Study are summarized in Table 2. These comparative results should be understood against the backdrop of several more general findings:

(a) patients in both RAS and EIO groups improved considerably in almost every area of outcome;

(b) there were very few instances of dramatic recovery from which the investigators could infer effects on core schizophrenic issues;

(c) an unexpected departure from the study design was the finding that RAS and

EIO therapists provided similar levels of support, consisting of suggestions, reality testing, encouragement, and warmth.

The results obviously failed to confirm either the strength or the breadth of more favorable effects that had been hypothesized for EIO treatment. Rather, RAS therapy exerted a preferential action on rates of re-hospitalization and on role performance (i.e., occupational functioning, and to a lesser extent social adaptation). In contrast, EIO therapy appeared to exert preferential, albeit more modest action in the area of ego functioning and cognition (i.e., in adaptive regression and decreased thought disorganization).

These findings are generally consistent with the focus and intention of the two treatment modalities. EIO treatment was directed more toward reducing disturbances in interpretation of events and toward promoting self-knowledge and understanding, while RAS therapy was more concerned with the practical issues of daily living. In this way, the results provide confirmation of a broader thesis that how one interacts as a therapist has differential and specific effects. This was seen in spite of the heavy crossover between EIO and RAS conditions in the use of supportive techniques, which diminished the distinctness of the two treatments.

CURRENT PERSPECTIVES ON CLINICAL PRACTICE

Our understanding of critical factors in individual psychotherapy with schizophrenic patients has gradually grown along two lines of development which

TABLE 2 *Boston Psychotherapy Study. Summary of results of hypothesis testing based on group contrasts at 24 months*

	Results favor:		
	EIO	RAS	Neither
Cognitive functioning			
Thought disorganization			×
Insight			×
Ego functioning	×		
Interpersonal relationships			×
Signs and Symptoms			×
Major Role Performance			
Social Functioning			×
Self-sufficiency			×
Occupational functioning		×	
Medications			×
Hospitalization		×	

have proven difficult to integrate. One is rooted in clinical experience, the other in empirical research. The clinical perspective has often taken for granted the question of efficacy, focusing on *how* psychotherapy works, whereas the bulk of the empirical literature has focused on *whether* psychotherapy works, often neglecting the process questions which are of concern to practicing therapists. The result of this divided attention is evident when considering the three broad areas of concern to the clinician: (a) the setting or antecedent conditions for psychotherapy; (b) processes and techniques in psychotherapy; and (c) outcomes and assessments of the effects of psychotherapy. The research literature has the most to contribute to the latter of these areas, the least to contribute in regard to technique, and an intermediate impact on our thinking about the conditions for psychotherapy. In contrast, the clinical literature has contributed most to the understanding of processes and techniques in psychotherapy.

The setting and antecedent conditions for psychotherapy

There is widespread agreement that the initial qualities of the participants, patient and therapist, and the setting or environment in which they work influence the process and outcome of psychotherapy, but specification of these factors has proven elusive.

Patient factors

The selection of patients most suitable for intensive individual psychotherapy has been considered important, in recognition of both the immense variability in ego capacity manifested in schizophrenic patients and the limited resources for providing such treatment, even in those centers where such treatment has been most highly regarded.

Some groups of patients have never been considered likely to benefit from intensive psychotherapy. This determination rests on the basis of clinical experience, since such patients have generally been excluded from research protocols. Patients with chronic and unremitting psychoses or concomitant neurologic or learning disabilities are most clearly treated best by other methods. Most clinicians would extend this contraindication for intensive individual psychotherapy to patients who are persistently socially aversive and uncommunicative or who are behaviorally unmanageable over extended periods of time. Structured milieu programs (42), behavioral modification (43), and social skills training (44) are directed at enforcing more adaptive behaviors and at the suppression of the verbal or behavioral expressions of disorganized or unrealistic mental states characteristic of this kind of patient. The individual practitioner's role is often to provide the continuity in the therapeutic relationship needed to plan treatment effectively and to give confidence and reassurance to these patients, who are among those least able to face a stranger when in trouble. The exploration of emotionally loaded issues and expression of feelings will usually be overwhelming for such patients, and is deliberately avoided in this approach to treatment. These conclusions do not derive directly from psychotherapy research, but are consistent with research on the impacts of both institutional and family practices (45).

When specifying factors which suggest that a patient would be most likely to profit from psychotherapy, clinicians have been relatively consistent in emphasizing the following: (a) acute onset of the illness; (b) a known or discrete precipitant to psychosis; (c) the psychosis being ego-dystonic; (d) the patient displaying pain or depression; and (e) a history of employment or academic success outside the nuclear home (41). These factors overlap considerably with those which are taken as indicators of good prognosis in general, regardless of the choice of treatment. It may well be that the experience which led clinicians to see this kind of profile as favorable for psychotherapy is not as specific for psychotherapy as was previously thought. Indeed, findings of the Boston Psychotherapy Study suggested that patients with these characteristics tended to drop out of the study in disproportionately high numbers (40) or to engage preferentially in the less intensive supportive treatment. Patients with positive signs of schizophrenia, namely disorganization, hallucinations or delusions, and high levels of anxiety and agitation, seemed especially apt to welcome supportive psychotherapy, while such patients were often intolerant of expressive insight-oriented psychotherapy.

In the Boston Psychotherapy Study, patients who were not so acute in their presentation, and whose mental statuses were characterized by negative signs of schizophrenia, were more readily engaged by the EIO psychotherapists and more apt to remain in EIO treatment. In many instances more acute symptoms had been relieved by other treatment, but apathy, anhedonia and affective impoverishment, social isolation, and discouragement remained as deeply dissatisfying residual areas of impairment. The patients who remained in EIO treatment had higher levels of education, which may speak to the ability and discipline needed for repeated attendance or to a greater intellectual capacity and interest in studying complex and covert problems. The greater amount of previous psychotherapy found in the group who stayed in EIO therapy may also be a factor which contributed to these capacities.

Patients who remained in EIO treatment also tended to express a high level of need to understand and integrate their psychotic experiences. This preference for or tolerance of a particular form of therapy (EIO versus RAS) may be related to the finding that patients manifest distinct styles of recovery from psychosis, tending toward either integration or sealing over (46). When the treatment offered clashes with a patient's defensive style, the clinician ends up working against increasingly stiff resistance, and the patient is more apt to leave treatment.

Another perspective which may explain the amenability of patients with negative symptoms to EIO treatment has to do with levels of stimulation. The degree of stimulation that a patient can tolerate may be a guide to treatment choice (47). The Boston findings are consistent with this perspective, in that those patients who were most agitated seemed to be flooded with stimulation and to benefit from the more structured and directive RAS treatment which reduces stimulation. In contrast, the patients who tended to become engaged in the more provocative and stimulating EIO treatment were relatively low in affective arousal; they may respond positively to therapy which shakes them out of apathy and despair.

Therapist factors

Most observers agree that intensive psychotherapy with schizophrenic patients makes special demands on the therapist, and efforts have been made to define characteristics of optimally effective therapists. Attributes of the optimal therapist which are frequently cited include the capacity for tolerating intense affects, symbiotic demands, primary process communications and high levels of confusion encountered in work with schizophrenic patients (48, 49). A therapist's own experience of pain in life (50) or 'being a little crazy' (20) have also been seen as helpful. The value of personal therapy or analysis and the use of consultation are almost always noted.

The best known empirical study and one of the earliest was that of Whitehorn and Betz (51) which led to the conclusion that 'Type A' therapists who scored high on vocational aptitudes for law and accounting were more effective than 'Type B' therapists who scored high on aptitude for mathematics or teaching physical science, but after subsequent research the validity and meaning of this 'A-B' typology has remained poorly defined (52). Some pessimistic interpretations of more recent outcome research have suggested that perhaps only exceptionally 'gifted' therapists could successfully lead to the substantial resolution of schizophrenic pathology (e.g., 33, 38). However, both the Boston study (31) and McGlashan's follow-up study (53) showed that even for exceptionally experienced and motivated therapists success was unusual, and seemed to depend on factors other than the intuitive 'gifts' of therapists. The more successful therapists in the Boston study were those who had a belief in the value of limiting regressions, were more comfortable sharing personal experience, and had a strong commitment to a well-defined treatment approach. Cognitive clarity and personal authority and confidence emerged as important attributes. These characteristics may be experienced by schizophrenic patients as reassuring by diminishing the amount of complexity to which they are exposed and by encouraging confidence that they are in safe hands and likely to improve if they sustain the therapy relationship. Motivated and experienced therapists who felt that treatment involved 'working through' the psychological meaning of extensive regressions or who were unable to articulate a clear strategy or theory for their approach were unlikely to be successful. The Boston findings failed to confirm earlier findings that ineffective therapists were unable to tolerate anger (54) or independence (37).

Of equal importance to any personal qualites a therapist may have is the issue of how well 'matched' he is with a particular patient, but both clinical and research literature are lacking in specificity regarding the critical dimenensions. A prior study (55) suggested that similarities in background and personality enhance the likelihood of engagement, and that the therapist's personal comfort with a patient's dominant affects was central to matching. In the Boston study, exceptionally good outcomes were associated with an unusual intensity of the engagement of the participants, seemingly due to fortuitous 'matches' rather than the patient's unique qualities or the therapist's exceptional skills.

The environment or setting for the psychotherapy

One important determinant of whether exploratory psychotherapy will be useful is whether a patient is living in a situation which is reasonably supportive of his undergoing an exploration into himself. When such treatment takes place in the hospital, the milieu must support psychotherapy both theoretically and pragmatically (56). The treatment setting must provide a sense of safety and security, and a climate in which adequate contact between patient and therapist can take place. While it is often useful to create a 'T-A split' between the role of therapist and that of administrator (57), a structure for regular communication between the therapist and others on the treatment team is essential. In the Boston Psychotherapy Study, it was noted that intensive psychotherapy conducted in a milieu which was not clearly supportive of that form of treatment led to higher early dropout rates (40) or to persistent difficulties in engagement in the process of therapy (58).

In outpatient settings, attention to a patient's living situation may be even more critical. Although the bulk of treatment in the current era takes place in outpatient settings of various kinds, little research information on the interaction of setting variables with psychotherapy is available, since all of the major empirical investigations of psychotherapy have been studies of inpatients. However, other studies have documented the heightened impact of the family environment (59) and the broader social network (60) on the schizophrenic patient. It has become increasingly clear that the therapist must consider what interventions may be needed to influence the patient's environment (e.g., family interventions, or the use of a halfway house or day treatment) and make an effort to secure the support and trust of the patient's family. Whereas mechanisms for doing this have been established over years of practice in inpatient settings, models for accomplishing these goals in outpatient settings are still evolving and in need of refinement.

Techniques and processes

The extensive clinical literature on psychotherapy of schizophrenia has focused most prominently on the description of the processes which develop in the psychotherapeutic interaction and the technical approaches which may be used to manage them.

Theory and technique

Most authors stress the importance of theory as a guide to technique (e.g., 16, 21, 56). Conversely, the clinical data obtained in the psychotherapy situation has often served as the basis for development of theories of the psychodynamics and etiology of schizophrenia, and has been applied to the more general development of theory regarding primitive defense mechanisms and pre-oedipal development of object relations. Whereas it is universally accepted that therapeutic strategy must be linked to theory, there is some danger that adherence to unproven theories can distort perception. It has been argued (e.g., 61) that theoretical bias has limited clinicians' open consideration of research findings and the development of new technical approaches on an empirical basis.

Controversy over the relative importance of conflict, deficit, transactional and systems theories have contributed to divergent recommendations regarding technique. In spite of this divergence, a number of general attitudes and specific technical approaches can be delineated which are widely enough cited to constitute a common or usual strategy for treating schizophrenic patients in psychotherapy (57).

General principles and attitudes

The recognition that the relationship between patient and therapist is itself the most important agent of change is the most widely underscored principle, and many other principles rest on this assumption. Continuity and consistency of relationship are considered vital to the viability of therapy. This includes both an attachment that can be maintained over time (56, 62, 63) and a relatively consistent attitude and technical approach (64). The Boston Psychotherapy Study provided support for these principles, finding that therapists who had a consistent and coherent approach to their patients were more successful in treating them.

Therapy with schizophrenic patients evokes powerful countertransference responses, and the therapist needs to examine and manage his responses to be optimally useful to the patient. In spite of the common reactions of depression, discouragement, hatred, contempt, fear and lust (17, 18, 65) the therapist does well to maintain an optimal distance from the patient, neither too detached nor overinvolved (66, 67) and to be optimistic in the face of the patient's negativism (68). At the same time, the therapist must temper therapeutic zeal, rescue fantasies, and excessive expectations, for patients often feel they cannot live up to them, or that they are being used by the therapist who must have a 'success' on his own terms (15). Similar balance must be maintained between the need for the therapist to tolerate the bizarre and confusing and the need to serve as a bridge to reality for the patient (14, 62). The therapist must maintain respect for the patient's privacy and autonomy, which are of added importance among schizophrenic patients, who commonly fear closeness and the loss of control.

The therapist must respect the patient's time frame, and proceed at the pace that a patient allows (56, 69). The slow and repetitious nature of the process requires tolerance on the part of the therapist, but in some instances persistently bland or boring interactions can be brought into therapeutic focus (63).

Specific technical approaches

Heterogeneity in both patients and therapists is such that an enormous number of specific problems and approaches to their management can be described, and a rich clinical literature has addressed these problems over the years. Several broad and basic therapeutic strategies can be defined which capture the elements emphasized most prominently in the literature.

The establishment of a relationship is universally regarded as the first step in treating a schizophrenic patient, and one which brings the therapist into confrontation with the barriers to interpersonal relationship which constitute one of the hallmarks of schizophrenic psychopathology. Different aspects of the process are captured in Sullivan's reference to 'participating' (70), Arieti's (16, 67) emphasis on 'establishing relatedness', or Searles' (18) focus on the development of a 'therapeutic symbiosis', but there is general agreement on the need to deeply engage the patient, whose defenses are often mobilized against such engagement. The means of overcoming these resistances have been widely debated, but the importance of consistency and directness are widely agreed upon, and there is a general consensus that attitudes of anonymity and neutrality fostered by adherence to a psychoanalytic ideal are counterproductive with this particular patient group (49). Most therapists suggest a patient and non-intrusive approach, rather than a more direct interpretive approach like that suggested by Rosen (10). Pao (65), for example, suggests that in the early stages of treatment interpretation is often overwhelming to the patient and impedes the development of a trusting relationship.

A second broad area of therapeutic technique involves active listening and feedback to the patient with the aim of expanding his awareness of an organization of his own experience and that of others. McGlashan (57) referred to this function as 'elucidating the patient's experience in the here and now'. Most authors emphasize the importance of helping the patient to acknowledge feelings, especially loss, anger, and sadness (21, 27, 49). Psychotic symptoms may be explored, but the object is to understand the 'here and now' conflicts or stresses which give rise to them. Attention is focused on what led to the disorder in thinking rather than its content (14). In this role, the therapist is often acting as 'comforter, inquisitor, and teacher' (71). Schulz (56) mentions several technical positions which contribute to this overall function: integrating outside experiences with treatment sessions, listening and interpreting at different levels, educating the patient to observe, asking and answering questions rather than sitting back in silence. Stanton (72) identified specific target areas in the patient's ego function which such techniques aim to improve: (a) enlarging the patient's grasp of context and recognizing its relevance; (b) discovering undesirable patterns of interpersonal relating and how they come about; and (c) understanding the nature of the patient's difficulties in accepting new information about himself.

A third constellation of technical recommendations revolves around concepts of structural or ego growth through identification or internalization of ego capacities of the therapist in an intensified transference-countertransference interaction. The inadequate ego of the patient is seen as requiring support or augmentation from an important other person, and the therapist deliberately tries to serve that function, with the expectation that gradually the 'borrowed ego' may serve as a template for ego development in the patient. Bearing painful feelings which overwhelm the patient's ego (21) is central to this task. Some theoreticians emphasize also the 'containment' of projective identifications (18, 73, 74) and the growth fostered in the patient when the therapist is able to accept the patient's intense feelings, to survive them, and to detoxify them through his analytic understanding (57). The particular activities which contribute to this aspect of ego developing therapeutic function are difficult to specify. A relatively silent or unarticulated process may take place in which the actions of the patient give rise to tension in the therapist which he comes to recognize and manage in such a way that his own tension and the patient's tension are reduced. Gradually the capacity for the experience and tolerance of affect is built up in the patient.

Interpretation which aims to provide insight is the cornerstone of psychoanalytic psychotherapy. In work with schizophrenic patients, interpretation is often seen as gaining prominence only in the later phase of therapy (16, 65). In this later and more interpretive phase, the patient is putting into perspective his feelings and his ways of managing them, which may include his psychosis, and the aim is some resolution of the transference (18, 66, 75). The literature also emphasizes particular approaches to interpretation which take into account the schizophrenic's limited ego capacities. It is generally felt that interpretations should focus on links between stresses and symptoms rather than the content of psychotic productions (14). Many authors suggest emphasis on defensive operations and the more immediate experience of the 'here and now'. The manner in which interpretations are given and their timing should be tailored to the schizophrenic's shortened attention span, idiosyncratic thinking and concreteness. Interpretations should therefore be concise and use language familiar to the patient. It is useful to check back with the patient on how he understood what was said. Timing of interpretation takes on added importance in these patients, who may be overwhelmed by intrusiveness or affective overstimulation.

Implications of research on processes and techniques

Empirical research is only modestly informative about the style and techniques which are most apt to facilitate favorable changes in schizophrenic patients. The clearest and strongest conclusions concern the development of an alliance between a patient and the therapist. Rogers and his coworkers (34) found that those schizophrenic patients who perceived a high degree of empathy and congruence in their therapist (i.e., the therapist appeared genuine and responded as a 'real person') showed the better outcomes. They also found that the patients' views of the relationship correlated much better with outcome than the therapists' views. In the Boston Psychotherapy Study a prospective evaluation of therapeutic alliance defined it in terms of affective involvement in the treatment and a shared collaborative goal. Only a minority of the patients were able to form good alliances (15.4% at one month and 29.8% at six months), and once an alliance was formed, it remained essentially unchanged for the duration of the study (76). If therapists were unable to secure a good alliance in the first six months, it was unlikely that they would subsequently achieve this. Since patients who formed good alliances were more apt to stay in psychotherapy, take medications as prescribed and to have better outcomes, the results underscore the importance of forming such an alliance and the need to consider discontinuation of a therapy when an adequate alliance has not developed by the end of six months.

Other analyses of Boston Psychotherapy Study data focused on defining variations in the patient-therapist interactions within the EIO condition and determining whether they correlate with 2-year outcome (77). The three major technical aspects of EIO therapy (each of which was comprised of a number of intercorrelated component activities) which accounted for most of the variance among EIO therapists were therapist's dynamic exploration, directiveness, and support. The strongest finding was an association between the degree to which a therapist was skillfully involved in dynamic exploration (i.e., the extent to which the therapist was judged to show a sound psychodynamic understanding and accurate attunement to the patient's underlying concerns and motives), and large reductions in patient denial, retardation and apathy, and global psychopathology. The complex process variable of dynamic exploration has some components which overlap with the variables of therapist empathy and sensitivity which Truax and Carkhuff (78) found to be associated with better outcome in the Rogers study. Of particular note is the finding that the exploratory techniques affected some of the negative symptoms of schizophrenia which are often refractory to treatment (79). In addition, improvement on measures of retardation and apathy was greater when therapists also focused to a greater extent on patients' relationships (outside the therapy relationship).

The strong role of supportive and directive techniques deserves attention, for although they are not prominent in the clinical literature on psychodynamic psychotherapy, they were used as much by EIO therapists as were more exploratory techniques, and variations in their use exerted an influence on outcome. Supportive and directive techniques were associated with more substantially decreased anxiety and depression. In contrast, greater reliance on exploratory techniques, especially if directed at the therapy relationship itself, was associated with diminished improvement on measures of anxiety and depression.

In summary, the research findings offer support for only some of the therapeutic strategies and processes emphasized in the clinical literature. The strongest support is for the emphasis on the essential first task of establishing a relationship with the patient. There are also indications of the importance of the therapist's attention to undercurrents, as reflected in the complex variable of dynamic exploration in the Boston study or the variables of empathy and sensitivity in the Rogers study. Empirical studies have not captured or assessed the more complex transference-countertransference interaction and interpretive process characterizing the middle and late phases of therapy. On the other hand, the empirical findings suggest the importance of elements which are relatively neglected by the clinical literature. Supportive and directive aspects of psychodynamic psychotherapy apparently play a greater role in determining outcome than has been usually acknowledged. This finding is consistent with results of studies of other populations (80, 81) and points to the need for further study of these elements of treatment.

Outcomes and assessments of the effects of psychotherapy

Clinicians want to know that they can expect psychotherapy to accomplish and how to assess progress during the course of treatment. There has long been a tension between the ideal of a sweeping resolution or 'cure' for schizophrenia and the acceptance of more modest expectations, which may include results more acceptable to the patient than to others (14). The complexity and diversity of areas of dysfunction in most schizophrenic patients and the results of outcome studies have led to a narrowing of expectations for the impact of psychotherapy. A number of authors have concluded that the effects of psychotherapy may be experienced in a limited sector of the patient's functioning (61, 82, 83). Even if more substantial changes in a patient's overall condition may sometimes take place (49), however, the expectation that broad gains in social and occupational function will result from psychotherapy may obscure the view of more subtle but important benefits. Greater specificity of target symptoms is needed to assess progress in those areas where psychotherapy exerts its greatest influence.

The findings of the Boston Psychotherapy Study suggest that intensive psychotherapy is most likely to exert a beneficial influence on negative or deficit symptoms, and on patients' subjective experience of understanding and accepting their illnesses. Some authors may devalue these benefits in comparison to more measurable improvement in terms of recidivism or return to occupational function. However, the symptoms most affected by psychodynamic psychotherapy are those which are most often refractory to other forms of treatment and which in the long term contribute to the discouraging and demoralizing aspects of the illness. As an anonymous recovering patient indicated (84), regardless of what one thinks causes schizophrenia, the patient's experience includes fractured relationships, feeling at war within his own mind, and an unsteady belief that he is 'a person, not just a visitor looking in on the world'; psychotherapy addresses these problems most directly.

SUMMARY AND CONCLUSIONS

In recent years the practice of psychodynamic or exploratory psychotherapy with schizophrenic patients has become less common. This is in part due to a decrease in the influence of the psychoanalytic perspective on the mainstream of psychiatry, but it is more particularly a response to the limited efficacy shown in empirical outcome studies. It seems clear that psychotherapy given to randomly assigned patients cannot be shown to have broad and substantial advantages over other forms of treatment, and the era of such evaluations should come to a close. The cost of providing intensive psychotherapy for these severely disturbed patients leads some observers to conclude that this treatment choice should be even more sharply limited than it already has been. We too believe that individual psychotherapy for schizophrenic patients should be used selectively. Moreover, available information can and should be used to determine when this treatment should be chosen and to help understand the particular role which psychotherapy may play in a multidimensional approach. Selectivity in the use of psychotherapy entails attention to the particular aspects of the patient's psychopathology which are being addressed and the timing of intervention in the course of the illness, as well as recognition of the importance of matching the patient and therapist.

Multidimensional conceptualization of mental illness from a 'biopsychosocial' perspective (86) and the recognition of the multiple tasks of psychiatry (83) encourage the targeting of aspects of the patient's psychopathology by particular treatment strategies. Psychiatry can be characterized as having a medical perspective, a rehabilitation perspective, an educative-developmental perspective, and a societal-legal perspective (83). Each of these perspectives can be applied to the analysis of goals for specific kinds of patient at certain points in the course of illness. The psychodynamic approach may address the educative-developmental tasks most directly, and its use may be determined by the importance of that aspect of functioning to the patient and by the availability of other tools to address concomitant needs. Future research might specify goals for particular groups of patients and refine assessment procedures for more specific domains of outcome.

Whereas Kraepelin (86) defined dementia praecox in terms of a deteriorating course, more recent evidence (87 – 89) has led to an appreciation of greater variability and better prognosis in the lifelong course of schizophrenia. Psychotherapists have usually resisted an overly deterministic view, but they have generally emphasized the value of initiating psychotherapy in the acute phase, before the development of a downhill course. Accordingly, most research has focused on acute patients. This traditional wisdom of early psychotherapeutic intervention should be reconsidered in light of more recognition that patients may often improve and be more amenable to re-engagement in a social milieu during later phases in the course of illness. The Boston Psychotherapy Study, like most others, excluded more chronic patients from consideration, but the findings of greater engagement in EIO therapy by patients who were struggling with apathy, withdrawal, and emotional blunting or demoralization, rather than more acute symptoms, suggest that processes which develop later in the course of the illness may provide an entree into and indication for intensive psychotherapeutic treatment. For many patients a psychotherapeutic approach with characteristics like those of the RAS therapy of the Boston study may be the best choice early in the course of the illness. For a subgroup of these patients, therapy with more characteristics of the EIO treatment might follow. The sequencing of various treatment approaches in a particular patient's course should receive more attention, both in clinical settings and in systematic evaluations of treatment process and outcome.

Whereas it has been important for empirical research to use random assignment of patients to treatment groups, in the natural world, where psychiatric practitioners encounter a more diverse population diagnosed as schizophrenic, the matching of a patient to a therapeutic modality or to a particular therapist is anything but random. The subjective, emotional responses of schizophrenic patients and their therapists to this process have received scant attention in the research literature, in spite of wide agreement on the importance of matching. Although some authors (e.g. 90) argue that the elements contributing to the matching process are not measurable or quantifiable, efforts to study this aspect of individual psychotherapy are important and should be pursued.

Individual psychodynamically oriented psychotherapy has enriched our understanding of schizophrenic psychopathology and of healing processes which ameliorate the psychic pain of the schizophrenic patient. The trend in recent clinical and research contributions is toward specifying more focal indications, goals, and methods for psychotherapeutic treatment. Tasks for the future include further delineation of the interaction of psychodynamic psychotherapy with other treatment modalities and the approaches to psychotherapy which may be taken at different junctures in the course of illness. For the field as a whole, the place of psychotherapy has become more limited. But for the particular patient and his therapist, psychotherapy is a means of expanding beyond the limits of human understanding and relatedness which schizophrenia imposes on the individual.

REFERENCES

1. Freud S (1911) Psychoanalytic notes on an autobiographical account of a case of paranoia. In: *The Standard Edition of the Complete Psychological Works of Sigmund Freud, Vol. 12,* pp. 3–82. Hogarth Press, London.
2. Freud S (1914) On narcissism. In: *The Standard Edition of the Complete Psychological Works of Sigmund Freud, Vol. 14,* pp. 73–102. Hogarth Press, London.
3. Tausk V (1933) On the origin of the 'Influencing Machine' in schizophrenia. *Psychoanal. Q., 2,* 535.
4. Federn P (1952) In: *Ego Psychology and the Psychoses.* Basic Books, New York.
5. Klein M (1932) The significance of early anxiety situations in the development of the ego. In: *The Psychoanalysis of Children, 3rd ed.* Hogarth Press, London.
6. Segal H (1950) Some aspects of the analysis of a schizophrenic. *Int. J. Psychoanal., 31,* 268.
7. Fairbairn R (1952) *Object Relations Theory of the Personality.* Basic Books, New York.
8. Rosenfeld HA (1966) *Psychotic States: A Psychoanalytic Approach.* Universities Press, New York.
9. Sechehaye MA (1951) *Symbolic Realization.* International Universities Press, New York.
10. Rosen JN (1963) *The Concept of Early Maternal Environment in Direct Psychoanalysis.* Doylestown Foundation, Doylestown, PA.
11. Meyer A (1950) Fundamental conceptions of dementia praecox. In: *Collected Papers of Adolph Meyer, Vol. 2.* Johns Hopkins University Press, Baltimore.
12. Sullivan HS (1953) *The Interpersonal Theory of Psychiatry.* W.W. Norton, New York.
13. Sullivan HS (1962) *Schizophrenia as a Human Process.* W.W. Norton, New York.
14. Fromm-Reichmann F (1948) Notes on the development of treatment of schizophrenics by psychoanalytic psychotherapy. *Psychiatry, 11,* 263.
15. Fromm-Reichmann F (1967) *Principles of Intensive Psychotherapy.* Phoenix Books, Chicago.
16. Arieti S (1955) *The Interpretation of Schizophrenia.* Basic Books, New York.
17. Will OA (1968) Schizophrenia and psychotherapy. In: Marmor J (Ed), *Modern Psychoanalysis.* Basic Books, New York.
18. Searles AF (1965) *Collected Papers on Schizophrenia and other Subjects.* International Universities Press, New York.
19. Whitehorn JC (1944) Guide to interviewing and clinical personality study. *Arch. Neurol. Psychiatry, 52,* 197.
20. Day M, Semrad EV. (1978) Schizophrenic reactions. In: Nicholi A (Ed), *The Harvard Guide to Modern Psychiatry.* The Belknap Press, Cambridge, MA.
21. Semrad EV (1954) The treatment process. *Am. J. Psychiatry, 110,* 426.
22. Semrad EV (1969) *Teaching Psychotherapy of Psychotic Patients.* Grune and Stratton, New York.
23. Adler G (1979) The psychotherapy of schizophrenia: Semrad's contributions to current psychoanalytic concepts. *Schizophr. Bull., 5,* 130.
24. Feinsilver DB, Gunderson JG (1972) Psychotherapy for schizophrenics – is it in-

dicated? A review of the relevant literature. *Schizophr. Bull., 1,* 11.
25. Dyrud JE, Holzman P (1973) The psychotherapy of schizophrenia: does it work? *Am. J. Psychiatry, 130,* 670.
26. Schooler NR (1978) Antipsychotic drugs and psychological treatment in schizophrenia. In: Lipton MA, DiMascio A, Killam KF (Eds), *Psychopharmacology: A Generation of Progress.* Raven Press, New York.
27. Gunderson JG (1979) Individual psychotherapy. In: Bellak L (Ed), *Disorders of the Schizophrenic Syndrome.* Basic Books, New York.
28. Mosher LR, Keith SJ (1980) Psychosocial treatment: individual, group, family, and community support approaches. *Schizophr. Bull., 6,* 10.
29. Heinrichs DW, Carpenter Jr. WT (1981) The efficacy of individual psychotherapy: a perspective and review emphasizing controlled outcome studies. In: Arieti S, Brodie HK (Eds), *American Handbook of Psychiatry, Vol. 7,* pp. 586–613. Basic Books, New York.
30. Stanton AH, Gunderson JG, Knapp PH, Frank AF, Vanicelli ML, Schnitzer R, and Rosenthal R (1984) Effects of psychotherapy in schizophrenia, I. Design and implementation of a controlled study. *Schizophr. Bull., 10,* 520.
31. Gunderson JG, Frank AF, Katz HM, Vanicelli ML, Frosch JP, Knapp PH (1984) Effects of psychotherapy in schizophrenia, II. Comparative outcome of two forms of treatment. *Schizophr. Bull., 10,* 564.
32. Fairweather GW, Simon R, Gebhard ME, Weingarten E, and Reahl JE (1960) Relative effectiveness of psychotherapeutic programs: a multicriteria comparison of four programs for three different patient groups. *Psychol. Monogr., 74,* 1.
33. Grinspoon L, Ewalt JR, and Shader RI (1972) *Schizophrenia: Pharmacotherapy and Psychotherapy.* Williams and Wilkins, Baltimore, MD.
34. Rogers CW, Gendlin EG, Kiesler DJ, Truax CB (1967) *The Therapeutic Relationship and Its Impact: Study of Psychotherapy with Schizophrenics.* The University of Wisconsin Press, Madison.
35. Karon B, O'Grady B (1969) Intellectual test changes in schizophrenic patients in the first six months of treatment. *Psychother. Theory Res. Pract., 6,* 88.
36. Karon BP, VandenBos GR (1972) The consequences of psychotherapy for schizophrenic patients. *Psychother. Theory Res. Pract., 9,* 111.
37. Karon BP, VandenBos GR (1981) *Psychotherapy of Schizophrenia: The Treatment of Choice.* Jason Aronson, New York.
38. May PRA (1968) *Treatment of Schizophrenia: A Comparative Study of Five Treatment Methods.* Science House, New York.
39. Frosch JP, Gunderson JG, Weiss R, Frank A (1983) Therapists who treat schizophrenic patients: characterization. In: Steirlin H, Wynne L, Wirsching M (Eds), *Psychosocial Intervention in Schizophrenia, An International View.* Springer-Verlag, Heidelberg.
40. Katz HM, Frank A, Gunderson JG, Hamm D (1984) Psychotherapy of Schizophrenia: what happens to treatment dropouts. *J. Nerv. Ment. Dis., 172,* 326.
41. Gunderson JG, Hirshfeld R (1975) Selecting schizophrenic patients for individual psychotherapy. In: Gunderson JG, Mosher LR (Eds), *Psychotherapy of Schizophrenia.* Jason Aronson, New York.
42. Linn NW, Caffey EM, Klett CJ, Hogarty GE, Lamb HR (1979) Day treatment and psychotropic drugs in the aftercare of schizophrenic patients. *Arch. Gen. Psychiatry, 36,* 1055.
43. Paul GI, Lentz RJ (1977) *Psychosocial Treatment of Chronic Mental Patients: Milieu versus Social Learning Programs.* Harvard University Press, Cambridge, MA.
44. Wallace CJ, Nelson CJ, Liberman RP, Aitchison RH, Lukoff D, Elder JP, Ferris C

(1980) A review and critique of social skills training with schizophrenic patients. *Schizophr. Bull., 6,* 42.

45. Gunderson JG, Carrol AS (1983) Clinical considerations from empirical research. In: Steirlin J, Wynne L, Wirsching M (Eds), *Psychological Intervention in Schizophrenia: An International View.* Springer-Verlag, Heidelberg.
46. McGlashan TH, Levy ST, Carpenter Jr. WT (1975) Integration and sealing over. *Arch. Gen. Psychiatry, 133,* 14.
47. Carpenter Jr. WT, Heinrichs DW (1980) The role for psychodynamic psychiatry in the treatment of schizophrenic patients. In: Strauss JS, Bowers M, Downey TW, Fleck S, Jackson S, Levine I (Eds), *The Psychotherapy of Schizophrenia.* Plenum, New York.
48. Gunderson JG, Mosher LR (1975) *Psychotherapy of Schizophrenia.* Jason Aronson, New York.
49. Lidz T (1980) The developing guidelines to the psychotherapy of schizophrenia. In: Strauss JS, Bowers M, Downey TW, Fleck S, Jackson S, Levine I (Eds), *The Psychotherapy of Schizophrenia.* Plenum, New York.
50. Friedman RJ, Gunderson JG, Feinsilver DB (1973) The psychotherapy of schizophrenia, an NIMH program. *Am. J. Psychiatry, 130,* 674.
51. Whitehorn JC, Betz BF (1954) A study of psychotherapeutic relationships between physicians and schizophrenic patients. *Am. J. Psychiatry, 111,* 321.
52. Razin AM (1971) The 'A-B' variable in psychotherapy: a critical review. *Psychol. Bull., 75,* 1.
53. McGlashan TH (1984) The Chestnut Lodge Follow Up Study, II. Long-term outcome of schizophrenia and the affective disorders. *Arch. Gen. Psychiatry, 41,* 586.
54. Shader RI, Grinspoon L, Harmatz J, Ewalt JR (1971) The Therapist Variable. *Am. J. Psychiatry, 127,* 1009.
55. Gunderson JG (1978) Patient-therapist matching: a research evaluation. *Am. J. Psychiatry, 135,* 1193.
56. Schulz CG (1975) An individual psychotherapeutic approach with the schizophrenic patient. *Schizophr. Bull., 1,* 46.
57. McGlashan TH (1983) Intensive individual psychotherapy of schizophrenia. A review of techniques. *Arch. Gen. Psychiatry, 40,* 909.
58. Frank AF, Gunderson JG (1987) Matching therapists and milieus: effects on engagement and continuance in psychotherapy. *Psychiatry, 47,* 201.
59. Vaughn CE, Leff JP (1976) The influence of family and social factors on the course of psychiatric illness: a comparison of schizophrenic and depressed neurotic patients. *Br. J. Psychiatry, 129,* 128.
60. Hammer M, Makiesky-Barrow S, Gutwirth L (1978) Social networks and schizophrenia. *Schizophr. Bull., 4,* 522.
61. Carpenter Jr. WT (1986) Thoughts on the treatment of schizophrenia. *Schizophr. Bull., 12,* 527.
62. Will OA (1975) Schizophrenia: psychological treatment. In: Freedman AM, Kaplan HI, Sadock BJ (Eds), *Comprehensive Textbook of Psychiatry, 2nd ed.,* pp. 939–955. Williams and Wilkins, Baltimore, MD.
63. Strauss JS, Carpenter Jr. WT (1981) *Schizophrenia.* Plenum Press, New York.
64. Boyer LB (1980) Office treatment of schizophrenic patients: the use of psychoanalytic treatment with a few parameters. In: Boyer LB, Giovacchini PL (Eds), *Psychoanalytic Treatment of Schizophrenic, Borderline and Characterological Disorders,* pp. 129–170. Jason Aronson, New York.
65. Pao P (1979) *Schizophrenic Disorders.* International Universities Press, New York.
66. Lidz T (1973) *The Origin and Treatment of Schizophrenic Disorders.* Basic Books, New York.

67. Arieti S (1974) An overview of schizophrenia from a predominantly psychological approach. *Am. J. Psychiatry, 23,* 182.
68. Knight R (1946) Psychotherapy of an adolescent catatonic schizophrenic with mutism. *Psychiatry, 9,* 323.
69. Rako S and Mazer H (1980) Semrad: *The Heart of the Therapist.* Jason Aronson, New York.
70. Mullahy PF (1980) Harry Stack Sullivan. In: Kaplan HI, Freedman AM, Sadock BJ (Eds), *Comprehensive Textbook of Psychiatry, 3rd ed,* pp. 748 – 774. Williams and Wilkins, Baltimore, MD.
71. Khantzian EJ, Dalsimer JS, Semrad EV (1968) The use of interpretation in the psychotherapy of schizophrenia. *Am. J. Psychiatry, 23,* 182.
72. Stanton AH (1978) The significance of ego interpretive states in insight-directed psychotherapy. *Psychiatry, 41,* 129.
73. Bion WR (1961) *Experiences in Groups.* Tavistock, London.
74. Feinsilver DB (1980) Transitional relatedness and containment in the treatment of a chronic schizophrenic patient. *Int. Rev. Psychoanal., 7,* 309.
75. Semrad EV (1966) Long-term therapy of schizophrenia: formulation of the clinical approach. In: Usdin GL (Ed), *Psychoneurosis and Schizophrenia.* J.B. Lippincott Co., Philadelphia.
76. Frank AF, Gunderson JG (1990) The role of the therapeutic alliance in the treatment of schizophrenia: effects on course and outcome. *Arch. Gen. Psychiatry,* in press.
77. Glass LL, Katz HM, Schnitzer RD, Knapp PH, Frank AF, Gunderson JG (1989) Psychotherapy of schizophrenia: an empirical investigation of the relationship of process to outcome. *Am. J. Psychiatry, 146,* 603.
78. Truax C, Carkuff R (1967) *Toward Effective Counseling and Psychotherapy: Teaching and Practice.* Aldine, Chicago.
79. Strauss JS, Carpenter Jr. WT, Bartko JJ (1974) An approach to the diagnosis and understanding of schizophrenia: speculations on the processes that underlie schizophrenic symptoms and signs. *Schizophr. Bull., 1,* 61.
80. Luborsky L, Singer B, Luborsky L (1975) Comparitive studies of psychotherapies. *Arch. Gen. Psychiatry, 32,* 995.
81. Wallerstein R (1986) *Forty-two Lives in Treatment.* Guilford Press, New York.
82. Docherty JP (1984) O tempora, O mores: directions in research on the psychotherapeutic treatment of schizophrenia. *Schizophr. Bull., 10,* 621.
83. Adler DA (1985) A framework for the analysis of psychotherapeutic approaches to schizophrenia. *Yale J. Biol. Med., 58,* 219.
84. A Recovering Patient (1986) 'Can we talk?' The schizophrenic patient in psychotherapy. *Am. J. Psychiatry, 143,* 68.
85. Engel GL (1977) The need for a new medical model: a challenge for biomedicine. *Science, 196,* 129.
86. Kraepelin E (1919) *Dementia Praecox and Paraphrenia, 8th ed.* Livingstone, Edinburgh.
87. Bleuler E (1911) *Dementia Praecox, or the Group of Schizophrenias.* International Universities Press, New York (1950).
88. Ciompi L (1980) The natural history of schizophrenia in the long term. *Br. J. Psychiatry, 136,* 413.
89. Harding CM, Strauss JS (1985) The course of schizophrenia: an evolving concept. In: Alpert M (Ed), *Controversies in Schizophrenia.* Guilford, New York.
90. Muller C (1984) Psychotherapy in schizophrenia: the end of the pioneers' period. *Schizophr. Bull., 10,* 618.

CHAPTER 5

Individual reality-oriented supportive psychotherapy

HISHAM M. HAFEZ, ARLENE FRANK AND JOHN P. DOCHERTY

The role of individual psychotherapy in the treatment of schizophrenia has been the subject of much debate. Over the past two decades, systematic research has failed to demonstrate the efficacy of intensive insight-oriented psychotherapy for the vast majority of schizophrenic patients, in either the acute or the chronic phase of the illness (1). The value of supportive psychotherapy, on the other hand, has been generally acknowledged; most consider it to be an important component of the management of any schizophrenic patient (2). Empirical evidence regarding the value of supportive psychotherapy comes primarily from comparative outcome studies where supportive therapy served as the control, or 'treatment-as-usual' condition. In these studies, supportive psychotherapy was shown to be as effective as, and in some areas of function superior to, insight-oriented psychotherapy (1), yet until recently, it was often relegated to the status of a second-class treatment.

Part of the problem has been that, despite its wide application, supportive psychotherapy is not clearly defined (4); the goals of the treatment are often confused with the techniques used to achieve those goals. As a result, it is hard to evaluate its efficacy per se, to use empirical work to refine this therapy or to compare its utility to other forms of treatment. Lacking clear, empirically based guidelines for its use, clinicians attempting to prescribe supportive psychotherapy for a schizophrenic patient have been forced to rely on their own, often limited experience or the anecdotal reports of others who have attempted to define supportive psychotherapy and specify its ingredients. The available literature has the potential to confuse matters further, showing as it does that supportive therapy encompasses many approaches based on different schools (5), none with documented superiority (6) or even clear features that might distinguish one from another (7).

We believe that, in fact, much more is known about supportive psychotherapy and its role in the treatment of schizophrenia than meets the eye. In this chapter we will attempt to integrate what is known about supportive psychotherapy and offer guidelines for its use. We will show how crucial it is to clarify the ways in which a person with a schizophrenic illness needs to be supported, and how this information can be used to integrate supportive psychotherapy in a comprehensive management plan. While drawing on available research data, our focus throughout will be on the clinical realities of the treatment situation and on the issues of greatest concern to therapists, patients, and their families.

The clinician should appreciate that the outcome of schizophrenia is not uniform-

Handbook of Schizophrenia, Volume 4: Psychosocial Treatment of Schizophrenia.
M.I. Herz, S.J. Keith and J.P. Docherty, editors.

ly poor, and can be altered by psychosocial variables. This appreciation should combat a sense of therapeutic nihilism that can undermine treatment. Communicating to patients and their families a realistic sense of optimism would help counter the demoralization and sense of futility seen so often.

BACKGROUND

In a recent review, Winston et al. (8) concluded that despite its widespread use, especially among hospitalized or chronically ill patients, supportive psychotherapy is under-represented in the literature and is not adequately taught in training institutions. With few exceptions (9, 10), the image of supportive psychotherapy remains that of a simple-minded technique requiring no special training (11); the individuals receiving it often are devalued (12). This view becomes less credible if one considers the origin and history of supportive psychotherapy, including the fact that its roots lie in psychoanalytic psychology. As such, it is grounded in an established theory of psychotherapy, one which stresses the need for an in-depth understanding of the patient (12).

It is useful, however, to remember that 'in-depth understanding' need not, indeed should not, be taken solely to mean understanding of the patients' intrapsychic processes, conflicts, defenses, transference reactions, etc. Rather, it should include an appreciation of all those factors, intrapsychic, interpersonal, social, cultural, biological, genetic, and environmental, which have impinged on the patient and continue to influence the patient in his/her efforts to negotiate life and adapt to stresses, both internal and external.

In this respect, supportive and insight-oriented psychotherapy are not so different. It is the use to which the in-depth understanding is put that distinguishes the two. As the name suggests, insight-oriented therapy seeks to achieve and promote the development of insight, which in turn is thought to propel behavioral changes and adaptation. While the latter is certainly of great importance, it is often considered secondary to the former. In supportive therapy, by contrast, understanding first and foremost functions in the service of adaptation to current realities and the exercise of self control and responsibility. Without such changes, achievement of insight is a hollow victory, Klerman (13).

The role of the therapist in insight-oriented and supportive therapy also differs. In insight therapy, the therapist's skill resides in carefully laying the groundwork for accurate understanding to emerge and personal choice for the implementation of that understanding in life change, if any, to proceed. This process relies heavily on the presence of definite intellectual, emotional and social skills in the patient. In supportive therapy the prototype therapist is a 'mentor', a 'good parent' an 'effective coach'; i.e., instructive, predictable, safe, reliable, available and inspirational (14), comfortable with actively setting limits and with demonstrating concern, sympathy and unconditional support (15). Supportive therapy calls more imperatively on therapist skills and experience. Not only must an accurate understanding be developed – a 'psychosocial diagnosis' – but the therapist must decide which interpersonal plan of therapeutic *action* will enhance the adaptation of a patient, recognizing the limited ability to actively formulate such a plan on his or her own.

In recognition of the primary importance of a real, therapeutic relationship, and the need-fear dilemma experienced by so many schizophrenic patients, the therapist's main relationship task is to help the patient titrate the closeness of relationships (16). To this end, the therapist functions as a benevolent other who provides advice and serves as an 'auxiliary ego' or an 'auxiliary superego' (12, 17). Recognizing that all defenses have a protective function, and that schizophrenic patients may need more protection than most patients, should dampen therapists' enthusiasm for confronting or 'interpreting away' those defenses. It is a central premise of supportive therapy that more is to be achieved by selectively reinforcing those defenses that are most adaptive and actively discouraging the use of those defenses that most limit or interfere with everyday functioning. For example, when denial and/or avoidance are operative, the patient should be gently encouraged to examine difficult events that have transpired and to consider alternative reactions should such similar events occur again in the future. However, projective blame, inaction, or a sense of entitlement need to be discouraged (8). The containment of affect, especially negative affect, is an important goal of treatment (18), since the schizophrenic patient can easily become overwhelmed.

'Psychodynamic life narrative', usually reserved for intensive psychotherapy, can be utilized as a supportive intervention as well (19). In essence, it is formulation and integration of the patient's problems in the context of the patient's overall life experience. The patient's behavior is thus seen as understandable, and by implication as falling within the patient's control. The importance of supporting and encouraging the patient's efforts at active mastery and control cannot be stressed enough. To this end, the supportive therapist draws on all of the resources at his/her and the patient's disposal, including family, social and community supports.

RESEARCH EVIDENCE

The first controlled study of supportive psychotherapy with schizophrenic patients was Hogarty et al.'s study of major role therapy (MRT) (20). At first glance, it appeared that patients receiving this form of supportive therapy, which had as its aim the enhancement of coping and full involvement in social and occupational roles, had worse outcomes than patients not receiving this treatment, at least in terms of relapse rates in the first six months after discharge from the hospital. However, for those patients who survived the first six months, the supportive therapy had a salutary effect. Not only was relapse subsequently reduced, but as time went on, patients receiving MRT showed significant improvement in social role functioning compared to patients who did not receive the supportive therapy but received maintenance medication alone. This study provided compelling evidence that good long-term outcome is best achieved using a combination of medication and supportive therapy.

The benefits of supportive psychotherapy, when provided in conjunction with psychotropic medication, were demonstrated more recently in the Boston Interhospital Study of the Psychotherapy of Schizophrenia (1). Using a randomized, prospective design, reality-adaptive supportive therapy was compared to exploratory insight-oriented therapy. Both were provided by experienced therapists to non-chronic patients over a prolonged period of time. The supportive therapy had as its objectives symptom relief and adaptation via drug management, the strengthening of existing defenses, and focusing on current complaints and likely future problems. Technical emphasis was on reassurance, limits, clarification, direction, suggestions for environmental manipulation, and use of community resources. Transference was managed by encouraging positive components and avoiding negative aspects of the relationship (21).

It is noteworthy that after 2 years, patients receiving the supportive therapy were functioning as well in most outcome domains as patients receiving insight-oriented psychotherapy (22); and in some areas, i.e., occupational functioning and hospitalization time, those treated with supportive therapy were functioning better. The advantages assume even greater significance when it is remembered that the costs of the supportive treatment in time and money were far less than those of the intensive, insight-oriented treatment.

In light of the findings of these studies, it is somewhat surprising that more research on supportive psychotherapy with schizophrenic patients has not been forthcoming. There are those who see a need for more research focusing on the nuances of psychotherapy (23) and the differential impact and interaction of different psychotherapy modalities (24, 25). There are, however, a number of researchers who believe that the evidence is now conclusive as to the lack of efficacy of individual psychotherapy and that no further studies are needed (13). This view overlooks the clear positive findings regarding supportive psychotherapy and the dilemmas that clinicians still face and that could be addressed by empirical investigation.

THE CLINICIAN'S DILEMMA

The clinician faced with the task of treating a schizophrenic patient is confronted with many challenges. Bellack (26) has written elegantly about those challenges, and about the gap between research and clinical practice. He calls attention to the fact that despite improving methodology, research studies barely simulate the complexity of the clinical setting. This view has been echoed by Muller (27). He pointed to the discrepancy between the focused purposes of research studies and 'the reality between a patient and his doctor'. The clinical reality includes important idiographic questions and concerns like: What role may supportive psychotherapy (or any other modality) play in the treatment of a specific schizophrenic patient? How can different treatments be most effectively integrated for an individual patient? What form of treatment is most effective at what stage of illness? What is the relevance of the prescribed treatment to the schizophrenic patient's life and his/her developmental tasks?

Therapeutic relationship

Although research on the effects of individual psychotherapy has often yielded inconclusive results, one thing seems clear. The strength and quality of the relationship that is formed between doctor and patient is the single most important factor contributing to positive outcome. Clinicians have long known that schizophrenic patients need stable, caring, consistent relationships to negotiate a life altered by prolonged illness. Available research (28, 29) underscores this. Unfortunately, little research has been devoted specifically to the role of the therapeutic alliance in the treatment of schizophrenia (30) or to the factors that facilitate the development and maintenance of an alliance with a schizophrenic patient.

Conceptualization of the illness

Another important task for the clinician is to decide on how to conceptualize the nature of the schizophrenic illness. The conceptual model chosen will determine what data will be used, how the patients' problems will be formulated and, by extension, what treatment will be prescribed (31). For some, schizophrenia is a biological disturbance; for others it is a psychological deficit or the product of noxious environment stressors impacting on an enduring vulnerability (32). Even among advocates of a single conceptual model disagreements exist, and unifying themes are generally lacking (33). While theoretical debates continue, clinically important questions remain unanswered: What determines the course of schizophrenic illness? What predicts outcome? Why do some patients recover while others don't? We believe that in order to answer these questions, the clinician must keep in mind the distinction between the disease entity and the person afflicted with the illness. Schizophrenia and a patient suffering from schizophrenia are not synonymous; and an understanding of one without the other is thus bound to be at best incomplete, and at worst misleading. In this regard, it should be stressed that schizophrenia is a heterogeneous syndrome with a variable course and a wide range of outcomes. The recovery process is complex and is best regarded as an interactive phenomenon that involves the person, his/her skills, hopes, vulnerabilities, developmental challenges, illness characteristics (mode of onset, course, severity, response to treatment) and the environment, its stressors and the support it offers. It is on this interactive matrix that the clinician brings to bear his/her therapeutic tools. Therapeutic techniques should hence be selected on the basis of the highly individualized understanding and meaningful configuration of these interactive factors.

A PROPOSED FRAMEWORK FOR SUPPORTIVE PSYCHOTHERAPY IN SCHIZOPHRENIA

Despite the fact that a wide range of theoretical formulations of the psychological and psychosocial origins of schizophrenia have been offered, no single framework for the psychotherapy of schizophrenia has emerged as dominant. Additionally, there has been much disagreement among writers in the field on the appropriate focus, content, and techniques of treatment (33). To meet the needs of the greatest number of patients we have adopted a framework for treatment in which psychotherapy is viewed in its most generic form, i.e., as learning, unlearning and relearning in a supportive context. In this framework, the therapist is many things, but above all is a mentor for his/her patients (34). In this role the therapist becomes an agent, a model, a coach and an advocate. In order to function effectively in this role, the therapist needs an understanding not only of the biological and psychosocial bases of schizophrenia and the range of treatments available to combat it, but also an understanding of those patient and therapist characteristics that influence the course of the disorder and the outcome of its treatment.

Patient indications for supportive psychotherapy

Psychotherapy outcome studies indicate that even under optimal conditions only one in three schizophrenic patients can be expected to remain in psychotherapy for an extended period of time. If clinical suitability for psychotherapy is first determined, 80% of patients assigned to treatment continue to be engaged (35). Assessing 'suitability for psychotherapy', however, is often difficult. Some guidelines have been provided by a recent report from the Boston Interhospital study (36). This study examined the characteristics of schizophrenic patients who were most receptive to supportive versus insight-oriented individual psychotherapy, assessed by willingness to continue in it beyond six months. The investigators found that patients with positive symptoms of schizophrenia, considerable subjective distress, high motivation to change and optimism about their recovery prospects were most apt to remain in supportive therapy. By contrast, those with more negative symptoms, a history of good role performance, and much prior therapy were most likely to remain in insight-oriented therapy. This suggests that supportive therapy should be the first line of defense in work with a schizophrenic patient, and that insight-oriented therapy should be reserved for the later stages of treatment when the patient has reconstituted. Additional support for this view comes from the finding that fewer patients dropped out of the supportive therapy (25%) than the insight-oriented therapy (42%) during the first six months (1).

Therapist qualities and behavior

The therapist characteristics that facilitate work with schizophrenic patients are not fully understood. In one of the earliest studies on this subject (37), Whitehorn and Betz noted that some psychiatrists do consistently well with schizophrenic patients while others do not. Subsequent studies, however, found little support for the hypothesized Type A-B therapist distinction in predicting treatment outcome; interest turned to other therapist characteristics, such as level of experience. Experienced therapists have been found to be moderately more effective than inexperienced therapists (38), but again, the differences were not marked. Feinsilver and Gunderson (39) documented therapist correlates of patient continuation in treatment. They found that therapists who were less inclined to externalize problems and who were more interactive, were more successful in keeping schizophrenic patients in treatment. In a more recent report (36), Gunderson et al. found that regardless of the type of therapy offered (supportive or insight-oriented), patients were most likely to continue in treatment with therapists who were willing to share their own personal experiences, feelings, and reactions with their patients, who sought to limit regressions within therapy sessions, and who showed little tolerance for the expression of primitive impulses and demands, all hallmarks of supportive therapy. The patients also were more likely to continue with therapists who had a strong committment to a well-defined treatment approach, no matter what the type. Additionally, the match between the therapists' approach and the approach of the hospital milieu in which treatment was initiated predicted greater engagement and longer stays in treatment (40). Thus, reality orientation, focus on adaptive behavior, treatment adherence and congruence of the individual approach with the larger social system seem to be major, critical components of successful therapist behavior.

Nature of the patient-therapist relationship

The clinician's challenge is not only to promote engagement in treatment, but also to effectively communicate sustained interest and care to his/her patients. Work with schizophrenic patients involves a long-term commitment, and progress is often measured in years rather than weeks or months. Arieti (41) described how some patients who had spent years on the back wards of a state hospital and were dismissed as irreversibly chronic indeed recovered sufficiently to leave the hospital. A common denominator in these cases was the development of what he described as 'relatedness' to a staff member. This occurred in two phases. First, the patient received special consideration from a staff member. Second, the patient was able to help the staff member with his/her work on the unit. Arieti's observations, and those of Stanton and Schwartz, that even the most regressed patients could benefit greatly from human interaction, was one factor that led them to advocate psychotherapy as a treatment for schizophrenia.

'Relatedness', almost by definition, involves mutuality. As Arieti's observations suggest, relatedness with a schizophrenic patient will be impeded by rigid adherence to an authoritarian 'doctor-knows-best' model. Flexibility must rule the day. In the initial phases of treatment, flexibility can take the form of the clinician allowing the patient to lead the way and embark upon treatment at his/her own pace. The clinician can maintain consistency in responding to the patient's lead without imposing an arbitrary agenda for treatment or sacrificing his/her expertise. Contrary to popular belief, the clinician will not 'lose control' of the treatment, and the message conveyed to the patient will be one of interest in him/her as a person. This may also be achieved via a mutual sharing of the patient's and therapist's respective priorities, interests, e.g., hobbies or skills and past experiences, both good and bad. From this sharing a rudimentary alliance often emerges in the form of a basic attachment. Establishing a common ground for discussion can also serve as a prelude for establishing mutually agreed upon treatment goals. It is most useful to at least initially center those goals on the patient's everyday life, regardless of how trivial they may seem to an outside observer or even to the therapist. To the patient they are important.

Allowing, and even encouraging the patient to lead the therapist rather than vice versa should not be taken to mean that the therapist is absolved of responsibility for the treatment. For example, the therapist must be willing to act vigorously to prevent self-destructive behavior and to limit psychotic distortions whenever they emerge. But as always, the therapist should explain in a language understandable to the patient why he/she (the therapist) is acting as he/she does, and the therapist should, as far as possible, encourage the patient to explore his/her fears and reality misperceptions. In this way, the patient and therapist become true collaborators in the enterprise of treatment, a crucial prelude to therapeutic gains (42).

GOALS OF TREATMENT: WHAT TO SUPPORT

The goals of treatment often are determined by the theoretical framework of the therapist. In work with schizophrenic patients, where questions outnumber answers, rigid theory can hamper rather than enhance treatment. Effective treatment, including supportive therapy, should be guided by an appreciation of the long-term nature of the illness and its meaning to the patient, the need for multi-disciplinary treatment coordination, and the acceptance of a partnership between those giving treatment, the patient, and his/her environment in setting treatment goals and devising methods for achieving those goals. The clinician's task is to be familiar with the patient's needs, hopes, vulnerabilities, stressors, peculiar style of negotiating difficulties, and behavioral patterns that predict relapse. We believe that supportive therapy should be the responsibility of a knowledgeable clinician, functioning in what Wing (42) described as 'a care coordinator or key worker' role. This suggests that although the clinician possesses special expertise, he/she must always utilize that expertise in the service of the patient. Knowledge will go for nought if the clinicial cannot find a way to communicate it so that it has meaning to and relevance for the patient. Individualized treatment goals must, therefore, be arrived at through negotiations with the patient and his/her family. Certain central goals, however, should be established and individually tailored for all patients. These include combating demoralization and inducing hope, modeling and reinforcing adaptive functioning, supporting the active role of the patient in influencing the course of illness, educating the patient and his/her significant others to recognize prodromal events and symptoms, developing strategies to prevent relapse, and informing patients and families about the role of medication and its side-effects. These goals can best be achieved by keeping in mind the heterogeneous nature of schizophrenia, the non-linear course of the illness, the ways in which the patient can actively influence that course, and the important contribution that contextual factors can play in the treatment.

HETEROGENEITY OF THE DISORDER

Schizophrenia is a far more heterogeneous disorder than was initially suspected, even for subgroups strictly diagnosed using DSM-III criteria. Chronicity as an indigenous component of schizophrenia has been questioned (43), and numerous studies have seriously challenged the classical view of schizophrenia as an inevitability involving an unfavorable and irreversible course (43 – 46). Since schizophrenic deterioration has been shown to be associated with psychosocial variables, such as social understimulation, family and environmental stressors, it has been speculated by some (46) to be a kind of psychosocial 'artifact'. This view has received support from observations that recovery can occur even after long-term chronic states. What determines the outcome of the disorder is not fully understood. Strauss and Carpenter (47) have postulated an interactive development model, in which outcome is seen as a product of interaction between favorable and unfavorable environmental influences and the person's vulnerability. According to this model, symptoms, occupational and social performance and re-hospitalization are relatively independent dimensions of the patient's function that together constitute 'linked open systems' (48).

NON-LINEARITY OF COURSE OF THE DISORDER

Using data from the Yale longitudinal study, Strauss et al. (49) have offered a model for the course of the disorder based on a non-linear progression of recovery. According to their model, recovery proceeds in identifiable phases that include moratoria, change-points and ceilings. Each phase has characteristic subjective experiences, objective findings and specific patient-environment interactions. An intervention that is appropriate at one point may not therefore be appropriate at another; and an intervention that can have beneficial effects in one domain may have deleterious effects in another. For example, during a change point, symptom exacerbation might occur. Aggressive intervention by means of psychotropic medication or hospitalization could abort a fully fledged psychotic episode. However, it also might limit the potential for important learning and possible improvement. In formulating a medication strategy it is useful to remember that psychological decompensation is a phasic process that seems to be sequentially ordered, unfolding over time (50). Psychotic symptoms evolve over a period of days and even weeks, preceded by non-psychotic prodromal periods. Appreciation of this relapse process should encourage the clinician to explore that phenomenology of the patients' 'psychic instability'. Rather than simply making a determination of whether the patient is manifesting symptoms that could be treated pharmacologically, the clinician should ask questions like the following: What factors dislodged the patient from a state of equilibrium or remission? What is the extent of the deterioration and how is it interfering with the patient's everyday functioning? What various factors might promote restablization?

For an individual patient, the factors that set this process in motion may be highly personal and varied, including psychological factors, such as loss of a significant other, promotion at a job, or anniversary reaction, as well as biological factors, such as medication non-compliance or use of illicit drugs. Often these factors are interrelated. For example, a patient may discontinue drug therapy because it signifies being ill, despite evidence of the medication's efficacy. Simply encouraging the patient to resume the medication without exploring the implications of this from the patient's perspective will be advice that falls on deaf ears.

Similarly, it is not sufficient simply to inform patients and their families of common identifiable prodromal signs and symptoms, although this may be quite useful. It is important also to discuss the meanings of these signs and symptoms and to recognize that not all patients show all of the manifestations described. Different individuals may show unique clusters of changes which may be recognizable only to significant others. This underscores the value of acquiring a thorough knowledge of the individual patient's patterns.

THE ACTIVE ROLE OF THE PATIENT

Supportive therapy is sometimes miscontrued as a treatment based on the assumption that patients, especially psychotic patients, do not know what they want or need and that the clinician must therefore set the treatment priorities and actively take charge of the treatment. There is little doubt that with schizophrenic patients, more than with others, therapists must be active. The danger is that in doing so, the therapist will unwittingly overlook or discourage the patient's active participation in the treatment or recovery process. Even the most disorganized patient has some legitimate ideas about what he/she wants *and* needs. Unfortunately, the active role of the patient in the recovery from severe psychiatric illness has been relatively neglected. Conceptualization of the mentally ill person as a helpless victim of a disease, pathogenic family or social environment is so pervasive that good data on how a person may interact with or influence the disease process is lacking. Nonetheless, recent findings based on single case reports, autobiographical descriptions (51) and longitudinal studies provide valuable information on the active role of the patient in recovery from illness.

Strauss et al. (52) have described different features of the patient's role in the recovery from psychosis that range from minimal involvement, e.g., basic compliance with prescribed treatment regiment, to maximal involvement, e.g., full and active collaboration in the treatment process. Wing (42) has also identified factors partially under patient control that could serve as the basis for self-help and could influence the long-term course of schizophrenia. These factors include decisions about whether or not to take medication, knowledge of situations that trigger decompensation, and opportunities for utilizing one's talents and helping others to understand the illness. Taking a somewhat broader perspective, Brier and Strauss (53) have utilized self-control theory to describe self-regulation mechanisms utilized by patients with psychotic disorders. These mechanisms include self-monitoring, self-evaluation, and self-control. With appropriate guidance, all of these can facilitate recovery and enhance self-esteem. So too can inclusion of patients in the conduct of clinical evaluations usually carried out by clinicians alone. For example, Herz et al. (54, 55) demonstrated that patients and their families can be taught to act as substitute diagnosticians and recognize prodromal events and symptoms that herald florid decompensation. With this information, patients then can make use of an intermittent regimen of medication. By careful monitoring of prodromal signs, hospitalization rates are comparable to those of stable outpatients maintained on medication (20). All of these studies show how the centrality and importance of the patient's role in overcoming illness can provide the patient with a measure of autonomy and control over an otherwise inexplicable disease.

MODIFICATION OF THE SOCIAL MILIEU

The clinician should appreciate the role that the patient's social milieu may play in altering the course of illness and inducing relapse, or promoting recovery and stabilization. For example, emotional attitudes of relatives termed high expressed emotion (or EE) has been linked to relapse and to outcome of schizophrenia (56, 57); so too have noxious life events. Brown and Birley (58) found an increased occurrence of stressful life events in the weeks preceding relapse. This, coupled with the fact that a significant number of schizophrenic patients leave hospitals to return to live with families, led Wing (42) to argue for the need to incorporate the exploration of family interaction patterns into treatment plans. One of the tasks of a supportive therapist is to encourage specific strategies for nullifying noxious social and familial influences. The therapist should decide how noxious the social environment is and what intervention is needed. Helping the patient enroll in a partial hospitalization program or encouraging the patient to seek activity outside the home are but two examples of the ways in which the therapist can support the patient in his/her efforts to manage life stresses and avoid florid decompensations.

Vocational intervention

The supportive therapist would, of course, be remiss if he/she did not involve him/herself in the patient's vocational endeavors and problems. Although the precise role of work in the course of psychiatric disorders is not well understood, its importance is clearly established. Work serves four major functions: structure, self-esteem regulation, personal relationships, and reality contact. Each can be related in relatively direct fashion to symptom disturbances, and by extension to recovery.

For patients not at the point of being able to work, the focus must of necessity be on rehabilitation, another neglected area in clinical training and practice. Recently, Harding et al. (59) reviewed the difficulties in bridging the existing gap between treatment institutions and rehabilitation programs and suggested methods to make efforts in both areas more integrated. The clinician's willingness to help the patient negotiate an often cumbersome rehabilitation system, and if possible, be available for consultation with employers, would obviously be beneficial to the patient. It is essential for the therapist to make interventions that are contextually meaningful, i.e., that are relevant to the patient in his or her life situation.

The provision of coherence and coordination

It is useful for the therapist to consider him/herself as the core of the treatment process. In this role, the therapist, *through the supportive relationship,* establishes a coherence and center for the different therapeutic interventions, agents, and agencies which may be made available to the patient. The therapist also plays an *instrumental* role in coordinating the manifold sources of therapeutic effort which will be made available to the patient. Treatment for most schizophrenic patients must extend beyond the therapist's office. It must address the welfare, housing, disability determination and even legal difficulties of the patient, as they are appropriate to maintaining the patient's psychological equilibrium.

CONCLUSION

In this chapter we have reviewed the role of supportive individual psychotherapy in the treatment of schizophrenia. We have stressed the need for the practical use of available knowledge about the disorder and its course to guide treatment. We believe that collaboration between clinicians, patients, and their significant others is essential for accomplishing treatment goals. Collaboration between clinicians and researchers also is important, since we believe that treatment studies should not only advance our knowledge, but be clinically relevant as well.

The reader might have noticed that discussing supportive psychotherapy, we have used terms like 'explore', that are typically associated with insight-oriented therapy. This reflects our view that many of the distinctions between the two forms of therapy are artificial and impractical. It also reflects our belief that therapists should avoid dogma in order to make available to their patients the full benefits of their knowledge and therapeutic skills.

In closing, as we design treatment approaches for our patients, we will hopefully not overlook their basic needs as people, but will heed Sullivan's reminder that 'schizophrenics are more human than otherwise'.

REFERENCES

1. Stanton AH, Gunderson JG, Knapp PH, Frank AF, Vannicelli ML, Schmtzer R, Rosenthal R (1984) Effects of psychotherapy in schizophrenia, I. Design and implementation of controlled study, *Schizophr. Bull., 10,* 520.
2. Torrey EF (1986) Management of chronic schizophrenia outpatients. *Psychiatr. Clin. North Am., 9,* 143.
3. May PRA (1968) *Treatment of Schizophrenia: A Comparative Study of Five Treatment Methods.* Science House, New York.
4. Conte MR, Plutchik R (1986) Controlled research in supportive psychotherapy. *Psychiatr. Ann., 16,* 530.
6. Luborsky L, Singer B, Luborsky L (1978) Comparative studies of psychotherapies. *Arch. Gen. Psychiatry, 32,* 995.
7. Naftulin D, Donnelly F, Wolkon G (1975) Four therapeutic approaches to the same patient. *Am. J. Psychother., 29,* 266.
8. Winston A, Pinsker H, McCullough L (1986) A review of supportive psychotherapy. *Hosp. Community Psychiatry, 37,* 1105.

9. Alexander F (1953) Current news on psychotherapy. *Psychiatry, 16,* 113.
10. Wallace ER (1983) Supportive psychotherapy. In: *Dynamic Psychiatry in Theory and Practice.* Lea and Febiger, Philadelphia, PA.
11. Sullivan PR (1971) Learning theories and supportive psychotherapy. *Am. J. Psychiatry, 128,* 119.
12. Werman DS (1986) *The Practice of Supportive Psychotherapy.* Brunner/Mazel, New York.
13. Klerman GL (1984) Ideology and science in the individual psychotherapy of schizophrenia. *Schizophr. Bull., 10,* 608.
14. Alder E (1982) Supportive psychotherapy revisited. *Hillside J. Clin. Psychiatry, 4,* 3.
15. Stafford-Clark D (1970) Supportive psychotherapy. In: Price JH (Ed), *Modern Trends in Psychological Medicine II.* Appleton Century Crofts, New York.
16. Robinson MV, Flaherty JA (1982) Self-regulation of distance in supportive psychotherapy. *Clin. Soc. Work J., 10,* 209.
17. Pine F (1986) Supportive psychotherapy: a psychoanalytic perspective. *Psychiatr. Ann., 16,* 526.
18. Kernberg OF (1984) Supportive psychotherapy. In: *Severe Personality Disorders, Psychotherapeutic Strategies,* pp. 147 – 164, Yale University Press, New Haven, CT.
19. Viederman M (1983) The psychodynamic life narrative: a psychotherapeutic intervention useful in crisis situations. *Psychiatry, 46,* 236.
20. Hogarty GE, Goldberg SC, Schooler NR, Ulrich RF, Collaborative Study Group (1974) Drug and sociotherapy in the aftercare of schizophrenic patients, II. Two-year relapse rates. *Arch. Gen. Psychiatry, 31,* 603.
21. Gunderson JG, Frank AF (1985) Effect of psychotherapy in schizophrenia. *Yale J. Biol. Med., 58,* 373.
22. Gunderson JG, Frank AF, Katz HM, Vannicelli ML, Frosch JP, Knapp PH (1984) Effects of psychotherapy in schizophrenia, II. Comparative outcome of two forms of treatment. *Schizophr. Bull., 10,* 564.
23. Docherty JP (1984) O Tempora, O Mores. Directions in research on psychotherapeutic treatment of schizophrenia. *Schizophr. Bull., 10,* 621.
24. Carpenter WT (1984) A perspective on the psychotherapy of schizophrenia project. *Schizophr. Bull., 10,* 599.
25. May DRA (1984) A step forward in research on psychotherapy of schizophrenia. *Schizophr. Bull., 10,* 604.
26. Bellack L (1979) The schizophrenic syndrome: what the clinician can do until the scientist comes. In: Bellack L (Ed), *Disorders of the Schizophrenic Syndrome,* pp. 585 – 590. Basic Books, New York.
27. Muller C (1984) Psychotherapy in schizophrenia: the end of the pioneers' period. *Schizophr. Bull., 10,* 618.
28. Rogers CR, Gendlin EG, Kiesler DJ, Traux CB (1967) *The Therapeutic Relationship and its Impact. Study of Psychotherapy with Schizophrenics.* The University of Wisconsin Press, Madison, WI.
29. Grinspoon L, Ewalt JR, Scharder RI (1972) *Schizophrenia: Pharmacotherapy and Psychotherapy.* Williams and Wilkins, Baltimore, MD.
30. Frank AF, Gunderson JG (1989) The role of the therapeutic alliance in the treatment of schizophrenia: relationship to course and outcome. *Arch. Gen. Psychiatry,* in press.
31. Lazare A (1981) Hidden conceptual models in clinical psychiatry. In: Caplan AL, Englehendt HT, McCarthy JJ (Eds), *Concepts of Health and Disease: Interdisciplinary Perspectives,* pp. 419 – 431. Addison Wesley, Reading, MA.
32. Zublin J (1987) Possible implications of the vulnerability hypothesis for the psychosocial

management of schizophrenia. In: Strauss JS, Boker W, Brenner HD (Eds), *Psychosocial Treatment of Schizophrenia,* pp. 30 – 47, Hans Huber, Toronto.
33. Gunderson J (1979) Individual psychotherapy. In: Bellack L (Ed), *Disorders of the Schizophrenic Syndrome.* pp. 364 – 398. Basic Books, New York.
34. Possick S (1983) The therapist as a mentor. *J. Nerv. Ment. Dis., 171,* 314.
36. Frank A, Gunderson JG, Gomes Schwartz B (1987) The psychotherapy of schizophrenia: patient and therapist factors related to continuance. *Psychotherapy, 24,* 392.
37. Whitehorn JC, Betz BJ (1954) A study of psychotherapeutic relationships between physicians and schizophrenic patients. *Am. J. Psychiatry, 3,* 321.
38. Gunderson JG, Hirschfeld R (1975) Selecting schizophrenic patients for individual psychotherapy. In: Gunderson JG, Mosher L (Eds), *Psychotherapy of Schizophrenia: Current Theory, Research and Practice,* pp. 292 – 304. Jason Aronson, New York.
39. Feinsilver DB, Gunderson JG (1972) Psychotherapy of schizophrenia: is it indicated? A review of the relevant literature. *Schizophr. Bull., 6,* 11.
40. Frank AF, Gunderson JG (1984) Matching therapist and milieus: effects on engagement and continuance in psychotherapy. *Psychiatry, 46,* 201.
41. Arieti S (1974) *Interpretation of Schizophrenia,* 2nd ed. Basic Books, New York.
42. Wing J (1987) Psychosocial factors affecting the long-term course of schizophrenia. In: Strauss JS, Boker W, Brenner HD (Eds), *Psychosocial Treatment of Schizophrenia,* pp. 13 – 29, Hans Huber, Toronto.
43. Bleuler M (1972) Die schizophrenen Geistesstörungen im Lichte langjähriger Kranker und Familiengeschichten. Thieme, Stuttgart.
44. Tsuang M, Woolson R, Fleming J (1979) Long-term outcome of major psychoses, I. Schizophrenic and affective disorders compared with psychiatrically symptom-free surgical conditions. *Arch. Gen. Psychiatry, 36,* 1295.
45. Harding CM, Brooks GW, Ashikaga T, Strauss JS, Landerl PD (1987) Aging and social functioning in once-chronic schizophrenic patients 22 – 62 years after first admission: The Vermont Story. In: Miller N, Cohen CD (Eds), *Schizophrenia, Paranoia, and Schizophreniform Disorders in Later Life,* pp. 160 – 166. Guilford Press, New York.
46. Harding CM, Zubin J, Strauss JS (1987) Chronicity in schizophrenia: fact, partial fact or artifact? *Hosp. Community Psychiatry, 38,* 477.
47. Strauss JS, Carpenter WT (1981) *Schizophrenia.* Plenum, New York.
48. Strauss S, Carpenter WT (1974) The prediction of outcome in schizophrenia, II. Relationship between predictor and outcome variables. *Arch. Gen. Psychiatry, 31,* 37.
49. Strauss JS, Hafez H, Liberman P, Harding CM (1985) The course of psychiatric disorder, III. Longitudinal principles. *Am. J. Psychiatry, 142,* 289.
50. Docherty JP, VanKammen DP, Siris SG, Marder SR (1978) Stages of onset of schizophrenic psychosis. *Am. J. Psychiatry, 135,* 420.
51. A Recovering Patient, (1986) 'Can We Talk?' The schizophrenic patient in psychotherapy. *Am. J. Psychiatry, 143,* 68.
52. Strauss JS, Harding CM, Hafez H, Lieberman PB (1978) The role of the patient in recovery from psychosis. In: Strauss JS, Boker W, Brenner HD (Eds), *Psychosocial Treatment of Schizophrenia,* pp. 160 – 166, Hans Huber, Toronto.
53. Brier A, Strauss JS (1983) Self-control in psychotic disorders. *Arch. Gen. Psychiatry, 40,* 1141.
54. Herz MI, Melville C (1980) Relapse in schizophrenia. *Am. J. Psychiatry, 137,* 801.
55. Herz MI, Szymanski HV, Simon JC (1982) Intermittent medication for stable schizophrenic outpatients; an alternative to maintenance medication. *Am. J. Psychiatry, 139,* 918.

56. Brown G, Birley J, Wing J (1972) Influence of family life on the course of schizophrenic disorders or replication. *Br. J. Psychiatry, 121,* 258.
57. Vaughn CE, Leff JP (1976) The influence of family and social factors on the course of psychiatric illness. *Br. J. Psychiatry, 129,* 125.
58. Brown GW, Birley JLT (1968) Crisis and life changes and the onset of schizophrenia. *J. Health Human Behav., 9,* 203.
59. Harding CM, Strauss JS, Hafez H, Lieberman PB (1987) Work and mental illness, I. Toward an integration of the rehabilitation process. *J. Nerv. Ment. Dis., 175,* 317.

CHAPTER 6

Behavior therapy

VOLKER RODER, THAD A. ECKMAN, HANS D. BRENNER, NORBERT KIENZLE AND ROBERT P. LIBERMAN

INTRODUCTION

Treatment and rehabilitation strategies for individuals suffering from schizophrenia can now be designed on the basis of a conceptual blueprint that explains and predicts the course and outcome of this major mental disorder. The variables comprising this blueprint are: biobehavioral vulnerability; environmental protectors, potentiators and stressors; and personal protectors. Schizophrenia is viewed as a biomedical, stress-linked disorder which is moderated by supports conferred by the environment and the afflicted individual's level of competence and ability to cope with life's challenges.

This framework for understanding the variability in schizophrenic disorders, both between individuals and over time for a particular individual, emphasizes a dynamic and homeostatic interaction among determinants at the biological, environmental and behavioral levels. Depending upon the balance of factors at any one time, transient intermediate states of psychobiological overload and hyperarousal can develop and lead to prodromal symptoms or even to florid symptoms characteristic of the disorder. This multilevel and interactional model of schizophrenia is graphically represented in Fig. 1. It should be noted that the symptoms of schizophrenia with their associated social and occupational impairments may be manifested for varying durations and in varying degrees of severity. Also, depending upon the interplay among vulnerability, stress, protective, and potentiating factors, the correlation between psychopathology and psychosocial functioning may range from high to low.

The symptoms and impairments in social role functioning that comprise schizophrenic disorders can be viewed as being in equilibrium with influences converging from the biological, behavioral, and environmental levels. For example, the appearance or exacerbation of symptoms may occur in a psychobiologically vulnerable individual when:

(a) Stressful events such as drug abuse or loss of a job overwhelm the individual's coping skills.

(b) Potentiating factors, such as high levels of intrafamilial tension or an overstimulating treatment environment, evoke hyperarousal and deficiencies in the processing of information in an already compromised cognitive apparatus.

(c) The individual cannot meet the behavioral demands of everyday life because the protective effects of medication have been lost through non-compliance.

(d) Social problem-solving skills have withered through disuse and withdrawal, or,

Handbook of Schizophrenia, Volume 4: Psychosocial Treatment of Schizophrenia.
M.I. Herz, S.J. Keith and J.P. Docherty, editors.

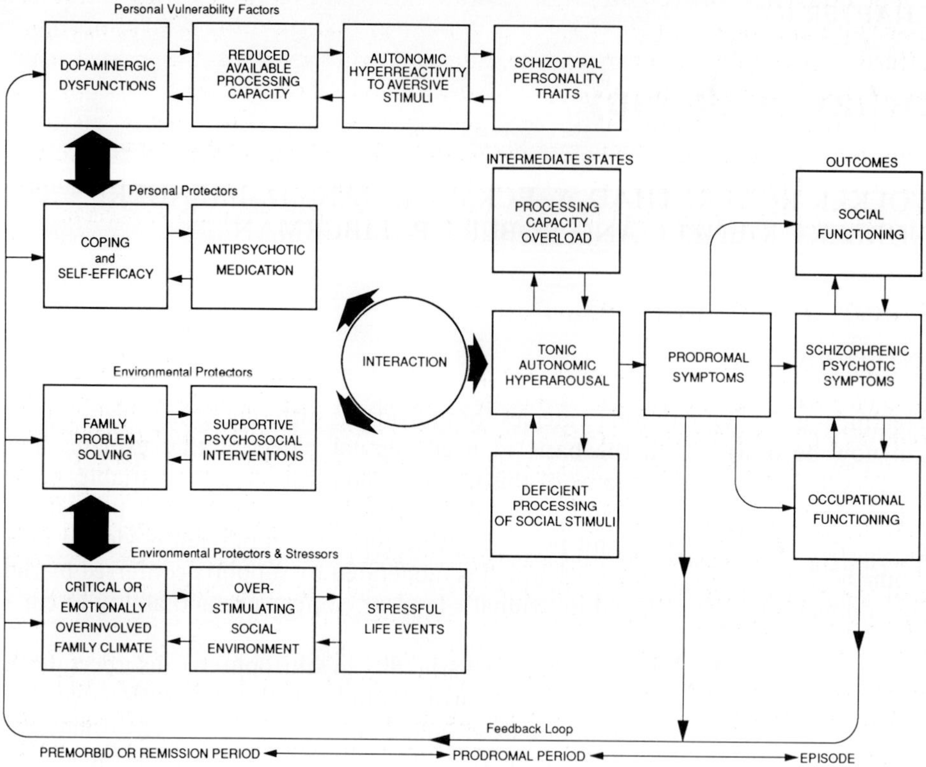

FIG. 1 *Multifactor model of schizophrenia.*

alternatively, have never been learned in the first place.

(e) The individual's social support network weakens or collapses.

The interactional and multilevel model of schizophrenia is bidirectional and does not consign the patient to being a passive figure. Thus, appropriate dosing of neuroleptic drugs can abort a relapse; social skills can be strengthened through training and can protect a vulnerable individual from succumbing to stressful life events. Family intervention and participation in a psychosocial self-help club can bolster social support and buffer the noxious effects of tension and stressors from the environment and even of heightened biological diathesis.

Instead of viewing the pathogenesis of schizophrenia as arising entirely and mechanistically from biological and environmental determinants, it is useful also to see individuals as active participants in the management and outcome of their disorder. The onset and course of schizophrenia are a reciprocal of the actions and behavioral repertoire of the individual, on the one hand, and biological and environmental processes on the other. A model of schizophrenia that encompasses 'stress-vulnerability-coping-competence' highlights the ability of the individual to exercise behavioral competencies that can have an effect on his social environment and on his brain function.

For example, a person with good social and assertiveness skills can galvanize assistance and support from friends and relatives that, in turn, will aid in coping efforts, community survival, and instrumental problem solving. Repeated many times over the course of months and years, these mastery experiences may also favorably affect neurotransmitter or other aspects of central nervous system function. For these conceptually based reasons, together with a substantial base of empirically validated outcome studies, behavior therapy and allied techniques have loomed large on the horizon of psychosocial interventions for schizophrenia.

EARLY BEHAVIORAL APPROACHES

Behavior therapy for schizophrenics began with a limited number of case studies in behavior modification and has progressed to elaborate, multimodal programs with reinforcement regimens for social learning (1). The first successes in the behavioral treatment of schizophrenic patients were reported by Ayllon and Michael (2) in 1959. Early workers in behavior modification defined psychotic dysfunctions as behavioral excesses or deficits. Efforts were directed at influencing symptoms by altering the antecedents and consequences of problematic behavior. It was assumed that the problematic behavior displayed by schizophrenics followed the same rules of learning as normal behavior (3). In the early days of behavior modification, researchers were not fully aware of the limitations that biological vulnerability imposes on the use of behavior modification procedures with schizophrenics (4).

The first attempts to influence schizophrenic behavior followed two strategies: the use of reinforcement contingencies to increase desirable behavior; and punishment and extinction procedures to reduce undesirable behavior. Studies designed to influence the language of schizophrenic patients were among the first experiments in which these techniques were used. The therapeutic goal common to these efforts was defined as reducing the frequency of psychotic language while increasing the frequency of appropriate language. Several authors reported successes with this approach (5 – 7). Furthermore, these operant procedures evaluated in early studies helped garner new information which led to the development of new therapeutic techniques. For example, it was shown that material reinforcers were generally more effective than verbal or social reinforcers in the treatment of schizophrenic patients (8). It was also found that the reinforcers commonly used in psychiatric settings, such as cigarettes, coffee and sweets, did not produce the desired behavioral changes in a number of cases. Thus, experiments evaluating the effects of secondary reinforcers, or tokens, were initiated (9). Furthermore, a difficult problem, still common today, was encountered – therapy successes rarely lasted longer than the therapy itself, and newly learned behavior patterns did not generalize readily to other classes of behavior. These problems compelled researchers to investigate further the specific nature of schizophrenia as basic principles of learning were applied in the design of new treatments.

Behavioral experiments were conducted in which symptomatic behavior was suppressed by training the patient to replace symptoms with incompatible behavior patterns. Diverting conversation proved effective in reducing hallucinations, while leisure-time occupations provided a means of reducing the frequency of psychotic monologues and bizarre behavior (1, 10). These studies showed that it was possible to provide even severely impaired chronic schizophrenic patients with an improved and more socially appropriate behavioral repertoire.

Paul and Lentz (11) demonstrated that substantial treatment effects could be achieved by using an elaborate, carefully planned and controlled, and sufficiently long therapeutic program encompassing a broad spectrum of behavior change modalities. In their study, Paul and Lentz compared three therapeutic procedures: standard psychiatric state hospital treatment; an up-scale milieu therapy program based on principles of the 'therapeutic community'; and a social learning program which made use of modeling, shaping, problem-solving techniques and a token economy. The psychosocial treatment programs explicitly aimed to rehabilitate the patients by helping them to improve self-care, interpersonal and communication skills. An effort was made to decrease the frequency of bizarre and unsuitable behavior as well. In order to ensure reintegration into the community upon discharge, treatment incorporated a 'maintenance' aftercare program following in-patient hospitalization.

The results of the study by Paul and Lentz indicated that the milieu therapy program was superior to traditional psychiatric treatment in every respect, while the social learning program proved to be even better than milieu therapy. The superiority of the social learning program was demonstrated most clearly with respect to the acquisition of cognitive, social and instrumental skills. The social learning program surpassed the other treatments in achieving all of the therapeutic goals established in the program. Severely disabled, chronic patients improved their adaptive skills, increased community tenure, reduced the frequency of psychotic and bizarre behavior and demonstrated a reduced need for antipsychotic medication (12). Since 1977, when Paul and Lentz published these results, a number of clinical researchers have achieved similarly dramatic changes in the behavior of chronically mentally ill persons (10, 13 – 18).

SOCIAL SKILLS TRAINING

There are many sources of empirical data that recommend social skills training as a means for improving patients' competence and ability to cope with stressors. A number of studies have highlighted the importance of premorbid and postmorbid social competence as a predictor of outcome in major psychiatric disorders (19, 20). These findings suggest that social skills training might improve long-term prognosis by upgrading the postmorbid social competence of chronic patients. Second, the magnitude of deficits in social and living skills has been well documented in chronic psychiatric patients. For example, in one study, major functional deficits in social and personal areas were found in more than 50% of a sample of chronic psychiatric patients (21). A multi-hospital study of schizophrenic patients placed in foster homes after relatively brief hospitalizations found that relapse rates at one year after discharge were significantly higher among those patients who had pre-release deficiencies in social skills (22).

Methods of social skills training

Many psychosocial programs claim to provide social skills training. However, it is important to distinguish between non-specific group activities that engage patients in 'socialization', and methods which deliberately and systematically use behavioral learning techniques in a structured approach to skills building. While socialization activities can lead to acquisition of skills through incidental learning during spontaneous social interactions (23), social skills training uses procedures based on well-established principles of human learning to train specific interpersonal skills and to promote the generalization and maintenance of these skills. The procedures that have been developed to train interpersonal skills have been empirically tested and 'packaged' for ready access by practitioners (24, 25). In the remainder of this chapter, the definition of social skills training will be limited to those methods which harness the specific principles of human learning to promote the acquisition, generalization, and durability of skills needed in interpersonal situations (26).

The learning disabilities experienced by many chronic psychiatric patients require the use of highly directive behavioral techniques for training social skills. For example, most chronic patients have attentional and information-processing deficits. They show hyperarousal or underarousal in psychophysiological testing, and they experience overstimulation from emotional stressors or even from therapy sessions that are not carefully structured and modulated. Chronic patients often fail to be motivated by the customary forms of social and tangible rewards available in traditional therapy. In addition, they generally lack conversational ability, a basic building block for social competence. Schizophrenics, in particular, are deficient in social perception and have difficulty generating alternatives for coping with everyday problems such as missing a bus, making an appointment, or getting help with bothersome drug side-effects. Patients tend to make less eye contact, have more verbal dysfluencies, and use less vocal intonation, all of which may impair social learning.

It is important to tailor social skills training procedures to the needs of the individual patient, as all patients present different constellations of social abilities and deficiencies. Several training models are presently available to the clinician. Longest in use is a 'standard package' for training skills, which includes providing detailed instructions to the patient, modeling appropriate use of the skills, role-playing interpersonal situations, and reinforcing and providing corrective feedback to the patient (27). However, this approach is ineffective for patients with severe attentional deficiencies. A model using 'attention focusing' procedures that simplify the learning of complex skills has been effective in training conversational skills in some seriously regressed and thought-disordered chronic psychiatric patients who are otherwise not amenable to social skills training (27).

Chronic psychiatric patients have been found to be deficient in basic problem-solving skills (28, 29). In this social skills model, components of problem solving are the focus of training. Interpersonal communication is viewed as a three-stage process, requiring:

(a) *Receiving skills* – attending to and accurately perceiving cues and contextual elements of interpersonal situations.

(b) *Processing skills* – generating response alternatives, weighing the consequence of each alternative, and selecting optimal options.
(c) *Sending skills* – using the chosen option for an effective social response, integrating both verbal and non-verbal skills.

In a subsequent development of this problem-solving model, the scope of the approach has been expanded to a variety of areas of social and independent living in addition to basic communication skills (24). Training 'modules' are being developed which include the areas of medication management, symptom management, recreation for leisure, home maintenance, grooming and self-care, social problem solving, and money management, among others. The modules are constructed to teach patients specific functional skills, solve problems that may be encountered while attempting to use newly learned skills, and practice the skills in the natural environment. Patients can enrol in one or more of these modules, depending upon the ex-

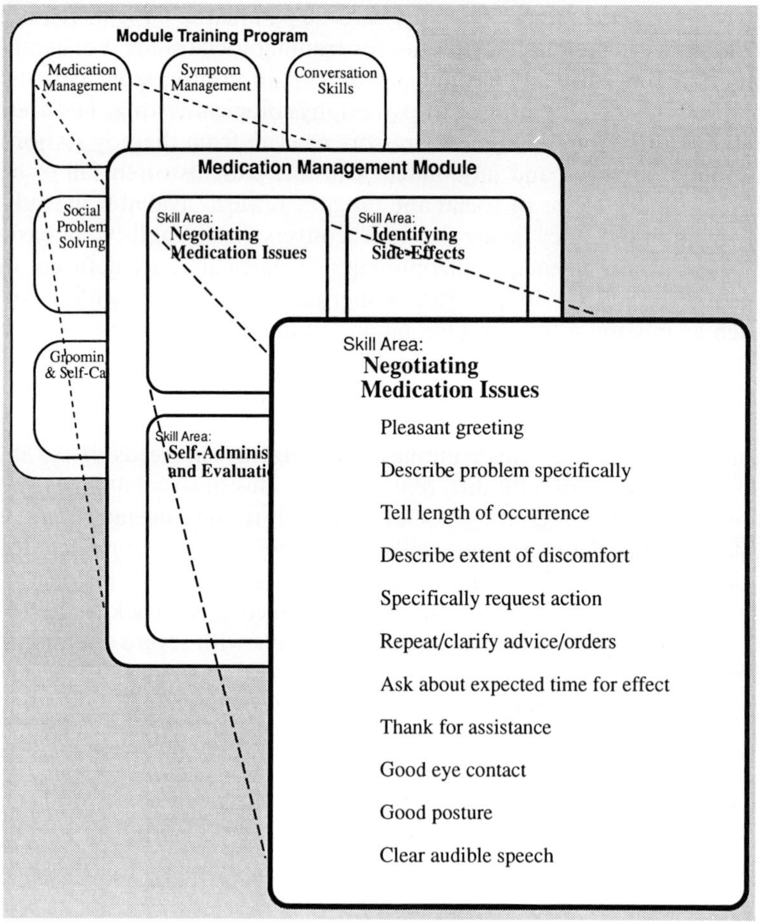

FIG. 2 *Modular training program structure.*

tensiveness of their deficits and the nature of the goals established for their treatment.

This model of social skills training offers considerable promise for those patients who have the cognitive capacity for learning social skills in hour-long sessions in small groups. Each module is divided into separate skill areas, each area having specific behaviors that are taught to achieve personal effectiveness and competence, as shown in Fig. 2. For example, the *Medication Management Module* contains skill areas on: (a) learning about the benefits of antipsychotic medication; (b) acquiring the skills of medication self-administration; (c) coping with the side-effects of medication; and (d) negotiating medication issues with health-care providers.

Each module is composed of a prescriptive clinician's guide, a videotape for demonstrating the skills to be learned, and a patient's workbook. Skills are trained by using a combination of focused instructions, videotaped demonstrations, role-played rehearsals, social and videotape feedback, and practice in the natural environment via in vivo exercises and homework assignments. The steps in this modular approach to training problem-solving skills are shown in Fig. 3.

Modular skills training procedures

Patients proceed through each skill area in a specific sequence of learning exercises and activities, starting with an introduction that aims to highlight the values and advantages of the module.

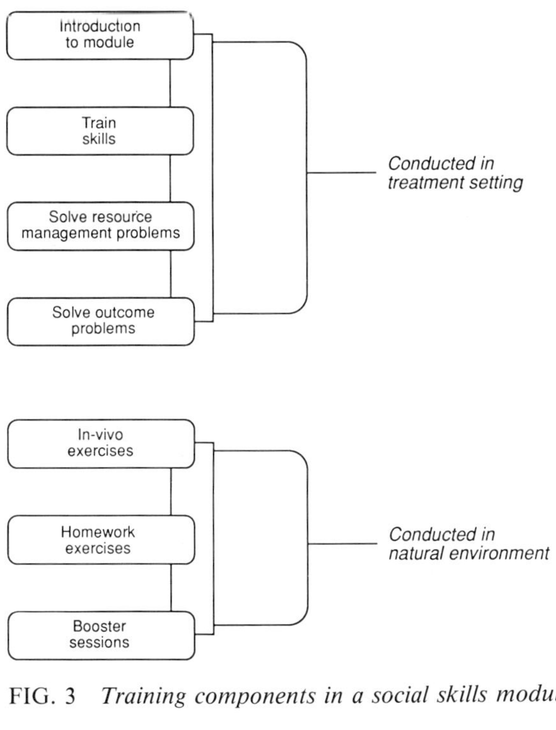

FIG. 3 *Training components in a social skills module.*

Introduction to the module

The objective of the first learning activity in the module is to help patients identify the goals of the module, the consequences that will occur if the goals are achieved, and the steps needed to achieve each goal. Additionally, patients are introduced to the language that will be used in various aspects of training. The introductory exercise consists of a brief description of the module and the following set of questions:
(a) What is the goal of this module?
(b) What is the problem?
(c) If you achieve the goal, what will happen?
(d) Do you have time, money, skills, people to help?
(e) What are the steps required to achieve the goal?
The purpose of the introduction is to inculcate realistic and favorable expectations and instill motivation to continue module training. The major goal at this point is to encourage the patients to think and talk about the material they are to learn. The therapist concentrates primarily on establishing a highly reinforcing environment, rather than on the correctness of patients' responses. However, if patients respond incorrectly to any question, the trainer asks an additional set of ever more leading questions designed to prompt patients to give the correct answer.

Training skills

Following the introduction, training progresses through the various skills that patients have identified. Training involves two basic sets of procedures. First, patients view a videotape demonstration of the correct performance of the skill. The tape is periodically stopped and patients are asked questions to assess their attentiveness and comprehension of the information presented in the videotaped demonstration. Incorrect answers result in replaying the videotape and highlighting the information needed to correctly answer the question when it is repeated.

Next, patients are asked to practice in a role-play exercise the skills they have just learned. This performance is videotaped for subsequent review by patients and the therapist. The therapist evaluates the performance and provides positive feedback and suggestions for improvement. The role-play is then re-enacted and the process is repeated until the patient exhibits mastery.

Problem solving

The training protocol recognizes that patients may encounter obstacles that make it difficult for them to achieve expected outcomes as they perform newly acquired skills. Training in problem-solving skills is designed to teach them methods that they can use to overcome these obstacles. The problem-solving model employed is a five-step procedure that includes a definition of the problem, generation of alternative responses to solve the problem, evaluation of these alternatives in terms of their potential positive and negative consequences, choice of an alternative based upon this evaluation, and implementation of the chosen alternative. Patients are taught how to overcome two types of obstacles: resource management problems and outcome problems.

The training in solving resource management problems is designed to teach patients methods of gathering the resources necessary to implement a particular medication management skill. For example, even if training in the Medication Management Module has taught an individual the skills needed to request a change in medication, the patient must have access to certain resources such as a telephone to make an appointment and transportation to visit the doctor. A set of resource management problems is presented during training of each skill in the module. The therapist describes a skill and asks the following series of questions:

(a) What is your goal in using this skill?
(b) What resources must you have in order to carry out the skill?
(c) How would you obtain these resources?
(d) If you were to obtain these resources, what positive consequences would happen?
(e) If you were to obtain these resources, what negative consequences might happen?
(f) Do the positive consequences outweigh the negative consequences? If yes, role-play the method generated by the patient. If no, what else would you do?

The training in solving outcome problems teaches patients how to respond when the environment fails to provide the expected outcome following the performance of a particular skill. For example, if an individual arrives for an appointment with the doctor only to find that the doctor has been called away to an emergency, what must he do to solve the problem? The training methods, which are similar to those used during the training in resource management problems, are illustrated in detail below. Training begins as the therapist describes an obstacle which might be encountered as patients attempt to use their skills. Patients are then asked a series of questions which engage them in the problem-solving model. The questions are:

(a) What is the problem?
(b) Do you have the time, money, skills, and people to help?
(c) What can you do to solve the problem?
(d) Is the chosen method feasible?
(e) If you use the chosen method, will you be likely to achieve your goal?
(f) If you were to use this method, what positive consequences would happen?
(g) If you were to use this method, what negative consequences would happen?
(h) Do the positive consequences outweigh the negative consequences? If yes, role-play the alternative generated by the patient. If no, what else would you do?

Promoting generalization

It is extremely important that patients have the opportunity to practice newly learned skills in the natural environment as an additional step toward programming for generalization. Skills that can only be used in the context of the clinic are of little use to the patient. *In vivo* exercises are used to facilitate the transfer of training. Essentially, the patient performs the skills in his or her world. However, a therapist accompanies the patient in order to prompt and reinforce the patient's performance, as well as to provide corrective feedback. These exercises are arranged to present increasingly difficult situations, which requires extending skills beyond the training provided in the clinic. An example in the Medication Management Module is an exercise in which the patient (and therapist) generate questions regarding the patient's antipsychotic medication and then ask a program nurse to answer the questions. Following this, the patient may be encouraged to ask the same or similar questions of the ward physician or a local pharmacist. In each of these in vivo exercises, the therapist helps the patients 'fine-tune' their performances while identifying needed resources and anticipating obstacles which may be encountered during the exercise.

Homework provides patients with an opportunity to perform independently the skills they have learned. Because it is the goal of the module to teach patients to function independently, this represents the ultimate step in training. Wherever possible, patients are asked to return from the assignment with tangible evidence that the assignment was completed. For example, if the assignment is to obtain information from a pharmacist about one's medication, the patient can verbally report the information to the therapist and bring back the pharmacist's business card. The role of the therapist in these exercises is to provide feedback to patients regarding their performance.

Effectiveness of social skills training

Reviews of the empirical studies done on social skills training with schizophrenics have shown that a wide range of skills can be learned and maintained over short-term follow-up periods (30, 31). In one controlled clinical trial, 28 carefully diagnosed male schizophrenic patients were randomly assigned to either intensive social skills problem-solving training or to holistic health therapy. A multidimensional evaluation was conducted before and after nine weeks of inpatient treatment and for 24 months of follow-up in the community. Patients exposed to social skills training evidenced significantly greater acquisition, generalization, and durability of social skills; their social adjustment in the community was rated as better by relatives; and they experienced fewer relapses and rehospitalizations (32). Similar results have been obtained from skills-training programs in Italy (33) and in Switzerland (34).

While social skills training programs are relatively new, they have clearly shown success. The Medication Management Module and the Symptom Management Module, for example, have been evaluated in a controlled experimental study where patients' skills were measured before treatment, after treatment, and at a six-month follow-up. Findings demonstrated that patients doubled their knowledge and ability to use the skills taught as a result of module training, and that there was no significant erosion of skills at follow-up (35). Equally important, it has been demonstrated that line clinicians find these modules to be 'user-friendly' and that they are able to deliver the modules faithfully without extensive training (36).

Social skills training has made considerable progress in enhancing skill levels of psychiatric patients. However, more work is needed in assessing strategies for promoting generalization and long-term change. While the issue of generalization presents a major task for applied clinical researchers, some work has been accomplished. For example, response generalization has been assessed in a number of clinical studies and the results reveal evidence of generalization to untrained situations on role-play tests (37 – 40). The reason that response generalization has been repeatedly observed in these assessments may lie in the strengthening of classes of responding as a by-product of training numerous related behaviors. In social skills training, a number of different role-play scenes and responses are practiced, resulting in various forms of the target skill being prompted and reinforced. For instance, an unassertive patient might practice sending burnt food back in a restaurant, confronting a person who cut in front of him in line, and saying 'no' to unreasonable requests, among other scenes. This method of training 'multiple exemplars' of a particular skill has been recommended as a way to promote generalization (41).

With schizophrenics and other severely impaired populations who suffer from cognitive deficits and a lack of initiative, generalization usually occurs only to a limited extent unless systematic efforts are made to transfer trained skills to naturalistic settings. One way to establish a solid link between training and naturalistic settings is by issuing homework assignments. Assignments to use trained skills in other settings and with other individuals have been used with positive results by a number of clinical researchers (38, 42, 43). This tactic has proved to be more effective when accompanied by prompts and reinforcement in settings outside the training milieu. Friends, family members, nursing staff personnel and peers can aid this process by prompting and reinforcing new social behaviors until they are established. Once the trained skills are well established and maintained by natural consequences in the environment, prompts and external reinforcement may be withdrawn. Gradually delaying reinforcement and making its delivery more variable will minimize the likelihood that newly learned patterns of behavior will be disrupted (44).

Training should not be separated from the patient's everyday world, but rather, fully integrated with it. Whenever possible, therapy should be taken out of the clinical setting and practiced in homes, wards, schools, stores, restaurants, and other environments where it is desirable to perform the target behaviors. Potent reinforcers (i.e., praise, money, edibles and privileges) should be initially tied to successful performance of the behavior so that it is 'worth doing'. Only after the behavior is thoroughly ingrained and under the control of natural contingencies should prosthetic reinforcement be removed.

While it has been amply demonstrated that behavioral training produces incremental improvement in social competence, only a few studies have demonstrated that such interpersonal strengthening actually reduces the probability of relapse or symptom exacerbation and increases community tenure and quality of life (32, 45). Skills training embedded within a family therapy context may prove to have greater impact on the long-term clinical status of chronic patients, such as in preventing relapse (38, 46). Much more outcome research must be done to document the extent to which social skills training adds benefits to schizophrenic patients' long-term clinical and symptomatic outcomes, over and above the judicious use of antipsychotic medication. Because many patients have limited potential for acquiring and generalizing functional skills sufficient for fully independent living, there is continued value in developing rehabilitation approaches that emphasize environmental prostheses and social support.

COGNITIVE THERAPY IN THE TREATMENT OF SCHIZOPHRENIA

While recognition of the clinical significance of cognitive disorders in the treatment and rehabilitation of schizophrenia has increased, no current conceptualization of the vulnerability-stress model provides a sufficiently specific account of these information processing disorders. Thus, there is little real understanding of the processes mediating pre-existing or residual cognitive deficits and manifest psychotic behavior. As a result, relevant therapeutic recommendations are general and vague (e.g., avoiding overstimulation; reducing the quantity of information; providing clear and unambiguous information; and structuring, simplifying, and clarifying interactions between the patient and the general treatment milieu). At best, these non-specific suggestions may facilitate information processing, but they do not directly affect the actual cognitive disorder (19, 47).

A number of cognitive deficits have been cited in the literature as basic processes of schizophrenia, including disturbances in the selection between relevant and irrelevant stimuli, the maintenance or flexible allocation of focused and sustained attention, and the availability of stored information for comparison processes to recognize and identify stimuli. Other disorders mentioned by researchers include impaired capacity for abstract thinking, unusual concept formation, inadequate concept modulation, errors in syllogistic and analogical inference, and disturbances in the choice of response arising from mutual interference of competing reactions. Physiological correlates of these cognitive dysfunctions have been reported by investigators studying the psychophysiology of schizophrenia (48, 49).

Many investigators have based their research on perceptual disorder models which assume that the basic cognitive deficits of schizophrenia occur in the early stages of information processing (50). In these models, deficits such as selective attentional dysfunctions are assumed to be the cause of inadequate concept formation and impaired response selection. Conceptual disorder models, on the other hand, posit that deficits at later stages of processing reactively lead to perceptual disorders via poor overall organization of information (51). However, perception and conceptualization are likely to be connected in the course of information processing by a circular process, in which each interactively complements and controls the other (52). As a consequence, it is probably the directing, evaluating and integrating operations that are impaired, rather than isolated sub-processes.

In the field of cognitive psychology, it is undisputed that such disorders of information processing can affect not only higher mental functions such as judgment, but also emotions and overt behavior. For instance, the unavailability of information stored in long-term memory can lead to an inadequacy which could become so extreme that the individual has experiences that seem foreign or externally produced. However, descriptions of such relationships have remained largely on a general level (53).

When cognitive disturbances in schizophrenia are considered within the framework of the stress-vulnerability model (46, 47, 54, 55), one is compelled to abandon a purely linear concept of etiology, i.e., that schizophrenia results from a 'core psychological deficit'. Therefore, a systems approach is preferred.

In the stress-vulnerability model, cognitive disturbances are considered to be vulnerability characteristics (56) and a cause of an increased susceptibility to stress (54, 57, 58). While the concept of vulnerability is not well differentiated, investigators generally agree that vulnerability comprises a broad spectrum of components ranging from biological deviations to deficits in social competence.

Deficits in information processing are likely to reduce the potential for adapting to autonomous biological changes and environmental demands. From a systems point of view, these deficits are best viewed as mediating variables within a positive feedback loop between biological and psychosocial factors that can lead to acute psychotic behavior (59, 60). Based on this systems viewpoint, relationships between the features described are best understood within a hierarchically organized model which has been presented in detail elsewhere (60). In this model, depicted in Fig. 4, overt behavior results from an integration of specific processes on the elementary functional levels of attention, perception, concept formation, and attribution, whether that behavior represents micro-social forms of interpersonal interaction or macro-social patterns that fulfill the demands of social roles. Schizophrenia is characterized by dysfunctions or deficits at all these functional levels (53).

Because of the hierarchical organization of behavior, deficiencies at elementary

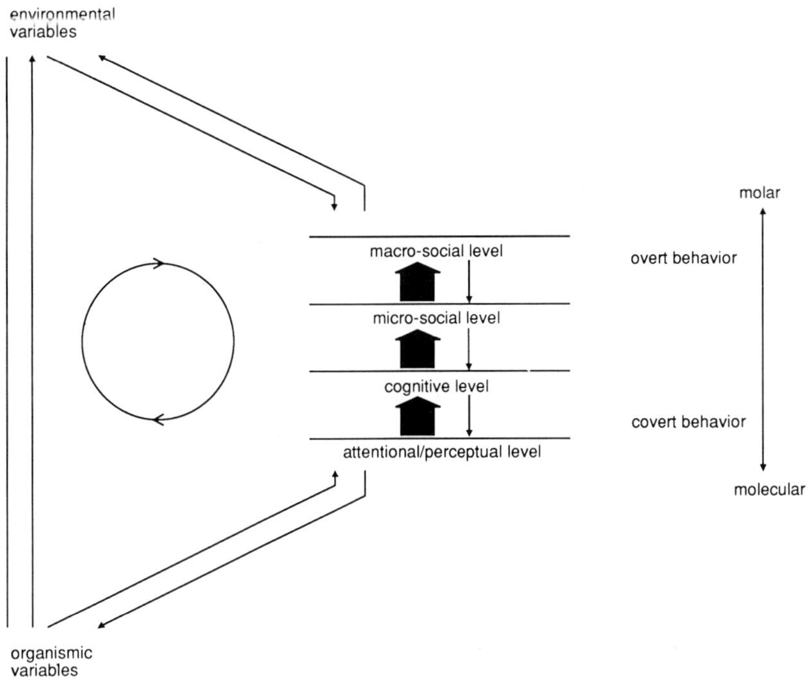

FIG. 4 *Hierarchical model of information processing and social behavior.*

levels lead to disturbances at complex levels. Some disturbing influences are sufficient unto themselves, while others must accumulate or interact among themselves or with environmental or organismic variables. For example, an individual having difficulties with the control, intensity, and processing of information will display reduced tolerance for interpersonal strains, especially if the interaction is ambiguous. When attentional and perceptual disorders are present, the subject experiences these strains as being more complex than would be the case if his information processing ability was undisturbed. Discrepancies arising between perception and interpretation prevent their integration, which further intensifies the cognitive deficiencies. An additional increase in the level of arousal can indirectly provoke an even greater deterioration, e.g., if the patient's environment reacts to the emergence of such disorders with irritation or rejection. If these interactions between impaired attentional functions, situational interpretation, emotion, and arousal enter into a vicious circle, they can ultimately lead to a total breakdown of systematic information processing.

The breakdown of information processing is seen as a target for therapeutic intervention. Cognitive treatments are being developed to address information processing deficits in schizophrenics (59, 60). Two important conclusions can be drawn with regard to these new cognitive treatments. First, cognitive therapy should aim at reducing these disorders by focusing directly on the attentional/perceptual and cognitive processes themselves. Interventions at elementary cognitive levels might affect treatment outcome at complex levels. Second, cognitive therapy must aim at breaking up two vicious cycles – the connections between impaired attentional/perceptual and conceptual processes and their integration on the one hand, and the positive feedback between cognitive dysfunctions and psychosocial stressors on the other. Because cognitive and social functions interact, effective therapy of cognitive disorders cannot take place in a quasi-experimental setting detached from everyday life, if meaningful therapeutic results are to be achieved (59, 60).

There are fundamental differences between these treatments and the currently popular methods of cognitive behavior therapy which focus mainly on the phenomenological aspects of psychopathology. Cognitive behavior therapy methods aim more at establishing self-control and extending the behavioral repertoire (8). For example, schizophrenic patients have been trained to use self-instruction and thought-stopping procedures to reduce delusions and hallucinations (61). Such treatments indirectly address cognitive deficits by teaching specific strategies.

However, few empirical studies have evaluated the impact of direct training of disordered cognitive functions (62, 63). Most of the existing research in this area has been in the form of case studies. Spaulding and his associates (59) demonstrated the successful reduction of distractibility. In two case studies, auditory and visual attention were directly trained using 'dichotic listening' and 'visual distraction' methods. In a similar case study, a multi-step training procedure was reported to improve general attention (64).

Roder and his co-workers (71) developed a systematic program for the integrated treatment of attentional, perceptual, cognitive, communication and social disorders of schizophrenic patients. The treatment program consists of five sub-programs in which groups of five to seven patients first practice selected, focal cognitive processes, followed by more general social and problem-solving skills. The five sub-programs are: *Cognitive Differentiation, Social Perception, Verbal Communication, Social Skills* and *Interpersonal Problem Solving.* A complete set of treatment materials has been devised and empirically tested for each sub-program (65 – 70).

An integrated cognitive treatment program

The various sub-programs which comprise the integrated cognitive treatment program are displayed schematically along cognitive and social dimensions in Fig. 5. The emphasis in treatment gradually shifts from cognitive processes to social skills, yet the two dimensions are inseparably linked at every stage of therapy. In the sub-programs focusing on cognitive aspects, the material becomes progressively more and more complex and realistic. At the same time, group interactions are qualitatively and quantitatively intensified, and emotionally charged contents are introduced slowly.

All sub-programs provide training in basic cognitive functions such as selective attention, shift of attention, focused and sustained attention, and sustained responsiveness. Specifically, the first sub-program, *Cognitive Differentiation,* is concerned with functions such as concept formation, abstraction abilities, concept modulation, recall and recognition, and the formation and use of associatively linked concept hierarchies. In this program, a deficit is demonstrated when a class or concept

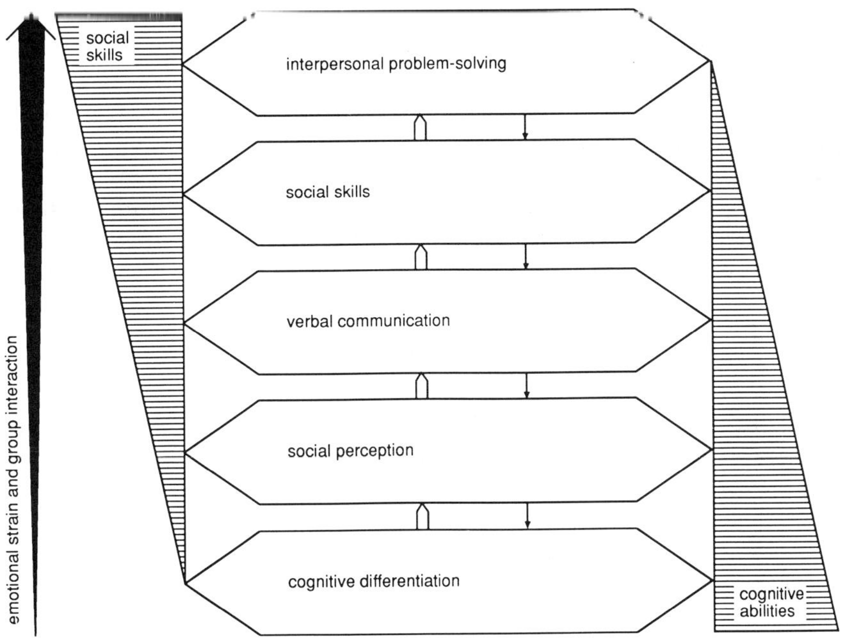

FIG. 5 *Integrated cognitive therapy program.*

is formed according to unessential features, which leads to unusual and overgeneralized combinations. Deficits are also demonstrated when concrete modes of thought become fixated.

Training in cognitive differentiation begins with exercises in concept formation, using small cards on which several systematically varying characteristics are presented. The second step consists of exercises focused on verbal concept systems (synonyms, antonyms, definitions, concepts with different meanings according to context, and hierarchies of concepts). The third and final step provides practice in systematic strategies for concept identification.

The second sub-program, *Social Perception,* concentrates on the processes of stimulus discrimination and interpretation. This program makes use of previous experiences in the perception and evaluation of social interactions. The deficits that this program is designed to remedy are those that affect size constancy, depth perception, figure-ground discrimination, contrast perception, and assessing probability by context and familiarity.

The third sub-program, *Verbal Communication,* is based on numerous findings about impaired communication in the families of schizophrenics. Impaired communication stems from ambiguous or contradictory information, talking at cross-purposes, and disqualifying another person's opinion. These impairments often arise whenever conversation becomes emotionally charged. The training objective is to enable group members to attend to the contributions of others, to understand another's thoughts while maintaining one's own, to establish connections between one's own thoughts and those of others, as well as in training the associative-semantic processes involved in the production of speech.

Training begins with the literal repetition of given sentences, followed by repeating the meaning of spontaneous phrases. Next, patients practice producing standard basic questions ('who, where, what, why, how') and the corresponding answers. Training continues with free questioning and answering. In the concluding step, the group engages in free communication, which is repeatedly observed for the types of communication difficulties described above.

The remaining two sub-programs are essentially the procedures used to train social and problem-solving skills described in the section on social skills training above.

Training in social perception

To illustrate the cognitive training approach, the *Social Perception* sub-program will be presented in more detail, because it fuses cognitive, communication and social therapeutic elements in a particularly graphic manner. Like the other sub-programs, *Social Perception* is structured to increase the demands made on the group from the moment therapy begins; i.e., by progressing from simple and subordinate tasks to more complex and difficult tasks. The therapeutic material consists of slides illustrating scenes which vary in the intensity of feelings and emotions expressed by the people depicted on the slide, as well as the degree of ambiguity presented in each situation. At the beginning of the sub-program, simple and well-structured slides of individuals expressing relatively little emotion are shown to the patients. During the course of the sub-program, slides showing emotionally more stressful and complex social interactions are introduced. This means that the amount of information processed by the patient increases progressively. The therapeutic procedure follows three main steps as each slide is presented. First, specific features depicted in the slide are described and summarized repeatedly by the therapist or by the least dysfunctional patients. Then, each individual's interpretations are discussed by the group, repeatedly referring to details raised during the discussion, until a consensus interpretation is reached. This exercise is designed to foster a subjective perception in each individual while simultaneously relating these experiences to the group's opinion. Cognitive restructuring of the perceptual field and explicit treatment of cognitive dissonances initially present are essential for the success of this process. Finally, each member of the group is asked to state succinctly the theme of the slide in question. This step allows the therapist to ascertain how adequately the content of the picture has been grasped. With more complex pictures, which permit differing interpretations, the group collects several meaningful interpretations, attempting to encourage each member to accept as many of these as possible before the slide's theme is stated. The advantages and disadvantages of each interpretation are discussed and carefully compared.

To achieve consensus, it is helpful to ask each group member to suggest additional information necessary to support a particular interpretation. Again, a consensus for each possible interpretation is attained. The therapist is directive and supportive, using methods derived from learning theory, such as self-reinforcement, self-control, and informational reinforcement. The therapist encourages interaction among the patients. Furthermore, special attention is given to help patients improve their self-concepts.

Evaluation of cognitive training

Several controlled studies have evaluated the cognitive training program in different clinics and have shown it to be effective (67, 71). While data support the treatment's efficacy, how and why the intervention succeeds is less clear. The 'pervasiveness hypothesis' – that cognitive disorders exert a pervasive influence extending into the levels of overt behavior and that interventions working toward their reduction must be similarly pervasive – is in need of additional empirical support. Cognitive therapy interventions appear to have a 'springboard' character; that is, the reduction in cognitive deficiencies seems to foster improvement and differentiation of self-image or self-perception, which then leads to improved social skills (72).

Cognitive treatment in schizophrenia is in need of further methodological development. For example, if the purpose of cognitive treatment is to correct cognitive deficits, then these deficits must be more stringently defined than has heretofore been the case. Until the present, most models and theories of cognition in schizophrenia have attempted to explain the fundamental nature of observable or measurable disorders, as have other areas of schizophrenia research. These models do not specify how such disorders can arise and exactly what definable effects these disorders would have on the higher functional levels of behavior.

BEHAVIORAL FAMILY MANAGEMENT

Employing the same learning principles and techniques as those integral to social skills training, a three-pronged module has been developed for enhancing the communication and problem-solving skills of families containing a schizophrenic member (73). Despite the development of community mental health programs and the widespread use of neuroleptic drugs, families continue to serve as the principal care-givers for schizophrenic patients. While the burden of providing emotional, social and instrumental support for schizophrenics has always fallen mainly on the patients' relatives, this has become even greater since the deinstitutionalization movement of the past 20 years. Based upon intensive interviews with 80 relatives of schizophrenics, a report entitled *'Schizophrenia at Home'*, which summarized the problems described by the relatives, was issued (74). Problems fell into three major categories: (a) distress caused by the patients' symptomatic and socially impaired behavior; (b) anxiety and 'burn-out' experienced by the relatives; and (c) disturbances in the relatives' own social network.

From the point of view of relatives, schizophrenic family members living at home display two types of behavior that are distressing and difficult to cope with: social withdrawal and solitary patterns; and aggressive, bizarre and disruptive behavior. These patterns are found in varying degrees at different points in time during the course of the illness. Social isolation to the point of rarely exchanging conversation is the more common pattern; it generates helpless frustration in relatives whose sustained social support for such patients requires a modicum of responsiveness. Another facet of isolated behavior is the apathy and indolence of the chronic schizophrenic. Inactivity frequently galls relatives because they view the patients as physically able, so they do not understand the absence of constructive activity.

Relatives speak of being constantly on a knife edge or 'feeling in constant dread of relapse and flare-ups of symptoms'. Guilt, exhaustion, depression, anxiety and anger are frequent experiences of relatives that, in combination with the patients' deviance, do much to explain the high 'expressed emotion' in families – a factor that has been found to predict relapse (75 – 78). High expressed emotion, consisting of criticism, hostility and emotional overinvolvement, is an understandable reaction of concerned family members who are at a loss to know how to help their schizophrenic relatives. Overinvolvement can lead to a family giving up its attachments to the outside community and to spending inordinate amounts of time at home with the patient. Criticism and hostility can lead to rejection of the patient, and ultimately, to a breach of the relationship.

Elements of behavioral family management

The three facets of behavioral family management include education about schizophrenia and its treatment, training in communication skills, and training in a step-wise and systematic problem-solving process. The initial sessions are used to educate relatives and patients about schizophrenia – its causes, course and management. Detailed information is presented, and patients and their families are invited to discuss their own experiences and to express their own feelings and concerns.

These sessions function to relieve some of the guilt, confusion, and helplessness experienced by family members, as well as to foster realistic expectations about treatment outcome and to emphasize the importance of maintaining medication regimens. The impact of schizophrenia upon each family member and problems of management are discussed. The educational seminars are presented in a semi-didactic style, with visual aids and written materials. The patient is encouraged to take the role of 'expert' and to describe his or her experiences to the family.

Following these information-giving sessions, the objective then becomes training in communication and problem-solving skills. Each session is devoted to the identification of problems facing the entire family, with training in relevant communication skills. The therapist demonstrates effective and ineffective communication skills in brief role-plays. This is followed by guided practice with feedback to teach four types of communication:

(a) Expressing positive feelings and giving positive feedback;
(b) Making requests of others: expressing expectations and setting rules;
(c) Using active listening skills to learn the needs and emotions of others;
(d) Expressing directly negative emotions, such as feelings of anger and disapproval.

The initial phase of enhancing communication skills of family members focuses on the expression of positive feelings through prompting mutually rewarding behavior and empathic listening. The aim of the early stage of family therapy is to create a warm milieu where family members are able to recognize and reinforce specific positive behavior in one another. In addition, they learn to identify areas of specific behavior they would like others to change, as well as to make appropriate requests for such changes. Finally, they develop the ability to sit together and discuss problems in an empathic, non-judgmental manner. Expression of strong negative feelings is taken up after positive communication and interaction has been established. Communication skills are important precursors to a successful problem-solving discussion.

Once families have developed adequate communication skills, they are in a position to learn improved problem-solving methods. The ability to specify a problem and to discuss it in detail can only be carried out by families competent in communication skills. Patients and their families are taught to do the following:

(a) Pinpoint and specify problems in living.
(b) Develop several options or alternative responses.
(c) Evaluate each option in terms of its possible consequences.
(d) Choose options that maximize satisfaction and seem reasonable.
(e) Plan how to implement that option (or options) as a family.
(f) Provide mutual support in the implementation of the chosen option.
(g) Review the problem after the option has been implemented.

These problem-solving steps are repeatedly used to analyze and focus on a wide range of family problems, especially those that are associated with tension and conflict. The repetitive practice of problem solving, together with repeated practice of the four basic communication skills, are aimed at inculcating durable, general problem-solving strategies.

Families are provided with forms that outline the steps, with spaces for completion of problem solving. Particular importance is attached to the detailed planning of the problem solution, with all anticipated difficulties discussed fully. Each family member takes a turn at chairing the family problem-solving sessions and recording details of the problem, all suggested solutions, and step-by-step plans to carry out the chosen 'best' solution. A folder is kept by each family in which members file all problem-solving records. This folder is kept in an accessible place in the home so that any family member can refer to it at any time. Sometimes problem-solving plans may be displayed on a family notice board or on the refrigerator door to prompt family members of the tasks they have agreed to undertake to assist with the problems.

In addition to the structured problem-solving approach, families are trained in the use of a range of behavioral strategies for dealing with specific problems that arise. These may include contingency contracting for parental discord, token economy programs for enhancing constructive daily activity, social skills training for interpersonal inadequacy, or behavioral management strategies for anxiety and depression. In these instances, all family members are usually involved in the execution of the specific strategy.

The behavioral family management module was designed for use with individual families and with multiple family groups and can be adapted for use with families of patients with other major mental disorders. It has been offered over nine weekly, two-hour sessions; alternatively, it has been provided for over a two-year period for more definitive skill building, with weekly sessions for three months, bi-weekly sessions for six months, then monthly maintenance sessions. In two empirical evaluations and controlled studies, it has been shown to reduce family tensions, conflicts and expressed emotion, markedly reduce relapse rates and re-hospitalization, enhance problem solving and coping, improve social adjustment of patients and reduce family burden. Cost-effectiveness analyses indicated that a home-based version of behavioral family management was more effective and less costly than comparison clinic-based treatment of individuals (46, 79).

VOCATIONAL SKILLS TRAINING

Work is vitally important to nearly everyone. Beyond a source of income, it provides opportunities for social contacts and greatly influences self-image and self-esteem. This is as true for mentally ill people as it is for healthy people. Mentally ill persons in particular stand to benefit from work as a source of self-esteem. However, economic realities often produce a different picture. A study conducted in 1982 showed that the unemployment rate among chronically mentally ill persons was 70% (80)! The situation today has not improved. Determining ways to support psychiatric patients in finding and keeping jobs so that they feel productive and useful to the community is an urgent task.

Successful job rehabilitation, however, can only be achieved if the patient possesses a number of general, self-regulative and interpersonal skills (1). These include:

(a) Punctuality and participation.

(b) Personal hygiene.
(c) Utilization of leisure time and breaks.
(d) Accepting professional approval.
(e) Accepting professional criticism.
(f) Starting a conversation.
(g) Assisting fellow workers.
(h) Setting priorities among several given tasks.
(i) Asking for assistance of fellow workers.
(j) Following general work regulations.
(k) Following specific orders.
(l) Making job-related proposals.

An example of a vocational skills training program is the Job Finding Club at the Brentwood Veterans Administration Hospital in Los Angeles. The Job Finding Club combines several successful behavioral techniques in a packaged program devised by Azrin and Basalel (81). Key elements in the program include: (a) the use of an environment conducive to motivating patients in their job search; (b) the use of reinforcement strategies; (c) a breakdown of the tasks involved in finding a job; and (d) the training of skills needed to find a job. Adapting this approach to meet the needs of the psychiatrically disabled necessitated increasing the structure of the program, including daily goal-setting activities and developing remedial training in job-seeking skills.

There are three distinct segments in the Job Finding Club: training in job-seeking skills; the job search itself; and follow-up and job maintenance. While the program is not time-limited, participants spend an average of 24 days in the program. The methods used in the Job Club are:

(a) *Teaching job-seeking skills:* finding job leads; contacting employers; using the telephone; completing applications; writing resumés; job interviews; using transport; appropriate grooming.
(b) *Sustaining the job search:* daily goal setting; frequent counselor-patient contact; incentives; prompting; generous praise for effort; peer support; liaison with other treatment personnel.

The Job Club is a supportive and structured setting in which counselors teach psychiatric patients how to find their own jobs. Job-finding skills are trained using principles of learning and patients are motivated to persist in job seeking through praise, encouragement and other incentives.

Training in job-seeking skills

During the first week of the program, patients participate in an intensive, six-hour-per-day workshop designed to assess and train basic job-finding skills. The curriculum includes identifying sources of job leads, contacting job leads, completing employment applications and resumés, participating in job interviews, and the use of public transportation. Instruction is competency-based, with trainers using programmed materials, didactic instruction, role-playing and *in vivo* training exercises. Wherever possible, the program uses materials and situations that the patient will face during the job search. For example, patients practice completing bona fide job applications and contacting actual sources for job leads. Patients' progress is continually monitored and additional instruction is provided to those who fall behind or present special training needs.

Job search

After completing the job-seeking skills workshop, patients begin the job search. The program provides work areas, secretarial support and current job leads. These leads are gleaned from newspaper advertisements, telephone directories, employment notices, civil service announcements and weekly visits by state job placement counselors from two different agencies. Patients participate on a full-day basis.

A daily, intensive goal-setting session is conducted with each patient to plan job-search activities. During this session, counselors and patients identify the most advantageous options for the day's job search. They also develop outcome expectations for the daily activities, set a time line for accomplishment of the task, and carry out problem solving of potential stumbling blocks which may be encountered during the day. Patients are expected to keep a log of their daily job-seeking activities and account for their time in the program.

Another component of this phase involves teaching patients how to manage daily problems, including the stress of looking for employment. Supportive, goal-directed counseling is provided as needed. This may include assistance in finding housing and reliable transportation in the community, adjusting to work hours and learning to interact with others. This phase lasts until the patient secures a job or leaves the program.

Job maintenance activities

Job Club graduates may attend a weekly session which teaches methods to deal with problems that may threaten job security. Training adheres to a problem-solving model of specifying solutions to an identified issue and then role-playing those solutions and obtaining corrective feedback before the patient uses the approach in his work setting. Training issues are identified by the participants and may include learning how to get along with others on the job, managing psychiatric symptoms and improving daily living situations. Graduates may also return to the program if they lose their jobs or wish to upgrade their positions.

Evaluation of the Job Club

Fifty-seven percent of the 97 patients who participated in the program during the first eight months of operation secured employment, and another 10% entered full-time job training programs. Twelve percent of the patients voluntarily dropped out of the program during the first week of job-finding skills training, and an additional 10% of the patients dropped out after the first week when they were engaged in the actual job search. Eleven percent of the patients were returned to their wards by Job Club staff because of symptom exacerbations that interfered with participation.

Participants averaged 23.9 working days in the program, ranging from 1 to 140 days. The average program stay for patients who found jobs was 12 days longer than for those who left the program before obtaining employment.

Almost 60% of the jobs secured were in clerical, sales and service occupations. Eleven percent were in the professions and 12% involved factory work or construction. Job leads came from newspaper advertisements (39%), rehabilitation counselors (22%), and friends and relatives (14%). There was no relationship between the type of job obtained and the source of the job lead (82).

Six-month follow-up data were collected on 74% of the 65 patients who entered jobs or job training following the program. The percentage of people employed 30, 60, 90 and 180 days after leaving the program was 80%, 75%, 80% and 67.5%, respectively. Ten patients switched jobs during this time; of these, six returned to the Job Club for assistance. Of the patients who switched jobs, two were fired or laid off, five left their job for a better position, two found new work after symptom exacerbation forced them to leave their original positions, and one patient moved to a new location where he found work.

Of the thirteen patients who were unemployed at the six-month follow-up, four had lost their jobs because psychiatric symptoms interfered with their work, four had quit because they were dissatisfied with their positions, three had been fired, and one had lost his job because of medical illness requiring hospitalization. Of the 25 patients who left the Job Club without a successful placement, none had found a job six months later.

Job outcomes have remained highly favorable during the three years since the Club began. More than 300 patients have been referred. Of these, 65% obtained jobs or entered full-time vocational training. Of these, 65% were still employed at six-month follow-up. Ten percent of patients were returned to their referring units because they were not ready to undertake a job search. Twenty-five percent dropped out of the Job Club before obtaining employment. Age and symptoms of mental disorder correlated with the ability to find jobs. Older patients and patients with positive symptoms were less likely to obtain a job. Previous work history and education did not predict the likelihood of finding employment, but did affect the type of job secured.

CONCLUSIONS

Behavioral training methods comprise a major strategy for the rehabilitation of schizophrenic patients. Building cognitive and functional skills in patients with major mental disorders is based on the assumption that increasing coping and competence can override stress and vulnerability in the improvement of psychosocial functioning. For maximum efficacy, skills training should incorporate principles and procedures of human learning and information processing. Several models of skills training and cognitive treatment have been designed and evaluated, each of which has proved to be effective in elevating the social competence of schizophrenic patients. The most basic model involves role-playing by the patient and modeling, prompting, feedback and reinforcement by the therapist. Newer models of training which incorporate problem-solving techniques provide general strategies for dealing with a wide variety of social situations. These models use role-playing to enhance behavioral performance, but also strengthen the patient's abilities to perceive and process incoming social messages and meanings. Similar procedures have also been successfully implemented in the context of family therapy and vocational rehabilitation.

It is essential that skills training be embedded in a comprehensive program of rehabilitation that features continuity of care, supportive community services, therapeutic relationships and judicious prescription of psychotropic medications. The aim of rehabilitation is not to cure disease, but to enhance a deficient individual's functioning, level of adaptation and quality of life. The necessary design and validation of a fully effective technology for skills training will require tools from a variety of disciplines. Despite the best efforts at training social, vocational, family and independent living skills, some patients with major mental disorders require a responsive and compensatory environment to allow them to function with a reasonable quality of life in the community. Designing environments to compensate for residual behavioral and social deficiencies and which encourage patients to use skills learned in systematic training programs is the next major task facing clinical researchers and rehabilitation practitioners.

REFERENCES

1. Wong SE, Massel HK, Mosk MD, Liberman RP (1986) Behavioral approaches to the treatment of schizophrenia. In: Burrows JD, Norman TR, Rubinstein G (Eds), *Handbook of Studies on Schizophrenia,* Part 2, p. 239. Elsevier Science Publishers, Amsterdam.
2. Ayllon T, Michael J (1959) The psychiatric nurse as a behavioral engineer. *J. Exp. Anal. Behav., 2,* 323.
3. Ullman LP, Krasner L (1969) *A Psychological Approach to Abnormal Behavior.* Prentice-Hall, Engelwood Cliffs, NY.
4. Liberman RP, Teigen J, Patterson R, Baker V (1983) Reducing delusional speech in chronic, paranoid schizophrenics. *J. Appl. Behav. Anal., 6,* 57.
5. Rickard HC, Digman PJ, Horner RF (1960) Verbal manipulation in a psychotherapeutic relationship. *J. Clin. Psychol., 16,* 364.
6. Ayllon T, Haughton E (1964) Modification of symptomatic verbal behavior of mental patients. *Behav. Res. Ther., 2,* 87.
7. Moss GR, Liberman RP (1975) Empiricism in psychotherapy: behavioral specification and measurement. *Br. J. Psychiatry, 126,* 73.
8. Meichenbaum D, Cameron R (1973) Training schizophrenics to talk to themselves: a means of developing self controls. *Behav. Ther., 2,* 451.
9. Wincze JP, Leitenberg H, Agras WS (1972) The effects of token reinforcement and feedback on the delusional verbal behavior of chronic paranoid schizophrenics. *J. Appl. Behav. Anal., 5,* 247.
10. Wong SE, Terranova MD, Bowen L, Zarate R, Massel HK, Liberman RP (1987) Reducing bizarre stereotype behavior in chronic psychiatric patients: effects of supervised and independent recreational activities. *J. Appl. Behav. Anal., 20,* 77.
11. Paul GL, Lentz RJ (1977) *Psychosocial Treatment of Chronic Mental Patients: Milieu*

Versus Social-Learning Programs. Harvard University Press, Cambridge, MA.
12. Glynn S, Mueser KT (1986) Social learning for chronic mental inpatients. *Schizophr. Bull., 12,* 4.
13. Baker R, Hall JK, Hutchinson K, Bridge G (1977) Symptom changes in chronic schizophrenic patients on a token economy: a controlled experiment. *Br. J. Psychiatry, 131,* 381.
14. Fullerton DI, Cayner JJ, McLaughlin-Reidel T (1978) Results of a token economy. *Arch. Gen. Psychiatry, 35,* 1451.
15. McCreadie RG, Main CJ, Dunlap RA (1978) Token economy, pimozide and chronic schizophrenia. *Br. J. Psychiatry, 133,* 179.
16. Nelson GL, Cone JD (1979) Multiple baseline analyses of a token economy for psychiatric inpatients. *J. Appl. Behav. Anal., 12,* 255.
17. Stoffelmayr BE, Faulkner GE, Mitchell WS (1979) The comparison of token economy and social therapy in the treatment of hard-core schizophrenic patients. *Behav. Anal. Modif., 3,* 3.
18. Turner SM, Hersen M, Bellack AS (1977) Effects of social disruption, stimulus interference and aversive conditioning on auditory hallucinations. *Behav. Modif., 1,* 249.
19. Liberman RP (1982) Behavior therapy in psychiatry. In: Grinspoon L (Ed), Psychiatry Update 1982: The American Psychiatric Association Annual Review, American Psychiatric Press, Washington, DC.
20. Presly AS, Grubb AB (1982) Predictors of successful rehabilitation in longstay patients. *Acta Psychiatr. Scand., 66,* 83.
21. Sylph JA, Ross HE, Kedward HB (1978) Social disability in chronic psychiatric patients. *Am. J. Psychiatry, 134,* 1391.
22. Linn MW, Klett J, Caffey FM (1980) Foster home characteristics and psychiatric patient outcome. *Arch. Gen. Psychiatry, 37,* 129.
23. Test MA, Stein LI (1977) Special living arrangements: a model for decision-making. *Hosp. Community Psychiatry, 28,* 608.
24. Foy DW, Wallace CL, Liberman RP (1983) Advances in social skills training for chronic mental patients. In: Craig KD, McMahon RJ (Eds), *Advances in Clinical Behavior Therapy.* Brunner/Mazel, New York.
25. Liberman RP, Evans CC (1985) Behavioral rehabilitation for chronic mental patients. *J. Clin. Psychopharmacol., 5 (Suppl.),* 8s.
26. Liberman RP, King LW, DeRisi WJ, McCann M (1975) Personal Effectiveness: Guiding People to Express their Feelings and Improve their Social Skills. Research Press, Champaign, IL.
27. Liberman RP, Massel HK, Mosk M, Wong SE (1985) Social skills training for chronic mental patients. *Hosp. Community Psychiatry, 36,* 396.
28. Platt JJ, Spivack G (1972) Problem-solving thinking of psychiatric patients. *J. Consult. Clin. Psychol., 28,* 3.
29. Edelstein BA, Couture E, Cray M (1980) Group training of problem solving with psychiatric patients. In: Upper D, Ross SM (Eds), *Group Therapy: An Annual Review, Vol. 2.* Research Press, Champaign, IL.
30. Wallace CJ, Nelson C, Liberman RP, Aitchison RH, Lukoff D, Elder JP, Ferris C (1980) A review and critique of social skills training with chronic schizophrenics. *Schizophr. Bull., 6,* 42.
31. Liberman RP, Jacobs H, Boone S, Foy D, Donahoe CP, Falloon IHR, Blackwell G, Wallace CJ (1986) New methods for rehabilitating chronic mental patients. In: Talbott JA (Ed), *Our Patients' Future in a Changing World.* American Psychiatric Press, Washington, DC.

32. Wallace CJ, Liberman RP (1985) Social skills training for patients with schizophrenia: a controlled clinical trial. *Psychiatry Res., 15,* 239.
33. Delsabella G, Meneghelli S (1983) Un training di abilità sociali per la riabilitazione di pazienti psicotici cronici. *Riv. Sper. Freniatr., 5,* 1194.
34. Brenner HD, Kraemer S, Hermanutz M, Hodel B (1988) Cognitive treatment in schizophrenia. In: Straube E, Hahlweg K (Eds), *Schizophrenia: Models and Interventions.* Springer-Verlag, New York.
35. Wirshing W, Eckman TA, Liberman RP, Marder SR (1990) Skill training of chronic schizophrenics: management of risk of relapse. In: Tamminga CA, Schulz SC (Eds), *Proceedings of the Second Annual International Congress on Schizophrenia.* Raven Press, New York, in press.
36. Eckman TA, Liberman RP, Phipps, CC, Blair KE (1990) Teaching medication management skills to schizophrenic patients. *J. Clinical Psychopharmacol., 1,* 33.
37. Bellack A, Hersen M, Turner V (1976) Generalization effects of social skills training in chronic schizophrenics: an experimental analysis. *Behav. Res. Ther., 14,* 391.
38. Liberman RP, Lillie F, Falloon IRH, Harpin EJ, Hutchison, W and Stoute BA (1984) Social skills training for relapsing schizophrenics: an experimental analysis. *Behav. Modif., 8,* 155.
39. Goldsmith JC, McFall RM (1975) Development and evolution of an interpersonal skill training program for psychiatric inpatients. *J. Abnorm. Psychol., 84,* 51.
40. Kelly JA, Urey JR, Patterson JT (1980) Improving heterosocial conversational skills of male psychiatric patients through a small group training procedure. *Behav. Ther., 11,* 179.
41. Stokes TF, Baer DM (1977) An implicit technology of generalization. *J. Appl. Behav. Anal., 10,* 349.
42. Finch B, Wallace CJ (1977) Successful interpersonal skills training with schizophrenic inpatients. *J. Consult. Clin. Psychol., 45,* 885.
43. McGovern KB, Burkhard J (1976) Initiating social contact with the opposite sex. In: Krumboltz JD, Thoreson CE (Eds), *Counseling Methods.* Holt, Reinhart and Winston, New York.
44. Kazdin AE (1975) *Behavior modification in applied settings.* Dorsey Press, Homewood, IL.
45. Hogarty GE, Anderson CM, Reiss DJ, Kornblith SJ, Greenwald DP, Jabna CD, Medonia MJ (1986) Family psychoeducation, social skills training, and maintenance chemotherapy in the after-care treatment of schizophrenia, I. One year effects of a controlled study on relapse and expressed emotion. *Arch. Gen. Psychiatry, 43,* 633.
46. Falloon IRH, Boyd J, McGill CW (1984) *Family Care of Schizophrenia.* Guilford Press, New York.
47. Ciompi L (1986) Auf dem Weg zu einem kohärenten multidimensionalen Krankheits- und Therapieverständnis der Schizophrenie: konvergierende neue Konzepte. In: Boker W, Brenner HD (Eds), *Bewältigung der Schizophrenie: Multidimensionale Konzepte, Psychosoziale und Kognitive Therapiën, Angehörigenarbeit und Autoprotektive Strategien.* Huber-Verlag, Bern, Stuttgart, Toronto.
48. Straube E (1983) Kann die psychologisch-physiologische Grundlagenforschung einen Beitrag zur Therapie und Prognoseforschung liefern? In: Brenner HD, Rey ER, Stramke WG (Eds), *Empirische Schizophrenieforschung.* Huber-Verlag, Bern, Stuttgart, Vienna.
49. Oehman A (1981) Electrodermal activity and vulnerability to schizophrenia: a review. *Biol. Psychol., 12,* 87.
50. Broga MI, Neufeld RWJ (1981) Evaluation of information sequential aspects of schizophrenic performance, I. Framework and current findings. *J. Nerv. Ment. Dis., 169,* 558.

51. Dingemans P, Space LB, Cromwell RL (1983) Repertory grid, consistency and schizophrenia. In: Adams-Webber J (Ed), *Personal Constructs: Theory and Application.* Academic Press, Toronto.
52. Magaro PA (1980) *Cognition in Schizophrenia and Paranoia: The Integration of Cognitive Processes.* Lawrence Erlbaum, Hillsdale, NJ.
53. George L, Neufeld RWJ (1985) Cognition and symptomatology in schizophrenia. *Schizophr. Bull., 11,* 264.
54. Zubin J (1986) Mögliche Implikationen der Vulnerabilitäts-hypothese für das psychosoziale Management der Schizophrenie. In: Boker W, Brenner HD (Eds), *Bewältigung der Schizophrenie: Multidimensionale Konzepte, Psychosoziale und Kognitive Therapien, Angehörigenarbeit und Autoprotektive Anstrengungen.* Huber-Verlag, Bern, Stuttgart, Toronto.
55. Hahlweg K (1986) Einfluss der Familieninteraktion auf Entstehung, Verlauf und Therapie schizophrener Störungen. In: Nordmann E, Cierpka M (Eds), *Familienforschung in Psychiatrie und Psychotherapie.* Springer-Verlag, Berlin.
56. Nuechterlein KH, Dawson ME (1984) Information processing and attentional functioning in the developmental course of schizophrenic disorders. *Schizophr. Bull. 10,* 160.
57. Spring B (1981) Stress and schizophrenia: some definitional issues. *Schizophr. Bull., 7,* 24.
58. Ciompi L (1984) Modellvorstellungen zum Zusammenwirken biologischer und psychosozialer Faktoren in der Schizophrenie. *Fortschr. Neurol., Psychiatrie Grenzgeb., 52,* 191.
59. Spaulding WD, Storms L, Goodrich V, Sullivan M (1986) Applications of experimental psychopathology in rehabilitation. *Schizophr. Bull., 12,* 560.
60. Brenner JD (1986) Zur Bedeutung von Basisstörungen für Behandlung und Rehabilitation. In: Boker W, Brenner HD (Eds), *Bewaltigung der Schizophrenie: Multidimensionale Konzepte, Psychosoziale Therapien, Angehorigenarbeit und autoprotektive Anstrengungen.* Huber-Verlag, Bern, Stuttgart, Toronto.
61. Alford GS, Fleece L, Rothblum E (1982) Hallucinatory-delusional verbalizations: modification in a chronic schizophrenic by self-control and cognitive restructuring. *Behav. Modif., 6,* 421.
62. Jacobs LI (1982) Cognitive therapy for schizophrenia in remission. *Curr. Psychiatr. Ther., 21,* 93.
63. Jacobs LI (1984) Cognitive therapy: enhancing remission in psychosis. *Psychiatr. Hosp., 15,* 89.
64. Adams HE, Brantley PJ, Malatesta V, Turkat JD (1981) Modification of cognitive processes: a case study of schizophrenia. *J. Consult. Clin. Psychol., 48,* 460.
65. Brenner HD, Rey ER, Stramke WG (1983) *Empirische Schizophrenieforschung. Experimental psychologische Ergebnisse und Beispiele ihrer Anwendung in Behandlung und Rehabilitation.* Huber-Verlag, Bern, Stuttgart, Vienna.
66. Brenner HD, Boker W, Muller J, Spichtig L, Wurgler S (1987) On auto-protective efforts of schizophrenics, neurotics and controls. *Acta Psychiatr. Scand., 75,* 405.
67. Brenner HD, Hodel B, Kube G, Roder V (1987) Kognitive Therapie bei Schizophrenen: Problemanalyse und empirische Ergebnisse. *Nervenarzt, 58,* 72.
68. Brenner HD, Boker W, Hodel B, Wyss H (1989) Cognitive treatment of basic pervasive dysfunctions in schizophrenia. In: Schulz SC, Tamminga CA (Eds), *Scientific Focus.* Oxford University Press, New York.
69. Kraemer S, Sulz KHD, Schmid R, Lassel R (1987) Kognitive Therapie bei standardversorgten schizophrenen Patienten. *Nervenartz, 58,* 84.
70. Hermanutz M, Gestrich J (1987) Kognitives Training mit Schizophrenen. *Nervenarzt, 58,* 91.

71. Roder V, Brenner HD, Kienzle N, Hodel B (1988) *Integriertes Psychologisches Therapieprogramm (IPT) für Schizophrene Patienten.* PVU, Munich, Weinheim.
72. Brenner HD (1988) On the importance of cognitive disorders in treatment and rehabilitation. In: Strauss JS, Boker W, Brenner HD (Eds), *Psychosocial Treatment of Schizophrenia.* Huber-Verlag, Toronto, Lewiston, New York, Bern, Stuttgart.
73. Falloon IRH, Liberman RP (1983) Behavioral family interventions in the management of chronic schizophrenia. In: McFarlane W (Ed), *Family Therapy of Schizophrenia.* Guilford Press, New York.
74. Creer C (1978) Social work with patients and their families. In: Wing JK (Ed), *Schizophrenia: Towards a New Synthesis.* Academic Press, London.
75. Brown G, Birley JLT, Wing JK (1972) Influence of family life on the course of schizophrenia. *Br. J. Psychiatry, 121,* 241.
76. Vaughn CE, Leff JP (1976) The influence of family and social factors on the course of psychiatric illness. *Br. J. Psychiatry, 129,* 125.
77. Vaughn CE, Snyder KS, Liberman RP, Falloon IRH, Freeman W, Jones S (1982) Family factors in schizophrenic relapse. *Schizophr. Bull., 8,* 425.
78. Vaughn CE, Snyder KS, Jones S, Freeman W, Falloon RIH (1984) Family factors in schizophrenic relapse: a California replication. *Arch. Gen. Psychiatry, 41,* 22.
79. Snyder KS, Liberman RP (1981) Family assessment and intervention with schizophrenics at risk for relapse. In: Goldstein MJ (Ed), *New Directions for Mental Health Services, 12.* Jossey-Bass, San Francisco.
80. Goldstrom I, Manderscheid R (1982) The chronically mentally ill: a descriptive analysis from the uniform client data instrument. *J. Community Support Serv., 2,* 4.
81. Azrin NH, Basalel V (1980) *Job Club Counselor's Manual: A Behavioral Approach to Vocational Counseling.* University Park Press, Baltimore, MD.
82. Jacobs HE, Kardashian S, Krienbring RK, Ponder R, Simpson AR (1984) A skills-oriented model for facilitating employment among psychiatrically disabled persons. *Rehabilit. Counsel. Bull., 28,* 87.

CHAPTER 7

Behavioral family therapy with schizophrenic disorders

IAN R.H. FALLOON

BACKGROUND

The value of family-based management of schizophrenia has been recognised for many years. In the 1913 edition of his textbook of psychiatry, Kraepelin (1) advocated early discharge of patients to their families once the most disturbing features of schizophrenia had diminished. He noted, with surprise, that many difficult patients behaved themselves remarkably well on return to the home environment. A decade later, Sullivan (2) developed a family-orientated milieu approach to inpatient care of schizophrenia.

The value of psychological intervention in the management of the florid phase of schizophrenia has been obscured by the advances in drug therapy. The effectiveness of neuroleptic drugs in controlling florid episodes has undoubtedly enhanced the quality of the milieu of the acute hospital ward. As a result, any additional benefits from psychological intervention have been difficult to measure in such settings. The recent work of Mosher and his colleagues (3) suggests that the benefits are not negligible. Furthermore, a substantial proportion of patients show only limited benefits from drug therapy, with persistence of florid symptoms.

Once the florid phase of schizophrenia has been controlled, the value of neuroleptic drugs is somewhat less dramatic. Even when compliance with drug taking is carefully controlled by giving depot injections, between 30 and 40% of cases suffer recurrent florid episodes in the first year after recovery (4). This rate continues to increase in the second year of follow-up, and five-year outcome shows even less value from continuous neuroleptic administration (5).

Thus, the major benefits from drug therapy appear to be in controlling florid episodes and in preventing recurrent episodes during the early months of aftercare. The emergence of serious side-effects, some irreversible, has led to further concern about excessive reliance on neuroleptic therapy in the long-term management of schizophrenia. Perhaps a more important criterion of successful outcome is the quality of life of the index patient and those involved in the patient's care. Optimal drug therapy may reduce clinical morbidity, but it cannot win friends for a lonely person, or provide satisfying employment or interesting leisure pursuits. Psychological interventions are needed to facilitate these goals. To date, however, the psychological interventions that have been employed do not appear notably cost-effective (6). Moreover, most studies have contrasted psychotherapies with drug

Handbook of Schizophrenia, Volume 4: Psychosocial Treatment of Schizophrenia.
M.I. Herz, S.J. Keith and J.P. Docherty, editors.

therapy in terms of reducing *clinical* morbidity – an unequal contest. Few have attempted to examine combinations of drug and psychological treatment that may prove additive or even synergistic, in conditions that resemble optimal clinical practice. In this chapter, I would like to describe some of the recent applications of psychological interventions that derive from learning theory principles. The focus will be on interventions that involve the family unit as the key resource in the long-term rehabilitation and care of schizophrenia.

EARLY DEVELOPMENTS

The earliest published study of behavioral interventions with families of persons with schizophrenia involved a programme of behavioral social work (7). This study of 12 chronic cases suggested the need for improved consumer education and social casework as well as behavior modification of handicapping symptoms. Only five cases proved suitable for behavioral interventions, which were applied with the collaboration of family members, and with limited success, particularly where delusional thinking persisted.

Around the same time, Liberman and his colleagues were developing a comprehensive behavior therapy programme of community-based management of all mental disorders (8). An important aspect of this project was mental health education for the patients and community carers. This included seminars to educate consumers about the nature and clinical treatment of schizophrenia. In 1975, Liberman joined forces with Falloon, Lillie and Vaughn at the Institute of Psychiatry in London to conduct a pilot study that incorporated behavioral family therapy and social skills training for the rehabilitation of severely handicapped patients who were living with family members who were rated high on the expressed emotion index (9). This study suggested that clinical and social morbidity could be reduced by these methods, and promoted further interest in psychosocial intervention programmes in the U.S. and U.K.

An extremely ambitious controlled study of this combined social skills training and behavioral family therapy was conducted under Liberman's direction in California (10). The aim of this programme was to assist adult male chronic schizophrenia sufferers to leave home and to sustain independent living in the community. The results suggested that the behavioral approach was more effective at achieving these aims than an alternative humanistic approach. There was evidence that family attitudes became more supportive as a consequence of the family intervention, but the complexity of the intervention programme prevented any clear-cut indication of the relative merits of the social skills training and family therapy components (11).

STRESS, VULNERABILITY AND RELAPSE PREVENTION

The second generation of studies that employed behavioral interventions were based more directly on a stress-vulnerability model of schizophrenia. This model suggests that persons with vulnerability to schizophrenic disorders, particularly those who have experienced previous episodes of these disorders, are at a high risk of experiencing recurrent episodes or unremitting symptoms when they are exposed to life stresses that pose a persisting threat to the coping capacity of that person. In other words, stress may trigger episodes and delay remission in individuals who have a vulnerability to develop schizophrenia (12).

Two stress factors have been associated with a relapsing course of schizophrenia in replicated research. These are: life events (13–15) and household tension (16–18). Both these factors appear to interact with the coping functions of the patient, including premorbid social functioning (especially work functions, and the ability to reduce face-to-face contact with stress-provoking family members, and regular adherence to drug regimens).

However, in households where family tension was low, these interactions proved non-significant. Indeed, some factors showed paradoxical effects. For example, a low degree of contact between index patients and low-tension households tended to increase the risk of recurrent episodes, while a high degree of contact ensured maximal clinical benefits. This suggests that, rather than viewing household tension as a negative factor in recovery from schizophrenic disorders, it may be more accurate to consider that the presence of a supportive social environment has health-enhancing qualities that help reverse the trend to a chronic, deteriorating course (19). It is also worth noting that a mere 15% of cases were exposed to the factors associated with a high probability of chronicity in the Camberwell family studies, i.e., index patient in *high contact* with a *high-expressed emotion* household member, and *not taking medication regularly*

The association between household support and the pathogenic association with major life events has not been defined in schizophrenia. In depressive disorders, the development of depression is less likely after a major life event where the index patient is in contact with a confiding person (20). Because major life events are defined by the level of continuing stress that is apparent a week after the event, it is evident that a household that is highly efficient in assisting its members to cope with stressful events may be capable of minimizing the threat these stresses might otherwise pose.

The behavioral family therapy interventions that were devised to facilitate the efficient management of environmental stress within a household living group aimed to counter the detrimental effects of everyday household tensions and stressful life events. Furthermore, the approach aimed to maximize the social functioning of all household members in order to improve the quality of life of patients and carers alike. The prevention of acute episodes of schizophrenia was considered less important than the sustained restoration of effective community functioning of all household members. This approach tended to run the risk of provoking more frequent episodes of schizophrenia, and demanded close monitoring of the index patient's clinical profile, so that intensive intervention could be provided at the earliest sign of a recurrence of florid symptoms. It was recognized that major exacerbations of clinical morbidity tended to be associated with disruption of social rehabilitation, whereas minor exacerbations were a minimal impedance to social functioning.

In addition to assisting the patient and family to minimize clinical and social morbidity, behavioral family therapy sought to reduce vulnerability to schizophrenia by expanding the coping capacity of the index patient. As well as training in stress management approaches, index patients participated in social skills training, cognitive restructuring, anxiety and depression management and compliance training, where deficits in any of these areas tended to increase the risk of morbidity associated with the schizophrenic disorder. Negative symptoms were regarded as just as disabling as positive symptoms, and strategies aimed to minimize the risk of both aspects of the disorder. Strategies based upon operant conditioning paradigms were particularly useful where negative symptoms were prominent. All these behavioral strategies were employed within a family problem-solving framework. The index patients and family members collaborated to apply the strategies on a daily basis after receiving training in the skills by the therapists.

This partnership between therapist, patient and family member(s) is a key ingredient of behavioral psychotherapy that facilitates the acquisition of functionally relevant skills. However, the training in skills is not restricted to those associated with the disabilities and handicaps of the index patient. Every household member is invited to participate in the family therapy, to set their own goals and to employ similar strategies to overcome their own functional deficits, which in some cases present greater handicaps than those of the index patient. In other words, *every* household member, including the index patient, is considered a client in their own right. The family unit is considered as the key support system for each member of the household, with disabilities in each person affecting each other household member, and detracting both from the stress management potential and from the rehabilitative capacity of the family unit. It is recognized that the family support system is not the only important system that may be operating within the index patient's social network, and that the interpersonal support that is provided in work, social and leisure systems may be highly relevant, and in some cases, prove of greater significance than the support of the household living group. Behavioral family therapy attempts to address these important extrafamilial support systems.

THE USC STUDY

A two-year controlled outcome study of behavioral family therapy in the community management of schizophrenia was conducted between 1978 and 1983 at the University of Southern California. This study compared 39 patients who were living with their parents and were randomly assigned to one of two treatment conditions: behavioral family therapy (BFT), and individual supportive therapy (IST). Three patients dropped out of the study in the early stages of therapy, leaving 18 closely matched patients and families in each group. Assignment to treatment was delayed until patients had been fully stabilized on optimal maintenance doses of neuroleptic medication after an acute episode of schizophrenia. The doses of medication were kept at the minimum level sufficient to maintain symptom stability throughout, by pharmacotherapists who were blind to the psychological treatment conditions and who had access to plasma assays of the drugs and serum prolactin levels.

The initial phase of intensive therapy consisted of weekly 1-hour sessions for 3 months, tapering to bi-weekly sessions until nine months, when monthly booster sessions continued until at least 24 months. In this way, each patient received 40 sessions during the two years after achieving stabilization. Therapists treated equal numbers of cases in each condition and were responsible for all case management, including 24-hour emergency care, throughout the study.

A battery of clinical, social and family measures was administered to family members at random assignment, and after three, nine and 24 months. In addition, continuous monitoring of symptoms, drug ingestion, plasma levels of neuroleptics, life stresses and family coping behaviors were made by blind/independent raters throughout the two years of study treatment.

All patients and family members were English-speaking, aged between 18 and 45 years and had a DSM-III diagnosis of schizophrenic disorder. One-third had experienced their first episode of schizophrenia at entry to the study. Patients were considered to have a high level of vulnerability to a chronic or relapsing course of the disorder as a consequence of living in a home environment characterized as 'high expressed emotion' or severe family burden.

The behavioral family therapy approach

The BFT was conducted primarily in the family home for the first 9 months, and consisted of 5 key components: (a) assessment of each family member's functioning; (b) education to enhance patient and family understanding of the nature and treatment of schizophrenia; (c) communication training to facilitate problems and goal-oriented discussion; (d) problem-solving training to enhance the efficiency of problem resolution and goal achievement; (e) specific behavioral strategies to assist patients and families to resolve specific disabilities.

Family assessment

Continued measurement of specific problems and goals is the key variable that distinguishes behavioral family therapy approaches from other methods. The problems and goals of each household member were assessed at baseline and throughout treatment. This enabled the therapist to direct interventions towards all sources of household tension, not merely those that were related to the index patient or his/her disorder. In addition, the specific framework and strategies the family unit employed in its efforts to cope with problems and goals were continually assessed in terms of their strengths and weaknesses. Everyday issues, as well as major life events, were considered.

The family assessment formed a framework to tailor the intervention to the specific strengths and deficits of each family unit, with particular emphasis on restoring the optimal functioning of each member of the household.

Education about schizophrenia

The initial two or three sessions were devoted to providing the patient and family with a straightforward explanation of the nature of schizophrenia and its treatment.

Handouts were provided and the index patient was invited to describe his/her experiences of schizophrenia and its treatment. Throughout treatment, revision of this education was conducted whenever indicated; for example, where a patient displayed reluctance to continue taking neuroleptic drugs. The early warning signs of an impending exacerbation were clearly delineated, so that patients and family members could take immediate action to avert a florid episode of schizophrenia. It was stressed that schizophrenia is a biological disorder that is made worse by stress. Thus, its successful management depends on the continuation of optimal biological (drugs) and stress management (BFT) interventions.

Communication training

The goal of communication training in BFT is to facilitate family problem-solving discussions. The ability to define problems or goals in a highly specific fashion, to reinforce progress towards objectives in small steps, to prompt behavior change without coercion, and to listen with empathy enables problems and goals of all kinds to be dealt with in an optimal fashion. Most families can improve their interpersonal communication substantially and benefit from several sessions of communication training. The skills are trained through repeated practice among family members, with instructions, coaching and reinforcement of progress. Homework practice is a key component in ensuring that the skills are not restricted to practice within the therapy sessions, but generalize to everyday interaction.

Problem-solving training

The six-step method used in this study differs from that employed in several other BFT methods (21). The main difference is that the therapist aims to teach the family to conduct their own structured sessions of problem solving. The therapy sessions are merely used as workshops, where the family learns the skills that they apply later in their own problem-solving discussions.

The steps employed include: definition of the problem or goal, choosing five or six possible solutions using a brainstorming method, evaluating the pros and cons of each solution, choosing the solution that best suits the resources and skills of the family, detailed planning of implementing the best solution, review of the effectiveness of the plan, and continued efforts until resolution has been achieved. Families are assisted in developing a regular family meeting, at least weekly, with a chairperson and secretary to administer the meeting, and to report back on their efforts at each therapy session. A guidesheet outlining the six-step method is used to record family discussions, and assists the therapist in his/her review. Skills training is provided where family members are deficient in their use of one or more steps of the method. The therapist avoids becoming personally involved in suggesting or choosing solutions, leaving that to the family.

Specific behavioral strategies

There are relatively few occasions where families are unable to devise effective strategies to resolve their problems or achieve their goals. However, where a family appears to be struggling to come up with an effective strategy, and there is a well-validated procedure for the management of that particular issue, the therapist may offer that procedure to the family as one possible solution. Common examples of this include: the use of operant reinforcement procedures to enhance motivation to perform tasks that are not inherently reinforcing, such as household chores and work activities; desensitization procedures for specific anxiety-provoking situations; cognitive-behavioral strategies for depressive disorders; social skills training for coping with difficult interpersonal situations; coping strategies for persistent hallucinations or delusions; strategies for sexual dysfunction. Although the six-step method is preserved, the therapist outlines the strategy in detail for the family and assists them in its implementation.

A second occasion when the therapist may become involved directly in the problem solving is when a major crisis impedes family ability to conduct their own problem solving in a calm, constructive manner. On these occasions, the therapist may choose to chair the problem-solving discussion in order to facilitate rapid stress reduction and thereby prevent symptomatic exacerbation.

Finally, when family members fail to adhere to the recommended treatment programme, thereby producing strong negative feelings in the therapist, he or she may choose to express his/her feelings directly to the family, and to chair a problem-solving discussion that aims to relieve his/her distress. Issues such as failure to complete homework tasks, missing sessions, and not adhering to prescribed drug regimens, are amongst the issues that engender high levels of therapist distress.

The individual supportive therapy approach

The IST method was designed to resemble excellent patient-focused psychological treatment for persons recovering from a florid episode of schizophrenia. Functionally relevant goals were set, and counseling that involved problem solving between the therapist and the patient was provided to assist the patient in achieving those goals. Family members were interviewed at regular intervals, provided with guidance on managing the patient's problems, particularly at times of crisis, when emergency sessions were provided on a 24-hour basis. Some behavioral strategies were employed for specific patient problems. No specific training in problem solving was provided for any family members.

Results of the study

The first question for the behavior therapist is whether the specific goals of the therapy were achieved in a specific manner. The main goal was that of changing the problem-solving efficiency of the family unit. Measures of family problem solving indicated that after the first intensive, three-month phase, the quantity of problem-solving statements in the BFT condition had trebled, whereas no significant change in the numbers of family problem-solving statements was noted after three months of IST (22). Perhaps more significantly, the quality of family problem solving that was observed by independent assessors who interviewed the families about everyday stressful events showed a significant linear improvement over the first nine months of treatment in families receiving BFT. No benefits were noted for IST families. Similar levels of stresses were encountered by families in each condition. Thus, it is reasonable to conclude that the BFT was associated with specific improvements in family problem-solving functions.

Having achieved specific changes in the ability of families to cope with a wide range of stressful life situations, it was hypothesized that this would result in parallel clinical benefits. The evidence for this is impressive. First, BFT patients experienced fewer major episodes of schizophrenia during the two-year period. Three BFT patients (17%) experienced a total of seven major episodes, while 83% of IST patients experienced 41 major episodes of schizophrenia and in addition 11 major depressive episodes. These observations were supported by blind ratings of psychopathology that indicated that not only were the florid symptoms of schizophrenia more stable in BFT patients, but there was a sustained improvement from baseline levels, suggesting that BFT may have promoted further symptom remission (23). A trend (almost reaching statistical significance) was noted on the BPRS withdrawal factor, that suggested that the BFT was associated with a reduction in negative symptoms of schizophrenia. At the end of two years, half of the BFT patients showed no evidence of any mental disorder on PSE interviews. By contrast, 83% of IST patients still showed evidence of schizophrenic symptoms at two years, although they too showed a trend towards remission, albeit on a much slower course. Thus, the benefits of BFT appear genuine, and not attributable to a comparative deterioration of the IST group, nor were these benefits associated with differences in the drug treatment received by patients in the two conditions. Indeed, BFT patients tended to have lower doses of neuroleptics than IST patients, and although the latter had more difficulty maintaining adequate compliance, this was remedied through the use of intramuscular preparations and other compliance strategies.

The achievement of clinical stability and remission is an important goal in the rehabilitation of a chronic disorder. However, a more crucial goal from the patient's perspective is the restoration of social functioning. The reader should be reminded that clinical stability is readily achieved by removing schizophrenia sufferers from community living into less stressful settings (24). BFT, with its emphasis upon achieving functional goals for patients, was associated with social benefits. BFT patients doubled the time they spent in constructive work activities compared with the two years before the study. Blind ratings of measures of social performance showed significant improvements over the two-year study period, as well as significantly greater benefits than those achieved by IST patients. The greatest comparative benefits for BFT were in the areas of work activity, household tasks and friendships outside the family (25).

The family members of persons suffering from chronic disorders tend to lead impoverished lives, and experience considerable distress themselves (26). An effective management approach would be expected to reduce levels of burden upon caregivers. BFT was associated with increased satisfaction for relatives as well as patients, even when the benefits for individual patients were limited. The burden associated with the care of the patients was reduced over the two years, so that only 17% of family members reported moderate or severe levels of burden at this point.

On the other hand, almost two-thirds of families who received IST continued to complain of moderate or severe burden at two years. Together with the earlier evidence of enhanced management of a wide range of family stresses, this suggests that the benefits of BFT extended beyond those for the index patients, and were experienced by the family as a whole.

Although the number of subjects in this study was too small to allow detailed multivariate analysis, the data supported the conclusion that the specific changes in family problem-solving behavior that were induced by behavioral family therapy were associated with the clinical and social benefits (27, 28).

Furthermore, increasingly efficient family problem-solving behavior generalized to a wide range of family stresses, and appeared to have an impact upon major life events. BFT families appeared to use their problem-solving behavior to reduce the stressful impact of life events (29). In the course of the first 12 months in the study, the 18 families suffered only three life events that were associated with high levels of long-term threat, as defined by Brown and Harris (20). Thus, the benefits of the behavioral family therapy appeared to derive from a reduction in both the stress of everyday household difficulties and the stress associated with major life events. This combined effect appeared to be sustained throughout the less intensive second year of the study, although the data were incomplete and a comprehensive analysis was not conducted. It is probable that the continued benefits in both clinical and social morbidity were achieved as a result of continued use of the structured problem-solving approach in the management of stress and the promotion of social functioning.

LATER STUDIES

The third generation of behavioral family therapy studies is now well under way. These studies are of two types: first, attempts to employ the BFT methods with different clinical and social populations; second, attempts to analyze the relative contributions of the major components of the approach. Because most of these studies are awaiting final data analysis and publication, I will concentrate on the study methods, rather than their outcomes.

The Brown study

James Curran and his colleagues at Brown University have undertaken a study that examines the efficacy of BFT when it is applied initially on an acute inpatient unit when the index patient is floridly disordered (30). This controlled study sought to compare BFT with the standard hospital treatment procedures, and extended beyond hospital discharge to at least the first 12 months of the aftercare phase. The methods employed communication and problem-solving skills training as well as family education; very similar to the approach used in the USC study. The involvement of the multidisciplinary team in the patient's clinical management was stressed. Videotaped feedback was used in the communication skills training.

Early reports of this study suggest that BFT was a useful addition to inpatient therapy and that this contributed to a smooth transition from hospital back to the community. The final results of this study are eagerly awaited.

The Rochester study

Robert Cole and Anthony Lehman and their colleagues at the University of Rochester have employed the BFT approach in the rehabilitation of young institutionalized patients. This study compared individually oriented community skills training with and without BFT. The family sessions continued for 12 months after discharge. The assessment procedures focused on the community functioning of the index patient, including his/her quality of life.

The UCLA Hispanic and VA studies

Two replications of the USC study are in progress in Los Angeles under the auspices of the NIMH-founded Mental Health Clinical Research Center for the Study of Schizophrenia. The first aims to apply BFT to Spanish-speaking families in East Los Angeles. Several families in the earlier study (28) were of Mexican-American origin, but the entry requirements excluded those families who used Spanish as their primary language in the home. It was apparent that many of these families learned the methods slowly on account of their unsophisticated command of English. It is likely that therapy provided in Spanish may enhance acquisition of efficient problem solving. BFT appears to be effective in a wide variety of cultural settings, and the flexible matrix of behavioral analysis encourages the therapist to adapt the therapy to the specific strengths and weaknesses of individual family units.

The Brentwood VA study aims to compare BFT in a clinic setting with BFT at home. While optimal learning is likely to occur when skill training is provided in the environment where the skills are used, similar benefits have been found in clinic-based BFT programmes. The added expense involved in therapist travel is substantial (31) and may reduce the numbers of cases that could be treated in a clinic setting. Undoubtedly some families would benefit minimally from a clinic-based approach, whereas others will tend to prosper in this setting. This study promises to answer some of these issues.

The NIMH treatment strategies in schizophrenia collaborative study

This is an extensive study of the relative efficacy of neuroleptic drugs and family interventions in the aftercare of schizophrenia. Five centers: Payne Whitney Clinic; Hillside Hospital (Long Island); Emery/Grady University; San Francisco General Hospital; and Medical College of Pennsylvania (EPPI) have been selected for the study. Therapists at each center have been trained to stabilize patients who have experienced a recent episode of schizophrenia with optimal doses of neuroleptic drugs before randomly allocating them, double-blind, to fluphenazine decanoate in one of three dosages: (1) continued optimal dose; (2) one-fifth of the optimal dose; (3) targeted doses of fluphenazine associated with periods when early warning signs of an impending episode are detected.

Random allocation to BFT or a supportive family intervention is made independently. All families are invited to participate in an educational workshop and a monthly educational support group, and receive crisis support when needed. The BFT is similar to that employed in the USC Study, with one significant modification: the therapists are not behavior therapists and have not been trained to apply sophisticated behavioral programmes, such as depression or anxiety management, social skills training or token economies, within the family problem-solving framework. Thus, the method concentrates almost entirely on enhancing the general problem-solving functions of the family units.

BFT is provided for at least 12 months after stabilization and continues throughout episodes of florid schizophrenia or hospital admissions, in a manner similar to the USC study.

The main hypothesis being tested in this study is that BFT, with its effectiveness in enhancing stress management, may reduce the need for higher doses of neuroleptic medication and hence the detrimental effects associated with these drugs. However, the large number of cases entering the study will enable a wide range of secondary issues to be explored. These include: the association between therapist competency and therapeutic outcome; the association between problem-solving skills and outcome; the specific benefits of more intensive, targeted family therapy; the cost-effectiveness of these approaches; and predictors of therapeutic efficacy.

The Max-Planck study

This study, under the direction of Dr. Kurt Hahlweg, has been developing methods to assess the quality of BFT and the association between therapist skills and therapeutic outcome. BFT is a highly specified treatment approach that enables therapists to be trained to a high degree of repeatability. It also allows a trained observer to rate the precise therapist skills and therapeutic goals in a highly reliable manner. Thus, the task of comparing the application of the method with its efficacy is relatively straightforward.

The Salford study

Dr. Nicholas Tarrier and Dr. Christine Barrowclough have recently completed a study that aimed to assess the relative contributions of education and behavior rehearsal to the effectiveness of the BFT approach (32). They randomly assigned 64 patients who were living with at least one relative (one half parental; one half marital or other) to one of four treatment conditions: (a) BFT with behavior rehearsal; (b) BFT with discussion; (c) education only; (d) routine treatment. All patients had suffered a recent episode of florid schizophrenia that had led to inpatient treatment. Nineteen further cases who were living in low-expressed emotion households were assigned at random to either educational treatment or routine treatment.

The BFT intervention differed from that developed by Falloon and Liberman in that the focus was on teaching the family members skills to assist their coping with the problem behaviors associated with schizophrenia (both florid and deficit symptoms). This approach resembled the specific behavioral strategies component of the

USC approach (see Chapter 12) (33). The goal of treatment was to lower expressed emotion by changing family members' coping styles and attitudes, and by changing the patient behaviors that elicited those stressful responses.

The BFT interventions were conducted over a nine-month period and were both significantly more effective in reducing clinical morbidity (i.e., relapse rates) than the two sessions of family education. The latter appeared to have little effect on relapse rates when applied on its own. A lowering of the expressed emotion index appeared specific to the BFT, and the levels of criticism and emotional overinvolvement were both reduced significantly after nine months. These changes were associated with reduced clinical morbidity. An unexpected result was the finding that the group receiving education only showed significant improvements in five areas of social functioning, whereas the BFT groups showed significant improvements in only one area of functioning. Although improved social functioning was a clear goal of many index patients, the focus on lowering stress and expressed emotion may have resulted in slower progress towards social rehabilitation than that observed with routine treatment, where more rapid and uncontrolled return to high levels of social performance may have contributed to a higher rate of florid episodes. The results of the USC study were somewhat consistent with this study. It was noted that family members' negative perceptions of the index patient's social disability tended to change more dramatically after BFT than the reductions in the actual levels of disability (29). However, in the earlier study, reductions in criticism and intrusive behavior by family members were associated with improvements in social functioning (27).

Another major difference was the finding that the effects of the BFT did not carry over to the second year of treatment (34). However, regular booster sessions were not continued throughout this period in the Salford study. The need to continue BFT indefinitely, albeit at relatively low intensity, is highlighted by these contrasting results.

The Buckingham early intervention study

Evidence that BFT reduces the morbidity of established cases of schizophrenia raises the possibility that initial episodes of schizophrenia might be aborted if similar interventions could be targeted to persons where there is a high vulnerability to the disorder. The current absence of clear biological measures of vulnerability means that clinical features must be employed. It has been noted that schizophrenic disorders tend to have a variety of prodromes that precede the florid disorder by weeks, months, and in some cases, years. The Buckingham study aims to detect these prodromes through screening by primary care physicians, who work in close collaboration with highly trained mental health professionals. The detection of a suspected prodromal state leads to immediate intervention with a continuation of BFT and targeted low-dose neuroleptics. The BFT focuses on stress management and educating the index patient and care-givers to recognize the symtoms of schizophrenia. The drugs are discontinued as soon as the prodromal features have remitted.

Early results support the feasibility of this approach, with over 20 cases being successfully managed in this way. Only one new case of schizophreniform disorder has been detected, whereas between 10 and 25 cases would have been expected from community surveys of the incidence of schizophrenia.

The combination of BFT, for early intervention as well as for the prevention of chronicity, in a comprehensive mental health service has tended to reduce the public health burden of schizophrenia to a minimal level. Epidemiological data to support these tentative conclusions are being compiled, and will be presented in due course.

FUTURE DEVELOPMENTS

The studies summarized in this chapter represent a substantial body of work. The conclusions tend to offer strong support for the value of BFT methods in the community management of schizophrenia. Early intervention, prevention of disability and the rehabilitation of handicaps all appear to be facilitated when this relatively straightforward psychological treatment approach is combined with optimal neuroleptic pharmacotherapy. Until all the studies in progress have been completed and their data fully analyzed, it would be premature to claim that the approach was anything more than a promising innovation. Several important issues remain somewhat obscure and further studies are clearly needed.

Among the unanswered questions are:

(a) How essential is the relatively complex communication skills training element of BFT? Could the method be almost as effective if families were only taught the structured six step problem solving method? In clinical practice, the behavioral family therapist often excludes many elements of communication skills training when families appear capable of conducting a problem solving discussion without excessive hostility or dominance by one or more members. However, in some families, grossly inadequate interpersonal communication by one or more family members necessitates a considerable amount of interpersonal skills training before the family can conduct effective problem-solving discussions without therapist assistance. This issue has been studied by Hahlweg and his colleagues (35) in the context of behavioral marital therapy, and would be worthy of a similar research enterprise for BFT in schizophrenic disorders.

(b) Is BFT more effective when combined with social skills training for the index patient? Although most BFT approaches tend to employ social skills training for the index patient (and other family members) within the context of family problem solving, this is seldom a consistent approach. The Pittsburgh Study (36) suggested that the combination of a stress-reducing family intervention with social skills training produced maximum benefits. A study that compared BFT with and without social skills training would help establish the merits of adding SST on a consistent basis.

(c) The manner in which families are assessed for behavioral treatment lacks consistency. Some studies have relied on non-behavioral assessment procedures, such

as the Camberwell Family Interview and its expressed emotion ratings, while others have conducted individual behavioral assessments of all family members, and behavioral tests of family problem solving. All behavior therapy approaches rely heavily on highly specific goals and continual monitoring of progress towards these goals. Further work on the development of efficient ways of assessing families is crucial to the application of these methods in everyday clinical practice where elaborate research assessments are not feasible.

(d) What is the long-term outcome of BFT? Do families retain their enhanced problem-solving skills indefinitely, or are booster sessions necessary? How frequently should booster sessions be provided? Unpublished evidence from the USC study suggested that the BFT remained effective for at least a year after regular sessions were discontinued (i.e., over the third year of follow-up). However, in subsequent years the benefits were less evident, particularly as index patients moved out of the home and spent less time in contact with their family unit. This finding is similar to that described earlier for patient contact with low-stress family units – a reduction in regular contact doubled the risk of recurrent episodes of schizophrenia. Although some patients develop excellent ability to monitor their own stress levels and to conduct their own problem-solving to cope with stresses, for others the added assistance provided by concerned household members is vital. It seems important to recognize that the *vulnerability* to schizophrenia is a lifelong feature in most cases, and that long-term contact that provides a flexible approach to stress management, combining drug and psychological interventions, is essential to minimizing the morbidity of all sufferers of schizophrenia. Long-term outcome studies of modern programmes of management of schizophrenia are needed before we can make definitive claims for the lasting benefits of our new intervention programmes.

(e) Primary prevention programmes have focused on the vulnerability factors found in children who have a high risk of developing schizophrenia, by dint of their parents having the disorder (37). BFT is a relatively straightforward approach that could provide additional protection for high-risk groups in a cost-efficient manner. The promising early results of the Buckingham project give impetus to further applications of BFT in prevention programmes.

(f) Many effective psychological interventions fail to demonstrate the promise they show in controlled trials. This is due largely to a lack of effective training programmes to ensure that the methods are faithfully replicated in clinical settings. It is essential not only that therapists receive supervised training in the specific skills of the interventions, but also that the delivery system in which those skills are applied is geared to promote the new approach. The application of BFT to schizophrenia requires early, accurate diagnosis, optimal pharmacotherapy, and 24-hour case management of crises. It is most readily applied within a multidisciplinary team approach.

A training programme that assists in developing all aspects of the family-based approach has been developed and is being evaluated both in Britain and in the U.S.A. This program incorporates workshop-based training in therapy skills, with audiotaped supervision, and on-site consultations with the multidisciplinary team. Therapist skills are assessed, in a reliable fashion, as well as the effectiveness of the application of these skills in achieving the goals of therapy. Further studies of the training process are needed to enhance its efficacy so that this cost-effective approach can be widely disseminated to clinical services.

CONCLUSIONS

It is concluded that BFT is a highly promising approach to the community management of schizophrenic disorders. It incorporates a self-help model of stress management, with education about the disorder, and behavioral rehabilitation strategies. This appears to result in a reduction in clinical and social morbidity, as well as increasing benefits for care-givers. The highly specified nature of the intervention strategies has facilitated the transfer of BFT to routine clinical practice in a variety of settings.

A substantial body of research is currently under way that aims to elucidate the most effective components of the approach and to refine the method. Several further studies are needed before the relative benefits of BFT can be fully understood. At the moment it seems likely that at least some aspects of the approach add to the benefits of optimal drug treatment in enhancing the quality of life of sufferers of schizophrenia and those people that help to care for them.

REFERENCES

1. Kraepelin E (1913) *Clinical Psychiatry*. William Wood, New York.
2. Sullivan HS (1927) The onset of schizophrenia. *Am. J. Psychiatry, 7,* 105.
3. Mosher LR, Menn A, Matthews S (1975) Soteria: evaluation of a home-based treatment for schizophrenia. *Am. J. Orthopsychiatry, 45,* 455.
4. Schooler NR, Severe JB (1984) Efficacy of drug treatment for chronic schizophrenic patients. In: *The Chronically Mentally Ill: Research and Services,* pp. 125 – 142. Spectrum, New York.
5. Shepherd M, Watt D, Falloon I, Smeeton N (1989) Outcome and prediction from a five-year follow-up of an epidemiologically representative sample of schizophrenics. *Psychol. Med. Monogr.,* Suppl. 15.
6. Mosher LR, Keith SJ (1980) Psychosocial treatment: Individual, group, family, and community support approaches. *Schizophr. Bull., 6,* 10.
7. Hudson BL (1978) Behavioural social work with schizophrenia patients in the community. *Br. J. Soc. Work, 8,* 159.
8. Liberman RP and Davis J(1975) Drugs and behavioral analysis. In: Hersen M, Bellack AS, Miller P (Eds), *Progress in Behavior Modification,* pp. 307 – 330. Academic Press, New York.
9. Falloon IRH, Liberman RP, Lillie FJ, Vaughn CE (1981) Family therapy for relapsing schizophrenics and their families: a pilot study. *Fam. Process 20,* 211.
10. Liberman RP, Mueser KT, Wallace CJ (1986) Social skills training for schizophrenic individuals at risk for relapse. *Am. J. Psychiatry, 143,* 523.
11. Liberman RP, Falloon IRH, Aitchison RA (1984) Multiple family therapy for

schizophrenia: a behavioral problem solving approach. *Psychosoc. Rehabil. J., 7,* 60.
12. Falloon IRH, Liberman RP (1983) Interactions between drug and psychosocial therapy in schizophrenia. *Schizophr. Bull., 9,* 543.
13. Birley JLT, Brown GW (1970) Crises and life changes preceding the onset or relapse of acute schizophrenia: clinical aspects. *Br. J. Psychiatry, 116,* 327.
14. Leff JP, Hirsch SR, Gaind R, Rohide PD, Stevens BC (1973) Life-events and maintenance therapy in schizophrenic relapse. *Br. J. Psychiatry, 123,* 659.
15. Leff J, Vaughn C (1980) The interaction of life events and relatives' expressed emotion in schizophrenia and depressive neurosis. *Br. J. Psychiatry, 136,* 146.
16. Brown GW, Birley JLT, Wing JK (1972) Influence of family life on the course of schizophrenic disorders: a replication. *Br. J. Psychiatry, 121,* 241.
17. Vaughn CE, Leff JP (1976) The influence of family and social factors on the course of psychiatric illness: a comparison of schizophrenic and depressed neurotic patients. *Br. J. Psychiatry, 129,* 125.
18. Vaughn CE, Snyder KS, Jones S, Freeman WB, Falloon IRH (1984) Family factors in schizophrenic relapse: a California replication of the British research on expressed emotion. *Arch. Gen. Psychiatry, 41,* 1169.
19. Falloon IRH, Pederson J, Al-Khayyal M (1986) Enhancement of health-giving family support versus treatment of family pathology. *J. Fam. Ther., 8,* 339.
20. Brown GW, Harris TO (1978) *Social origins of depression.* Tavistock Press, London.
21. D'Zurilla TJ, Goldfried MR (1971) Problem solving and behavior modification. *J. Abnorm. Psychol., 78,* 107.
22. Doane JA, Goldstein MJ, Miklowitz DJ, Falloon IRH (1986) The impact of individual and family treatment on the affective climate of families of schizophrenics. *Br. J. Psychiatry,* 148, 279.
23. Falloon IRH, Boyd JL, McGill CW, Williamson M, Razuni J, Moss HB, Gilderman AM, Simpson GM (1985) Family management in the prevention of morbidity of schizophrenia, I. Clinical outcome of a two-year longitudinal study. *Arch. Gen. Psychiatry, 42,* 887.
24. Lamb HR, Goertzel V (1971) Discharged mental patients: are they really in the community? *Arch. Gen. Psychiatry, 24,* 29.
25. Falloon IRH, McGill CW, Boyd JL, Pederson J (1987) Family management in the prevention of morbidity of schizophrenia: social outcome of a two-year longitudinal study. *Psychol. Med., 17,* 59.
26. Hatfield AB (1978) Psychological costs of schizophrenia to the family. *Soc. Work, 24,* 355.
27. Doane JA, Falloon IRH (1985) Assessing change in family interaction: methodology and findings. In: Falloon IRH (Ed), *Family Management of Schizophrenia,* pp. 153 – 170. Johns Hopkins University Press, Baltimore, MD.
28. Falloon IRH (1985) *Family Management of Schizophrenia: A Study of Clinical, Social, Family and Economic Benefits.* Johns Hopkins University Press, Baltimore, MD.
29. Hardesty JP, Falloon IRH, Shirin K (1985) The impact of life events, stress, and coping on the morbidity of schizophrenia. In: Falloon IRH (Ed), *Family Management of Schizophrenia: A Study of Clinical, Social, Family and Economic Benefits,* pp. 137 – 152. Johns Hopkins University Press, Baltimore, MD.
30. Curran JP, Faraone SV, Graves DJ (1988) Behavioral family therapy in an acute inpatient setting. In: Falloon IRH (Ed), *Handbook of Behavioral Family Therapy,* pp. 285 – 315. Guilford Press, New York.
31. Cardin VA, McGill CW, Falloon IRH (1985) An economic analysis: costs, benefits and effectiveness. In: Falloon IRH (Ed), *Family Management of Schizophrenia,* pp.

115 – 123. Johns Hopkins University Press, Baltimore, MD.
32. Tarrier N, Barrowclough C, Vaughn C, Bamrah JS, Porceddu K, Watts S, Freeman H (1989) The community management of schizophrenia: a controlled trial of a behavioural intervention with families to reduce relapse. *Br. J. Psychiatry, 153,* 532.
33. Falloon IRH, Boyd JL, McGill CW (1984) Family Care of Schizophrenia. Guilford Press, New York.
34. Tarrier N, Barrowclough C, Vaughn C, Bamrah JS, Porceddu K, Watts S, Freeman H (1989) Community management of schizophrenia. A two-year follow-up of a behavioural intervention with families. *Br. J. Psychiatry, 154,* 625.
35. Hahlweg K, Baucom DH, Markman H (1988) Recent advances in behavioral marital therapy and in preventing marital distress. In: Falloon IRH (Ed), *Handbook of Behavioral Family Therapy,* pp. 413 – 448. Guilford Press, New York.
36. Hogarty GE, Anderson CM, Reiss DJ, Kornblith SJ, Greenwald DP, Javna CD, Madonia MJ (1986) Family psycho-education, social skills training and maintenance chemotherapy in the aftercare treatment of schizophrenia. *Arch. Gen. Psychiatry, 43,* 633.
37. Newton J (1988) *Preventing Mental Illness.* Routledge and Kegan Paul, New York.

CHAPTER 8

Psychoeducational family management of schizophrenia

GERARD E. HOGARTY, DOUGLAS J. REISS AND
CAROL M. ANDERSON

Approximately one decade ago, the field of clinical psychiatry had reached something of an impasse in its efforts to advance the community care of schizophrenic patients following the resolution of psychosis and hospital discharge. Results from a number of integrated drug and psychosocial studies were available which, on casual inspection, seemed contradictory, but which, upon a more condidered evaluation, provided insights from which a new generation of psychosocial interventions has developed.

On the one hand, the efficacy of maintenance antipsychotic medication, relative to placebo, had been clearly established, but relapse rates nonetheless, averaged 40% by one year post-discharge and often reached 50% by two years (1). The corresponding relapse rates of 65% among placebo recipients at one year and 80% by two years clearly documented the fact that as many as 30% of patients remained free from an interim psychosis when maintained on maintenance chemotherapy, but that medication alone afforded an incomplete approach to forestalling the relapse of 40 – 50% of patients. Intuitively, medication non-compliance seemed to be the primary reason for schizophrenic relapse among drug-assigned patients. However, results from one of our earlier trials (2), from an NIMH Collaborative Study (3), as well as from an independent investigation conducted in England (4), led to the conclusion that the rate of relapse, at least in the first year post-discharge, was nearly identical whether or not patients were maintained on injectable fluphenazine decanoate or whether they received an oral equivalent with which they could covertly non-comply. Other reasons for drug relapse had been offered (1), extending from drug dysphoria to supersensitivity psychosis, but few explanations captured the attention of investigators as much as the potential influence of adverse environmental events on vulnerable schizophrenic patients.

RATIONALE FOR FAMILY PSYCHOEDUCATION/MANAGEMENT

Within the *therapeutic environment*, experiences which appeared overstimulating (5, 6) or which reflected increased expectations for interpersonal or instrumental role performance (7 – 9), were associated with the reappearance of psychotic symptoms. Patients who were particularly vulnerable to these expectations in one of our

Handbook of Schizophrenia, Volume 4: Psychosocial Treatment of Schizophrenia.
M.I. Herz, S.J. Keith and J.P. Docherty, editors.

earlier trials were characterized as having less insight, and were more withdrawn and conceptually disorganized (7). For those patients who did not relapse while receiving placebo tablets, psychosocial intervention appeared to contribute to impairments in social adjustment (10). In the *natural environment* of patients, precipitation of relapse ranged from cultural differences (11,12) (perhaps once again reflecting expectations for performance), through aspects of family life (13) to the presence of independent life events in the weeks or months preceding a new episode. The latter, particularly interpersonal losses and conflicts, have repeatedly been shown to be associated with the relapse of medicated schizophrenic patients (14 – 18).

If, then, the considerable relapse observed anomg drug-maintained schizophrenic patients could be traced to environmental stimuli, the observation more likely spoke to some profound difficulty in the patient's ability to negotiate even ordinary life experiences, rather than to some pathognomonically noxious psychosocial experience. In point of fact, no psychosocial event has been identified which, in itself, appears sufficient to 'cause' schizophrenia in a previously unaffected individual. Rather, an extensive body of knowledge (ref. 19, Ch. 1) accumulated over the past 5 decades provided ample evidence for the problems faced by many schizophrenic patients in the perception, processing and response to stimuli and in the associated regulation of arousal. Whether these elementary deficits were directly connected to the cognitive dysfunctioning which underlies psychosis, or whether they were indirectly influenced by such phenomena as cerebral cell loss, functional hypofrontility or altered neurotransmission seemed less important than the implicit message that the psychosocial experiences believed to exploit these deficits might be more appropriately managed by principles of clinical practice relevant to schizophrenia (19), Antipsychotic medication did seem able to regulate arousal and enable patients to deploy attention more correctly (20), but the prophylactic effect was apparently incomplete in the face of overwhelming environmental stress (16). Available psychosocial strategies seemed largely atheoretical, and when applied non-specifically, they also appeared to contain stimuli capable of evoking the psychotic process (5 – 10). As such, we reasoned the following:

> 'If either the demands of the environment *or* the underlying deficits were sufficiently severe, then these factors operating alone, or more likely together, might represent a sufficient cause of schizophrenic relapse, even when the receipt of antipsychotic medication was assured. Conversely, antipsychotic drug regulation of attention and arousal and/or the provision of a more benign, stimuli-modified environment operating alone or together might possibly result in a reduction of schizophrenic relapse.' (21, p. 634).

In 1978 a grant from the National Institute of Mental Health (Schizophrenia Research Branch) was received which provided the opportunity to test whether a family education/management strategy, (specifically addressed to aspects of the family environment believed to be risk factors in schizophrenic relapse), was more or less effective than either maintenance chemotherapy and support or a patient-centered behavioral approach, applied alone or in combination with family education and management. The thrust of the family education and management strategy was to lower the emotional climate of the home while maintaining reasonable expectations for patient performance, i.e., by striking a balance between over- and understimulation. The intervention sought to increase the stability and predictability of family life by decreasing the family's guilt and anxiety, increasing their self-confidence and providing a sense of cognitive mastery through the provision of information concerning both the nature and course of schizophrenia, as well as specific management strategies thought to be helpful in coping with schizophrenic symptoms on a day-to-day basis. If effective, this process might decrease the intensity of interaction between the patient and family members and diminish the possibility of patients being overstimulated by even the common elements of family life. The goals of this family model are approached in a series of interventions that, while sequential in nature, are at times overlapping. A full description of the method and process had been published elsewhere (19).

THE CONTENT OF FAMILY PSYCHOEDUCATION/MANAGEMENT

Phase I: Connecting with families

Phase I involves interventions which concentrate on establishing a working relationship with the patient and family. This phase, designed to occur as early as possible during the period of acute psychosis, lays the foundation for the entire process of treatment and has four primary goals:

(a) Develop a working alliance between the clinician, the patient and the family.
(b) Maximize and emphasize family strengths and resources rather than focus on weaknesses and deficits.
(c) Gain an understanding of life experiences which might contribute to the stress level of a patient or other family members.
(d) Establish the rules and expectations of treatment through the creation of a contract which embodies specific, attainable and mutually agreed upon goals.

Families usually experience pain, frustration, anger, confusion and embarrassment in dealing with their acutely ill member. Providing families with an opportunity to share their feelings and thoughts initially helps to decrease emotional intensity. Since years of coping with schizophrenia often leaves the family with a sense of hopelessness, treatment must emphasize the family's strengths and ability to effect change for the patient and themselves.

Much of the focus of this initial phase of treatment is upon the development of a positive working relationship between the clinician and all members of the family, including the patient. The process evolves by using early sessions to review the course of illness and past treatment experiences, including their impact on the lives of individual family members. The connecting process is further facilitated by making a specific effort to help family members recognize that they were not involved in causing this illness, but that they do have the ability to positively influence its subsequent course.

In order to enhance the importance of the family's involvement in the treatment process, the clinician should establish him/herself as the family's ombudsman. In the past, most treatment systems have primarily focused on the patient, and have rarely sought family input. To help reinforce the family's emerging sense of mastery, and in order to maintain their desire to be involved, it is important to keep family members informed of treatment decisions, answer their questions and communicate their concerns to the treatment team.

Phase II: The survival skills workshop

Phase II is a day-long, multiple family 'survival skills' workshop held at our Institute which provides basic information about schizophrenia. Convened early in the treatment process, the workshop is designed to decrease the family's anxiety, sense of helplessness, and feelings of stigma or isolation. Knowledge, we feel, can be a stress reducer by allowing a person to develop a sense of cognitive mastery. Information about schizophrenia is given in a way that is clear and understandable. The content includes topics related to the phenomenology, epidemiology, pathophysiology, onset, course, treatment and outcome of the illness. Schizophrenia is first described from the perspective of the patients' internal experience and then related to the external manifestations of the illness in order to help families better understand the behaviors of their patient.

In keeping with the theoretical underpinnings of this treatment model, data which suggest a cognitive and perceptual impairment and an ensuing sensitivity to stimulation are emphasized. The mechanisms of action, main effects, and possible side-effects, of antipsychotic medication in regulating these processes are emphasized. This information lays the groundwork for the presentation of a series of techniques which family members can use to facilitate the patient's progress and help avoid decompensation, and diminish their own tendency to react emotionally to each change in the patient's behavior. Family members are encouraged to refocus some of their energy on their own lives apart from the patient.

Although family members are told that while there are no research data which demonstrate that families 'cause' schizophrenia (22), it is stressed that there is evidence that families do have the resources to influence the course of the illness (13). Within this framework, a number of management techniques are introduced to the family.

It is emphasized that behaviors which will be asked of family members during treatment might be difficult to implement. They will, nevertheless, be encouraged to:

(a) Revise their expectations for patient performance, at least temporarily.
(b) Set priorities as to what goals and behaviors are to be focused upon, while selectively ignoring others.
(c) Decrease extreme involvement with the patient, whether the involvement be positive or negative.
(d) Diminish conflict and criticism by setting limits on behaviors or rituals that are disruptive or upsetting to other family members.
(e) Keep communication clear and simple.
(f) Increase their involvement with the family's own social support network or other potentially positive activities outside the nuclear family.

(g) Support the patient's medication regime.

The workshop also offers the opportunity for families to discuss and integrate their past experiences with the illness, and to be helpful to others coping with the same problems. The process of de-isolation for the family begins in the workshop as families are exposed to other families struggling with similar issues, and continues as patients and family members are invited to meet periodically as a multiple family group.

The response to the workshop is often dramatic. The atmosphere between staff and families becomes more cooperative, family members gain a greater understanding of the nature of schizophrenia, and the principles of treatment and management become 'reasonable' and better accepted. Unilateral views of the patient as being either 'hopeless' or 'deliberately obstructional' frequently change. Often we see the understandable criticism and overinvolvement which might follow upon misinformation . . . or no information . . . diminish following a workshop. However, the workshop is only one component of the treatment process. Although information is a valuable resource in helping a family to cope with schizophrenia, it appears to us to be an insufficient tool in itself. Many families appear to need continuing intervention that allows change to occur at a modulated pace, offers support over the long haul, and authoritative guidance in integrating information into day-to-day experiences.

Phase III: Ongoing treatment for the first year

Phase III involves individual family sessions. The purpose of these ongoing sessions are multiple, but all relate to the themes of the initial sessions and the survival skills workshop. Primarily, these sessions are designed to help patients survive in the community by:

(a) Helping each family to apply the principles outlined at the workshop by offering ongoing support and suggestions to the family and patient about how to do so over the 'long haul'.

(b) Beginning and maintaining a gradual process of reintegration of the patient into usual family routines and roles.

Since each family has different issues, the tasks of the clinician are to individualize the treatment by using the unique strengths of a given family as well as deal with the specific prolems of the individual patient and family identified earlier in the contract. Throughout this period, the clinician must also be able to deal with those issues which are common to most patients and families coping with schizophrenia: the patient's vulnerability to overstimulation; the patient's tendency not to comply with medication programs; the frustration inherent in living with the ramifications of a debilitating chronic illness; the natural tendencies of family members to center their lives around an ill member; and the patient's apparent lack of motivation and energy. Successful negotiation of these issues is primarily accomplished by careful attention to the themes of gradual resumption of responsibility by the patient and appropriate maintenance of interpersonal, generational, and family-community boundaries.

Family sessions during this phase generally occur every two weeks and are highly structured, with each session having four basic components: (1) the social contact; (2) a review of previously assigned tasks; (3) the identification and resolution of interim or new problems; and (4) the assignment of a new task. The use of small tasks as 'homework' helps to prolong the impact of the sessions and gives the family and the patient both a focus and a sense of progress over time. The content of sessions varies, but there are certain topics that are consistent from family to family, including: strategies for living together; recognition and use of prodromal signs; medication compliance; and the patient's gradual resumption of responsibility.

This latter theme is often one of the most difficult to address because of patients' tendencies toward excessive sleep, inactivity, amotivation, and withdrawal during the first six to ten months post-discharge. Experience has shown that these 'negative' symptoms are highly resistant to aggressive intervention in the early months of convalescence, making it very difficult to set an appropriate pace for the patient's gradual resumption of responsibilities. A rapid pace appears highly stressful and provocative of positive symptoms, while too slow a pace could promote further withdrawal and isolation.

In addition to posing a prolem for the professional in terms of treatment, this stage of the illness is exceptionally frustrating and often difficult for families to tolerate. In the absence of postitive symptoms, it sometimes becomes hard for family members to remind themselves of the severity of the illness. It is too often easy for families, as well as professionals, to believe that the patient could do more, if he or she only tried. The assumption that the patient's lethargy and amotivation are 'voluntary' often leads to increased pressure on the patient to be more active and function more effectively. This, in turn, has the potential of increasing environmental stress, often leading to an affective dysregulation in the patient and an increase in cognitive symptoms. Even when this process does not occur, family members can become increasingly discouraged with the patient and the treatment process, feeling that nothing is changing and wondering whether it is worth their time and effort.

At these times, it is essential to re-emphasize the themes of the psychoeducational workshop by stressing the frequency of decreased functioning during this phase of illness and the need for a very gradual return to the normal responsibilities and demands of everyday life. Such reminders help family members to increase their tolerance and control. Individual family sessions are used to work on scaling down goals and expectations that are too ambitious. The early priorities of treatment are reiterated and emphasized: (a) the need for an extended period of recuperation in order to avoid precipitating relapse; and (b) the need for patients to gradually resume roles and responsibilities within their families. Thus during the first few months following hospital discharge, emphasis is placed on allowing the patient to restabilize within his or her home while gradually assuming responsibility for the small chores which often lead to a re-establishment of normal household functioning. To help achieve this objective, structured tasks are assigned during each session utilizing the following principles:

(a) The task-related goal is divided into small behavioral units. For example, the goal of increased patient responsibility may be approached with the initial task of drying the dishes once a week, while another family member washes.
(b) Each successive task is directly related to the success of the previous one. The

previous task mentioned would then be followed either by increasing the number of days on which the task is to be performed *or* by asking the patient to expand the task on one day, e.g., wash *and* dry the dishes.

(c) Feedback from the patient and family is requested following task assignment in order to clarify possible misunderstandings and to help in creating future tasks.

(d) Progress is assessed by an 'internal yardstick', i.e., how well the patient is doing compared to his or her *own* recent past performance, rather than to the accomplishments of peers or siblings.

Although the attention to detail inherent in these tasks seems slow and cumbersome, it sets a pace that enhances the possibility of success and minimizes the probability of failure. As the patient becomes more motivated and capable, the tasks increase in terms of complexity and time demands. In this entire phase, it is the clinician's responsibility to set a pace that minimizes the stress level of patient and family, yet which never completely accepts the status quo.

In minimizing the stress level in the home, conflictual issues of importance to any family member are placed on the agenda for discussion during a session. Family members are helped to set limits on behaviors that upset or inconvenience other family members. These limits can be reassuring to patients, helping them to establish structure, as needed, over time. Often the patient has valid issues or complaints as well, frequently related to a need for privacy and 'space'. These, too, are addressed in the sessions.

Families are encouraged during this phase to adopt an attitude of 'benign indifference'. They are helped to minimize the negatives of nagging, rejection, fights and conflicts, as well as the positives of extreme concern, encouragement, and enthusiasm. Family members are more comfortable in accepting this philosophy as they feel they can better identify what are truly problem behaviors. Considerable time is spent in helping the patient and family identify what might constitute prodromal signs of a new episode.

Finally, it should be noted that due to the wide variability in the chronicity of patients, this phase may extend from a few months to a few years.

Phase IV: Social and vocational rehabilitation

Phase IV is a continuation of Phase III and involves patients from the time they are successfully functioning within the family, through their reintegration into the social/vocational world. It is based on the assumption that, although patients and families can be helped to cope better and deal with problems that arise at home, many schizophrenic patients have limited resources available for independently seeking successful employment or social activities. Traditional rehabilitation programs are often too complex and stimulating for the patient to negotiate successfully. Geared primarily for the physically disabled patient, these programs often tend to be unaware of the cognitive problems and deficits of patients recovering from schizophrenia, particularly their vulnerability to competing demands and expectations for role performance beyond the limits imposed by the illness.

For these reasons, the rehabilitative approach of Phase IV remains consistent with the overall philosophy of the entire family program. It incorporates the following components:

(a) Flexible, individualized vocational and/or social programming that accommodates the patient's stress and tolerance level.
(b) Realistic goals, developed with the patient's input, that take into consideration past, present and potential levels of functioning.
(c) Patients entering the vocational and social realm at a stage which is commensurate with the patient's level of functioning and one at which success can likely be experienced.
(d) Changing only one thing at a time in the patient's overall treatment and rehabilitation program. If there is a crisis or the patient is experiencing internal or external stressors, no other social or vocational changes are made until the crisis is resolved.

Flexibility in all phases allows for movement backward as well as forward, dependent upon the patients' or other family members' response to environmental changes. A negative response is viewed not as resistance or failure, but rather as an indication that the pace is too rapid or that the new step was too complex. The clinician usually assumes responsibility for the timing of decisions which appear to lead to 'failure'. The treatment program's response is to help the patient re-stabilize and then to attempt a smaller incremental step.

The areas of social and vocational rehabilitation are difficult ones to negotiate for the patient with schizophrenia. In the past, patients often remained isolated and dysfunctional, less as a result of the acute symptoms of their illness than due to a lack of the skills necessary to negotiate the complexities of maintaining a social and vocational life.

However, with patience and a carefully laid out step-by-step approach, reintegration into both settings is possible for many patients, although not without difficulty (see below). Some success is possible if the principles of temporarily lowered expectations, the provision of a relatively low-stimulation environment, making only one change at a time, and keeping goals tangible and immediate can be applied in a flexible manner.

Phase V: The final stages of treatment

Phase V occurs when and if patients have shown progress in accomplishing their goals of treatment, and when they have maintained these gains over an extended period of time. At this point, the patient, family, and clinician have four options:

(a) Treatment can continue to focus on the goals of the original contract.
(b) Treatment can move to a focus on the more traditional topics of family therapy.
(c) Treatment can move to a less frequent maintenance condition in order to ensure continued functioning and the sense of a stable lifeline;
(d) Treatment can be terminated.

For those patients who have been ill for many years, it is generally not advisable to consider termination. Some ongoing supportive contact, however minimal, is recommended, since many of these patients are likely to have at least mild, periodic exacerbations of their symptoms. At times of crisis, an already existing relationship with professionals makes it possible for patients or their families to receive help before a severe episode occurs.

EFFECTS OF THE FAMILY PSYCHOEDUCATION/MANAGEMENT APPROACH

Our psychoeducation model was tested among 103 consecutively admitted RDC shizophrenic patients who resided in high-expressed emotion (EE) households prior to their index hospital admission (21). Patients were randomly assigned at intake to the family psychoeducation approach, to a patient-centered social skills training program, (designed to respond to patient behaviors which were believed to elicit high-EE attitudes), to a combination of these two treatments, or to a control condition of supportive therapy. All patients were kept on maintenance antipsychotic medication, most often fluphenazine decanoate, and remained in the study for two years post-discharge or until relapse. Of the 103 patients, 13 patients and/or their families were designated as 'partial takes' to treatment, having failed to meet full criteria for treatment exposure. (Eleven of these 13 patients relapsed during the process of engagement.) For the entire sample, a clear main effect of treatment on relapse was observed for both the family intervention and the social skills intervention in the first year. An additive effect was observed when treatments were combined. Further, among patients known to be faithful compliers with medication, a main and additive effect of family treatment was obtained which clearly demonstrated that psychosocial interventions provide an effect not possible with drug treatment alone. Data for the 90 patients who faithfully complied with treatment are illustrative (21): 19% of family intervention patients relapsed in the first year, as did 20% of social skills recipients and 38% of drug-treated controls, but *no patients* relapsed in the combined family treatment/social skills condition. Furthermore, 25% of families in the control and social skills alone conditions changed from high to low EE, but 39% of families in the two family conditions did so as well. In no case did a patient relapse if the family household changed from high to low. Unlike British studies, we observed neither an effect of face-to-face contact on relapse nor an effect of treatment on the amount of face-to-face contact.

These relapse results were quite similar to the results of other recent family intervention studies reported by Falloon et al. (23) and Leff et al. (24) at nine months. (While the Leff approach is quite similar to our own, the Falloon model appears to endorse more behaviorally oriented, problem-solving strategies for family members.)

In contrast to the two-year follow-up reports descriptive of the Leff et al. (25), Falloon et al. (26) and Wallace and Liberman (27) studies, our program chose to place patients under controlled treatment conditions for the entire two-year period post-discharge. By two years, a clear main effect of the family psychoeducation approach had persisted, but the effect of social skills training on relapse (but not on adjustment) had all but disappeared. Among patients in the two family conditions, approximately one quarter had relapsed by two years, but one half of the social skills alone recipients and nearly two-thirds of controls had experienced a relapse by 24 months. Again, the effect of family intervention persisted among the subsample of 75 patients who faithfully complied with medication during the period of study.

At the moment, differential treatment effects on adjustment are being analyzed. Preliminary results indicate selective but important effects of the family and social skills approaches on different adjustment parameters, particularly on aspects of personal well-being and symptomatology. However, one is not overwhelmed by the number of patients who experience a restoration of instrumental role functioning. A recent review (28) representing the past decade of integrated drug and psychosocial studies, suggested to us that psychosocial interventions might be necessary in order for certain patients to achieve the potential which a good premorbid competence confers. However, it remains entirely unclear whether any gains beyond the forestalling of further decompensation accrue to poor premorbid patients. Studies which do cite gains in personal and social adjustment often represent end-point analyses which include both relapsed and non-relapsed patients. However, since most variance on symptom and adjustment measures is a function of relapse, then if relapsed patients are included in an analysis where it had previously been determined that major relapse differences between treatments exist, then a test of treatment effects on adjustment becomes a redundant test of relapse.

Delay versus prevention of relapse

As reassuring as results have been, neither of our psychosocial interventions could be construed as having *prevented* schizophrenic relapse. Rather, both exert a time-limited, albeit important effect in *forestalling* decompensation. The phenomenon of 'delay' rather than 'prevention' has provided an opportunity to examine more closely the circumstances at least, which were associated with late relapse.

To begin, medication non-compliance continues to appear to be associated with relapse. Twenty-eight of the 103 patients failed to comply with medication at some time during the study; 26 of them relapsed, (although it was not always clear whether non-compliance preceded or followed the psychotic episode). Psychosocial interventions not only reduced medication non-compliance (20%) compared to controls (40%), but the effect of psychosocial interventions (family psychoeducation, at least) on the remaining compliant patients was, as noted above, highly significant. Still, 54% of the late relapsing experimental subjects were drug-non-compliant: three of six social skills relapses; one of two family treatment relapses; three of five combined treatment relapses (and six of seven controls). Furthermore, one drug-compliant patient relapsed in the family condition when the family withdrew from treatment in the second year, and one medication-compliant patient relapsed in the combined treatment group where the patient failed to comply with social skills training. As such, the long-term effects of integrated drug and psychosocial interventions might usefully be enhanced by the development of more effective means of engaging patients and families in treatment *over time*. One approach, recently introduced by us, is the provision of a 'mini-workshop' at the beginning of the second year of treatment, with the goal of maintaining reasonable expectations and reinforcing the positive effects of continuing treatment.

More important to us in the analysis of late relapses, both off and on medication, was the experience of experimental subjects who improved sufficiently during the first year to begin a social and/or vocational rehabilitation program in the second year of treatment. Entry into the broader social field, particularly following referral to a collaborating rehabilitation agency, was associated with a new schizophrenic episode among most of the 13 experimental subjects who relapsed (even though many others succeeded). This is not a new experience for us, since an earlier trial of vocational rehabilitation (Major Role Therapy) years before had led to a similar increase in relapse among selected patients exposed to a high-expectation rehabilitation intervention (7). However, years of consultation with and training of the rehabilitation staff in the present program seemed insufficient to avoid the kinds of vocational demands which appeared capable of exacerbating the illness in some patients. Up to the time of referral to school or vocational rehabilitation agency, or emancipation from the family, the success of family psychoeducation and social skills training seemed to us to suggest that schizophrenic patients could be 'trained' to accommodate to a more protected, safe and less stressful family environment; one which essentially remained under the control of therapists. Once a move beyond the family was made, the effects seemed not to persist, an observation compatible with the long-term outcomes of other family and social skills programs (21, 25, 27). Our visceral response was to conclude that skills learned in one setting 'failed to generalize' to another. However, the process of schizophrenic decompensation might not be so simply reasoned. Weinberger (29), for example, has recently suggested a model of schizophrenic pathophysiology which implicates impairments in dorsolateral, prefrontal cortex (DLPFC) as the source of both problem-solving difficulties, hypo-functioning of the mesocortical dopaminergic system (e.g., negative symptoms), and a compensatory hyperfunctioning of the mesolimbic dopaminergic system which might underlie positive symptoms of schizophrenia. The model represents a major challenge to psychosocial intervention theorists. If DLPFC impairment is significant, will the patient require the support of a problem-solving 'alter ego' throughout the age of risk (i.e., the presence of a supportive therapist)? Or is it possible, through the application of a disorder-relevant, cognitive habilitation strategy to equip patients with problem solving or coping skills which they can utilize on their own in a variety of settings beyond the therapist's influence? If the former position is correct, then future psychosocial efforts will be directed to refinements in clinical practice more appropriately described as principles of 'human engineering' than psychotherapy. In many regards, the process of family psychoeducation thus developed is more an exercise in environmental manipulation than one directly focused on the resolution of intrapsychic or interpersonal conflict. In Pittsburgh, we have recently embarked upon a long-term program designed to test the *second* hypothesis. Following patient recovery from an acute episode, attention in this new program is focused upon the earliest 'pre-prodromal' affective and psychophysiologic cues which might herald a subsequent psychotic episode. In the context of clinically controlled 'probing', potentially detrimental affects and cognitions are identified and a graduated series of internal coping strategies is being taught in a repetitive, serial learning program. The intent is to provide patients with better generalized coping strategies that might not only forestall relapse in those environments which remain beyond therapeutic control, but that could offer patients a fuller social and vocational experience without compromising their clinical state.

PROBLEMS IN CONTEMPORARY FAMILY PSYCHOEDUCATION INTERVENTIONS

For many recent programs (21, 23, 24, 27), a criterion of admission had been patient residence in a household defined as stressful, usually high expressed emotion. Given the confound between expressed emotion gender and marital status (30), the result too frequently has been to over-sample schizophrenic patients who arc young, male, unmarried and residing in parental households. It is clear from experience, however, that patients and families characterized as low in expressed emotion could profit equally from family education/management programs. Unfortunately, the results of contemporary studies largely ignore low-EE female subjects who, if young, divorced or separated, experience significant exacerbations of psychotic illness (30). Patients who live in alternative residential placements have been similarly ignored within the present generation of novel psychosocial interventions.

Elsewhere, it is with some dismay that we note a development wherein any attempt to provide information to a family (seemingly, at times, the provision of a pamphlet or two), is characterized as 'psychoeducation'. For us, knowledge of the illness is only the cognitive scaffold upon which day-to-day survival and coping skills are formulated and implemented with the continuing assistance of a trained professional. We do realize that efforts are underway both in this country (31) and abroad, (J. Leff, personal communication) to test whether a formal psychoeducation program plus a regularly convened relatives' group is as effective as ongoing family education and management. Our opinion (unsupported by any facts), is that this approach might not be appealing to a significant number of families, who want and seek continuing professional counsel regarding the implementation and management of a long-term maintenance program.

Otherwise, there appear to be legitimate needs and concerns voiced by family members which could be profitably addressed in future programs. Some families feel that family psychoeducation programs are being 'forced' upon them, either to the exclusion of other needed residential alternatives, or as a means of shifting the burden of care from professionals to families in order to contain the rising costs of mental health services. In no instance have we or others, to our knowledge, urged a family to embark upon a program of education and management which they felt was unwanted. Yet, as one family member indicated, the coercion is often subtle. If the community has failed to provide alternative residential placements, then they become reluctant consumers of family psychoeducation by default. Our response to these concerns is to advise families to avail themselves of the requisite knowledge and coping skills available, if for no other reason than to secure a greater feeling of personal comfort and mastery for themselves. At the same time, they should pursue and solicit alternative community residential placements, particularly if residence with the patient over time is not viewed as helpful or desirable to either them or their loved one.

Finally, legal issues of estate and long-term financial planning, identification of various community resources and other informational needs, not necessarily addressed by available psychoeducational programs, could be richly expanded upon in the future. Perhaps, understandably, the information content of initial programs represented professional value judgments as to what families wanted and needed, rather than to base the education component upon a direct sampling of family opinion. Foremost among these modifications might be the knowledge base and management skills useful for families who have experienced their first episode of schizophrenia, as opposed to families dealing with more chronic forms of the illness. Important differences in premorbid adjustment, treatment response, course and outcome might be profitably developed in parallel formats for various families. At the moment, we have little data which would enable us to determine which of the many components of family psychoeducation/management actually account for the observed, positive effects of treatment. Continuing research in this area could be most fruitful.

REFERENCES

1. Hogarty GE (1984) Depot neuroleptics: the relevance of psycho-social factors. *J. Clin. Psychiatry, 45*, 36.
2. Hogarty GE, Schooler NR, Ulrich RF, Mussare F, Herron E, Ferro P (1979) Fluphenazine and social therapy in the aftercare of schizophrenic patients. *Arch. Gen. Psychiatry, 36*, 1283.
3. Schooler NR, Levine J, Severe JB, Brauzer B, DiMascio A, Klerman GL, Tuason VB (1980) Prevention of relapse in schizophrenia: an evaluation of fluphenazine decanoate. *Arch. Gen. Psychiatry, 37*, 16.
4. Falloon I, Watt DC, Shepperd M (1978) A comparative controlled trial of pimozide and fluphenazine decanoate in the continuation therapy of schizophrenia. *Psychol. Med., 8*, 59.
5. Van Putten T, May PRA (1976) Milieu therapy of the schizophrenias. In: West LJ, Flinn PE (Eds), Treatment of Schizophrenia, pp. 217–243. Grune and Stratton, New York.
6. Linn MW, Caffey EM, Klett CJ, Hogarty GE, Lamb R (1979) Day treatment and psychotropic drugs in the aftercare of schizophrenia patients. *Arch. Gen. Psychiatry, 36*, 1055.
7. Goldberg SC, Schooler NR, Hogarty GE, Roper M (1977) Prediction of relapse in schizophrenic outpatients treated by drug and social therapy. *Arch. Gen. Psychiatry, 34*, 171.
8. Linn MW, Klett CJ, Caffey EM (1980) Foster home characteristics and psychiatric patient outcome. *Arch. Gen. Psychiatry, 37*, 129.
9. Wing JK, Brown GW (1970) Institutionalism and Schizophrenia. Cambridge University Press, London.
10. Hogarty GE, Goldberg SC, Schooler NR (1974) Drug and sociotherapy in the aftercare of schizophrenic patients III. Effects on adjustment. *Arch. Gen. Psychiatry, 31*, 609.
11. Warner R (1983) Recovering from schizophrenia in the third world. *Psychiatry, 46*, 197.
12. Sartorius N, Jablensky A, Korten A, Ernberg G, Anker M, Cooper JE, Day R (1986) Early manifestations and first contact incidence of schizophrenia in different cultures. *Psychol. Med., 16*, 909.

13. Hooley JM (1985) Expressed emotion: a review of the critical literature. *Clin. Psychol. Rev., 5*, 119.
14. Leff JP, Hirsch SR, Gaind R, Rohde, Stevens BC (1973) Life events and maintenance therapy in schizophrenic relapse. *Br. J. Psychiatry, 123*, 659.
15. Brown GW, Birley JLT (1968) Crises and life change and the onset of schizophrenia. *J. Health Soc. Behav., 9*, 203.
16. Leff JP, Kuipers L, Berkowitz R, Vaughn CE, Sturgeon D (1983) Life events, relatives' expressed emotion and maintenance neuroleptics in schizophrenic relapse. *Psychol. Med., 13*, 799.
17. McEvoy JP, Howe AC, Hogarty GE (1984) Differences in the nature of relapse and subsequent inpatient course between medication-compliant and noncompliant schizophrenic patients. *J. Nerv. Mental Dis., 172*, 412.
18. Bartko G, Maylath E, Herczeg I (1987) Comparative study of schizophrenic patients relapsed on and off medication. *Psychiatry Res., 22*, 221.
19. Anderson CM, Reiss DJ, Hogarty GE (1986) Schizophrenia and the Family: A Practitioner's Guide to Psychoeducation and Management. Guilford Press, New York.
20. Spohn HE, Lacoursiere RB, Thompson K, Coyne L (1977) Phenothiazine effects on psychological and psychophysiological dysfunction in chronic schizophrenics. *Arch. Gen. Psychiatry, 34*, 633.
21. Hogarty GE, Anderson CM, Reiss DJ, Kornblith SJ, Greenwald DP, Javna CD, Madonia MJ (1986) Family psychoeducation, social skills training, and maintenance chemotherapy in the aftercare treatment of schizophrenia. *Arch. Gen. Psychiatry, 43*, 633.
22. Hirsch SR, Jeff JP (1975) Abnormalities in Parents of Schizophrenics. Oxford University Press, London.
23. Falloon IRH, Boyd JL, McGill CW, Razoni J, Moss HB, Gilderman HA (1982) Family management in the prevention of schizophrenic relapse. *New Engl. J. Med., 306*, 1437.
24. Leff J, Kuipers L, Berkowitz R, Eberlein-Vries R, Sturgeon D (1982) A controlled trial of social intervention in the families of schizophrenic patients. *Br. J. Psychiatry, 141*, 121.
25. Leff J, Kuipers L, Berkowitz R, Sturgeon D (1985) A controlled trial of social intervention in the families of schizophrenic patients: two-year follow-up. *Br. J. Psychiatry, 146*, 594.
26. Falloon IRH, Boyd JL, McGill CW, Williamson M, Razoni J, Moss HB, Gilderman AM, Simpson GM (1985) Family management in the prevention of morbidity of schizophrenia. *Arch. Gen. Psychiatry, 42*, 887.
27. Wallace CJ, Liberman RP (1985) Social skills training for patients with schizophrenia: a controlled clinical trial. *Psychiatry Res., 15*, 239.
28. Schooler NR, Hogarty GE (1987) Medication and psychosocial strategies in the treatment of schizophrenia. In: Meltzer HY (Ed), Psychopharmacology: The Third Generation of Progress, pp. 1111 – 1119. Raven Press, New York.
29. Weinberger DR (1987) Implications of normal brain development for the pathogenesis of schizophrenia. *Arch. Gen. Psychiatry, 44*, 660.
30. Hogarty GE (1985) Expressed emotion and schizophrenic relapse. In: Alpert M (Ed), Controversies in Schizophrenia, pp. 354 – 363. Guilford Press, New York.
31. Schooler NR, Keith SJ (1983) Treatment Strategies in Schizophrenia Study Protocol. National Institute of Mental Health, Rockville, MD.

CHAPTER 9

Multiple family groups and the treatment of schizophrenia

WILLIAM R. McFARLANE

INTRODUCTION

Multiple family therapy originated nearly three decades ago in attempts by Laqueur (personal communication) and Detre et al. (1) to develop a psychosocial treatment approach for hospitalized schizophrenic patients. Unlike family therapy during its early period, the emphasis in work in multiple family groups was more pragmatic than theoretical. The earliest reported experiences with the modality arose, in fact, from a need to solve ward management problems. Laqueur noted improved ward social functioning in patients who insisted on attending a group organized for visiting relatives. Detre and his colleagues started a multiple family group (MFG) in order to encourage cooperation between resident psychiatrists and social workers on an acute inpatient service, but quickly found a high level of interest in the group among patients and family members alike, as well as improvements in family communication and morale. From these beginnings, the modality has grown steadily, and most of the focus has continued to be the major psychiatric disorders. Indeed, there seems to be an especially effective congruence between specific clinical management problems in schizophrenia and characteristics of the multiple family group. This chapter will present recent empirical data that explains some of that congruence and goes on to describe a new variant that attempts to capitalize further on the unique nature of the multiple family group.

This new form of multiple family group brings together aspects of psychoeducational (Chapter 8), family behavioral (Chapter 7) and multi-family approaches to create a new model, the psychoeducational multiple family group (PEMFG). As such, it is a second-generation treatment model which incorporates the advantages of each of its sources, diminishes their negative features and leads to a number of synergistic effects which appear to enhance efficacy. Like the psychoeducational family approach of Anderson et al. (2), the model presented here has attempted to reflect contemporary understanding of schizophrenia from biological, psychological and social perspectives, on the assumption that an effective treatment should address as many known aspects of the illness as possible, at all relevant system levels.

The general character of the approach can be summarized as consisting of three components, roughly corresponding to the phases of the group. In the first phase, the content of the model follows Anderson's, with its emphasis on joining in a collaborative alliance with family members, conducting an educational workshop and

Handbook of Schizophrenia, Volume 4: Psychosocial Treatment of Schizophrenia.
M.I. Herz, S.J. Keith and J.P. Docherty, editors.

focusing on preventing relapse for a year or so after discharge from an acute hospitalization. Unlike the single-family psychoeducational approach, the format for treatment after the workshop is a multi-family group in which patients are present.

The second phase involves moving beyond stability to gradual increases in patients' community functioning, a process that uses MFG-based problem-solving, structured similarly to Falloon's behavioral approach, as the primary means for accomplishing social and vocational rehabilitation; this occurs during the second year of the PEMFG. During this phase, the group may be used to intervene in families where overinvolvement is present and might impede the rehabilitation effort.

The third phase consists of deliberate efforts to mold the group into a social network, one that might persist for an extended period and satisfy family and patient needs for social contact, support and control and for a context in which to continue psychopharmacologic treatment and routine case management.

THEORETICAL AND EMPIRICAL FOUNDATIONS

In the following discussion, theoretical and empirical bases for the PEMFG model are presented, with reference to seven treatment objectives and organized by the three phases outlined above.

Phase I. Prevention of relapse

Social network expansion

The social networks and social supports of schizophrenic patients have been well studied, less so those of their families. The findings seem consistent across studies: patients, and very often their families, are more isolated than their peers. Pattison et al. (3), Hammer et al. (4) and Garrison (5) found smaller network size for patients. Garrison also noted that the family members of the most severely ill patients seemed to be isolated and preoccupied with the patient. Brown et al. (6) noted that 90% of the families with high expressed emotion were small in size and socially isolated. A pilot study by McFarlane (unpublished) replicated this finding, except that isolation correlated only with overinvolvement, and only for mothers of patients. Anderson et al. (7) did not find the same association, but did demonstrate that family network size diminished with length of illness, a finding consistent with a study by Lipton et al. (8) in which network size for patients appeared to decrease in the period immediately following a first episode. Tolsdorf (9) found smaller network size at first admission, suggesting that schizophrenic patients and their families have already lost social supports before the onset of manifest symptomatology. A typical survey of families (10) demonstrated that families report having withdrawn from their own social circles, and vice versa.

Beyond size, other characteristics of networks have been found to affect, and to be affected by, schizophrenia. For instance, when density is low – that is, when the various clusters in a network are not known to each other independently of the patient – network shrinkage is more likely. Indeed, lower density and fewer social contacts are associated with relapse and rehospitalization (11, 12). Interestingly, Dozier et al. (13) concluded from her data that moderate density was correlated with the lowest rates of rehospitalization; i.e., high density in a small network probably leads to excessive burden and reduced endurance in its caretaking, non-patient members.

It seems likely that ongoing access to social contact and support might prevent the deterioration of a chronic condition, and perhaps improve its course. Conversely, it seems likely that attenuated social support leads to the loss of adaptive coping capacity among family members, exacerbates the effects of care-taking burdens, increases potential for preoccupation with the patient (overinvolvement) and increases family tension. For instance, Schoenfeld et al. (14) documented reduced hospitalization after an intervention which increased network involvement with the patient and family and simultaneously increased network density. As we will see, embedding patients and their families in an *ongoing* healing community could be expected to mediate the impact of life events, thereby preventing relapse and fostering recovery in chronic psychiatric disorders. That is similar to the conclusion of Mosher and Keith (15) after reviewing the more effective psychosocial treatments: they all 'provide the most comprehensive, corrective [and] sustaining social support systems'. Therefore, in the PEMFG, the creation of a therapeutic social network, including families, is both a goal and the means for conducting other aspects of the treatment.

Reduction of stigma

A sizeable body of literature has accumulated, documenting the effects of caring for a relative with schizophrenia, much of which has been concerned with stigma. In one study, two-thirds of the wives of patients tried to conceal their husband's illness from friends (16), while in another, very little concealment or shame was reported (17). The difference appears to relate to degree of chronicity. This fits in with clinical experience, in which relatives of younger patients may feel more shame and personal stigma than those of older patients. On the other hand, stigma on the part of friends and more distant relatives may play a role in the shrinking network phenomenon. In the pilot study by the author mentioned above, stigma experienced by mothers of patients was associated with overinvolvement with the patient, but only in the presence of a larger social network. From these and other studies, it does not appear that the stigma experienced is universal among family members, but it may be important as a factor in shaping the social network, on the one hand, and relationships in the family on the other. Many families feel stigmatized and may become more isolated and enmeshed as a consequence.

Nearly all families experience severe burden, the extent of which seems to be at least partly a function of the number and density of social supports available. One study found inverse relationships between (a) satisfaction with the total social network and the degree of burden experienced, and (b) network density and burden (18). Higher levels of experienced stigma and burden seem likely to increase the tension in family environments and secondarily increase the tendency toward patient relapse and social and vocational dysfunction.

Reduction of expressed emotion (EE)

The multi-family group was chosen to reduce EE because of previously observed tendencies for members of different families to develop remarkably tolerant and supportive relationships toward the patients in the group, while patients often seem to prefer the mixture of family and non-family membership. The ambient tone is often quite close to the 'emotional expression' described by Spiegel and Wissler (21), who found that a positive, accepting feeling toward patients in family members was predictive of a longer remission interval.

Alleviation of communication deviance

Singer et al. (22) described what is probably the only family characteristic that is even close to being specific to schizophrenia, a factor that they termed 'communication deviance'. It usually means that relatives, especially in conversations with each other in test situations, manifest higher degrees of either vague/amorphous or anxious/fragmented communication patterns than relatives in other psychiatric conditions. Because it appears to have a linguistic structure similar to formal thought disorder, some have presented empirical evidence that it may represent a subclinical manifestation of a heritable disorder of attention (23).

The implication of these findings is that the treatment format must in some way compensate, through technique or social structure, for difficulties that patients and their family members may have in sustaining a conversational focus during a social or therapeutic meeting. Furthermore, to the degree that communication problems are a function of social isolation, it is important to offer social contact that reinforces communicational effectiveness. As we will see, the PEMFG approach attempts to address these issues specifically, – both in the structure of the treatment, by exposing participants to a large group in which many individuals will communicate normally – and in technique, by providing an extra measure of structure and predictability, with an emphasis on clear communication and task completion without distraction.

Phase II. Improved psychosocial functioning

Family support for gradual increases in social and vocational performance

Negative symptoms and social and vocational disability seem to be largely untouched by neuroleptic medication. Indeed, a recent study has found that negative symptoms are associated with reduced dopamine metabolism, making dopamine blockade suspect as an effective treatment for this crucial aspect of the disorder (24). The PEMFG model is based on several findings and one theoretical principle that suggest a more promising outcome than previous psychiatric rehabilitation programs.

A central consideration in this model is that schizophrenic patients have difficulty when asked to make discrete transitions from one context to another, especially from home to work, school or peer relationships. These transitions can be seen as requiring more control of arousal and greater information processing capacity than most patients may possess. Thus, it could be argued that family members need to be present initially to provide a kind of social bridge to non-family contexts, much as occurs in traditional village societies. Reiss and Costell (25) documented this family-to-society acculturation process in multifamily groups for hospitalized adolescents. Using direct interactional measurement techniques, they found that, even when the adolescents sat in a group separate from their parents, cues from family members and the social structure of the senior subgroup determined speech dominance patterns and other structural aspects of the adolescent subgroup.

Empirically, Falloon (26) and his colleagues found that behavioral family intervention was most successful when families developed more effective coping strategies; they suggested that this factor contributed more to outcome than changes in expressed emotion. Because that approach relies on a problem-solving strategy, it seems likely that the larger the pool of available solutions from which to choose, the greater the likelihood of a workable solution. A multi-family group allows for the gradual bridging of family and non-family ties, and can be organized to contain a great variety of personal experiences, including those of the participating relatives and of the clinicians.

In some families, it appears that overinvolvement by relatives may impede functional progress, especially when it requires greater interpersonal and physical distance between patient and relative. While dependency-inducing interaction was considered ubiquitous in families of schizophrenic patients in psychodynamic and family systems theories of etiology, the experience of the clinicians who have worked in the author's research projects, within a psychoeducational framework, is that this kind of interaction is rare *after families are reassured and supported in dealing with the illness.* For instance, Miklowitz et al. (27, 28), found that only one-third of families rated high on emotional overinvolvement (EOI), and that EOI was associated with single mothers, with sons as patients, poor premorbid adjustment in the patient, high levels of residual symptomatology and higher levels of communication deviance. Doane et al. (29) noted that EE was predictive of poor social and vocational functioning in the absence of relapse. The direction of influence is unclear from these studies, but a positive feedback interaction in which poor premorbid functioning predisposes to parental overinvolvement, which in turn exacerbates poor adult functioning, seems a likely possibility.

To the extent that EOI might hinder functional improvement, a successful intervention would have to address this process, if it were present. However, unlike critical comments, EOI may reflect a long-standing behavioral pattern in the family (30) and therefore may be slower to change as a result of direct intervention. Because one study suggests that EOI is also associated with social isolation and stigmatic rejection among relatives (McFarlane, unpublished), a more benign approach would seem to involve expanding social networks and reducing feelings of stigma among relatives, while offering substitute extra-familial relationships. Since direct confrontation by the therapists would be perceived as blaming, suggestions or criticisms should come from other families who have been struggling with the same issues. As we will see, the PEMFG approach offers ample opportunities for each of these more indirect intervention strategies.

Phase III. Creation of a social network

Long-term outcome, social support and continuity of care

A study by Hogarty and Ulrich (31) suggested that relapse risk declines with time, especially during the second year after an episode. This result is consistent with the finding of Harding et al. (32) that after two or three decades, symptomatology and functioning substantially improves in nearly three-quarters of chronic cases. We have little or no data on what happens between two and twenty years, but the two studies appear to reflect a gradual decrease in symptomatology and risk for relapse over long periods of time. The Harding reports suggest that ongoing social and clinical support may have accounted for some of the positive outcome, most probably because it was available for up to five years after discharge. It is noteworthy that earlier psychosocial intervention studies by Pasamanick et al. (33) and by Stein and Test (34) found that deterioration began after the test treatments were discontinued, by the end of the second year. There is no data on long-term outcome in family psychoeducation trials, except for one report of a follow-up study of patients who had participated in a controlled trial of family crisis intervention (35). This study revealed that relapse was remarkably rare three to six years after termination of therapy. In an ongoing study of my own, half the patients treated in PEMFGs have not relapsed up to six years after discharge.

The research on social networks and Harding's work imply that continuity of social context may be as important to outcome as is continuity of care. For instance, Steinberg and Durrell (36) found that the vast majority of first episodes in an Australian sample occurred after separation from home and family – on entering college or the military. It is widely recognized that therapist departure, even for vacation, is often a precipitant of relapse. The data on life events and their relation to relapse suggests a strong association, and most of the events involve disruption of social support or the membership and organization of a social network. The principal weakness of single-family models of treatment is that they are vulnerable to the vicissitudes of the therapist's professional career, which often leads to disruption before the end of the three- to five-year stabilization/adjustment period, even though a new therapist assumes responsibility for the case. In short, the design of a psychosocial treatment requires some means for ensuring as much continuity of social support and clinical care as possible. Because multi-family groups readily persist for years, they provide the kind of continuity that in other treatment approaches is too often disrupted by therapist turnover and departure of members of the individual family. The PEMFG is resilient, in the sense of being less vulnerable to changes in the participation of any one member.

MECHANISMS OF ACTION OF PSYCHOEDUCATIONAL MULTIPLE FAMILY GROUPS

The effects of the approach can be grouped by therapeutic interventions, depending on whether they proceed from direct and overt behavior of the therapists or from more covert, intrinsic multifamily group processes.

Educational and directive mechanisms

These arise directly from the psychoeducational aspects of the approach. The process of establishing a collaborative alliance with family members, providing information about schizophrenia and giving instruction in family management is designed to reduce guilt, anxiety and confusion in family members and thereby to reduce family tension. Furthermore, the content of the family management advice is specific to certain aspects of schizophrenic psychophysiology, particularly a vulnerability to stimulation and stress. Thus, teaching family members to give the patient psychological space, to reduce expectations, to set limits on extreme behavior and to use a straightforward and more positive communication style with the patient are all designed to reduce pressure and create a more emotionally neutral, supportive environment that reduces the risk of relapse. By encouraging family members to maintain or develop their own social support network, it is hoped that they will be better able to sustain an optimal home environment over a prolonged period. In essence, the family is recruited as a therapeutic ally. In the PEMFG version, by being involved consistently in a group-centered problem-solving process, other families and patients are engaged as collaborators in the treatment effort. (For a more extensive discussion of the conceptual and technical particulars of the psychoeducational and behavioral approaches, see Chapters 7 and 8 in this volume.)

Process-dependent mechanisms

As we saw in the preceding section, there appear to be four family factors that are associated with the disorder. These are: expressed emotion (EE); communication deviance (CD); social isolation; and stigma/burden. A presumed biologically based vulnerability interacts with the family environment in complex ways, many of which involve reciprocal feedback processes. Moreover, some family factors appear to interact with one another. Isolation appears to be associated with high EE (6); high EE seems associated with CD (37); it seems possible that isolation and CD tend to coexist (38). In addition, one has to assume, based on these same studies, that families with schizophrenic members are markedly heterogeneous: some may manifest all of these phenomena to an extreme degree (and may have other problems, such as marital dysfunction, as well); some, at the other extreme, may show only minor difficulties, in particular those that appear to be reactive to the illness.

A multiple family group induces several intrinsic processes which enhance the efficacy of the psychoeducational therapies. What follows is a description of those processes or mechanisms of action and their respective effects on schizophrenia-associated family factors.

Resocialization

In PEMFGs, families are provided with an artificial social support system in addition to encouragement to maintain or expand their natural network. An MFG satisfies the technical requirements for a natural social network: the other family members are not kin and are heterogeneous as to age, sex, personality, ethnicity and class, yet they share a vital common experience and concern: mental illness in one member of the family. The family's network increases in the MFG, because the other families provide many different, more varied relationships, real and potential. These are on the whole much less intense than family relationships and usually remain less intense than most close friendships. Density changes, because all the families in the group become interconnected. With time and therapists' encouragement, the MFG can become a natural network, whose formal characteristics are very similar to those that arise spontaneously. Given the evidence that many families of schizophrenic individuals are socially isolated, and that isolation may be associated with high EE and relapse frequency, it seems possible that resocialization of the family may be a key element in achieving the goals of PE approaches. The fact that family members of schizophrenic patients have begun to band together in self-help organizations (39, 40) is a testament to the need for, and value of, illness-induced network expansion. Note that the other MFT mechanisms below depend totally on therapeutic network expansion for their effectiveness.

Stigmatic reversal

Anderson, Falloon, Leff and others have noted that education appears to reduce the family's sense of shame and guilt. It has long been recognized that relief and higher morale result from group members sharing their difficulties openly and discussing the experience of living with a schizophrenic offspring with others who are in similar straits. In this process, there is often such a profound sense of relief and acknowledgment that stigma appears to be reversed, replaced by a kind of pride in being able, as a group, to begin to understand and master the illness that until then has been a great burden. If they have experienced social rejection or discrimination as a consequence of the illness, the group becomes a source of social acceptance. To the extent that the PEMFG induces improved social functioning among the patients, it becomes a source of pride, a sense of achievement, improved morale and cognitive mastery in family and patients alike.

A PEMFG can have equally positive effects on family burdens. The subjective aspects are somewhat relieved by the shared realization of the possible effects of schizophrenia on individual family members. The perception that other patients do improve in treatment produces a sense of impending relief. By ventilating specific anxieties and receiving support and encouragement, family members experience an increase in moral that allows them to carry on. As for objective burdens, group members trade experiences and advice, develop new coping strategies, arrange to relieve one another, and bring political pressure on the therapists and their institutions to provide sorely needed services. Finally, to the extent that the group succeeds in developing new family coping strategies, *both the sense and the reality* of burden are reduced. These phenomena of reversal of stigma and reduction of burden go a long way toward explaining the enthusiasm and loyalty that families come to feel about a PEMFG, and the high rates of retention that have usually been noted.

Modulated disenmeshment

The social structure of an MFG provides a non-intrusive alternative to the problem of family overinvolvement, a key aspect of high EE. Family members can develop new, less intense and more functional and satisfying relationships in the group, *while preserving intra-family bonds.* With time, these new relationships gradually attenuate enmeshed interaction, particularly between parents and their schizophrenic offspring. The either-or choice presented by more straightforward PE approaches (i.e., overinvolvement vs. disengagement) is avoided in PEMFGs by providing readily available substitutes for intra-family relationships, while in no way attempting to disqualify or interrupt them. The rate of disenmeshment can be controlled by the family, so that change can proceed at a non-threatening pace. Note that this process imitates nature: most young adults gradually increase their interpersonal distance with their parents, at a rate that is tolerable to all family members. In both generations, parent-child interaction is replaced by extra-familial social interaction and relationships.

Furthermore, rigidity in family relationships is difficult to preserve indefinitely in an MGF, because group interaction tends to be increasingly complex and unpredictable, usually in positive ways. Cross-family relationships wax and wane, depending on circumstances, and gradually dissolve family boundaries. This process is almost universally welcomed, with the partial exception of highly secretive families with tendencies toward paranoia. Family members are often surprised and relieved by the different ways their intimates behave in the MFG; particularly the patients, who usually behave more responsibly and responsively in the group than at home.

Beyond these indirect effects, specific processes tend to occur which reduce overinvolvement. In a well-established group, relatives are often blunt in their criticism of overprotective, disengaged or rejecting behavior in other families. Such comments are usually received with acceptance and sometimes appreciation, but only because the source is a fellow sufferer. These confrontational interactions are tolerated because someone almost always steps forward to support emotionally the individual receiving criticism.

Another subtype of this process could be termed 'cross-parenting'. Relatives who have become involved in tense, overstimulating relationships with their patient-offspring, will show remarkably sensitive and supportive attention to the patient member of another family. That attention may be quite therapeutic for the recipient, but seems as well to become the basis for new and more adaptive interaction with that parent's own child. At the same time, the recipient's relatives see that other kinds of behavior are not only possible, but evoke a very different response in their supposedly intractable and disabled offspring. Thus, an MFG allows family members to try new, more adaptive relational styles with members of other families before attempting to use them within their own family. The group-based problem-solving approach used in the PEMFG approach is a structured variation on this mechanism, in which therapists actively involve other families' members in dealing with the sensitive and complex issues encountered as families began to implement the family management guidelines. It is a natural extension of processes that occur spontaneously in MFG's: cross-family problem-solving methodology seems to enhance cross-parenting, and vice versa.

A third form of disenmeshment, certainly the least threatening, is 'indirect restructuring'. Family members are remarkably attuned to the structural and interactional problems in other families. In many instances, especially when the problem-solving method is used, they appear to apply the concrete solutions arrived at in the PEMFG, as well as their implicit lessons, to their own family, without having to explicitly acknowledge the similarity. Of course, the same process can occur overtly, but for some families that may be too threatening. It seems that family insight may not always be essential to therapeutic change, but exposure to other families in a process of mutual change may be, and will not occur in single-family approaches.

Communication normalization

Improvements in family communication were the first and most consistently reported therapeutic effects of multiple family therapy. The PEMFG model, with its overt emphasis on certain prescribed modes of communication, is a synergistic combination of seemingly intrinsic MFG therapeutic processes and a structured communication skills methodology. Harrow (41) and colleagues demonstrated the effects of MFT empirically: more family members spoke spontaneously, more problem solutions were offered, more family issues were openly discussed and more comments made about others' interactions than in conventional patients' groups. Patients themselves spoke more. The apparent efficacy of a PEMFG in improving patients' social performance seems to relate to this aspect: the group is an ideal setting for schizophrenic patients to practice being in a complex social environment without being expected to perform normally until they are able.

These results do not address directly the specific issue of communication deviance. As to whether MFGs affect CD, there is no clear answer in the literature; the question is hardly raised, in fact. It is the author's impression, clinically, that CD does diminish in an MFG if the family remains in the group for several months. It often seems as if the group process evokes societal norms for speech and discussion, which then influences members to conform to them. In addition, the majority of family members do not manifest CD, and tend to set norms that are more linguistically adaptive. This process is an example of the well-studied and powerful influence of groups in enforcing conformity to group and societal norms for behavior and the structure of thought (42–45).

SPECIFIC TECHNIQUES IN PSYCHOEDUCATIONAL MULTI-FAMILY GROUPS

The four types of intervention delineated here are the foundation for implementing the psychoeducational approach within the MFG context. The overall strategy is to maximize the impact of the PE portion of the model by exploiting the unique social structure of the MFG. Thus, putting into practice the family management guidelines, doing problem-solving, working on social and vocational rehabilitation, encouraging disenmeshment and beginning the social nework-building process are carried out as interactions involving as many members of the group and as many different families as possible. The emphasis in the descriptions below is on the direction of interaction, rather than the verbal content, because it is the social structure which is of critical importance to efficacy.

Self-triangulation

This approach involves serial individual and family interviewing. The clinicians interact with specific individuals within a family or focus on one family as if in a single-family context. They intentionally interpose themselves between the members of different families, directing interaction through themselves and inhibiting interaction between families or individuals.

This form of intervention has several uses. Primarily, it establishes a clear social structure by emphasizing the leadership role. The clinicians allay uncertainty about what family members are supposed to do by setting a clear direction, controlling and initiating interaction. The leaders use this approach at times when the families would most be likely to expect strong leadership and when the leader's role lends authority to advice and suggestions based on the family management principles. In the early meetings of the group, this method builds cohesion in the group and allays anxiety. Specific applications of value in the PEMFG model will be outlined here.

Relating a problem to a family management guideline

The clincicians will need to use leader-family member intervention to link patient-related problems presented by a family to the appropriate family management guideline. This kind of move will be necessary in the early phases of the group, before families have begun to fully grasp the problem-solving model used in the PEMFG approach. The directive, authoritative mode is used primarily for teaching group members to assume much of the responsibility in determining which guideline is most relevent and how to implement it.

Eliciting information

It is essential in successful problem solving to elicit specific information about the problems families present in the PEMFG. The leaders will usually need to take the initiative in defining the problem in limited, specific and behavioral terms.

Directing problem-solving sequences

Active involvement in guiding structured problem solving is a legitimate use of this type of intervention early in the group or at points of unusual difficulty. Deliberate problem solving comes naturally to few families, with or without schizophrenia. Therefore, in the first few attempts to use this approach, the leaders remain central, tracking and guiding the sequence, making explicit what step is in focus and when the process seems complete. Wherever possible, the leaders should avoid the temptation to provide the 'definitive' solution to a particular dilemma.

Blocking interruption

A primary therapeutic intervention in any MFG is the blocking of interruption of one group member by another, especially the interruption of the patient by a well member of his/her family. The implication of an interruption is that the interruptee appears to be socially and/or cognitively incompetent. When repeated over days and years, the effect of this all-too-common interaction is to establish a social ineptness as the fixed characteristic of the schizophrenic patient. Negative consequences may follow from some patients' habitually interrupting their relatives. Experience has taught that simply insisting that everyone be allowed to complete his or her thoughts without interruption seems to reverse the expectation, and gradually the actuality, that the schizophrenic patient is completely incompetent in a social situation. Here, remarkable progress can be seen simply through consistent validation of the patient's potential for more active and appropriate social participation.

Addressing poor attendance

It is the leaders' responsibility to assure the maximum effectiveness of the PEMFG by intervening when poor attendance by a family or crucial members of a family threatens the viability of the group. Although progress in a PEMFG seems not to be critically affected by less-than-perfect attendance, families which consistently miss more than half of the meetings are likely to make little headway. Also, a spouse or parent who misses more than half of the sessions can block progress. Furthermore, it is absolutely necessary that the key relatives, at minimum those living on a day-to-day basis with the patient, attend the educational workshop. With the above as rules of thumb, the leaders will need to contact, by telephone or home visit, families that consistently miss sessions, and emphasize the therapeutic importance of full attendance in the group and the need to carry out the entire treatment to achieve a result.

Controlling extreme affect, negativity and violence

Very rarely, individual families will become involved in extreme disagreements, with strong expressions of feeling and even threats of violence. Sometimes a family may be so critical that symptomatic exacerbation in the patient is provoked. The leaders carry the final responsibility for group interaction and the well-being of all its members; they must intervene directly and quickly when indicated.

Group interpretation

The clinicians occasionally take a complementary position to the entire group in order to lay ground rules, share personal reactions, point out commonalities in the families or in subgroups (mothers, parents, etc.), set group themes and, very infrequently, make conventional group interpretations.

The main function of this type of intervention is to validate the group as a group or, more specifically, to validate the families' contributions to each other and to the group as a whole as being therapeutic for the patients. The group is explicitly defined as the instrument of change and improvement. Thus, these group-oriented techniques serve as the technical bridge between leader-centered/educational and group-centered/problem-solving processes. Experience suggests that group-dynamic interpretations are to be avoided, especially those having to do with group member-to-leader transference.

Laying ground rules

It is advisable to make explicit the rules of the group at the outset of the post-workshop phase of the PEMFG. At a minimum these include the following.

(a) Attendance at each meeting is expected of all members of the family who have significant contact with the patient. The patient is expected to attend as much as possible, but is not required to attend against his or her will, nor when feeling vulnerable emotionally.

(b) Families should attempt to share their difficulties openly when they see fit. There is no pressure on anyone to disclose anything that is thought to be inappropriate.

(c) Group members should feel free to interact with members of other families; this is encouraged and is the key to the effectiveness of the group. Comments or suggestions are to be taken as attempts to be helpful; no one is obliged to accept what is said.

(d) No physical interaction will be allowed during the sessions. Participants should try to maintain emotional control. Interrupting others' comments is discouraged.

These rules are described straightforwardly, with invitations for discussion if desired. Their main function is to clarify the minimum expectations for participation in the group, so that they are explicit and available for reference later.

Setting and eliciting themes

A primary task for the leaders is to reflect to the families the shared feelings, issues, problems or problem solutions that emerge in the discussion. Whenever it is meaningful, these should be defined as a common experience for all families with a schizophrenic member, emphasizing that each family is involved in a struggle that other families are sharing. That reality can then be linked to their inherent expertise and value to each other, as collaborators with each other and with professionals to achieve the highest level of recovery possible for the patients.

Obviously, one indication for setting themes is their actual emergence in the group. Re-definition of an emergent theme will often enhance the focus on problem solving. Common examples have to do with anxiety, confusion, despair and conflict, within families and individuals. As much as possible, these problematic affects and interactions are redefined as nearly universal responses to the disorganizing influence of schizophrenia on patients and families alike. That theme is then generalized to all the families and, in a limited way, to the clinicians.

Praise for inter-family assistance

One of the key uses for a group interpretation is to recognize and reward efforts of family members to provide emotional support and to help one another think through problem solutions. The leaders should make a point of acknowledging all atttempts to provide assistance, even if they are not fully accepted or immediately successful. The rationale for this intervention is the time-proven value of positive reinforcement in shaping individual and group behavior: it is one of the simplest methods of encouraging further inter-family interaction.

Handling intra-group social conversation

As opposed to dynamically oriented group therapy, random discussion of everyday topics, grousing, joking, i.e., general socializing, is considered neither defensive nor diversionary in a PEMFG. Up to one-quarter of the session may be given over to this kind of interaction, as long as it is across family boundaries and there is no urgent crisis to be dealt with. The value of socializing lies in its function as the foundation for the group becoming a social network. Thus, some interaction that is not patient- and illness-focused needs to be encouraged so that the members of the group have an experience of each other as peers and friends. Most sessions of a PEMFG should begin with general socializing, which seems to foster better concentration on therapeutic work later in the meeting. The leaders should validate such interaction and explicitly encourage it at appropriate times. Also, they should feel free to judiciously join in the discussion, particularly if the topic is relatively neutral and does not involve disclosure of any sensitive personal information.

Cross-family linkage

While this technique is less varied in form than the others described here, it is crucial for accomplishing the core tasks of PEMFG: applying the guidelines, problem solving, and social/vocational rehabilitation. This is the technique that fosters therapeutic work between families, work which appears to be at least as effective as efforts by professionals trained in the single-family psychoeducational approaches. It is often more congenial to families than professional intervention, perhaps because the families in the group know that the others have had the same sorts of experiences: they come with a built-in credibility.

In essence, the clinicians use their relationships with family members, built up during the connection phase, to promote relationships across family boundaries. As in a natural network, these are intended not to be transferential, but real social bonds in which there is sanction for sharing, open feedback and therapeutic work between families. The aim is the creation of a task-oriented social network, in which structured problem solving and individualized application of the family management guidelines constitute the overt vehicle for both cross-family linkage and managing the patient's illness. The most common context in which this intervention is used is within the problem-solving approach. For instance, a question or issue is raised by a member of a specific family, let us call it the index family, with the expectation that one of the cilincians will answer of deal with it. Another applicable situation is when the index family is discussing a problem among themselves, implicitly expecting the clinicians to intervene with a suggestion or a process intervention. Yet another use is when members of two families are discussing an issue but not making any progress toward an acceptable solution.

A specific sequence of maneuvers constitute the usual technique in these situations. First, the clinician may discuss with the index family for a brief period what the problem is, to clarify it and to make sure everyone has contributed to the definition of the problem. Then, the clinician turns to a member of another family and briefly discusses the situation in the index family. Some discussion between clinician and member(s) of the other families can then proceed, focusing on the various options open to the index family or other ways of understanding their interaction. The next step involves asking specific members of the group to share their suggestions with the index family directly. The clinician may ask them to describe their thoughts in more detail, especially when the previous discussion has involved weighing alternatives or complex observations, or lengthy descriptions of the other families' solutions to similar problems.

The next step, which may follow the first step directly, is to encourage a full discussion between two families, or with members of several families, as to what might be helpful. In general, these directive interventions should be short and to the point, with the implication that the clinicians are not likely to intervene to make further suggestions. A concluding intervention should be carried out if the index family does not acknowledge the other families' input, or if the discussion ends before the index family has developed a prospective plan. Here, members of the index family discuss group members' ideas. If the index family asks for professional guidance, the clinician should defer to other families, and save any indicated corrections until later, after the groundwork has been laid by the families. During the subsequent inter-family discussion, the clinician needs to assume a more reflective stance, gently encouraging families to continue, keeping the discussion on track and, if necessary, intervening to structure the problem-solving sequence.

Cross-parenting

This type of cross-family linkage seems to be of therapeutic value to the social functioning of patients within, and with time, outside the group. The parent in one family engages the patient member of another family in either unstructured socializing or focused discussion of a problem affecting that patient. This most often occurs spontaneously, but it can be engineered when a particular parent is known to manifest a particular style in coping and problem solving that differs dramatically from that used by a particular patient's relatives. Even when the content of the 'cross-parent's' comments is quite similar to what the actual parent may have been saying, the style is usually one of symmetrical joining and friendly advice, without overt or covert criticism. In some instances the cross parent may have vital information that is not available to the patient's own parents or even to the clinicians. This frequently happens around job openings, or other subjects pertaining to concrete occupational issues raised during the social/vocational rehabilitation phase.

Another important use for cross-parenting linkage is to help a relative who is unable to accept the seriousness and reality of his/her own patient-relative's illness. As was noted above, a conversation with another family's schizophrenic member will usually convince the most denying parent, sibling or spouse that their ill family member is not lazy, malingering or exaggerating his/her mental disorder. The technique here is non-specific, involving framing the issue as understanding the effects of the illness, gentle encouragement of the two individuals to interact, some urging if the patient is unusually recalcitrant and, if necessary, intervening to help the senior generation listen. Blocking the patient's relatives' interruptions is sometimes needed, since they may want to speak for the patient or interpret what they think s/he means.

INTER-FAMILY MANAGEMENT

Once family members have developed relationships across family boundaries, the clinicians use a non-specific technique to regulate and enhance the group process. In essence, the clinicians use this approach in mature groups for guiding and facilitating inter-family conversation, group-based problem solving and social network development. The position adopted is non-hierarchical, more detached, collegial and unobtrusive. The specific objective is to enhance and reinforce inter-family contacts and thereby to promote the process of quasi-natural social network development. There are several identifiable applications for this approach.

(a) Reinforcing , primarily through praise, families' support or constructive confrontation with each other.
(b) Regulating group tone, or even the overall direction of interaction, through reminders of guidelines, comments about dropped subjects of importance and hints to follow up on previous problem-solving efforts.
(c) Expanding a conversation between members of two families to include others.
(d) Disagreeing, in rare situations, with the general direction of a problem-solving process and suggesting alternatives.
(e) Concluding, summarizing or modifying cross-family interventions, when family members have successfully engaged one another across family lines in mutual problem solving.

PHASE-ORIENTED TECHNIQUES IN PSYCHOEDUCATIONAL MULTIPLE FAMILY GROUPS

Because the first two phases of a PEMFG (i.e., connecting and the educational workshop) are similar to interventions in single-family psychoeducation, as described by Hogarty (see Chapter 8), we will review here only those later phases in which the MFG format requires specific techniques.

Community re-entry

Preferably, a PEMFG assumes a long-term, closed-membership group format, the form that has consistently shown the greatest efficacy. Much of that effectiveness depends on the formation of a close-knit social network among the families in the group, a process that takes time and consistency of membership to evolve. This format also seems best suited to the chronic course of the illness. Because the PEMFG begins as an educational workshop, with a clear message that the illness is chronic and responds best to gradual, long-term efforts toward recovery, there is a natural congruence with a closed, low-intensity and long-term group format.

Multiple family groups that are conducted with a relatively stable membership typically go through phases, much as do all persistent social networks. An effective PEMFG moves from one extreme (leader-centered) to the other (group-centered) over a two- to three-year course. That process is inherent to this type of group, but experience suggests that it is more effective to exaggerate these extremes in groups for schizophrenic patients and their families. In the beginning, the group is markedly dependent on the clinicians, with respect to both process and content. By the last phase, the leaders' interventions become more dispensable.

As in the single-family psychoeducational model, the emphasis in roughly the first year after the workshop is on achieving a stable recompensation of the patients. Generally, this involves reducing family tension, dealing with medication noncompliance and avoiding or attenuating stress. Technique in the early sessions of the re-entry phase involves beginning with predominately leader-group member interactions, i.e., self-triangulation and group interpretation. Discussion initially focuses on general methods of fostering recovery and explanations of the family guidelines. Only when spontaneous cross-family interaction begins to take place should the orientation become more group-centered. Group members' dissatisfaction with leader-centered process, manifested by directing comments to one another or openly initiating more group discussion of the workshop content and/or guidelines, is a good indication that the group is sufficiently cohesive to allow a more intensive inter-family process.

Then, the process gradually shifts to individualized implementation of the family guidelines, using a more task-oriented and group-centered leadership style. The leaders use whatever issues are of concern as a vehicle for teaching the problem-solving approach, which increasingly focuses on one family in rotation. Other family members contribute possible solutions and 'pros and cons' to the problem-solving process. Repeated discussion of the key family guidelines occurs in relation to almost all problems raised by families. The activity of the leaders shifts from initiating therapeutic work to facilitating and tracking it.

Increasingly, the patients contribute as equal partners in socializing and problem solving, especially when the clinicians consistently seek their input. This stage should be characterized predominately by the use of cross-family linkage techniques. Specific kinds of interaction can be encouraged as subgroups begin to form.

For instance, facilitating discussions of relatives' reactions to the patients' illness, followed by the patients' describing their own subjective experiences, is usually deeply moving, while it begins to break down the barriers between families, and between patients and their own relatives. This type of sequential subgroup discussion gradually diminishes family boundaries and brings the group much closer to being a natural network.

Social and vocational rehabilitation

As in the comparable phase of single-family psychoeducational family work, the second major post-workshop phase, beginning at about 12 months and lasting from 6 – 18 months, focuses on the gradual resumption of responsibility by the patients in the PEMFG. Their own families and the other families in the group collaborate in the effort to enhance the schizophrenic members' psychosocial functioning. The leaders explicitly frame this as the task for the group and gradually turn over much of the actual implementation to the group, so that family members work with each other across family boundaries.

The dominant technique to be used throughout this phase is cross-family linkage within a problem-solving format. Cross-parenting interaction is fostered to enhance the sense of maturity and competence in the patients. The goal is that the family and the PEMFG serve as a bridge of support and encouragement as the patient gradually emerges from the family environment into the more pressured non-family world of work and social activity.

A specific function that the PEMFG can serve in this phase is to reduce family members' overinvolvement, especially excessive protectiveness and tendencies to avoid challenging the patient to take on more independent role. The means for achieving this are relationship substitution and, in rare instances, direct confrontation across family boundaries (see *Modulated disenmeshment,* above). If it becomes clear that family members are overcompensating and interfering with the rehabilitation process, leaders can encourage members of other families to work with the involved family to gradually raise their expectations for the patient.

THERAPEUTIC STYLE AND GROUP CLIMATE

The optimal tone for therapists to adopt in PEMFGs is rooted in emerging concepts regarding cognitive deficits and arousal dyscontrol as core deficits in schizophrenia, deficits which may be shared in a subclinical form by some family members. A major modification of conventional multiple family therapy technique is the educative mode, used extensively in the workshop and the first months of the group. The therapists in this period adopt a much more directive, expert role than that used in most other therapies.

In addition, the leaders will need to adopt a low-key approach that may at times border on the tedious. A quiet confidence, coupled with a willingness and ability to lead the group unobtrusively will set an optimistic and non-provocative tone. The rationale for this low-keyed, accepting and understanding outlook is to set an example for the families of an optimal low-expressed-emotion style. Further, this deliberately calm approach is necessitated by the fact that a MFG tends to become overly intense, especially in the beginning, in ways that are similar to the high expressed emotion that characterizes high-risk families.

Some inter-family intensity can be constructive, but at al later a stage and under carefully controlled conditions, e.g., in cross-family constructive criticism. A gradual increase in intensity is seen as therapeutic, because it helps the schizophrenic patient become tolerant of somewhat higher degrees of emotional activity. Even then, therapists need to remain calm and in control, to avoid overstimulating patients or offending family members.

Thus, during the re-entry phase especially, therapists should create a group tone that is low in complexity, intensity, challenge and rapid change. Further, by acknowledging and validating the relatives' and the patients' experiences, an accepting, non-judgmental and understanding approach can be established as a model for family interaction. It is important that the therapists also acknowledge and allow for the cognitive and social skills deficits of the patients, without appearing to be condescending. Whenever possible, humor and lightness of mood should prevail. During the rehabilitation phase, a more focused therapeutic style should be adopted, paying serious attention to achieving the goal of re-establishing the patients as participants in the outside community.

TREATMENT EFFECTS

Outcome studies of multiple family group treatment were quasi-experimental or impressionistic during the period from 1960 to the advent of the psychoeducational treatment models. In spite of the lack of rigorous design, the consistency of these reports lends them a certain credence, especially since the effects on relapse match those measured in more recent experimental studies. Table 1 summarizes relapse outcome as reported in the literature to date.

In an attempt to more accurately assess outcome and to differentiate the contributions of various elements of the multiple family group, the author has undertaken two studies using experimental designs and standardized measurements. In the first study, 40 patients with a diagnosis of schizophrenia or schizoaffective disorder, mainly schizophrenic, by the Research Diagnostic Criteria (51) were randomly assigned during an acute inpatient hospitalization to one of three conditions:

TABLE 1 *Relapse outcome in uncontrolled trials of multiple family groups*

Principal author	Sample size	% Sample relapsing	Months
Berman (46)	?	0	12
Levin (47)	19	0	< 12
Lurie (48)	?	19	24
		12	36
Lansky (49)	10	10	24
Falloon (50)	14	21	12

TABLE 2 *Relapse rates in three forms of family intervention*

	Months after treatment start:				
	N	12	24	36	48
Single-family psychoeducation	17	23.5%	47.1%	58.8%	76.5%*
Multi-family psychoeducation	16	12.5%	25.0%	37.5%	50.0%*
Multi-family therapy	7	42.9%	42.9%	42.9%	57.1

* P = 0.01, Cox's regression.

psychoeducational multiple family group, dynamically oriented multiple family therapy, or single-family psychoeducational treatment, without inter-family contact. The design varied two elements, the psychoeducational treatment strategy and inter-family social support, in the hope of distinguishing separate and possibly additive effects. Table 2 presents relapse data.

Using Cox's proportional hazards regression model, the PEMFG approach yields significantly lower relapse rates (P = 0.01) than the single family format across the entire study period, which is presently from 48 to 72 months in length. Of the earliest PEMFG cohort of ten patients, six have remained in remission for five years or more. Interestingly, although the first-year relapse rate in the dynamically oriented group was in the range of rates for neuroleptics alone, long-term, 60-month outcome has matched that of the psychoeducational groups. What is suggested by the data is that there is a specific multi-family group effect which appears to prevent or forestall relapse from roughly one year after an index episode to an as yet undetermined end point.

The second study is a large, multi-site experimental replication of the single family/multiple family comparison, using psychoeducational approaches in both treatment conditions, with nearly 90 patients in each modality. At present, relapse data suggests that the findings for short-term (12 months) outcome will be nearly identical to that in the earlier study: multi-family relapse rates were 19% and single-family rates were 28%. What is of perhaps greater interest is that the sites are six public hospitals widely distributed across New York State, the patients have a severe and chronic history and the clinicians are regular permanent staff of the respective facilities. That is, it now appears that the PEMFG model can be shown to be effective in a wide variety of settings, most of them suffering from staff and resource shortages, when carried out by clinicians who usually manage patients with the greatest disabilities and the poorest prognosis.

REFERENCES

1. Detre T, Sayer J, Norton A, Lewis H (1961) An experimental approach to the treatment of the acutely ill psychiatric patient in the general hospital. *Conn. Med., 25,* 613.
2. Anderson CM, Hogarty GE, Reiss DJ (1986) Schizophrenia in the Family. Guilford Press, New York.

3. Pattison EM, Llama R, Hurd G (1979) Social network mediation of anxiety. *Psychiatr. Ann., 9,* 56.
4. Hammer M (1963 – 64) Influence of small social networks as factors in mental hospital admission. *Human Organ., 22,* 243.
5. Garrison V (1978) Support systems of schizophrenic and nonschizophrenic Puerto Rican women in New York City. *Schizophr. Bull., 4,* 561.
6. Brown GW, Birley JLT, Wing JK (1972) Influence of family life on the course of schizophrenic disorders: a replication. *Br. J. Psychiatry, 121,* 241.
7. Anderson CM, Hogarty G, Bayer T, Needleman R (1984) Expressed emotion and social networks of parents of schizophrenic patients. *Br. J. Psychiatry, 144,* 247.
8. Lipton FR, Cohen CI, Fischer E, Katz SE (1981) Schizophrenia: a network crisis. *Schizophr. Bull., 7,* 144.
9. Tolsdorf CC (1976) Social networks, support and coping: an exploratory study. *Fam. Process, 15,* 407.
10. Biegel DE, Yamatani H (1986) Self-help group for families of the mentally ill: research perspectives. In: Goldstein MZ (Ed), Family Involvement in the Treatment of Schizophrenia. American Psychiatric Association Press, Washington, DC.
11. Sokolovsky J, Cohen CI (1981) Toward a resolution of methodological dilemmas in network mapping. *Schizophr. Bull., 7,* 109.
12. Cohen CI, Sokolovsky J (1978) Schizophrenia and social networks: ex-patients in the inner city. *Schizophr. Bull., 4,* 546.
13. Dozier M, Harris M, Bergman H (1987) Social network density and rehospitalization among young adult patients. *Hosp. Community Psychiatry, 38,* 61.
14. Schoenfeld P, Halevy J, Hemley-van der Velden E, Ruhf L (1986) Long-term outcome of network therapy. *Hosp. Community Psychiatry, 37,* 373.
15. Mosher LR, Keith SJ (1979) Research on the psychosocial treatment of schizophrenia: a summary report. *Am. J. Psychiatry, 136,* 623.
16. Yarrow M, Schwartz C, Murphy H, Deasy L (1955) The psychological meaning of mental illness in the family. *J. Soc. Issues, 11,* 12.
17. Freeman H, Simmons O (1961) Feeling of stigma among relatives of former mental patients. *Soc. Probl., 8,* 312.
18. Potasznik H, Nelson G (1984) Stress and social support: the burden experienced by the family of a mentally ill person. *Am. J. Community Psychol., 12,* 589.
19. McGuiness D, Pribram K (1980) The neuropsychology of attention: emotional and motivational controls. In: (Eds), The Brain and Psychology, pp. 95 – 139. Academic Press, New York.
20. Tecce JJ, Cole JO (1976) The distraction-arousal hypothesis, CNV and schizophrenia. In: Mostofsky DI (Ed), Behavior Control and Modification of Psychological Activity. Prentice-Hall, Englewood Cliffs, NJ.
21. Spiegel D, Wissler T (1986) Family environment as a predictor of psychiatric rehospitalization. *Am. J. Psychiatry, 143,* 56.
22. Singer MT, Wynne LC, Toohey MC (1978) Communication disorders and the families of schizophrenics. In: Wynne LC, Cromwell RL, Matthysse S (Eds), The Nature of Schizophrenia. Wiley, New York.
23. Wagener DK, Hogarty GE, Goldstein MJ, Asarnow RF, Browne A (1986) Information processing and communication deviance in schizophrenic patients and their mothers. *Psychiatry Res., 18,* 365.
24. Van Kammen DP, Van Kammen WB, Naum LS, Sepala T, Linnoila M (1986) Dopamine metabolism in the cerebrospinal fluid of drug-free schizophrenic patients with and without cortical atrophy. *Arch. Gen. Psychiatry, 43,* 978.

25. Reiss D, Costell R (1977) The multiple family group as a small society: family regulation of interaction with nonmembers. *Am. J. Psychiatry, 134,* 21.
26. Falloon IRH, Boyd JL, McGill CW, Williamson M, Razani J, Moss HB, Gilderman AM, Simpson GM (1985) Family management in the prevention of morbidity of schizophrenia. *Arch. Gen. Psychiatry, 42,* 887.
27. Miklowitz DJ, Goldstein MJ, Falloon IRH (1983) Premorbid and symptomatic characteristics of schizophrenics from families with high and low levels of expressed emotion. *J. Abnorm. Psychol., 92,* 359.
28. Miklowitz DJ, Strachan AM, Goldstein MJ, Doane JA, Snyder KS (1986) Expressed emotion and communication deviance in the families of schizophrenics. *J. Abnorm. Psychol., 95,* 60.
29. Doane JA, Falloon IRH, Goldstein MJ, Mintz J (1985) Parental affective style and the treatment of schizophrenia. *Arch. Gen. Psychiatry, 42,* 34.
30. Leff JP, Kuipers L, Berkowitz R (1983) Intervention in families of schizophrenics and its effects on relapse rates. In: McFarlane WR (Ed), Family Therapy in Schizophrenia, pp. 173 – 189. Guilford Press, New York.
31. Hogarty GE, Ulrich RF (1977) Temporal effects of drug and placebo in delaying relapse in schizophrenic outpatients. *Arch. Gen. Psychiatry 34,* 297.
32. Harding CM, Brooks GW, Ashikaga T, Strauss JS, Breier A (1987) The Vermont longitudinal study of persons with severe mental illness, I Methodology, study sample, and overall status 32 years later. *Am. J. Psychiatry, 144,* 718.
33. Pasamanick B, Scarpetti F, Dinit S (1967) Schizophrenics in the community: an experimental study in the prevention of hospitalization, pp. 301 – 306; 341 – 345. Appleton-Century-Crofts, New York.
34. Stein LI, Test MA (1978) Alternatives to Mental Hospital Treatment. Plenum Press, New York.
35. Kopeikin HS, Marshall V, Goldstein MJ (1983) Stages and impact of crisis-oriented family therapy in the aftercare of acute schizophrenia. In: McFarlane WR (Ed), Family Therapy in Schizophrenia, pp. 69 – 98. Guilford Press, New York.
36. Steinberg HR and Durell JA (1968) A stressful social situation as a precipitant of Schizophrenia. *Br. J. Psychiatry, 114,* 1097.
37. Doane JA, West KL, Goldstein MJ, Rodnick EH, Jones JE (1981) Parental communication deviance and affective style. *Arch. Gen. Psychiatry, 38,* 679.
38. Hammer M, Makiesky-Barrow S, Gutwirth L (1978) Social networks and schizophrenia. *Schizophr. Bull., 22,* 522.
39. Hatfield AB (1987) Social support and family coping. In: Hatfield AB, Lefley HP (Eds), Families of the Mentally Ill, pp. 191 – 207. Guilford Press, New York.
40. Lamb HR, Oliphant E (1978) Schizophrenia through the eyes of families. *Hosp. Community Psychiatry, 29,* 803.
41. Harrow M, Astrachan B, Becker R, Detre T, Schwartz A (1967) An investigation into the nature of the patient-family therapy group. *Am. J. Orthopsychiatry, 37,* 888.
42. Asch S (1952) Social Psychology. Prentice-Hall, Englewood Cliffs, NJ.
43. Festinger L (1957) A theory of social comparison processes. *Human Relat., 7,* 117.
44. Hackman JR (1976) Group influences on individuals. In: Dunnette M (Ed), Handbook of Industrial and Organizational Psychology. Rand-McNally, Chicago.
45. Schachter S (1951) Deviation, rejection and communication. *J. Abnorm. Soc. Psychol., 46,* 190.
46. Berman KK (1966) Multiple family therapy: its possibilities in preventing readmission. *Ment. Hyg., 50,* 367.
47. Levin EC (1966) Therapeutic multiple family groups. *Int. J. Psychother., 19,* 203.

48. Lurie A, Ron H (1972) Socialization program as part of aftercare planning. *Gen. Psychiatr. Assoc. J., 17,* 157.
49. Lansky MR, Bley CR, McVey GG, Botram B (1978) Multiple family groups as aftercare. *Int. J. Group Psychother., 29,* 211.
50. Falloon IRH, Liberman RP (1983) Behavioral family intervention in the management of chronic schizophrenia. In: McFarlane WR (Ed), Family Therapy in Schizophrenia, pp. 117 – 137. Guilford Press, New York.
51. Spitzer RL, Endicott JE, Robins E (1981) Research Diagnostic Criteria (RDC) for a Selected Group of Functional Disorders. Research Assessment and Training Unit, New York State Psychiatric Institute, New York.

CHAPTER 10

Group therapy

ULF MALM

INTRODUCTION

The five-treatment study by May (1) established that the main method of treatment for the acute psychotic episode in schizophrenia is neuroleptic medication. However, May (2) also maintained that drug therapy alone is not sufficient for achieving a satisfactory long-term outcome in most schizophrenic patients.

Perhaps the greatest limitation of exclusive reliance on drugs is the inability of this mode of treatment to develop interpersonal skills and to improve social role re-adaption. Outcome research has shown that the combination of psychosocial intervention and antipsychotic drugs was more beneficial than either treatment alone (3). One psychosocial approach is group psychotherapy (4). There is no widely accepted difference between the two concepts ‘group therapy’ and ‘group psychotherapy’. For the sake of brevity, I have chosen the term group therapy.

In schizophrenia, communication disturbances are an intrinsic handicap of psychosis – in fact, they are part of the diagnostic criteria, like autism and thought disturbances. Everyday communication comprises interaction between people singly or in groups. To help a patient using formal psychotherapy, there are good clinical and theoretical reasons for aiming at reducing communicative handicaps and towards the transition of the improved communicative capacity into life in society.

The *Comprehensive Textbook of Psychiatry* (5) maintains that formal psychotherapy should be reserved for outpatients in remission with good reality contact and the ability to communicate and grasp and understand rational reasoning. Generally speaking, I agree, but it may be of advantage to establish a working alliance between patient and therapist and begin group therapy while the patient is still in hospital. In order to discharge the hospitalized patient with an established contact with reality and rational reasoning, not only support, but also a certain degree of communicative capacity is needed. In other words: the ability to communicate is a prerequisite for the patient’s ability to fulfill the other criteria.

REVIEW OF THE LITERATURE

Group therapy research

The literature on the outcome of group (psycho)therapy is summarized in seven reviews (5 – 11). The research findings have been summarized by O’Brien (12): quite

Handbook of Schizophrenia, Volume 4: Psychosocial Treatment of Schizophrenia.
M.I. Herz, S.J. Keith and J.P. Docherty, editors.

quite disturbed schizophrenic patients may benefit from group therapy if this is combined with psychopharmacological treatment. O'Brien also states that results of treatment research speak in favor of group therapy as being more efficient than individual therapy in schizophrenia. Most efficacy studies involved outpatients, with follow-up after the completion of therapy. Group therapy has been used in the treatment of schizophrenia for more than 60 years. Based on clinical experience, different advantages of group therapy in relation to individual therapy have been described. For the patient, being part of a group means sharing experiences with other people and tends to decrease anxiety, improve reality testing, improve the ego and decrease the need for hospital care. The schizophrenic can learn to master his basic lack of confidence in other people while being in a safe group situation. Several authors have reported a remarkable improvement in social function.

Furthermore, O'Brien emphasises the importance of the therapy group in providing socializing experience to the patients. The survey of the literature in the *Comprehensive Textbook of Psychiatry* (5) indicates that group therapy focusing on real-life planning, problem solving, relations, social roles, interaction, and co-operation with regard to medical treatment and side-effects probably gives the best results.

Although no comprehensive theory exists for process or therapeutic factors, some research data (Luborsky, personal communication) and long clinical experience suggest that a working alliance between patient and therapist, and the group interaction process, are associated with a good outcome. Group therapy is a practical and adequate method of providing continuity in the transition between institutional and open care. The therapy group functions as a secondary social network, adding to the patient's individual contacts with the psychiatrist and nurse. Kanas (13) points out the need for further research in the field of group therapy of schizophrenics, including comparison of the value of interaction-oriented versus insight-oriented approaches.

The interaction between neuroleptics and psychosocial therapies

As the schizophrenic person experiences social encounters as stressful (14), even a single trivial encounter stands a good chance of ending up in disturbed interpersonal communication, and sometimes in a psychotic reaction. The role of neuroleptic drugs is to protect the individual against such reactions. Drugs act by providing neurochemical protection from overstimulation and overarousal, preventing relapse, and reducing positive symptoms and signs.

IDEAS ABOUT CHANGE AND RATIONALE

Ideas about change

The patient's capacity to communicate during social interaction is very important in rehabilitation strategies. This is evident when one explores the patient's psychotic world, in understanding and insight, in the working alliance between patient and therapist, in group therapy and other kinds of psychotherapy, and in many role functions within the family and in society. Empirical psychotherapy studies have not demonstrated any simple or direct associations between single process variables and effects; the pattern is complex and interactional (15, 16). From experience of psychotherapy, we learn that it takes a long time for people to change, and that it is not necessary to actually attend psychotherapy all the time that it takes for the change to occur. Change can thus be related to the patient's communicative capacity, the therapy group, and social interaction in everyday life.

Rationale

It seems reasonable to tailor goals and methods for group therapy in schizophrenia according to the patient's possibilities and needs due to symptoms and signs (DSM-III-R) and illness-generated handicaps (17, 18). The essential problems of the illness concerning ego disturbances should be penetrated and changed by, for example, strengthening the patient's social identity in the group and his experience of being an independent individual and deciding about, governing and being responsible for his own actions in the therapy group. The therapy group should work primarily with concrete 'here-and-now' material and make possible interpretations from this (i.e., interpretations on the surface), as schizophrenia is accompanied by difficulties of abstract symbolic thinking.

The therapist should also be well aware of the schizophrenic patient's attentional dysfunction. The cognitive disorders in the sense of information processing deficits deserve special attention. Other basic symptoms are concerned with autism, with, for example, affective contact disturbances. This means that it is difficult for the patient to express in words his psychotic experience in particular and his everyday experience in general: he has a low communicative capacity, and this is a hindrance to psychotherapy of his psychotic experience. A logical result of this will be that the group therapist monitors the interaction between the members of the group and stresses, and works with verbal, cognitive and emotional communication. Bleuler (19) emphasized the affective contact disturbance as one main problem area for the patient with schizophrenia. This influences other people's experience of the patient as well as the patient's experience of the environment, and may generate emotional messages to others. In natural social contexts, this may be an important reason for the patient's social isolation and withdrawal from communication with others.

Re-entry into the world of reality must take place together with other human beings. Some degree and some quality of communicative capacity is then necessary. Even if the patient still has primary handicaps like delusions, he may partly be able to handle them after first describing, and them regaining them in a mode understandable for himself (reverie). This wording and insight oriented process is carried out with the help of interpretations. The interpretations are related to the therapist's theory and are shaped accordingly. This means that the patient, cooperating with others with similar experiences and with the therapist, could find ways to reduce the anxiety-provoking influence of various perceptional disturbances and delusions and prevent these from causing breaks in the contact with reality, hence modifying their social consequences. Communication is also necessary in order to talk about, describe and obtain help with relevant and important matters in life outside the group, i.e., 'there-and-now'. To build up the patient's ego consciousness, considering the continuity dimension of the ego or in connection with psychodynamic or cognitive interpretations of context, it is relevant to talk about childhood and adolescent experiences, i.e. 'there-and-then'.

The sensitivity of schizophrenic patients means that they react to encounters with other people, as well as life events, with a high degree of emotional tension, anxiety and arousal. Their sensitivity may lead to increased communicative disturbances, such as splitting or autism. The group therapy session must therefore have an outer structure making it possible for the group therapist to monitor the group plainly and directively and also to support an afflicted member of the group. In this connection we also may consider the group therapist's need for distinct and clearly identifiable goals for the group session.

COMMUNICATION-ORIENTED GROUP THERAPY: A CLINICAL APPLICATION OF RESEARCH FINDINGS

Design of the study

Mosher and Keith (10) conclude that there is an urgent need for comparative studies in which group therapy starts as soon as the patient's psychosis has subsided, but while he or she is still in residential care, and is continued into the post-hospital period.

One such comparative study was carried out by Malm (20). The purpose of the study was to test the hypothesis that addition of one year of communication-oriented group therapy to a regimen of neuroleptics and social skills training leads to greater improvement than neuroleptics and social skills training only. The study was a controlled comparison over two years. Diagnostic criteria were autism, thought disturbances and ego disturbances, and the patients' disorders were probably representative of a fairly broad spectrum of semi-chronic schizophrenic syndromes.

Eighty consecutive patients who fulfilled the inclusion criteria were randomly allocated to the control and therapy groups, using one randomization list for women and one for men. Patients who recovered after the first month of treatment with neuroleptics alone were excluded. Of the 40 patients in each group, 34 completed the two-year study. Of the 34 patients in the therapy group, 23 completed one year of group therapy. Treatment started in residential care and continued in open care. All patients received fluphenazine depot and social skills training. The assessment concerned symptoms and signs, social function in the community, life events, course-of-illness variables such as relapse rate, and a global evaluation of remission.

The goals

The general goals are ego support and social remission. The specific goals are: to increase self-awareness, to increase interpersonal communicative capacity (both verbal and emotional), to increase the social role repertoire, and to reduce negative social consequences of psychotic symptoms. Furthermore, the group should provide a socializing experience for the patient.

Group therapies may have different goals, such as insight or support, but most are a kind of ego-supportive and educational psychotherapy. The therapy used here belongs to the latter category, but places the emphasis on improvement of communication.

Inclusion criteria

All schizophrenic patients may participate, e.g., be exposed to communication-focused group therapy. However, only a few of the severely disturbed patients, namely those with continuous severe psychotic symptoms, such as splitting, hallucinosis and withdrawal, seem to benefit from the therapy.

Preliminary treatment before starting group therapy

The patient who is found to have frequent signs of thought disorders such as incoherent speech, or who reports perception disturbances like auditory hallucinations, should be prescribed a neuroleptic drug. At this point, the main goal of neuroleptic drug therapy is reduction of Type I positive psychotic symptoms. A reduction of positive symptoms at this point may well be the key to subsequent rehabilitation.

In an elementary individual therapy approach, the verbal dialogue between the patient and the therapist focuses on expression and self-understanding of the patient's psychotic identity disturbance. Concurrently, the functioning of the patient is improved by social skills training. Little by little, the patient learns to talk in individual encounters of up to about an hour with two members of the rehabilitation staff. This is about the right time for the patient to enter communication-oriented group psychotherapy (20) with the focal goals of improving his adaptive communicative capacity and increasing his social role repertoire.

The role of the therapists

O'Brien (12) points out that different authors, in theoretical reports on psychodynamic theory concerning group therapy and schizophrenics, have discussed multiple transference and the importance of confrontation in relation to exploration. They maintain that it is not necessary to 'uncover' unconscious impulses in the treatment of schizophrenics and that the therapy should be oriented towards the relevant reality. The therapist fulfills this aim by giving the schizophrenic a healthy group-social experience.

Therapists starting from different theories may interpret the group process differently. Thus, some therapists stress the expression of weaknesses in ego consciousness, others stress transactions, and some point out the importance of structure and cognitive functions. Good results seem to have been achieved both by therapists with various theoretical starting-points and by therapists with little initial formal psychotherapeutic training. The role of the professional is to tailor exposure and changes to a level the patient can tolerate. The therapist should remember that the interaction process is more important than the content, however rich the content may seem as material for analysis. The group therapist should have at least 3 years' clinical experience of working with schizophrenics. He may work alone or together with another therapist. If two therapists lead a group, one should be male and the other female.

The therapist may work according to his own personal style, but he should react actively in the group, primarily showing concern, i.e., being empathic. He should stick close to a manual for group therapy, i.e., structure the activities of the group by choosing themes, stimulating interaction, pointing out expressions of ego consciousness among the participants and stress-modulating verbal and emotional communication. He should also, together with the group, try to develop a social role repertoire for the individual patient and penetrate separation problems. After each session, the group therapist should summarize, using themes and sociograms emanating from the communication between the participants.

The study by Malm (20) also provided empirical evidence that communication-oriented group therapy is teachable. The method has also proved to be applicable in various treatment settings, both in hospital and in open care. Experience from many studies shows that therapists, even those who originally doubted the value of therapy in schizophrenia, spontaneously say that the group therapy has increased their enthusiasm for psychotherapy in schizophrenics. It is also less tiring for the therapist to work with a group than with individual therapy.

The group therapy is planned in coordination with other treatment methods. It may be applied by a group therapist (or two working together) who has no conventional psychotherapeutic training. This was also elucidated in Malm's study (20). In this study, six group therapists with no previous psychotheurapeutic training carried out the group therapy. On the other hand, with formally trained group therapists, even better treatment effects can be achieved. The communication-oriented group therapy method meets the need for a robust and unsophisticated routine method that can be used for most schizophrenic patients and can be applied at almost any psychiatric treatment centre, both in hospitals and in outpatient care.

The need for psychotherapy manuals

If psychotherapy is to be used in routine treatment, it must be based on robust techniques that are reproducible and easy to apply by therapists working in different rehabilitation settings and in individual personal styles, with varying levels of education in psychotherapy. Thus, there is a need for a basic manual on how to carry out group therapy with schizophrenic patients (Luborsky, personal communication). The original 1972 manual for communication-oriented group therapy by Ottosson and Malm was revised in 1985 and 1987.

The gateway process

We consider it possible to reach schizophrenic patients in psychotherapy and to establish a therapeutic alliance. At the same time we maintain that the therapist-patient relationship is different from that in the treatment of neurosis. The most important difference between neurotic and psychotic transference is the fact that the psychotic patient has lost his inner object representation and cannot distinguish between 'the self and the objective world'. The psychotic patient projects his delusions onto the therapist. Before the patient starts group therapy, the method and goals should be explained to him and a one-year contract drawn up in individual consultations with the group therapist(s) and consultant psychiatrist. These individual encounters also lay the foundation for a working alliance between the group therapist and the patient. The patient should be aware of the fact that the group therapy session will be audio tape-recorded. The therapist should explain why recordings are necessary: i.e., the therapist and his supervisor need to be able to follow up and monitor the therapy in the best ways possible.

The group setting

The therapy group should consist of up to eight patients, male and female – at least two of each sex. New participants may enter during therapy. The group therapy may thus be of a closed or semi-open type. The group should be homogeneous with respect to diagnosis, i.e., schizophrenic syndrome according to DSM-III-R. The group should always know why someone is absent. If someone is unable to be present, he should notify the group in advance and give the reason why. If he is delayed, e.g., in a traffic jam, he should inform the group of the reason at the next session. Participants should be seated on chairs in a circle, with no table in the middle. The group should preferably meet in the same room for all sessions. The scheduled duration of the single session is 60 minutes. The group meets once a week. If the majority of the group members are inpatients, the therapist might consider two sessions a week. Altogether, the therapy for each of the participating patients should comprise 40 sessions in one year.

Audio tape recordings

The main purpose of the tape recordings is to allow the therapists to clarify or check what was said or happened during the session, but part of the tape may sometimes be useful to the supervisor by providing essential original material.

Basic techniques

Focus for a single session. During the initial exploratory and warming-up phase of each session, the therapist should listen for a theme assessed as being of relevance and importance to the group. When he decides on a theme, the therapist should, often without announcing the theme directly to the group, apply his interventions consistently according to the theme. Sometimes it may be possible and suitable for the group to choose the theme.

In the management of the group session, the therapist must try to get the members of the group to say what is happening among them in the therapy session and how they feel ('here-and-now'). The therapist must also encourage the members of the group to discuss things and events that are important in their lives outside the therapy session ('there-and-now').

Approval should be shown when a patient expresses ego awareness, for example if he or she indicates a sense of responsibility for his or her actions, or speaks of him or herself as 'I'. The therapist should show his approval of expressions of verbal or emotional communication. The therapist should make particular efforts to get the patient to speak clearly, speak to and not about the others, indicate with words that he has been listening to what someone else has said. The therapist should also show approval when a patient shows signs of interest in other members of the group as a whole. The therapist should be restrictive with disapproval, for example of lack of ego awareness or initiative, and primarily express approval of positive elements.

The theme. The beginning of each session should be explorative and the therapist should listen for a relevant subject which he considers important to the group. He should also consider the relevant group process and single participants' vulnerability. The therapist should perform his interventions for that session consistently with the theme. Some examples of themes: silence as communication (should people talk only when they have important things to say); sharing fantasies; physical contact and sexual feelings; deeper contact with others; anxiety in the group; feelings about giving and taking between people; loneliness; leaving home; entering the community; making new friends; feeling unreal; talking to one's parents. The same group theme sometimes recurs frequently in various disguises.

Focus on the patient. This technique aims at involving a withdrawn or shy patient in the group process and making him a member of the group. The therapist identifies a patient expected to benefit from, and be able to stand, being in the center of the group's interest. He gives the patient the support he needs to talk about himself or to tell the group his opinions on a certain subject for up to a quarter of an hour. When the patient finishes his introduction, the therapist initiates a round-the-group reaction. The therapist should comment on important aspects of the patient, especially if he has not been sufficiently clear in words. The therapist is thus mainly responsible for structure and assessment of extent and how thorough the penetration of the patient in focus should be, e.g., regarding risks of social overstimulation.

Round-the-group. The intention behind the round-the-group technique is to develop interaction between members of the group and encourage them to explore and express in words their emotional problems. Each member has the opportunity to discuss his personal reactions to either the theme of the session or another member of the group.

The therapist decides who is to start in the round-the-group presentation. Usually, each patient takes his turn and the therapist encourages the participant in focus to develop his spontaneous and immediate feelings towards the theme or the patient speaking. When the affective reactions appear, the therapist should monitor the group process towards a rational cognitive penetration of the emotional material regarding both the single patient and the group. The therapist should conclude the session by openly summing up the content and interactional process, bearing in mind the psychoeducative aspects.

Verbal interaction. The group therapist should appear active and directive, should stress interaction between members of the group and try to encourage the members to speak. His behavior should be empathic. By being attentive or consciously inattentive, he should monitor the group process. The attention should be transformed into words, e.g., he should repeat or elucidate a statement made by a participant. The therapist might use interpretations here. If a participant, in an important context, has been expressing himself vaguely, an interpretation is a preferable alternative to a question. The therapist should also show his attentiveness in his gestures and body carriage. Support, assurance, and acknowledgement should be given as expressions of the therapist's comprehension, or stress the group's apprehension.

The therapist should show his or her approval or disapproval primarily in verbal comments (i.e., by repeating or rephrasing what the members of the group have said). In addition, the therapist can indicate his or her attentiveness by listening and gesturing. Approval may be an expression of the therapist's own opinion or may emphasize the opinion of the group.

If interpretations are made, they should mainly be superficial, i.e., emanate from relevant concrete material from the process or the participants. Support, assurance and acknowledgement should always follow an expression of ego consciousness, e.g., feelings of responsibility for activities in the group. In particular, the therapist should help the participants to speak plainly, speak to and not about others, and to indicate in words that they are emotionally engaged with or have listened to someone else in the group.

Emotional communication. In these respects, the therapist also functions as an example to the participants. He should support and acknowledge expressions of or attempts to express emotional communication, whether it is a matter of one participant's interest in someone else in the group, or in the group as a whole, or any personal involvement.

The therapist should be careful not to express dislike of, for example, emotional expressions of ego weakness, but he may show dislike of, and manage correctively, observed symptoms disturbing the group, like delusions, hallucinations or stereotype behavior.

Socializing experiences. The therapist should also focus in some sessions on socializing group experiences, for this reason he may encourage everyday conversation and interaction rather than individual conflict-oriented themes or problem solving activities. The therapist may encourage lonely patients to meet outside the group as well. Any psychopathology like hallucinosis or stereotype behavior, as well as remaining primary handicaps like information-processing deficits or attentional dysfunction, should be commented on by the therapist in order to make not only the individual patient but also the group conscious of other people's reactions, and thus make way for sharing and understanding by the group. The therapist should then focus on consequences and stimulate the group to find ways to reduce psychopathology and to handle the interactional problems in the therapy group. The therapist associates to adaptive behavior in natural settings in the community.

Closing a group session. The end of a session should relate to the goals of therapy, i.e. to survival in the community, social role repertoire and improved communicative capacity. The therapist may, in his summary, confront the group with e.g., delusions or stereotype behavior in an attempt to create understanding in the group and make the patient aware of psychopathological phenomena. The therapist should also get the members of the group to help one another find ways of reducing psychopathological phenomena and their social consequences in extra-therapeutic situations. The therapist should conclude by summarizing, possibly together with the group (i.e., reflecting technique) what has been most important during the session with regard to the theme, interaction, communication, solution or interpersonal problems in the group, or relevant situational problems. Immediately after the session, the group therapist(s) organizes his impressions and activities. Common psychodynamic concepts, sociograms for visualizing communication and the audio tape-recording are useful tools for this purpose.

Withdrawal from group therapy. About one out of 8 patients in a therapy group does not complete the whole course of group therapy. The few patients who refuse to continue with group therapy usually drop out early in the therapy, most often within the first five sessions. They almost always consider themselves too healthy compared to other members of the group. However, the most common reason for a patient's leaving before the final session is that the therapist considers that the patient experiences too much instant anxiety in the group setting, often related to psychotic symptoms. If the therapists decide that group therapy is for the moment not beneficial or that the patient does not now meet the inclusion criteria for group therapy, the first step is to give the patient a few weeks' holiday from group therapy. During this time, the patient should be met in individual encounters by one of the group therapists or by his individual therapist, and he should also be given an appointment with his doctor. If the anxiety symptoms cannot be dealt with by increased individual support or changed medication, the patient should stop the group therapy and continue individual therapy and social skills training for at least six months. One of the main goals during this time is to prepare the patient for entry to a new therapy group later on. If the individual therapist also works as a group therapist, one idea to be considered is to take the patient into his own therapy group in due course.

Whatever the reason for withdrawal, the patient and the group therapist should explain them jointly to the therapy group. For the group, this means a separation situation that has to be dealt with both immediately and later in the therapy group.

Summary of main features

Aims. Adaptive communicative capacity and social role repertoire; communication about feelings and thoughts; managing remaining symptoms and primary handicaps, e.g., strengthening existing defences and use of neuroleptics for symptom reduction.

Direction of content. Interaction and social roles in the group; relations with important persons and their expectations; problem solving and real-life planning; exploration of feelings and conflicts.

Focus on therapy. Concrete material; interpretations based on current awareness; group socializing experiences; separation.

Temporal focus. Present; future; occasionally 'there-and-then'.

Techniques. Support; assurance; limitations; explanations; attention-stressing verbal expressions; individual interpretations, group interpretations; common experience to shared experience; theme; patient in focus and round-the-group. Transference and projective identification. Encouraging positive transference; identifying but subduing, negative transference; containing and meeting with projective identification; reverie (p. 193).

Countertransference in the therapist. Expressing positive feelings; controlling negative feelings; degree of transparancy may vary according to the therapist's personal style.

Supervision

The group therapist should participate in regular supervision. Once a week, the supervisor and the group therapist should review the group therapy sessions and problems related to the clinical application of the group therapy manual. The therapist and the supervisor should use tape-recordings as one source of original material. Another important reason for the supervision is to take care of the therapist's own reactions, as for instance projective identification and his role as container, and finally, in order to be instructed about, e.g., reverie function.

The supervisor might also participate as observer in some sessions, particularly when the group therapist handles his first group. Once a month might be suitable. On these occasions, the supervisor and the group therapist might summarize each session together (the group therapist normally does this on his own). Group supervision is a good alternative to individual supervision. The group therapists from up to three groups (six therapists) should meet for about one hour a week. The supervisor should have several years' experience of working with schizophrenics, have training in group therapy and be familiar with the treatment setting of which group therapy is a part.

The therapist should normally encourage positive transference and actively subdue negative transference but he might, after consultation with the supervisor, consider penetration of negative transference. Emanating from the single patient's style, the degree of transparency may vary. This concerns control of frankness about the therapist's own life and thoughts.

GROUP THERAPY AND OTHER PSYCHOSOCIAL THERAPIES

It is possible, and may also be of advantage to some patients and in some situations, to give individual therapy concurrently with group therapy. The individual therapy is thus directed towards helping the patient to utilize group therapy. Short-term intensive psychotherapy could also be used, e.g., crisis intervention, in threatening psychotic relapse, or in connection with separation situations as, for instance, when the therapy group has ended. According to our experience, individual therapy may be applied by another member of the same rehabilitation team, but it also seems possible for the group therapist to act as individual therapist.

Concurrent family intervention (21 – 24) is especially indicated for patients living with their family, particularly in high-expressed-emotion families. Family therapy is directed mainly towards the family milieu and atmosphere, and is thus complementary, but not alternative, to individual and group therapy. Family intervention can be carried out while the patient continues in group therapy.

Concurrent social skills training (25) and group therapy are complementary to each other, as the social exercises allow the patient to experience different areas of communication and participate in social interaction.

A GLIMPSE INTO CLINICAL PRACTICE

Example

The therapy group of eight patients and two therapists sit down and the weekly session begins. One of the patient participants tells the group that he has been to a party, but left early. He says he went home alone because he was upset. During the initial warming-up phase, the group therapist decides that the theme for today's session will be 'loneliness'. This subject, chosen by the therapist, is not announced to the group. Instead, the therapist starts to be attentive to the patient who left the party, and encourages him to describe in more detail what went on at the party. The intension is to bring out the participant and focus on the interpersonal context in which the maladaptive behavior began. The therapist now focuses on the verbal communication about the event from the party patient to the other members of the group. Meanwhile, the other therapist acts supportively and empathically. When the party patient has finished his story, the first therapist adresses the group as a whole and asks everybody to discuss their reactions to what their group-mate told them. The therapist decides who is to start speaking about his or her thoughts and feelings. The procedure is to go round the group one by one. By making use of what the members of the group have said, the therapist points out to the party patient that other members of the group have had apparently similar experiences – the therapists attempt to identify the shared aspects, but the therapists also emphasize that different opinions have been expressed as to whether the patient should have left or remained at the party.

Next, the therapists turn to the group as a whole and suggest that 'we have all been upset in some social grouping', for instance at a party. The therapists then direct the group to express fantasies about why people sometimes become upset in social groupings. After having listened to the reactions of the members of the group, the therapists ask the group to identify the consequences of leaving a party. 'If you leave parties, you will not be able to make friends, and this will only add to your loneliness'. While members of the group react to this, the therapists are attentive both to verbal ways of communication and to emotional messages. These may have been adequate or incongruous. Firstly, the therapists comment on this by relating the comments to what is going on here-and-now in the group. Secondly, the therapists also associate to some earlier event in the life of the therapy group when one member of the group was upset and wanted to leave the group early, well before the scheduled end. The therapists point out the similarities as well as the differences between a therapy group and a natural group setting.

Finally, the nature of the feared consequences is explored, i.e., the fantasies that mobilized the retreat from the party: 'what do you imagine would have happened?'. The therapists then direct the therapy group towards a rational cognitive penetration of their feelings and actions. Using the common group experiences, the group is advised to seek adaptive social role alternatives to retreat in the future.

Using the original party episode as a starting point, the therapist describes contacts and reactions, always talking in simple words and checking that what she says is understood by the members of the group. The therapists also show their approval of the party patient and emphasize his expressions of ego awareness. The therapists also point out that the therapy group can serve in future as a supportive network for its members in their efforts to make social entries into the community. All members of the group are asked to describe briefly their reactions to the group session – a mirror technique is thus used.

Finally, the therapist summarizes the theme, the reactions of the individual patients and the interactional process. The possible problem-solving alternatives are discussed and their implications for the future are repeated. The session ends when the scheduled hour has passed.

In the supervision session some days later, the therapists and the supervisor discuss whether the therapists in the therapy group were successful in their efforts to carry out interventions in accordance with the manual for communication-oriented group therapy. The therapists present a simple sociogram indicating the communication and interaction between the individual members of the group. Some episodes of projection as well as certain interpretations are discussed.

The two therapists then analyze a brief audio tape excerpt in order to clarify how mutual interactions had transformed some mystifying remarks and incongruous emotional expressions from the party patient into words. At the end of the session their efforts to clarify had been rewarded by the group. Most of the members of the group showed signs that they had understood what had been going on in the group session.

Author's comments

The supervisor pointed out that the therapist in this session had mostly worked with consequences of events, exploration, the integration of 'here-and-now' material with 'there-and-then' material, problem solving, reality, orientation and support. The group therapy becomes a transition and step-by-step extension of the process between patient and therapist because the theme was dealt with together with group-mates, and in a socializing context.

The examples from clinical practice have been chosen to make it easier for the reader to compare with the individual therapies in the Boston study (26). Certain similarities, as well as differences, between the group and individual psychotherapies in schizophrenia are apparent.

OUTCOME

Benefits

General effects

In the study of communication-oriented group therapy in schizophrenia, significantly more patients achieved clinical and social remission after one year of group therapy than a control group receiving optimal routine treatment ($P < 0.005$) (Table 1). Significant symptom reduction was found in both the therapy group and the control group. Almost all patients could be discharged in both groups. The relapse rate was about 15% in both groups (20).

Specific effects

Certain significant differences between the therapy and control groups for less psychotic patients were found at the two-year follow-up. Those specific effects for group therapy patients were concerned both with symptoms related to communication and with those related to social functioning in the community. The score for the observed emotions symptoms factor (mainly negative symptoms) in the 'less psychotic' patient sample was thus more reduced in the therapy group than in the

TABLE 1 *Global evaluation of change from index admission to two years later*

Remission	Patients					
	All		Less psychotic		More psychotic	
	T	C	T	C	T	C
Clinical remission	4	0	3	0	1	0
Social remission	13	7	11	6	2	1
No remission	17	27	7	22	10	5
Remission vs. no remission			P < 0.005			

T, therapy group; C, control group.

control group. Furthermore, the two-year outcome showed that the addition of group therapy increased the improvement in factors and items related to emotional communication and anhedonia, and increased free-time activities, entries and re-entries into the social field (20).

Side effects

In schizophrenia, increased social interaction may cause, for example, increased anxiety, increased positive symptoms or withdrawal. However, there were no differences between the therapy and control groups in the inner tension item (corresponding to anxiety), the psychotic factor or the withdrawal item (20).

Analysis of positive and negative symptoms and signs indicates equal outcome, and the global rating of remission was also similar. Thus, no support for any adverse effect of group therapy was obtained. The incidence of psychotic relapses was also similar to that in other controlled studies.

Goldberg et al. (27) found that the relapse rate of patients with poor prognostic signs was increased by individual therapy for those patients not on medication early in the treatment process. No corresponding increase could be shown in this study on group therapy. Nonetheless, it is advisable to be careful in the therapy of patients with overt psychotic symptoms. Continuity of care from residential to outpatient care should be the major factor in preventing an overload of emotional stimuli.

Outcome, coping skills and social entries

When the change was evaluated globally in terms of clinical and social remission, there were substantially more remissions, mainly social in the 'less psychotic' therapy group (Table 1) (20). Intrapsychic changes included improvement of the symptoms with regard to emotional communication. Interpersonal changes appeared in the patient's primary social network in the form of development of new, and revival of old social contacts. This may be interpreted as a result of changes in inner psychodynamic structure, where primary defences like splitting and projective identification (which prevent communication) are compensated by a more adaptive communicative capacity leading to an improvement in coping skills.

Negative symptoms and signs corresponding to 'die affektive Grundstörung der Schizophrenie (Parathymie)' contribute to the social isolation among schizophrenics (E. Bleuler) (19). They influence both how others see the patient and the patient's expressions of emotional communication. Disturbed emotional communication is probably an essential factor underlying the disturbed social function. The difference in the observed emotions factor and the inability to feel item may thus explain why the number of entries and re-entries into the social field increased more in the therapy group. The total treatment regimen may have given the patients the support and capacity necessary to manage these social interactions. This is particularly applicable to the patients in the therapy group, who both participated in group therapy sessions and experienced a larger number of entries and re-entries (20). Various outcome criteria thus indicate that communication-oriented group therapy leads to practical benefits in extra-therapeutic situations.

The therapy group, together with the psychiatrist, will provide continuity between hospital and open care. One aim is now to guide the patient into his family and other primary social network. The patient uses the therapy group to develop adaptive social roles for the remaining primary handicaps and expectations linked to future social remission. In the community, verbal communication is taken for granted in most interpersonal roles. This applies to families as well as to the initiation of social contacts. There must be a transitional stage between therapy and society. Small groups are suitable for this purpose.

Ego-supporting and resource-mobilizing group and individual therapies may help the patient to function in the normal social field. Selected patients may benefit from inidividual expressive insight-oriented psychodynamic therapy (26). When the patient has achieved social remission, occupational therapy aiming at vocational rehabilitation begins. The patient has gradually, usually after 1 – 2 years of rehabilitation, attained a communicative capacity which he can utilize in primary social networks, replacing therapy, to organize his daily life (Fig. 1). Nevertheless, most patients will need psychosocial support and prophylactic antipsychotic treatment.

SOCIAL NETWORKS

Outcome research has shown that the advantages of combined psychosocial and neuroleptic treatment, compared to either treatment alone, are primarily in the in-

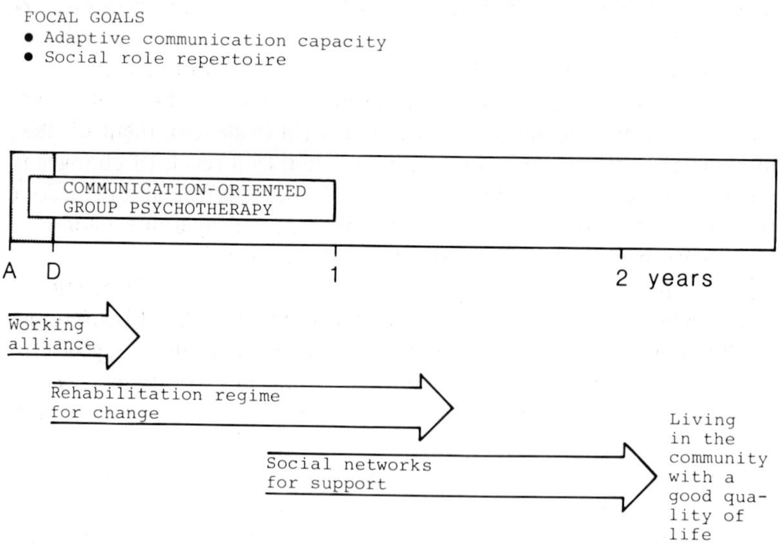

FIG. 1 *The focal goals of communication-oriented group therapy are to increase the patient's interpersonal communicative capacity and social role repertoire. In order to build social networks, the group therapy should be a coordinated part of a rehabilitation regime aimed at living in the community. A, admission to hospital; D, discharge to open care.*

terpersonal sphere of change and increased adaptive capacity for social role functions leading to future functioning in a real-life environment. Of course, the patient will need support in his own home after achieving the goals of the rehabilitation programme. A shared home with support from staff, such as a large shared apartment or hostel in the community, might be a suitable transitional form of living. Most patients want a home of their own and a primary social network like a family. This transition should take place simultaneously with the arrangement of the secondary social network of hospital and social care. We must prevent loneliness, perhaps with clubs like Fountain House, which has proved to be a very effective way of providing community-based rehabilitation for communication and work.

This brings us to the question of the importance of work to people. To work may be a way of being normal and contributing to society and earning one's living. On the other hand, the important thing with work might be that it structures one's existence with regard to both time and content. However, it is an empirical fact that only few schizophrenic patients in Western post-industrial societies are employed. This can be explained to a great extent by the labor market in post-industrial societies like Sweden. In the 1970s, the employment security legislation and the rules for obtaining study grants made it extremely difficult for individuals with a long history of illness to get a job or be accepted for vocational training. For these reasons, we should not automatically consider employment as the most common way of organizing the schizophrenic patient's life.

It is time to reconsider the general rehabilitation goals of the 1950s, which maintain that the patient should return to the state he was in before his illness. We should instead aim our rehabilitation at changing the adaptive capacity of the patients. Expectations of, and prerequisites for, the rehabilitation of handicapped persons may change – handicaps may not necessarily last for ever, and social support might increase. The importance of the concept *repeated* or *renewed rehabilitation* must thus be pointed out. Repeated rehabilitation is based on the fact that new goals and needs in the patient arise as changing goals and improvement are stabilized (Bennet, personal communication).

FUTURE DIRECTIONS

To summarize international experience: it is possible for schizophrenics to participate in psychotherapy. Different theoretical theurapeutic backgrounds and various types of psychotherapy (individual, group, family, environmental) seem useful. Future research will therefore seek possible common therapeutic factors in different categories of psychosocial treatment methods. Most important might be to carry out therapy according to psychotherapy manuals, and to select methods that have proved successful in empirical outcome studies with schizophrenic patients. The actual category, milieu, individual, group or family might be of lesser importance.

Clinical experience and theoretical considerations tell us that the patient's need for rehabilitation is best met by the use of two or more kinds of psychotherapy on the basis of individual specific needs and entry criteria. These psychotherapies may be carried out simultaneously or sequentially. Individual and personalized rehabilitation demands are, e.g., specific symptoms, social dysfunction, and goals for quality of life (28, 29).

TABLE 2 *Main features of a rational strategy for the rehabilitation of schizophrenic patients*

Modes of treatment and focal goals	Shortest usual duration
Working alliance(s)	Several years
Individual therapy directed at the patient's expression and self-understanding of the psychotic experience	Some months
Symptom reduction by antipsychotic drugs	Some weeks
The focal goals of the milieu therapy and social skills training are concerned with the patient's survival in the community	Some months
Relapse prevention by minimum maintenance doses of (depot) neuroleptics	1 – 2 years
The focal goals of individual psychotherapies are ego support and reality adaptation, and influencing the inner psychodynamic structure of the patient	Periods of about 6 months
The focal goals of communication-oriented group psychotherapy are to increase the interpersonal communication capacity and the social role repertoire of the patient	1 year
Family education programme	6 weeks
The focal goal of psychoeducative family intervention is change in the emotional style of the family system	3 months
Body awareness therapy focused on non-verbal communication	6 months
Vocational rehabilitation in order to regain an external structure of daily life and organize personal time and pattern of living	6 months
Social networks	No time limitation
Total	2 years

The table gives examples of the coordinated treatments and their usual time schedules.

The strategy outlined in Table 2 reflects the fact that rehabilitation in schizophrenia requires several coordinated specific treatment methods, each with focal goals. The methods are used in a rational order, considering the patient's communicative capacity and social network as well as continuity of care, thus, timing is important. The process in each method is directed according to the therapist's empathetic understanding of the needs of the patient, the symptom picture, and accessibility to therapy.

CONCLUSION

It is now generally agreed that schizophrenics can be 'reached' in psychotherapy.

The ideas behind change are comprehensive and take into consideration psychotherapeutic methods as well as neuroleptic treatment, and may be based on the single patient's communicative ability.

There are now strong arguments, including evidence from empirical outcome research, for using communication-orientated group therapy as an elementary psychotherapeutic approach.

Surveys of the literature on efficacy research in psychotherapy in schizophrenia indicate that group therapy, in combination with neuroleptic treatment, gives the best effect if it is focused on social planning, practical problem solving, social relations and cooperation with psychopharmacological treatment. Group therapy emphasizes social interaction processes.

Group therapy is an important factor for continuity between hospital and open care, and can promote the transition from psychiatric care to independent living in primary social networks.

A small semi-open group is the best form; 4 – 8 participants meeting once a week for 60 minutes. A full course of therapy lasts one year and will thus comprise about 40 sessions. The therapist uses certain basic techniques to structure the session.

The therapeutic philosophy behind communication-oriented group therapy not only constitutes a clinical application of research findings, considering other simultaneous treatment methods, but has also met the need in psychiatric care for a robust routine method that is teachable and can be carried out by therapists with no formal training. The general goal of this supportive psychotherapy is social remission, while specific goals are improved ego consciousness, improved verbal and emotional communication and the development of an adaptive social role repertoire.

ACKNOWLEDGEMENTS

Thanks to Sven Jonas Dencker, Dick Lindberg, Lennart Lundin, and Göran Persson for their important contributions and comments. Special thanks to Brenda Morris for advice on the final design of the paper.

REFERENCES

1. May PRA (1968) Treatment of Schizophrenia. A Comparative Study of Five Treatment Methods. Science House, New York.
2. May PRA (1976) Rational treatment for an irrational disorder: what does the schizophrenic outpatient need? *Am. J. Psychiatry, 133,* 1008.
3. Dencker SJ, Malm U (1984) Combination of neuroleptics and psychosocial therapies in schizophrenia. *Nord. Psykiatr. Tidskr., 38,* 27.
4. Kaplan HI, Sadock J (Eds) (1983) *Comprehensive Group Psychotherapy, 2nd ed.* Williams and Wilkins, Baltimore.
5. May PRA, Simpson G (1980) Schizophrenia: overview of treatment methods. In: Kaplan HI, Freedman AM, Sadock BJ (Eds), *Comprehensive Textbook of Psychiatry, 3rd ed, Vol. 2,* pp. 1251 – 1258. Williams and Wilkins, Baltimore.
6. Meltzoff J, Kornreich M (1970) *Research in Psychotherapy.* Atherton Press, New York.
7. Luborsky L, Singer B, Luborsky L (1976) Comparative studies of psychotherapies: is it true that 'Everybody has won and all must have prizes'? In: Spitzer RL, Klein DF (Eds), *Evaluation of Psychosocial Therapies.* The Johns Hopkins University Press, Baltimore.
8. Gunderson JG (1976) Recent research in psychosocial treatments of schizophrenia. In: Jørstad J, Ugelstad E (Eds), *Schizophrenia 75. Psychotherapy, Family Studies, Research.* Universitetsforlaget, Oslo.
9. Parloff MB, Dies R (1979) Group psychotherapy outcome research. *Int. J. Group Psychother., 27,* 281.
10. Mosher LR, Keith SJ (1980) Psychosocial treatment: individual, group, family, and community support approaches. *Schizophr. Bull., 6,* 10.
11. Kanas N (1986) Group therapy with schizophrenics: a review of controlled studies. *Int. J. Group Psychother., 36,* 339.
12. O'Brien CP (1983) Group psychotherapy with schizophrenia and affective disorders. In: Kaplan HI, Sadock BJ (Eds), *Comprehensive Group Psychotherapy, 2nd ed,* pp. 242 – 249. Williams and Wilkins, Baltimore.
13. Kanas N (1986) Therapy group with schizophrenics: response to Dr. Parloff. *Int. J. Group Psychother., 36,* 597.
14. Royal College of *Psychiatrists (1980) Psychiatric Rehabilitation in the 1980s.* Royal College of Psychiatrists, London.
15. Horowitz MJ, Marmar C, Weiss DS, DeWitt KN, Rosenbaum R (1984) Brief psychotherapy of bereavement reactions: the relationship of process to outcome. *Arch. Gen. Psychiatry, 41,* 438.
16. Pilkonis PA, Imber SD, Lewis P, Rubinsky P (1984) A comparative outcome study of individual, group and conjoint psychotherapy. *Arch. Gen. Psychiatry, 41,* 431.
17. Anthony WA, Jansen MA (1985) Predicting the vocational capacity of the chronically mentally ill: research and policy implications. *Am. Psychol., 39,* 537.
18. Hogarty GE (1988) Treatment resistance of schizophrenic patients to social and vocational rehabilitation: the nature of the problem and a model of treatment. In: Dencker SJ, Bender W, Kulhanek F (Eds), *Treatment Resistance in Schizophrenia.* Vieweg-Verlag, Braunschweig/Wiesbaden.
19. Bleuler E (1916) Lehrbuch der Psychiatrie. Springer-Verlag, Berlin.
20. Malm U (1982) The influence of group therapy on schizophrenia. *Acta Psychiatr. Scand., Suppl. 297,* Vol. 65. Munksgaard, Copenhagen.
21. Goldstein MJ, Rodnick EH, Evans JR, May PRA, Steinberg MR (1978) Drug and family therapy in the aftercare of acute schizophrenics. *Arch. Gen. Psychiatry, 35,* 1169.

22. Leff J, Kuipers L, Berkowitz R, Eberlein-Vries R, Sturgeon D (1982) A controlled trial of social intervention in the families of schizophrenic patients. *Br. J. Psychiatry, 141,* 121.
23. Falloon IR, Boyd JL, McGill CW, Razoni J, Moss HE, Gilderman AM (1982) Family management in the prevention of exacerbations of schizophrenia. A controlled study. *New Engl. J. Med., 306,* 1437.
24. Anderson DM, Reiss OJ, Hogarty GE (1986) Schizophrenia and the Family. Guilford Press, New York.
25. Liberman RP, Massel HK, Mosk M, Wong SE (1985) Social skills training for chronic mental patients. *Hosp. Community Psychiatry, 36,* 396.
26. Gunderson JG, Frank AF, Katz HM, Vanucelli ML, Frosch JP, Knapp PH (1984) Effects of psychotherapy in schizophrenia, II.Comparative outcome of two forms of treatment. *Schizophr. Bull., 10,* 564.
27. Goldberg SC, Schooler NR, Hogarty GE (1977) Prediction of relapse in schizophrenic outpatients treated by drug and sociotherapy. *Arch. Gen. Psychiatry, 34,* 171.
28. Malm U (1988) Good routine treatment in schizophrenia. In: Dencker SJ, Bender W, Kulhanek F (Eds), *Treatment Resistance in Schizophrenia,* Viewig-Verlag, Braunschweig/Wiesbaden.
29. Morris B (1986) Rehabilitation of the schizophrenic patient. In: Burrows GD, Norman TR, Rubenstein G (Eds), *Handbook of Studies in Schizophrenia, Part 2,* pp. 129 – 139. Elsevier, Amsterdam.

CHAPTER 11

A system approach to the care of persons with schizophrenia

LEONARD I. STEIN, RONALD J. DIAMOND AND ROBERT M. FACTOR

INTRODUCTION

Schizophrenia is a chronic disease that we do not know how to prevent or cure. The other chapters in this volume, however, give testimony that we know a good deal about influencing the course of the illness. There are chapters describing specific interventions such as individual and group therapy, work with families, and strategies for prescribing medication. In addition, there are chapters describing programmatic approaches, such as hospitalization, partial hospitalization and emergency services. Despite these specific interventions and programs, large numbers of persons with schizophrenia continue to experience frequent relapses and have a poor quality of life even when in remission (1 – 3).

One can ask whether this problem is due simply to a lack of sufficient resources to provide greater numbers of these specific interventions and programs. We believe that lack of resources may contribute to the problem; however, we also believe there are some major problems with how these interventions and programs are organized: they are uncoordinated, they are non-collaborative, and they often compete with one another (4 – 6). Together they comprise a 'non-system' of mental health care, where a few patients get more than they need, many patients get less than they need, and some get nothing at all. Patients may get lost in this non-system, and no one feels obliged to look for them. Patients may refuse to follow a program's rules and be terminated from treatment by staff who believe that they had no other choice. Patients are moved from the community into the hospital and from the hospital back into the community in such a way that the hospital, the community, the patient, and the family all feel mistreated. A major problem with this non-system is that it is episode-oriented rather than oriented to providing continuous care. This non-system fails the patient and undermines the potential effectiveness of the professionals working in it.

We need a system approach where the specific interventions and programs operate in a coordinated fashion to provide continuous and comprehensive care. Initially, many hoped that good case management alone could bring this to patients. However, without the infra-structure to make a non-system into a system, case management becomes a Herculean, if not impossible, task. In a system approach,

Handbook of Schizophrenia, Volume 4: Psychosocial Treatment of Schizophrenia.
M.I. Herz, S.J. Keith and J.P. Docherty, editors.

specific treatments, programs, and other services, ranging from housing to financial, are established and integrated to provide comprehensive care for the population of a designated area.

This chapter is divided into the following sections: (a) The rationale for a system approach to schizophrenia, based on the clinical issues of helping persons with schizophrenia make a stable and satisfactory life in the community. (b) Organizational principles that must be followed in order to have a system approach. (c) Clinical principles of community treatment that must be implemented within a system framework to ensure optimum patient care. (d) A description of the system of care operating in Dane County, Wisconsin as an example of how the organizational and clinical principles can be put into operation.

RATIONALE FOR A SYSTEM APPROACH

To live and function well in any community, anyone, including a patient, requires a number of things, including money, suitable living arrangements, socialization, a vocation or avocation, crisis resolution services, medical services, and mental health services (7). When a patient with schizophrenia is institutionalized, the institution provides all of these requirements. Moreover, the staff operate three shifts a day, seven days a week, to ensure that the patient and these necessities are brought together. However, when the patient is discharged, a dramatic change in the patient's care occurs. Although the patient's requirements remain essentially unchanged, now only mental health treatment is provided. All the other requirements for survival in the community have to be obtained by the patient. Even when a detailed discharge plan has been made which includes all the requirements, the patient no longer has a team to ensure that the patient and these requirements are brought together. The consequence of this change is that a person discharged from a mental hospital has a 60% chance of being readmitted within two years (8).

In the United States over the last 25 years, the number of patients placed from state hospitals into the community has risen dramatically, while the readmission rate to mental hospitals has also risen, from about 150,000 patients to about 400,000 yearly. In essence, what was accomplished was the replacement of one inadequate mode of care (keeping people institutionalized for long periods) with another inadequate mode of care (having patients revolve in and out of the hospital) (9). Under the current system, the patient comes into the hospital, receives short-term help, is released into the community, runs into new problems, has a new crisis, and has to be readmitted.

A logical question to ask about this pattern is: Why cannot the typical patient with schizophrenia function successfully in the community after release from the hospital? On discharge, the patient has been stabilized and relieved of many of the positive symptoms of schizophrenia. Why then can he not organize and maintain for himself the necessities of life, the way the rest of us do? The answer involves issues to which we have not paid sufficient attention. In spite of optimal medication regimens, many people with schizophrenia continue to suffer from significant long-term impairments. These impairments are the result of a combination of factors, including negative symptoms of schizophrenia; persistent positive symptoms of schizophrenia; character pathology; and organic pathology. Whatever their cause, however, these impairments seriously interfere with the patient's ability to organize and maintain the necessities of life, which are requirements for a stable adjustment in the community.

Specific long-term impairments include high vulnerability to stress (a small amount of stress can cause the patient extreme anxiety or regression into psychosis), difficulty with interpersonal relationships, marked dependency (the patient has been dependent on hospitals or family for long periods), deficiency in coping skills (e.g., the ability to shop in a supermarket, use public transportation, budget money), and poor transfer of learning. This problem with transfer of learning is particularly significant. We have found that even when substantial time is spent in the hospital teaching patients the skills that they need, patients do not use these skills after discharge. This is in part because they have difficulty generalizing what they have learned in the hospital setting to the new community setting. Perhaps even more importantly, many people with schizophrenia find that anything new is highly stressful. Therefore, they tend to avoid new situations and new experiences, even though they may have mastered the skills required to cope with the new situation.

Thus, the schizophrenic patients' long-term impairments are a major barrier to their developing a sustained and adequate life in the community. To help them requires a broadly defined approach that includes services in all need areas – from mental health to social services. Furthermore, all care should be provided in the context of a system to ensure that every patient with schizophrenia receives comprehensive and integrated services.

ORGANIZATIONAL PRINCIPLES

Just having a collection of different programs that provide different services is not enough to have an effective system of care. A system of care must organize these services to bring together the patients and the services to meet their needs. The principles of organizing the system are as important to the final goal of providing effective treatment as are the clinical principles that guide the front-line clinician (10). Listed below are five organizational principles that must be followed in order to have a system of care:

(A) For every service area (conceptually similar to catchment area) there must be one central authority that is responsible for planning the service system. In developing its plan, the central authority should solicit participation from a broad range of professionals from the mental health, social service, rehabilitation, housing, and government financing areas, and from consumers, families of consumers and other interested citizens.

(B) This central authority must have control of all the public funds and use that money to fund all needed services. This control over funding must include funding of state hospital services. There are a variety of models that the central authority could use to fund needed services. For example, if the central authority were county government, the county could provide the services by having a county mental health clinic, a county-run psychosocial club, etc. Another possibility would be for the county to contract for all services rather than provide them itself; or it could do a combination of both. The authors are biased towards contracting for services rather than providing them, based on our experience in Dane County, Wisconsin, and our knowledge of systems in other parts of the country. The problem with the central authority providing services is that it suddenly finds itself having a dual allegiance. It experiences tremendous political pressure to listen to the needs of its own civil service employees as well as pressure to provide needed services to the patients these employees were hired to serve. Unfortunately, at times the wishes of the employees and the needs of the patients come into conflict with each other. When contracting for services, there is less pressure to feel an allegiance to contractees, which leaves the authority more free to give its primary allegiance to the patients it must serve.

(C) The central authority must be responsible for the care of all patients in that central authority's area. In order to fulfill this responsibility, every patient is assigned either to a case manager or to a core service team that, among other things, fulfills case management responsibilities. The case manager, whether this is an individual clinician or an entire core service team, assumes responsibility for all aspects of the care that patient may require in order to live satisfactorily in the community. We have found that while the more stable patients with schizophrenia can be well served by an individual clinician functioning as the case manager, more difficult patients with more pressing needs and more frequent crises require an entire team to share case management responsibilities. These responsibilities include either providing all the services needed, or arranging for missing services to be provided by another agency. In all cases, the case manager remains responsible for making sure that needed services are provided. This broadly based care, as noted above, includes psychiatric treatment, rehabilitation, housing, finances, etc.

(D) Since schizophrenia is an illness of very long duration, the system must not have arbitrary time limits for segments of its treatment. To put this another way, the length of time a patient receives services must depend on that particular patient's needs, and not on an arbitrary time span. This has not been the practice for most services in the United States, where services have been provided on a time-limited basis with the expectation that the patient will transit through the services and at some point will no longer need any service at all. Of course, a system must do all it can to help patients in the transition from more intensive to less intensive services if it is going to help patients improve, and at the same time use its resources as economically as possible; however, to set arbitrary time limits is clinically inappropriate.

(E) The central authority must ensure that services are balanced and thus must not allow itself to become aligned with one or another of the professions that are competing with each other for status and funds. The central authority must recognize that rehabilitation, psychiatry, self-help groups and others can complement one another and are all needed to contribute to the service package. The central authority must face the difficult task of making funding decisions based on clinical needs and resist making them primarily in response to political pressures.

CLINICAL PRINCIPLES OF TREATMENT

Effective treatment of a person with schizophrenia must include working with both the patient and the community in which that patient lives. Even the most innovative and potentially effective treatment will fail if the treatment process does not actively involve the community. Clinical principles of treatment must start with consideration of how to work with the patient, but must go on to consider how to work with the community (11). We will start by discussing clinical principles of working with the patient, and will then go on to discuss principles of working with the community.

Working with the patient

An assertive approach

Frequently, patients with schizophrenia do not seem to be motivated to stay involved with treatment. What is often most frustrating about their willingness to be involved is that it is highly variable. There are times when a patient will seek help; at other times the same patient does not want to have anything to do with the treatment program. When treaters accept being fired by a patient with a shrug of their shoulders and a comment that 'unmotivated people can't be helped' the treaters show poor clinical judgment. Lack of or variability in motivation is part of the basic illness. If this lack is accepted passively, there is a high probability that in a relatively short period of time the person will again regress into psychosis, be hospitalized, and be referred back at discharge to start all over again.

Programs must be assertive in keeping patients involved. If someone does not show up for an appointment or for his job (in a system of care this information should be quickly available), we will go out and find the person. We may have to go to his home or drive along the street we know he frequents. When we find him, we try to learn what he perceives his problem to be and then try to explain how we may be helpful to him. The patient may say no the first few times we try, but in our experience, with persistent effort, he will eventually come back into the program. This approach has markedly reduced dropouts from our programs.

Individually tailored programming

As noted earlier, patients have a wide variety of needs. To help provide these needs in the most efficient way possible, we individualize treatment programs. This process must start with careful assessment. We carefully assess patients in a broad range of areas, from housing and finances to socialization and medication. The patient's skills, motivation, goals and supports must all be carefully considered. We then design a program to ensure that the patient has what he needs in order to make a stable adjustment to community life (12 – 15).

Ongoing monitoring

In order to know how and when to intervene with a patient with schizophrenia, it is necessary to have very current and accurate knowledge of how the patient is faring in his efforts to live in the community. Early intervention, which is crucial to effective treatment, is impossible without this knowledge. Thus, careful monitoring of each patient is a critical element of effective treatment, and we then change the treatment plan to meet each patient's changing needs.

Titered support

In their training, many mental health professionals are made almost phobic about giving patients psychological support, believing this will lead to overdependency. Although overdependency can be a problem, most people with schizophrenia are going to be dependent on us, to a greater or lesser degree, for the rest of their lives. The appropriate strategy is to increase independence to the greatest degree possible but not beyond what the patient can tolerate. To do this requires good clinical judgment. The amount of support we give is highly variable and depends on the patient's current clinical need (16). For example, there will be some days when we will give a person a great deal more support than we would two days earlier or two weeks later. In summary, patients need support, and good clinical judgment must be utilized in order to titrate the support so that patients get what they need but not more. Despite the danger of encouraging too much dependence, the common problem in community settings is that patients get too little rather than too much support, or that the support is inconsistent and unreliable. When thinking about giving support to persons with schizophrenia, a good rule of thumb is, 'when in doubt, give the support'.

In vivo services

We noted earlier that many of our patients do not easily transfer learning from one place to another very well. For example, we used to teach patients how to cook in the model kitchen in the hospital and to shop in the supermarket near the hospital. After discharge, we visited patients and found to our surprise that they were not shopping in their local supermarkets or using the stoves in their kitchens. We tried to find out why and learned that when they went to their local supermarket they found that the aisles were labeled A, B, C and D instead of 1, 2, 3 and 4. Some patients went ahead and tried finding what they wanted but the products were not in the aisles where they expected them to be. It was not long before they began to feel that people were staring at them, and they left the supermarket as fast as they could and did not go back.

We learned from these kinds of experiences to assess patients' skills carefully, to determine which ones might be generalized, and to teach these in a group setting.

But for those patients who were not able to transfer their learning, we had to go to their homes and neighborhoods and teach them how to shop in *their* supermarkets, to cook in *their* kitchens, to use the specific bus routes *they* needed to get from home to their supported work placement, and so on.

Capitalizing on patient's strengths

We have learned that patients do much better if we pay attention to their strengths instead of spending all of our time on their pathology.

> Paul was a 35-year-old single man with a fixed paranoid delusional system. A variety of psychotropic medications at different dosage levels had been tried, but despite them Paul remained delusional. However, his delusion was quite circumscribed, and his reality-testing for activities of daily living was good. Even when actively delusional, he had no history of being either verbally or physically threatening or violent.
>
> Paul had a good work history prior to developing his paranoid psychosis. He was a skilled auto mechanic and, because of his energetic nature, he completed a lot of good work. However, since becoming symptomatic, he had been unable to keep a job. At times he would get agitated when his delusional thinking became more than he could tolerate, and he would begin talking loudly to himself. This was not tolerated well by employers or fellow employees, and repeatedly he would be fired.
>
> The treatment staff concluded that to help Paul keep his job, they would need to give a good deal of support to his employer and actively teach the employer to also pay attention to Paul's strengths rather than his deficits. After a search, they found an employer who was willing to give Paul a try. They gave the employer some information about Paul's psychiatric problem and assured him that Paul was not dangerous. The staff also assured the employer that they would be available to help any time he felt he needed their assistance. Further, they suggested that he focus primarily on Paul's work effort and that he try to ignore Paul's habit of talking to himself.
>
> During Paul's first week of work, the employer called the staff several times when Paul started talking to himself more loudly than usual. Each time, the staff came immediately, assessed Paul, and reassured the employer that the situation was in hand. As the weeks progressed, Paul became less anxious in his work, and the employer became less anxious with Paul. The calls from the employer decreased significantly. Months later, Paul continued to work, and the staff continued to respond to the employer's very infrequent requests for an immediate assessment of the patient. Thus, focusing on a patient's strengths rather than just on pathology can bring large dividends in a rehabilitation effort.

Relating to patients as responsible citizens

It is extremely important for staff to adopt this attitude in order to work effectively with patients as well as with the community. The staff must believe that the people they are working with are citizens of the community; that they are living in the community because they have a right to and not because the community is allowing them to be there, that patients are indeed free agents able to make decision and be responsible for their actions. These attitudes influence clinical behaviors.

One area where this is important is that of medication. Patients are frequently ambivalent about taking medication. We find we get better compliance if we relate to patients as responsible persons. As much as possible, we collaborate with them regarding medication decisions (17). While we will certainly try to influence a patient's decision, we do not fight with them or attempt to control them regarding medication decisions when we do not have the power to do so. We are willing to negotiate about dosage and are willing to set a range within which patients can control their own dosages according to their needs. At times, we agree to patient's requests for small changes in medication that we believe might be pharmacologically insignificant (though some patients do respond markedly to very small dose changes) because we know they give patients a real and important sense of control and participation in their treatment (18). This approach makes them a part of the treatment process and respects them as responsible persons.

Another important clinical reason to treat patients as responsible citizens is that many of them have learned that they can use their illness as an excuse for their behavior. We disabuse our patients of that notion. We tell them that we believe that they are ill, otherwise we would not be prescribing medication or providing other treatment, but that we do not believe they should use their illness as an excuse for unacceptable behavior. We tell them that we will do everything we can to see to it that their positive behaviors are rewarded, but also that we believe that their negative behaviors should get the same consequences that we would receive had we behaved that way.

For example, we had one patient who believed he should be re-hospitalized whenever he became even mildly stressed or anxious. His way of doing that would be to go into a supermarket, take some soda and candy, and walk through the line without paying for it. If he were not apprehended, he would simply walk back in and take more until someone called the police. He would then get into the police car, and half a block down the road would say to the policeman, 'Oh, by the way, I'm a patient at Mendota State Hospital.' At this point, the policeman would sigh with relief, turn the car sharply around and give him a free taxi ride to the hospital. The policeman not only thought he was doing a good thing; he also avoided having to take him downtown, book him, write a detailed report, show up in court, and so on. To avoid the problem of the police taxiing the patient to the hospital, we had to work very closely not only with the police but also with the district attorney and the judges to see that this kind of minor crime was handled as it would be for any other citizen. The next time this patient shoplifted at a supermarket he went before a judge; the judge gave him the same stern lecture he gives to all first offenders of this crime. The judge told him, 'If you ever do this again you will spend three days in the county jail or have a $50.00 fine.' For most people (and most patients) this would be sufficient to stop the behavior. However, this patient shoplifted again, and since he didn't have $50.00 he spent three days in the county jail. Our staff spent a good deal of those three days in the jail as well, working not only with the patient but also with the jailers to make sure everyone got through the three days all right. With this approach, we found that the patient's maladaptive style of coping with stress dropped precipitously.

We do not advocate this approach for people who break the law in the midst of a psychotic episode. We must use good clinical judgment to determine when this approach should be used (19). Because we do this with patients whom we know well, we have little difficulty in determining when our patients are consciously breaking the law as a maladaptive coping strategy and when they are doing things because they are really out of touch with reality.

Crisis resolution available twenty-four hours a day

Patients do not limit their crisis to normal business hours, nine to five, Monday through Friday. Indeed, hospital admissions are more likely to occur between 5 p.m. and 8 a.m. or at weekends and holidays – periods of time when patient's usual support systems and services are generally less available (20). Thus 24-hour-a-day,seven-day-a-week crisis resolution services are a necessary part of a comprehensive treatment system for seriously ill patients. Round-the-clock availability of community-based crisis services ensures that a support system is always available to the patient.

Besides providing better clinical treatment, an additional benefit is that these services markedly reduce the use of the hospital. In our system, effective crisis resolution services and judicious use of hospitalization have saved hundreds of thousands of dollars yearly in inpatient costs. We have been able to redirect these saved dollars to community-based services, and this is largely responsible for making it possible to operate our other community-based program.

Working with the community

Providing support to the community members who are in contact with our patients, including family members, landlords, storekeepers, employers and community agencies, is just as important as working with the patients themselves. These community members' attitudes about and modes of relating to patients are significant factors in influencing how well our patients do. The following are the principles we use in working with the community.

An assertive approach

Just as appropriate assertiveness is crucial in working with patients, it is also crucial in working with the community. For example, if one lets things slide with a landlord or an agency to the point where the decision has been made to evict or terminate the patient, it is then usually too late to repair the problem. The patient has lost a resource, and the results of this loss are not only stressful to the patient but create a great deal of work for the staff. The clinician or team who function as the patient's case manager must closely monitor the relationship that the patient has with the community and intervene early if a difficulty arises.

Utilize a wide variety of community resources

There are many public agencies that advertise themselves as providing services to the citizens of the community, but which had never contemplated that they would be asked to provide those services to psychiatric patients. We recommend making use of those agencies to provide services to psychiatric patients. For example, until a few years ago, the Visiting Nurse Service (VNS) of Dane County had virtually no psychiatric patients on their caseload. Now they have quite a number of psychiatric patients. They give many of our depot neuroleptic injections, they visit and provide support to patients in their homes, and they serve an important monitoring function. The best way to know how a patient is doing is to visit his home and see, and this is exactly what the VNS is set up to do. Thus, the VNS has become a tremendous asset to us.

When we first approached the VNS, they were not jubilant about the thought of doing what they are now quite happy to do. They said, 'We really don't know much about treating psychiatric patients and will probably do them more harm than good. Our staff do not have proper training.' We replied that we understood their anxiety and would have one of our staff members accompany one of their staff members until their staff felt comfortable without our presence. They agreed and we gave them the support and on-the-job training they needed. Now, none of our staff members has to be with the VNS. An added bonus is that the VNS has become a strong advocate for community treatment. We have had the same experience with other agencies who have not had prior experience with seriously mentally ill people. Once they get to know the patients and work with them over a period of time, they come to know patients as people; prior prejudices or myths that they might have had evaporate.

Not all community agencies will be this responsive. At times, it might be necessary to push agencies into working with clients with a psychiatric disability. Many agencies receive public, charitable or other funding that prohibits discrimination based on disability, and many communities have laws against discrimination based on disability. If one is truly interested in getting the community to work with and accept these patients, there are times when one has to be willing to press very hard, to be assertive and even pushy to make sure that mentally ill individuals have the same rights and the same access to community resources as other citizens. It is difficult for any staff to do this unless they truly believe that these patients have a right to these services, a right to live in the community, and that the staff do not have to feel humbly grateful to the rest of the community for allowing the patients to be there. Ideally, staff should feel this to the depth of their souls so that they can imbue and instill these values in both their patients and in the other members of the community. We emphasize that agency cooperation is not obtained by simply demanding it. Staff must provide sufficient support and education to those agencies in order to gain their cooperation.

Provide support and education to community members

In addition to agencies, it is important to provide support and education to families, to landlords, shopkeepers, employers, and to anyone else with whom patients come into significant contact. Rather than attempting to mount a mass education program, we decided to educate and support community member every time there was a problem between a patient and a community members. For example, if we learned that one of our patients was having trouble with a shopkeeper, we would get together with the shopkeeper with several goals in mind. First, we would teach the shopkeeper to relate to our patient in a very straightforward and unambiguous manner. We would also use the event as an opportunity to teach about chronic mental illness. We would give the shopkeeper a realistic appraisal of that particular patient's dangerousness and discuss how chronically mentally ill people are no more dangerous than the general population of the same age, sex and socio-economic status (21 – 23). We would then help the shopkeeper understand why a community-based approach made more sense than institutional care, and we would emphasize that, although we might not approve of some of their behaviors, as good citizens we must be willing to tolerate deviant behaviors that are not against the law. Finally, we would leave the shopkeeper our card with our name and phone number on it and urge him to call us any time, twenty-four hours a day, seven days a week, if he experienced any problems or questions relating to our patients. Although problems remain, we found that providing this kind of education and support has helped our patients to achieve greater community acceptance.

Retain responsibility for patient care

People with serious mental illness require an array of different services. These services may not all be provided by a single agency, much less a single person. There must therefore be coordination among the various providers, and someone must take responsibility for maintaining continuity of care for the patient. In the past, mental health practitioners have relied on traditional referral and on interagency communication to attain coordinated and continuous services for patients. Unfortunately, this has not worked well: too often, services have been poorly coordinated, incomplete, and patients have 'fallen through the cracks'. Although referral and interagency communication are necessary, they are not sufficient. The keystone of coordinated and continuous services is having a fixed point of responsibility for patient care. Even though there are many agencies providing services, one agency must remain responsible to see that all the services are delivered (24). There are a number of case manager models. Although we use individual case management with the most stable patients, we use team case management for the more difficult ones to provide services that are available when needed without causing staff burnout.

All programs have patients who tax their limits, and at some point a decision might be made to terminate work with a patient. In addition to ensuring coordination, retaining responsibility for patient care means that the patient is not transferred or expelled from one program until he is well connected with another. If we cannot easily or quickly find another program, we continue to work with the patient until we do find one. Retaining responsibility also means we recognize that many of our patients have lifelong disorders which require lifelong help. Thus, we make a commitment for life to a patient. The amount of service we may give during that lifetime varies tremendously. Some patients do so well that all they need is a phone call once a month just to find out how they are doing. Other patients require daily contact in their home, and for most patients the amount of input varies over time. To operate as efficiently as possible we do our best to give the patient just what he needs, when he needs it, and where he needs it. In summary, retaining responsibility is crucial and it means ensuring that there is good agency coordination, that patients are not dropped from programs, and that treatment continues as long as the patient requires it (25, 26).

Work with the family

We believe that the families of our patients have carried a double burdon for too long. They have carried the burden of having a member of their family stricken with a severe chronic illness. Unfortunately, they have also carried the burden of mental health professionals telling them that they were responsible for that illness, that the mother was schizophrenogenic, or that the husband-wife relationship was pathological and caused a schizophrenic child, or that the whole family was sick and that the identified patient was carrying everyone's pathology so that the rest of them could appear well (27). Although these theories may be interesting, they are post hoc and have very little data to support their causal features. There are ample data that support a bio-psycho-social etiology of schizophrenia, with the biological component being very important. In any case, we help neither the patient nor the patient's family by making either one feel guilty or responsible for the illness. Working effectively with the patient often requires the cooperation of the family, and a high level of guilt or hostility towards treaters markedly reduces cooperation (28, 29). Often, it is useful to have the patient move from his family's home – a process termed constructive separation (30). This may be difficult to do, but it is almost impossible if the family is made to feel guilty. When working with families, we do the following. (a) We do our best to try to persuade them that we do not hold them responsible for the illness. (b) We try to assess whether it is useful for the patient to continue to live at home with the family. In some cases separation is a good thing and in some cases it clearly is not. We use emotional over-involvement, criticality, and intolerance by the family towards the patient as indicators of whether to suggest a constructive family separation (31, 32). (c) Whether we separate patients from their families or not, we continue to work closely with the family using a psychoeducational approach (33, 34).

THE MENTAL HEALTH SYSTEM IN DANE COUNTY, WISCONSIN: AN EXAMPLE OF A SYSTEM OF CARE

In 1974 the Mental Health Center in Dane County was similar to the majority of mental health centers in the United States. At that time, most centers expended most of their resources in providing psychotherapy to patients with neurotic and characterological problems, while patients with major mental illness received very limited services. In 1974, the Executive Director and Medical Director of the Mental

Health Center in Dane County left, and their replacements felt strongly that the Center had its clinical priorities reversed. These new administrators set about to change the Center from essentially a large outpatient psychotherapy clinic to a multi-programmed clinic that had serving the needs of the seriously mentally ill as its highest priority. Changing complex systems is a slow process, but the system continues to evolve.

The description of the Dane County system which follows provides an example of how the organizational and clinical principles described earlier in this chapter can be operationalized. Other communities may use similar organizational and clinical principles to construct a mental health system that utilizes a different mix of programs than those in Dane County to respond to the needs of the seriously ill (35). In all cases, however, effective systems faced with limited resources must start by defining their priorities. They must develop some way of constructing an integrated and coordinated system of care rather than a collection of independent programs. Finally, the system must be designed to meet the needs of the patients, especially the patients who are most in need of help to survive in the community. The mental health system in Dane County can be taken as one example of a system that largely fulfills the above objectives.

Dane County has a population of 340,000. Approximately 200,000 live in Madison, with the remainder living in small towns and on farms. The system of care in Dane County for chronic psychiatric patients is nationally recognized, and it has been designated by the National Institute of Mental Health as the National Training Resource Center for community support programs. The county has identified approximately 1,500 individuals suffering from 'chronic mental illness' (CMI) who receive care from the publicly funded system. The county has used its normal funding mechanisms creatively in order to develop a broad-based, multi-agency system of care for the CMI population. It is important to note that the system is not especially well-endowed with the funds needed to run a model program. It spends approximately $24 per capita per year on public mental health services compared to the U.S. average of $30 per capita (36).

Dane County has a philosophy and a commitment to work with all the chronically mentally ill persons in the community who require services. Since resources are finite, it must expend them as efficiently as possible. Thus, the county provides only those services that each patient requires in order to make a stable adjustment to community life, and it uses the least expensive service or combination of services to accomplish that goal. Obviously, the intent is not to give everyone the same service, but to give as little as necessary in order to achieve the goal. It also means that priorities must be carefully set, so that those resources are available for patients most in need. If resources were limitless, the goal would be expanded to help everyone achieve his or her highest potential of social and vocational functioning and to help everyone maximize the quality of his or her life. If resources were extremely limited, the goal might be simply to ensure that people were adequately fed, clothed, and housed and that they were not harming themselves or others. Given the resources in Dane County, the goal is to ensure that patients have as few relapses as possible, that they live as stable a life as possible, that they live as independently as possible, and that they enjoy a decent quality of life. While limiting goals may sound harsh, it is necessary if all patients are to be offered services. If goals were not kept in mind and resources were not conserved carefully, just one segment of people with psychiatric disorders could use all the resources and other people with high needs would be left with no services at all.

Patient characteristics: influencing selection of services

A major problem is how to determine the kinds of clinical services that a particular patient needs in order to live in the community and how to identify the program or programs in the system that can provide those services. Grouping patients by diagnosis or even by the overall severity of their illness is less useful when making these decisions than is thinking about the specific service needs of individual patients (37, 38). The Dane County system uses a typology that allows clinicians to think about patients on a number of different dimensions. Seven characteristics – willingness to come in for services, medication compliance, need for structured daily activities, ability to self-monitor, frequency of crisis, need for professional psychological support, and degree of case management services required – are directly related to the kind of programming that each patient requires in order to live successfully in the community.

Willingness to come in for services

Patients vary in their willingness to come in for services. Some are unwilling to come in at all, while others are unreliable and frequently miss appointments. In many communities around the country, these patients are called 'unmotivated' or 'treatment-resistant' and are not treated until they become so sick as to qualify for involuntary hospitalization. In Dane County, unwillingness to come in for services has been conceptualized as part of the illness; thus, it requires a specialized response. We designed a program especially for this population which, among other things, has the ability to do assertive outreach. Obviously, a program that has to go to patients requires a higher staff-to-patient ratio than a program that serves patients who are willing to come in for services.

Medication compliance

Patients who respond to medication but are not willing to take it reliably require a treatment approach that includes monitoring them very carefully and using a wide variety of incentives, augmented by legal coercion when necessary, to ensure that they take needed medicaton.

Need for structured daily activities

Many patients in the system have a social network of their own or a way of adequately structuring their own time and do not require a professional team to provide structured daily activities. However, other patients require special help in structuring their daily activities.

Ability to monitor oneself

Patients who can recognize that an increase of irrational thoughts and hallucinations is a signal that their disease is getting worse and that they should therefore seek help can be treated by a program that provides less intensive follow-up than is needed for patients who are less able to monitor themselves. Other patients interpret their irrational thoughts and hallucinations as a signal that they are in personal danger and thus respond by staying in their room and discontinuing their normal social and treatment contacts. They often become isolated and withdrawn, and, if they are not intensively followed, they will emerge only when their symptoms become very overt.

Frequency of crises

Patients who have frequent or severe crises need treatment from a program equipped to provide intensive and extensive crisis intervention and resolution services. Patients who have few crises do not need such a program.

Need for professional psychological support

Some of the chronically mentally ill have a well-established folk network that gives them sufficient psychological support to maintain stability. Many patients, however, required professional psychological support in order to maintain stability. These patients require more intensive services.

Degree of case management services required

Some patients are able to negotiate complicated social and bureaucratic systems well enough and do not require much in the way of specialized case management services. Others require help in everything from budgeting money to shopping for food. Again, the intensity and hence the cost of services varies according to individual needs.

Comprehensive community services

As noted earlier, a large number of programs at the Mental Health Center and at agencies outside the mental health system work together to provide an array of services designed to meet the diverse needs of the CMI population. The descriptions that follow give the reader an idea of what is available.

Crisis resolution services

The Dane County Mental Health Center provides twenty-four-hour-a-day, seven-day-a-week crisis resolution through a mobile team that can assist persons in crisis by going to where they are. The Center also staffs a 24-hour-a-day telephone service that works closely with the mobile crisis team. Together, the mobile crisis team and the crisis phone unit form an integrated crisis service (39). The telephone service receives calls from all parts of the community, including persons in need, families, police, and other mental health providers including the emergency rooms of the general hospitals. The telephone service provides direct help and consultation, often acts as an information bank for other mental health professionals, and refers calls that require immediate attention to the mobile crisis team.

Crisis teams operate, by definition, in the midst of crisis. The person in crisis, their family, and the community are often all upset. The crisis staff has to be prepared to deal with resistance and conflict. A patient or family member may come in demanding hospitalization when it is not clinically indicated. A store owner might demand that we get someone off the street in front of his store when the patient has a legal right to be there. At times, hospitalization is indicated and used, but more often, careful assessment along with the development of a carefully developed and concrete treatment plan will permit outpatient crisis resolution to be successful with minimal risk. An important part of this is the availability of staff 24 hours a day to continually reassess the crisis plan as required.

From its inception the crisis team was developed with a strong outpatient orientation. The job of the crisis team is to work with the patient and the community to stabilize the immediate crisis, and then continue to provide whatever service is necessary until the crisis is resolved or until a transfer to ongoing treatment can be arranged. As such, the crisis team in Dane County is very different from many emergency services that act only to assess the need for emergency hospitalization, but are not designed to assume any responsibility for true crisis resolution. The crisis team is at the center of the Dane County mental health system, and considerable effort has gone into making sure that it is effective.

The crisis team consists of five full-time equivalent (FTE) telephone workers, eight FTE crisis workers, a secretary, 20 hours per week of staff psychiatrists, and 30 hours per week of psychiatric resident time. The experience of the crisis team over the last 15 years of its operation has reinforced the conviction that most people who come into a crisis service or into an emergency room do not need hospitalization. What they do need is a careful assessment, the development of a clear treatment plan, and monitoring to make sure that the treatment plan is actually put into practice. With such monitoring, the team can assess whether an ongoing treatment plan is effective, and modify it as needed.

Often, the person in crisis is someone who is already in the system receiving active treatment for a mental illness. In such cases, the crisis team has immediate access to the person's clinical record and treatment plan. The availability of good clinical records is critical to an accurate risk assessment, as well as to the development of effective treatment options. Records include a history of past suicidal or assaultive behavior, some information about the person's support system, a description of what has helped in the past, medication history, and often a specific treatment plan for how to deal with a crisis that might arise. If such information is not available, the person's case manager is contacted for further information and for joint treatment planning with the crisis team.

Sometimes the crisis is precipitated by the stress of concrete needs that are unmet – stabilizing a psychotic decompensation in a person with schizophrenia following their eviction starts with finding emergency housing for the night. At other times, the ability to intervene rapidly with psychotropic medication is critical. In still other situations, rapidly involving the person's support system, be it friends of family or employer, proves to be a critical step in crisis resolution. Developing a community-based treatment plan requires much more time from the crisis staff than hospitalizing the patient. Staff must have the time to do the job. Staff must also have the space to do the job. Too often in other communities, patients with a psychiatric emergency must be seen in a busy, noisy and confusing medical emergency room where the staff is under pressure to 'dispose' of the patient as rapidly as possible. The Dane County crisis team sees patients at the Mental Health Center as well as going into the community. In addition, they are also called to see people in hospital emergency rooms. Arrangements have been made at local hospitals so that when the crisis team is called to see a patient in the emergency room, the crisis team can use a comfortable conference lounge adjacent to the emergency room so that the pressure and noise of the emergency room can be avoided.

Crisis stabilization often requires more than a single contact. At times, the needs of the person in crisis require a follow-up session later the same day to assess medication effects, to hold a family session, or just to re-evaluate how things are going after a few hours and provide some additional support. It often requires working with a person in crisis for days to weeks, and at times even months, until more definitive treatment can be planned and implemented. The staff must be flexible, and follow the clinical needs of the person in crisis rather than any preset policies. Going out for a bite to eat with a client, calling a landlord, involving family in another area or helping to arrange for emergency housing may all be part of crisis resolution. Mobilizing community resources often plays an important role. This may involve working with the client to call his employer or his estranged wife, but may also include calling food pantries for emergency food or planning with the client to apply for welfare and then helping to ensure that the application goes smoothly. Dane County has also developed an array of emergency housing options, from 48-hour crisis beds within one of the local hospitals, to crisis forster homes where a client can stay for a few days to two weeks.

The police are the community resource most commonly involved with mental health crises. Very often the police are the first people called by the community when a crisis erupts. An officer's primary focus, however, is on keeping the peace. He or she is under pressure to settle the problem quickly and definitively so that it does not recur, and to return to other duties as soon as possible. Having few other options, police officers will often bring people who are mentally ill and causing a disturbance to a crisis unit or an emergency room, hoping that the person will be hospitalized as an alternative to jail. In many communities, police officers may be kept waiting by mental health staff for hours, or an emergency room may refuse to see the patient. Problems may also result if the person is released rather than hospitalized, for the police officer may be faced with the possibility of being called back to the same situation a few hours later.

It is of critical importance that the crisis staff have a good working relationship with the police. The relationship between the crisis unit and the police in Dane County has been consciously developed and nurtured ever since the crisis service was first established. The crisis staff see the police as important professional coleagues and work with them in a collaborative fashion. Over the years we have worked to enhance the skills and sensitivity of the police. We provide 40 hours of mental health training for each new police cadet class, and new police recruits come to the crisis unit for a shift, just as new crisis workers and psychiatry residents ride along with the police for a shift. We expect them to give us their highest priority when we request their help, and we give them our highest priority when they request our help. When the police bring someone into the crisis unit, the crisis worker will often invite the officer to sit in on the evaluation in cases where there does not seem to be a problem with confidentiality or authority. This helps make the assessment and the treatment plan a joint endeavor. It often leads to more creative options than if there were only the traditional choices of hospital or jail for someone who is mentally ill but has committed a misdemeanor. This sense of collaboration, whether the officer is directly involved in the assessment or not, is particularly important in our system, since most of the people brought in by the police are neither hospitalized nor jailed.

The structure of the crisis service is designed to facilitate its operation. Both the mobile crisis team and the telephone crisis staff share a large open space, lined with desks and telephones and adjacent to the record room of the Mental Health Center. This facilitates cross-communication and makes sure that multiple staff are immediately involved in any crisis that comes in.

An important part of the crisis service is the ability to act as a central information bank. Clinicians who know that one of their patients is at increasing risk to develop a crisis can provide the crisis unit with a 'crisis alert' that includes a brief description of the problem, a brief but concrete plan of action, an assessment of risk factors including past suicidal or assaultive behavior, and the appropriate people to contact. Ongoing treatment plans for patients who are chronically in crisis are also kept on file with the crisis service.

A final, important role of the Crisis Service is its function as the gatekeeper for all county-funded hospitalization. In Wisconsin, each county is financially responsible for any indigent patient without insurance or medical assistance who is admitted to a psychiatric unit, whether the admission is to a private hospital or the state hospital. In Dane County, the Crisis Service must authorize such hospitalization or the county will refuse to pay for them. If an indigent patient presents at a hospital for admission, the hospital staff calls the crisis team, who come over to do an assessment. Payment for the hospitalization is only authorized if a community-based treatment plan cannot be developed. Even if the hospitalization is authorized, it is usually for a specified number of days so that the Crisis Service can remain involved, monitor the status of the patient in the hospital and the development of the treatment plan, and develop a community-based plan as soon as this is feasible (40).

Mobile community treatment: a training in community living replication

The Mobile Community Treatment (MCT) program was designed specifically to work with the most difficult-to-treat patients in the system. This program is a direct replication of the Training in Community Living (TCL) program (41). The patients targeted by this program suffer from schizophrenia and other major mental illnesses and have a history of repeated hospitalization. These patients often resist coming in regularly for services; thus, they need assertive outreach. They are often not compliant with medication; this, too, requires a specialized approach. Many need to have some daily structure provided. Most are poor at monitoring themselves; thus, they require frequent external monitoring. They tend to have frequent and sometimes severe crises. Their folk network is absent, overwhelmed, or tenuous; thus, they required professional psychological support. Finally, they have significant deficits in coping skills, and they are not able to negotiate the system; thus, they require a great deal of case management services.

The MCT program was developed to help severely ill schizophrenic patients live in the community, to decrease their need for psychiatric hospitalization, and to enhance their quality of life. Much of the program is oriented toward providing help with the normal tasks of daily living, teaching patients coping skills so that over time they can accomplish things on their own, and providing a support system for patients who have little in the way of social support or human contact. Much of the treatment involves practical activities such as helping a patient maintain his apartment, going shopping with him for groceries, or teaching him how to use a washing machine at a local laundromat. Verbal interaction between staff and patients is important, but it is easier for many of these patients to form relationships when staff spend time helping them to meet their concrete needs than it is when contact is restricted to talk in a therapist's office. Two key parts of the program are assertive outreach and a strong case management system that assures that patients' needs are being met, that problems are recognized early in their development, and that patients do not drop out of treatment.

The MTC program operates two shifts a day, from 8:00 a.m. until 10:30 p.m. seven days a week; night-time emergency backup is provided by the Mental Health Center's Crisis Resolution Service. The MCT program currently has nine full-time personnel plus a program manager, a program secretary, and approximately 30 hours of psychiatric coverage a week to treat 200 patients. (Our own experience has convinced us that our patient-to-staff ratio is too high. To work effectively with the 'difficult-to-treat' patient, we recommend an optimal patient-to-staf ratio of 10 to 1 and a maximum of 15 to 1. We are in the process of decreasing the number of patients followed by MCT to its original size of 120 while maintaining the current staffing level.) Many patients need very intensive services if they are to survive in the community. The MCT staff can dispense medication seven days a week, hand out spending money on a daily basis, arrange for food vouchers at restaurants or go grocery shopping, or accompany the patient to a new volunteer job. Over time, some patients become relatively stable and need less intensive services. These patients may stop in once a week to make contact with staff or come in every two weeks for a depot anti-psychotic injection. Even these relatively stable patients need close monitoring in order to prevent decompensation and re-hospitalization.

One important priority of the MCT program is to work closely with other parts of the patient's support system. For example, many patients also have a welfare worker or receive visits from the Visiting Nurse Service. Sometimes, the waitress in the restaurant where the patient eats every day is in a better position to help monitor the patient and detect early signs of crisis than the MCT staff members who see the patient less often. Employers and landlords are much more willing to be helpful when they receive support and assistance from the MCT staff. Finally, families – even families who have been considered resistant to traditional family therapy – are often an important and positive part of the patient's treatment when a psychoeducational approach is used. We respect confidentiality and autonomy when working with these extended support systems, but find that helping the patient to coordinate the other people and programs in his life is critical in maintaining community stability.

The patients followed by the MCT program are frequently in and out of crisis, often have extraordinary needs, and require staff who are more available than any single clinician could be. Therefore, a team case management system, rather than an individual case management system, is used to provide continuity of care and to protect individual staff persons from the burden of sole responsibility. It is critically important for the entire staff to know all the patients, to be kept up to date on their current status and treatment plans, and to share responsibility.

Both formal and informal mechanisms have been developed to ensure that communication and coordination within the team function smoothly and that patients are not lost through the cracks in the system. Every staff-patient contact, from a patient's brief daily visit to pick up medication to contact in an emergency room following a suicide attempt, is described in a daily log so that staff members starting their shift can scan all the events of the last several days. During the daily afternoon shift change meeting, every patient in the program is reviewed at least briefly with both day and evening staff present. Every patient has a treatment plan. Some plans involve daily staff contact; others require much less. Patients who have missed appointments, who need a special service, or who need some kind of follow-up can be identified, and specific staff assignments can be made. Longer staff meetings once a week allow time for treatment planning on new or problematic patients. While only those staff working on a given day are present during daily shift changes, the schedule allows most staff to attend the weekly meeting to ensure that everyone is kept current on any problems and that everyone is actively involved in the treatment-planning process. All staff, from the program secretary to the psychiatrist, actively share information so that the entire team functions as a coordinated unit. While team coordination takes staff time to implement, it is critical if the program is to be effective. Here are three examples of typical daily occurrences:

> John failed to come in for his fluphenazine decanoate injection scheduled for today. In the past MCT staff have gone out to bring John in when he has missed. Recently, he has been taking more responsibility for his own life; he has been coming in regularly for his injections, and he has generally been doing well. Since John has been demonstrating more responsibility, staff are reluctant to go out and bring him in, since that would undermine his movement toward autonomy. Thus, a new treatment plan needs to be developed. A few minutes of discussion between the three staff members and the psychiatrist who are working this morning results in a new plan. Staff are scheduled to go grocery shopping with John in three days. Thus, staff will wait to see whether John comes in on his own for the injection. Staff will bring him in for his injection

after grocery shopping if he has not come in before then. John's missed appointment is logged along with the new treatment plan. Both will be discussed at the afternoon shift change and followed up at the next weekly staff meeting.

Susan has not been doing well over the past several days. MCT has been in close touch with a contact person at her volunteer job. While she attended yesterday, she was more disorganized than usual. She missed attending the job several days last week. She normally comes into the MCT program every day to take medication in front of staff, have a brief contact, and pick up daily spending money. She missed coming in this morning, and she is now not answering her phone. This has occurred before, and a treatment response has already been planned. This afternoon, staff will stop by her apartment and the coffee shop where she spends time. If they cannot find her, they will schedule further follow-up on the next shift's assignment sheet. The most likely precipitant is stress between Susan and her boyfriend. Staff have usually been able to talk Susan through these periods, but plans are made to increase her anti-psychotic medication during the stressful period if it becomes necessary.

David has a history of many psychotic decompensations and long hospitalizations. He had been stable for the last three years, working full-time as a dishwasher, living in his apartment, and owning his own car. He had been taking medication on his own, although he does have a limited guardian who has legal power to force him to take medication if it becomes necessary. Several weeks ago, David broke off contact with his parents, started to become suspicious and angry, and began to have trouble at work, both in doing the job and in arguing with his co-workers. David's MCT treatment plan specifies weekly contact, but with the impending decompensation contact has been increased to daily meetings in an attempt to help him deal with stress at work, structure his time away from the job, and monitor him more closely. MCT staff have already established contact with David's family and work supervisor. When David's behavior became erratic, attempts were made to support his family and his supervisor and to make sure that he would be placed on medical leave rather than be fired from his job. As David became more paranoid, he refused first to take an increased amount of medication, then to take any medication at all. At first, MCT staff brought oral medication to David's apartment on a daily basis. When David refused it, his guardian obtained a court order requiring the police to bring David to the Mental Health Center for an injection of a depot neuroleptic. Shortly after the first injecton, David agreed to take oral medication with daily staff supervision.

Most of the patients who are admitted to the MCT program have been ill for years, and they are likely to require the specialized services of the program for an indefinite period of time. A follow-up study of the first 50 patients admitted to the program revealed that 35 were still active three years after admission. Of the other 15 patients, some had moved to other cities, some had been transferred to other programs, two had committed suicide, and three had proved impossible to maintain in the community, even with MCT. Since the most treatment-resistant patients in Madison had been referred to MCT, the fact that only three of the first 50 patients needed long-term institutional care is particularly impressive. The outcome of the thirty-five patients still followed by MCT is also impressive. In the three years before they entered the program, these 35 patients collectively used 5,793 hospital days. In the three years after entering the program, this same group collectively required 792 hospital days. Evaluation studies of other replications of the Training in Community Living Program have shown similar outcomes (42).

Support network

The Support Network program is the Mental Health Center of Dane County's psychosocial rehabilitation unit for chronically mentally ill adults. As with other clubhouse-type programs, the program has adopted many of the principles developed at Fountain-House in New York City. It has a strong vocational emphasis and provides basic skill training, social support, and a way of structuring time (43). People who attend the programs are considered 'members', and the program is arranged such that it cannot function without the very real service that the members provide. Telephones are answered by members, meals are cooked by members, minor maintenance of the building is performed by members, and even some of the outreach to members who have not been attending is done by other members. Professional staff are responsible for providing structure and supervision, but once the culture is established even much of this falls to the members to maintain. Professional staff are freed up to spend much of their time providing case management services for clients as well as some outreach services, both of which are critical to minimize dropout from the program and to maintain community stability.

The program operates seven days and four evenings a week. As a replacement for the extended families and support system that many of the members lack, the program is open for holidays such as Thanksgiving and Christmas. It is dedicated to providing people suffering from severe and persistent mental illness with effective and comprehensive services that can assist them to lead more independent, healthy, successful and fulfilling lives in the community. The program works with those patients who are relatively stable, who have at least some motivation, and who are able to tolerate group activities. The program is organized into units, each unit having a major area of responsibility. All of the units are connected with a range of vocational opportunities, including transitional employment positions (TEPs) in the community. The basement unit is responsible for meals – arranging menus, buying food, cooking and serving it, and cleaning up after the lunches and dinner that are served to approximately 70 members a day. The first floor unit runs the phone and the reception area, keeps track of the attendance of members, and does much of the paperwork required to operate the Support Network program. The second floor unit puts out both the daily and weekly newspapers, makes posters and takes care of publicity for special events, and puts out special educational booklets such as one on 'the value of work'. The second floor unit also produces a weekly video program which is broadcast on the city public access cable TV channel.

An additional part of the program is the medical unit. Historically, there has been some tension between programs that operate on the basis of a 'rehabilitation model' and those that operate from a 'medical' model. In most clubhouse programs, 'treatment' services such as monitoring and prescribing psychotropic medication are disconnected from the clubhouse and provided by a separate staff at a separate site. Support Network has worked instead to integrate medical services within the rehabilitation framework (16, 44). Information about medication is shared among medical staff and members. The emphasis of the medical unit, as in the other units of the program, is for members to gain a sense of expertise and competence. Members not only learn about their medication and their illness, but are also encouraged to acknowledge and share their own expertise about medications, side-effects, their experience about how the medications affect them, and what techniques they have learned to deal with symptoms of the illness (16, 45). Members working in the medical unit are taught to take the screening blood pressures of other members, and are becoming more involved in administering health care questionnaires.

Adult clinical services and 'Meds Plus'

The adult services program is an outpatient clinic that provides services to many different kinds of patients. Approximately 40% of the patients have chronic schizophrenia. Many schizophrenic patients do well without elaborate services – they neither want nor need more than brief contact, support, and monitoring. These patients come in every two to four weeks to see the 'Meds Plus' nurse for medication monitoring under the supervision of a psychiatrist. They are seen initially for an evaluation by a psychiatrist and at one to three-month intervals thereafter, depending on need. For some of these patients, more intensive involvement might become too intrusive and might disrupt a rigid but precarious stability. Other patients come in once every two to four weeks for supportive counseling, medication monitoring, and prescription renewal. Some groups, some case management services, and some crisis intervention services are available from the patient's regular therapist; if a patient temporarily requires more intensive services, the crisis resolution service assists.

It is important to reassess the needs of these patients on a regular basis. A patient who has been stable with minimal support might need much more intensive help if his parents become unavailable or if his support system changes in some other way. Other patients who were not interested in vocational rehabilitation might become much more open to this kind of help as they grow older. Other program units and other kinds of assistance need to be available for the patients who require more than this minimal level of service. At the same time, in a system with very scarce resources, we cannot afford to utilize a slot in a more expensive program if minimal support is all that is needed or wanted.

Inpatient system

Hospitalization is one important element in a comprehensive community system of care (46, 47). Just as with a medical intensive care unit (ICU), the psychiatric hospital plays a critical, at times life saving role in the treatment of seriously ill patients. Just as with the medical ICU, however, the role of the hospital is limited in that it provides a dramatic but circumscribed intervention as one part of ongoing treatment that continues for years in the community. It is crucial, therefore, for the primary locus of care to remain in the community.

Dane County uses the psychiatric units of four general hospitals, a Veterans Administration hospital, an acute unit in the state hospital, and a county hospital. As we noted earlier, the crisis resolution service acts as gatekeeper by authorizing funding for admission of indigent patients to all these units (except the VA hospital). In addition, each hospitalized patient continues to be monitored closely by the Mental Health Center staff who have been assigned to the case. A weekly list of all inpatients is provided to these staff members monitoring progress and length of stay, indicating who is in the hospital for what reasons and for how long. Patients who had been followed at the Mental Health Center before their hospital admission continue to be the ongoing responsibility of their community-based case manager throughout their hospital stay. Patients who are new to the system are provided with case management services by the Crisis Resolution Service until more definitive treatment can be arranged. The case manager stays actively involved with the patient, helps to develop a treatment and discharge plan, often is involved in family meetings or hospital staffings, and uses the time in the hospital to develop the clinical relatonship prior to discharge. As a result of these practices, patients in the hospital are not forgotten, and hospital stays are relatively brief.

We have found that some patients who require hospitalization can be stabilized in a very short period of time. A special crisis bed program has been developed for patients who we expect can be stabilized and discharged in less than 48 hours. These beds are physically located in the inpatient units of one of the private hospitals, but are administratively connected with the emergency room. This permits very rapid and easy admissions and discharges without the need for all the paperwork of a full hospital admission. Often, this allows a patient to be held overnight while medication is started, until an emergency family meeting can be arranged, or just provide supervised time until the immediate crisis situation can cool off. These very brief admissions are typically used for patients whom the Mental Health Center staff already know, and who have received a medical work-up in the past. Patients admitted to a crisis bed have a treatment plan marked off in hours instead of in days, and the entire staff is aware that a further treatment decision must be made before the end of the 48-hour period. Patients requiring hospitalization past the 48-hour period can have their status transferred to a regular bed on the same psychiatric unit, but this is required only rarely.

Vocational services

Dane County provides a wide variety of opportunities for vocational services. The county has two sheltered workshops, and one-third to one half of the client population at each workshop are chronically mentally ill persons. Increasingly, however, vocational programs have been arranged to help provide psychosocial support so that patients can maintain real jobs in the community. These have included a variety of transitional employment and supported employment programs. Transitional employment programs (TEP) find jobs that are 'owned' by some part of the mental health system. That is, a component of the mental health system becomes the employee and has the responsibility to make sure the job gets done. Mental health staff first learn and if necessary initially work the job and then become 'job coaches', going on-site to train the patient and provide whatever support is needed. TEPs all pay at least minimum wage. They are designed so that patients hold the jobs for a transition, usually three to six months, before rotating to another transitional job or finally obtaining a permanent job in the community (48).

Supported employment is different from transitional employment in that it is designed for patients who are not able to keep up the pace of a fully competitive job (49 – 51). Special arrangements have been made to allow people in these slots to be paid based on their productivity, even if that is less than minimum wage. There is no time limit for patients in supported employment, and while some patients are ready to move on after a few months, most stay on the same jobs for long periods of time. Together, these options allow people who have never held a job before, or who have not held a job for many years, to successfully enter the community workforce and be paid for it. Prevocational resources are also available, including an innovative program that helps chronically mentally ill persons to find and keep volunteer jobs in the community (52).

Living arrangements

The vast majority of the 1,500 chronically mentally ill persons in Dane County between the ages of 18 and 65 live in independent settings. Approximately 300 of them receive specialized help with their living arrangements. The type of help ranges across a very broad continuum, consistent with our philosophy of trying to supply what is needed, but not more nor less. At the most supportive end is a small number of patients – approximately 65 – in highly structured group homes or halfway houses with twenty-four-hour staff supervision. Another 50 patients live in adult foster homes, where one or two patients live with a family. Approximately 175 patients live in cooperative apartment projects or scattered-site supported apartments, where clients live independently with off-site staff support. Staff are available to help patients find apartments, find room-mates, budget money, and help with shopping, cooking, cleaning and other necessities of apartment life. A special budget makes it possible to lend patients enough money for a security deposit when necessary. Staff also monitor how well patients are doing so that any problems with the living situation can be corrected, if possible before they lead to eviction or to psychiatric decompensation. Another 200 patients have similar home visiting services provided by their case managers. The rest of the chronically mentally ill population live in their own apartments of with their families with less need for regular in-home support (53).

The support and training that the staff provide to each patient who need supported housing are provided in the patient's own living unit, which is consistent with our philosophy of providing in vivo services. Our experience in Dane County demonstrates that most chronically mentally ill patients can live independently if they are provided with appropriate support services. We have found that it is very difficult to predict a priori which patients will be able to thrive in their own apartments. Even very ill patients should be given a chance in a more independent setting before a group home is assumed to be required. Many patients with major disabilities actually do better in their own apartments with outside staff support than they do in more traditional group homes, probably because there are fewer rules, they have more control of space, and more autonomy. In Dane County, patients may remain in supported living arrangements for as long as they need. While some patients only stay in a group home or a supported apartment for a few months before moving on to a more independent setting, many others in the same supported living situation may stay for years.

In addition to long-term supported housing, we have also developed short-term crisis residential options that we can use as an alternative to hospitalization, or that can allow us safely to discharge patients from hospital sooner than if they had to return directly to an unsupervised apartment or problematic home situation.

These crisis foster homes are run by foster parents who are specially selected and trained by the Crisis Resolution Unit staff. Foster parents have a contract to take patients referred by the Crisis Resolution Unit into their homes for a period of up to two weeks. When a patient is staying in a crisis foster home, the Crisis Resolution Unit staff consult daily with the foster parents on the status and management of the patient (54, 55).

Coordination of services

Every mental health system has some patients who tend to fall through the cracks. They are patients who do not fit well into any existing programs, and they are often difficult to work with for any of a large number of reasons. For example, they may have a problem with substance abuse, histories of violence or other forms of acting-out toward themselves or others, difficult personality disorders, to name just a few. At the Mental Health Center of Dane County, an intake Committee is responsible for coordinating the treatment of these difficult-to-treat patients by assigning them to one or more program units of the Mental Health Center. The managers of the various programs and the Medical Director of the Center sit on this committee.

New patients are often presented to the Intake Committee by the manager of the Crisis Resolution Service, which is initially responsible for their care. New patients are usually stabilized, by the Crisis Unit staff before they are brought to the Committee for transfer to one or more of the center's ongoing programs. There is generally some discussion about where the patient best fits, based on the patient characteristics for selection of services outlined earlier in this chapter. The Committee addresses questions such as the needs of the patient, the goals of treatment for the patient, and the ways that services can be organized to meet these goals. If the patient's needs fall on the border between two services, he is usually assigned to the less intense service on a trial basis. If the patient begins to show signs that he or she cannot live in the community with the support of the less intense service, he is transferred to the more intensive service.

The Committee also discusses transfers of patients already within the system. For example, the manager of the MCT program may present a patient who, she feels, is now sufficiently stable to begin to work with the Support Network psychosocial program, which is a less intensive service. Eventually, after a connection is firmly in place, the case management responsibility for that patient may also be transferred from MCT to Support Network, although this may take months or even years. Likewise, a patient in the Support Network program may be presented for transfer to the MCT program because the patient's condition has worsened, and the patient thus requires more intensive services and assertive outreach. If there are disagreements within the staff of any program about the appropriateness of a patient for that program, the intake Committee makes the final decision about the assignment. It is common for patients to receive service from two or more programs. In cases of such shared treatment plans, it becomes crucial to have a clear understanding of who is responsible for what. In our system, every patient has a case manager or case management team that is responsible for planning, coordinating and assessing that patient's treatment. These case managers are clinicians who know the patient well and continue to be clinically involved with the patient. We use team case management for the most unstable and difficult patients, and individual case management for the more stable patients.

Coordinating services through the Intake Committee has worked very well. Services are cooperative with one another, primarily because their willingness to help out is repaid when other services show a willingness to be helpful to them.

Budget strategies

Limited resources cannot support both a large hospital population and a comprehensive system of community-based services. Fortunately, having a comprehensive system of community services dramatically reduces the need to use the hospital and produces a superior long-term clinical result (56). The system of care in Dane County, which is responsive to those in the community who are in greatest need, could not have been developed if mechanisms for controlling inpatient costs were not available. In the United States, 70% of public mental health expenditure supports hospital services, while only 30% is left for community services, although the community is where the vast majority of the patients reside (57). In sharp contrast, in Dane County, 17% supports inpatient care, while 83% supports community-based services (58). From our experience, one could argue that there is already enough money in the national system to provide good care, if only that money were distributed more rationally.

Most public mental health systems in the United States utilize separate budgets for community-based programs and hospital-based programs. Such traditional funding strategies reinforce the separateness of inpatient and community-based services and allow them to remain, at best, only loosely connected systems. In addition, separate budgets inevitably lead to conflict between inpatient and community programs, with each part of the system fighting for a larger share of the available resources. The consequence is that there are no fiscal incentives to provide or develop less expensive clinical alternatives to hospital care, even if they are more clinically desirable. For example, a community-based program may find that they could stabilize a patient if they could provide extra staff to work overtime with a patient in his home, thus avoiding displacing the patient and also saving the cost of an expensive hospitalization. Likewise, developing a crisis residential home might decrease the need to hospitalize some patients. But, in both cases, the money saved by this decreased hospital utilization is not passed back to the community program; the money to fund these interventions may not be available, and the fiscal incentives to create them in the first place are lacking. In fact, with separate budgets, the incentives are in the opposite direction. Trying to keep the patient in the community is expensive in terms of staff time and energy, but hospitalizing the patient is 'free' in terms of the community's budget. In turn, the hospital administrator fights to keep his budget intact, feeling that the money is needed to take care of all of the patients requiring hospital services. Because of increasing readmissions, the hospital finds more and more pressure for its services. Hospital administrators find it difficult to support community-based services at the expense of their own budgets, especially when even more hospital beds are required to relieve overcrowding caused by the inadequate community treatment. Unfortunately, as noted above, the inability to shift resources from the hospital to the communities prevents the community from developing programs and coordinated treatment systems that would allow a decrease in hospital utilization.

In Wisconsin, the budgeting strategy is different in a crucial way. Instead of two independent mental health budgets, one for inpatient and one for community-based services, that compete for funds, there is one mental health budget. In each county, a county mental health board receives all of the money available from state, county and federal sources for providing mental health services. This board also carries all the responsibility for providing both inpatient and community-based mental health services to residents of the county. For example, Dane County contracts for services with a wide range of community-based providers, placing emphasis on community based services for the chronically mentally ill population and for persons in crisis. The dollar literally follows the patient: if an indigent patient is hospitalized in any hospital, including the state hospital, the county pays the bill. If hospitalization can be avoided, the county keeps the money that was saved and uses it to further enrich community programs. In addition, Dane County plans budgets for inpatient costs on the basis of the previous year's usage. If inpatient costs exceed the budgeted amount, then community program budgets for the following year must be cut to pay for the higher inpatient costs (59).

These strategies are facilitated by Dane County's practice of contracting for most services rather than providing services directly. The service providers are mostly non-profit agencies, not county agencies, and thus are not encumbered by civil service regulations. Staff positions at those agencies depend on the agencies doing their job well. Everyone working in these community agencies is acutely aware that, if the hospital is not used wisely, the inpatient bill will go up, agency budgets will be cut, and jobs will be lost. This provides a real incentive to work with many very difficult patients, rather than extruding them from the system through long-term hospitalization. In Dane County, there is an average of 50 county-funded patients between 18 and 65 in the hospital at any given time. About 15 of these patients are in an acute unit at one of the private hospitals or at the state hospital, and about 35 are in a long-term unit at the county hospital. For a population of 340,000 people, this very low hospital utilization is only possible because of the comprehensiveness of the community services, which results in keeping patients stable. Because the need to use hospital-based services varies inversely with the comprehensiveness of community-based services, the emphasis on community-based care is self-reinforcing.

The county uses two mechanisms to keep hospital costs at an appropriate level and ensure sufficient funds for comprehensive community-based treatment: gatekeeping hospital admissions, and controlling the length of stay. The Crisis Resolution Service has been authorized by the county mental health board to screen all requests for hospitalization of patients whose treatment costs would be borne by the county, and to authorize or withhold payment for inpatient care. If the Crisis Resolution Service staff believe that hospitalization is appropriate, they will authorize payment for hospital and professional fees for a specific number of days. The Service staff then monitor the progress of the hospital treatment. They work closely on treatment and discharge planning with the permanent case manager and the hospital staff to assure that the hospital stay is no longer than necessary. If the Service staff believe that hospitalization is not necessary, the Service assumes part or all of the clinical responsibility for the treatment in the community. Over the past five years, the Crisis Resolution Service has averted approximately 75% of potential hospital admissions.

Involuntary treatment and commitment legislation

Involuntary mental health commitment has gone through a number of cycles over the years. Until fairly recently, the civil rights of persons labeled as mentally ill were abrogated to the point that almost anyone deemed 'in need of treatment' could have that treatment forced upon him. In the 1970s, beginning with the cases of Lessard vs. Schmidt, and O'Connor vs. Donaldson, the pendulum swung back to allow mental health commitment only if the person were not only mentally ill and a fit subject for treatment, but also clearly and imminently dangerous to either himself or someone else (60). In all cases, however, it was assumed that commitment would be to a hospital. The hospital was the central locus of treatment – patients went into the hospital when they were ill and needed treatment and were discharged when that treatment was completed. Unfortunately, what really happened is that patients were committed to the hospital, stabilized on medication and then released to inadequate care in the community where they received insufficient support for either psychological or instrumental needs. The result was frequent relapse, rehospitalization and the development of the revolving-door syndrome.

With the change of the primary locus of treatment from the hospital to the community, there needed to be changes as well in involuntary treatment. In Wisconsin, the commitment laws were changed at the same time that the legislation to establish the county mental health boards was passed. Commitment is no longer to a hospital, but rather to the county boards who then decide where treatment should take place. Because the grounds for involuntary treatment are very limited in Wisconsin and require mental illness plus imminent dangerousness, most people treated involuntarily initially require the structure and security of the hospital. Commitment can last up to six months, and in some cases may be extended through an additional court hearing. In Dane County, we find it is usually possible to keep the period of acute hospitalization very short, usually under two weeks, even with committed patients. Following discharge, the patient continues to be under commitment, only the locus of treatment changes from the hospital to the Mental Health Center. Often the commitment order requires the person to come into the center at regular intervals and continue on medication. If the person does not follow this order, the court can issue an order to the police, who help with enforcement. The enforcement may require that the person return to the hospital, but this is very unusual. More commonly, the very presence of the commitment order is enough for the patient to stay in treatment. In rare cases, the police may be required to bring a patient into the mental health center to forcibly receive medication. This is uncomfortable for all concerned, both patient and staff, but it happens infrequently and is in fact no different from the kind of coercion that is regularly applied within the hospital.

In states where commitment is only to a hospital, people have been repeatedly committed and hospitalized, but have never achieved any stability in the community. We find that when commitment is extended into the community, some patients can stabilize their lives for the first time. For example, Susan was a woman in her thirties who had lived through a cycle of repeated commitments and stabilizations for years. Between hospitalizations, she would be evicted from one apartment after another, until finally she would end up on the street immediately prior to the next commitment. She responded well to medication in the hospital but absolutely refused to take it after discharge. When she was committed under the new statute, she was discharged from the hospital after 20 days. However, she was told that if she refused to come in for medication as ordered by the court the police would pick her up and bring her in to the Mental Health Center. She was given the choice of coming in every day to have medication supervised by staff, or to come in every two weeks to have the medication given as a long-acting injection. At the same time, the staff from the MCT program helped her obtain an apartment with a room-mate and a volunteer job. With her new stability and the help of the MCT staff, she re-established connections with her family and began going home for dinner for the first time in many years. Throughout this time, she came in for medication every day, always promising that the day that her commitment expired she would never take it again. By the time her commitment expired, she had a nice apartment, a circle of friends and activities, a friendly relationship with her family, and a reason to want to prevent yet another relapse. Without ever explicitly talking about it or promising to stay on the medication, both she and the staff continued the working relationship, medications and all, even after the commitment expired.

A number of writers have been concerned with the special civil rights issues associated with community commitment laws. Specifically, they fear that judges may be more willing to commit someone to community treatment than to hospital treatment and that the availability of community commitment statutes might increase the number of people committed (61 – 64). We share this concern. We feel that the civil rights of people who are mentally ill must be protected, and that the laws governing community commitment should be the same as those governing any other kind of involuntary treatment. In fact, as noted above, in Wisconsin there is no separation of hospital and community commitment – there is only commitment, and it is then up to the clinicians and the county mental health board to determine the least restrictive place of treatment if the court finds that commitment is necessary. In the Wisconsin system, the availability of community-based involuntary treatment increases, rather than decreases, the civil rights of patients. In addition, the law establishes commitment to a system of care. Commitment either to a hospital or to outpatient treatment alone supports the fragmentation of care between hospital and community, rather than integrating it.

There has also been some discussion in the literature about whether involuntary community treatment laws are effective in helping patients live stably in the community. The two available research studies (65, 66) have suggested that such laws are not very useful. However, both studies were done in areas where effective community support was not available. It seems unreasonable to expect that treatment in the community would be effective if community treatment programs were absent or inadequate. Our own experience is that, when we must resort to involuntary treatment, the ability to continue treating through the first few months of community tenure allows many people to achieve community stability who could not achieve it in any other way. This is not to say that commitment, either to the hospital or to the community, is needed that often. The more community options there are available, the less often the clinical staff is forced to become coercive.

Conclusion

Medical training pays lip service to the ideal of 'treating the whole person', and no one would disagree that patients benefit from such an approach. Sadly, treating the whole person is the exception rather than the rule. Fortunately for patients suffering from most diseases, the more limited approach, although not ideal, does not lead immediately to catastrophic consequences. Not so with schizophrenia: there are few other diseases that show such a clear relationship between the disease's clinical picture and biological, psychological and social factors. When any of these is neglected, the patient is very apt to experience a relapse into psychosis.

Treating the whole person with schizophrenia is what we have discussed in this chapter. To do this requires having services available that attend to the wide range of patient's needs, and organizing them into a comprehensive and integrated system of care. We have developed such a system in Dane County, and the results have been highly gratifying. Of the approximately 1,500 identified chronic mentally ill persons in the county, the great majority live in high quality, independent settings. Case management is assertive, and few people are lost to treatment. As a result, patients remain stable most of the time, and hospitalization rates in Dane County have been dropping for the past several years, whereas hospitalization rates have been increasing in the United States as a whole. In addition, length of hospital stay is short, and use of involuntary treatment is relatively low. Finally, and very importantly, Dane County has used a rational funding mechanisms to facilitate the provision of a range of programs that vary in intensity, and thus in cost. This has allowed Dane County to provide cost-effective services that support a reasonable quality of life for its citizens with schizophrenia.

REFERENCES

1. Bassuk E, Gerson S (1978) Deinstitutionalization and mental health services. *Sci. Am., 238,* 46.
2. Kirk SA, Therrien ME (1975) Community mental health myths and the fate of former hospitalized patients. *Psychiatry, 38,* 209.
3. Allen P (1974) A consumers view of California's mental health care system. *Psychiatr. Q., 48,* 1.
4. Talbott JA (1988) The chronic mentally ill: what do we know and why aren't we implementing what we know? *New Dir. Ment. Serv., 37,* 43 – 58.
5. Mechanic D, Aiken LH (1987) Improving the care of patients with chronic mental ill ness. *New Engl. J. Med., 317,* 1634.
6. Mosher LR (1983) Alternatives to psychiatry hospitalization: why has research failed to be translated into practice? *New Engl. J. Med., 309,* 1579.
7. Peterson R (1978) What are the needs of chronic mental patients? In: Talbott JA (Ed.), *The Chronic Mental Patient,* pp. 39 – 49. American Psychiatric Association, Washington, DC.
8. Talbott JA (1984) The chronic mental patient: a national perspective. In: Mirabi M (Ed.), *The Chronically Mentally Ill: Research and Services,* p. 3. Spectrum Publications, New York.
9. Goldman HH, Adams NH, Taube CA (1983) Deinstitutionalization: the data demythologized. *Hosp. Community Psychiatry, 34,* 129.
10. Bachrach LL (1984) Principles of planning for chronic psychiatric patients: a synthesis. In: Talbot JA (Ed.), *The Chronic Mental Patient: Five Years Later,* pp. 165 – 182. Grune & Stratton, New York.
11. Test MA, Stein LI (1976) Practical guidelines for the community treatment of markedly impaired patients. *Community Ment. Health J., 12,* 72.
12. Harris M, Bergman HC (1987) Differential treatment planning for young adult chronic patients. *Hosp. Community Psychiatry, 38,* 638.
13. Anthony WA (1979) The rehabilitation approach to diagnosis. *New Dir. Ment. Health Serv., 2,* 25.
14. Freddolino PP, Moxley DP, Fleishman JA (1988) Daily living needs at time of discharge: implications for advocacy. *Psychosocial Rehab. J., 11/4,* 33.
15. Liberman RP (1982) Assessment of social skills. *Schizophr. Bull., 8,* 62.
16. Straus JS, Glazer W (1982) Treatment of the so-called chronically psychiatrically ill. In: Masserman J (Ed.), *Current Psychiatric Therapies,* pp. 207 – 217. Grune & Stratton, New York.
17. Diamond R (1983) Enhancing medication use in schizophrenic patients. *J. Clin. Psychiatry, 44/2,* 7.
18. Wilson W, Diamond RJ, Factor RM (1985) A psychotherapeutic approach to task-oriented groups of severely ill patients. *Yale J. Biol. Med., 58,* 363.
19. Stein LI, Diamond RJ (1985) The chronic mentally ill and the criminal justice system: when to call the police. *Hosp. Community Psychiatry, 36,* 271.
20. Mendel WM, Rapport S (1969) Determinants of the decision for psychiatric hospitalization. *Arch. Gen. Psychiatry, 20,* 321.
21. Cohen CI (1980) Crime among mental patients: a critical analysis. *Psychiatr. Q., 52,* 100.
22. Steadman HJ (1981) Critically reassessing the accuracy of public perceptions of the dangerousness of the mentally ill. *J. Health Soc. Behav., 22,* 310.
23. Teplin LA (1984) Criminalizing mental disorder: the comparative arrest rate of the men-

tally ill. *Am. Psychol., 39,* 794.
24. Test MA (1979) Continuity of care in community treatment. *New Dir. Ment. Health Serv., 2,* 15 – 23.
25. Bachrach LL (1981) Continuity of care for chronic mental patients: a conceptual analysis. *Am. J. Psychiatry, 138,* 1449.
26. Test MA (1981) Effective community treatment of the chronically mentally ill: what is necessary? *J. Soc. Issues, 37,* 71.
27. Lidz T et al. (1958) Intrafamilial environment of the schizophrenic patient, VI. The transmission of irrationality. *Am. Med. Assoc. Arch. Neurol. Psychiatry, 79,* 305.
28. Hatfield AB, Fierstein R, Johnson DM (1982) Meeting the needs of families of the psychiatrically disabled. *Psychosoc. Rehabil. J., 6,* 27.
29. Bernheim KF, Switalski T (1988) Mental health staff and patient's relatives: how they view each other. *Hosp. Community Psychiatry, 39,* 63.
30. Marx AJ, Test MA, Stein LI (1973) Extrahospital management of severe mental illness: Feasibility and effects of social functioning. *Arch. Gen. Psychiatry, 29,* 505.
31. Greenley J (1986) Social control and expressed emotion. *J. Nerv. Ment. Dis., 174,* 24.
32. Leff JP, Vaughn C (1985) Expressed emotion in families: its significance for mental ill ness. Guilford Press, New York.
33. Anderson CM, Reiss DJ, Hogarty GE (1986) Schizophrenia and the family. Guilford Press, New York.
34. Bernheim KF, Lehman AF (1985) Working with families of the mentally ill. W.W. Norton, New York.
35. Bachrach LL (1981) Discussion: the role of model programs in the care of chronic mental patients. In: Talbott JA (Ed.), *The Chronic Mentally Ill,* pp. 300 – 314. Human Sciences Press, New York.
36. Torrey EF, Wolfe SM (1986) *Care of the seriously mentally ill: a rating of state programs.* Public Citizen Health Research Group, Washington, DC.
37. Factor RM, Stein LI (1986) An empirical typology of the chronically mentally ill: a commentary. *Community Ment. Health J., 22,* 25.
38. Mariotto MJ, Gordon IP (1984) The utility of assessment for different purposes. In: Mirabi, M (Ed.), *The Chronically Mentally Ill. Research and Services,* p. 73. Spectrum Publications, Jamaica NY.
39. Cesnik B, Puls M (1977) Law enforcement and crisis intervention services: a critical relationship. *Suicide Life-Threatening Behav., 7,* 211.
40. Cesnik B, Stevenson K (1979) Operating emergency sevices. *New Dir. Ment. Health Serv., 2,* 37.
41. Stein LI, Test MA (1980) Alternative to mental hospital treatment. *Arch. Gen. Psychiatry, 37,* 392.
42. Stein LI, Diamond R (1985) *New. Dir. Ment. Health Serv., 26,* 29.
43. Beard JH, Propst RN, Malamud TJ (1982) The Fountain House model of psychiatric rehabilitation. *Psychosoc. Rehabil. J., 5,* 47.
44. Backes R, Cohen J et al. (1987) Paper presented at the 12th Annual Conference on The Integration of Medical Services into the Fountain House Model. Toronto, Ontario, Canada.
45. Diamond RJ, Little M (1984) Utilization of patient expertise in medication groups. *Psychiatric. Q., 56,* 13.
46. Talbott AJ, Glick ID (1986) The inpatient care of the chronically mentally ill. *Schizophr. Bull., 12,* 129.
47. Diamond RJ (1979) The role of the hospital in treating the chronically disabled. *New Dir. Ment. Health Serv., 2,* 45.

48. Bond G, Dincin J (1986) Accelerating entry into transitional employment in a psychosocial rehabilitation agency. *Rehabil. Psychol., 31,* 143.
49. Anthony WA, Blanch A (1987) Supported employment for individuals who are psychiatrically disabled: an historical and conceptual perspective. *Psychosoc. Rehabil. J., 6,* 5.
50. Isbister F, Donaldson G (1987) Supported employment for individuals who are mentally ill. *Psychosoc. Rehabil. J., 11,* 45.
51. Bond G (1987) Supported work as a modification of the transitional employment model for clients with psychiatric disabilities. *Psychosoc. Rehabil. J., 11,* 55–73.
52. Keys L (1982) Former patients as volunteers in community agencies. A model work rehabilitation program. *Hosp. Community Psychiatry, 33,* 12.
53. Blanch AK, Carling PJ (1988) Normal housing with specialized supports: a psychiatric rehabilitation approach to living in the community. *Rehabil. Psychol., 33,* 47.
54. Polak PR (1978) A comprehensive system of alternatives to psychiatric hospitalization. In: Stein LI, Test MA (Eds.), *Alternatives to Mental Hospital Treatment,* p. 115. Plenum Press, New York.
55. Brook BD et al. (1976) Community families: an alternative to psychiatric hospital intensive care. *Hosp. Community Psychiatry, 27,* 195.
56. Stein LI, Test MA (1985) The evolution of the training in community living model. *New. Dir.Ment. Health Serv., 26,* 7.
57. Kiesler CA (1982) Public and professional myths about mental hospitalization. *Am. Psychol., 37,* 1323.
58. Stein LI, Ganser LJ (1983) Wisconsin's system for funding mental health services. *New Dir. Ment. Health Serv., 18,* 25.
59. Stein LI (1987) Funding a system of care for schizophrenia. *Psychiatr. Ann., 17,* 592.
60. Halleck SL (1980) *Law in the Practice of Psychiatry: A Handbook for Clinicians.* Plenum Medical Book Company, New York.
61. Mulvey EP, Geller JL, Roth LH (1987) The promise and peril of involuntary outpatient commitment. *Am. Psychol., 42,* 571.
62. Geller JL (1986) The quandaries of enforced community treatment and unenforceable outpatient commitment statutes. *J. Psychiatry Law.* Spring/Summer 1986, 149.
63. Geller JL (1987) Rights, wrongs and the dilemma of coerced community treatment. *Am. J. Psychiatry, 143,* 1259.
64. Schwartz SJ (1987) Compelling treatment in the community: distorted doctrines and violated values. *Loyola Los Angeles Rev., 20,* 1329.
65. Bursten B (1986) Posthospital mandatory outpatient treatment. *Am. J. Psychiatry, 143,* 1255.
66. Miller RD, Fiddleman PB (1984) Outpatient commitment: treatment in the least restrictive environment? *Hosp. Community Psychiatry, 35,* 147.

CHAPTER 12

Emergency room evaluation and management of schizophrenia

ANDREW EDMUND SLABY AND ROBERT MOREINES

Emergency room evaluation and treatment of schizophrenia entails recognition of signs and symptoms suggestive of the disorder, establishment of differential diagnosis to exclude illness which may present as schizophrenia but require a different therapeutic approach, management of the acute symptoms, and appropriate disposition for long-term care. Early recognition and treatment of a patient undergoing a schizophrenic decompensation reduces pain to patients and families and reduces or actually obviates need for hospitalization.

DIAGNOSIS

Diagnosis is based on history and constellation of symptoms. There are no pathogenetic or core symptoms despite early impressions of Bleuler and Schneider to the contrary (1). Gradual social withdrawal coupled with deterioration in school and gainful employment, family history, age of onset in adolescence or twenties, and symptoms discussed in the chapters on diagnosis *suggest*, but do not prove, schizophrenia. Patients may have a history of schizophrenia but been misdiagnosed and treated. The fact that some patients previously diagnosed as schizophrenic have been found to respond to lithium, valproic acid or carbamazepine raises ethical concerns regarding hasty assumptions and subsequent treatment with neuroleptics exposing the patients to the risk of tardive dyskinesia (1 – 7). Absence of response to conventional treatment in the past without a history of trials of other medications may indicate misdiagnosis. Flat affect is not always or exclusively seen with schizophrenia. Affect may, in fact, be blunted by neuroleptics.

Family history of affective illness does not mean that a patient is not schizophrenic. Greater lifetime prevalence of affective illness alone contributes to the higher observed incidence of affective illness in families of documented schizophrenics (8, 9). Schizophrenic patients have a family incidence of affective illness comparable to controls (i.e., approximately 7%) (8). A history of bipolar illness raises more doubts than unipolar illness, although affectively ill individuals with mood-incongruent delusions appear more frequently in families of schizophrenics (10).

Emergency room clinicians' suspicions should be heightened when patients present who have experienced a sudden switch from religious and political insouciance

Handbook of Schizophrenia, Volume 4: Psychosocial Treatment of Schizophrenia.
M.I. Herz, S.J. Keith and J.P. Docherty, editors.

to extreme philosophical and religious concern or overpassionate political zeal. Sexual interest may diminish or proliferate without regard to object. Auditory hallucinations are seen but any variety may occur. Command hallucinations are not necessarily a harbinger of violence (11), but they do increase risk if the voices dictate self- or other destructive behavior.

A well-documented course consistent with schizophrenia and history of a neuroleptic-responsive disorder does not mean that hypothyroidism, a hallucinogen or an antihypertensive medication, or seizure disorder is not prompting current symptoms and presentation.

Particular problems arise in diagnosis of the disease in blacks (12). White therapists, unfamiliar with norms among minority groups, overdiagnose the illness in blacks, other minorities, and low-income groups. Poverty, discrimination, and alienation from mainstream society causes a suspiciousness resembling paranoia. Reluctance to trust or form a positive therapeutic alliance in the emergency situation is misinterpreted as flattened affect or schizoid unrelatedness. Unfamiliar mannerisms may be seen as bizarre; unfamiliar language construed as a thought disorder. Styles of relating that are incongruent with predominant subcultural norms may be misinterpreted as affectual disturbance or as inappropriate.

Recent evidence suggests that what have historically been construed as negative symptoms (i.e. social withdrawal, anergy, disorientation, and blunted affect) respond selectively to clozapine. Negative symptoms are more frequently seen with neuronal loss, dilated cerebral ventricles (2, 13, 14) and frontal lobe dysfunction, raising the suspicion that ultimately this subtype of schizophrenia may be distinguished as a separate clinical entity from the form with positive symptoms and increased dopamine transmission. Identifying these symptom clusters and recommending diagnostic specific treatment has become more an emergency psychiatric task, as minimal hospitalization and community care models of management of schizophrenia evolve which utilize non-physician therapists. In this type of care, the ratio of psychopharmacological consultants to patients does not allow as intense an evaluation of a patient as can be accomplished in the emergency room with unmedicated patients. Diagnosis is important for predictive validity in medication, prognosis, social management and genetic counseling.

Differential diagnosis

Addison's disease
Adjustment disorder with mixed disturbance of emotions and conduct
AIDS
Alcohol hallucinosis
Alcohol idiosyncratic intoxication
Alzheimer's disease
Amphetamine or similarly acting sympathomimetic intoxication or delusional disorder
Arteriosclerotic brain disease
Atypical psychosis
Bipolar disorder
Brain stem/diencephalon neoplasm

Brief reactive psychosis
Cannabis intoxication or delusional disorder
Cimetidine intoxication
Cocaine intoxication or delusional disorder
Collagenosis
Cushing's disease
Delirium
Delusional disorder
Dysthymia
Electrolyte imbalance
Encephalitis
Frontal lobe neoplasm
Hallucinogen hallucinosis or delusional disorder
Heavy metal poisoning
Huntington's chorea
Hyperthyroidism
Hypothyioidism
Induced psychotic disorder
Inhalent intoxication
Major depression
Menningitis
Mental retardation
Migraine equivalent
Multi-infarct dementia
Multiple sclerosis
Obsessive-compulsive personality disorder
Opioid intoxication or withdrawal
Panhypopituitarism
Paranoid personality disorder
Periodic catatonia
Pernicious anemia
Phencyclidine or similarly arylcyolohexlamine, intoxication or delusional disorder
Pick's Disease
Schilder's disease
Schizoaffective disorder
Schizoid personality disorder
Schizophrenia, catatonic
Schizophrenia, disorganized
Schizophrenia, paranoid
Schizophrenia, undifferentiated
Schizophreniform disorder
Schizotypal personality disorder
Sedative, hypnotic, or anxiolytic intoxication or withdrawal
Steroid intoxication and withdrawal
Subdural hematoma
Syphilis
Temporal lobe epilepsy
Temporal lobe neoplasm
Traumatic brain damage

Withdrawal delirium
Subdural hematoma

MANAGEMENT

After it has been reasonably determined that schizophreniform symptoms are due to schizophrenia or schizoaffective disorder, therapeutic interventions specific to the acute management of schizophrenia are initiated. It is imperative to maintain an agnostic stance as to the absolute certainty of diagnosis. Mimics and concurrent illness may only with time provide what is required for the validation of diagnosis. Ironically, psychopharmacotherapy may contribute to obfuscating a non-schizophrenic illness by its attendant impact on affect, thought, and motor function.

Psychopharmacotherapy

Historically, the approach to the management of an acute exacerbation of schizophrenia has been rapid tranquilization with neuroleptics. While this is effective and relatively safe in most cases, it exposes patients to the risk of tardive dyskinesia. Recent trends include lower-dose antipsychotics, neuroleptics combined with benzodiazepines and the use of droperidol or propranalol, particularly with violent patients. Psychopharmacotherapy is initiated only after medical mimics of schizophrenia have been reasonably ruled out, and proper precautions have been taken to protect patient, staff, and other patients from the presumed schizophrenic's danger to self or others when present.

Neuroleptics

Rapid neuroleptization has historically been the approach to management of schizophrenia in the emergency situation after medical mimics have been ruled out and an evaluation has been made to ascertain if hospitalization is required because the patient is an immediate danger to self or others or because social supports are insufficient to assure compliance with initial treatment on an outpatient basis. High-potency low-dosage antipsychotics are given every half hour to hour while monitoring blood pressure, heart rate, degree of sedation, and extrapyramidal side effects. Frequent choices are haloperidol, thiothixene, fluphenazine, perphenazine and trifluoperazine. If haloperidol or thiothixene are chosen, 5 – 10 mg is given orally or intramuscularly every half hour or hour for 5 – 6 hours. Doses in excess of 100 mg have been given. Thioridazine may be used in tablet or liquid form with a cooperative patient requiring sedation in addition to the antipsychotic effect. Doses in excess of 800 mg are dangerous, due to ocular side-effects. Both thioridazine and chlorpromazine are associated with anticholinergic side-effects, including psychosis and severe hypotension which may further complicate treatment. Increased temperature and muscular rigidity may herald the malignant neuroleptic syndrome even in the acute situation. Concurrent use of diphenhydramine (Benadryl) or 1 – 2 mg of benztropine mesylate (Cogentin) given intramuscularly or orally will reduce the likelihood of akasthisia and dystonic reactions, but are themselves anticholinergic and are associated with constipation, dry mouth and blurred vision. There is no significant increase in onset of action when benztropine is given intravenously (5). If there is no improvement after six hours, the patient will need to be hospitalized.

Risk associated with higher doses of neuroleptics has led to modification of the the technique of rapid tranquilization (15). Doses higher than the equivalent of 10 – 20 mg of haloperidol are thought to be without advantage and are associated with increased extrapyramidal side-effects. Repeated small doses intramuscularily, with target goals such as amelioration of agitation or compliance with oral medication, are recommended. Augmentation with benzodiazepines reduces the need for larger doses of neuroleptics. No antipsychotic has been demonstrated to have specific advantage for any subtype of schizophrenia. A maintenance dosage equivalent to 300 mg of chlorpromazine is recommended. ECT or carbamazepine may be required for violent patients.

Exacerbations of chronic schizophrenia require less medication than those initially medicated. Ten to twenty milligrams of haloperidol, thiothixene, fluphenazine or trifluoperazine or 100 to 200 of chlorpromazine or thioridazine may be sufficient to ameliorate symptoms. If oral medication is refused, parenteral medication should be given. Additional medication is required for sleep during an acute episode. One hundred milligrams of chlorpromazine or thioridazine or 10 mg or perphenazine, thiothixine, fluphenazine, haloperidol or trifluoperazine per hour until asleep can be given. Medication should be continually re-evaluated during the acute phase until an appropriate dose is achieved, at which time divided doses may be given during the day and at bed-time. Eventually, all medication may be given at bed-time. A benzodiazephine may be added for panic or anticipatory anxiety.

Long-acting haloperidol or fluphenazine should be considered if a patient is unreliable and cessation of medication results in re-hospitalization. Generally, a dose is given every two weeks. If a patient is given this in an emergency situation and he/she has not had it before, a test dose of 1/10 cc. should be given subcutaneously while monitoring blood pressure and general response. This is to test for allergy to fluphenazine as well as the vehicle (i.e., decanoate or enanthate) and the sesame seed oil base. If there is no indication of sensitivity after half an hour, the calculated dose (usually between 25 – 75 mg) is given subcutaneously or intramuscularly.

High-potency neuroleptics, while better tolerated with less extrapyramidal symptoms at low doses may be effective but require longer to work (two weeks vs. one week) (16). Patients maintained on low-dose neuroleptics (e.g., 5 mg vs. 25 mg) of fluphenazine decanoate every 2 weeks have a greater incidence of symptomatic exacerbation (especially during the second year of treatment) which may be managed by temporarily increasing the dosage. High-potency neuroleptics are acutely tolerated in higher doses in the acute situation, but over time do not show a significantly greater response rate. A selected group may respond to megadoses (17, 18).

Choice of neuroleptics is based on patients' known sensitivity to adverse effects, side-effect profiles, and therapeutic response to a particular drug (17, 18). Sedating antipsychotics are recommended for agitated patients and non-sedating drugs for withdrawn patients. The full impact of antipsychotic medication is usually not seen for 4 – 6 weeks. Studies of serum levels are difficult to interpret, given the heterogeneity of patient population and the number of metabolites of many of the drugs. This is compounded by the length of stay on drugs and interaction with other drugs altering absorption or metabolism. A therapeutic window may exist for haloperidol. Low neuroleptic serum levels on standard doses suggest need for megadoses. Concomitant use of anti-Parkinson agents leads to some decrease in blood levels of neuroleptics.

Elderly schizophrenics are particularly prone to developing Parkinsonian symptoms (e.g., drooling, rigidity, resting tremor, mask-line faces and bradykinesia) and are at increased risk for tardive dyskinesia on neuroleptics if treatment is prolonged (19). Low-potency neuroleptics such as chlopromazine and thioridazine (and its injectable analogue mesoridazine) have the lowest incidence of extrapyramidal side effects, but orthostatic hypotension, sedation and anticholinergic effects will be prominent in older people (20). Photosensitivity is seen in 3% of elderly patients treated with chlorpromazine (19). Initial tranquilization with small doses reduces risk in this group. Side-effects in the acute situation, such as sedation, urinary hesitancy and retention, impaired bowel motility, visual problems, and dry mouth leading to ulcers and poorly fitting dentures is seen in greater frequency with older patients (20). Salzman (21) reviewed 60 studies with a total of 5,000 elderly patients and found that neuroleptics have a consistent, modest therapeutic effect. There is no superiority of any one class of antipsychotics in treating this group. Sedation causes older patients to become confused and thereby increases agitation. Falls and serious injury result from syncope due to orthostatic hypotension. Tardive dyskinesia and other abnormal involuntary movements are more common in older people. Low-potency neuroleptics contribute to sedation and orthostatic hypothesion; high-potency drugs to extrapyramidal side-effects. Older people should receive 0.25 mg of haloperidol or thiothixene or 10 mg of thioridazine four times a day mixed with orange juice. Trazadone, 200 – 400 mg, has been used for treating agitated behavior with organic brain syndromes with minimal side-effects (e.g., sedation and gastrointestinal discomfort), and serves to calm older agitated schizophrenics. Thioridazine causes retinopathy at doses above 800 mg/day, and of all neuroleptics it is the most likely to cause impotence and retarded ejaculation. Loxapine is reported to have a more rapid onset of tranquilization (60 vs. 95 min) when given intramuscularly than thiothixene, with the same clinical improvement (22). No difference was found on oral administration. Side-effects are minimal with intramuscular use. Dystonia is the most common adverse effect with oral use. Thiothixene is equipotent to haloperidol and is associated with fewer extrapyramidal complications.

In all instances of rapid neuroleptization, use of, choice of, and dose of neuroleptics is contingent upon the identification of target symptoms and awareness of the specific side-effects one wishes to avoid, given the patient's age and medical condition (23). The least amount required to suppress symptoms is given after discussing, where possible, with patient and family, the expected side-effects, to help forge a therapeutic alliance, ensure compliance, and reduce fear that a side-effect such as akasthisia may represent evolving psychosis. Early intervention with targeted pharmacotherapy can minimize subsequent problems of institutionalization, long-term substantial-dose neuroleptic exposure, undesirable interaction between drugs and negative symptoms of schizophrenia, masking of diagnostic indicators, and iatrogenic increase in positive symptoms of schizophrenia (24). Skilful use of psychosocial supports and environmental engineering facilitates functioning with minimal use of pharmacotherapy at times of crisis and little or no use interepisodically. The targeted approach entails early detection of warning or prodromal signs so that minimal psychopharmacotherapy is used with least restrictive care settings. Early treatment in the course of an acute episode serves to avoid the need for hospitalization.

The role of clozapine in the acute situation has yet to be determined. This drug, widely used in Europe and the Orient, has only recently become available in the United States. There are no reports of tardive dyskenesia with it (19).

Neuroleptic malignant syndrome. Neuroleptic-induced catatonia and the neuroleptic malignant syndrome (NMS) are relatively rare side-effects of neuroleptic use seen in the emergency situation. The catatonic state accompanied by immobilizing muscle rigidity and catatonic stupor and muscle rigidity with NMS may be mistaken for an acute episode of schizophrenia. Amantadine (100 – 200 mg/day), bromocriptine, or L-dopa are used to treat neuroleptic-induced catatonia (19). Hyperthermia, tachycardia, diaphoresis, associated extrapyramidal signs and blood pressure instability, coupled with increased serum creatine phosphokinase, confirm diagnosis. Further use of neuroleptics aggravates the condition, with a reported mortality of 20 – 25% in severe cases. Death results from pulmonary complications and acute renal failure due to muscle breakdown. This syndrome can last for weeks after cessation of neuroleptic treatment and is most commonly seen with neuroleptics with high dopamine-blocking activity, such as fluphenazine or haloperidol. Pre-existing brain disease and febrile illness contribute to its development (19). The dopamine agonist bromocriptine (2.5 – 10 mg orally every 8 h) and dantrolene sodium (1.25 – 1.5 mg/kg intravenously or 50 mg every 12 h orally) are effective treatments in many cases.

The use of neuroleptics in the acute situation should be restricted to those instances in which efficacy is clearly documented (25). Emergency psychiatrists should be aware that, just as diagnosis arrived at in the emergency setting may be carried without further evaluation or question by physician and non-physician chronic care givers, so too maintenance therapy may continue for years after the emergency contact, using the drug prescribed in the emergency room at the dose given. Obviously, anyone who writes prescriptions should continue to query the need for a neuroleptic and monitor onset of tardive dyskinesia, agranulocytosis, neuroleptic-induced catatonia, and NMS, but this is often not so in practice. The emergency psychiatrist cannot and must not assume that the visit is the first stage of continuing evaluation and quality care unless he/she has guaranteed to the best possibility that quality care will be provided by the agency or person to whom the patient is referred.

Droperidol. Droperidol is a safe butyrophenone neuroleptic, structurally and pharmacologically related to haloperidol, but with a more rapid onset when given intramuscularly, a shorter duration of effect, and a lower incidence of extrapyramidal symptoms. Sedation is somewhat greater (26, 27). Five milligrams of the drug intramuscularly is considered rapid and reliable for acute agitation. Because it lacks the pronounced cardiovascular effects of some phenothiazines, it is widely used in Europe. In America, its sedative and antiemetic properties have contributed to its use in anesthesia. It is particularly good when the aim is to control violence. Rapid control is achieved, with reduction of tension, anxiety, bizarre behavior, hostility and excitement, with only mild sedation. The onset of action is usually within 5 minutes. The recommended dosage is up to 10 mg intravenously or intramuscularly. Even with 10–20 mg little orthostatic hypotension or extrapyramidal side-effects are seen. Essentially no side-effects are seen in most cases, with the majority of combative schizophrenic patients sedated in 15 minutes with 10 mg or less (27).

Lithium

Neuroleptics are the mainstay of treatment of acute schizophrenic episodes, but a number of other drugs have roles. Lithium is of value in management when onset or exacerbations are acute and course is remitting, regardless of acute psychotic symptoms (28). Lithium is felt to augment neuroleptic potency, thereby obtaining effect at lower doses. Increased use of lithium over the past decade has resulted in an increase in diagnoses of mania and a decrease in diagnoses of paranoid schizophrenia for both first and re-admissions (29). Treatment response is a critical element in data on which diagnosis is based. Lithium has been found to be helpful alone and in concert with neuroleptics, but has limited value in most emergencies (30). It appears most effective when onset is acute, premorbid functioning is good, and psychotic excitement and irritability is present but response is difficult to predict. In some instances a worsening of symptoms may occur and cause presentation in the emergency room. In these instances a toxic confusional syndrome may be mistaken for a worsening of initial symptoms or an exacerbation of an ongoing process. It is particularly important in managing schizoaffective illness along with neuroleptics, although it has been used successfully alone for what often appear to be poor prognostic subtypes (30).

Benzodiazepines

Benzodiazepines in general, and lorazepam, clonazepam, and alprazolam in particular, have been found to be efficacious in management of agitation, combative behavior, and mania seen in acute schizophrenic episodes, thereby reducing the amount required of, or totally eliminating the need for, neuroleptics in some instances (31). Lorazepam has been found to be particularly useful, although some patients become more agitated or suffer respiratory distress or arrest if they have concurrent pulmonary disease. Lorazepam is preferred to other injectable benzodiazepines because of its rapid absorption and shorter elimination half-life. One to two milligrams of lorazepam is given with each 5 mg of haloperidol or thiothixene (31). Mean and total doses of neuroleptic are reduced when parenteral lorazepam is given in conjunction with the neuroleptic.

Lorazepam alone has been reported to be effective in treating catatonia in the acute situation, much as intravenous amobarbital was used in the past for the same condition (32). Definitive treatment with neuroleptics or lithium may be required. Neuroleptic-induced catatonia itself responds to benzodiazepines (33). Two to four milligrams of lorazepam may be sufficient to reduce psychotic agitation without neuroleptics. Hallucinations do not appear to diminish. There is less pain at the injection site, no risk of dystonia or orthostatic hypotension, decreased risk of seizures, fewer adverse reactions, and greater safety with agitated patients with CNS trauma or anticholinergic toxicity using benzodiazepines rather than low-potency neuroleptics (33). Lorazepam alleviates extrapyramidal adverse effects and akathisia as well as insomnia and anxiety. Benzodiazepines have a particular advantage in agitated schizophrenics with ischemic heart disease to which neuroleptics pose a threat. Stupor, mutism and other psychomotor disturbances seen as part of a schizoaffective process also respond (34). Mutism, rigidity, posturing, negativism and staring into space, as well as violence and psychomotor aggitation, have been found to respond to lorazepam (35 – 39). Lorazepam, a facilitator of the gamma-aminobutyric acid (GABA) system, is thought to act both in the limbic system and in certain layers of the cerebral cortex (38). Lorazepam acting as a GABA facilitator probably alleviates a dopamine blockage in the mesostriatal and mesolimbic systems, thereby stimulating the motor system and releasing the inhibited catatonic behavior.

Lorazepam does not alter hepatic enzymes or the absorption or first-pass distribution through the liver and therefore there is no reason to suspect that lorazepam will influence serum neuroleptic levels pharmacokinetically (35). Benzodiazepines have been found to be at least as effective as antipsychotics in reducing time in seclusion (37). These effects appear to be achieved without the disinhibition of behavior described with some benzodiazepines. Tardive dyskinesia, NMS and laryngeal spasm are not seen with benzodiazepines. Onset of action is earlier than with neuroleptics (reported to be one to three weeks) or the antimanic effects of lithium (reported to be 5 – 10 days) making it ideal for low-risk immediate treatment of schizophrenic and manic symptoms and schizoaffective disorder (36). Lorazepam is well absorbed orally, intramuscularly and intravenously and has a relatively short elimination half-life (approximately 15 h), has no known active metabolite, and is excreted through the kidneys. Its pharmacokinetic properties make dosing more amenable to rapid changes in clinical picture. This allows it to be used in patients with compromised liver function. The major contraindication to lorazepam use is respiratory disease (40), because of its depressant effects alone or in combination with neuroleptics, in particular loxapine. Drug-induced delirium or psychoses or ataxia are rare effects at therapeutic doses (40).

Schneideran first-rank symptoms have also been reported on withdrawal from benzodiazepines (41). Intravenous diazepam has been reported to be helpful in alleviation of catatonic symptoms although worsening of psychoses is seen as a potential side effect (34). High-dose alprazolam (3.0 – 8.0 mg/day) has also been suggested for management of selected cases of schizophrenia alone (42) or in conjunction with neuroleptics (43) for the treatment of both positive (e.g., hallucinations, delusions) and negative (e.g., inappropriate affect, withdrawal) symptoms of schizophrenia. Clonazepam, the benzodiazepine anticonvulsant, decreases agitation and logorrhea in schizoaffective disorder (44) in doses of 0.5 – 16 mg per day. Clonazepam has a rapid onset of action, is highly sedative, and will be tolerated at high doses (45). The drug acts by increasing 5-hydroxytryptamine synthesis.

In summary, benzodiazepines produce sedation without the anticholinergic, extrapyramidal or hypotensive effects of neuroleptics. Sedation is the main side-effect.

Other psychotropic agents and electroshock

Other agents used to treat acute psychoses have little value in an emergency setting, given their latency of onset of action, but they may be important when acute symptoms persist requiring other modes of primary or supplementary treatment or electroshock. Monoamine agonists and antagonists (e.g., clonidine, propranolol), neurotransmitter precursors (L-tryptophan), cholinergic agents (e.g., physostigmine), magnesium sulfate, anticonvulsants (e.g., carbamazepine, phenytoin, sodium valproate), calcium channel blockers (e.g., verapamil), and opiate agonists and antagonists (e.g., methadone, naloxone) have all been reported to be successful in selected cases of treatment of acute psychosis (46). Unfortunately, identifying the treatment-resistant case that will respond to one of these alternatives is still in a nascent phase.

Barbiturates and bromides were the first drugs used in lieu of restraints at the beginning of the century. While intravenous administration of sodium amobarbital and short-acting barbiturates rapidly ameliorates disruptive behavior, oversedation can lead to aspiration, respiratory depression, and death. Barbiturates are still used, but drug interactions and dependence limit their use (31).

Wet packs are rarely used today, but electroshock is in some instances indicated when acute psychotic symptoms are unresponsive to various modes of psychopharmacological intervention, symptoms such as severe self-destructive behavior require its use for immediate relief, and medical conditions such as cardiorespiratory instability limit the use of medication.

L-Tryptophan as a serotonin precursor is said to have some inhibiting effects within the nervous system (46). Propranolol, the beta-blocker, has been found to be effective in the management of intractable violence, especially at higher doses. Like lithium, it has a longer latency of impact.

Anticonvulsants such as diphenylhydantoin, carbamazepine and valproate work to assuage schizophrenic symptoms that represent a *forme fruste* of epilepsy as well as working alone as adjuncts in managing severe schizophrenic symptoms although they may be decidedly more effective in treating treatment-resistant bipolar disorder (46). The calcium channel antagonist verapamil appears to have little role in the treatment of resistant schizophrenia. Hostility and uncooperative behaviors and a syndrome of heightened emotional tone has been reported with its use (47).

Evaluation of homicidal and suicidal risk

Severely psychotic schizophrenic patients may be so disturbed that they present an immediate danger to self or others. This is particularly true in severely depressed schizoaffective patients and both schizophrenic and schizoaffective patients who have mandatory hallucinations motivating them to kill themselves or others. This reality may be so great that considerable sedation, patient monitoring, seclusion, restraints, or ECT may be required to prevent harm. Current threats should be placed in the context of a patient's history as provided by relatives and current therapist (if any) and in what can be gleaned regarding previous threats, attempts and gestures. Patients who have talked about harming themselves for 20 years without any attempts are different from those who have progressively become more psychotic and/or depressed (48 – 55).

Ambulance teams cannot forcibly bring in a patient who is not committed. If, however, patients threaten to kill themselves or others, the police may be called and the patients brought to an emergency room. The presence of severe suicidal ideation or a history of a major previous attempt with exacerbation of symptoms requires hospitalization. Antidepressants take considerable time at therapeutic levels to impact (one to three weeks) and longer (6 weeks) to reach maximum effect. Depressive symptoms will not readily abate in the emergency room. Any sudden remission of self-destructive impulses may be ominous and suggest that a plan may have crystallized to assuage the pain of psychosis by death. In some instance, a schizophrenic patient who was depressed and suicidal may have been mistakenly diagnosed as depressed and prescribed a thymoleptic, resulting in intensification of schizophrenic symptoms without reduction of suicide risk.

Patients with the superimposition of a toxic psychosis on schizophrenia and/or lack of social supports coupled with mild self-destructive urges may require hospitalization, whereas those with moderate suicidal ideation and good social supports in continuing outpatient care may not. Paranoid patients pose a particular threat. They are secretive and may kill themselves or others to avoid or defend themselves against their punitive assailants. Families of schizophrenics, even with the best conscious intentions, may unconsciously deny the seriousness of a patient's condition and the extent of his or her potential for violence. In other instances, there may be an unconscious desire to have a patient commit suicide, and a family may neglect to observe the patient or ensure that he or she takes medication. In their ambivalence they may fail to support compliance with medication and follow-up care, so that a patient may be re-hospitalized or commit suicide and remove the burden to the family. Schizophrenia must be constantly re-evaluated for suicidal potential, regardless of immediate risk. Depression is a common correlate of resolving psychosis and may have as a feature suicidal ideation or action.

Environment

A quiet environment and calm coordinated staff serves to contain disorganized behavior with a minimum need for medication or physical restraint. Distractions such as screams of patients in pain, shadows, and paging systems may be perceived in a paranoid manner. The amount of neuroleptics used in units with well-trained staff has been shown to be less than that on control wards (39). The presence of other agitated or delirious patients serves to kindle evolving psychosis. Keeping acutely ill patients apart serves to calm escalating behavior. Restraints tend to be used on patients, particularly young males, who are perceived as potentially violent. Leather restraints are deemed more humane than strait-jackets (which more severely limit movement), poseys, or gauze (which may be twisted to the extent that circulation is compromised, resulting in gangrene). A leather restraint should be released on a single limb every 15 minutes so that all four limbs have been non-secure for a 15-minute interval each hour. Food, drink, toilet privileges, and personal hygiene must be attended to as needs dictate. Verbal intervention, strong therapeutic milieu, and antipsychotic medication reduce the need for restraint. Required relaxation may reduce the need for the restraint (39). Seclusion is deemed by many to be less restrictive than restraints and sufficient to ameliorate many instances of dangerous or self-injurious behavior, disorganized or bizarre behavior, inappropriateness, rule-breaking, and destruction of property.

The site of emergency treatment shoud be free of objects that can be used to harm self or others. An alarm to obtain help should be present and a ready exit for patient or staff available if violence that cannot be contained erupts. A patient should not be touched if paranoid, as a violent episode may be instigated. If a clinician feels uncomfortable interviewing a patient, a security guard or other clinician should be present or the patient should be interviewed in an area where both patient and clinician are in view of others who can provide help should the need arise. A full pharmacopeia of psychotropic options should be available, including liquid, pill, intramuscular, and intravenous (e.g., droperadol) medication. Providing a schizophrenic with a choice between oral liquid (to prevent 'cheeking') and intramuscular medication may reduce acting-out by allowing a modicum of control when patients feel they are disintegrating.

Non-pharmacological means of restraint are required early in the course of acute management while a benzodiazepine, neuroleptic, or barbiturate reaches sufficient serum level to sedate. While evaluation of an organic process is pending, the generalized EEG slowing seen with some psychotropics may confuse the picture or precipitate a medical emergency such as a cardiac or respiratory condition or generalized allergic response. Records must indicate need for restraint, document that less restrictive means are ineffective, and show that reassessment has occurred for continuing need and to prevent adverse side-effects (e.g., gangrene) (54).

Other measures to reduce potential violence include meeting patients outside the office to determine whether prudence dictates that a patient should not be seen alone, and leaving a door open during the interview.

Contact with therapist

Patients seen with an exacerbation of a chronic process often have a permanent therapist. Therapists should be contacted to provide clues to the reason for acute psychotic episodes and to management. A therapist's vacation or leaving may be the cause of presentation as an emergency. Current medication, medical problems, and allergic history can be obtained, and social manipulations or medication dose and type can be ascertained that may most rapidly assuage intensity of symptoms. Therapists may have names and addresses of relatives or friends who provide an alternate disposition if it is felt a patient should not go home but still is not sick enough for hospitalization. If available, a therapist talking to a patient on the telephone or coming to the emergency room may be sufficient to calm the patient. Contemplated changes in medication and the decision to hospitalize if indicated should be discussed with therapists. Baseline hallucinatory and self- or other-destructive status can be obtained and the current picture evaluated in the context of chronic symptom patterns.

Family intervention

Families may facilitate or impede patients' functioning outside an institutional context. At times of stress, all individuals tend to be curt, defensive, anxious, and short-tempered. Family members have a greater amount of diagnosed and undiagnosed schizophrenic and related illnesses (e.g., schizotypal and schizoid personality), which sometimes make rational efforts to form a therapeutic alliance difficult. Relatively healthy families' guilt may militate against a smooth working relationship when time and resources are limited. Families can provide useful historical information which facilitates differential diagnosis from affective disorders, drug-induced states, and other medical conditions as well as complementing a therapists' information on baseline symptoms and social functioning. They will also provide information on what medication the patient has been prescribed and the degree of compliance with therapeutic recommendations. A family member's presence may facilitate physical examination and acceptance of required clinical examinations (e.g., serum screens), tranquilization, and hospitalization if required. After evaluation, clinicians should explain diagnostic considerations, present presumed diagnosis, symptoms targeted for management, and treatment options to patients and their families so that they may actively participate in the formation of a treatment plan.

Patients' and families' lack of understanding of the nature and course of illness and the role of medication and its side-effects are common causes of refusal of medication. Rapport with patients and families enhances early and appropriate engagement in treatment and minimize non-compliance if side-effects emerge. It further promotes a rapid return to the emergency room if symptoms re-emerge or do not abate over the course of a week, requiring either more medication or a protective care setting. A few moments with a patient and his/her family may obviate problems over taking medication in the emergency situation, hospitalization, and follow-through on outpatient therapy.

The cost-benefit ratio of use of medication (i.e., increase risk of hospitalization vs. tardive dyskinesia) should be discussed with families. Most side-effects of neuroleptics are minor, while untreated major psychosis has serious physical, economic, and social consequences. It is sometimes so painful, that death is hardly worse.

The therapist should advise a patient's family as well as the patient of the name of the therapist, the therapist's location and telephone number, the medication the patient has been prescribed, and the medication's expected duration of use before full impact, its side-effects, and how its side-effects should be managed. The patient should be advised to have his/her family attend the first appointment with the usual therapist or a new one following the emergency.

If hospitalization is required against a patient's will, a patient's family alone or together with security guards and other clinical staff may be required to assure that patients reach their destination. If a patient is referred for outpatient care, a family will need to be instructed as to medication regimen and the need to monitor ingestion. Liquid medication may be required where patients cheek drugs in pill form. The importance of continued medication and the need to monitor the emergence of side-effects and to continue in treatment should be discussed with families as well as patients. Signs of decompensation and increased risk of suicide or homicide should be presented and process of hospitalization outlined. If intolerable situations arise at home, work or school, a temporary increase in medication doses may be required. Cessation of medication is the most common cause of relapse. Discontinuation of medication, however, may be due to an unconscious need to be hospitalized because of an intolerable situation such as completion of college, facing the job market, or marriage.

Families should be taught both how to give medication and how to reduce immediate stress to avert hospitalization at times of crisis. If the presentation of the crisis is not the first, a careful review of medication history must be undertaken. Is the patient on none, too little, too much, or the wrong medication? All four are causes of presentation as well as lack of involvement in a treatment plan specific to patients' strengths and weaknesses. Some patients need case managers, others, with considerable family support and resources, may require only medication maintenance without a major psychosocial skills training supplement.

Some families and patients may be instructed in how to use minimum-dose medication for maximum functioning. This provides a decrease in psychic pain without oversedation and unnecessarily contributing to the development of tardive dyskinesia. Drug holidays for a fixed amount of time each month or interepisodically is another way of reducing risk of tardive dyskinesia and assuaging patient and family fears of psychopharmacotherapy.

Families may need to help structure patients' environments so that rent is paid, job attended, and normal hygiene maintained. A family may be counseled to support a decision to commence use of long-acting fluphenazine or haloperidol if compliance is inconsistent or a patient particularly paranoid.

Psychoeducation in the emergency situation is time-limited but critical to assure follow-up care. The chronicity of the illness must be stressed, as well as how to recognize signs of exacerbation as well as the emergence of schizophrenia de novo in other relatives (57 – 60). Successful psychopharmacotherapy serves to obfuscate the seriousness of the problem and help family or patient deny the need for continuing care to avoid harm to self and others, regression and hospitalization. Once a patient becomes severely psychotic, hospitalization may be the only option for containing the behavior. It is obviously impossible to make any realistic plans for families to participate in therapy if they deny the illness. At times of crisis, there may be such overwhelming self-flagellation that a family may need help to focus and look forward rather than backward to ascertain what must be done immediately and in the future. It helps neither the family nor the patient to recount a litany of psychological indescretions in the past.

Family help in continuing care is best when medication schedules are simple (e.g., once a day) and psychotropic drugs are used that have the least side-effects that might contribute to discontinuation. Family members should seek help from others interested in the well-being of the patient, such as other relatives, friends, clergy, and internist, to assure continuing involvement in the treatment plan.

A note should be made in the patient's records that all side-effects of medication have been discussed with the family and the patient and family have consented to the treatment as informedly as they can, given the reality of the condition.

Social support

In many instances, a patient does not have a family, or family members impede rather than enhance social functioning. In such instances, the role of family may be assigned to caring others or to clinicians assigned to a patient's case. The social support network of deinstitutionalized chronically mentally ill help moderate life stresses and reduce the need for re-hospitalization. Critical variables at a time of crisis which are valuable for prognosis are the number of individuals in the network, the roles assumed in each relationship, and the nature of behavioral exchanges (61).

Social supports may play a greater role in successful treatment outside an institution. Patients whose families or supports are hostile and critical fare less well than those whose families are accepting and warm. The greater the number of supports, the less the pressure is on any one person and the less the likelihood of emergence of anger. Support groups of other family members who are experiencing chronic mental illness help to dissipate the stress of the burden of care.

Specific questions should be asked as to whom the patient sees, for how long and how frequently, what a patient does with them, and what they talk about. A support person not only helps to reduce stress and to reality-test, but also may recognize early symptoms of decompensation. For schizophrenics with little manifest symptomatology, small network size predicts re-hospitalization (61). For example, if a patient depends on one person to supervise medication, personal hygiene, food preparation and social interaction, and that one person becomes dysfunctional, a patient may be re-hospitalized. A protective web is formed when a patient has a number of individuals who serve many roles in his/her life. Another factor is a patient's ability to initiate seeking help as needed rather than depend on others to provide it spontaneously. The less dependent and the more instrumental, the lower the rate of re-hospitalization at low symptom levels (61). Obviously, when symptoms are great, the number in social network, multiplicity of roles played by a supportive member, and the degree of instrumental behavior by a patient become less important.

Hospitalization

An attempt should always be made to manage a patient outside the hospital if this appears possible. If rapid tranquilization calms but does not totally assuage symptoms, a 3 – 5-day trial period outside a hospital may be attempted if a patient is compliant and not suicidal or homicidal. This eliminates the stigmatization of hospitalization and counters the regressive tendency encountered in patients undergoing a psychotic break. A minimal hospitalization model of care is not only economically advantageous to the family, but it also serves to maintain extant social supports in the community where a patient must ultimately function to survive.

The goal of crisis intervention is to rapidly restore an individual to asymptomatic functioning and to facilitate individual growth. Individuals, ideally, should be better for having been through a crisis that allows them and those close to them to become aware of what their resources are and what their liabilities are and how the latter can be minimized. Hospitalization is to be avoided whenever possible. This entails knowing what resources are available in a community and how they may be brought to bear on extra-hospital resolution of a crisis. Social support is sought to facilitate mastering the stressful situation in the form of cognitive guidance and emotional support that compensate for the reduction in problem-solving capacity resulting from stress-induced emotional arousal. Successful non-hospital care entails a sophisticated awareness of how each individual may uniquely rally his or her defenses to facilitate functioning in times of stress.

Transportation

In most states, unless a patient willingly consents to transportation to another institution, this is not possible without a physician's certification of need for emergency hospitalization. Appropriate sedation should be provided in all instances, using agents that will not result in a medical crisis en route such as respiratory depression, an acute dystonic reaction or laryngeal spasm. Time should be allowed to assess the emergency of side effects, and ambulance drivers informed of possible difficulties. Suicidal and homicidal patients should be humanely but adequately restrained. Search for hidden lethal objects and concealed drugs is completed before embarkment.

Patients who are not in imminent danger are allowed to be cooperative before they are labeled dangerous. Oral medication is provided to calm patients who themselves voice concern over fear of eruption. This allows patients to feel they have some control over what is happening to them. Patients should never be deceived about their destination. Psychiatrists should not collude with a family's deception. The cost may not only be credibility but also future compliance, and greater agitation over fear of uncertainty. Ambulance policy may entail that a patient be restrained. If so, patients and families should be informed that this is necessary. If patients are violent and need to be forcibly restrained, this should not be undertaken until a sufficient number of personnel are present to avoid incident. Family members and patient's friends may or may not be of great value in calming a patient. Once in restraint, most patients rest assured that their behavior is controlled and are calm.

A female escort should always accompany a woman patient en route. A delusional patient may fantasize that she has been sexually abused. A chaperone serves to protect both patient and ambulance crew.

Acutely psychotic patients do not require immediate arrival at a hospital. A speeding ambulance with rapidly blinking lights and loud siren serves to increase risk of accident and to agitate a patient with significant negative therapeutic impact. A patient must be medically and surgically cleared if disposition is from a general hospital to a psychiatric facility at great distance. Not all intense anxiety is of psychotic origin. Some is due to internal bleeding, cardiac arrthymias, hypotension and pulmonary embolism.

Prognosis

Patients' families, friends, and referring agents may ask about patients' prognosis after an emergency evaluation. Reasonable prognostications depend on the extent of historical data provided and the accuracy of diagnosis. In a sleep-deprived state, a patient with bipolar illness (which is generally a good prognosis) may appear schizophrenic if the course without treatment has been longer than six months (62, 63). Complex partial seizures may remit rapidly on anticonvulsants, without any further problems. The prognosis of a schizophrenic is better with acute onset, an affective component, confusion, good work and school history, clear precipitant, lack of family history of schizophrenia, a family history of affective illness, lack of dilated cerebral ventricles, and supportive social relationships found in anamnesis and on physical and clinical examination (64–66). Factors subsequent to acute treatment that impact on prognosis are degree of medication compliance, dosage of drug (less may be more), drug dysphoria, development of a supersensitivity psychosis, and environmental stressors. Critical and hostile family members or close personal contacts of the patient can vitiate the best efforts of a sentient therapist and skilled psychopharmacologist. Targeted interventions (using neuroleptics only during periods of acute psychosis) minimize drug-induced impairment but may hasten recrudesence. The argument for early intervention targeted therapy in the emergency situation (24) is based on the need to avoid side-effects (e.g., tardive dyskinesia, NMS), and the fact that continuing medication may serve to perpetuate negative symptoms during stability. Over-medication may make differential diagnosis difficult (e.g., identifying migraine-equivalent or complex partial seizures) and may contribute to a supersensitivity or rebound psychosis. High-dose treatment and rapid loading is not superior to more limited psychopharmacological intervention. Both the heterogeneity of schizophrenia and the fact that patients vary in therapeutic window of efficacy contribute to a need of more considered medication to maximize interepisodic functioning. Prodromal symptoms such as dysphoric affect, sleep problems, suspiciousness, and increasing psychosis warn of impending decompensation. A supportive family, patient cooperation, and medication-responsive exacerbations allow the use of a targeted approach.

Targeted psychopharmotherapy is not possible when there are no characteristic prodromal symptoms, when a relapse may have serious consequences (e.g., homicide or suicide), when there is no support system, when a patient or family is non-cooperative and lacks insight, and when a stable state is not possible without medication. Family involvement is very necessary if a targeted approach using a predictable pattern of exacerbation is employed (67). Symptoms most frequently mentioned as appearing or worsening before psychotic episodes are tenseness, nervousness, decreased appetite, trouble concentrating, difficulty sleeping, social withdrawal and neuroleptic-sensitive depression (67).

Unmedicated schizophrenia has a relapse rate of approximately 10% per month (68). Rates are much lower (2.5 – 10-fold decreases) in patients with maintenance antipsychotic medication. Initial treatment with drugs improves prognosis (68). Characteristics of poor-outcome schizophrenia include negative symptoms, poor response to neuroleptics, family history of schizophrenia, cerebral ventricles that are asymmetrical, and complete dependency on others (69 – 81). Patients with negative symptoms show more impairment of affect, social relations, spontaneous thinking, attention and motor activity at onset of illness, and have by history less education and a poorer work history (13). Negative symptoms are not felt, due to prolonged hospitalization, severity of illness, drug side-effects, or progression of illness. Schizophrenic patients show more thought disorder throughout the course of illness than good-prognosis patients (73).

Marengo and Harrow (73) found that 40% of a sample of 41 schizophrenic patients had a persistent thought disorder 4 years following index hospitalization. Another 37% showed an episodic thought disorder course. Persistent thought-disordered patients suffered higher rates of unemployment and re-hospitalization than non-thought-disordered and episodically thought-disordered patients.

A humble, caring demeanor on the psychiatrist's part can assuage patient and family concerns and maintain a sense of hope that is required to maximize the possibility of a good outcome.

REFERENCES

1. Andreasen NC, Akiskal HS (1983) The specificity of Bleulerian and Schneiderian symptoms: a critical reevaluation. Diagnosis and treatment of affective disorders. *Psychiatr. Clin. N Am., 6,* 41.
2. Andreassen NC (1987) The diagnosis of schizophrenia. *Schizophr. Bull., 13,* 9.
3. Parker S, Engelsman F (1983) A symptom-based approach to the diagnosis of schizophrenia. *Am. J. Psychiatry, 28,* 484.
4. Mukheyee S (1983) Reducing American diagnosis of schizophrenia: will the DSM-III suffer? *Br. J. Psychiatry, 142,* 414.
5. Slaby A, Lieb J, Tancredi LR (1985) *The Handbook of Psychiatric Emergencies,* 3rd ed. New York Medical Examination Publishing Co., Flushing.
6. Lipkowitz MH, Idopuganti S (1985) Diagnosing schizophrenia in 1982: the effect of DSM-III. *Am. J. Psychiatry, 142,* 634.
7. Adler LW, Pulver, AE (1986) Diagnosing schizophrenia. *Hosp. Community Psychiatry, 37,* 636.
8. Kendler KS (1986) Affective illness in the families of schizophrenic patients: what does it mean diagnostically. *Arch. Gen. Psychiatry, 43,* 714.
9. Kendler KS (1986) Kraepelin and the differential diagnosis of dementia praecox and manic-depressive insanity. *Compr. Psychiatry, 27,* 549.
10. Farmer AE, McGaffin P, Goltesman, II (1987) Twin concordance for DSM-III schizophrenia: scrutinizing the validity of the definition. *Arch. Gen. Psychiatry, 44,* 634.

11. Hellerstein D, Frosch W, Koenigslierg HW (1987) The clinical significance of command hallucinations. *Am. J. Psychiatry, 144,* 219.
12. Jones BE, Gray BA (1986) Problems in diagnosing schizophrenia and affective disorders among blacks. *Hosp. Community Psychiatry, 37,* 61.
13. Lindenmayer JP, Kay SR, Opter L (1984) Positive and negative subtypes in acute schizophrenia. *Compr. Psychiatry, 25,* 455.
14. Andreasen NC, Olsen S (1982) Negative vs. positive schizophrenia: definition and validation. *Arch. Gen. Psychiatry, 39,* 789.
15. Ortiz A, Gershan S (1986) The future of neuroleptic psychopharmacology. *J. Clin. Psychiatry, 42, (Suppl 7),* 3.
16. Van Putten T, Marder SR (1986) Low-dose treatment strategies. *J. Clin. Psychiatry, 47, (Suppl)* 12.
17. Kane JM, Woessner, Sarantakos, S (1986) Depot neuroleptics: a comparative review of standard, intermediate, and low-dose regimens. *J. Clin. Psychiatry, 47, (Suppl)* 30.
18. Kane JM (1987) Treatment of schizophrenia. *Schizophr. Bull., 13,* 133.
19. Stoudemire A, Fogel BS (1987) *Principles of Medical Psychiatry.* Grune & Stratton, New York.
20. Raskind MA, Riese SC (1986) Antipsychotic drugs and the elderly. *J. Clin. Psychiatry, 46, (Suppl),* 17.
21. Salzman C (1987) Treatment of the elderly agitated patient. *J. Clin. Psychiatry, 48,* 19.
22. Dubin WR, Weiss KJ (1986) Rapid tranquilization: a comparison of thiothixene with loxapine. *J. Clin. Psychiatry, 47,* 294.
23. Buskirk J, Mendel W (1987) Treating the newly diagnosed schizophrenia. *Psychiatr. Ann., 17,* 207.
24. Carpenter W (1986) Early targeted pharmacotherapeutic intervention in schizophrenia. *J. Clin. Psychiatry, 47,* 23.
25. Coyle JT (1982) The clinical use of antipsychotic medications. *Med. Clin. N. Am., 66,* 993.
26. Resnick M, Burton BT (1984) Droperidol vs. haloperidol in the initial management of acutely agitated patients. *J. Clin. Psychiatry, 45,* 298.
27. Hooper JI, Minter G (1983) Droperidol in the management of psychiatric emergencies. *J. Clin. Psychopharmacol., 3,* 262.
28. Donaldson SR, Gelenberg AJ, Baldessarini RJ (1983) Treatment of schizophrenia: a progress report. *Schizophr. Bull., 9,* 505.
29. Parker G, O'Donnell M, Walter S (1985) Changes in the diagnosis of the functional psychosis associated with the introduction of lithium. *Br. J. Psychiatry, 146,* 377.
30. Barklage NE, Jefferson JW (1987) Alternative uses of lithium in psychiatry: studies show promising results in a variety of disorders. *Psychosomatics, 28,* 239.
31. Salzman C, Green AI, Rodriguez-Villa F et al. (1986) Benzodiozepines combined with neuroleptics for management of severe disruptive behavior. *Psychosomatics, 27,* 17.
32. Greenfeld D, Conrad C, Kincure P et al. (1987) Treatment of catatonia with low-dose lorazepam. *Am. J. Psychiatry, 144,* 1224.
33. Ward ME, Saklad SR, Ereshefsky L (1986) Lorazepam for the treatment of psychotic agitation. *Am. J. Psychiatry, 143,* 1195.
34. Wetzel H, Heuser I, Benkert O (1987) Stupor and affective state: alleviation of psychomotor disturbances by lorazepam and recurrence of symptoms after RO15-1788. *J. Nerv. Ment. Dis., 170,* 240.
35. Greenberg WM, Triana JP, Karajgi R (1986) Lorazepam in the treatment of psychotic symptoms. *Am. J. Psychiatry, 143,* 932.
36. Lenox RH, Modell JG, Weiner S (1986) Acute treatment of manic agitation with

lorazepam. *Psychomatics, 27,* 28.
37. Beck DA, Hannah AL (1986) Intramuscular lorazepam to restrain violent patients. *Lancet i,* 206.
38. Salam SA, Gillai AK, Beresford TP (1987) Lorazepam for psychogenic catatonia. *Am. J. Psychiatry, 144,* 1082.
39. Campbell R, Simpson GM (1986) Alternative approaches in the treatment of psychotic agitation. *Psychosomatics, 27,* 23.
40. Cohen S, Khan A (1987) Respiratory distress with use of lorazepam in mania. *J. Clin. Psychopharmacol., 7,* 199.
41. Roberts K, Vass N (1986) Schneiderian first-rank symptoms caused by benzodiazepine withdrawal. *Br. J. Psychiatry, 148,* 593.
42. Kulik FA, Wilbur R (1987) High-dose alprazolam in schizophrenia. *J. Clin. Psychopharmacol., 6,* 191.
43. Wolkowitz OM, Pickar D, Doran AR et al. (1986) Combination alprazolam-neuroleptic treatment of the positive and negative symptoms of schizophrenia. *Am. J. Psychiatry, 143,* 85.
44. Victor BS, Link WA, Binder RL et al. (1984) Use of clonazepam in mania and schizoaffective disorder. *Am. J. Psychiatry, 141,* 1111.
45. Chouinard G, Young SN, Annable L (1983) Antimanic effect of clonazepam. *Biol. Psychiatry, 18,* 451.
46. Cohen BM, Lipinski JF (1986) Treatment of acute psychosis with non-neuroleptic agents. *Psychosomatics, 27 (Suppl),* 7.
47. Pickar D, Walkowitz OM, Doran AR, et al. (1987) Clinical and biochemical effects of verapamil administration to schizophrenia patients. *Arch. Gen. Psychiatry, 44,* 113.
48. Yesavage JA (1983) Dangerous behavior in Vietnam veterans with schizophrenia. *Am. J. Psychiatry, 140,* 1180.
49. Yesavage JA (1984) Differential effects of Vietnam combat experience vs. criminally on dangerous behavior by Vietnam veterans with schizophrenia. *J. Nerv. Ment. Dis., 171,* 182.
50. Yesavage JA (1983) Inpatient violence and the schizophrenic patient: a study of Brief Psychiatric Rating Scale scores and inpatient behaviors. *Acta Psychiatr. Scand., 67,* 353.
51. Yesavage JA (1982) Inpatient violence and the schizophrenic patient: an inverse correlation between danger-related events and neuroleptic levels. *Biol. Psychiatry, 17,* 1331.
52. Yesavage JA (1983) Relationships between measures of direct and indirect hostility and self-destructive behavior by hospitalized schizophrenics. *Br. J. Psychiatry, 143,* 173.
53. Yesavage JA, Werner PD, Becher JMT, et al. (1982) Self and dangerousness: social class differences between acute schizophrenics and their parents in relation to measures of violence. *Br. J. Psychiatry, 141,* 267.
54. Yesavage JA, Becker J, Werner PD, et al. (1982) Serum level monitoring of thiothixene in schizophrenia: acute single-dose levels of fixed doses. *Am. J. Psychiatry, 139,* 174 – 178.
55. Yesavage JA, Becker JMT, Werner PD, et al. (1983) Family conflict, psychopathology, and dangerous behavior by schizophrenic inpatients. *Psychiatry Res. 8,* 271.
56. Skodol AE, Karasu TB (1978) Emergency psychiatry and the assaultive patient. *Am. J. Psychiatry, 135,* 202.
57. Kety SS (1983) Mental illness in the biological and adoptive relatives of schizophrenic adoptees: findings relevant to genetic and environmental factors in etiology. *Am. J. Psychiatry, 140,* 720.
58. Kendler KS, Gruenberg AM, Strauss JS (1981) An independent analysis of the Copenhagen sample of the Danish Adoption Study of Schizophrenia, III. The relation-

ship between paranoid psychosis (delusional disorder) and the schizophrenia spectrum disorder. *Arch. Gen. Psychiatry, 38,* 985.

59. Kendler KB, Greenberg AM, Strauss JS (1981) An independent analysis of the Copenhagen sample of the Danish Adoption Study of Schizophrenia, II. The relationship between anxiety disorder and schizophrenia. *Arch. Gen. Psychiatry, 38,* 973.
60. Kendler KS, Gruenberg AM, Strauss JS (1981) An independent analysis of the Copenhagen sample of the Danish Adoption Study of Schizophrenia, II. The relationship between schizotypol personality disorder and schizophrenia. *Arch. Gen. Psychiatry, 38,* 982.
61. Sokalove RL, Trimble D (1986) Assessing support and stress in the social networks of chronic patients. *Hosp. Community Psychiatry, 37,* 370.
62. Solovay MR, Thenton ME, Holeman PS (1987) Comparative studies of thought disorders, I. Mania and schizophrenia. *Arch. Gen. Psychiatry, 44,* 13.
63. Shenton ME, Solovay MR, Holzman P (1987) Comparative studies of thought disorders, II. Schizo-affective disorders. *Arch. Gen. Psychiatry, 44,* 21.
64. Szymanski HV, Simon JC, Gutterman N (1983) Recovery from schizophrenic psychosis. *Am. J. Psychiatry, 140,* 335.
65. Keefe RSE, Mohs RC, Lasonczy MF, et al. (1987) Characteristics of very poor outcome schizophrenia. *Am. J. Psychiatry, 144,* 889.
66. Andreasen NC (1982) Negative symptoms in schizophrenia: definition and reliability. *Arch. Gen. Psychiatry, 39,* 784.
67. Herz M (1985) Prodromal symptoms and prevention of relapse in schizophrenia. *J. Clin. Psychiatry, 46,* 22.
68. Davis JM (1985) Maintenance therapy and the natural course of schizophrenia. *J. Clin. Psychiatry, 11,* 28.
69. Keefe RSE, Maks RC, Losonczy MF, et al. (1987) Characteristics of very poor outcome schizophrenia. *Am. J. Psychiatry, 144,* 889.
70. Parkorny AD (1983) Prediction of suicide in psychotic patients: report of a prospective study. *Arch. Gen. Psychiatry, 40,* 249.
71. May PRA, Van Putten T, Yale C (1980) Predicting outcome of antipsychotic drug treatment from early response. *Am. J. Psychiatry, 137,* 1088.
72. May PRA, Van Putten T, Jenden DJ, et al. (1981) Chlorpromazine levels and the outcome of treatment in schizophrenic patients. *Arch. Gen. Psychiatry, 38,* 202.
73. Marengo JT, Harrow M (1987) Schizophrenia thought disorder at follow-up: a persistent or episodic course? *Arch. Gen. Psychiatry, 44,* 657.
74. Soris SG, Harmon GK, Endicott J (1981) Postpsychotic depressive symptoms in hospitalized schizophrenic patients. *Arch. Gen. Psychiatry, 38,* 1122.
75. Roy A (1981) Depression in the course of chronic undifferentiated schizophrenia. *Arch. Gen. Psychiatry, 38,* 296.
76. Sakurol Y, Takahashi R, Nakahara T, et al. (1980) Prediction of response to and actual outcome of chlorpormazine treatment in schizophrenic patients. *Arch. Gen. Psychiatry, 37,* 1057.
77. Tsuang MT, Woodson RF, Fleming VA (1980) Premature deaths in schizophrenia and affective disorders: an analysis of survival curves and variables affecting the shortened survival. *Arch. Gen. Psychiatry, 37,* 979.
78. Tsuang MT, Woodson RF (1978) Excess mortality in schizophrenia and affective disorders. Do suicides and accidental deaths solely account for this excess? *Arch. Gen. Psychiatry, 35,* 1181.
79. Tsuang MT (1978) Suicide in schizophrenics, manics, depressive and surgical controls: a comparison with general populations suicide mortality. *Arch. Gen. Psychiatry, 35,* 153.

80. Canton CIM (1982) Effect of length of inpatient treatment for chronic schizophrenia. *Am. J. Psychiatry, 139,* 856.
81. Wilder JF, Levin G, Zwerling I (1966) A two-year follow-up evaluation of acute psychotic patients treated in a day hospital. *Am. J. Psychiatry, 122,* 1005.

CHAPTER 13

The role of hospitalization

M.I. HERZ AND M.A. MOSTERT

INTRODUCTION

This chapter will deal with the role of hospitalization and alternatives to hospitalization in the comprehensive treatment of schizophrenic patients. Prior to World War II, virtually the only treatment schizophrenic patients received was in long-term governmental hospitals. The majority of schizophrenic patients in the United States were housed in state hospitals which offered custodial care for patients, who often spent many years and sometimes their whole lives in these facilities.

Historical Perspective

In the late 1950s and early 1960s, the management and treatment of schizophrenic patients was re-evaluated and revised due to a number of major developments which led to a change in therapeutic practice. Beginning in the 1950s there was a great deal of concern about the postulated deleterious effects of state hospital care on patients. Goffman (1), in 1961, studied a large public mental hospital. He determined that the treatment provided there was termed custodial, but in effect was equal to neglect, exploitation, dehumanization and the creation of iatrogenic symptoms. He used the term 'total institution' to describe the basically antitherapeutic atmosphere of large governmental psychiatric institutions such as state hospitals in which every aspect of the patient's life was controlled by the institution. Gruenberg (2) described the effects of long-term hospitalization in these facilities and coined the term 'social breakdown syndrome'. He attributed many of the pathological behaviors of patients to the antitherapeutic milieu of large state hospitals.

The civil rights movement also began in the early 1960s. In addition to involvement with minorities, there was increasing concern about the rights and welfare of psychiatric patients. Many civil libertarians and psychiatrists began to equate hospitalization itself with poor treatment of psychiatric patients. Initially, they had focused on state hospitals as being antitherapeutic, but then generalized to all hospital care including general hospitals and private psychiatric hospitals. They believed that the hospital was responsible for much of the symptomatology and impaired role functioning, and that if psychiatric patients were allowed to remain in the community (the natural environment), their lives would be normalized.

Treatment in the community became the watchword, and in 1963 the National Institute of Mental Health provided a strong impetus for the development of federally funded Community Mental Health Centers in the United States under the Com-

Handbook of Schizophrenia, Volume 4: Psychosocial Treatment of Schizophrenia.
M.I. Herz, S.J. Keith and J.P. Docherty, editors.

munity Mental Health Centers Act of 1963. Essential components were inpatient hospitalization, partial hospitalization, outpatient care, 24-hour emergency services, and consultation and education services to local community groups and agencies. A major aim of community mental health centers was to provide flexible, comprehensive and continuous care to patients within their local communities as a preferred substitute to long-term custodial care in large state hospitals. Unfortunately, many state hospitals indiscriminately discharged large numbers of chronic patients into the community prior to the development of community resources to treat these patients effectively. As a result of poor planning prior to hospital discharge and scarce community treatment resources, many patients have been left to languish in the community under the worst environmental conditions with little or no treatment available. Some have questioned whether patients are benefiting or being harmed by deinstitutionalization.

The major tranquilizers were introduced in the 1950s, with the result that schizophrenic and other psychotic patients became more accessible and amenable to therapeutic intervention. Antipsychotic medication was able to diminish the length and severity of acute episodes, leading to a further questioning of the need for long-term hospitalization. In addition, many patients could be maintained in the community with less likelihood of relapse.

Studies of family dynamics were carried out along with other studies of the influence of social factors in schizophrenia. At that time investigators believed that in some families there was a dynamic equilibrium which functioned to maintain the labeled patient in the sick role. They believed that during periods of stress, the family needed a scapegoat, the sick member, to blame for all family problems, and to extrude him. Some family therapists believed that it would be more therapeutic for the family to deal with the patient at home in the family situation rather than have the patient hospitalized. They believed that a 'closing of ranks' occurred while patients were hospitalized which made it difficult for patients to re-enter the family after hospital discharge, since their family roles had been assumed by others. Family therapists reasoned that if a patient remained at home, at least in the evenings and weekends, and attended a day hospital or had outpatient treatment, the whole family would be more strongly motivated to engage in the therapeutic process because they would have to deal with the family member in an ongoing way. It was expected that family members' role relationships could be examined within a family therapy situation and a new, healthier equilibrium would be established for all members. Further, it was believed that if only the patient changed and the family remained the same, the patient would return to the same pathogenic environment which played a major role in precipitating the original psychotic decompensation.

Some of the assumptions of these early family therapists have been questioned. No family dynamic has been found which is uniquely associated with the development of schizophrenia. Psychiatrists began to recognize that families had to bear a large burden living with a schizophrenic member. It became clear that the whole family could not be viewed as the patient. There was a designated patient in the family with the defined diagnosis of schizophrenia, which probably has a genetic component leading to vulnerability to the illness. However, recent studies have shown that some families exert a good deal of stress on the patient (3). On the other hand, it has become evident that family members do experience considerable stress themselves, and need to be involved in the treatment process. Family members can be useful collaborators in helping patients when psychoeducational and family problem-solving strategies are employed.

Since the therapeutic benefits of hospitalization were being questioned, studies were conducted to evaluate the outcome of various types of hospital therapeutic programs. The emphasis on outcome shifted from a concern about how well a patient adjusted to the hospital milieu to an evaluation of the patient's post-hospital adjustment in the community, including employment and social relations. Anthony et al. (4), in a review article, stated that it did not seem to matter whether hospitalized psychiatric patients received eclectically oriented group therapy, psychoanalytically oriented therapy, milieu therapy, pharmacotherapy or somatotherapy. Regardless of the type of traditional therapy patients received, the recidivism and employment rates were not differentially affected. It appeared that there was very little transfer of learning which took place while in the hospital to role functioning in the community. Thus, many psychiatrists concluded that patients should be treated briefly in inpatient hospitals when necessary, and then transferred to a day hospital if it were appropriate, followed by outpatient treatment; the definitive learning should take place outside the hospital rather than in the hospital.

In recent years in the United States there has been a growing trend toward decreasing the length of inpatient hospitalization stay for patients with serious mental illnesses. However, many psychiatrists believe that the trend toward short-term hospitalization is a mistake. They believe that the definitive treatment of a severe psychiatric illness requires the use of the hospital not only for control and stabilization of acute symptoms, but also to facilitate the patient's growth and maturation in a controlled environment using psychotherapy, milieu therapy, and pharmacotherapy. Others, who are advocates of community care, believe that the hospital should be used primarily to control acute symptoms. Once the patient's symptoms have been partially stabilized, enabling him to cooperate with his treatment, he can then be moved to less restrictive modalities of treatment, such as day hospitalization. In other words, treatment of a particular illness episode may involve inpatient hospitalization, day hospitalization, and outpatient care, in contrast to the more traditional model of definitive treatment of the episode only in the hospital. To use the analogy with physical illness, one may say that short-term hospital proponents believe in early ambulation in order to discourage regression and atrophy of skills.

STUDIES OF THE EFFECTS OF DEINSTITUTIONALIZATION

The introduction has described increasing disenchantment with the hospital as an appropriate place for treating individuals with schizophrenia. A number of writers provided vivid descriptions of the dehumanizing conditions in large state mental hospitals. The thesis propounded by Goffman (1) was that institutionalization actually made patients worse, but his method of proof was descriptive rather than scientific. It remained for other investigators to provide more rigorous explorations of his thesis.

Wynne (5) rated verbal behavior of institutionalized individuals, comparing those with schizophrenia to non-psychiatric patients with chronic physical illness. Short-stay patients averaged about two years and long-stay patients about 14 years in the hospital. Patients were carefully matched for family history, marital status, education, social class, IQ, and a number of other variables. Wynne found that both schizophrenic and non-psychiatric patients showed deterioration in most of the tests used as length of stay increased. This was felt to be a product of the impoverished social environment of large public institutions, which are usually understaffed, underfinanced, and overcrowded. However, this was a cross-sectional study, looking at patients at only one point in time rather than prospectively, and the number of patients studied was small: 13 short-term and 11 long-term schizophrenic patients, and 38 non-psychiatric patients, equally divided into short- and long-term groups. The authors also wondered whether length of stay may have been confounded with severity of illness despite efforts to control these variables. Schizophrenic patients were given more tests than non-schizophrenic patients; comparisons between the two groups were not made. At that time it was not possible to find a control group of schizophrenics living in the community, since the standard treatment was lengthy institutionalization, so the effect of hospitalization is difficult to separate from the natural course of illness on the basis of this study alone.

Honigfeld and Gillis (6) used the 80-item Nurses' Observation Scale for Inpatient Evaluation (NOSIE-80) to explore whether length of institutionalization was related to functional deterioration. The scale was completed by a pair of raters based on a three-day observation period. Six hundred and ten male patients, almost all of whom were schizophrenic, were assessed after a 28-day period on placebo. Average length of stay ranged from less than one to more than 47 years. Since age and length of hospitalization were correlated, the data were corrected in order to separate out these two factors. Items on the NOSIE-80 were separated into four positive factors (social competence, social interest, cooperation, and personal neatness), three negative factors (irritability, paranoid depression, and manifest psychosis), and a global factor reflecting the patient's total assets. Results showed a consistent tendency for positive ratings to decrease and negative ratings to increase as length of stay increased. This occurred despite a tendency for positive factors and global assets to increase as patients aged. Manifest psychosis increased with both age and length of stay. The authors concluded that the effects of institutionalization run counter to the natural course of the illness, which tends to improve as the patient ages. They argued that prolonged institutionalization should be replaced with brief hospitalization using alternative milieu therapies. However, one cannot help but wonder whether long-stay patients may in fact have been more severely ill than short-stay patients, confounding interpretation of these results.

Wing and Brown (7 – 9) reported results of a naturalistic study of the social environment in three British mental hospitals over an eight-year period. Three hundred and thirteen schizophrenic women were selected for follow-up. The authors hypothesized that 'social poverty' of the hospital environment was associated with 'clinical poverty', or an increase in negative symptoms. Social poverty was measured, for example, by counting the number of the patient's personal possessions, examining how her time was structured, and surveying nurses' opinions about patients, such as whether they thought the patient could do useful work in the hospital. Of all social indices, the length of time spent doing absolutely nothing correlated best with the patient's clinical condition, tending to support the association of social poverty with clinical poverty. Follow-up showed that social improvement, achieved by the gradual introduction of a milieu approach, was accompanied by clinical improvement. These improvements were most related to the introduction of occupational therapy and work programs. Wing believed these results showed that schizophrenic patients are extremely vulnerable to social understimulation, whether in the hospital or in the community. However, in providing appropriate treatment for these individuals, a delicate balance must be struck between a protective environment and social enrichment, which may prove overstimulating and provoke a relapse.

Length of stay

Concerns about the development of institutional behaviors, possible dependency on the hospital setting, and practical issues such as cost and bed availability have led a number of investigators to explore the relative benefits of 'short' and 'long' hospital stays.

A non-experimental study by Burhan (10) was prompted by a bed shortage at his facility. One hundred diagnostically mixed patients in need of admission were randomly assigned to his ward, where they stayed an average of 15 days compared to the institutional average of 46 days. He provided intensive outpatient contact of six months after discharge. When compared with over 1,000 patients admitted to other wards during the study, his patients had fewer readmissions (3% versus 14% at one year and 8% versus 38% at two years) and the overall cost of both inpatient and outpatient care was less than the cost of inpatient care alone for the control group. No information was provided on diagnosis or changes in psychopathology with treatment.

Caffey and associates (11, 12) reported on a VA collaborative study of 201 predominantly middle-class male schizophrenics. A pilot study had concluded that short hospital stays were relatively safe. Exclusion criteria included primary alcoholism, medical conditions which could be expected to delay discharge, hospitalization within the last year or for more than half of the last five years, no home to which to return, dangerousness to self or others, and high nuisance potential in the community. Subjects were randomized into one of three groups. Group A had usual hospital and outpatient care. Group B aimed for discharge within 21 days with special outpatient follow-up. Group C had usual inpatient care and special outpatient follow-up. Follow-up care for groups B and C was delivered by hospital staff, lasted for one year and usually included maintenance on antipsychotic drugs. The type and frequency of treatment was at the treating physician's discretion, but visits at least once a month were recommended to provide continuity of care. Families of short-stay patients were visited in their homes during the admission by a social worker for education and preparation for discharge after a brief stay.

Average lengths of stay were as follows: group A, 75 days; group B, 29 days; group C, 83 days (12). Despite equal initial levels of pathology, at three weeks group B showed the least pathology, although only ratings of retardation and motor disturbances were significantly better. At the time of discharge, group B showed the most pathology, which may be expected as individuals in this group had less time since the onset of the episode to recover. Readmission rates for the three groups for the year following discharge were not significantly different: A, 34%; B, 34%; C, 23%. Neither was there a statistically significant difference in the mean time out of hospital for those subjects who required readmission: A, 119 days; B, 140 days; C, 141 days. The similarity in time spent in the community for groups B and C suggests the value of a consistent aftercare program. Even so, the frequency of outpatient contacts was the same in all groups. Ratings of community adjustment provided by family members tended to favor group C, whose members were engaged in significantly more free-time activities at 6 months than other subjects. However, at 12 months they were rated as more negativistic. This study demonstrated no difference in outcome between short-stay and long-stay patients.

Herz et al. (13 – 16) conducted a study of 175 newly admitted patients who had families, randomly assigning subjects to one of three treatment groups: (1) standard treatment: the patient stayed as long as the therapist deemed necessary; (2) brief-day treatment: the patient was offered transitional day treatment after an inpatient stay of about one week; and (3) brief-out treatment: the patient stayed in the hospital for one week with no transitional day care. All patients were offered outpatient care, and were followed for up to 24 months after discharge. Day treatment took place on the same ward where subjects were treated as inpatients, and care was delivered by the same treatment team. If patients required readmission during the study period, they were assigned to the same treatment group as at the index admission. Exclusion criteria included diagnoses of alcoholism, drug abuse, or antisocial personality. Sixty-three percent of the study group carried a diagnosis of schizophrenia.

The average length of inpatient stay was 11 days for both brief groups and 60 days for the standard group. There were no differences in rates of speed of recovery or readmission rates between the three groups. Despite equal levels of psychopathology, there was more impairment in role functioning at 3 and 12 weeks in the standard group; this makes sense, as most standard subjects were still in the hospital at this time. Interestingly, both brief groups received significantly less medication during the first 12 weeks than did the standard group. Brief-stay patients also spent half as many days (4) in the intensive care unit as the standard patients (11). The level of expectation communicated to patients and their families that it would be a brief hospital stay may have been a significant factor in producing this result.

Assessments of patient psychopathology by research interviewers and families generally agreed. There were few differences between groups with regard to the effect of patients on families. Brief group families did report more unpleasantness or uncooperativeness and negativism at 3 weeks, which was to be expected given that patients in the brief groups were at home and still resolving an acute psychotic process at that point. The main positive effect for families of brief-stay subjects was that patients could return to work sooner, thus relieving financial stress. Family distress, usually taking the form of anxiety, trouble sleeping, and worry about the future, was similar whether patients were in the hospital or at home. By six months, dysphoric symptoms in families in all groups had substantially diminished. Satisfaction with the treatment program was high for all groups. However, at 24 weeks twice as many (21%) families of standard subjects as families of brief subjects (10%) believed that their relative should be back in the hospital, despite the fact that there were no observable differences in the level of family burden.

At two years, standard patients had spent significantly more days in the hospital (average 115.5) than had brief-day (26.8) or brief-out patients (46.8). The difference between brief groups was not statistically significant. Those patients in the brief-day group who actually used day treatment (about half) spent an average of 43 days in day treatment over the study period. There were no differences in readmission rates between groups. Diagnosis of schizophrenia and younger age tended to be predictive of readmission, regardless of treatment group.

With regard to psychopathology and role functioning, differences between groups were most striking at one year. Ratings on the Global Assessment Scale were highest (best) for brief-day patients, and lowest for standard patients. Psychopathology, as measured on the Psychiatric Status Schedule, was greatest in the standard group. The brief-out group showed more behavioral disorganization, interview belligerence, negativism and speech disorganization than did the brief-day group. Role functioning was also poorest in the standard group, with only 46% working at six months, compared to 64% of brief-out patients and 52% of brief-day patients. At 24 months, the proportions failing to perform any occupational role were as follows: standard 40%, brief-out 31%, and brief-day 20%.

Assessments of role functioning and psychopathology by family informants at one year generally agreed with the above findings; brief-day patients showed the least psychopathology and impairment in role functioning, and standard patients the most. For example, the standard group had higher scores than the brief-day group on subjective distress, social isolation, disorganization, reality testing, and parental role functioning. The brief-out group had higher scores than the brief-day group in impairment in occupational role functioning and marital role functioning. Furthermore, independent raters found that families of standard patients had a significantly greater level of burden at one year than did families of brief-day patients. During the second year of the study, families of standard patients were less likely to have a favorable attitude toward the treatment staff and were more likely to think that their relative should be back in the hospital. However, family attitude and burden were less predictive of readmission than were patient's global assessment ratings.

In a series of articles, Glick and Hargreaves (17 – 20) compared the outcome of 141 schizophrenic subjects randomly assigned to short-term (21 – 28 days) or long-term (90 – 120 days) hospitalization. Outpatient treatment was not under the investigators' control. Both groups were markedly improved at four weeks, with the short-term group having a slight advantage. Long-term patients were functioning better at discharge than were short-term patients; this is readily explainable by the fact that long-term patients had had a longer time in which to recover. There was no comparison of both groups at four months, when the long-term group was being discharged and the short-term group had already been in the community for a few months. There were no significant differences between groups in severity of symptomatology, as opposed to measures of functioning, by the time of discharge. At one year, global outcome ratings favored the long-term group. However, this better outcome may not have been related to the experimental variable, short- versus long-term hospitalization. Long-term patients made more outpatient psychotherapy visits and received more antipsychotic medication as outpatients. The long-term group differed from the short-term group in that they had on average one more year of education, had higher socioeconomic status, and had better premorbid adjustment. These differences between groups in outpatient treatment and sociodemographic and prognostic variables could very likely account for the difference in seeking and remaining in aftercare which the authors suggest was a function of long-term treatment. In the Herz et al. study there was no difference in aftercare between groups. The inpatient, day hospital and outpatient services were all part of the same comprehensive community mental health service.

When subjects were separated according to pre-hospital functioning, long-term hospitalization proved to result in a better outcome at two years for those with good pre-hospital adjustment, particularly for women. Those with poor pre-hospital functioning improved equally, regardless of length of stay, although there was a trend for them to do better with short-term hospitalization. There were no differences between groups in the number of readmissions, the number of subjects hospitalized, or the mean number of days in hospital. This study has limited generalizability because of significant baseline differences between study groups. Also, there is a problem with the study design: other studies have suggested that a smooth transition to appropriate outpatient care is essential in facilitating the recovery of individuals treated only briefly in the hospital. In this study, hospitalization was not viewed as part of a comprehensive health service delivery system.

In a series of articles, Mattes, Rosen and colleagues (21 – 24) compared outcome for 126 patients assigned to 'short' (average 86 days) or 'long' (average 179 days) stay on an analytically oriented inpatient ward with a strong milieu philosophy and primary emphasis on psychotherapy. Assignment to one of the two groups was not strictly random; rather, it was based on administrative requirements. Clinical condition did not enter into this decision. Twenty-one percent of the long-term and 25% of the short-term group had a diagnosis of schizophrenia. There was no separate analysis of results for schizophrenics, except to say that there was no difference in outcome for this diagnosis between short- and long-stay groups. Short-stay patients showed a greater improvement at the time of discharge in cognitive and affective disturbance. More short-stay patients participated in reality-oriented group therapy focused on problems in self-expression and interpersonal relations; improvement was correlated with the use of this treatment modality. Long-stay patients were more likely to have private individual therapy following discharge, were more frequently re-hospitalized, and spent more time in hospital. The authors suggest that a type of conditioning may occur in the long-stay patients, in which they learn to perceive the hospital as a solution to their problems and continue to use this as a solution following discharge. Interestingly, all the patients who proved to be unmanageable were on long-stay units; the authors suggest that the prospect of long-term analytic therapy may cause unstable patients to decompensate. Another likely possibility is that long hospital stays may foster regressive behavior in vulnerable individuals.

The most recent controlled study of brief versus standard hospitalization, by Hirsch, comes from England (25). Two hundred and twenty-four patients, about 50% of whom were schizophrenic, were randomized to brief care or standard care. Patients younger than 16 or suffering from 'a diagnosable severe brain or physical disorder' were excluded. Every attempt was made to discharge brief care patients within eight days. The median stay was found to be nine days for brief care and 17 days for standard care. The mean stays were not statistically significantly different. Patients assigned to either group who stayed less than four days were excluded from the analysis unless they had been assigned to brief care and transferred to a day hospital according to the research protocol. Out of the original group, 127 were interviewed at admission (others refused or were unavailable for other reasons), and of these, follow-up data at three months was available for 106. No differences in clinical outcome between brief and standard groups were found at two weeks or at three months, as measured by the Present State Examination and interviews with informants. Most of the improvement in both groups took place within the first 2 weeks. Patients' behavior proved to be no more distressing to informants (usually family members) for brief-care patients than for those of standard-care patients at assessment points. Fewer brief-stay patients were re-hospitalized in the year following study entry. However, for many brief-stay patients, the day hospital was substituted for inpatient care; more brief care patients than control patients were admitted to the day hospital in the following year (47% versus 34%). The authors concluded that community resources such as day hospital are crucial to the success of shortened hospital stays. Interestingly, the authors found that their study contributed to a shortening of standard hospital stays at their hospital both during the study period and in the subsequent years. This study replicates the findings of Herz et al., particularly in supporting the use of transitional day hospitalization. Both the standard and brief lengths of stay in this study were shorter than in the other studies. The standard length of stay is in keeping with statistics on the average length of stay on acute inpatient units in the United States today, while the length of stay of brief patients, nine days, is much shorter.

No major studies of length of hospitalization have been published since 1979. Since then, the average length of stay on psychiatric wards has dropped considerably. As an example, one of the more recent retrospective entries on this subject in the literature (26) contrasts readmission data for a short-stay unit with a mean stay of six days with a teaching unit with mean stay of 29 days. This is a far cry from studies describing 'short' stays in the neighborhood of 90 days, or even 28 days. Schwartz and Vallance found fewer subsequent days in the hospital for the short stay group, but a larger proportion of patients initially assigned to the short-stay unit required transfer for long-term care (11% versus 1.5%).

All the above studies show that for the vast majority of patients a lengthy stay has no advantages over a brief stay. In fact, as Mattes (27) points out in his review of the literature on length of stay, long stays seem to have an addictive quality. Patients with previous long stays are the most likely to be readmitted, seeking the same solution to their difficulties. The factors determining length of stay often have more to do with hospital and treatment variables than with the patient's clinical condition (28). Hospital variables may include pressure on bed space, unit treatment philosophy, hospital discharge policies, and psychiatry resident rotations. Community variables such as the availability of family, outpatient treatment, a place to live, work, and financial support are also important. Of course, the length of stay financed by insurance companies can be a determining factor. Continuity of care through linkage to ambulatory resources in the community is essential to the success of brief hospitalization. As the studies by Herz and Caffey show, adequate aftercare is more important than length of stay in determining outcome. Outpatient and day programs must continue the healing process to achieve and then maintain stabilization.

Long-term hospital care

A small minority of patients do not respond favorably to brief hospitalization, even with the most persistent efforts of dedicated staff. Reibel and Herz (29) described nine out of 112 patients in the large study by Herz and colleagues who could not be treated briefly. Failures were more likely to be younger, single, and schizophrenic. They had more previous hospitalizations, showed more overt anger, and tended to be more impaired in their roles as parents or housekeepers. Particular patient problems which made it difficult to maintain study failures outside the hospital included the following: persistent poor judgement and impulsive behavior, antisocial behavior, and continued psychotic disorganization. At least one individual was lost in the community between the criminal justice and psychiatric care systems. Problems in families which prevented early discharge included acute intense crises and chronic dysfunctional interactions. Schizophrenic patients who decompensated after marrying and having children also needed a lengthy hospitalization.

The 1981 reorganization of the Massachusetts Mental Health Center, which cut the inpatient component down to a small Intensive Care Unit with an average length of stay of 10 days, was found to leave a small minority of chronic patients without appropriate long-term care. Gudeman (30) calculated that approximately 15 long-term beds are required for a catchment area of 100,000; 7.5 of these beds would be occupied by patients with schizophrenia. He separated patients requiring long-term care into the following categories: (1) elderly patients with a combination of dementia, psychosis, and medical illness who are dangerous to themselves or others; (2) psychiatrically ill mentally retarded patients with assaultive and aggressive behavior; (3) brain-damaged individuals with serious loss of impulse control; (4) psychotic and assaultive schizophrenics; and (5) chronic schizophrenics with socially unacceptable behavior which makes them vulnerable to exploitation. Since the treatment needs of these groups are obviously different, Gudeman proposed specialized long-term facilities to serve each group.

Alternatives to hospitalization

A number of studies have addressed the question of whether hospitalization can be dispensed with altogether, for the reasons discussed in the introduction. Partial hospitalization as an alternative will be discussed in the next chapter. The hypothesis entertained by this group of investigators whose work will now be reported is that most patients who are acutely ill or in long-term inpatient care can be managed in the community if the appropriate programs are in place. Alternatives for chronic inpatients will be discussed first.

Alternative care for chronic patients

In an uncontrolled study Weinman (31) showed that a majority of long-term inpatients who required considerable supervision and showed such institutional behaviors as apathy, isolation and dependency could be successfully returned to the community. They received a 12-week orientation which stressed activities of daily living. Community 'enablers' with minimal training spent 10 hours weekly with patients after they were placed. These patients had fewer readmissions than did a group of chronic patients discharged according to traditional policy. The absence of randomization, adequate controls and careful description of study methods makes it difficult to generalize from this study, although it does suggest that this type of approach may be feasible.

In 1970 Linn and colleagues embarked on a four-year cooperative study involving five Veterans Administration hospitals to determine whether hospitalized patients could be managed in foster care as an alternative to inpatient care (32). Foster care was chosen rather than return home on the premise that families sometimes breed pathology or fail to provide sufficient support to the newly discharged patient. Subjects, who were all male, were required to carry a psychiatric diagnosis and be cleared by social work staff for study participation in order to be included in the study. Criteria used by social work staff were not reported. The average duration of hospitalization at entry was 45 months. Seventy-one percent of the 569 subjects were schizophrenic; most of the rest suffered from organic mental disorders. Thirty-three percent of the sample were current or past alcohol abusers. Patients were randomized to foster care or continued hospitalization and then paired. Measures of mood, functioning and adjustment were carried out when one of the pair entered foster care and again four months later. Experimental patients required an average of 44 days preparation time before discharge to foster care. Seventy-three percent of experimental patients were eventually placed in foster care. Of those who were not placed, half had deteriorated and about one quarter had left the hospital against advice. At four months, fully 88% of experimental patients were still residing in the community. Twenty percent of the group required admission during the four-month follow-up period. Compared to inpatients, foster care patients showed a significant improvement in functioning and overall adjustment, but there was a trend for them to become less active than patients in the hospital. Experimental failures had a history of more previous hospitalizations and were more dysfunctional. Patients with diagnoses of organic mental disorder or alcohol abuse were more likely to fail at foster care. Although this study is limited by the short follow-up period, it does demonstrate that many long-term inpatients can successfully survive the critical first few months outside the hospital.

Marx et al. (33) conducted a randomized study in Madison, Wisconsin, designed to determine whether current inpatients judged to have a high potential for continuous institutionalization or a recidivist pattern could be maintained in the community in a special program: 'total in-community treatment'. Sixty-one patients, 48 of whom were schizophrenic, were randomly assigned to one of three treatment groups: Community Treatment Group (CTG), Research Unit Controls (RUC), and Other Unit Controls (OUC). RUC patients were treated by the same staff as experimental patients. All patients were judged to be incapable of sustained community living. After a maximum of eight days, experimental patients were discharged to residence in the community, where they received intensive assistance from study staff in activities of daily living, problem-solving, finding work, and socializing. Staff members were available around the clock. Members of the community were encouraged to regard the patient as responsible and provide him or her appropriate feedback about behavior. The treatment lasted five months, and patients were to be followed up two years after treatment ended. During the treatment period the mean number of days in the hospital was as follows: CTG, 6; RUG, 103; and OUC, 99. At the end of treatment there were no differences in psychiatric symptomatology or self-esteem. CTG patients were living and working in a more independent fashion than control patients at this point. There was a positive response from the community, which learned to tolerate these severely disabled individuals; neither individuals nor agencies were alienated by the treatment program. This study demonstrated the feasibility of treating severely ill patients in the community, and served as the basis for another study of alternative treatment by Stein and Test (34) which will be described later.

Alternative care for acutely ill patients

The next group of studies explores the management of acutely ill patients in the community. One of the earliest (35) was a naturalistic study of two demographically similar neighboring English towns, one of which had its conventional hospital-based psychiatric service replaced with a community-based service. Forty-five percent of patients were psychotic. The burden to families turned out to be higher for the community-based service, but this finding was confounded by the fact that the hospital-based service actually had more social work staff available to visit families and provide advice and support. The burden was heaviest on relatives' mental health, with half of family members reporting symptoms. One-third restricted social and leisure activities, and one-tenth reported loss of income. Families said that about one-third of children were disturbed by the ill patient. Organic psychosis and personality disorder were the most difficult diagnoses for families to deal with, leaving open the question of how well schizophrenic patients could do with this approach. The many questions left open by this uncontrolled analysis remained for subsequent researchers to explore.

In 1961 Pasaminick and associates (36) began a controlled trial at the Louisville

Institute Treatment Center comparing the effectiveness of home care versus conventional hospital treatment for 152 schizophrenic patients who were considered in need of hospital treatment. Subjects assigned to home care were further divided into groups receiving placebo or active medication, in order to determine the impact of medication on preventing re-hospitalization. Patients who were homicidal, suicidal, or who did not have a family willing to care for them at home were excluded from study participation. Over the three-year study period, home care patients received visits from public health nurses which were weekly for three months, and then gradually tapered to monthly. After the index admission, patients initially assigned to conventional inpatient care spent 75% of the study period out of the hospital; 46% required readmission during this time. All patients improved equally in the first 6 months, regardless of treatment group, with little improvement thereafter. All raters, including psychiatrists, nurses, and relatives, agreed in their assessments. No group of patients was found to have superior long-term results; patients typically returned to the low level of functioning they had shown before the acute exacerbation of illness resulting in the index admission. For example, only one-third of the male home care patients held stable employment throughout the study and half of the female patients were unable to function effectively at home in some major area. Placebo home care patients tended to be more burdensome to their families, and were less successful in remaining in the community. Only 34% of placebo home care patients remained in the community throughout the entire study period, compared with 77% of drug home care patients. Pasaminick and associates drew rather pessimistic conclusions about the treatment of schizophrenia: almost regardless of treatment assignment, the functioning of patients in the community is quite poor, resulting in continuous burden to their families and to society and the need for constant attention, even when their most florid symptoms have subsided.

Davis and associates (37) performed a long-term follow-up on 90% of these patients five years after the conclusion of the study. No statistically significant differences were found among groups in time spent in hospital or the extent of clinic care received. Only a little more than one fourth of all patients were employed in any occupation. Placebo patients were more likely to be on welfare, probably because of the greater disability they had shown during the study period. There were no differences among groups in psychopathology, community adjustment, domestic performance, or social participation. Patients who were able to avoid re-hospitalization during the study period were less sick during the follow-up period, had shorter readmissions during the follow-up period, were more regular in clinic attendance and more compliant with medication, and had more cooperative families. 'Intrapsychic' or endogenous problems were the usual precipitants of re-hospitalization, rather than visible external stresses. In fact, study successes were more likely to have experienced interpersonal problems, which were not related to readmissions. Patients who were successful in staying out of the hospital were more likely to be married, were less dependent on significant others, and were slightly more competent in task performance. The authors reiterate their conclusions from the earlier study, that in order to be successful in the community, patients with schizophrenia must have continuous supervision and medication, as well as social services and emotional support for their families to alleviate personal and family disorganization. Their assessment of the ability of any type of care to be truly effective in schizophrenia was quite pessimistic: regardless of whether patients are treated in the hospital or in the community, the overall outcome is equally poor, with prominent deficits in role functioning and capacity for any type of creativity. The system of community care, in which patients were considered to be responsible for their own treatment, including going to appointments and taking prescribed medication, was judged by the authors to be inadequate in meeting the needs of these impaired individuals and their families. Active reaching out to patients and family members in their homes was considered essential for effective treatment.

Langsley (38) reported on follow-up for 350 acutely ill patients randomized to either admission to a university hospital or outpatient family crisis therapy (FCT). At six months, FCT patients were less likely to be hospitalized than controls, and when they were, it was for a shorter time. They also returned to jobs or primary functioning an average of three weeks before hospitalized patients. There were no differences in outcome between experimental and control groups at 18 months. Unfortunately, no information was provided about exclusion criteria, diagnosis, severity of illness, demographic variables, or drug therapy. When families of 50 schizophrenic patients were compared with those of 50 non-schizophrenic patients (39), it was discovered that families of non-schizophrenics were more able than families of schizophrenics to use family therapy to become more efficient and more able to work together to solve problems. The use of family therapy in schizophrenia is discussed in greater detail in other chapters.

Brook and colleagues (40) used a crisis hostel as an alternative to inpatient care, in a non-randomized study conducted at the Fort Logan Mental Health Center in Colorado. Forty-nine patients were accommodated over six months in a house accommodating a maximum of four residents. Half were schizophrenic. Staff stayed with patients as necessary, and patients were encouraged to socialize and to work. The mean stay in the hostel was 5.75 days. Interestingly, when compared with patients admitted to the hospital before the hostel opened, hostel patients had lower doses of medication. The readmission rate after six months was also lower.

In a subsequent study of alternatives to hospitalization also conducted at Fort Logan (41), there were three options for home care: (2) boarding with 'healthy' host families with 24-hour nursing coverage and a psychiatrist on call; (b) an 'intensive observation apartment' for acutely psychotic or suicidal patients, staffed by mental health personnel and volunteers; and (c) home day care in the home of a family sponsor. Methods of choosing between these options were not discussed, and results were lumped together. The control hospital treatment was not described in detail. Eighty-five patients considered in need of admission were randomized to home (37 patients) or hospital care (38 patients). The same clinical team provided treatment for both groups. There were no exclusion criteria. Twenty-seven percent of the home care group and 34% of the hospital group were schizophrenic. However, 10 cases randomized to home care could not be treated there due to violent or suicidal behavior and other management problems. Most of these patients were paranoid; six of the ten were schizophrenic. They were removed from the analysis of results. Data was collected at admission, at discharge, and four months after discharge. The average time spent in treatment was the same for both groups, but the amount of time was not reported. Follow-up showed that home care patients were more satisfied with their treatment outcome, including overall treatment effectiveness and staff concern and competence. Home care patients rated higher on goal attainment and self-disclosure at follow-up. It was the authors' clinical impression, however, that chronic patients preferred the more structured, dependent role they have in an institution to the community treatment system designed for this study. Interpretation of the results of this study is difficult, given the exclusion from the results of patients who could not be managed in home care, the short follow-up period, and the absence of data on important variables such as length of treatment.

Mosher (42, 43) explored the possibility of treating acutely ill patients in a supervised residence (Soteria House) instead of in the hospital. Subjects were schizophrenics judged to be in need of admission who were aged 16 – 30, were not currently married, and had no more than one previous hospitalization lasting no more than two weeks. Three clinicians had independently made a diagnosis of schizophrenia according to DSM-II on every subject. Criteria for admission to the study were chosen to select for patients who were likely to become chronic (unmarried individuals with early onset of illness) and to exclude those who had learned the hospital patient role and therefore would be resistant to alternative treatment. Control patients were admitted to the inpatient service, which was oriented to short-term care, consistent use of antipsychotic medication and linkage to aftercare. There were no significant differences between groups on demographic variables. Six patients lived in Soteria House, which was staffed by six paid non-professional staff, a project director, and a quarter-time psychiatrist. Psychosis was viewed as having the potential for being a growth experience. Patients were therefore given no medication for six weeks, after which time they were treated with chlorpromazine if they remained paranoid or had a history of insidious onset of illness. Staff attempted to relate to patients as peers. Followup data was available on 33 experimental patients and 30 controls two years after the index admission. The average length of the initial admission was 28 days in the hospital for controls and 166 days in Soteria House for experimental patients. Two patients could not be managed at Soteria House and were transferred to the hospital. Sixty-seven percent of controls, compared with 53% of experimental patients, required admission to the hospital during the follow-up period; this difference was not statistically significant. The length of stay for readmissions was not reported. All controls were treated with medication, compared with only 8% of study patients. Maintenance medication was used by only 4% of study patients, but 43% of controls. Readmission rates were not significantly different. Control patients made greater use of outpatient facilities; 40% of experimental patients had no subsequent contact with the regular mental health system. Experimental patients achieved a significantly higher occupational level than did controls, and were more likely to be living independently at 2 years (58% versus 33%). The authors acknowledge certain limitations to their study: follow-up care was not controlled, raters were not blind to treatment assignment, and follow-up was difficult for this group of young, highly mobile individuals. They concluded that withholding medication from this selected group of patients did no harm; however, data is not presented about the length of the acute episode for both groups.

Fenton and colleagues (44, 45) conducted a study of home care versus hospital care. They screened patients considered by non-study staff to be in need of admission, excluding those with organic mental disorders (20%), alcohol or substance abuse, chronic physical illness, and threat of suicide or homicide (16%). Patients who did not have a significant other (9%), lived too far away, did not speak English, or had lived in the community for less than six months were also excluded. Overall, 55% of those screened were accepted and randomized to home care (N = 78) or hospital care (N = 84). The average hospital stay on the inpatient ward was 28 days, with follow-up by an inpatient psychiatrist or registered nurse. Sixty-two percent of home care patients were managed exclusively outside the hospital; 30% were hospitalized for an average of 1.8 days. Home care patients received home visits and pharmacologic intervention as necessary from study staff, who were on call 24 hours a day. Schizophrenics made up 44% of the home care group and 39% of the hospital care group. Follow-up was available on 50% of patients up to one year. There were no differences in clinical symptoms, role functioning or family burden, although families of home care patients had to assume more responsibility in the first month. Over the course of one year, home care patients were hospitalized for an average of 14.5 days, hospital patients 41.7 days. About 24% of both groups were readmitted at some point. Home care patients required more outpatient visits (contacts with the home care treatment team) in the first 3 months, mostly in the first month, averaging 7.7 contacts compared with fewer than one outpatient visit for hospital patients. In the second six months, home patient contacts amounted to one-third of those utilized by hospital patients. Results for schizophrenics were not separated out. This study demonstrates that many severely disturbed patients can be managed in the community.

Stein, Test and Weisbrod (34, 46–48) reported on various aspects of their comparison of inpatient and community care. Subjects were patients seeking admission at a state hospital. The only exclusions were diagnoses of organic mental disorder or primary alcoholism. Patients were randomly assigned to experimental and control treatment; each group consisted of 65 subjects. The assigned treatment was discontinued after 14 months, with an additional 14-month follow-up. For the experimental treatment, Training in Community Living (TCL), ward staff were transplanted to the community. Staff was available 24 hours daily. Patient programs were individually tailored, with a focus on patient strength rather than pathology. There was active outreach for patients who missed appointments. The control condition consisted of inpatient treatment along with partial hospital and outpatient care as necessary. The median inpatient stay for the control group was 17 days. Analysis of the results showed that experimental patients spent more time than controls in independent living and had fewer subsequent admissions during the study period (6% versus 58% for controls). They extract significantly more time employed and more time in sheltered workshops, but there was no difference in competitive employment rates, although experimental patients earned more. Experimental subjects were more satisfied, rated higher on measures of self-esteem, and showed less symptomatology. They were more compliant with medication than controls. Despite spending more time at risk living independently in the community, experimental patients spent less time in psychiatric, penal, and medical institutions:

9% of their time during the first year of the study versus 20% of the time for controls. Control subjects made greater use of emergency room facilities. Overall, the burden to families was similar for both groups during the whole study period, but during the first four months, families of experimental subjects experienced a greater decrease in burden. The authors point out, however, that their measures of burden were limited and somewhat subjective, and the sample size was fairly small (50 in each group for analysis of burden). The advantages shown by the experimental subjects during the period of active study involvement were not sustained during the follow-up period, during which both groups received standard treatment. There was a gradual increase in hospital use by experimental patients and a decrease in the proportion working, although their wage advantage continued. Satisfaction with treatment and symptomatology in the experimental group rapidly converged with these ratings of the control group. The authors conclude from this evident regression with the end of intensive treatment that treatment programs for the chronically ill should be ongoing rather than time-limited; unfortunately, many aspects of community treatment are not usually reimbursable by third-party payers. They list the following guidelines for exclusion from their Training in Community Living program: imminent suicide or homicide risk, significant medical problems, and severe psychosis.

The most recent controlled study of community care as an alternative to hospitalization, by Hoult and colleagues, comes from Australia (49 – 52). As in the Stein and Test study, exclusions were kept to a minimum: alcoholism, drug abuse, organic mental disorder, and mental retardation. Acutely psychotic or suicidal patients were not excluded. Neither were patients required to have families willing to participate; a friend who was in contact with the patient on a regular basis was sufficient. One hundred twenty patients were randomized immediately after assessment in the admissions office. Three quarters of the group were psychotic, and 65 patients met DSM-III criteria for schizophrenia. The majority of the group were chronic patients. Of those with schizophrenia, 17% had no previous admissions and 38% had spent more than one year in the hospital. Fewer than one-fifth held a full-time job; half were dependent on social services for financial support. There were no differences between groups on demographic, social or psychiatric variables.

The control treatment consisted of a hospitalization averaging about 3 weeks, with group, recreational and occupational therapy, followed by aftercare in a community mental health center. Experimental patients were returned to the home setting, or placed in alternative accommodations if the home situation was problematic. Alternative placement often helped relatives see their contributions to the patient's current crisis. Staff members were available 24 hours a day, and often stayed with the patient for several hours initially. Visits by staff members were frequent in the first few days, when they frequently took patients out to provide family members some respite from their ill relative. Later, staff members accompanied patients on tasks of community living, providing in vivo training. Experimental patients were hospitalized if they were uncooperative, if their behavior was intolerable to the community, or if drugs proved too sedating (some patients fell asleep in the admissions office and could not be sent home). Initial treatment was involuntary for 60% of the group. Independent ratings were obtained at four-month intervals over 12 months. Twelve-month follow-up was available on more than 80% of the group.

Over the follow-up period, experimental patients spent an average of eight days in the hospital, compared to 53 days for controls. Looking at results for schizophrenia only, 32% of experimental patients were admitted during the study period; this figure includes initial admissions. One hundred percent of the controls with this diagnosis were admitted, according to study design. Of the ten home care patients who were admitted, six were discharged within a week; the remaining four patients were all chronically ill and had previously been hospitalized for more than one year. At 12 months, experimental schizophrenic patients had a superior clinical outcome, with only 32% versus 59% of controls remaining psychotic. Experimental patients had statistically significantly fewer symptoms on the Present State Examination. Two-thirds of both groups were taking antipsychotic medication at the end of the study period; community treatment had no effect on the need for medication. Neither were there any differences in employment status at the endpoint. There were two deaths in the control group, one from a cerebrovascular accident, and the other from drowning (a possible suicide). There were no deaths in the experimental group, despite the fact that there was a trend for community treatment to be less successful in reducing suicide threats.

Both patients and families found the experimental treatment to be more helpful. Experimental patients were no more burdensome to the community than were controls. Standard treatment was 26% more expensive than the experimental treatment ($5,669 versus $4,489). Eighty-one percent of costs for experimental patients were incurred in the community, compared with 7% of treatment costs for controls. Hospitalization accounted for 79% of costs for control patients. This well designed study showed that many severely ill patients can be managed more effectively and less expensively in the community than in the hospital, as long as staff is actively involved in providing services where the patient needs them (in the community) and is able to respond immediately to changes in the patient's condition. Hoult (52) identifies the following principles of care: (a) intensive initial contact to develop a bond with patient and family; (b) willingness to actively involve patient and family or caregivers in treatment; (c) consistent care by one team; (d) a personal case manager; (e) readiness to assertively reach out to the patient and relatives; (f) help with practical problems of living; (g) around-the-clock availability; and (h) ongoing rather than time-limited service. The persistently low level of functioning and continued need for antipsychotic medication found in most schizophrenic patients attests to the need for responsive, continuing maintenance treatment.

Program characteristics

A large VA collaborative study by Collins and Ellsworth (53, 54) attempted to define inpatient program variables that correlate best with community adjustment. One hundred and ninety-one setting and treatment characteristics were selected for study on the basis of available literature and the investigators' clinical experience. Methodological problems of earlier milieu treatment studies were outlined and the study design structured to best avoid these problems, which included failure to control for patient variables, use of poorly selected outcome measures, reporting of chance findings due to small sample size, confusing correlation and causality, and inability to control for placebo effects. About one third of more than 34,000 patients screened on 79 wards at 18 Veterans Administration Medical Centers were selected for follow-up. Women, uncooperative and highly disturbed individuals, and chronic patients residing on the wards were excluded. The response rate for follow-up questionnaires sent out three months after release from the hospital was 41% for patients and 30% for significant others. There was no difference in community adjustment between responders and non-responders, as determined by telephone interviews with subjects who did not return ratings. Outcome was measured by the Veterans Adjustment Scale, which was completed by the patient, and the Personal Adjustment and Role Skills Scale, which was completed by the patient's significant other. Both included global measures of improvement since the index admission. None of the program characteristics studied was significantly predictive of good outcome, but consistent trends suggested a number of principles. Better outcome was associated with wards having a mixture of acute and chronic patients and less opportunity for patients to withdraw from social interactions. For example, having chairs in a circle in the dayroom tended to predict worse outcome, because this usually meant that patients were sitting a circle around a television, interacting very little with one another. Effective treatment characteristics included increasing patient activities, optimal medication practices, less ward emphasis on order and organization (i.e., more flexibility), and more stability of shift assignment for nursing staff. Open and less restrictive interactions between patients and staff were better, e.g., patients calling staff by their first names. In summary, important variables had to do with an optimal level of social activity and interaction on the ward. It should be noted that with a response rate of only 41% of patients and 30% of significant others in this correlational study, a selective bias could have been introduced.

Milieu therapy

The therapeutic community was originally developed by Maxwell Jones (55) and others in England for an inpatient population very different than that found on contemporary brief-stay acute care inpatient wards and hospitalization was much longer. Most patients were nonpsychotic and had personality disorders. Treatment decisions were made in large groups of staff and patients, using a democratic process. Distinctions between staff and patients were blurred, such that the behavior of both patients and staff members could be discussed openly. No privileged communications were allowed. The hospital ward was seen as a therapeutic community where the patient could learn a healthy social role.

The relatively unstructured, permissive environment in the therapeutic community may not best serve patients with acute schizophrenia, who are usually disorganized and too regressed to participate in meaningful social activity (56). These patients may do better in a protective,structured, low-stimulus environment. Even Jones (57) subsequently admitted that his original expectations of the ability of patients with schizophrenia to function in the therapeutic community were too great. Moreover, achieving the requisite democracy of the therapeutic community means doing away with role expectations of staff members trained in different disciplines. A study by the senior author (58) showed from questionnaires filled out by all community members, including both staff and patients, that this model is difficult to implement. Most members showed attitudes more consistent with a hierarchical model. There was significant conflict among role groups in perception of some role functions, and practically no responsibility assigned to patients. Role-blurring and role confusion resulted in conflict, competition, hostility, and anxiety. Differences in training, responsibility, status, and function cannot be ignored (56). On the positive side, the concept of the therapeutic community has contributed to reducing the dehumanizing effects of institutionalization by promoting patient participation in ward management and decision making.

'Milieu therapy' assumes simply that the proper inpatient environment can be therapeutic. The therapeutic community described above is only one such approach. Components of the milieu may include various combinations of occupational and recreational therapy, group activities, vocational and educational rehabilitation, patient government, and individual and group psychotherapy. Somatic therapies are typically included, but may be de-emphasized by enthusiasts of this approach (59).

Evidence for the efficacy of milieu therapy in schizophrenia is limited. We will cite only a few of the controlled studies. In an often-cited study, Greenblatt et al. (60) compared a state hospital setting with an enriched milieu at the Massachusetts Mental Health Center for 115 chronic schizophrenic patients both on and off antipsychotic medication. After six months, patients on medication showed significantly greater improvement than those off medication, regardless of treatment setting. Despite the lack of evidence for greater therapeutic efficacy of the active milieu, there were more discharges from the active milieu. This finding can be explained by the greater availability of social services and a day hospital for patients treated in the active milieu. Follow-up at 12 – 18 months showed that patients who had received both drugs and milieu therapy continued to improve, leading the authors to conclude that drugs and an active milieu have an additive effect, with milieu showing its effects over a longer time course than that needed for antipsychotic drugs. This conclusion is easily disputed, given that follow-up treatment was not controlled, and other research has shown that long-term outcome is probably more dependent on the effectiveness of ongoing outpatient care than on a relatively brief inpatient experience.

An extensive review of controlled studies of milieu therapy in schizophrenia by Van Putten and May (59) concluded that this approach adds little to the treatment of acutely psychotic individuals once gross neglect is corrected; the patient is receiving adequate doses of antipsychotic medication; and the confounding effects of prognosis on outcome are removed. By itself, milieu therapy is not a very powerful treatment. The sometimes higher release rate for patients assigned to milieu therapy is usually attributable to vigorous discharge planning rather than any inherent superiority of the milieu. Van Putten and May believe that milieu therapy can actually be toxic for certain kinds of patients: those who are acutely disorganized or who show chronic deficits in attention, arousal and perception. They are overstimulated by the increased activity of milieu therapy. The 'defective filtering' hypothesized to occur in schizophrenia causes patients to be overwhelmed in a complex, high-stimulus environment. Intensive treatment settings inevitably produce enormous variance in outcome because some patients get better and some get much worse.

Van Putten and May believe that milieu therapy may be more useful for either acute or chronic patients who respond poorly to antipsychotic agents. They also suggest that for some good-prognosis patients, drugs can have an adverse effect; these individuals may be better treated with milieu alone. They conclude that less expensive and simpler interactional approaches and practical help with housing and employment are more useful than traditional therapies that focus on insight.

Only two major studies of the effectiveness of milieu therapy have appeared since Van Putten and May's comprehensive review. May and Tuma (61, 62) provided follow-up for 228 moderately ill first admission schizophrenic patients who had been randomly assigned to one of five treatment groups: (a) individual psychotherapy; (b) antipsychotic drug treatment; (c) individual psychotherapy plus drug; (d) electroconvulsive therapy (ECT); and (e) milieu alone. Each patient received treatment for 6 – 12 months before being judged a treatment failure. Discharge rates ranged from a low of 58% for milieu to more than 95% for drug alone or in combination with psychotherapy. Sixty-five percent of psychotherapy patients and 79% of ECT patients were discharged. 'Successes' were discharged to uncontrolled community follow-up. Almost all study failures responded when treated with antipsychotic drugs and group psychotherapy. If readmission was required, patients again received the treatment assigned initially, unless it had been judged unsuccessful, in which case drugs and group psychotherapy were used. The total number of days of hospitalization following discharge from the initial admission for patients treated with psychotherapy or milieu was consistently larger than for other groups during the first three years of follow-up. Psychotherapy plus drug and ECT had the lowest number of days of hospitalization for those patients followed for five years. Psychotherapy alone had significantly more days of hospitalization over the first three years compared to drug, psychotherapy plus drug, and ECT treatment, but not compared to milieu. Results were similar when only results for successfully treated patients were considered. Psychotherapy had a consistently negative, and drug therapy a consistently positive effect. Milieu patients tended to do better than psychotherapy patients, but worse than the other groups. The relatively good outcome for milieu may have much to do with the likelihood that only good-prognosis patients could get better with this approach, given its low release rates. Gunderson (63) has criticized this study for the absence of a description of the milieu treatment. Although staff-to-patient ratios were high, nothing is said of patient participation, groups, or staff expectations. This study has also been criticized for its use of inexperienced therapists (psychiatry residents), which leaves open the possibility that more experienced therapists may have achieved better results.

Paul and Lentz (64) studied a chronically institutionalized schizophrenic population which had been rejected for community placement. None of the patients had been hospitalized for less than two years. The mean age was approximately 45. Patients were divided into three groups: social learning, milieu therapy, and usual state hospital treatment. The social learning program used a token economy and other behavioral strategies. The 28 patients in each group were further randomized to active medication or placebo, on the theory that many chronically ill patients do not respond to antipsychotic medication and only suffer from its side-effects. Six months into the study there were no differences between patients on placebo and those on active medication.

Significant improvements in global functioning occurred in both psychosocial treatment groups, with the social learning program achieving better results than milieu therapy in a number of areas, producing lower rates of inappropriate behavior and cognitive distortion and higher scores on self-care and instrumental role functioning. The two programs were equally effective in controlling schizophrenic disorganization and improving interpersonal skills. Fifteen percent of patients in both groups achieved stable increases in functioning. A smaller proportion kept dropping back to low levels of functioning. After six months 100% of social-learning patients were improved, compared to 75% of milieu therapy patients. No patients in either group deteriorated from baseline assessment. Improved patients were more likely to be female and to have been hospitalized for a shorter period of time. In the next two years of the study, milieu patients only maintained earlier gains while social learning patients continued to improve. At thirty months, 11% of milieu and 25% of social learning patients had been promoted to vocational training. In the next year and a half, milieu patients as a whole lost some of the gains they had made, while social learning patients managed to maintain theirs. The authors attributed this to continuing struggles with an inflexible bureaucracy. In the last six months, new measures were introduced for dealing with assaultive behaviors and program effectiveness returned.

During the four-and-a-half-year study period, the control group of state hospital patients remained remarkably stable. At the end of the study the proportions of patients achieving discharge were 98% for social learning, 71% for milieu therapy, and 45% for the hospital comparison. Re-hospitalization rates for the next year were 10%, 30% and 50%, respectively. In summary, social learning procedures were significantly more effective than either milieu therapy or conventional state hospital treatment in improving behavior and achieving release. The authors point out (64, p. 435) that even Maxwell Jones became disillusioned with the effect of the therapeutic community on the desocialized chronic patient, concluding that small groups focused on a simple task may be more productive for this population. Follow-up on patients discharged to the community showed an initial loss of function for patients in the two psychosocial treatment groups during the first six months, with some recovery of function after psychosocial consultation. This reinforces the point made previously, that maintaining improvement in the chronic patient requires continuing intervention in the community; there is no such thing as a definitive cure and there is questionable transfer of learning which took place in the hospital to community functioning.

Gunderson (63) disputed the conclusions of Van Putten and May. Reviewing some of the same studies, he concluded that negative results for milieu therapy are a result of inadequacies in the milieu as well as of using poor-prognosis or chronic schizophrenics as subjects. He felt that nonchronic patients can benefit from intensive milieu therapy. In support of this thesis he cited, among others, the study of Soteria House by Mosher and colleagues which is described above in the section on alternatives to hospitalization. This position is somewhat circular, as good-prognosis patients can be expected to do well almost regardless of treatment; it is not a very powerful argument in favor of milieu therapy. From a review of studies attempting to define characteristics of effective milieus, Gunderson distilled the following qualities: (a) distribution of responsibilities and decision-making power among all staff members; (b) clarity in treatment programs, roles, and leadership; and (c) a high level of staff-patient interaction. There appears to be a contradiction between characteristics (a) and (b). How can responsibilities and decision-making be shared among all staff members while maintaining clarity in roles and leadership? Gunderson further suggested that iconoclasm and a sense of missionary zeal contribute to effectiveness. This is reminiscent of the Hawthorne effect, in which dedicated researchers produce improvement in their subjects simply through their enthusiasm, rather than any uniquely beneficial effects of the experimental treatment. Again, this says little for the unique effectiveness of milieu therapy.

In 1977 the senior author became medical director of the Georgia Mental Health Institute. He subsequently reorganized the acute inpatient ward to replace a milieu therapy model with a medical model (65). It was theorized that the medical model could take advantage of some of this culture's positive transference to the hospital, which is viewed as a place where one receives care. Staff members were clearly identified with white coats and name tags. Daily morning medical rounds were introduced. Schedules of activities were clearly posted and patients were provided with information booklets about treatment and also with newspapers, clocks, and calendars. Large community meetings and other unstructured meetings were abolished and an organized activity program was developed. Individual sessions focused only on here-and-now issues, primarily on discharge planning. After reorganization, the average length of stay dropped from 21 days to 14 days, with the readmission rate unchanged. Higher-functioning patients were no longer subjected to longer stays while the inpatient therapist explored dynamic issues. Patients were more accepting of these changes than were staff members, some of whom left in order to return to previous modes of relating to patients, such as in insight-oriented psychotherapy.

Conclusions

The research we have reviewed on hospital treatment of schizophrenia, as well as alternatives to hospitalization, supports a number of conclusions. Studies on length of stay suggest that short stays are best, particularly for chronic patients, who are prone to develop institutional behaviors during long hospital stays. Wing and Brown (7) showed that the longer a patient had been in the hospital, the more likely it was for him to be reluctant to leave. Role functioning is best preserved when the patient is returned to the community as soon as possible.

Alternatives to hospitalization are feasible for the majority of patients (66, 67), given appropriate support in the community, including the use of either a crisis outreach team or a partial hospital program (to be discussed in the next chapter). Unfortunately, such approaches have not been adequately supported by third-party payers, although Hoult (52) has reported that the Department of Health of the Australian province of New South Wales has recommended development of community-based teams to provide crisis care, treatment and rehabilitation of the severely mentally ill along the lines of his study of alternatives to hospitalization. At the moment, over 70% of money spent on mental health is for hospital care (67), to the detriment of outpatient services, which often lack the resources to provide preventive care, far less alternative care.

Given that hospital care for exacerbations of schizophrenia is the norm, how can it best be used? First, hospital treatment should be geared to the patient's deficits, rather than to development of skills, which is a more appropriate goal for outpatient treatment. Treatment in the hospital should therefore emphasize the provision of structure and protection for acutely ill patients. The treatment program should be more activity-oriented and place less stress on developing insight. The importance of the milieu remains to be determined, but is probably more important for long-term care. Hospitalization can provide protection and containment for the acutely psychotic patient, structure to counter psychotic disorganization, respite for weary family members and other caregivers, intensive diagnostic assessment, and carefully controlled and monitored pharmacotherapy to bring psychosis under control. As Gudeman (30) has shown, a small percentage of severely ill schizophrenic patients cannot be managed outside the hospital and require long-term care with programming tailored to their special needs.

REFERENCES

1. Goffman E (1961) Asylums. *Anchor Books, Garden City,* NY.
2. Gruenberg EM (1962) Objective appraisal of deterioration in a group of long-stay hospital patients. *Millbank Memorial Fund Q., 40,* 90.
3. Leff J, Vaughn C (1981) The role of maintenance therapy and relatives' expressed emotion in relapse of schizophrenia: a two-year follow-up. *Br. J. Psychiatry, 139,* 102.
4. Anthony WA, Buell GJ, Sharratt S, Althoff M (1972) Efficacy of psychiatric rehabilitation. *Psychol. Bull., 78,* 447.
5. Wynne RD (1964) The influence of hospitalization on the verbal behavior of chronic schizophrenics. *Br. J. Psychiatry, 109,* 380.
6. Honigfeld G, Gillis R (1967) The role of institutionalization in the natural history of schizophrenia. *Dis. Nerv. Syst., 28,* 660.
7. Wing JK, Brown GW (1970) *Institutionalism and Schizophrenia.* Cambridge University Press, Cambridge.
8. Wing JK (1977) The management of schizophrenia in the community. In: Usdin GE (Ed.), *Psychiatric Medicine.* Brunner/Mazel, New York.
9. Brown GW, Bone M, Dalison B, et al. (1966) *Schizophrenia and Social Care: A Comparative Follow-up Study of 339 Schizophrenic Patients.* Oxford University Press, London.
10. Burhan AS (1969) Short term hospital treatment: a study. *Hosp. Community Psychiatry, 20,* 369.
11. Caffey EM, Jones RD, Diamond LS, Burton E, Bowen WT (1968) Brief hospital treatment of schizophrenia – early results of a multiple-hospital study. *Hosp. Community Psychiatry, 19,* 282.
12. Caffey AS, Galbrecht CR, Klett CJ (1971) Brief hospitalization and aftercare in the treatment of schizophrenia. *Arch. Gen. Psychiatry, 24,* 81.

13. Herz MI, Endicott J, Spitzer RL (1975) Brief hospitalization of patients with families: initial results. *Am. J. Psychiatry, 132,* 413.
14. Herz MI, Endicott J, Spitzer RL (1976) Brief versus standard hospitalization: the families. *Am. J. Psychiatry, 133,* 795.
15. Herz MI, Endicott J, Gibbon M (1979) Brief hospitalization: two year follow-up. *Arch. Gen. Psychiatry, 36,* 701.
16. Endicott J, Cohen J, Nee J, Fliess JL, Herz MI (1979) Brief vs. standard hospitalization. *Arch. of Gen. Psychiatry, 36,* 706.
17. Glick ID, Hargreaves WA, Goldfield MD (1974) Short vs. long hospitalization: a prospective controlled study, I. The preliminary results of a one-year follow-up of schizophrenics. *Arch. Gen. Psychiatry, 30,* 363.
18. Glick ID, Hargreaves WA, Raskin M, Kutner SJ (1975) Short vs. long hospitalization: a prospective controlled study, II. Results for schizophrenic inpatients. *Am. J. Psychiatry, 132,* 385.
19. Glick ID, Hargreaves WA, Drues J, et al. (1976) Short vs. long hospitalization: a prospective controlled study, IV. One-year follow up results for schizophrenic patients. *Am. J. Psychiatry, 113,* 509.
20. Hargreaves WA, Glick ID, Drues J, Showstack JA, Feigenbaum E (1977) Short vs. long hospitalization: a prospective controlled study, VI. Two-year follow-up results for schizophrenics. *Arch. Gen. Psychiatry, 34,* 305.
21. Mattes JA, Rosen B, Klein DF (1977) Comparison of the clinical effectiveness of 'short' versus 'long' stay psychiatric hospitalization, II. Results of a 3-year post-hospital follow-up. *J. Nerv. Ment. Dis., 165,* 387.
22. Mattes JA, Rosen B, Klein DF, Millan D (1977) Comparison of the clinical effectiveness of 'short' versus 'long' stay psychiatric hospitalization, III. Further results of a 3-year post-hospital follow-up. *J. Nerv. Ment. Dis.,* 395.
23. Mattes JA, Klein DF, Millan D, Rosen B (1979) Comparison of the clinical effectiveness of 'short' versus 'long' stay psychiatric hospitalization, IV. Predictors of differential benefit. *J. Nerv. Ment. Dis., 167,* 175.
24. Rosen B, Katzoff A, Carillo C, Klein DF (1976) Comparison of the clinical effectiveness of 'short' versus 'long' stay psychiatric hospitalization, I. Inpatient results. *Arch. Gen. Psychiatry, 33,* 1316.
25. Hirsch SR, Platt S, Knight A, Weyman A (1979) Shortening hospital stay for psychiatric care: effect on patients and their families. *Br. Med. J., 1,* 442.
26. Schwartz C, Vallance M (1987) Length of stay. *Hosp. Community Psychiatry, 38,* 201.
27. Mattes JA (1982) The optimal length of hospitalization for psychiatric patients: a review of the literature. *Hosp. Community Psychiatry, 33,* 824.
28. Erickson R, Paige A (1973) Fallacies in using length-of-stay and return rates as measures of success. *Hosp. Community Psychiatry, 24,* 559.
29. Reibel S, Herz MI (1976) Limitations of brief hospital treatment. *Am. J. Psychiatry, 133,* 518.
30. Gudeman JE, Shore MF (1984) Beyond deinstitutionalization: a new class of facilities for the mentally ill. *New Engl. J. Med., 311,* 832.
31. Weinman B, Sanders R, Kleiner R, Wilson S (1970) Community based treatment of the chronic psychotic. *Community Ment. Health J., 6,* 13.
32. Linn MW, Caffey EM, Klett CJ, Hogarty G (1977) Hospital versus community (foster) care for psychiatric patients. *Arch. Gen. Psychiatry, 34,* 78.
33. Marx AJ, Test MA, Stein LI (1973) Extrahospital management of severe mental illness. *Arch. Gen. Psychiatry, 29,* 505.
34. Stein LI, Test MA (Eds.), (1978) *Alternatives to Mental Hospital Treatment.* Plenum

Press, New York.

35. Grad J, Sainsbury P (1968) The effects that patients have on their families in a community care and a control psychiatric service – a two-year follow up. *Br. J. Psychiatry, 114,* 265.
36. Pasaminick B, Scarpitti FR, Dinitz S (1967) *Schizophrenics in the Community.* Appleton-Century-Crofts, New York.
37. Davis AE, Dinitz S, Pasaminick B (1974) *Schizophrenics in the New Custodial Community: Five Years After the Experiment.* Ohio State University Press, Columbia.
38. Langsley DG, Machotka P, Flomenhaff K (1971) Avoiding mental hospital admission: a follow-up study. *Am. J. Psychiatry, 127,* 1391.
39. Langsley DG, Pittman FS, Swank GE (1969) Family crises in schizophrenics and other mental patients. *J. Nerv. Ment. Dis., 149,* 270.
40. Brook BD (1973) Crisis hostel: an alternative to psychiatric hospitalization. *Hosp. Community Psychiatry, 24,* 621.
41. Polak PR, Kirby MW (1976) A model to replace psychiatric hospitals. *J. Nerv. Ment. Dis., 162,* 13.
42. Mosher LR, Menn A, Matthews SM (1975) Soteria: evaluation of a home-based treatment for schizophrenia. *Am. J. Orthopsychiatry, 45,* 455.
43. Mosher LR, Menn AZ (1978) Community residential treatment for schizophrenia: two-year follow-up. *Hosp. Community Psychiatry, 29,* 715.
44. Fenton FR, Tessier L, Struening EI (1979) A comparative trial of home and hospital psychiatric care: one-year follow-up. *Arch. Gen. Psychiatry, 36,* 1073.
45. Fenton FR, Tessier L, Struening EI, Smith FA, Benoit C (1982) *Home and Hospital Psychiatric Treatment.* University of Pittsburgh Press, Pittsburgh.
46. Stein LI, Test MA (1980) Alternative to mental hospital treatment, I. Conceptual model, treatment program, and clinical evaluation. *Arch. Gen. Psychiatry, 37,* 392.
47. Test MA, Stein LI (1980) Alternative to mental hospital treatment, III. Social cost. *Arch. Gen. Psychiatry, 37,* 409.
48. Weisbrod BA, Test MA, Stein LI (1980) Alternative to mental hospital treatment, II. Economic benefit-cost analysis. *Arch. Gen. Psychiatry, 37,* 400.
49. Hoult J, Reynolds I, Charbonneau-Powis M, Coles P, Briggs J (1981) A controlled study of psychiatric hospital versus community treatment: the effect on relatives. *Aust. N.Z. J. Psychiatry, 15,* 323.
50. Hoult J, Reynolds I, Charbonneau-Powis M, Weekes P, Briggs J (1983) Psychiatric hospital versus community treatment: the results of a randomized trial. *Aust. N.Z. J. Psychiatry, 17,* 160.
51. Hoult J, Reynolds I (1984) Schizophrenia: a comparative trial of a community orientated and hospital oriented psychiatric care. *Acta Psychiatr. Scand., 69,* 359.
52. Hoult J (1986) Community care of the acutely mentally ill. *Br. J. Psychiatry, 149,* 137.
53. Collins JF, Ellsworth RB, Casey NA, Hyer L, Hickey RH, Schoonover RA, Twemlow SW, Nesselroade JR (1985) Treatment characteristics of psychiatric programs that correlate with community adjustment. *J. Clin. Psychol., 41,* 299.
54. Ellsworth RB, Collins JF, Casey NA, Schoonover RA, Hickey RH, Hyer L, Twemlow SW, Nesselroade JR (1979) Some characteristics of effective psychiatric treatment programs. *J. Consult. Clin. Psychol., 47,* 799.
55. Jones M (1953) *The Therapeutic Community.* Basic Books, New York.
56. Herz MI (1972) The therapeutic community: a critique. *Hosp. Community Psychiatry, 23,* 69.
57. Jones M (1968) Beyond the Therapeutic Community: *Social Learning and Social Psychiatry.* Yale University Press, New Haven, CT.

58. Herz MI, Wilensky H, Earle A (1966) Problems of role definition in the therapeutic community. *Arch. Gen. Psychiatry, 14,* 270.
59. Van Putten T, May PRA (1976) Milieu therapy of the schizophrenias. In: West LJ, Flinn D (Eds.), *Treatment of Schizophrenia: Progress and Prospects.* Grune and Stratton, New York.
60. Greenblatt M, Solomon M, Evans AS, et al. (1965) *Drug and Social Therapy in Chronic Schizophrenia.* Charles C. Thomas, Springfield, IL.
61. May PRA, Tuma AH, Dixon WJ (1976) Schizophrenia – follow-up study of results of treatment, I. Design and other problems. *Arch. Gen. Psychiatry, 33,* 474.
62. May PRA, Tuma AH, Yale C, Potepan P, Dixon WJ (1976) Schizophrenia – a follow-up study of results of treatment, II. Hospital stay over two to five years. *Arch. Gen. Psychiatry, 33,* 481.
63. Gunderson JG (1980) A reevaluation of milieu therapy for nonchronic schizophrenic patients. *Schizophr. Bull., 6,* 64.
64. Paul GL, Lentz RJ (1977) *Psychosocial Treatment of Chronic Mental Patients: Milieu Versus Social Learning Programs.* Harvard University Press, Cambridge, MA.
65. Herz MI (1979) Short-term hospitalization and the medical model. *Hosp. Community Psychiatry, 30,* 117.
66. Braun P, Kochansky G, Shapiro R, Greenberg S, Gudeman JE, Johnson S, Shore MF (1981) Overview: deinstitutionalization of psychiatric patients, a critical review of outcome studies. *Am. J. Psychiatry, 138,* 736.
67. Kiesler CA (1982) Mental hospitals and alternative care: noninstitutionalization as potential public policy for mental patients. *Am. Psychol., 37,* 349.

CHAPTER 14

The role of partial hospitalization

M.A. MOSTERT AND M.I. HERZ

HISTORY

The first day hospital was introduced in the Soviet Union out of economic necessity. Dzhagarov (1) used day hospitalization to alleviate a shortage of inpatient beds for seriously ill psychiatric patients, most of whom were schizophrenic. The first day hospital in the western hemisphere, established by Cameron (2) in Montreal in 1946, was deliberately used as an alternative to inpatient treatment. Cameron believed that day hospitalization was more beneficial for many patients. In 1948 day hospital treatment was introduced in England (3). The first program in the United States was opened at Yale in the same year, with the Menninger Clinic following the next year. A steady growth in the number of day programs has continued since that time. In the United Kingdom, the number of new patients treated in partial hospitals increased from 5,700 to almost 27,000 from 1961 to 1966 (4). In the United States, the growth of partial hospital programs was catalyzed by the passage of the Community Mental Health Centers Act of 1963, which mandated day hospitalization as an essential component of federally funded community mental health centers. The growth in the number of programs in the United States is shown in Table 1.

Availability of day treatment services has gradually expanded throughout the United States. In 1963, half of the facilities were located in four states (California, New York, Ohio, Pennsylvania). By 1972, 15 states accounted for two-thirds of programs, but only one state (North Dakota) had no day program. In 1971, the average census in a Community Mental Health Center (CMHC) day program was 18, but this was lower in rural areas. The average stay per episode was 30.2 days, and the average annual number of episodes per CMHC was 154 (5). By 1980 (6) partial care was provided by 44% of mental health organizations, with most partial care services being provided by federally funded CMHCs. Although the number of partial care admissions per 100,000 population increased from 35.0 in 1971 to 73.6 in 1976, the rate declined to 64.6 in 1981 (7). By 1983, the admission rate had increased to 76.3 per 100,000. Table 2 shows a compilation of data on admissions and admission rates. Factors contributing to the levelling-off of growth will be discussed at the end of the chapter.

Handbook of Schizophrenia, Volume 4: Psychosocial Treatment of Schizophrenia
M.I. Herz, S.J. Keith and J.P. Docherty, editors.

FUNCTIONS

Acute day hospital

Partial hospitalization serves different functions in the treatment of schizophrenia depending on the phase of illness, i.e., acute symptom exacerbation, recovery phase, and plateau phase (8 – 10). Partial hospitalization can serve as an alternative to inpatient treatment for many acutely ill patients. It provides structure and a variety of treatment modalities which facilitate recovery from an acute episode. There are a number of potential advantages over traditional inpatient care. First, there are social advantages. Partial hospitalization allows the patient to remain in his community, thus preserving his usual social support network and social role function-

TABLE 1 *Partial care services, United States*

Year	Number of partial care services
1963	114
1967	500
1970	778
1971	932
1975	1378
1976	1447
1978	1571
1980	1648
1981	1489
1984	1817

(Adapted from 5, 6, 7, 52) Note: Figures are not strictly comparable because of definitional changes in some years.

TABLE 2 *Partial care admissions*

Year	Number	Rate per 100,000 population
1967	26,595	–
1969	55,486	27.8
1971	71,522	35.0
1975	155,538	73.6
1976	163,326	77.2
1979	172,331	77.6
1981	146,978	64.6
1983	177,332	76.3

(Adapted from 5, 7, 52) Note: figures are not strictly comparable due to definitional changes in some years.

ing. It is not necessary to 'put the patient away', extruding him from his usual environment. Avoiding hospitalization permits the patient to feel less 'sick', and obviates the added burden of social stigma with accompanying lessened self-esteem. Further, hospitalization is more likely to lead to regression and more dependence on the institution with more impairment of social and vocational functioning. These advantages apply to both first-break and chronic patients who are acutely ill. Second, there are clinical advantages. The diagnostic work-up and treatment takes place while the patient remains in his natural environment, thus facilitating transfer of new learning to this environment after discharge. Third, day hospitalization is less expensive than inpatient care (11 – 17).

Recovery: time-limited day hospital

For the patient in the early stages of recovery, whose acute symptoms have subsided to the point where he is better able to cooperate with treatment, partial hospitalization can reduce the length of inpatient stay and can provide a smooth transition from inpatient to outpatient care (18). One transitional option is part-time presence on the inpatient ward. For example, the patient may stay at home at night and at the weekend, but participate in structured inpatient programming during the day. In another type of transition, the patient is transferred to a free-standing day hospital whose programs are better tailored to his increasing functional capacity. This option may be useful for patients who need more structure than an occasional outpatient visit provides. It may also be of benefit in fostering an alliance between the patient and continuing caregivers which may not be achievable if the patient is abruptly shifted from an inpatient ward to infrequent outpatient treatment. The development of an institutional transference (to the outpatient facility) can similarly be encouraged in patients who have difficulty forming a bond with a single caregiver (19). Many proponents of brief hospitalization find this transitional function extremely useful. To draw an analogy with physical illness, transitional day hospital can be likened to early ambulation to discourage regression and atrophy of skills (20).

During the recovery phase, the primary function of partial hospitalization is to foster return to baseline clinical status. The therapeutic focus should be on achieving health through increasing social and pre-vocational role functioning as well as working on increasing patients' coping skills. The patient should not be pushed too much during the early recovery phase, as his equilibrium is fragile. It appears to take about six months before the patient reaches a stable plateau of functioning (21, 22). During this period of recovery, staff members should help the patient re-establish ties in the community, actively working with families and social agencies. Astrachan et al. (8) characterize this as a boundary function. To facilitate re-integration into the community, some experts believe the program should be located away from the hospital, because patients tend to equate hospitals with illness. There is less need for medical input during the recovery phase because the patients are relatively stable symptomatically. The partial hospital program schedule for this phase of illness is modeled on the workday: five days a week for six to eight hours a day. Duration of attendance is limited, in keeping with the goal that the patient will achieve maximal functioning in the community.

Maintenance: continuing day treatment

A large number of schizophrenics never make the transition to independent living, requiring ongoing structured programming to prevent atrophy of their limited social skills and minimize the risk of relapse. Without day treatment at least two or three days per week they may regress to marginal social niches, joining the ranks of the homeless or locking themselves away from meaningful social interaction. Expectation of these patients by the day program staff should be less demanding and more flexible: attendance need not be daily or all-day, but patients should be encouraged to follow a regular schedule, since many of them are in need of an external structure in order to function. Programming should be low-key, limiting the intensity of stimulation to protect patients from becoming overwhelmed and disorganized. Staff should have a high tolerance for symptoms and realistic expectations, such as preservation of minimal social functioning and self-care and decreasing the relapse rate. The staff-patient ratio is lower than required for rehabilitative-phase programs, and even less medical input is necessary. Patients need to remain in this type of program on a continuing basis with no time limit.

We have hitherto described phase-specific functions of partial hospitalization. Whether these functions should take place in separate locations is a matter of debate. Many agencies currently separate acute and recovering patients from chronic patients. The Veterans Administration created the 'day hospital' for the former and 'day treatment' for the latter in the 1960s (23, 24). In Britain, acute patients are treated in 'day hospitals', whereas chronic patients are treated in 'day centres' (4). The arguments for separating the two populations are various (8, 9, 24). Treatment can be better tailored to individual needs. Patients who are aiming for rehabilitation and re-entry into the community may feel held back by chronic patients. Chronic patients may feel frustrated by the progress of their better-functioning peers. Homogeneous cliques may develop, stymying healthy group interaction. Staff may become frustrated by the lack of improvement in many of the chronic patients who need maintenance treatment, and as time goes on there is a build-up in the number of chronic patients because they never improve enough to be terminated from the program. Empirical support for separating acute and chronic patients comes from Beigel and Feder's 1970 study (9) of 176 partial hospital patients, 42% of whom were schizophrenic. The day hospital program in question was oriented toward treatment of acute illness. The only patient variable which predicted likelihood of completing the program was the acute/chronic distinction. Chronic patients were less likely to complete the program and be discharged to aftercare. They tended to be transferred to inpatient services, leave against advice, or be discharged because of disruptive behavior. Beigel and colleagues speculated that chronic patients see active treatment as a threat to regressive and dependent needs.

Those supporting combining acute and chronic populations (25) argue that cost considerations may preclude the provision of separate programs. There may be insufficient referrals to maintain separate programs. Staff working exclusively with chronic patients may be more susceptible to burnout (26), although this should be less problematic if treatment goals are clearly defined. It is clearly not always easy to determine whether a patient belongs in a good or poor prognosis category. Furthermore, worse-functioning patients can benefit from the modeling of better-functioning individuals. Lefkovitz (27) suggests 'stratified programming', consisting of phase-appropriate levels under one roof as a solution. Unfortunately, manpower needs would be high, and staff may very well resist such an unwieldy arrangement. The current reality is that most programs separate acute and sub-acute patients from chronic patients; finer distinctions are rare. In the next sections we will describe research pertaining to the functions of partial hospitalization discussed thus far.

SUMMARY OF RESEARCH ON PARTIAL HOSPITALIZATION

Acute phase: alternative to inpatient care

In 1964 Zwerling and Wilder (28) demonstrated the feasibility of substituting day hospitalization for inpatient care for seriously disturbed psychiatric patients. Two-thirds of the patients considered in need of inpatient care who were randomized to the day hospital were actually accepted for treatment at the day hospital. Those patients not accepted for day treatment had diagnoses which included organic mental disorders and other unspecified conditions; they remained as inpatients. Forty percent of patients treated in the day hospital required at least a few nights of boarding on the inpatient service. This study showed that a significant proportion of acutely ill patients who would ordinarily have been hospitalized could be treated in a day hospital. When the patients were followed up at two years, Wilder et al. (29) found no great differences between patients randomized to day hospital versus inpatient care. One obvious limitation of this study is that a third of those randomized to the day hospital never actually received that treatment, making it difficult to draw clear conclusions from the results.

With the feasibility issue established, the next important question is the efficacy of partial hospitalization. Herz et al. (30) undertook a prospective study in which patients were randomized to full-time hospitalization or day care on the same inpatient ward at the New York State Psychiatric Institute. Forty-five patients were assigned to each group, out of a total of 424 admissions screened. Patients were excluded from participation if they were 'too sick' (31% were suicidal, homicidal, potentially violent, extremely disorganized) or 'too healthy', indicating that the patient was no longer in need of either inpatient or day hospital treatment (20% of those screened), or if family factors or physical illness necessitated inpatient care. According to this paradigm, all patients randomized did receive the assigned treatment. Evaluations, which included the Psychiatric Status Schedule (PSS) and the Psychiatric Evaluation Form (PEF), were performed at admission, at two and four weeks, and at follow-up, which averaged a little less than two years after entry into the study. The average inpatient stay before randomization was three days. Daytime programming was geared toward 'activation' of patients, and included individual, group, family, milieu, and somatic therapies, as well as vocational rehabilitation. Day patients and inpatients participated in daytime program together. Forty-nine percent of the total study group was schizophrenic, 45% of the day group and 57% of the inpatient group. Incidentally, most of the patients deemed 'too ill' to participate were schizophrenic. Patients in the inpatient group were somewhat younger, of a higher social class, more frequently American-born, and had more previous admissions than those in the day group. Average length of stay proved to be much shorter for day patients: 48.5 days compared to 138.8 days for inpatients. At that time the tradition at the New York State Psychiatric Institute, where the study was carried out, favored long-term hospitalization. Twenty-two percent of day patients were boarded overnight for at least one night during the first four weeks. At every time point in the study there were a larger proportion of day patients than inpatients residing in the community. Staff members initially feared that day patients would be readmitted sooner, but this proved not to be the case: inpatients had a consistently higher average readmission rate, which was fully double that of day patients from three to nine months after entry into the study. As for measures of psychopathology, at two weeks there were practically no differences between groups. At four weeks, evaluations of psychopathology done by the treating physician using the PEF showed a small but statistically significant advantage for day patients. It is interesting that the four-week ratings by therapists give so much of an advantage to day patients, given that therapists, especially psychiatric residents, were particularly apprehensive about the use of day treatment for patients who would ordinarily have been admitted to the hospital. There was another clear difference between groups at four weeks: 63% of day patients, compared with only 45% of inpatients, were involved in any occupational role. On long-term evaluations, day patients had a clear advantage on measures of daily routine-leisure time impairment and housekeeper/role impairment. The authors acknowledge that information about medication use and effects of the two types of treatment on the family were not addressed.

Michaux and Chelst (31) conducted a non-randomized study of day hospital versus inpatient treatment: inpatients did not have a locally available day program. The day hospital was located in a rural area, limiting generalizability to urban areas. At the time of discharge, inpatients experienced greater symptom reduction, whereas day patients showed a better social recovery. These differences were most pronounced in schizophrenics, and negligible for other diagnoses. These differences were reproduced, although less strongly, two months after discharge. The authors attribute the greater symptom relief in inpatients to the more structured environment, but neglect to note in their results any possible differences in drug treatment. At one-year follow-up, symptom reduction was virtually identical in both groups. Social performance, including employment, was better in the day patients. In a subsequent analysis of the same study population, Sappington and Michaux (32) point out some inequities in the study groups: hospitalized subjects tended to be more disturbed, and day patients tended to come from a higher social class. The authors concluded that the overall relapse data from this study does not significantly favor either treatment.

Washburn and Vannicelli (33, 34) explored day hospital as an alternative to inpatient care in a private setting. After two to six weeks of initial evaluation on an inpatient unit, 59 female patients were randomized either to continue inpatient care or enter the day hospital. They were compared with 34 'usual' day hospital patients. An additional 106 patients refused or were unable to participate; there did not appear to be any significant differences in demographics between refusers and participators. Suicidal and 'destructive' patients were excluded. Patients were predominantly middle-class, and 50% were schizophrenic. Follow-up measures done every six months over the two-year study period showed that day patients showed greater improvement from baseline up to 18 months than did inpatients in measures of subjective distress, community adjustment and burden. Day patients and their families were more satisfied with treatment than inpatients. In the second six months of follow-up, inpatients spent more days in the hospital than did day patients. There were no differences in number of roles attempted or in role functioning. Differences between the two groups disappeared between 18 and 24 months after entry into the study. Again, results for schizophrenics were not separated out. Results for this study are difficult to interpret because no data were provided on length of stay in the experimental settings. Also, since study patients were evaluated for up to six weeks as inpatients, this is not truly a study of day hospitalization as an immediate alternative to inpatient treatment for acutely ill patients, but rather use of day hospital as a transition from inpatient care.

In a subsequent analysis (34) the presumably sicker experimental patients randomized to the day hospital were compared with the usual day hospital patients referred from the community or the hospital. Although baseline measures of psychopathology showed that experimental patients were in fact more ill, at one year they were rated as healthier than usual day patients. Because control patients were significantly older than experimental patients, the authors speculate that controls were more chronic and therefore less capable of improvement. During the first three months experimental patients spent more days attached to the hospital, required more social work time, and incurred higher costs. Despite the greater efforts that initially had to be expended on the experimental patients, this analysis showed that patients who were more ill than those usually selected could do well with day hospital treatment.

In a non-randomized study, Penk et al. (14) obtained ratings from community informants on 37 pairs of patients who were matched for age, severity of illness, type of illness, and coping resources who were treated either as inpatients or in day hospital at a VA facility. Forty-eight percent of patients were schizophrenic. Measurements were obtained before and two months after treatment. Compared with inpatients, day hospital patients did better on measures of social activity, employment, depression and anxiety. Symptomatic improvement was identical. This study is limited by the absence of randomization, the short follow-up, and the use of a single source in rating patient improvement. The authors concluded that day hospitalization is an important alternative to inpatient treatment for many patients.

In an uncontrolled study, Fink et al. (12) compared 43 day hospital patients and 43 inpatients with comparable symptoms who were treated at a private non-profit psychiatric hospital with an associated day hospital. Patients who were suicidal, homicidal, or who needed 24-hour supervision were excluded. Outcome data was collected at 12 months from interviews with patients and significant others. The Psychiatric Evaluation Form and a subjective distress and role functioning scale were used. There were no statistically significant differences between groups in gender, marital status, severity of illness, or proportion without previous inpatient admissions (70% of day patients and 65% of inpatients). Average length of treatment was significantly different: 24.7 days for day patients and 37.8 days for inpatients. Length of attachment to the day hospital was longer for day patients because discharge was delayed by a gradual tapering off of the frequency of attendance; the result was an average of 60 days from admission to final discharge for day patients versus 37.8 days for inpatients. Twelve-month follow-up was available on 65% of the study population; no differences in outcome were evident. One encouraging result was that the lower initial cost of day treatment was not offset by higher aftercare costs. In the 12-month study period, costs for psychiatric care for the day group were only slightly more than half of the cost for the inpatient group. This study is obviously subject to criticism because of the absence of randomization. It may be that there were possible unrecognized selective factors which were responsible for some patients being admitted to inpatient care while others were referred for day treatment.

Early recovery phase: transition from inpatient care

Studies which compare the efficacy of brief and standard duration hospitalization tend to support the use of partial hospitalization as an adjunct to shortened inpatient treatment. Herz and colleagues (21, 35 – 38) randomized 175 patients to (a) standard inpatient treatment (N = 63); (b) brief hospitalization with the availability of transitional day care (N = 61); and (c) brief hospitalization without subsequent day care (N = 51). All patients received follow-up outpatient treatment. Sixty-three percent of the study group was diagnosed as schizophrenic. In the standard option, therapists decided the length of stay. The study design called for brief patients to be discharged within one week if possible. Day care took place on the inpatient ward, with regular inpatients. Study patients were required to be living with a responsible adult, excluding 31% of those eligible. Other exclusions were serious medical illness, substance abuse, antisocial behavior, and adolescent behavior disorders. Measurements were obtained at admission, at three weeks, every three months during the first year and every six months during the second year. When patients required readmission, they received the same treatment as initially assigned. The three study groups were comparable at baseline except that the brief-out group had more male and fewer married subjects. Fifty-two percent of patients in the brief-day group actually attended day care for at least one day; of the remainder either day hospitalization was not considered necessary or patients refused it when offered.

The average number of days of hospitalization over the first three months was 15 for the brief-out group, 14 for the brief-day group, and 42 days for the standard group. Initial and three- and 12-week follow-up measurements found essentially no significant differences in levels of psychopathology between the three groups. The brief-day group initially made greater use of social service time than did the other groups, for unclear reasons. This group was most likely (74%) to be actively involved in outpatient treatment at six months compared to brief-out (65%) and standard (57%) groups. The brief-day group spent an average of 43 days in day care. Family members of patients in standard and brief-day groups were more likely to complain at the time of discharge that patients had been discharged too soon; it appeared that a longer initial hospitalization, or other intensive treatment, was more likely to produce family intolerance of symptomatology. At two-year follow-up, brief-day patients tended to do best in role functioning. Only 20% were unable to perform any occupational role at 24 months, compared with 31% of brief-out and 40% of standard patients. Of those expected to work, the proportion actually working was lowest for the standard group at all time points, amounting to 40% at 24 months. Although brief-out patients had an advantage at six months (64% of brief-out patients were working compared to 52% of brief-day patients), the proportion working at 24 months was similar in both brief groups (55% of brief-out and 57% of brief-day patients). Family informants' descriptions of patients' psychopathology and role functioning showed more differences than did direct evaluation. When sources of assessment were combined, the overall level of psychopathology and the degree of impairment in role functioning was generally least for the brief-day group, and most for the standard group. Interestingly, 63% of those in the brief-day group who actually received day care were readmitted, compared with only 10% of those who did not. This suggests that patients who were more ill tended to use the option of day care. Overall there were no significant differences in readmission rates between the three groups over two-year study period.

Endicott (38) conducted further analyses of the results of this study to determine whether certain patients did better with a particular treatment assignment. The conclusion was that the three treatment types were equivalent in outcome, with patient variables being more important in determining prognosis. Poorer prognosis was associated with younger age, male sex, more previous admissions, diagnosis of schizophrenia, baseline low Global Assessment Scale score (lower is worse) and overt anger. Angry patients did best with the brief-day option and worst with brief-out. The only recommendation which contradicts conventional wisdom was that a long stay is contraindicated for patients with a high number of previous admissions. It may be that chronic patients are more likely to regress with longer hospitalizations, with loss of motivation to perform social and other roles.

In another randomized study of brief versus standard length of stay, Hirsch et al. (39) obtained almost identical results. Although day treatment was not built into his study, it was available. He found that patients assigned to brief stays made greater use of day hospital facilities than did patients receiving standard care. Forty-seven percent of brief patients versus 34% of standard patients used day hospitalization in the year after the index admission. About 50% of his study population was schizophrenic. Consistent with his finding that there is no difference in outcome between standard and brief stays, he concluded that lowering the number of inpatient days would necessitate an increase in the number of places available in day hospitals.

Recovery phase: rehabilitation

Weldon (40) randomized 30 newly discharged schizophrenic patients to either day hospital or outpatient psychotherapy, which consisted of combinations of medication clinic, group therapy and individual therapy. Patients were assessed for symptomatology and community adaptation at entry and at three months. There were no differences in symptom scales, but at three months all of the day hospital patients were working or in job training, compared to only 20% (three out of 15) of the outpatients. Unfortunately, the small size of this study and the short follow-up limit the generalizability of these results. This result may demonstrate more about the goals of this particular day hospital, in particular the goal of occupational rehabilitation, than it shows about day hospitals in general.

Plateau phase: continuing treatment

Meltzhoff and Blumenthal (41) conducted a controlled study comparing a VA day hospital with outpatient care. They demonstrated that day care was superior to outpatient care for the marginally adjusted schizophrenic patient. Over the 18 months of the study, only 19% of the day patients were re-hospitalized, but 76% of the control group returned to hospital. The authors found that day patients either held their own or improved in their adjustment to the community as shown in assessments of self-concept, relationships with families, and general mood, whereas the outpatients showed a decline in these areas. Neither group showed any improvement in non-familial personal relationships or motivation for new achievement.

Aiming to explore the effects of drugs alone versus drugs plus milieu therapy, Guy et al. (42) randomly assigned patients referred to a day center to either day treatment plus drugs or drugs alone. Results were also obtained on non-study day treatment patients. Patients were diagnostically mixed (43). The population of schizophrenics was noted to have more affective symptoms than did comparable inpatients. Ratings on 92 patients included the BPRS, the Springfield Symptom Index, and three global clinical judgments of psychiatric status and improvement. Twenty percent of patients terminated before starting treatment; this group tended to be more severely ill. Overall, day patients had a better outcome: 80% were rated improved, compared to 54% of outpatients. Day patients also had greater symptom reduction on global measures. Time spent in the hospital over the succeeding year was less for day patients. Interestingly, schizophrenics did relatively better in day treatment than non-schizophrenics; symptoms most responsive to treatment were suspiciousness, unusual thought content, and hostility. Patients remaining in day treatment for more than three months improved more than those who spent less time in treatment. For schizophrenics, emotional withdrawal improved equally with outpatient or day treatment. Residence with spouse, less than one month of previous hospitalization, and age more than 20 predicted better response to day treatment in the schizophrenic group. Young chronic patients tended to show increased rage and projection with day treatment. The investigators speculate that this group was overstimulated by day treatment. Drugs alone were judged to be a better treatment for non-schizophrenic patients. The result of this study clearly demonstrate that day treatment is not an appropriate mode of therapy for neurotically anxious and depressed patients, who can be predicted to do better with outpatient chemotherapy. But for schizophrenic patients with schizoaffective features, Guy and colleagues concluded that day hospitalization is the treatment of choice.

Guidry et al. (15) performed a retrospective review at a Veterans Administration day treatment center geared to chronic patients. Using each patient as his own control, he showed that there were fewer inpatient days during the period of day treatment compared to a period of previous treatment. Sixty-one percent of this sample were schizophrenic. There are obvious limitations to this method, as the patient's clinical condition may not have been comparable for the two time periods.

Linn and colleagues (16) designed a prospective, randomized study comparing day treatment (DTC) and outpatient drug management (ODM) at ten VA hospitals. Subjects were chronic schizophrenics specifically referred to day treatment, the VA program for chronic patients. About one quarter were judged to have poor potential for rehabilitation. None had prior day treatment experience. About 8% of the referred patients were turned down due to poor motivation or lack of transportation. Patients were followed for two years, with ratings obtained every six months and when hospitalized. A variety of measures were utilized for 80 DTC and 83 ODM patients. The study showed DTC patients had better social functioning and fewer symptoms than ODM patients after two years. DTC patients also demonstrated a more favorable attitude toward the hospital and other people. The advantage which DTC patients had over ODM patients was most pronounced at 24 months. However, there was no difference between the two groups in days spent in the community as contrasted with days in the hospital. These results suggest that for this chronic population, time-intensive treatment works better than brief visits for medication management in maintaining maximal functioning. The overall cost of both inpatient and outpatient treatment over the two-year period was higher on average for DTC patients.

Further analysis of differences between programs showed that DTCs whose patients had consistently less successful outcomes were also more expensive. Less successful programs had more social work and psychologist hours, which may have accounted for the higher cost. There were fewer part-time staff members. Patient turnover was more rapid, with a greater number of admissions, discharges and readmissions both to the DTC and to the hospital. Fewer hours were devoted to recreational and occupational therapy. There was more group therapy and family counseling, and there were more interview rooms. Programs with poorer outcomes did not assign patients to individual case managers, and lacked clear methods of evaluating patient progress. They tended to have less experience of treating schizophrenic patients. Linn concluded that programs with a high turnover and intensive treatment may have caused relapse in some patients; these two factors could not be sorted out in the analysis. However, both may have contributed to making the environment overstimulating. Patients who risked relapse in these programs appeared to be those with motor retardation, emotional withdrawal and anxiety.

Outcome: program variables

Little work has been done evaluating the relative efficacy of different types of programming in the partial hospital setting. One such study (44) compared two day programs, one of which used a behavioral model, the other a milieu treatment model. Forty percent of patients in the former program were diagnosed as schizophrenic, and 35% in the latter. On entry into the study, Goal Attainment Scaling, in which specific goals of treatment are arrived at by consensus between patient, family, and therapist, was performed. Interviews were repeated at three-month intervals, with subsequent ratings on five-point outcome scales. Median length of attendance was 39 days for the behavioral program, and 28 for milieu therapy. Outcome was better for the behavioral program, but the difference was not significant. The authors found that individual differences between therapists had an impact on their study: one therapist at the milieu center was actually doing behavioral therapy. When this therapist's caseload was removed from the analysis, the results at six-month follow-up approached statistical significance. Length of attendance tended to correlate with outcome score, although some of the highest GAS scores (higher is better) were associated with the shortest attendance. Results for schizophrenics were not separated out. As the authors point out, variation in the behavior of therapists was a problem for this study. Also, Goal Attainment Scaling may have had some therapeutic value in itself. This study is also limited by the lack of randomization and differences in the populations at the two centers, particularly on crucial demographic variables. Thirty-seven percent of 'behavioral' patients were married, compared with 23% of 'milieu' patients. Also, only 53% of behavioral patients had previous admissions, compared with 73% of controls. The prognostic importance of both marital status and history of previous admissions may have affected differential outcome between the two groups. Despite its limitations, this study is still an important first step in determining which treatment approaches are most effective in the day hospital setting.

Patient selection

Hogarty (43) provided a discouraging assessment of selection of patients for day treatment. Analysis of 146 admissions of the Baltimore Psychiatric Day Center over a 14-month period showed that the average patient was a white married woman with a high-school education, living with her spouse, who was typically a skilled or semi-skilled worker. When compared to inpatients, day patients were more likely to have a history of community-level treatment, were of a higher socioeconomic class, had less severe symptoms, were more depressed, had more personal discomfort, had more neurotic conflicts and had greater social competence. Inpatients were more likely to be hostile, belligerent and negativistic. Where legal commitment or police admission was involved, or where the family had been unable to utilize outpatient mental health services, hospitalization inevitably resulted. With regard to symptomatology, hospitalized schizophrenics had more thought disorder, whereas those at the Day Center had more affective disturbance. This analysis shows that preconceptions about who should go where can be major determinants of choice of treatment, and underscores the need for randomization in any study comparing full-time and day treatment. It should be pointed out that the Baltimore Day Treatment Center was autonomous, not part of a Community Mental Health Center or hospital program. This factor could have influenced types of referral to the program.

A more recent study by Bowman et al. (45) continues to show bias in patient selection. It was found, predictably, that a psychiatrist in charge of a day program tended to refer patients there, whereas inpatient psychiatrists preferred to hospitalize. Paranoid patients tended to require involuntary treatment, and therefore were more likely to be hospitalized. Hospitalized patients were older on average, had transportation problems, required a longer stay, had less insight (i.e., staff and patients' views were discrepant), and there was family pressure to admit. Day patients were more often employed, families were perceived as being more helpful, and the patient was happier with his placement.

Program components

Program components and staffing patterns in partial hospital programs vary according to the function they serve. Casarino et al. (46) provide a summary of standards and guidelines for partial hospitalization compiled by the American Association for Partial Hospitalization. Programs designed for acute care or as an alternative to hospitalization have staffing patterns similar to the day shift of inpatient wards, as well as similar programming. At the other end of the spectrum, programs providing chronic maintenance care have lower staff-to-patient ratios, along with less need for medical and more highly trained professional personnel. Table 3 shows the average distribution of staff in free-standing psychiatric partial care organizations in 1984.

Most programs include a combination of occupational therapy, recreational therapy, group meetings, and vocational rehabilitation, as well as individual

TABLE 3 *Staffing of free-standing partial care organizations; distribution of full-time equivalent positions*

Position	Percent
Patient care staff	72.5
BA level	33.1
Social workers	17.8
Less than BA	12.3
Psychologists (PhD, EdD, MA)	4.3
RNs	2.1
Psychiatrists	1.8
Physical health professionals and assistants	1.0
Other MDs	0.1
Administrative, clerical, and maintenance	27.5

(Adapted from 53).

meetings with case managers, social workers and psychiatrists. Group meetings may be educational, therapeutic, or promote socialization through discussion. Discussion groups may focus on current events, music appreciation, art, or gender-specific issues. Meltzhoff and Blumenthal (41) recommended that the content of groups change according to patients' interest. Their chronic study population was found to be resistant to 'therapy' groups. Since such groups can evoke strong affects, this observation is in keeping with Linn and colleagues' (15) finding that chronic patients do poorly in overstimulating situations. Family involvement should be an important component of any partial hospital program and should include psychoeducational and practical problem-solving approaches.

Behaviorally oriented programs have an educational emphasis to their programming, with close attention to specific behavioral goals which are often tailored to individual patients, as in Goal Attainment Scaling (44). Falloon and Talbot (47) describe one such program. Groups typically meet for socialization skills training, and make extensive use of role-playing and rehearsal of desired behaviors. Specifics of these and other treatment modalities are discussed elsewhere in this volume. As we have previously noted, there has been very little research addressing the comparative efficacy of different treatment approaches, for example, behavioral versus milieu therapies.

Economics

(a) Comparison of partial hospitalization and inpatient care

Most studies have found that day treatment is more cost-effective in the long run than inpatient treatment, but the extent of the savings is difficult to ascertain since methods used to assess costs vary enormously. Guillette et al. (13), in a study done for Aetna Life and Casualty, found the cost of treating 31 patients in day hospital for a total of 1654 days to be $155,611. This is clearly cost-effective, the authors state, because the cost of keeping patients in the hospital for that much time would be $411,150, at $150/day. This argument for cost effectiveness works only if inpatient stays are as long as day hospital stays; in fact, the former are currently much shorter than the latter. On a per diem basis, costs are lower for day care than for inpatient care: only one shift is required instead of three, only one meal is necessary rather than three, the staff-to-patient ratio is lower, lodging is not required, fewer professional hours are needed, and so on.

Another study which followed patients for two months after discharge (14) found an average daily direct cost of $33.26 for day hospital patients and $43.16 for inpatients at a VA facility. The difference between indirect costs was more striking: $39.02 versus $73.49. Unfortunately, the means of calculating these costs was not explained.

Fink's (12) study of inpatients and day patients with similar symptom levels at a private non-profit psychiatric hospital showed costs for both inpatient and outpatient treatment in the 12 months after the index admission to be lower for day patients: an average of $2,334 versus $4,159 for inpatients.

Endicott (11) reported on costs for the Herz (21, 36, 37) study of brief hospitalization with or without transitional day care compared to traditional inpatient care. Inpatient costs were significantly higher for the traditional inpatient group, reaching $7,482 over the two-year study period. Inpatient costs were lower for the brief-day group ($1,742) compared to the brief-out group ($3,475 for combined inpatient and day treatment), brief-out patients had a slight advantage. Additional costs incurred by the traditional inpatient group included a higher cost for medication because doses were higher (despite the same severity of illness), and a higher actual cost of inpatient care because twice as many days were spent in intensive care compared with patients who were briefly hospitalized. For unclear reasons, patients in transitional day treatment utilized more social service time, almost twice as much as the other groups, during the first two weeks. More patients in this group were married and had small children. However, these direct costs paint only part of the economic picture. At six months, the proportion of patients who could be expected to work who were actually working was lowest for the standard inpatient group, at 46%. Fifty-two percent of those receiving transitional day care and 64% of those who received brief hospital care only were working at this time point. Moreover, family reports at 24 months reveal further economic disadvantages of traditional inpatient care: 13% reported a family member missing work because of the patient's condition, 38% reported needing financial assistance because of the patient, and 31% were on welfare. The comparable figures for brief-day patients were 7%, 28% and 20% respectively, and for brief-out patients 1%, 16% and 13%. Overall, brief hospitalization followed by transitional day hospital was much less expensive over time than traditional inpatient care, but it was more expensive than brief hospitalization alone. Initially, day hospital appears to hinder return to expected role functioning, but to a lesser degree than does inpatient care.

Gudeman (17, 48) compared operating costs before and after restructuring the Massachusetts Mental Health Center from a traditional inpatient and outpatient format to a small inpatient intensive care unit, day hospital as an alternative to inpatient care, and an inn for patients without appropriate lodging. Costs decreased by 13.5% in the first six months, during which staff time was decreased by 15.6%.

(b) Comparison of day treatment and outpatient care

Some studies find day treatment to be more expensive than outpatient care. Linn's comparison of day treatment and outpatient medication management in Veterans Administration hospitals showed that total cost of psychiatric care over the two year study period was $5,895 for day treatment versus $4,437 for medication alone (16). However, she also showed that day programs which had better results tended to be less expensive, partly because they used less professional staff time and less intensive treatment methods, which were better tolerated by this chronic population. She estimated a substantial cost savings if the methods used by the more successful centers were uniformly adopted. Guidry's (15) much less scientifically valid smaller retrospective study, which also used a VA day treatment center population, showed that there were fewer inpatient days while patients were in day treatment. For example, the duration of hospital stay was four times as long before day treatment. With a cost of $8 a day for day treatment and $152 a day for inpatient care, he calculated that the reduction of inpatient care with day treatment produced a net saving of almost $1.4 million for his group of 65 patients.

Effect on families

The effect of partial hospitalization on families has not been well studied, although the consensus seems to be that families must be more involved in treatment when day care is used as an alternative to inpatient care. In their study of brief versus standard length inpatient care, Herz and colleagues (36) found that the objective burden was higher initially on families of patients who received brief care. At three weeks after admission to the study, twice as many significant others in standard length and brief treatment combined with day care complained that patients had been discharged too soon, as compared to families of patients who had received brief care with outpatient follow-up. At 24 weeks after entry into the study there was no difference between groups, but fully one quarter of families still felt that the patient came home too soon. In general, longer hospitalization appeared to produce more family intolerance of patient symptoms and behavior. Furthermore, families of patients who received brief treatment were under less financial strain during the two-year study period, partly because patients were better able to return to expected occupational roles sooner.

UNDERUTILIZATION

As Tables 1 and 2 show, after an initial period of enthusiasm, there appears to have been a drop-off in the utilization of partial hospitalization, despite the overwhelming evidence from studies cited above that it can be as effective as full-time inpatient treatment, at a lower cost. A recent survey of partial hospitalization in New York State revealed that there were no acute facilities substituting day hospital for inpatient care. The sources of this underutilization are many (12, 49). Hospitals are under financial pressure to keep inpatient beds occupied. Many third-party insurance programs do not pay for partial hospital treatment. As noted above, particular patient characteristics predictive of response to day programs have not been well defined. Furthermore, both clinicians and families persist in the assumption that day care imposes a greater burden on families than does inpatient care, although this is not supported by the literature. Clinician bias is another potent force in limiting care in day settings; psychiatrists who work in a particular setting prefer to refer patients to that setting. Therefore, unless a physician is familiar with day treatment, he is unlikely to refer a patient to such a program (12, 45, 50). Leibenluft and Leibenluft (51) also cite the lack of awareness about this treatment modality on the part of employer groups negotiating benefits, resulting in low consumer demand.

Leibenluft and Leibenluft (51) conducted an extensive survey of reimbursement for partial hospitalization. Information was obtained from nine of the 11 largest commercial insurers, seven of the ten largest Blue Cross and Blue Shield plans, and seven of the best-established HMOs. Information on Medicare and Medicaid coverage was obtained from a review of relevant regulations and discussion with officials at the Health Care Financing Administration. The survey found that 42% of private insurance policies reimburse partial hospitalization, whereas 28% do not, and 30% do not specify. Those who do not usually reimburse for a day of partial hospitalization as an outpatient visit, with high co-payments and low annual maximum allowances. Three private insurers were found to have developed pilot projects using partial hospitalization as an alternative to inpatient care. One of these, by Empire Blue Cross and Blue Shield, was discontinued because of the low number of patients enrolled. Participants in this project who were contacted cited the scarcity of day programs for acutely ill patients and the desire of hospitals to keep their inpatient beds filled as reasons for discontinuation. Four out of the seven HMOs reported covering partial hospitalization, typically on a 2 : 1 ratio with inpatient coverage. Partial hospitalization is commonly used by HMOs as a method of decreasing the length of inpatient stay, but may be used to avoid hospitalization. Of the remaining 3 HMOs, one did not cover partial hospitalization, and two had a variety of policies. One HMO has plans for a pilot program consisting of a step-down unit staffed like a day hospital program with sleeping facilities. It should be noted that although 26 states have mandated private health insurance benefits for mental health, only seven mandate the inclusion of benefits for partial hospitalization, and one requires that such coverage be available to policyholders.

Coverage of partial hospitalization by Medicare has been somewhat confused over the last few years, with conflicting directives and complicated relationships between allowances for physician and non-physician care. Outpatient psychiatric services provided by a physician are currently subject to a cap of $1,100. Since 1987, coverage is allowed if it can be demonstrated that the patient will deteriorate or require hospitalization if partial hospitalization is discontinued. With regard to Medicaid, about 75% of states and territories provide some type of reimbursement for partial hospitalization. Officials from a number of states evidenced confusion about the extent of Medicaid coverage in their areas. Leibenluft and Leibenluft point out that policies of private insurers, Medicare, and Medicaid tend to favor the use of hospital facilities for treatment of acutely ill patients. Use of partial hospitalization is greater among HMOs, as it is demonstrably more economical for a capitated system. The authors favor the use of active incentives to promote the use of partial hospitalization, possibly taking the form of requiring the clinician to justify the use of inpatient rather than partial hospital facilities. Reimbursement of partial hospitalization at the same level as outpatient care makes no sense. Finally, the authors endorse consolidation of money budgeted for the care of the chronically mentally ill, as suggested by Talbott and others, in order that more rational allocation of funding will remove the incentives for inpatient care and facilitate the use of partial hospitalization when appropriate.

The goals of many partial hospitalization programs are unclear, with the criteria for admission and discharge remaining unspecified. Under these circumstances, patients stay a long time and programs which may be geared for acute treatment begin to be used for maintenance care. Such never-ending programs deter acceptance by third-party payers. Ultimately, though, the economic advantage of partial hospitalization should increase utilization of these programs. With the advent of

Health Maintenance Organizations and capitation payments we predict that partial hospitalization will become more popular than more expensive inpatient care.

CONCLUSIONS

The research described above shows clearly that partial hospitalization is an effective form of treatment for schizophrenic patients. For most acutely ill patients, it is at least as effective as inpatient care in bringing about recovery, while being less disruptive to the patient's social and instrumental functioning. Even when hospital care is necessary, transitional day treatment facilitates return to optimal role functioning in the community. With the trend toward briefer hospital stays, day treatment can provide a structured environment in which patients who are not yet fully recovered can achieve full remission. For chronically ill patients with marginal functioning, a day treatment program with limited expectations can help to prevent regression and atrophy of social skills and minimize the tendency to relapse more effectively than can outpatient care.

With regard to future research on partial hospitalization in schizophrenia, researchers should take care to specify the phase of illness being treated. Careful delineation of treatment program components which are being studied is needed to expand our knowledge of the efficacy of various therapeutic approaches, e.g., social skills training. It would be particularly helpful to third-party payers to better define the goals of day treatment so as to better predict the appropriate length of stay. Determinations of cost effectiveness under current conditions, with attention to indirect costs and benefits in the form of improved occupational functioning and reduced burden to families, will be useful in improving reimbursement and utilization of this form of treatment.

REFERENCES

1. Dzhagarov M (1937) Experience in organizing a day hospital for mental patients. *Nuropathologia i psikhiatria (Neuropathology and Psychiatry), 6*, 137.
2. Cameron DE (1947) The day hospital. *Modern Hosp., 69,* 60.
3. Bierer J (1951) *The Day Hospital: An Experiment in Social Psychiatry and Synthoanalytic Psychotherapy.* Washburn and Sons, London.
4. Bennett DH (1969) The day hospital. *Bibl. Psychiatr. Neurol. (Basel), 142*, 4.
5. Taube CA (1973) Day care services in federally-funded community mental health centers. Statistical Note No. 96. *National Institute of Mental Health, Rockville, MD.*
6. Redick RW, Witkin MJ, Bethel HE, Manderscheid RW (1985) Changes in inpatient, outpatient, and partial care services, United States, 1970–1980. *Statistical Note No. 168.* Division of Biometry and Epidemiology, National Institute of Mental Health, Rockville, MD.
7. Redick RW, Witkin MJ, Bethel HE, Manderscheid RW (1985) Trends in number of additions to mental health organizations, United States, 1971, 1975, and 1981. *Statistical Note No. 173.* National Institute of Mental Health, Rockville, MD.
8. Astrachan BM, Flynn HR, Geller JD, Harvey HH (1970) Systems approach to day

hospitalization. *Arch. Gen. Psychiatry, 22*, 550.
9. Beigel A, Feder SL (1970) Patterns of utilization in partial hospitalization. *Am. J. Psychiatry, 126*, 101.
10. Klar H, Frances A, Clarkin J (1982) Selection criteria for partial hospitalization. *Hosp. Community Psychiatry, 33*, 929.
11. Endicott J, Herz M, Gibbon M (1978) Brief versus standard hospitalization: the differential costs. *Am. J. Psychiatry, 1*, 5.
12. Fink EB, Longabaugh R, Stout R (1978) The paradoxical underutilization of partial hospitalization. *Am. J. Psychiatry, 135*, 713.
13. Guillette W, Crowley B, Savitz S, Goldberg SD (1978) Day hospitalization as a cost effective alternative to inpatient care: a pilot study. *Hosp. Community Psychiatry, 29*, 525.
14. Penk WE, Charles HL, Van Hoose TA (1978) Comparative effectiveness of day hospital and inpatient psychiatric treatment. *J. Consult. Clin. Psychology, 46*, 94.
15. Guidry LS, Winstead DK, Levine M, Eicke FJ (1979) Evaluation of day treatment effectiveness. *J. Clin. Psychiatry, 40*, 221.
16. Linn M, Caffey E, Klett J (1979) Day treatment and psychotropic drugs in the aftercare of schizophrenic patients. *Arch. Gen. Psychiatry, 36*, 1055.
17. Gudeman JE, Dickey B, Evans A, Shore MF (1985) Four-year assessment of a day hospital-inn program as an alternative to inpatient hospitalization. *Am. J. Psychiatry, 142*, 1330.
18. Koltun LV (1972 – 1973) Possibilities of stabilizing remissions in schizophrenics transferred from a psychiatric hospital to a day hospital. *Soviet Neurol. Psychiatry, 5*, 109.
19. Fox RP (1973) Therapeutic environments: a view of nondyadic treatment situations. *Arch. Gen. Psychiatry, 29*, 514.
20. Herz MI (1975) Partial hospitalization. In: Freedman AM, Kaplan HI, Sadock BJ (Eds.), *Comprehensive Textbook of Psychiatry*. Williams and Wilkins, Baltimore, MD.
21. Herz MI, Endicott J, Spitzer RL (1977) Brief hospitalization: a two-year follow-up. *Am. J. Psychiatry, 134*, 502.
22. Hogarty GE, McEvoy JP, Munetz M, DiBarry AL, Bartone P, Cather R, Colley SJ, Ulrich RF, Carter M, Madonia MJ (1988) Dose of fluphenazine, familial expressed emotion, and outcome in schizophrenia. *Arch. Gen. Psychiatry, 45*, 797.
23. Freeman P (1962) Treatment of chronic schizophrenia in a day center. *Am. J. Psychiatry, 7*, 259.
24. Ognyanov V, Cowen L (1974) A day hospital program for patients of day hospital and inpatient psychiatric treatment. *J. Consult. Clin. Psychology, 46*, 94.
25. Lamb HR (1967) Chronic psychiatric patients in the day hospital. *Arch. Gen. Psychiatry, 17*, 615.
26. Klein J (1974) The day treatment center for chronic patients; the politics of despair. *Mass. J. Ment. Health, 4*, 10.
27. Lefkovitz PM (1979) Patient population and treatment programming. In: Luber RF (Ed.), *Partial Hospitalization: A Current Perspective*. Plenum Press, New York.
28. Zwerling I, Wilder JF (1964) An evaluation of the applicability of the day hospital in treatment of acutely disturbed patients. *Isr. Ann. Psychiatry and Rel. Discip., 2*, 162.
29. Wilder J, Levin G, Zwerling I (1966) A two-year follow-up evaluation of acute patients treated in a day hospital. *Am. J. Psychiatry, 122*, 1095.
30. Herz MI, Endicott J, Spitzer RL (1975) Brief hospitalization of patients with families: initial results. *Am. J. Psychiatry, 132*, 413.
31. Michaux MH, Chelst MR, Foster SA, Pruim RJ, Dasinger EM (1973) Post-release ad-

justment of day and full-time psychiatric patients. *Arch. Gen. Psychiatry, 29*, 647.
32. Sappington AA, Michaux MH (1975) Prognostic patterns in self-report, relative report, and professional evaluation measures for hospitalized and day care patients. *J. Consult. Clin. Psychol., 43*, 904.
33. Washburn S, Vannicelli M, Lonabough R, Scheff B (1976) A controlled comparison of psychiatric day treatment and inpatient hospitalization. *J. Consult. Clin. Psychology, 44*, 665.
34. Vanicelli MD, Washburn SL, Scheff BJ, Longabaugh R (1978) Comparison of usual and experimental patients in a psychiatric day center. *J. Consult. Clin. Psychol., 46*, 87.
35. Herz MI, Endicott J, Spitzer RL (1975) Brief hospitalization of patients with families: initial results. *Am. J. Psychiatry, 132*, 413.
36. Herz MI, Endicott J, Spitzer RL (1976) Brief hospitalization: a two-year follow-up. *Arch. Gen. Psychiatry, 36*, 795.
37. Herz MI, Endicott J, Gibbon M (1979) Brief hospitalization: two-year follow-up. *Arch. Gen. Psychiatry, 36*, 701.
38. Endicott J, Cohen J, Nee J, Fliess JL, Herz MI (1979) Brief vs standard hospitalization: for whom? *Arch. Gen. Psychiatry, 135*, 713.
39. Hirsch SR, Platt S, Knights A, Weyman A (1979) Shortening hospital stay for psychiatric care: effects on patients and their families. *Br. Med. J., 1*, 442.
40. Weldon E, Clarkin JE, Hennessy JJ (1979) Day hospital versus outpatient treatment: a controlled study. *Psychiatry Q., 51*, 144.
41. Meltzhoff J, Blumenthal RL (1966) *The Day Treatment Center.* Charles C. Thomas, Springfield, IL.
42. Guy W, Gross GM, Hogarty GE, Dennis HA (1969) A controlled evaluation of day hospital effectiveness. *Arch. Gen. Psychiatry, 20*, 329.
43. Hogarty GE, Dennis H, Guy W, Gross GM (1968) 'Who goes there?' – a critical evaluation of admissions to a psychiatric day hospital. *Am. J. Psychiatry, 124*, 94.
44. Austin NK, Liberman RP, King LW, DeRisi WJ (1976) A comparative evaluation of two day hospitals. *J. Nerv. Ment. Dis., 163*, 253.
45. Bowman EP, Shelley RK, Sheehy-Sheffington A, Sinanon K (1983) Day patient versus in-patient: factors determining selection of acutely ill patients for hospital treatment. *Br. J. Psychiatry, 142*, 584.
46. Casarino JP, Wilner M, Maxey JT (1982) American Association for Partial Hospitalization (AAPH) standards and guidelines for partial hospitalization. *Int. J. Partial Hosp., 1*, 5.
47. Falloon IRH, Talbot RE (1982) Achieving the goals of day treatment. *J. Nerv. Ment. Dis., 170*, 279.
48. Gudeman JE, Shore MG, Dickey B (1983) Day hospitalization and an inn instead of in-patient care for psychiatric patients. *New Engl. J. Med., 308*, 749.
49. Mosher LR (1983) Alternatives to psychiatric hospitalization. Why has research failed to be translated into practice? *New Engl. J. Med., 309*, 1579.
50. Fottrell EM (1973) A ten years' review of the functioning of a psychiatric day hospital. *Br. J. Psychiatry, 123*, 715.
51. Leibenluft E, Leibenluft RF (1988) Reimbursement for partial hospitalization: a survey and policy implications. *Am. J. Psychiatry, 145*, 1514.
52. National Institute of Mental Health (1987) Mental Health, United States, 1987. In: Manderscheid RW, Barrett SA, (Eds.), DHHS Publ. No. (ADM) 87 – 1518. US Government Printing Office, Washington, DC.
53. Redick RW, Witkin MJ, Atay JE, Fell AS, Manderscheid RW (1987) Staffing of specialty mental health organization, United States, 1984. Statistical Note No. 183. National Institute of Mental Health, Rockville, MD.

CHAPTER 15

Models of supportive living: community residential care

RICHARD D. BUDSON

Comprehensive treatment of patients with schizophrenia often requires the provision of community residential care. These rehabilitative programs may be provided as aftercare following hospitalization or as alternatives to inpatient care, preventing hospitalization entirely. In practice, patients with schizophrenia who are not severely disabled are usually in programs where there are patients with other diagnoses as well. These include, especially, the borderline and other character disorders, and the affective disorders, including both unipolar depression and bipolar manic-depressive illness. However, those programs designed for the most disabled patients usually have schizophrenics as the preponderant diagnostic group. Taken as a whole, programs for patients with psychotic disorders are usually designed for different levels of disability. Some are designed for long-term patients, and others for patients recovering from first acute breakdowns. There are special programs for adolescents as well as for the elderly. Some programs may be 'social push', others may be 'low intensity'. Different types of patients, then, can be placed in any one of a variety of community residential programs which have been specifically conceived and planned to serve their particular needs. Thus, a spectrum of services is available in a range of different community residential programs.

Certain basic ideological principles are generally applicable to all community residential programs. These principles, conceptualized by this author in 1973 (1) were identified as rectifications of major deficiencies in the existing practices of the traditional state or private psychiatric hospitals. It was believed that the large, impersonal ward, run on a universal medical model, and imposing its own standards of conduct in a remote physical setting generally reinforced pathology and perpetuated the 'patient' state. The end result was too often an institutionalized chronic schizophrenic patient, withdrawn and hopeless, maintaining a bizarre symptomatology. The psychiatric community residence was seen as explicitly alleviating these four problems by providing a small, family-based program, naturally open to the mores of the community and located truly within it. Thus, the community residence provided a rich contrast to the stark environment of the psychiatric hospital. In this new setting, rehabilitation of patients, preparing them for life and work within the community, could be carried out with a new vigor and purposefulness.

With these basic principles in mind, clinicians and mental health administrators work to develop various programs to meet the clinical needs of various patient

Handbook of Schizophrenia, Volume 4: Psychosocial Treatment of Schizophrenia.
M.I. Herz, S.J. Keith and J.P. Docherty, editors.

types. The job of starting such programs, however, is usually complex and difficult. There are legal, political, and financial obstacles which must be understood, faced, and overcome. Furthermore, a rapidly changing health care industry scene has had profound effects on the very motivations for setting up these programs. For the first time there is, in some instances, an economic motivation to develop these programs.

LEGAL, FINANCIAL, AND HISTORICAL PERSPECTIVES

The nature of these programs requires that they often be located in existing large homes within relatively cohesive residential neighborhoods. Consequently, the very establishment of these homes can be a difficult and frustrating process due to community opposition stemming from fear of mental illness. To make matters worse, there are usually inadequate public financial resources available to expedite program development. The intermix of these factors effects a complex of administrative challenges, the solutions of which will vary from place to place.

The legal issues of zoning and building code requirements are usually decided at the local community level. Local resistance to the starting of a new program can be expressed through overly restrictive determinations of building inspectors, as well as through the denial of requests for special permits from local zoning appeals boards. It may well be that the rapid development of the Alliance for the Mentally Ill as a potent and expanding advocacy group in the United States may have some positive impact upon the very difficult problem of community resistance to these programs.

Other legal issues are licensing and the requirement for a determination of need certificate. These issues are usually decided by state agencies which may or may not be supportive and helpful, depending on state policy which, in turn, is responsive to the prevailing political climate within the electorate.

Contributing to the complexity of finding operational monies for these programs is the fact that the financing of mental health care, in general, is in a state of flux. Until recently, only in the public sector has there been support and subsidy of these programs. However, this support has been extremely uneven, depending upon the politics of an individual state, or the nature of the federal administration. State subsidies directly fund the programs themselves, while federal subsidies support the clients in the form of Federal Supplemental Security Income. Some programs have also received federal subsidies through the Community Support Program funded by the NIMH. Until recently, financing the private sector has been primarily limited to patients paying out-of-pocket, with the exception that rare private insurance companies have included community residential care in their benefit packages, often because it was included in a partial hospitalization benefit which was mandated by state legislation.

New on the scene, and potentially very significantly so in relation to community residential care, is the development of Health Maintenance Organizations (HMOs) which are funded on a capitation basis. Through this mechanism, a health service provider contracts to provide necessary services for an annual, fixed amount of funds per subscriber. In this situation, it is incumbent upon the provider to keep costs low. Since a community residential program is often able to care for an inpatient who cannot otherwise be discharged at only one-quarter to one-fifth of the cost of inpatient hospitalization, a strong incentive exists for health care providers to develop such services. Consequently, we may be on the threshold of a rapid development of privately operated community residential programs serving HMOs throughout the United States.

In addition, even the traditional health insurance companies are beginning to have all their benefits subject to 'health care management'. In this instance, experienced psychiatric nurses from a central office of the insurance company monitor the progress of the inpatient care and, in the ideal situation, collaboratively develop a plan with the hospital clinician, for the patient's earliest discharge from the hospital. Often this will involve 'conversion of benefits' with a trade-off of a multiple of hospital days for community residential care days. The movement of the health insurance companies in this direction, combined with similar HMO strategies, heralds a significant movement of patient care in the direction of community residential care.

Once a program is in operation, complicated and unique administrative situations can arise, such as legal quandaries regarding the rights of a program to exclude a disruptive resident. A major problem arises if housing law, invoking tenant's rights and regulations regarding eviction, is to be the determining law affecting community residential programs. Under that condition, unruly and uncooperative patients are able to drag the program's management into lengthy struggles in housing court, simultaneously creating a disruptive nuisance within the facility affecting all of the program's participants. An important solution to this legal issue is that the program may be legally considered to be *not* primarily *housing* but rather a mental health *service* which has a right as well as a clinical responsibility to exclude disruptive and uncooperative residents or patients. Several court decisions are beginning to establish that the latter is the case. New programs need to incorporate into their administrative structure the execution of a contract defining the program as providing a service. There are mutual obligations and responsibilities by both parties in this arrangement – service to be rendered by the program and adherence to programmatic policies by the client.

Historical perspective suggests that some of these legal and financial issues are problems because the establishment of community residential programs for the mentally ill is a relatively new entity on the mental health scene. They have been developed in the United States only in the last 20 years. Thus, their legal identity and financial place in the health care delivery system is in a process of evolution. Building codes in many states are just being drafted for these facilities, zoning bylaws do not usually take them into account, and the health care industry is just beginning to realize their potential as a cost-effective way to deliver quality service.

When viewed from a long-term historical perspective, the principles guiding these facilities do not represent an entirely new departure in mental health care. In fact, the roots of their clinical philosophy can be found in the origins of moral treatment as it was established by members of the Society of Friends for insane Quakers in the eighteenth century in England. William Tuke, a successful wholesale tea and coffee merchant, responding to the impetus of a Quaker's death in St. Luke's

Asylum which had conditions he considered to be intolerable, took the initiative to found The Retreat near York in May 1796. One can find in the *Description of the Retreat* (at York), by William's grandson, Samuel Tuke (2), many of the principles also described in my own work, *The Psychiatric Halfway House: A Handbook of Theory and Practice* (3). The commonality which bridges almost two centuries is the conviction that family values brought to bear in a homelike environment are helpful to the rehabilitation of mental patients. As described by Samuel Tuke in 1813, The Retreat espoused these values, which were common with our current thinking: staff eating and living in the same quarters with patients; a focus on enhancing the self-esteem of the patient; a sense of the importance of productive work to mental health; a family-like set of values and known consequences to aberrant antisocial behavior; and a presumption that the patient, as any developing person in a family, wished to be well thought of. In the eighteenth century, moral treatment at The Retreat replaced conditions at the local lunatic asylum where,

> 'It was believed . . . that the general treatment of insane persons was, too frequently, calculated to depress and degrade, rather than to awaken the slumbering reason, or correct its wild hallucinations.' (2, p. 23).

At The Retreat, the building housing the patients was located in a nice area in the country, without bars on the windows, and with thick shrubbery replacing iron gates around the facility. In recent years, I have similarly described the community residence as replacing long-term hospital care which to the patient's detriment sustained an environment which was based on a universal medical model where all activity was viewed in terms of the patient's pathology rather than being focused upon building his or her strengths.

TYPES OF COMMUNITY RESIDENCES

There are nine different types of residential facilities currently in use or being developed throughout the United States. Three of these predominate in usage, and are true rehabilitative programs often affiliated with psychiatric hospitals or mental health agencies: the transitional halfway house, the long-term group residence, and the cooperative apartment (satellite housing, landlord supervised apartments, post-halfway house accomodations). In addition, acute intensive care community residences are planned to serve the needs of HMOs and health care management of insurers. Five other types of facilities, only some of which are genuine rehabilitative programs, make up the remainder. Two types of programs are rare, but are of clinical and historical interest: lodge programs and total rural environments (work camps). Many patients, especially from the Veterans Administrative system, are placed in foster care (family care). Even more patients are placed in board-and-care homes and nursing homes, especially in the large cities, although these situations are often only barely rehabilitative.

Transitional halfway house

The transitional halfway house has been defined by the National Institute of Mental Health as a 'residential facility in operation seven days a week with round the clock supervision (often a staff member living on the premises) and providing room, board, and assistance in the activities of daily living'. These facilities have been traditionally operated by non-profit corporations in large old houses, with 10 – 20 residents, who generally participate daily in a planned program outside the dwelling. Although some facilities are increasingly acting as an alternative to hospitalization, the 'halfway house' has conventionally been used as just that – a transitional facility from hospital to the community. Programs of substantive quality usually provide individual counseling, house meetings, and recreational activities with emphasis on mutual support and understanding among house residents. This type of facility is more likely to have a relatively younger population whose problems are of more recent onset, and whose potential for reentry into the community and total independent living is quite high (4 – 12).

Long-term group residence

In the long-term group residence the residents are usually sufficiently lacking in living skills, or sufficiently symptomatic, to require a higher on-site staff/resident ratio than is present in the high-expectation halfway house. Furthermore, due to the severe nature of the patient's disability, the length of stay in these facilities may exceed one year, in contrast to the transitional facility, which may be only six to eight months. This type of program is designed to care for those difficult patients who otherwise would be detained indefinitely in a psychiatric inpatient setting. The majority of these patients usually have schizophrenia.

Cooperative apartments program

Unique to the cooperative apartments programs is the fact that they have no on-site staff and are usually comprised of groups of four per unit. Regular staff visits from the sponsoring mental health agency provide oversight of the success of the adjustment of the residents to each other, as well as the compliance with a required outside daily program. These programs are often developed as outward community extensions of more intensely staffed residential programs. The apartments may be designed not only to broaden the scope of these core community care programs, but also to avoid various constraints – to minimize starting costs, lower operating costs, avoid community opposition, and circumvent restrictive building codes. These programs are among the least expensive for the patient (13 – 16).

Fairweather found that patients known to each other in the hospital can more easily move into the community as a group. The group also establishes economic independence by organizing itself to operate a self-sustaining business. The hospital staff prepares the group for both the living and business aspects of the community program prior to leaving the wards. 'Patients function together as a cooperative, communal society, running the household and working together to earn money

(17 – 20).' Greenblatt lamented that these programs were not replicated commensaturately with their clinical success. They may have less current significance, as their usefulness is for hospital groups of patients who have become well known to each other through months of hospitalization together (21).

Intensive care community residences

Intensive care community residences may prevent hospitalization altogether, or significantly shorten the length of stay of hospitalization. These facilities have nursing personnel available through the waking hours and around-the-clock counseling staff. A complement of other mental health professionals fill out the staffing including an attending psychiatrist, social worker, and rehabilitation counselor. It is considered to be feasible that open hospital wards could be replaced by these facilities, which would cost approximately only half as much as inpatient care.

Total rural environments

Total rural environments are non-hospital residential facilities which offer total supervised living, including daily on-premises farming chores. The focus of these programs is that of an operational farm which provides ongoing reality-based responsibilities with high attention to the fulfillment of rehabilitative goals. Such facilities are particularly suitable for those clients who, although not needing a hospital, cannot reliably or safely manage in a more independent community setting. Gould Farm in Monterey, Massachusetts and Spring Lake Ranch in Cuttingsville, Vermont have been pioneers in this area (22, 23). Here again, this type of program continues not to be replicated and is relatively rare.

Foster care

Foster or family care, one of the oldest community placements, entails the location of ex-patients in private homes. The Veterans Administration has relied more heavily upon foster care than the state systems. Up to four residents may be placed in one foster home. The patient is supervised by the family caretaker who is in turn supervised by a visiting social worker from the referring institution. One continuing problem with foster home care is the concern that it provides primarily a custodial function. A significant study on foster homes in Canada by Murphy et al. (24 – 26) showed that there was no, or only minimal improvement in social functioning or community participation.

Board and care homes

Board and care homes have been the recipient of many discharged mental patients from the public hospitals. They are generally proprietary rooming houses which provide a wide range of care depending upon the interest and motivation of the proprietor. Some of these facilities provide little more than room and board in dingy surroundings, with no semblance of a rehabilitative program whatsoever. Other programs have well-kept, pleasant surroundings, and close alliance and consultation with referring mental health agencies. Special efforts have been described on methods to improve these facilities which are so important to the public sector in several large metropolitan cities (27 – 30).

Nursing homes

Nursing homes are a major community residential site to which thousands of chronically mentally ill who are elderly or physically handicapped are sent. The nursing home was one type of supervised residential facility which was readily available when the pressure to discharge patients mounted. Indeed, nursing homes doubled from ten thousand in 1964 to almost twenty thousand in 1969. The Medicare/Medicaid Programs becoming available in these years accounted for much of this growth. However, these facilities continue to play a controversial role in the rehabilitation of the chronically ill in the community. In addressing this problem, Goldmeir, for one, had the opinion that,

> 'nursing homes appropriate for the patient's level of functioning have a definite role to play in a continuum of community mental health services'.

He felt that ideally these facilities,

> 'should serve those requiring a relatively high degree of personal, medically oriented attention . . .'

Various investigators have suggested that more developed activity programs were needed in nursing homes in order to prevent physical and self-care decline (31 – 34).

The reader should keep in mind that well-planned and financed services primarily use the four first-mentioned types of facilities: the transitional halfway house, the long-term group residence, the cooperative apartment and the acute intensive community residence. These will be described in greater detail later in the chapter. The remaining detailed clinical description of issues with which the clinician is faced relates primarily to these four types of facilities.

DIAGNOSTIC CONSIDERATIONS

Taken as a whole, community residential facilities care for patients with various diagnoses, in addition to schizophrenia. The community residence carries out specific therapeutic tasks and addresses issues characteristic for each diagnostic group. The primary determinant of the type of community residence to which the patient would be referred is usually the level of disability, irrespective of the diagnosis. Nevertheless, as stated above, the community residence for the most severely impaired chronic patients is likely to have a majority of schizophrenics. There are also diagnostic-specific facilities for special groups such as neuropsychiatric patients and eating disorders, where only one diagnostic group is served.

In all of these programs, the universal focus and goal of the community residence is relapse prevention, and a simultaneous strengthening of the patient's capacity to function in a healthy and adaptive manner.

The schizophrenics represent a major group of patients who are largely cared for in post-hospital community residential care programs. Use of the residence may follow an initial acute psychotic episode, or be subsequent to one of many hospitalizations for a long-term chronic patient.

Within the group of the most chronic schizophrenic patients there is a dilemma in balancing the need for some social relationships on the one hand with the need to avoid a noxious level of emotional intensity on the other. Wing (35) has adroitly addressed this problem in reviewing the work of Goldberg et al. (36) and Stevens (37). These studies identify that patients living in a sheltered environment relapse very quickly when they are exposed to a program of rehabilitation that asks too much of them. Then again, Wing describes the 'clinical poverty syndrome' characterized by social understimulation. He concludes that patients who suffer from schizophrenia,

> 'remain vulnerable to social stresses of two rather different kinds. On the one hand, too much social stimulation experienced by the patient as social intrusiveness, may lead to acute relapse. On the other hand, too little social stimulation will exacerbate any tendency already present toward social withdrawal . . . Thus the patient has to walk a tightrope between two different types of danger and it is easy to become decompensated either way'.

Contributing to this area of investigation is the concept of high and low 'expressed emotion' (EE), identified by Brown et al. (38) and more recently further developed by Vaughn and Leff (39). These investigators have found high re-hospitalization rates (58%) for patients returning to families with high EE which present attitudes of intrusiveness, disappointment and pressure on the patient to act normally, whereas patients returning to low-EE families (non-intrusive, tolerant of symptom behaviors, and understanding of the illness) had much lower relapse rates (16%). As C. Christian Beels (40) observed,

> 'There are patients who appear to survive crises with the help of friends, relatives and therapists. On the other hand . . . some patients are overwhelmed instead of supported by their social connections in ways that are not easy to define'.

This discrepancy of patient types in the schizophrenic group represents a dilemma in community residence program planning, as patients can be divided into two groups – those who can tolerate a social push program (which they may need to prevent desocialization) and those patients who must have a low-intensity program (who relapse in the face of any high-intensity program). Thus, program design and operation (as well as sophisticated patient referral) requires careful assessment so as to differentiate which patients should go to which program.

The chronic schizophrenic patient represents a special challenge for mental health workers in the despair and hopelessness which they encounter in the patient and his or her family. Techniques of creating a systematic therapeutic plan which creates achievable goals, an atmosphere of hope and which simultaneously help to prevent staff burnout, will be outlined below.

A common feature of all programs for schizophrenic patients is careful monitoring of antipsychotic medication. This is because many paranoid patients either deny their illness or have paranoid thoughts about their medication being poison – both of which impel the patient to stop taking the medicine. There should also be thoughtful alertness to adverse reactions to family visits or interactions, both of which can be regular precipitants of relapse in many patients. In addition, during the evaluation, a careful history is always taken to determine two clinical facts: first, the previous precipitants to relapse (these are often typical and predictable), and second, the previously noted early signs of impending relapse. Knowing the latter can give the clinicians and even fellow patients early warning that trouble is brewing, and thereby facilitate early intervention.

The one character disorder which programs must avoid is the patient who has antisocial features, and who, in particular, lies. There is no room for a person who cannot be trusted in a community residence. This is because the residence operates as a small family-modeled community where there is much interdependence upon all of the community members for the program to operate successfully. Time and again, we have had the clinical experience of the referring clinical team not being aware of, nor fully recognizing this psychopathic element in a patient's background, to the ultimate detriment of the recipient program – not to mention the poor result for the patient.

INDICATIONS FOR REFERRAL TO RESIDENTIAL CARE

The clinician needs to become familiar with those special clinical conditions which warrant consideration of community residential care. First, there are clinical considerations which are specific to the illness, such that the successful outcome requires community residential care. These include the illness's severity, its duration, the history of relapse, and the history of previous attempts at discharge to other sites. Second, less related to the precise nature of the illness, there are those aspects of the patient's life situation which are deciding factors leading to community residential referral. These factors include the life phase of the patient, such as whether the patient is adolescent, adult, or elderly; or the particular family situation such as whether the adult is single or divorced; or whether there is an intact family home.

An unrelenting schizophrenic illness is an example of severity of illness being the determinant factor. In this instance, the patient is left delusional regardless of all pharmacological and other psychotherapeutic efforts during hospitalization. Such a patient will need to be discharged from the hospital, as there is nothing more that can be done there. However, it may be impossible for a family to have this patient at home as he or she would require more supervision than the family could provide. A group residence would be the ideal solution for such a patient. The same argument would hold true for severe manic-depressive illness, unipolar depression or any of the personality disorders.

When a patient has a history of repeated relapse following discharge from the hospital either into the home or into other types of independent living, alternative plans for placement into a community residence ought to be considered. The usual history in this situation reveals either a particular noxious family situation or inadequate structure and supervision either at home or in more independent living. The isolation of living alone is particularly deadly for most patients with psychiatric illnesses. A community residential placement often goes a long way in preventing breakdown from this kind of isolation.

An example of a life-phase indication for community residential placement would be an adolescent who is in a home which itself contains so much pathology that it is a primary precipitant of his or her disturbed behavior. This youngster may have to be placed in an adolescent group home especially to afford him or her the opportunity for a more healthy development. A young adult who is recovering from a psychotic episode may need to work at developing the capacity to care for him- or herself away from the family home, as he or she is at the stage of development where the development of autonomy from the family home is essential. The elderly patient may be widowed and isolated, with a severe depression. This would suggest the possibility of a community residential stay in the post-crisis recovery period from which longer-term planning could be accomplished. Those people who have acute psychotic illnesses in the face of a recent divorce may have no intact home to which to return. Here again, a residential interim stay may give the patient and the treatment team time to plan a better living situation.

CLINICAL ATTRIBUTES UNIQUE TO COMMUNITY RESIDENTIAL CARE

Community residential care uniquely provides a setting which approximates the actual independent living situation of the patient in such a manner that there is likely to be replication of his or her characteristic pathologic behavioral patterns which presage psychotic relapse. These patterns are subject to unusually early therapeutic intervention because they occur under the direct observation of a trained staff. Furthermore, it should be noted that in the careful evaluation of the patient the early *signs* of impending decompensation unique to that patient are also elicited so that the staff is alert to the eventuality of their appearance. Examples of this would include a patient who characteristically suddenly begins to smoke cigarettes incessantly and drink large amounts of coffee in a manner representing significant change; or a patient who had previously been meticulous, neat, and punctual becoming messy and missing or being late for his or her obligations.

Clinicians with experience in this type of care believe that these subtle changes would most likely either be missed if the patient were only seen in outpatient visits or would be discovered so late in the course of decompensation that hospitalization could not be prevented. The rectifying therapeutic intervention can be made, therefore, much earlier than would otherwise be possible. This is also at a time when the patient has not yet become so psychotic as to prevent him or her from becoming a true collaborator in the endeavor of relapse prevention. This, then, is a new *learning* experience for the patient who can, in this unique setting, be engaged in the process of learning how to take care of his or her own illness – especially when decompensation is threatening. In this context, the patient gains mastery of the situation and the ego is given a chance to deal more effectively with more disruptive, primitive parts of the psyche. All of this represents a powerful therapeutic event which could not otherwise have occurred.

In addition to being alert to early *signs* of relapse, the staff learns, during the evaluation before admission, of previous *precipitants* to relapse. It then helps the patient to *avoid* known noxious situations which are avoidable; and it helps the patient to carefully *prepare* for such situations as are unavoidable. This again is a part of the education of the patient in self care – avoidance of that which can be avoided, and preparation for that which cannot. Furthermore, it should be noted that the close staff contact with the living situation of the patient also places the staff in a position to observe signs of unexpected strengths in the patient. These, then, can be exploited in a positive way, bringing new mastery of another sort to the patient.

Additionally, the community residence has an ideology which is different from the hospital which I have described above and in detail elsewhere (3). Community residential care, in contrast to the hospital, is conceived of as being small, family-modeled, integrated within the community, and an open society, whereas the hospital is seen as large, medically modeled, isolated from the community, and a closed society. In particular, the 'family-modeled social system' is the ideological basis regarding all phases of the community residence's life. This means, for one thing, that the community of patients is involved in decision making in the facility – from choosing wallpaper and fabrics in decorating the house to selecting food preferences, to choosing weekend activities, to having a role in deciding details of house policies. This kind of participation in the life of the house gives the patient an opportunity to have the beneficial experience of decision making, which is a preparation for independent living. This is in contrast to hospital practices, which usually keep the patient very remote from decision making regarding the hospital ward, which is the patient's milieu. The staff, too, is small, stable and committed to this philosophy. As in any home, they act as role models, as they tend to be more stable figures than are found on a hospital ward, and at the same time they are more open as real people to the residents of the facility.

Central to the milieu is the ideal of fostering a continual process of self-discovery and mastery of the ability to care for the self. This usually means learning about one's vulnerabilities and one's strengths, and learning how to minimize the former and enhance the latter to preserve health. This may mean grieving for the lost ego ideal and coming to terms with realistic goals. Secondly, the concept of altruism is stressed in the milieu, which in this context means caring about your fellow house resident. This caring fosters the development of true social relationships which, in turn, fosters the forming of an extended psychosocial kinship system (4). This social network made up of patients can help foster mutual caring among friends, which we believe has a profound effect in helping patients to stay well. As a result of all this education in the milieu, patients are prepared to note adverse changes in their friends and are able to act upon these observations either by intervening themselves or by calling for help.

The length of stay at the community residence can vary. However, if it is long enough, then significant rehabilitative gains can be accomplished. Time will have been provided for working on the newly developed self, time for working through new relationships with the family, time for gaining support while developing new work skills and life skills both within the residence and in the community.

Finally, a characteristic type of interpersonal dynamic is uniquely seen in community residential care. Within the context of the social matrix of the community residence, a patient often unconsciously repeats characteristic, stereotypic relationship patterns which reflect family patterns which have distorted his or her life relationships in a very detrimental manner. Staff of the community residence are experienced as and reacted to as parental figures. Fellow residents are experienced as and reacted to as siblings. Sibling rivalries, and jealousies, raging, distrustful, paranoid attitudes towards parents, or playing off one parent against another (often in characteristic sexual patterns) with one idealized and one demeaned – all of these are played out with house staff and residents. In this situation the staff has a golden opportunity to interpret these reactions, and to elucidate the nature of the distortions. House meetings with fellow residents can be instrumental in clarifying the distorted views a frightened, distrustful, or angry resident may have adopted. The patient is given a real opportunity in the context of the community residential milieu of finding a new life style, liberated from old patterns.

FOUR TYPES OF COMMUNITY RESIDENCE

It is important for the clinician to have a more in-depth idea of the therapeutic programs in four primary types of facilities: the transitional halfway house, the long-term group residence, the cooperative apartment, and the acute intensive community residence.

The high expectation transitional halfway house

The high-expectation transitional halfway house cares for some of the healthiest patients in their capacity to function in the community. It requires that the resident have a 30-hour-a-week daily program outside the house. This requirement may be met by competitive or volunteer employment, a school program (usually college, but possibly high school), or by the resident being in a psychiatric day center. An ethos of pride among the residents is created in the milieu through their compliance with this requirement. The self-satisfaction acquired in the residents' ability to function in the community creates a spirit of self-esteem and group cohesion which impels new members of the community to sustain this standard of health. It is clear, in spite of the resident's health as manifested in his or her capacity to fulfill the daily program, that a therapeutic program is needed. It must be remembered that these residents have a severe psychiatric disorder. The crucial difference here is that the schizophrenia or manic-depressive illness, the depression or the personality disorder is not so disabling as to prevent the patient from benefiting from a high-expectation program. At the same time, this kind of program is able to provide support for the schizophrenic, structure for the manic-depressive, limit-setting for the borderline personality disorder, and an alliance against suicide with the severely depressed.

Whereas these patients are all out of the facility during the day at their respective activities, the therapeutic life of the house takes place during the evening hours. We have had a motto, in fact, summarizing the essence of the program: 'Day-time is for work; evening is for support'. The clinical program includes dinner, family-style, each evening. Through this informal group setting, a great deal of emotional sharing and support occurs as the efforts, successes and failures of the day are naturally exchanged over the meal.

Additional programmatic features in the evening include a weekly house meeting. This is a time that the entire milieu gets together and reviews issues common to all. In addition, individual problems, where appropriate, may be reviewed so as to obtain group support for a resident going through particularly difficult times. In addition to the house meeting, each resident is seen by a primary clinician once per week in an 'administrative interview'. The individual interview should include a number of areas of inquiry which are, in fact, standard areas for a clinician working with a population of discharged mentally ill patients. The interviewer inquires about how the patient is feeling; how things are going with other clients in the residence; how things are going with the client's daily activity (job, day program etc.); how the client is physically, including medication side-effects; how things are with the client's family; how preparations are going for any impending change in the client's life, such as in work, housing, family, health; how things are going financially; how things are going with any other mental health system member. These areas of inquiry are all carefully monitored so that the clinician stays abreast of the pressure points which could ultimately lead to relapse.

The clinical team of the community residence can work collaboratively with an outside therapist of a patient, so as to enhance the psychotherapy in several ways. First, clinical information which is obtained from direct observation in the living situation can be made available to the psychotherapist to enhance his or her picture of how a patient is seen by others as opposed to possible distortions of self-portrayal. Secondly, the community residence provides a therapeutic environment which either prevents crises or manages crises if they arise, so that serious recurrent disruptions do not occur in the patient's life. This, then, enables the therapy to focus on psychodynamic issues instead of being caught up in the direct management of chaos in the patient's life to the detriment of the accomplishment of psychotherapeutic work.

Unique in the staffing of the high-expectation halfway house is a live-in person or couple who makes the facility his or her primary domicile. This permits them to become true role model figures in the facility. The degree of health of the clients permits such a live-in situation without undue burnout or hardship. At the same time, it should be noted that patients can come to the halfway house who are too sick to be able to go to an apartment program which has only visiting staff. For many patients, the reassurance, availability, and structure offered by live-in staff makes all the difference between community survival and return to the hospital. Additional staff include an executive director of the program who is a clinician, and other clinicians or counselors, as required by the size of the program. There needs to be a psychiatrist affiliated with the program with regard to pharmacological issues, but other clinicians may be social workers, psychologists or psychiatric nurses.

The halfway house is usually located off the hospital grounds and is best sited in an urban situation close to public transport and near first-level job opportunities such as fast-food restaurants, shops and stores. The program is often considered to be transitional as opposed to a facility for a long-term stay. The program is best located in a large old house with many bedrooms. Size varies according to available housing. Our experience has been very favorable with a program of up to 20 residents in a halfway house. This size allows for development of enough pooled ego strength in the population to foster a strong group process motivated toward positive rehabilitative goals. Other halfway house programs will vary from 12 – 20 residents.

The cooperative apartment

The cooperative apartment provides the most independent living situation of all of the residential care for the mentally ill. This is because its aim is to provide as much independent living as possible, whilst at the same time providing support, supervision, and structure which can make all the difference between successful community tenure and relapse. In this program the residents have to have the life skills to take responsibility for themselves in shopping, cooking, handling utilities, neighbor relations – all of those issues which are entailed in independent living. The staffing is usually only one social worker or other clinician supervising each two-family unit, totaling eight residents. The program includes a weekly psychiatric interview as outlined above, and two weekly group meetings – for each separate apartment and one with both apartments meeting together. A 30-hour-per-week program is required outside the house, exactly as at the halfway house.

It is important to note that the apartment program treats patients with various severity levels of pathology. The critical issue here is the capability of the patient to function appropriately in the community with only this amount of staff supervision. Thus, there may be a highly delusional schizophrenic patient who, at the same time, has all of his life skills, and the capacity to contain his actions so that they are appropriate. Psychiatric day care may be the daily program, or a sheltered workshop. Simultaneously, there could be in the same type of facility a very capable patient with a fully compensated mental status, who is still benefiting from staff support. The key to the ability of the program to operate with this low level of staff is first, the careful screening and knowledge of the patient developed during evaluation; and second, the carrying of an electronic page which assures the residents that help is *always* available. There is an advantage when the program is one of a network of facilities so that the staff on-call is shared with other professionals.

The long-term group residence

The long-term group residence is designed to care for the group of patients who are, in fact, the most severely impaired. These are the ambulatory schizophrenic patients who have not had a beneficial therapeutic result in spite of all pharmacological and psychotherapeutic efforts. Round-the-clock supervision and programming is required for these patients. Some are able to be rehabilitated and eventually move on to a more independent level of residence. Others, even though they may improve in their adaptation in this setting, may not be able to move to more independent living. Nevertheless, for these latter patients, there is no question but that prevention of hospitalization is a major accomplishment of this program.

The staffing in this type of program is usually around the clock shifts of counselors, usually two at a time on duty, with a single awake person on duty through the sleeping hours at night. A multi-disciplinary professional staff complement during the day facilitates the various rehabilitative components required in the program. Thus, included are: a psychiatrist, a psychiatric nurse, a social worker, a rehabilitation counselor and a psychologist.

Program components provided in the group residence include life skill as well as pre-vocational skill training. These skills include all of those involved in daily living and at home and at work – appropriate dress, maintenance of personal hygiene, manners at the dinner table, punctuality, reliability, management of money and those skills needed in the community such as use of transport, shopping, banking, and utilization of community resources such as sheltered workshops, libraries, community centers, and recreation and entertainment. The use of both work time and leisure time is a focus in community residential care. Sometimes, for long-term hospitalized patients, a program in an old superintendent's house or other on-hospital-grounds building is a good site. Alternatively, this program could be in a large old home in the community. It is useful for such a facility to be near a hospital, as this may help some residents feel more secure. In addition, they often continue to use various hospital services including psychopharmacological and rehabilitative services.

Much of the therapeutic work done in this level of facility is helping the patient to come to terms with the devastating nature of the illness of schizophrenia, and to make a positive adjustment to it. Peter Choras, at the McLean Hospital, has highlighted the steps entailed in this work (personal communication). First, the patient must *accept the illness* and the usefulness of medication to help control its symptoms. Nevertheless, it is stressed to the family that it is a chronic illness which cannot be cured. Next, the patient must engage in *mourning the lost ego-ideal.* The patient must come to terms with his or her limitations, and give up early aspirations which are no longer realistically attainable. The patient often goes through a secondary depression at this point. Tricyclic antidepressants may be a helpful adjunct-therapy at this stage. Next, upon resolution of the depression, Choras describes a need for the *development of ego-compromises.* Now the patient comes to terms with what he or she *can* realistically do. Vocational rehabilitation is an important adjunct at this stage of treatment. Vocational evaluation and careful placement in a sheltered work setting can be crucial in helping to build up a new self-esteem. Family work at this junction is also important, for it is vital that the family's expectations are similarly brought into alignment with the patient's realistic capabilities. Choras's final rehabilitative stage is described as the *testing of the new ego-ideal.* Here the patient adjusts to a new-found success. Often such success frightens the patient, who feels it to be synonomous with separation and abandonment. Reassurance from the milieu helps the working through at this stage. Families sometimes have a resurgence of unrealistically high expectations at this point and must remind themselves that this success is, in fact, commensurate with their loved one's capability.

The acute intensive care community residence

This facility is designed from the outset to take patients who have had either no hospitalization whatsoever, or a brief admission of no more than two weeks. It should be remembered that part of the impetus for these programs is the desire of HMOs and health care management companies to have a more economical system of care. Consequently, the program is designed to be as efficient as possible. It also requires staff who are experienced in treating very sick psychiatric patients, who have good judgment, and who can make decisions expeditiously with confidence. (It also should be noted that, although the impetus for this system is economic, this may, in fact, result in excellent care from the patient's point of view. What is different is that for the first time the health care industry is paying the bill. Previously, it was only very rarely that a third-party payer would pay for community residential care.)

Three important clinical tasks are accomplished during the hospitalization of a patient with an acute psychotic episode. First, the patient is carefully medically cleared, e.g., any underlying organic illness which may or may not have psychiatric components is identified and treated as necessary. Second, the patient's psychiatric symptoms are brought under control clinically, e.g., the patient is no longer violent, to either the self, others or destructive to property and is coherent enough to reason with. Third, an appropriate psychopharmacological regimen is established.

While the hospitalization continues, the acute intensive care residence uniquely requires that a clinician on its team be involved with the inpatient team from the time of admission, so that key elements are known at the time of referral to the residence: the precipitants of the episode; the nature of the successful interpersonal, milieu, and pharmacological interventions; the rationale of the psychopharmacological regimen; the status of the family's involvement, support, and capacity to receive the patient back home; the likely further sites for ultimate disposition of the patient.

With these tasks accomplished, the acute community residence can take the patient. The residence itself is unique in its more intensive staffing than other residences. Here, there are nurses on duty during the waking hours. This provides the capability to alter recently established pharmacological programs. Further, vital signs can be easily monitored as required in certain clinical situations. The social worker will work closely with the family's readiness to receive the patient back home. The entire milieu works with purpose and intensity to facilitate a rapid recompensation to a previous premorbid state.

The nature of this program lends itself to the management of acute initial psychotic episodes, and to acute psychotic exacerbations of previously chronic but well-managed cases. The intention is that the length of stay in this type of facility would generally not exceed approximately four to six weeks.

Relative costs of different program types

Experience has been that costs for these four programs run generally in multiples. In 1988 U.S. dollars: the cooperative apartment program costs about $25 – 30 per day; the halfway house program costs about $50 – 60 per day; the group residence costs about $100 – 130 per day, and the acute intensive care residence costs about $200 – 225 per day. All these costs are reflections primarily of the staffing intensity and size. The cost of the number of full-time-equivalents of staffing plus other significant costs (including rent or amortization of the building, food, utilities, taxes, secretarial and accounting services) divided by the number of residents determines the cost per resident. It should be noted that, whereas the acute intensive care facility costs as much as $225 per day, that cost is still only half of the prevailing inpatient daily costs.

SOME CLINICAL FEATURES OF COMMUNITY RESIDENTIAL CARE

In the previous section, some program-specific clinical considerations were discussed. In this section, some additional features are presented which are generally applicable to patients in various types of programs. The general assumption is that the patient has been hospitalized for several weeks to months prior to referral, and that the condition was not able to be managed in an acute short-term manner.

Evaluation at admission

The clinical team that referred the applicant should be present at the admission meeting along with some representatives of the auxiliary services. Therefore, meeting together to discuss the referral should be, in addition to the community residence staff: the applicant's therapist, representatives of the inpatient back up facility, the applicant's social worker and the vocational counselor. Any disagreements among the staff involved in prior treatment should be aired, as well as any differences that may crop up during the meeting between these prior caregivers and residence staff. Included in a list of critical issues to be reviewed are: history of the prospective resident; the dynamics that contributed to the acute illness; the family's relationship to the applicant; the community residence's approach to the family; the role of continuing psychotherapy; the status of medication; services required to ensure that medication is maintained and monitored; the applicant's physical health; his or her proposed outside daily program and transportation to that program; the history of peer relationships and interpersonal difficulties; arrangement for potential inpatient backup, if necessary; the applicant's special talents, interests, and strengths; and planning the applicant's transition from the inpatient unit into the community residence.

If at all possible, there should be no more than one significant change in the applicant's life at any time involving four key areas. These include the residential circumstances, the job or other daily program, therapy, and medication. Changes in these areas create a great deal of stress in the prospective resident. Careful support of and preparation by the patient is necessary for effective coping to occur. Providing a two-week interval between these changes is recommended. Otherwise, the clinician is often hard pressed to weigh the relative importance of the likely cause of an impending decompensation, rendering it all the more difficult to intervene therapeutically with the correct measure.

Suitability for the program is decided by the community residence clinical staff, together with the applicant's clinical team. Disqualifying conditions include poorly controlled destructive impulses toward the self, others, or property, ongoing substances abuse and sexual promiscuity. The characterological trait of lying habitually, as noted previously, also usually disqualifies a candidate.

The clinical program

If at all possible, it is preferable for a new resident to move in gradually, especially if there is a positive attachment to the inpatient milieu from which he or she is coming. This permits adjustment to the new environment and saying good-bye to the old.

Experience has shown that double bedrooms are preferable to singles. Living with room-mates facilitates socialization and creates a 'buddy' system, making the residence a safer place. Furthermore, room-mates, over time, increasingly tend to look after each other's wellbeing, e.g., a resident will come to the house staff if it is felt that the room-mate is in some secret difficulty. The problems can range from suicidal feelings, through drug problems, surreptitious avoidance of the daily program, or despondency over a lost lover or friend. Double occupancy, then, provides checks and balances with regard to the clinical program and its behavioral codes, helping prevent illicit drinking, sex, drugs or antisocial behavior.

When the resident first moves in, the responsible clinician makes a very strong effort to form a strong therapeutic alliance by getting to know the resident well. The likelihood of a good outcome is very much enhanced by the quality of this alliance. In collaboration with the patient, a problem list is developed which identifies all of his or her deficiencies followed by specific therapeutic measures designed to correct them. As appropriate, life skill development schedules are drawn up or outside activity schedules identified. The resident's share in domestic chores is identified and described. A schedule of weekly individual counseling sessions is followed. Sharing of the day's events among the residents occurs naturally at the nightly family-style dinner. Over time, by experiencing this house routine, the patient gradually becomes more confident of an emerging self which has grieved over a lost ego-ideal and has adjusted to a new notion of what is within realistic reach.

The house meeting can be viewed as a paradigm of the clinical program, and is included in the routine of all facilities. These meetings can be important therapeutic events in four ways. First, each patient, in spite of his or her shyness or isolation, is afforded an opportunity to speak about meaningful issues with an entire group. Second, through the feedback the patient gets from fellow residents, it is discovered that he or she is not so strange, nor is his or her problem so unique. He or she is not alone. Third, through the help of house-mates, the resident learns to master the problems themselves and to improve his capacity to talk about them effectively. Finally, by participating in the group meetings, the resident learns that he or she was not the cause, as feared, of another house-mate seeming to be unapproachable or hostile. Thus, each person's sharing diminishes isolation, enhances self-understanding, and promotes accessibility, and undermines unnecessary paranoia. Each gain for the individual carries a reciprocal gain for the whole group. Openness on the part of both the individual and the group facilitates a mutuality, a closeness, a common helping and support, that carries into the milieu, beyond the limits of the house meeting. This effect, too, is reciprocal: group solidarity and increasing pride in the milieu foster a feeling of strength and capacity in the group to do further meaningful work.

Crisis management

In a clinical crisis, the precipitating event must be identified and explored, along with the reason for the resident's particular vulnerability to the event. An effort is always made to help the resident understand how a present event has triggered a past painful experience. Hopefully, this will assist the resident to master the situation. Alternatively, the resident may have to directly confront the reality of a situation and deal with someone who is at the cause of the difficulty. Sometimes a small amount of anti-anxiety or antipsychotic medication, as appropriate, can help. Enlisting the support of a resident's family and/or significant others may be a very therapeutic move. This can be accomplished in a joint meeting to identify the nature of and solutions to the crisis.

In spite of these efforts, if the resident remains agitated or seriously depressed, requiring continuous special attention from staff, a brief hospitalization may often shorten the duration of the disturbance. If at all possible, such action should be taken with the cooperation of the resident, with the understanding that the community residence bed will remain available for immediate return upon the resolution of the crisis.

Leaving the community residence

The resident should depart, if at all possible, to a living situation within the context of an existing social network. Ex-residents should move into a living arrangement with known others such as other former house-mates, not live alone. A daily program of familiar activities should be in place. A therapeutic relationship with a significant trusted other, often a clinician, to whom the patient can turn in time of trouble is a crucial sine qua non of requirements before departure. The medication regimen should be stabilized and provisions made for medical monitoring where appropriate. Ideally, the ex-resident's relationship with the family of origin is also under control, so that old pathological patterns will not re-emerge without some provision for checking them and preventing relapse. Finally, it is desirable for there to be a continuing relationship with the community residence through an ex-resident program and personal ties to the house. Taking all these items into consideration, it is apparent that it is in the interest of the resident moving out to benefit from the greatest amount of stability and resources as possible.

CONCLUSION

This chapter has summarized some salient points regarding community residential care both as an important aftercare service following psychiatric hospitalization, and as an important alternative to hospitalization altogether. The potential for a rapid increase in the development of these facilities has been reviewed. The reader has been made aware of some of the administrative issues in starting these much-needed programs. The various types of programs have been briefly surveyed. The clinician has been furnished with a detailed description of which patients these programs can treat, and when he or she ought to consider a patient for referral. Their essential character, so reminiscent of the moral treatment of the eighteenth century, has been identified. A more thorough description of four primary types of program has been furnished, and various clinical topics pertinent to the successful management of these programs have been reviewed.

REFERENCES

1. Budson RD (1973) The Psychiatric Halfway House. *Psychiatr. Ann., 3,* 64.
2. Tuke S (1964) *Description of the Retreat.* Dawsons of Pall Mall, London.
3. Budson RD (1978) *The Psychiatric Halfway House: A Handbook of Theory and Practice.* University of Pittsburgh Press, Pittsburgh.
4. Budson RD, Jolley RE (1978) A crucial factor in community program success: the extended psychosocial kinship system. *Schizophr. Bull., 4,* 609.
5. Budson RD (1978) Community residential care for the mentally ill in Massachusetts: halfway houses and cooperative apartments. In: Goldmeier J, Mannino FV, Shore MF (Eds.), *New Directions in Mental Health Care: Cooperative Apartments.* DHEW Publ. No. (ADM) 78-685, pp. 4–19. National Institute of Mental Health Study Center, Adelphi, MD.
6. Budson RD (1981) Challenging themes in community residential care systems. *New Direct. Ment. Health Serv., 11,* 105–113.
7. Wechsler H (1960) Halfway houses for former mental patients: a survey. *J. Soc. Issues, 16,* 20.
8. Landy D, Greenblatt M (1965) *Halfway House.* U.S. Dept. of Health, Education, and Welfare, Vocational Rehabilitation Administration, Washington, DC.
9. National Institute of Mental Health (1973) *Reference Data on Halfway Houses for the Mentally Ill and Alcoholics, United States.* U.S. Government Printing Office, Washington, DC.
10. Rothwell ND, Doniger JM (1966) *The Psychiatric Halfway House: A Care Study.* Charles Thomas, Springfield, IL.

11. Raush HL, Raush CL (1968) *The Halfway House Movement: A Search for Sanity.* Appleton-Century Crofts, New York.
12. Glasscote RM, Gudeman JE, Elpers JR (1971) *Halfway Houses for the Mentally Ill.* Joint Information Service of the APA and NAMH, Washington, DC.
13. Goldmeir J, Mannino FV, Shore MF (Eds.) (1978): *New Directions in Mental Health Care: Cooperative Apartments.* Department of Health Education and Welfare Publication No. (ADM) 78-685. National Institute of Mental Health. Adelphi, MD.
14. Sandall H, Hawley T, Gordon GL (1975) The St. Louis Homes. *Am. J. Psychiatry, 32,* 617.
15. Chien C, Cole JO (1973) Landlord supervised cooperative apartments: a new modality for community based treatment. *Am. J. Psychiatry, 130,* 156.
16. Arce AA, Vergare MJ, Adams RS, Lazarus L (1982) *A Typology of Community Residential Services.* American Psychiatric Association, Washington, DC.
17. Mannino FV, Ott S, Shore MF (1977) Community residential facilities for former mental patients: an annotated bibliography. *Psychosoc. Rehabil. J., 1,* Winter, 1.
18. Fairweather GW, Sanders DH, Maynard H (1969) *Community Life for the Mentally Ill: An Alternative to Institutional Care.* Aldine, Chicago.
19. McDonald L, Gregory GW (1971) *The Fort Logan Lodge: International Community For Chronic Mental Patients.* National Institute of Mental Health Final Report, Grant No. 1-RO1 MH1 5853-02. National Institute of Mental Health, Rockville, MD.
20. Anthony WA (1972) Efficacy of psychiatric rehabilitation. *Psychol. Bull., 78,* 447.
21. Greenblatt M, Budson R (1976) A symposium: follow-up studies of community care. *Am. J. Psychiatry, 133,* 916.
22. Huessy HR (1966) Spring Lake Ranch – The pioneer halfway house. In: Huessy HR (Ed), *Mental Health With Limited Resources,* pp. 63 – 72. Grune & Stratton, New York.
23. Wechsler H (1961) Transitional residences for former mental patients: a survey of halfway houses and rehabilitation facilities. *Ment. Hyg., 45,* 65.
24. Murphy HBM, Engelsmann F, Tcheng-Laroch F (1976) The influence of foster home care on psychiatric patients. *Arch. Gen. Psychiatry, 33,* 179.
25. Goldmeir J (1977) Community residential facilities for former mental patients: a review. *Psychosoc. Rehabil. J., 1,* Summer, 1.
26. Linn MW (1981) Can foster care survive? *New Direct. Ment. Health Serv., 11,* 35.
27. Lamb HR (1981) Maximizing the potential of board and care home. *New Direct. Ment. Health Serv., 11,* 19.
28. Lamb HR (1980) Board and care home wanderers. *Arch. Gen. Psychiatry, 37,* 135.
29. Shadoan RA (1976) Making board and care homes more therapeutic. In: Lamb, HR et al. (Eds), *Community Survival for Long Term Patients.* Jossey-Bass, San Francisco.
30. Tunaka B, Shaefer I (1965) The community boarding house as a traditional residence during aftercare. *Curr. Psychiatr. Ther., 2,* 235.
31. Dobson WR, Patterson TW (1964) A behavioral evaluation of geriatric patients living in nursing homes as compared to a hospitalized group. *Gerontology, 1,* 135.
32. Epstein L, Simon A (1968) Alternatives to state hospitalization for the geriatric mentally ill. *Am. J. Psychiatry, 124,* 955.
33. Gaitz CM, Baer PE (1971) Placement of elderly psychiatric patients. *J. Am. Gerontol. Soc., 19,* 601.
34. Goldstein SE, Rogers L (1973) Community liaison with a mental hospital. *J. Am. Gerontol. Soc., 21,* 538.
35. Wing JK (1978) The social context of schizophrenia. *Am. J. Psychiatry 135,* 1333.
36. Goldberg SC, Schooler NR, Hogarty GE (1977) Prediction of relapse in schizophrenic outpatients treated by drug and sociotherapy. *Arch. Gen. Psychiatry, 34,* 171.

37. Stevens B (1973) Evaluation of rehabilitation for psychotic patients in the community. *Acta Psychiatr. Scand., 49,* 169.
38. Brown GW, Birley JLT, Wing JK (1972) Influence of family life on the course of schizophrenic disorders: a replication. *Br. J. Psychiatry, 121,* 241.
39. Vaughn CE, Leff JP (1981) Patterns of emotional response in relatives of schizophrenic patients. *Schizophr. Bull., 7,* 43.
40. Beels CC (1981) Social support and schizophrenia. *Schizophr. Bull., 7,* 58.

CHAPTER 16

Psychosocial management of substance abuse in schizophrenia

SAMUEL G. SIRIS AND JOHN P. DOCHERTY

In recent years, substance abuse has become increasingly recognized as an issue of substantial prevalence in schizophrenia and a prominent source of secondary morbidity (1 – 7). Between 20 and 25% of psychiatric patients admitted with a diagnosis of schizophrenia report recent substance abuse in response to specific questioning (4), and higher proportions of substance abuse can be uncovered if laboratory tests are also employed to detect abused substances (5). Nevertheless, the scientific study of appropriate interventions for this complication in the course of schizophrenia has lagged far behind the need.

Doubtless, there are a number of important reasons for this scientific lag. Schizophrenia and substance abuse are complex clinical conundrums, difficult to study properly in their own right, without compounding the difficulties by looking at the two types of disorder in their combined state. Unfortunately, the situation in the world of clinical treatment parallels that in research. Programs which treat psychiatric patients often do not wish to accept responsibility for patients who are also substance abusers, and often do not know how to treat them. At the same time, substance abuse treatment programs usually do not want to be burdened by patients carrying an Axis I psychiatric diagnosis, and are usually not appropriately staffed for such patients. The result is that patients carrying this co-morbidity frequently have no place to turn. Yet, 'dual diagnosis' cases exist: people are suffering, lives are going to waste, and the burden on the community is great.

SUBSTANCE ABUSE AS A COMPLICATION OF SCHIZOPHRENIA

It is the schizophrenia programs which have to learn how to treat substance abuse in schizophrenia. This is because the substance abuse is a complication of schizophrenia in these patients and not the other way around. There are special skills crucial to working effectively with schizophrenic patients which cannot be forgotten just because that patient is now abusing a substance. Although some of the specific therapeutic interventions from which patients with primary substance abuse seem to benefit may be applicable to schizophrenic patients prone to substance abuse, others of these interventions are often antithetic to what is beneficial for patients with schizophrenia (8 – 15). For example, primary substance abuse patients often need to be vigorously and dramatically confronted. They need to have their walls

Handbook of Schizophrenia, Volume 4: Psychosocial Treatment of Schizophrenia.
M.I. Herz, S.J. Keith and J.P. Docherty, editors.

of defensive denial broken down. These individuals' direct experience of the full impact of the devastation they are bringing on themselves is mobilized in an effort to restore more accurate reality testing and counteract the power of the abused drug. Interpersonal techniques, usually in the form of powerful group processes, are mobilized in this endeavor and focused unrelentingly on the patient to achieve this breakthrough. Of course, these are obviously interactions of exceptionally high expressed emotion (high EE). However, the most prominent single finding in the past two decades of psychosocial investigation of the course of schizophrenia is that a high-EE environment (i.e., an environment rated high for criticism, intrusiveness, and hostility) is strongly associated with psychotic relapse (16 – 18). The types of intervention which the treatment programs geared to primary substance abusers are required to make also constitute information overload for schizophrenic patients – another factor which is considered to predispose schizophrenic patients to decompensation (19, 20).

Additionally, primary drug treatment programs expect and require a high degree of autonomous functioning, socially and otherwise, on the part of their participants – generally far more autonomous functioning than most schizophrenic patients are capable of generating, and they generally require patients to be able to make use of metaphorical and other abstract communications which may exceed the capability of many schizophrenic patients to decipher. Vulnerable and easily scapegoated schizophrenic patients are quite at sea in such an environment. Primary drug treatment programs are in fact correct in not wanting to include patients with schizophrenia and expose them to stimuli which may be detrimental, and referring such patients to primary drug-treatment rehabilitation programs is certainly not the answer for most schizophrenic patients who have also been experiencing substance use and abuse.

The answer is to develop expertise in managing substance abuse within the context of expertise in managing schizophrenia itself. The substance abuse needs to be understood and worked with as a symptom – a potentially ominous symptom to be sure, filled with potential for further morbidity or social complications. Substance abuse is a difficult complicating symptom in schizophrenia, much as suicidality or irritability are difficult complicating symptoms which threaten additional psychiatric, medical, or social morbidity, and which therefore require specific attention in their own right. Special treatment tracks may need to be developed for the management of the symptom of substance abuse in the context of schizophrenia, but we should not exclude patients from our programs for being afflicted with the very illness we are trying to treat. If we are to treat this complication of schizophrenia, we cannot say, 'If you do this we will throw you out of the program', any more than we would say, 'If you insist on hallucinating we will throw you out of this program'. Schizophrenic patients will correctly hear this as 'If you allow me to become aware of the fact that you are having this symptom, I will reject you'. The patient will then generalize this to a feeling, indeed correct, that it is dangerous to let the therapist know what is really going on. In such an atmosphere, no meaningful therapeutic alliance can exist. The principles of effective treatment for substance-abusing schizophrenic patients begin with the building of a working therapeutic alliance. They then go on to include psychoeducational and behavioral techniques, including the providing and reinforcing of concrete alternatives.

THERAPEUTIC ALLIANCE

A strong therapeutic alliance is central to the success of useful psychosocial interventions in schizophrenia (21 – 24). The therapist needs to be able to speak, in a gentle, patient, and unambivalent way, to the healthy part of the patient and be saying (through his actions, which speak louder than his words) 'I am here, I am consistent, I am rational. I can deal with your truth and your experience without abandoning you, and I will try to help you.' The therapeutic alliance is the work of two experts, the therapist and the patient. The therapist is an expert on 'what all the books say' and what numbers of other patients have experienced. The therapist is also a communications expert in being able to converse with and get to know a person who has schizophrenia. The patient is an expert on what it is he experiences and what his life has been like. These two experts must work together. They must both be able to speak openly and honestly for this work to progress.

For a substance-abusing schizophrenic patient, as for many other patients, a useful analogy for the therapist in this alliance is that the therapist functions for the patient as a coach does for an athlete. The coach is highly invested in the athlete functioning as well as possible, and uses many aspects of special expertise to help train and prepare the athlete, yet the race itself is for the athlete alone to run. The world judges the race, and the athlete may judge himself, but a good coach does not judge the race. At most, the good coach may judge whether the athlete is doing his personal best.

Similarly, the therapist of a substance-abusing schizophrenic is not judgmental. He works with the patient to build adaptive behaviors and extinguish maladaptive ones. He rewards positive behaviors with praise, i.e., avoiding those situations which lead to substance abuse, avoiding substance abuse itself, developing alternative behaviors and sources of gratification. If the patient falters and abuses his substance, the therapist is permitted to show anger or disappointment (gently, to the extent the therapeutic alliance will support and in a manner which demonstrates concern for the patient's welfare – not as an expression of the therapist's frustration or chagrin). The anger or disappointment should not be in the context of 'You are bad' (a negative communication), but rather, 'You can do better than that' (a positive communication). Like a good coach, the therapist can and should show affect. Although schizophrenic patients may be 'allergic' to negative affect, they thrive on authentic positive affect. In anhedonic or undermotivated states, a gentle infusion of positive affect may be crucial. This can usefully take the form of a 'You can do it!' positive pep talk, as long as the therapy progresses by small steps and does not ask of the patient what the patient is not yet able to achieve: 'That's the way to go!', 'Nice job!' or 'You're doing very well at avoiding crack now, but remember, you've got to keep your guard up all the time!'. Patients should be encouraged and admired for their constructive alternative behaviors. This is useful because it moves at least part of the focus away from drugs to other areas, (i.e., the patient is not important or notorious for being a drug abuser, or even a wonderfully abstinent former drug abuser, but the focus can move on to something else concretely positive). Many patients, as they move away from the physical sensations created by drugs, turn to other positive, constructive physical activities such as jogging, bicycle riding, weight-lifting, etc. The therapist should be supportive about this with the patient. 'You really look like you're getting into shape'. 'How many repetitions are you up to now?' Again, this is not to impose unrealistic pressures or expectations on the patient, but simply to join him in the pleasures and self-esteem which derives from constructive endeavors.

All along, drug abuse is consistently and firmly discouraged. The framework of this is not because drug abuse is bad or immoral, but because it is maladaptive. The therapist helps the patient understand that drug-abuse experiences are a chemically induced deception. Instead, the therapist wants to work with the patient to achieve real experiences which will be more genuine and lasting, and which will not carry with them the risk of re-exacerbating the psychosis which was such a big part of the problem in the first place. The therapist understands that a brief experience of gratification may follow the ingestion of a substance, and that this brief pulse of gratification may be occurring in an existence which is otherwise experienced as being quite desolate. Nevertheless, the therapist remembers, and asks the patient to remember, that more enduring and more genuine gratifications can be built in other ways, and that this is the goal toward which the therapy is working.

DIFFERENTIAL DIAGNOSIS

There is no one single reason why a schizophrenic patient may abuse a substance. Therefore, a proper treatment of substance abuse will start with a differential diagnosis of what the predispositions are.

Self-medication

One reason why a schizophrenic patient may abuse a substance is in an attempt to find relief from an uncomfortable or unhappy state. In this version of the 'self-medication' hypothesis of substance abuse (4, 25, 26) the patient may be endeavoring to relieve dysphoria, anergia, or anhedonia. Indeed, it is noteworthy that the substances disproportionately chosen for abuse by patients with schizophrenia are psychostimulants. In their review of the literature, Schneider and Siris (7) found that amphetamines and cocaine were abused more by schizophrenic patients than by control groups in four out of eight studies (1, 2, 4, 27 – 31). They found that the majority of studies also showed more abuse of caffeine, cannabis, hallucinogens, inhalants and tobacco among patients with schizophrenia. On the other hand, most studies showed alcohol, opiates, and sedative hypnotics to be less likely to be abused by schizophrenic patients (7). In a sense, such a pattern for choice of substances of abuse is counterintuitive, inasmuch as psychostimulants are the substances which might most likely be associated with re-exacerbation of psychosis (4, 17, 31 – 38), and schizophrenic patients regard psychosis as a terrifying experience which they want to avoid. Therefore, there must be a powerful counter-reason pushing them to abuse psychostimulants. The inference, then, is that dysphoria, anergia, and anhedonia are such terribly unpleasant experiences for these patients that they may risk psychosis to self-medicate with psychostimulants. Of course, the possibility must also be considered that certain schizophrenic patients, suffering major confusion in the realm of understanding cause and effect, may not realize that abused substances have psychotogenic properties, and psychoeducational approaches in this area may be invaluable.

For their own part, the dysphorias of schizophrenia have their own differential diagnosis. Several of these are psychopharmacological in their etiology and management. Nevertheless, it is appropriate to mention them because members of the psychosocial treatment team may be the first to recognize them in a given patient. Also, they may occur in conjunction with other more psychosocial issues and impede the proper course of psychosocial help if they are left unaddressed.

Extrapyramidal neuroleptic side-effects

Akinesia is an extrapyramidal neuroleptic side-effect. It may occur in conjunction with muscle stiffness or lack of associated muscle movements which can make its diagnosis obvious. Associated muscle movements include not only such action as arm-swing while walking, but also such socially important behaviors as gesturing while talking, or changes in facial expression (which are a powerful component of maintaining the engagement of the other person) while talking or listening. Another insidious and subtle manifestation of akinesia may best be described as a loss of spontaneity (39 – 41). In this version of akinesia, a patient presents as a prototypic 'bump on a log' or 'as if starter motor is broken'. For example, when a show comes to an end on television, the patient with akinesia will continue 'through inertia' to watch whatever comes on next, whether he is interested in it or not. Obviously, the anhedonia and ennui which can result from this form of akinesia can be enormous. It is crucial to recognize because it can be treated through reduction of neuroleptic medications or aggressive treatment with appropriate antiparkinsonian medications to which it may promptly respond (41, 42).

Another extrapyramidal neuroleptic side-effect which can be associated with marked dysphoria is akathisia. This is a motor restlessness syndrome which can also be either dramatic and obvious or subtle and easily overlooked (43, 44). Again, this is a syndrome which may respond to a decrease in the neuroleptic dosage. It may also respond to antiparkinsonian medications (although it is less likely to respond to these than akinesia), beta-blockers such as propanolol, or occasionally benzodiazepines. The risk is that akathisia may be misidentified as an increase in psychosis, psychotic agitation, psychotic anxiety, or a predisposition to non-specific 'acting-out' behavior, and that this could lead to an increase in the dose of antipsychotic medications which, in turn, could lead to a worsening of these symptoms in a spiralling manner. Sometimes the patient is able to provide the valuable clue that the restlessness associated with akathisia has a distinctly physical quality, or seems to be centered in the legs, and this can help establish an otherwise difficult diagnosis.

Prodrome of psychotic relapse

A third dysphoria of schizophrenia is the dysphoria which is frequently a concomitant of the decompensation process into psychosis (20, 45). Incipient decompensation in schizophrenia is an event to be treated not only with increased attention to appropriate neuroleptic medication, but also with an increase in psychosocial supports to help ward off a more flagrant psychotic episode (46). Obviously, such a time would be the worst moment for a patient to self-medicate with a psychostimulant, which might be expected to hasten the decompensation process. Part of the intensification of psychosocial support at such a time for schizophrenic patients with a propensity for substance abuse is to be sure to safeguard them against that behavior. Other crucial psychosocial support at those times will involve stress reduction, concrete problem-solving help, and reduction to exposure to negative expressed emotion.

Depression and negative symptoms

Secondary depression in schizophrenia and negative symptoms in schizophrenia are two concepts which have been popularly described, but variously and at times somewhat loosely defined (47 – 50). Each involves the constructs of anhedonia and anergia – symptoms which might prompt a patient to attempt self-medication with illicit substances; and hypotheses with regard to the pathophysiology of these states are consistent with the use of at least some of these substances as self-medication. In terms of psychopharmacological management, it has been relevant to recognize secondary depression and negative symptoms in schizophrenia, because each may have relevance to the utility, or lack thereof, for specific medication treatment approaches (42, 50 – 56). Whether or not secondary depression in schizophrenia will respond to psychotherapeutic interventions such as those which have been devised and tested for primary depression (57 – 62), however, is a testable empiric question which has not as yet been addressed. The possibility of this occurring, though, might well be born in mind by persons involved in treating substance-abusing 'depressed' schizophrenic patients. Similarly, certain cognitive deficits may be prevalent in schizophrenic patients with negative symptoms (63). Psychosocial strategies for helping substance-abusing schizophrenic patients who manifest the 'negative symptom' syndrome will benefit by being informed with regard to the specific cognitive difficulties these patients may have in the areas of attention, organization of thought, and ability to generalize, so that patients may better be able to absorb the value of the interventions.

Disappointment and demoralization

Transient disappointment reactions, of course, can occur in patients with schizophrenia as they do with other people. These times are also times for increasing psychosocial support for patients who, in the past, have learned to self-regulate their affective state through the ingestion of illicit substances. At these times the psychosocial support should focus on problem solving and, possibly, concrete help in eliminating the situation which is generating the disappointment. The saving grace of transient disappointment reactions, of course, is that they are transient. If the patient can be supported and protected from ill-advised attempts to resolve the state (such as drug abuse or eliciting negative reactions from others in order to feel their presence or generate their attention), the transient disappointment reaction will run its own course and resolve.

Much more enduring than a transient disappointment reaction is the syndrome of demoralization (64) among patients whose self-esteem is already likely to be low. Schizophrenia is undoubtedly a major life-disrupting affliction. Even if patients are not told this directly, they quickly figure out from looking around them that, although there are treatments, schizophrenia is a disorder for which there is as yet no cure. Furthermore, it is a recurrent disorder, with terrifying and debilitating episodes recurring at unpredictable intervals and, often enough, 'just at the worst time' when some other important life event is in the process of taking place. Patients also learn that they are stigmatized, discriminated against, and often enough abandoned by friends or even family. In the name of 'therapy', mental health professionals will also often be telling them that what they need to do is to lower their expectations – lower vocational expectations, lower social expectations, and/or lower economic expectations. Instead of seeing themselves as a person with future, they may begin to see themselves as an embarrassment to all who know them and a drain on society. This is indeed a state of affairs worth being severely disappointed about, and not transiently so. It is understandable how an individual with a demoralization syndrome could turn to drugs out of a sense that 'it doesn't matter anymore anyway,' and as an escape from the intensely painful feelings which accompany his dilemma. Psychosocial therapy for the demoralization syndrome is a long-term enterprise. Losses and pessimism which are not acute cannot usually be acutely reversed. The fact that this enterprise is ambitious and costly makes it all the more important that clinical phenocopies which can be more easily treated, pharmacologically or psychotherapeutically, are ruled out first.

REHABILITATION

Psychosocial rehabilitation is central to the treatment of demoralization. Social and vocational skills which have been lost need to be refreshed and relearned. If these skills are absent, never having been present in the first place, a very careful assessment needs to be made of exactly which skills are 'rate-limiting' for the patient's progress, so that a focused effort can be made to help the patient develop them. In any case, the atmosphere should be optimistic, but not pressured. Growth and improvement should be expected, but the expectation of the pace of these gains should not be unrealistic. 'One step at a time and keep it moving gently forward' should be the watchword rather than progressing, and retrogressing, by great leaps and disruptive lurches. Patients should be encouraged to do whatever they are able to do, yet reassured that recovery takes time and that patience is valuable. Here, the wisdom of Solomon is often required to know how hard to 'push' a patient to progress. It is probably best to keep pushing gently while monitoring the patient's symptomatology, mental status, and objective progress for clues about how best to proceed. Sometimes the wisdom must come in the other direction as well: a patient may feel ready to move forward before we are confident he will succeed (i.e., the patient may quickly want to move back into a paying job). In this case we may not want to create another disappointment for the patient by allowing him to try something at which he will fail, but we also do not want to make an invalid out of a patient unnecessarily. Sometimes patients will surprise us with their strengths, and they should be allowed to do this. Strengths are as important, or maybe even more important than liabilities in this realm of endeavor. Determination and confidence are strengths, and patients should be allowed to use these to their best advantage to get themselves back into the mainstream of life; yet realism and good judgment must be the watchword as well.

The challenge for the therapist here is to make sure he keeps up with the patient and stays at the patient's side as the patient progresses, so that the progress is not a conflict and can occur with the continuing support of a constructive therapeutic alliance. In the counter-transference, as well as the transference, issues of dealing with 'parental' concern about autonomy are bound to surface. But at some point, the therapist has to let the patient get back into life, just as the parent at some point must (perhaps with his heart in his throat) let a child cross the street alone for the first time. But self-esteem gained through honestly autonomous successes and functioning can be a useful antidote for the temptation of achieving the same, albeit transitory, subjective state by inducing it pharmacologically with an illicit substance.

Indeed, lack of self-esteem or other manifestations of 'superego gratifications' can be substantial contributors to substance abuse. Certain substances, most notably cocaine, seem to generate the psychic equivalent of a 'superego' reward as a prominent component of their subjective response profile. An aspect of the pleasure, then, which a patient gets from ingesting such a substance is the equivalent of the gratification he would experience if his parents, his boss, his clergyman, his drill sergeant, his teacher, and his girlfriend all told him what a wonderful, powerful, handsome, clever, successful, good and special person he was. This factor is an important part of the reason why disapproval is such a flimsy weapon in attempting to help mold patients' behavior away from such drugs. The experience of disapproval by an authority can promptly be reversed by fresh ingestion of the substance. An alternative strategy is to emphasize what the patient is missing in life while he is involved in the drug use. Such an approach is behavior-oriented rather than value-oriented. For the schizophrenic patient, of course, work must be done to be sure that there actually are pleasures to be experienced in a life free from drugs – pleasures of sharing, mutuality, and intimacy; pleasures of creativity, success, and self-actualization; pleasures of self-esteem and self-respect. On the other hand, if all the patient feels able to anticipate in the 'real' world is loneliness and failure, it is difficult for him to counterbalance the lure to substance abuse. Social and vocational rehabilitation to make these pleasures obtainable in the real world, therefore, can be a crucial component of discouraging patients from attempting to find related pleasures in the fantasy world of pharmacologically induced emotional states. In treatment, the therapist will help the patient notice and label work-related and interpersonally related positive experiences and affects as they occur, and aid the patient in appreciating the joys and satisfactions which can flow from them.

Some have stated that a change of state itself is what dual-diagnosis, substance-abusing patients may be seeking when they abuse substances (14, 20). The schizophrenic patient lacks the control of mental life experienced in the normal state. Such a lack is often quite profound and a source of intense misery and self-disparagement for the patient. The patient may not be able to express even the simplest idea in a coherent way which he finds to be his own. This latter feeling, especially, the feeling of being oneself, of knowing and expressing the person one genuinely feels oneself to be, is painfully absent from schizophrenic patients. Yet enormous effort is expended in reaching for this feeling or in withdrawing from the disappointment of its loss. Psychoactive drugs may provide the schizophrenic with a way to obtain some semblance of control over these mental states; with a way to alter an oppressive misery which seemed unalterable.

BEHAVIORAL ISSUES

Another differential on the list of possible contributors to substance abuse among schizophrenic patients may involve their acting to elicit a reaction or to elicit an emotional response from their environment. If they are longing strongly enough for human interaction or affective input, they may experience even a negatively valenced interaction involving criticism and anger as preferable to continuing in an empty and lonely monotony. Needless to say, such an approach can be enormously counterproductive for such patients. Not only can many substances induce psychosis pharmacologically, but a barrage of negatively charged expressed emotion can also be a potent factor predisposing toward relapse (16–18). When a patient is acting with such a motivation, the therapist needs to empathize with the patient's cry for contact, acknowledge his loneliness and level of desperation, but reward by attention behaviors which are more adaptive than substance abuse. Even small steps and small behaviors can be rewarded. Although it is appropriate for the therapist to explain what he is doing in this regard as he does it, the therapist must realize that explanations are not the key ingredient. For the schizophrenic patient, actions speak louder than words. If the therapist's words and the therapist's behavior contradict, the patient is likely to respond to the therapist's behavior. If this pattern of contradiction persists and the therapist does not realize it, both patient and therapist will become frustrated and confused – while, in the meantime, the patient will continue to respond to the therapist's behavior, not the therapist's words.

Not only will the patient respond to the meaning of the therapist's behavior, but the patient will respond to the therapist's behavior as a reinforcer. The smile, the handshake, the pat on the back as encouragement for constructive behavior are also part of the therapist's arsenal. These, and other positive actions, are shapers of patient behavior in accordance with classic behavioral paradigms. 'Negative' reinforcers of maladaptive behaviors are harder to evaluate for their effect. This is because it is harder to be certain about just what is or what is not a negative reinforcer. A criticism or frown which would be expected to be a negative reinforcer, could in fact act as a positive reinforcer on the level that the patient may be lonely for any human contact, or be longing for attention. Additionally, negative expressions are naturally more difficult for therapists to manage, since most effective therapists see themselves as good, helpful, positive people. It is therefore difficult for negative expressions to be given (or received) without at least some ambivalence and/or confusion. Negative expressions also tend to stress the therapeutic alliance, the maintenance of which is crucial; whereas positive reinforcement tends much more to build and strengthen the therapeutic alliance.

It is also relevant to attend to the principles of behavioral techniques in helping patients avoid the use of street drugs. Patients can be educated and encouraged to avoid exposure to such proximal cues for substance abuse as particular street corners, particular people, particular music, particular paraphernalia, and particular other stimuli and situations which, alone or in combination, have come to be associated in the patient's mind with this mode of behavior. More effective, of course, than asking a patient to abandon a behavior is to help a patient substitute an alternative behavior for the one the patient and therapist are working to extinguish. Listening to alternative forms of music, going to sporting events, participating in various physical activities, or treating oneself to a special snack or meal can provide alternative gratifications.

GROUP AND FAMILY THERAPY

Group support can also be very helpful for a patient trying to make this sort of behavioral change. The mutuality of purpose of such a group cannot only reduce the loneliness and provide concrete encouragement, but can provide a larger sense of strength, purpose, and community to the endeavor. Groups take on a life of their own, and if a therapist can help stimulate a constructive set of group agendas, this can work importantly to counteract other group pressures and agendas the patient may experience which would otherwise pressure him toward substance abuse. The action of groups in regard to the therapy of non-schizophrenic substance abusers has been found to be invaluable in a number of regards. However, the specific adaptation of group techniques to the therapy of schizophrenic patients with substance abuse problems has only recently been initiated and is deserving of further development (65). Again, in this approach, it needs to be borne in mind that these patients are schizophrenic first, and only secondarily substance abusers. The knowledge and wisdom which has been developed with regard to the treatment of schizophrenic (and other psychotic) patients with group techniques needs to be preserved and applied to the special subpopulation of substance-abusing schizophrenic patients. Group techniques not only carry the virtue of economy in being able to spread a skilled therapist's expertise over as broad a number of patients as possible, but they can provide both group support and an expanded base of experience, understanding of the issues encountered, and relevant coping techniques.

Family therapy, including the techniques of psychoeducation, can also be a crucial modality for the substance-abusing schizophrenic patient. So often, substance abuse can be a red flag which spurs a family to a vehement judgmental response. While this is quite understandable, and may indeed be the most appropriate response for the patient with primary substance abuse, for the patient with schizophrenia it is then very likely to become part of the vicious cycle of relapse.

Psychoeducational techniques will probably never extinguish this reaction entirely, nor perhaps should they, but they do have the potential to soften it and keep it bracketed in a context that will remain constructive. These psychoeducational techniques will be aimed primarily at the schizophrenia, with substance abuse addressed as one among a number of complicating issues for the patient. Helping the family to develop a more adaptive approach to problem solving is at the core of this family intervention model. Falloon's six-step model for problem solving has proven to be one which works well for schizophrenic patients and their families (66, 67). This includes (a) defining the problem; (b) listing possible solutions; (c) evaluating these possible solutions; (d) selecting the optimal solution; (e) planning how to carry out that solution; and (f) evaluating the effectiveness of that solution – with the greatest emphasis being put on steps 1 and 5. Once again, a crucial issue involves making the problem a positive statement of need for a desired result, not an angry, negative, blaming statement. Thus the therapist helps the patient's family move toward statements like 'Bill needs more ways to build his self-confidence and feel that other people respect him', rather than 'All Bill does is shoot dope, and he embarrasses us'. To aid in this process, the therapist will endeavor to remain behavior-oriented rather than value-oriented, and help the family learn that approach which seems to be more useful in schizophrenia.

HOSPITALIZATION

One decision that the clinician will need to make – or hopefully that the patient and the clinician will be able to make together – involves when the patient is better off being hospitalized. As a general rule of thumb, the reason for a patient to be hospitalized is that he or she is not able to act in his or her own best interest without this degree of external structure, or that the effort involved in doing so is exhausting and unreasonable to continue expending. Thus, for example, hearing voices per se is not necessarily a reason to be hospitalized, whereas feeling it is a burdersome struggle not to be controlled by the voices, or being frightened that one might lose control, would be. In an important sense, the abuse of a substance can represent such a loss of control, but this can be a subtle determination. Using a substance per se is not necessarily a loss of control, but if a patient is abusing a substance in an uncontrolled way, i.e., he or she cannot stop or cannot regulate the behavior, then this is a clear indication for hospitalization in order to regain control. Obviously, if the patient is losing control of failing to regulate his life properly secondary to other symptoms or schizophrenia, this is also a reason for hospitalization.

One problem with hospitalizing a patient with substance abuse as the specific indication is that the patient may not feel that he is out of control at a time when his therapist thinks that he is. The resolution of that dilemma best rests with the therapeutic alliance. Before the issue arises, the patient and therapist should discuss the level of substance abuse which represents being 'out of control' and agree on that. This will constitute a level of substance abuse that the patient has clearly acknowledged is not behavior in which he wishes to engage and which the therapist agrees must be externally controlled. Obviously the therapist's position is to counsel firmly against *any* use of illicit substances, but the guidelines for hospitalization are not necessarily drawn at that same level. Sometimes, of course, especially at the outset of treatment, the patient and therapist may not have a sufficient pre-existing alliance to set such a clear contract. At these times the therapist can state, in a necessarily more unilateral mode, what the therapist believes to constitute out-of-control drug abuse behavior which, in the patient's best interest, would warrant the external control of hospitalization. The therapist can state that these are guidelines which the patient and therapist can discuss in the future and modify accordingly, but that not to act on them straight away would constitute what the therapist judges to be an unacceptable hazard to the patient's current and/or future welfare. Thus, although hospitalization may constitute a unilateral move on the therapist's part at such a point in time, it is an openly communicated move based on behaviors and adaptation rather than on values and judgmental attitudes. This communication, even if not acknowledged by the patient at the time, is a statement addressed to the patient's healthy ego. The issue, again, is not that drugs are immoral or corrupt, but that they are dysfunctional for the patient and that the patient needs to do everything possible to load the odds for his success, rather than vice versa. Other people may, perhaps, 'get away with' using substances, at least for a while. That is not the issue. The issue is that drugs will load the odds against the patient in important ways, and that is why the therapist, being on the patient's side, is against substance use.

Hospitalization, of course, offers a number of advantages when substance abuse is out of control. Firstly, substances are more difficult (although certainly not impossible) to obtain in the hospital. Secondly, the patient will be physically separated from others who may be directly fostering the abuse for their own purposes. Thirdly, many of the proximal cues for abuse may be removed, interrupting a stimulus-response paradigm. Fourthly, massive attention and support can be directed toward the patient for problem solving, self-esteem building, and human contact needs which may have contributed to the abuse. If physical dependency has developed, resources are available in the hospital to wean the patient off the pharmacological action of the substance without undue discomfort. The hospital is not a jail, and hospitalization is not a punishment. Rather, it is a protection, a place where the patient can seek asylum and structure, a place where he can regain control and internalize controls for his own benefit. Hospitalizations for such purposes need not be lengthy. In fact, making them overlong can partially defeat their purpose by encouraging the patient to become dependent on external structure and controls rather than on generating these for himself in an appropriate way. Nevertheless the patient will need to understand, and the therapist will need to explain to him, that assessing when the patient is well enough prepared for discharge (i.e., when the indications for hospitalization referred to above no longer substantially apply) is a difficult determination, that the patient can easily feel ready before he really is ready, and the therapist will take the very rational position of 'better safe than sorry'. Indeed, 'better safe than sorry' is a good philosophy for the patient to identify with – especially where substance abuse is concerned.

TESTING FOR SUBSTANCES OF ABUSE

'Better safe than sorry' should also be part of the therapist's philosophy when it comes to regular or randomized urine testing for substances of abuse. Substance abuse can easily present as a secretive problem which is readily denied, disguised or dismissed when it is really on its way to being out of control. By pursuing regular testing, the therapist can set an example of always 'keeping his guard up' against any substance abuse, much as the patient also needs to 'keep his own guard up'. This can make the testing another form of collaborative effort, and the therapist's continuing attentiveness to a persisting vulnerability can be a constructive model for identification by the patient.

In circumstances where the setting permits, testing for abuse can also be made a 'clinic policy'. This has the advantage of institutionalizing an activity which the patient may sometimes feel is an expression of the therapist's mistrust and which therefore might signify something counter to the therapeutic alliance. But even in circumstances where such testing does not fit under the umbrella of a clinic policy, the therapist can prospectively discuss urine testing on some sort of regular basis with the patient because 'the books' (such as this one) recommend it as the best thing to do. Again, of course, the issue, and the approach, is behavior and adaptation, not morality.

SUMMARY

The issue of substance abuse in schizophrenia represents a difficult clinical conundrum. Insufficient research has been done, and much more research needs to be done to determine clearly which are the best therapeutic approaches to be taken. What seems rational is that these dual-diagnosis patients need to be treated as persons with schizophrenia who also have the complicating symptom of substance abuse, rather than the other way around. Thus factors which have been learned with regard to the effective psychosocial treatment of schizophrenia, such as these patients' sensitivity to high levels of expressed negative emotion, need to be respected. Ego functions and adaptive capacity need to be bolstered and the therapist must pay careful attention to building a strong therapeutic alliance built on problem solving and behavior, not moral judgmentalism. A differential diagnosis of the etiology and contributing factors to the substance abuse symptom is important, and an integrated treatment plan will need to be developed, within the context of the therapeutic alliance, which addresses each of the factors that may be involved. Individual and group treatment, family psychoeducation, social and vocational rehabilitation treatments and strategic hospitalizations may all play an important role in addressing the issues related to treating substance abuse in schizophrenia.

ACKNOWLEDGEMENT

This work was supported in part by Grants MH-34309 and DA-05039 from the National Institute of Mental Health and the National Institute of Drug Abuse.

REFERENCES

1. Crowley TJ, Chesluk D, Dilts S, Hart R (1974) Drug and alcohol abuse among psychiatric admissions. *Arch. Gen. Psychiatry, 30,* 13.
2. McLellan AT, Druley KA (1977) Non-random relation between drugs of abuse and psychiatric diagnosis. *J. Psychiatr. Res., 13,* 179.
3. Hall RCW, Popkin MK, Stickney SK, Gardner ER (1978) Covert outpatient drug abuse. *J. Nerv. Ment. Dis., 166,* 343.
4. Richard ML, Liskow BI, Perry PJ (1985) Recent psychostimulant use in hospitalized schizophrenics. *J. Clin. Psychiatry, 46,* 79.
5. Gold MS, Dackis CA (1986) The role of the laboratory in the evaluation of suspected drug abuse. *J. Clin. Psychiatry, 47 (Suppl.),* 17.
6. Kofoed L, Kania J, Walsh T, Atkinson RM (1986) Outpatient treatment of patients with substance abuse and co-existing psychiatric disorders. *Am. J. Psychiatry, 143,* 867.
7. Schneier RF, Siris SG (1987) A review of psychoactive substance use and abuse in schizophrenia: patterns of drug preference. *J. Nerv. Ment. Dis., 175,* 641.
8. Rounsaville BJ, Glazer W, Wilber CH, Weissman MM, Kleber HD (1983) Short-term interpersonal psychotherapy in methadone-maintained opiate addicts. *Arch. Gen. Psychiatry, 40,* 629.
9. Woody GE, Luborsky L, McLellan AT, O'Brien CP, Beck AT, Blaine J, Herman I, Hole A (1983) Psychotherapy for opiate addicts: does it help? *Arch. Gen. Psychiatry, 4,* 639.
10. Allison M, Hubbard RL (1985) Drug abuse treatment process: a review of the literature. *Int. J. Addict., 20,* 1321.
11. Childress AR, McLellan AT, O'Brien CP (1985) Behavioral therapies for substance abuse. *Int. J. Addict., 20,* 947.
12. Kaufman E (1985) Family systems and family therapy of substance abuse: an overview of two decades of research and clinical experience. *Int. J. Addict., 2,* 897.
13. DeLeon G (1985) The therapeutic community: status and evolution. *Int. J. Addict., 20,* 823.
14. Millman RB (1988) Evaluation and clinical management of cocaine abusers. *J. Clin. Psychiatry, 49 (Suppl.),* 27.
15. Washton AM (1988) Preventing relapse to cocaine. *J. Clin. Psychiatry 49 (Suppl.),* 34.
16. Brown GW, Birley JLT, Wing JK (1972) Influence of family life on the course of schizophrenic disorder, a replication. *Br. J. Psychiatry, 121,* 241.
17. Vaughn CE, Snyder KS, Jones S, Freeman WB, Falloon IRH (1984) Family factors in schizophrenic relapse. *Arch. Gen. Psychiatry, 41,* 1169.
18. Koenigsberg HW, Handley R (1986) Expressed emotion: from predictive index to clinical construct. *Am. J. Psychiatry, 143,* 1361.
19. Miller JG (1965) Information overload and psychopathology. *Am. J. Psychiatry, 116,* 695.
20. Docherty JP, Van Kammen DP, Siris SG, Marder SR (1978) Stages of onset of schizophrenic psychosis. *Am. J. Psychiatry, 135,* 420.
21. Rogers CR, Gendlin EG, Kiesler DJ, Truax CB (1967) *The Therapeutic Relationship and Its Impact: A Study of Psychotherapy with Schizophrenics.* University of Wisconsin Press, Madison.
22. Grinspoon L, Ewalt JR, Schader RI (Eds) (1972) *Schizophrenia: Pharmacotherapy and Psychotherapy.* Williams & Wilkins, Baltimore.
23. Docherty JP (1989) The individual psychotherapies: efficacy, syndrome-based treatments, and the therapeutic alliance. In: Lazare A (Ed), *Outpatient Psychiatry:*

Diagnosis and Treatment, pp. 624–644. Williams & Wilkins, Baltimore.
24. Frank AF, Gunderson JG (in press) The role of the therapeutic alliance in the treatment of schizophrenia: relationship to course and outcome. *Arch. Gen. Psychiatry,*
25. Khantzian EJ (1985) The self-medication hypothesis of addictive disorders: Focus on heroin and cocaine dependence. *Am. J. Psychiatry, 142,* 1259.
26. Millman RB, Sbriglio R (1986) Patterns of use and psychopathology in chronic marijuana abusers. *Psychiatr. Clin. N. Am. 9,* 533.
27. Hekimian LJ, Gershon S (1968) Characteristics of drug abusers admitted to a psychiatric hospital. *J. Am. Med. Assoc., 205,* 125.
28. Rockwell DA, Ostwald P (1968) Amphetamine use and abuse in psychiatric patients. *Arch. Gen. Psychiatry, 18,* 612.
29. Breakey WR, Goodell H, Lorenz PC, McHugh PR (1974) Hallucinogenic drugs as precipitants of schizophrenia. *Psychol. Med., 4,* 255.
30. Prosser RA, Pickens R (1979) Catecholamines, drug abuse and schizophrenia. In: Pickens RW, Heston LL (Eds.) *Psychiatric Factors in Drug Abuse,* pp. 285–300. Grune & Stratton, New York.
31. Tsuang MT, Simpson JC, Kronfol Z (1982) Subtypes of drug abuse with psychosis: demographic characteristics, clinical features, and family history. *Arch. Gen. Psychiatry, 39,* 141.
32. Janowsky DS, Davis JM (1976) Methylphenidate, dextroamphetamine, and levamfetamine: effects on schizophrenic symptoms. *Arch. Gen. Psychiatry, 33,* 304.
33. Knudsen P, Vilmar T (1984) Cannabis and neuroleptic agents in schizophrenia. *Acta Psychiatr. Scand., 69,* 162.
34. Angrist B, van Kammen DP (1984) CNS stimulants as tools in the study of schizophrenia. *Trends Neurosci., 7,* 388.
35. Kleber HD, Gawin FH (1985) Cocaine. *Am. Psychiatr. Assoc. Annu. Rev., 5,* 160.
36. Hollister LE (1986) Health aspects of cannabis. *Pharmacol. Rev., 38,* 1.
37. Lieberman JA, Kane JM, Alvir J (1987) Provocative tests with psychostimulant drugs in schizophrenia. *Psychopharmacology, 91,* 415.
38. Chiarello PJ, Cole JO (1987) The use of psychostimulants in general psychiatry: a reconsideration. *Arch. Gen. Psychiatry, 44,* 286.
39. Rifkin A, Quitkin F, Klein DF (1975) Akinesia: a poorly recognized drug-induced extrapyramidal behavioral disorder. *Arch. Gen. Psychiatry, 32,* 672.
40. Van Putten T, May PR (1978) 'Akinetic depression' in schizophrenia. *Arch. Gen. Psychiatry, 35,* 1101.
41. Siris SG (1987) Akinesia and post-psychotic depression: a difficult differential diagnosis. *J. Clin. Psychiatry, 48,* 240.
42. Siris SG (in press) Pharmacological treatment of depression in schizophrenia. In: L. DeLisi (Ed), *Depression and Schizophrenia.* American Psychiatric Association Press, Washington, DC.
43. Van Putten T (1975) The many faces of akathisia. *Compr. Psychiatry, 16,* 43.
44. Siris SG (1985) Three cases of akathisia and 'acting out.' *J. Clin. Psychiatry, 46,* 395.
45. Herz MI, Mellville C (1980) Relapse in schizophrenia. *Am. J. Psychiatry, 137,* 801.
46. Siris SG (1988) Treatment planning: schizophrenic woman on neuroleptic medication suffers secondary depression. *Hosp. Community Psychiatry, 39,* 24.
47. McGlashan TH, Carpenter Jr WT (1976) Post-psychotic depression in schizophrenia. *Arch. Gen. Psychiatry, 33,* 231.
48. Crow TJ (1980) Molecular pathology of schizophrenia: more than one disease process? *Br. Med. J., 280,* 66.
49. Andreasen NC, Olsen S (1982) Negative vs. positive schizophrenia: definition and

validation. *Arch. Gen. Psychiatry, 39,* 789.
50. Siris SG, Adan F, Cohen M, Mandeli J, Aronson A, Casey E (1988) Post-psychotic depression and negative symptoms: an investigation of syndromal overlap. *Am. J. Psychiatry, 145,* 1532.
51. Carpenter Jr WT, Heinrichs DW, Alphs LD (1985) Treatment of negative symptoms. *Schizophr. Bull., 11,* 440.
52. Goldberg SC (1985) Negative and deficit symptoms in schizophrenia do respond to neuroleptics. *Schizophr. Bull., 11,* 453.
53. Herz MI, Szymanski HV, Simon JC (1982) Intermittent medication for stable schizophrenic outpatients: an alternative maintenance medication. *Am. J. Psychiatry, 139,* 918.
54. Carpenter Jr WT, Heinrichs DW, Hanlon TE (1988) A comparative trial of pharmacologic strategies in schizophrenia. *Am. J. Psychiatry, 144,* 1466.
55. Kane JM, Rifkin A, Woerner M, Reardon GT, Sarantakos S, Schiebel D, Ramos-Lorenzi J (1983) Low-dose neuroleptic treatment of outpatient schizophrenics, I. Preliminary results for relapse rates. *Arch. Gen. Psychiatry, 40,* 893.
56. Marder SR, Van Putten T, Mintz J, Lebell M, McKenzie J, May PRA (1987) Low- and conventional dose maintenance therapy with fluphenazine decanoate: two year outcome. *Arch. Gen. Psychiatry, 44,* 518.
57. Rehm LP (1977) A self-control model of depression. *Behav. Ther., 8,* 787.
58. Beck AT, Rush AJ, Shaw BF, Emery G (1979) *Cognitive Therapy of Depression.* Guilford Press, New York.
59. Bellack AS, Hersen M, Himmelhoch JM (1981) Social skills training compared with pharmacotherapy and psychotherapy in the treatment of unipolar depression. *Am. J. Psychiatry, 138,* 1562.
60. Lewinsohn PM, Anlonuccio P, Steinnetz J, Teri L (1982) *The Coping with Depression Course. A Psychoeducational Intervention for Unipolar Depression.* University of Oregon, Portland.
61. Klerman GL, Weissman MM, Rounsaville BJ, Chevron ES (1984) *Interpersonal Psychotherapy of Depression.* Basic Books, New York.
62. Docherty JP (1989) The individual psychotherapies: Efficacy, syndrome-based treatments, and the therapeutic alliance. In: Lazare A (Ed), *Outpatient Psychiatry: Diagnosis and Treatment,* pp. 624–644. Williams & Wilkins, Baltimore.
63. Bilder RM, Mukherjee S, Rieder RO, Pandurangi AK (1985) Symptomatic and neuropsychological components of defect states. *Schizophr. Bull., 11,* 409.
64. Frank JD (1973) *Persuasion and Healing.* Johns Hopkins University Press, Baltimore.
65. Hellerstein DJ, Meehan B (1987) Outpatient group therapy for schizophrenic substance abusers. *Am. J. Psychiatry, 144,* 1337.
66. Falloon IRH, Boyd J, McGill CW (1984) *Family Care of Schizophrenia.* Guilford Press, New York.
67. Falloon IRH, Gingerich S, Mueser K, Rappaport S. *Behavioral Family Therapy: A Handbook,* Unpublished manuscript.

CHAPTER 17

Homelessness and schizophrenia: a psychosocial approach

STEPHEN M. GOLDFINGER

The inclusion of this chapter in a volume on psychosocial treatment approaches to schizophrenia is an event of rather striking import, and one that should not occur without comment, since it documents the recognition of an epidemiological subpopulation of schizophrenics which has not previously been the focus of our clinical planning and concern.

Certainly, the association between homelessness and schizophrenia is not new. Yet the problems of the homeless mentally ill have never before been such a focus of attention. Curled up in doorways covered in cardboard boxes, wrapped in newpapers over heating grates or walking all night in multiple layers of clothing, homeless men and women have become an expected sight in our cities and towns. Mumbling to themselves, wildly gesticulating, responding to voices they alone hear, the signs of psychotic disorders in this population have become almost as expected as their presence.

What is happening? How extensive, in fact, is the problem of homelessness among schizophrenics, or schizophrenia among the homeless? How are we to understand the seemingly sudden emergence of this population on our national landscape? Will the answer lie in the consideration of economics, social policy, treatment interventions, or the nature of schizophrenia itself?

What treatment approaches to this population might be helpful? Are there models of psychosocial intervention that have already been tried, and how effective have they been? Of the skills and techniques we've adopted for other schizophrenic populations, what must be modified, and what discarded?

In order to develop rational treatment approaches for this population it is necessary first to understand something of the history and magnitude of the problem. Only by articulating the complexity of the contributing social, system and individual etiological factors will we be able to recognize those elements best addressed by psychiatric services, and avoid the assumption of responsibility for social problems whose scope and complexity lie outside the purview of our professional expertise and technical competence.

Handbook of Schizophrenia, Volume 4: Psychosocial Treatment of Schizophrenia.
M.I. Herz, S.J. Keith and J.P. Docherty, editors.

HISTORICAL ROOTS

Early reports

Just after the turn of the century, Alice W. Solenberger analyzed the case records of a thousand homeless men in Chicago (1). Her work is notable not only for its historical interest and the poignancy of its case descriptions, but also because of the way it adumbrates many of the questions central to our thinking about homelessness and mental illness today. Despite a language that sometimes appears archaic and her description of a social and treatment milieu that often appears foreign and outmoded, many of the conceptual and service delivery issues remain remarkably germane. The problems of transiency, discontinuity of care, and patient 'dumping' offer little to differentiate them from current concerns.

Ezra Susser and the research group at the Nathan Kline Institute in New York have begun exploring the issues of causal influence and the pitfalls of the misapplication of epidemiological work concerning those who are homeless and mentally ill. Working eighty years ago, Solenberger struggled with

> 'one of the first questions of interest about insane homeless men. . . whether they are homeless and vagrant because of their insanity, or insane because of their vagrancy.' (1, p. 89)

She provides case material documenting both viewpoints, of individuals who are no longer able to maintain themselves in pre-existing living situations after the emergence of psychotic symptoms and of those who through various possible etiologies (malnutrition, intolerable stress) only begin to demonstrate symptoms of mental illness after entering a life of vagrancy. One fact clearly remains the same:

> 'Whatever may have been the causes of their disorders, and by whatever chances or mishaps they may have drifted or been forced into the life of the road and the cheap lodging houses, unquestionably the sufferings of the insane, as they wander about uncared for, are very great.' (1, p. 95)

Amos Baker, a New York psychiatrist writing in 1918, reported his findings of the examination of 50 'vagrant' inmates of the Westchester County Penitentiary. He found 76% with evidence of psychiatric pathology. Of these, approximately a quarter suffered 'dementia praecox' (2). Baker compares this to the findings of Wilmans of Hidelburg who found that 104 of the 120 'old professional tramps sent to a hospital for the insane' were of 'long-standing unrecognized types of insanity' and to Bonhoffer, who in an examination of 404 'chronic vagabonds, found 74 percent mentally unsound' (2, p. 600). Baker believed that it was incumbent upon the physician to examine these patients and design individual treatment plans for them, rather than ascribing causality only to economic forces and responsibility only to penal systems and social service agencies.

Although a literature on vagrancy and insanity existed at the turn of the century, it was only during the 1930s that the problem of the undomiciled and unsheltered became the focus of significant national attention. Only more recently has the term homeless replaced the more derogatory characterizations of 'derelict', 'vagrant' and 'tramp' as the ranks of the hobo and flophouse resident have been swelled by the young, the disabled, by women and children, by the never employed and the newly jobless. This new and far more varied population requires a fresh terminology to differentiate it from the less widespread and broadly characterized vagrant of prior times (3).

ETIOLOGICAL ISSUES

Just as it is clear that the number of homeless individuals in the United States has dramatically increased in recent years, the over-representation of the chronically and severely mentally ill among them is also well established. The factors contributing to this disproportionate presence include decisions about mental health treatment policies, broad epidemiological issues, changes in federal entitlement program criteria and the clinical characteristics of schizophrenia itself.

Deinstitutionalization

Virtually all writers addressing the issue of the over-representation of the chronically mentally ill among the homeless cite deinstitutionalization as the primary contributing factor (4 – 13). During the period 1955 – 1983, the state hospital population was decreased by more than 433,000 individuals (5, 14). Certainly, many of the individuals who would have occupied these beds entered community-based treatment programs. However, it is also clear that many of them ended up on the streets. Hope and Young (15) note that during the fiscal year 1979 – 80, of those individuals released from state psychiatric centers in New York, 23% were sent to 'unknown' living arrangements. Citing Talbott (16), they point out that 38% of discharged patients received no referral for follow-up psychiatric services.

In addition to the lack of provision for clinical aftercare, many individuals are discharged from state hospitals to inadequate or short-term residences or to no sheltered living situation whatsoever. Appleby and Desai (17) reported on the residential status of patients admitted and discharged in the Illinois state hospital system. In 1980, they found that 16% of all of those admitted were undomiciled, and that 80% of the initial number of people homeless on admission were also discharged as undomiciled. Thus, state hospital facilities have not only reduced the number of severely mentally ill who are 'removed from circulation', but have actually contributed directly to the problems of homelessness by discharging people without adequate clinical services or living situations. As Wing points out (18), the fact that individuals are discharged to the community does not imply 'that they had made social contact with it' (18, p. 185).

Other cohort effects

Other demographic factors have contributed to the increase in the homeless mentally ill. The age of those living in shelters has been steadily decreasing (Ezra Susser, personal communication). The median age of the homeless in most studies of adult shelter users is between 37 and 40 (9, 14, 19, 20). As Bachrach points out (5), this may be a result of the 'baby boom', the 64 million individuals born between 1946 and 1961, who are, or have recently been at, the age of highest risk for the development of schizophrenia and other severe psychopathology.

The effects of this age cohort interacting with local and federal mental health policies can clearly be seen in the group frequently described as 'young adult chronic patients' (21, 22). This group of deinstitutionalized or, increasingly, never institutionalized young patients suffering from schizophrenia and other chronic illnesses share a number of clinical and service use characteristics with the homeless population. Unwilling to accept a docile, patient role, and unwilling to cooperate with behavioral expectations (22), they are frequently denied access to residential services. Treatment agencies, finding it far easier to work with more compliant and less impulsive individuals, may relegate the care of these young patients to emergency rooms and hospitals. More of them are finding their way into large shelters (23) whose rules are less confining and where the label of 'mental patient' can be traded for the less stigmatizing one of 'homeless'.

Housing and Marginality

During the period from 1980–1984, the funds committed by the Department of Housing and Urban Development to assist those with low incomes was decreased by 78% (24). During this same period of time, federal policy dramatically decreased the financial stability of the chronically mentally ill. During the years 1981–84, the Reagan administration attempted to save approximately $1 billion by dropping 700,000 individuals from the SSI programs for disabled persons. Those with psychiatric disability took a disproportionate share of the economic loss. Although only 11% of those on disability are psychiatrically disabled, a third of those who were discontinued during the cutbacks were mentally disabled (13, 15). Thus, in the very face of rising housing costs, at least 200,000 chronically mentally ill individuals lost their federal entitlement benefit income.

As Segal and others (25) have noted, the severely mentally ill frequently live without 'social margin', which these authors define as 'personal possessions, attributes or relationships which can be traded on for help in times of need' (25, p. 387). Without the availability of such resources, these individuals are particularly vulnerable to the impact of any disruption in their finances. Although many of those cut from the SSI rolls were subsequently reinstated, many were forced into a life on the street or in a shelter.

Vulnerability and schizophrenia

The very symptoms and other characteristics which are inherent in the pathology of schizophrenia contribute to this group's vulnerability to homelessness (26). As Lamb and Talbott state so simply and eloquently in their report on the American Psychiatric Association's perspective on the homeless mentally ill,

> 'the chronically and severely mentally ill are not proficient at coping with the stresses of this world.' (27, p. 499)

Paranoia, delusions and hallucinations may precipitate fights with building managers, landlords or others responsible for providing housing. Disorganization and confusion may result in poor money management and haphazard paying of bills, or behaviors considered irresponsible or undesirable by property managers. Withdrawal and internal preoccupation may result in a lack of attention to bodily hygiene, or to living spaces kept in a way deemed unsanitary and unacceptable. Poor judgment may result in dangerous activities, impulsivity in fights with those in authority. Decompensations may result in hospitalizations, during which housing arrangements are abandoned, with eviction as the eventual outcome. Without the continuity of a stable living situation, these individuals are more likely to discontinue their medication, furthering the spiral of decompensation.

SCOPE OF THE PROBLEM

Defining homelessness

In order to grapple with the scope of the problem of homeless schizophrenics, it becomes necessary to define what we mean by the term homeless. Initially, it may appear that there is a general consensus, as if we inherently 'know' what homelessness is. Baxter and Hopper, in one of the seminal works in the field, *Private Lives/Public Spaces* (4) define the homeless population as

> 'those whose primary nighttime residence is either in the publicly or privately operated shelters or in the streets, in doorways, train stations and bus terminals, public plazas and parks, subways, abandoned buildings, loading docks and other well-hidden sites known only to their users.' (4, pp. 6, 7)

This definition equates homelessness with shelterlessness, paralleling the approach of the Department of Housing and Urban Development (28) in their attempts to count the homeless in America during the winter of 1983–84. Others, such as Larew (29) regard homelessness predominantly in terms of its social and interpersonal elements, as

> 'a human condition of disaffiliation and detachment (unattachment) from the primary agents of social structure.' (29, p. 107)

It is generally agreed that homelessness, in fact, contains elements both of inadequate housing and of disconnection and isolation (5, 6, 30).

Questions naturally remain about when a housing situation is sufficiently inadequate for its occupants to be considered homeless – as in refugees living with 15 or 20 people in a single room, or migrant farm workers whose shacks may offer a little protection from the elements (31, 32). A consideration of the number of homeless people must also take into account the dimension of longitudinality. Many individuals live temporarily in institutional settings such as hospitals, jails or short-term drug and alcohol treatment programs, but have no home to which they can return. In an attempt to grapple with this issue, some researchers replace the term homeless with 'residential instability' (33). Roth, Bean and their coworkers (19, 34) provide an operational definition which accounts for physical location, length of stay, and social variables in determining residential status.

Definitional and methodological issues have resulted in widely divergent estimates of the number of homeless. Nationally, the Alcohol, Drug Abuse and Mental Health Administration published a report in 1983 (35) estimating that there were approximately 2 million homeless individuals in the United States. The following year, the Department of Housing and Urban Development (28) published an estimate of between 250 and 300 thousand homeless individuals, or approximately 15% of the ADAMHA number. The HUD study has come under severe criticism by both advocates and epidemiologists. Yet, even when expensive studies have been done by sophisticated epidemiologists in more circumscribed localities (20), the findings have been met with controversy and are refuted by those knowledgeable in the field (personal communication, Chicago Health Care for the Homeless Project).

Defining and counting the homeless mentally ill

Controversies over the absolute number of homeless individuals complicates establishing prevalence rates from mental illness in this population, as well as rates for schizophrenia. Even were we to be able to establish a perfect screening tool for psychiatric symptomatology, our calculations would be confounded. Given the uncertainty of the overall population's size (the denominator of the prevalence equation), estimates of those with psychiatric disorders must inevitably lead to relative, rather than absolute, prevalence rates.

The most widely cited prevalence estimate, that published in the report of the American Psychiatric Association Task Force on the homeless mentally ill concludes that

> 'in most universes of homeless people, between 25% and 50% have serious and chronic forms of mental illness.' (36, p. 88)

but does not go on to define serious and chronic forms of mental illness. In the Department of Housing and Urban Development survey cited above (28, p. 24), an estimate was given of 22%, but this is based on a survey of shelter operators, hardly a group sophisticated in their diagnostic skills. Other studies which are frequently cited rely on clinical samples for their overall population, naturally including a higher rate of the psychiatrically disabled than in the general population. Thus, for example, Lipton and colleagues drew on those presenting to the Bellevue Psychiatric Emergency Services (7), Arce et al. (8) on those referred to a shelter specializing in the psychiatrically disabled. Prevalence estimates derived from such skewed samples will clearly not represent the rates of mental illness among the overall homeless population.

Robertson (37) has reviewed 24 studies done between 1975 and 1985 on the prevalence of mental illness among non-clinically drawn homeless populations. (It is notable that only 25% of these were published in professional journals, while an additional 50% were only available from the authors.) She provides a thoughtful critique of the methodological problems inherent in making prevalence estimates in this population. In addition to difficulties with diagnosis and sampling biases, she enumerates several other sources of error. Among these are the use of a history of psychiatric hospitalization as a proxy for the finding of mental illness, the difference between using current versus historical evidence of symptomatology, and the source of diagnostic and historical information. More recent studies address many of these criticisms. Farr, Koegel and Burnhan completed 1 – 3-hour interviews with 379 homeless individuals for the Los Angeles Department of Health. The subjects were a stratified sample of individuals using Los Angeles shelters, free meal programs, day time drop-in centers or living on the streets. Psychiatric disorders were determined using the National Institute of Mental Health Diagnostic Interview Schedule (DIS) and the Center for Epidemiological Studies Depression Scale (CES-D). In addition, questions were borrowed from the Los Angeles Epidemiological Catchment Area Survey instrument, and other demographic and social information was collected (Farr RK, Koegel P, Burnham A, A Study of Homelessness and Mental Illness in the Skid Row Area of Los Angeles, L.A. County DMH, unpublished). Farr specifically defined the 'chronic mentally ill' as those who had a diagnosis of either severe cognitive impairment (organic brain syndromes), a diagnosis of schizophrenia, or a diagnosis of a major affective disorder. Those who had not suffered any symptoms for the last three years, or had a single episode of affective illness, were excluded. Using this criteria, the Los Angeles group found a prevalence of 28% of severe and chronic mental illness, and suggest that, with correction for self-reporting, the number would rise to approximately 33%.

In a much smaller study, Fischer and Breakey (9) examined 51 homeless persons drawn from a probability sample of those using a mission in eastern Baltimore. Using the DIS to diagnose mental disorders, they looked at the prevalence of various disorders over a one-month, six-month, and lifetime period. Using Farr's definitions, they found an 11.8% one- and six-month prevalence and a 23.5% lifetime prevalence of chronic mental illness among their sample. Finally, two other studies are worth noting because they draw on extremely large samples of homeless individuals. Crystal, Ladner, and Towber (10) report on the psychiatric status of 7,578 New York city shelter system clients between November 1982 and December 1983. They found that 24.9% of the shelter clients identified themselves as psychiatrically impaired, reporting 'current mental problems, current psychiatric outpatient status, or previous psychiatric inpatient status' (10, p. 63).

Wright and Weber (38) report their analysis of the largest series of clinical contacts with homeless individuals ever reported, 22,000 clients served in 16 American cities which provide Robert Wood Johnson Foundation-funded Health Care for the Homeless programs. Although a clinical population, the majority of individuals are seen for medical or social service problems. Using a combination of diagnosed psychiatric problems, a history of psychiatric disorders, or undiagnosed but recorded 'mental or emotional problems', they estimate a 32.9% rate of mental illness. They further estimate that at least half of these are chronically mentally ill.

Prevalence of schizophrenia among the homeless

Impediments to accurate diagnosis

The problems of making accurate psychiatric diagnosis in a sample population of the homeless are extraordinarily complex. Although the presence of significant mental illness may be ascertained based on gross disturbances of behavior or communication, making a diagnosis requires far more specific information. Establishing sufficient credibility with the population may require contact and presence over an extended period of time. The development of sufficient study subjects requires a fine mix of clinical sophistication and the ability to maintain a non-intrusive and non-threatening stance. The locations where homeless people congregate tend to be noisy and crowded, without the availability of privacy and subject to constant disruption and intrusions. Yet, in order to gather sufficient data, interviews must allow a sufficient period of time for the asking of multiple and complicated questions. In addition to these exogenous sources of difficulty, the very characteristics that might be used to make a diagnosis may require modification for a homeless population. Thus, such symptoms as 'marked impairment in personal hygiene and grooming', 'hoarding food', 'marked impairment in role functioning as wage earner', are all listed as part of the residual signs of schizophrenia (39, pp. 194 – 195). Yet, these may be indistinguishable from behaviors and characteristics present in many non-schizophrenic homeless individuals. Finally, the very instruments used for standardized diagnosis may not be well suited to diagnose major mental disorder in the homeless population (9).

Current data

There exists little in the way of well-designed and executed epidemiological studies of the prevalence of schizophrenia among the homeless. Studies prior to 1984, reviewed by Arce and Vergare (36) provide estimates ranging from 15 to 72%, but many of these studies are significantly more than 15 years old. More recent research efforts are all based on either clinical or other non-representive sample populations. Among the ten studies funded by the National Institute of Mental Health and summarized by Morrissey (Morrissey, JP and Dennis, DL (1986), NIMH-funded research concerning homeless mentally ill persons: implications for policy and practice, US Department of Health and Human Services, Administrative Document), only two have both completed their data analysis and used rigorous diagnostic evaluation tools. The Los Angeles study (unpublished) described above found a lifetime prevalence rate of schizophrenia of 13.1% and a 'current' (symptoms in past three years) prevalence rate of 11.5%. This remarkable finding represents a prevalence over 38 times that found in the Los Angeles Epidemiological Catchment Area survey of domiciled subjects. The Baltimore group (9) in its smaller and less representative homeless sample, found a six-month and lifetime prevalence rate of schizophrenia of 2%, or 5 and 3.3 times the respective prevalence rates of domiciled males in the Baltimore ECA. Sampling only the users of missions, this investigation may have evaluated a less severely disturbed group than those who do not, or cannot, avail themselves of regular shelter services. What is clear from these studies is that schizophrenia occurs in the homeless population at an order of magnitude higher than that among domiciled individuals.

The 'bottom line'

Combining findings on the prevalence of schizophrenia among the homeless with estimates of the size of the overall population results in some rather startling figures. Using the ADAMHA (30) estimate of two million homeless individuals and Farr's 11.5% prevalence rate of schizophrenia among the homeless gives us an estimate of 230,000 homeless schizophrenics in the United States. A lower end estimate, using the projection of 300,000 homeless Americans from the HUD report (28) and Fischer's (9) 2% prevalence rate gives us an overall estimate of 6,000 homeless schizophrenics.

Wright and Webber (38), reporting on 22,494 individuals served by the Health Care for the Homeless program, estimate that 7,400 of these suffer from mental illness. In a more closely studied subsample, they found that 36% of these psychiatrically impaired individuals were schizophrenic, giving a projection of 1224 homeless schizophrenics in their sample. The likelihood that the 18 small Health Care for the Homeless programs have served 20% of all homeless schizophrenics in the United States is obviously absurd. Given the increase in the numbers of homeless individuals, and the ongoing data that has accumulated to support the ADAMHA estimate, it is probably reasonable to assume that there are at least 100,000 individuals in the United States who are both homeless and diagnosable as schizophrenic.

THE CONTEXT OF CARE

Heterogeneity

As we now turn to clinical approaches, we must move as well from considerations of the aggregate to those of the individual. The very language we use, 'homeless schizophrenic', may lead us linguistically into the false assumption that this is somehow a homogeneous group. Although such labels provide a necessary shorthand for discussion, they should not mislead us as we begin to consider the organization of services for this population.

The population of homeless schizophrenics is a diverse group, with varying levels of function, degrees of impairment and chronicity of symptoms. Their homeless state may be a result of a recent loss of housing or reflect a long-standing condition. As individuals, homeless schizophrenics will reflect all the diversity of the larger homeless and schizophrenic populations. No one program design can be expected to meet their needs, no style of intervention can be appropriate for all. Neither schizophrenia nor homelessness are static processes, and interventions will need to reflect changing residential and functional states. Those services that would most closely meet the needs of an individual today may be unnecessary, and of little use, tomorrow. As Goldfinger and Chafetz point out,

> 'it is precisely because these patients are unable to utilize existing 'modal patient' services that they reappear over and over again at inpatient and emergency psychiatric facilities, cycle through our jails, or leave the shelters provided for them'. (40, p. 101)

The question of housing

Obviously, the existence of a population of homeless schizophrenics is predicated by their problem with housing. The availability of food, clothing, and shelter must be seen as a prerequisite for meeting any of their other treatment needs. This recognition of the primacy of the need for adequate shelter should be separated from its illogical pseudo-corollary: that the provision of adequate housing is sufficient to address the problems of homeless people with schizophrenia. Too often, in the attempt to underscore the importance of the need for shelter, those working with the homeless mentally ill have failed to adequately address this key point. Once housed, a severely incapacitated schizophrenic who was living on the street becomes a severely incapacitated schizophrenic living indoors.

One might argue that, once provided with a reasonable living space, the problems of the (formerly) homeless schizophrenic become the problems of any schizophrenic. Such an approach underestimates the impact of homelessness on an individual's life. For those who precipitously lose their customary living space, the sudden transition to a life on the street is likely to interrupt ongoing treatment and other supportive relationships and lead to a symptomatic exacerbation or decompensation. At minimum, the sudden loss of one's possessions and customary surroundings would lead to a crisis of adjustment, if not a full-blown psychotic episode. For those who have been living shelterless for an extended period, the effects will have been far more profound. Virtually every element of their behavior, interpersonal relatedness and expectations will have been affected. Their ability to trust their responses to attempts to approach them, their entire 'being-in-the-world' will have adjusted to, and been changed by, the situation of homelessness. We have learned that returning home for a combat veteran does not guarantee his resumption of life as previously led. Simply removing someone with chronic mental illness from the street to an apartment does not erase the scar of the battle of the streets.

'Engaging the disengaged'

This section takes its title from the classic 1980 paper by Segal and Baumohl (41), an exploration of the difficulties involved in forming relationships with the 'space cases' living on the streets of Berkeley. This population is frequently distrustful, suspicious of, and hostile to any offers of contact by psychiatric clinicians. Many homeless individuals have had extensive prior contact with the mental health system and have found their experiences disappointing, frightening, and humiliating. Often receiving service only when their symptoms become sufficiently dangerous or bizarre to warrant the attention of police, much of the treatment that they receive is involuntary care in emergency rooms and inpatient hospitals, where they have found such assistance as is offered a poor match for their needs. Frequently, they are arrested and jailed for petty crimes, (42) leading to a fusion of the penal and mental health systems in their minds (43). With few or no possessions, they may be entirely dependent on public assistance programs and private charity to provide for their needs. Within the welfare system, they are often met with hostility and rejection. The long lines, multiple forms, and endless questions may simply be beyond the capacity of those who are psychotic. When, in addition, one adds the desperation of knowing that such services may be one's only source of support, failure to negotiate the system carries grave consequences. Given the interpersonal deficits inherent in schizophrenic symptomatology, the ostracism and rejection, not only by the system but even at the hands of their less disturbed peers (41), intensifies their despair and isolation. The sense of disaffiliation and disenfranchisement so frequently noted among the homeless mentally ill is clearly the outcome of a cruel juxtaposition of clinical and system characteristics.

Like many other chronically mentally ill individuals of their age, a large number of the homeless refuse to accept the role of patient (21 – 23, 41, 44). To be a patient is to be compliant, dependent, defective and in need of help. Yet, in the experience of many, the treatment system is simply not dependable enough to justify sacrificing one's independence. Few caregivers recognize the strength and skills required for survival on the streets; fewer still acknowledge that understanding to the patient presenting for help. After the struggle of life on the streets (4), asking for help from a system which is so reluctant or unable to provide it is simply too demeaning.

Clinician responses

Designed for a significantly less impoverished and impaired population, existing mental health programs are frequently unable to provide the comprehensive multidimensional services this group requires. (31, 40, 45). Knowing that they are unable to meet such patients' needs, service providers may greet them with thinly or even undisguised hostility and rejection. Chafetz and Goldfinger, studying homeless people in a psychiatric emergency room, write

> 'an influx of undomiciled and ill-housed clients has placed a strain on staff of this service . . . In the words of one clinician, 'even before you see a client, if you know he has a family and a place to live, you feel relieved. If you know he has no where to live, your stomach goes into a knot' (33, pp. 95 – 96)

Breakey reports on a study showing that nursing staff on an inpatient psychiatric unit were twice as likely, when asked if they 'like' a patient, to respond negatively about homeless than about domiciled patients (Breakey, WR, Clinical care for the homeless mentally ill. Paper presented at the Annual Meeting of the American Psychiatric Association, 1987).

Staff frustration and dislike are not so easily masked as one might imagine; life as a homeless person frequently makes one exquisitely sensitive to abandonment.

Unfortunately, the inability of the service system or its providers to adequately address the needs of this population does not decrease those needs. It has, however, added to the burden of clinicians charged with engaging this population. The initiation of clinical contact must take into account the individual's prior history with the system and experiences with previous caregivers.

The role of involuntary commitment

One model of assuring that those at risk receive services has been the use of mass involuntary detention of the homeless mentally ill in several cities. These widely publicized 'street sweeps' generally involve the round-up of large numbers of homeless individuals, often put into effect when the outdoor temperature falls below a certain level. Touted by some as a humane gesture, such activities have been severely critized by many advocates for the homeless. This policy received national media attention when, after being involuntarily hospitalized, one patient challenged this plan in the courts (46).

It is incumbent on us to differentiate between such indiscriminant use of civil authority and the appropriate application of civil commitment criteria to schizophrenic individuals who are also homeless. Such an intervention cannot, however, be done without a careful assessment of the circumstances, symptoms and potential risks of the individual to be committed. Certainly, society has recognized that some of the severally mentally ill will, at times, be so significantly impaired as to pose a danger to themselves or others. In many parts of the country, an additional criteria, that of 'grave disability', allows for the involuntary commitment of individuals unable to provide food, clothing and shelter for themselves because of their mental disorder. The problems of applying a grave disability criterion to evaluations of homeless individuals leads to an examination of fundamental principles implicit in any model of involuntary treatment. Designed for a broader population, applying the standard of grave disability to a homeless population involves a series of clinical and ethical dilemmas. How are we to disentangle the extent to which the individual's inability to be fed, clothed and sheltered is a function of the severity of his symptomatology, given the large cohort of others in the same situation who do not suffer from psychiatric symptoms? Given the paucity of available services in many communities, are we assessing the individual's disability or the dysfunction of the public welfare system? Clearly, there are cases where a homeless individual is at severe risk because of schizophrenic symptoms. Overt delusions, hallucinations and impaired thinking may lead to starvation or hypothermia even in those with far greater resources. Differentiating the effects of economic, social and psychopathological contributants to the patient's grave disability remains one of the challenges confronting clinicians in this field.

Finally, an essential notion behind the concept of involuntary commitment is that one is committing a patient to treatment. For the few days of involuntary hospitalization, this may be true for many of the homeless individuals committed. But what lies beyond? As we have seen, discharge to a shelter or back to the streets is the most frequent disposition for homeless individuals after they have been hospitalized. The ethical questions raised by depriving individuals of their liberty, while denying them necessary long-term treatment, remain a serious subject of debate among service providers and advocates for this population.

PATIENT-CENTERED TREATMENT SERVICES

Mental health services may, for convenience, be divided into two types, those which are tied to specific sites, and those which follow patients regardless of the location of service. While many traditional public mental health programs employ the first model, such an approach is often poorly suited to the needs of homeless patients. Service-specific programs usually require that patients come to them, assuming a population that is willing and able to do so. Eligibility for service is often tied to residence in a specific geographic area, leading to the exclusion of transient or undomiciled individuals (5, 25). Clinical responsibility for the patient is fragmented, changing with each change of treatment site (44). Many of the most vulnerable and disabled patients, unable to tolerate the inconsistent and varying demands of such a system, resist any engagement with it at all (47).

A primary means of providing services to such 'system resisters' has been the development of outreach and case management services which make the patient, not the site, the locus of responsibility. Initiating and maintaining clinical contact wherever the patient is provides a source of continuity of person and treatment philosophy. Although such an approach is useful for many chronically ill populations, it is essential for work with the most distrustful, suspicious and alienated.

Outreach to the homeless schizophrenic*

Establishing a connection with the homeless schizophrenic individual seems to require more than anything else patience and sensitivity. Although there certainly are some who would welcome offers of referrals or treatment, for many trust can only be gained slowly and cautiously. Many outreach workers to this population agree that the first step is frequently merely establishing one's presence in locations where homeless people congregate, without attempts at interaction. Some workers then begin by offering some concrete assistance, generally in the form of food or coffee. Sometimes, this snack may be offered without further comment. Others may make non-intrusive inquiries about the individual's well-being. Frequently, such circumscribed contacts may go on for many months before further engagement is attempted. New York's Midtown Outreach Program's street-outreach team is a prototype of such services. Outreach workers carry large shopping bags offering fig newtons, coffee or clothing to individuals congregating in New York's train stations, parks, doorways or street corners. Along with their food or clothing, they are given a pamphlet and the program's phone number. Since staff visit the same sites

---

* Many of the ideas contained in this section are a result of a consensus conference 'Outreach Services for Homeless Mentally Ill People', sponsored by the National Institute of Mental Health and occurring under the auspices of the Intergovernmental Health Policy Project, George Washington University, Feb. 2–3, 1987.

on a daily basis, the workers become familiar faces to those they serve. Over time, staff may begin to ask after an individual's health and to offer the possibility of shelter or health care services. If the person appears in no immediate danger, however, they are free to reject any and all offers; many accept only 'Hellos' and cookies. Some difficult-to-engage individuals have required up to four years of virtually daily contact before accepting any other services (Marsha Martin, personal communication).

Mental health outreach workers attempting to make initial contact with prospective clients within shelters have a somewhat easier task. Simply by their presence in the shelter, such clients have demonstrated their willingness and ability to tolerate some interpersonal interaction. Because of their continued residence in the shelter, it is easier to maintain ongoing contact, compared to the far more transient life of those remaining undomiciled. Since clients are already fed, clothed and housed, shelter outreach workers must often rely of non-threatening forms of interpersonal contact to bolster their relationship. Thus Susser, as a prelude to providing psychiatric services in a New York City hotel, found himself running bingo games for the homeless mentally ill clientele (48).

Frequently, intervention with patients' medical problems serves as an effective 'carrot' to involve them in mental health care. Even if they will not actively seek it out, most homeless individuals will not refuse medical attention when it is offered (49). This is particularly true when they are experiencing pain or discomfort. Unlike mental health care, which some experience as making them feel worse, most associate medical care with feeling better. Therefore, offers of cough medicine, shampoo for lice infestations or dressings for foot ulcers are frequently a first step to being seen as someone who can provide help and relief.

Establishing a therapeutic relationship with a schizophrenic patient who has had little positive interaction with psychiatric care requires extraordinary clinical skills. As with the initiation of any treatment relationship, the clinician must remain exquisitely sensitive to subtle cues reflecting the patient's response to each intervention. Only through a combination of empathy and clinical experience can one determine the extent to which a specific interaction is being positively received. For some, offers of food or clothing approach the limits of their ability to tolerate interpersonal connectedness. For others, such offers may be seen as overly intrusive or as condescending. Although the modalities employed by outreach workers in an attempt to initiate relationships with clients may appear trivial to those more accustomed to the tools of clarification and interpretation, their use is a sophisticated clinical maneuver. The goal is not solely to provide the homeless person with calories or garments. Rather, these serve as vehicles to document one's concern, to demonstrate one's reliability and to acknowledge the preeminence of the client's needs. If playing bingo with patients is the most effective way to insinuate oneself into their lives in an acceptable and non-threatening way, then bingo may be well be the first appropriate clinical intervention.

Critical to effective outreach services is a recognition of the difference between what the homeless person perceives as their needs and what a clinical observer might believe is most necessary. A survey of mentally ill homeless individuals done in San Francisco illuminates some of these differences (50). The population sampled had all had two or more contacts with either psychiatric emergency or acute inpatient psychiatric facilities over the previous twelve months. Nonetheless, on the list of the 15 problems they cited most frequently, mental illness was ranked thirteenth, below their lack of a place to live, money, jobs, food, and places to go. It was also felt to be less of a problem than police harassment, robbery, alcoholism, assault, rape, physical illness, particular personal animosities and loneliness. Only drug addiction and being cold were mentioned less frequently. The group rated as their most significant need 'affordable housing', followed by financial entitlements, employment, free-time activities and social contacts, food, alcohol cessation, and only then supportive counseling. By recognizing these needs, and providing for those deemed most essential by each individual, outreach workers can begin to establish themselves as someone who listens and who understands.

Triage or treatment?

Originally conceived of as a short term service designed to triage previously undiscovered cases into a system of care, outreach often undergoes significant modification when applied to homeless schizophrenic populations. The concept of triage is predicated upon the availability of a spectrum of services to which an individual may be sent. It also presumes that the individual is able and willing to make use of these services. In many communities, there are simply no services available to this group; in others, they are inaccessible, inadequate, or oversubscribed. The path to establishing rapport and developing an interpersonal relationship is a strenuous one. Having finally developed a sufficient sense of trust, the patient may begin to share the extent and intensity of his or her needs. Yet, having achieved a willingness on the part of the patient to receive further services, are such services available? Affordable housing, the most frequently cited need of the population, rarely is. Entitlement programs often entail extensive waiting periods; in many parts of the country it may be a year between the time an SSI application is submitted and the time it is approved.

Having finally established some relationship of trust with an outreach worker, many patients are unable to extend this relationship to encompass other care providers. Changing one's world view to accept that there is another who is capable of understanding and caring about you, is one thing; altering all your previously held conceptions about treatment providers in general is a different matter. The outreach worker is frequently caught between a system unwilling to accept the care of his or her charge and a patient unwilling to accept the services of the system.

In recognition of this dilemma, many programs designed as outreach services have gradually undergone a transition to providing more long-term ongoing care. From an initial perspective of contact, evaluation, and triage, they have acccpted the role of primary provider merged into the function now commonly called case management.

Case management

Bridging the gaps

Regardless of our ultimate evaluation of the quality of state mental hospitals, they did provide psychiatric services, a place to live, food, clothing, and medical care. They offered a relative certainty about where the next night would be spent and a continuity of social milieu that allowed for the development of personal relationships. Since the advent of deinstitutionalization, such comprehensive and continuous services have rarely been made available at one site. Thus, any attempts at meeting these multiple needs must often be accomplished through patching together a variety of services offered by specialized and unrelated agencies. The needs of the homeless schizophrenic are even more complex and demanding than those of other deinstitutionalized populations, since, in addition to the usual array of medical, mental health and social services, they also require the provision of basic shelter and nourishment. The task of assuring that individuals receive comprehensive services for their complex needs, despite the multiple disconnected programs available, is the function of case management.

Therapists or brokers

Although there is substantial agreement about the necessity of case management services for adequate community care of the severely mentally ill (51 – 53) there is little consensus on what case management is. Generally, it is agreed that case management includes assessment, planning, linkage, monitoring, advocacy and follow-up (51, 52). Some conceptual models, however, view the case manager as primarily an office-based worker who, like a travel agent, serves as the intermediary between a client and multiple service agencies (51). Such a model is, of course, dependent on the existence of suitable services to which clients can be referred and on clients who are accepting of services. In contradistinction to this 'brokerage' model of case management is one which views case management as a clinical service involving a primary relationship between case manager and patient (54 – 56). Such a 'hands-on' approach to case management is essential in work with the homeless schizophrenic population. In communities with a sufficient array of available shelters, day treatment programs and outpatient clinics, a case manager

> 'can provide the glue that binds otherwise fragmented services into arrangements that respond to the unique and changing needs of clients'. (53, p. 9)

Gradually, as connections are formed with other programs, the case manager can begin to decrease the intensity of contact, making time available to treat other patients. Far too often, however, the case manager must serve not only as the primary, but as virtually the sole source of clinical care.

Such clinical case management is an extremely complex and demanding therapeutic activity. Within the framework of traditional psychotherapy, clinicians can rely on a series of contextual variables that help delineate the boundaries of therapy. Sessions of a specified length, a door that separates the site of treatment from the outside world, and the regularity and fixed frequency of appointments help define what is, and is not, part of the treatment. Case management, as we have defined it, knows no such boundaries. 'Sessions' may be of any duration, occur at any frequency, and take place at many different sites. The decision of how much the interaction should involve the attainment of hard goods and services, and how much will focus on more traditional, verbal interaction, is flexible and changes over time. Without the fixed definitions of what is acceptable, the clinician doing case management must rely upon his or her own resources for determining the intensity, structure, and context of each interaction. In addition to knowledge of a wide range of community resources, such work requires keen clinical judgment and a familiarity with multiple treatment modalities. It may initially involve the provision of food, clothing and access to a hotel room or shelter space. As the patient's survival needs are met, the case manager can begin to provide less tangible means of support, and interactions with the patient can begin to more closely resemble traditional therapeutic encounters. In some ways, such case management can be seen as the logical extension of supportive psychodynamic psychotherapy. In more traditional approaches, the technique may involve 'lending a bit of ego' to less functional patients. With the homeless schizophrenic, what is 'lent' may be more extensive, involving participation in planning and help in carrying out a wide variety of daily activities (57).

Who should do case management with homeless schizophrenic?

Without the fixed parameters of offices and appointments, the clinician doing case management is forced to draw upon his own clinical skills to an unusual degree. Although paraprofessionals have frequently been asked to do this work (52), it is best handled by more highly trained professional staff. Such individuals are better prepared to face complicated clinical decisions, and to address the extraordinarily strong transference and countertransference feelings it frequently evokes.

A frequent pitfall of this work is the tendency to overinvolvement. Recognizing the breadth and severity of a patient's needs, the case manager may attempt, too rapidly and too vigorously, to meet them all. Trained in a model which equates accomplishment with improvement, the naive case manager may push a patient into situations and expectations which cannot realistically be accomplished. Without the experience to recognize the slow pace of change in those with severe disorders, unrealistic optimism may be evoked by each demonstration of slight improvement.

Overidentification with the patient's pain and deprivation may lead to unrealistic attempts to tackle, and improve, all elements of the patient's life. Recognizing the gaps in the service system, the naive case manager may attempt to do all, and be all, for his or her patients (58). The working day becomes longer and longer, and the case load smaller and smaller, as the struggle to provide for the deficits of the system and the patient become an ever increasingly complicated and demoralizing task. Without proper supervision, such attempts frequently lead to disillusionment, frustration and depression.

A somewhat opposite and more insidious process may occur with even greater frequency. Workers who are initially dedicated and caring may, after a relatively brief period of time, develop a detached and cynical stance. After a brief assessment, the patients may be labeled 'manipulative', 'non-compliant' or 'sociopathic'. 'Not needing' or 'undeserving' of care, they are ignored or hastily referred to other agencies. Such behavior represents a frequent countertransference reaction. Faced with the extraordinary needs of a severely deprived population, the case manager nonetheless has few external resources upon which to draw. Fully exposing oneself to the depth of the patient's misery becomes too painful to tolerate. Rather than face the depression which might result, the case manager undergoes an unconscious defensive maneuver. By making the patient unsuitable for or undeserving of services, the case manager avoids dysphoric feelings evoked by the recognition of the mismatch between what is available and what is needed. By rejecting the patient as 'unworthy', the pain of this recognition is avoided. Naturally, however, such a stance leads to frustration and discomfort in the work, and often to the inability to continue involvement with the population.

Certainly, it is unrealistic to believe that professional education, let alone a particular degree, immunizes one from either of these countertransference responses. However, an essential feature of most psychotherapy training is a recognition of the primacy of the clinicians' internal states and responses as an element in the treatment paradigm. Thus, although such training will not prevent one from developing such feelings, it does help one learn how to keep the results of those feelings from having such an extensive impact on the therapeutic relationship. Although some authors feel that the nature of much case management work would keep it from being attractive to highly trained staff (52), others disagree (54, 56, 57).

Providing therapeutically oriented case management requires sophisticated conceptualizations and a great deal of clinical experience and judgement. Were it only passing out sandwiches, making phone calls or standing in line, it would indeed be an activity for untrained staff. If psychotherapy were just sitting in a room conversing, it would be, too. In fact, doing intensive supportive psychotherapy 'on the hoof' is among the most complicated of clinical endeavors. Doing it with a population so psychologically disabled and socially disenfranchised makes it highly rewarding one as well.

SITE-SPECIFIC TREATMENT SERVICES

Obviously, case management cannot exist in isolation. There will be times when patients need other services which can only be delivered at specialized treatment sites. Ideally, patients will be able to move freely between these programs as their clinical condition warrants while maintaining ongoing contact with a case manager. The degree to which intervention will require adaptation for a homeless population will vary at each site and depend not only on the clinical status of each patient, but also on the availability of further treatment options at other levels of care.

Emergency and inpatient services

In many ways, the role of acute care services for homeless schizophrenics differs little from its application to other schizophrenic populations. (see Chapters 12–14). However, given the intensity and severity of the confounding effects of social, economic, and residential concerns in this population, certain areas of the evaluation merit particular clinical attention.

Within emergency services based in public hospitals, there exists a significant overlap between homelessness and schizophrenia in the patients seen. Lipton and his co-workers, reviewing 100 consecutive undomiciled patients at Bellevue Hospital, found that 72% of them were diagnosed as schizophrenic (59). Chafetz and Goldfinger (33), examined the residential status of a random sample of patients presenting at the country psychiatric emergency services in San Francisco. They found that 46% of all patients seen evidenced some degree of residential instability. Of this group, 40% were diagnosed schizophrenic. Studying the group's symptomatology along 19 separate symptom scales, they found that the domiciled and undomiciled groups differed significantly only in the areas of social isolation and impairment in daily routine and leisure activities. Each of these 'symptoms' is virtually inherent in the life of those who are homeless. It was noted that the very sociodemographic characteristics of the population they studied may explain the lack of differentiation. All those served by public emergency services may be so much at risk for the loss of residence

> 'that the patients in all 3 groups – homeless, transients and stable – might be essentially the same patients, observed at different moments in time'. (40, p. 94)

One central concern in the acute evaluation of those presenting as psychotic and homeless is the need for careful differential diagnosis. There is a high incidence of alcohol and other drug abuse among the homeless, and a striking co-morbidity of substance abuse and mental illness in the population (38). Clinical evaluation should always include the possibility that psychotic symptoms are the result of an acute toxic phenomenon. As with all populations, care must be taken to rule out affective disorders presenting with psychotic features. Given the extraordinarily high over-representation of veterans, particularly Vietnam-era veterans among the homeless (*Soldiers of Misfortune.* Research and Liaison Unit, Office of the Comptroller, City of New York, Nov., 1982) clinicians should be alert for the presence of untreated post-traumatic stress disorder presenting with psychotic features.

Often, the areas requiring the most significant attention during acute hospitalization of homeless schizophrenics lie outside the circumscribed domain of psychiatry. Given these individuals' lack of access to ongoing health services (39), the period of psychiatric hospitalization may be their only contact with general medical care. Given the high incidence of physical illness in this population (38, 61, 62) the treatment of their non-psychiatric disorders often becomes a significant focus of attention.

The psychosocial evaluation, an essential part of any inpatient assessment, takes on particular importance with this population. One area of inquiry should include assessment of how individuals became homeless, with an eye to illuminating any remediable situations.

An exploration of the patient's willingness and ability to participate in various ongoing treatment options can often be effectively carried out during hospitalization. For those who are have not previously received psychiatric services, initial hospitalization can, of course, significantly influence their later treatment history. For those individuals who have not participated in outpatient care, hospitalization can provide the time to explore with them their reasons for refusing such treatment. Often, referral can be made to services which are more appropriate to, and accepting of, their needs. By providing an experience of compassionate, comprehensive and meaningful contact, the acute hospitalization can sometimes serve as a first positive experience with the organized psychiatric service system and help change some of the patient's negative perceptions about the nature of organized psychiatric care.

Medication clinics

Probably the most predictable discharge referral for homeless schizophrenics is to outpatient medication clinics. Although many in this population require ongoing pharmacotherapy, the rate of follow-through on such referrals, in the absence of a stable residence, is quite low. Case managers often provide the only means of assuring that these patients get to, and are accepted by, outpatient clinics (57). Regardless of the sophistication of the case manager, it is clear that these patients will virtually all require the additional services of a psychiatrist for their medication management.

Obviously, schizophrenia retains its characteristic responses to pharmacological interventions regardless of whether the patient is domiciled or homeless. Several clinical considerations however, may be unique to the evaluation and prescription of medication for this group. Even the differential diagnosis of homeless patients introduces a number of rather unique situations. Assessments of sleeping patterns, eating patterns and daily activities require a recalibration of baseline expected behaviors. Obviously, the interpretation of complaints of not sleeping well or eating well takes on a very different significance if one is sleeping on the street and eating in soup kitchens.

Prescribers must frequently alter their choice of medication and dosing frequency as a function of the unusual life situation of the homeless schizophrenic. Those sleeping outside often refuse anything other that low-dose neuroleptics. Given the constant threat of assault and robbery on the streets, they may reject any medication which alters their self-perceived sense of alertness and ability to respond rapidly to potential threats. Those sleeping in shelters face somewhat different problems. Frequently, shelters open quite late at night and require occupants to be out by early morning. Overly sedating medication may make it difficult for the patient to comply with this fixed time schedule, and may consequently lead to unilateral dosage reduction or discontinuance of some medication entirely.

Many homeless schizophrenics have already had multiple drug trials, and are familiar with a large number of neuroleptic medications. Often, patients will mention a particular medication that they found especially helpful, or at least less offensive. Although rather unorthodox, a variation on an approach suggested by Schatzberg and Cole (62) seems appropriate for this population. Within broad parameters, homeless schizophrenic patients should be allowed to choose the neuroleptic with which they are most comfortable, even if such a clinical stance may not lead to a patient being treated at the optimum dose of what would be considered the ideal drug. Given the frequency of non-compliance in this population, the alternative may be no neuroleptic whatsoever, a significantly less desirable outcome.

The fact that many homeless schizophrenics may only be seen by the physician on an intermittent and unpredictable basis obviously has implications for prescribing practices. Medications which might require extensive preliminary blood work or other diagnostic evaluation, or which necessitate routine serum monitoring, may be impractical for many of these individuals. The use of depot neuroleptics in this population poses unique advantages and problems. Certainly, it offers the option of providing relatively constant serum levels without the need for regular contact or daily medication. However, dosage regulation is obviously compromised, and extrapyramidal side-effects are more difficult to address. Although for those living in shelters it may be possible to establish regular follow-up, this is often highly impractical with individuals who are being seen only intermittently during street outreach or other unstructured contacts. There are clearly no overarching recommendations that can be offered: the risks and benefits must be decided on an individual clinical basis (64).

It is particularly important that homeless patients receive a thorough explanation of the potential side-effects of their medications. Such education should, of course, be a part of all prescription practice. However, alerting patients to the possibility of such side-effects as dystonic reactions and other acute symptoms becomes particularly important in a population who may not have access to medical care at the time symptoms emerge.

As a final note, clinicians should be aware of the relatively high street value of benzodiazopines. One strategy is to provide only a one- or two-day supply at a time. Probably, this class of drug should be used in this population only in situations where there is a compelling necessity which justifies such use.

Residential services

In the recommendations of the American Psychiatric Association Task Force on the Homeless Mentally Ill, the need for residential services was addressed immediately after the need for food, shelter and clothing (65). The recommendation called for 'an adequate number and ample range of graded, step-wise, supervised community housing settings' (pp. 5, 6). There is virtually nowhere in the United States where such an array of services is available for any group of chronically and severely mentally ill individuals. Nowhere is it available for those who are both mentally ill and homeless. In many respects, residential services for the homeless differ little from those for their domiciled counterparts (see Chapter 15). There has, however, been a proliferation over the last 10 years of specialized services which combine shelter and mental health care.

Shelter-based clinics

The simplest model for providing psychiatric care to the homeless population is to offer a mental health outreach health team or small mental health clinic within a shelter site. Although clearly a preferable alternative to the absence of any psychiatric care, such an approach suffers from the same problems as other outreach services. Without any specific organized programs within the shelter, and lacking access to more intensive treatment alternatives, it frequently provides an inadequate clinical 'patch', leaving essential problems unaddressed. Nonetheless, several programs have found ways to expand their meager resources and have developed novel approaches to engaging with and treating this population. Unlike street outreach workers, the advantage of a captive audience makes both patient tracking and continuity of care somewhat less problematic. The best of these programs have taken as their goal a model of psychosocial rehabilitation, and provide training in independent living and the development of skills necessary to make a transition back into the domiciled community. Although individual apartments for each patient may not economically feasible, one approach has been to work with cohorts of patients, preparing them to pool their resources and live together (66).

Regardless of how well designed such shelter-based services are, they cannot substitute for residential programs specifically planned for the chronically mentally ill homeless. The very nature of large 'general' shelters makes them even less suitable as living alternatives for the severely ill than they are for all other homeless people. Frequently housing dozens to hundreds of people in large open dormitories, they are virtually all noisy, crowded and full of activity. The level of sensory stimulation, uncomfortable to most occupants, is frequently intolerable to those with schizophrenia. By mixing homeless people of multiple backgrounds and functional capacity, they expose the most vulnerable to theft, intimidation and physical assault. Although possibly preferable to life on the streets, most residents find them degrading, dehumanizing and grossly inadequate (4, 12, 23). Thus, in a recent study in New York, public shelter users reported that their most serious problems in staying in public shelters were robbery, violence, noise and the lack of privacy. (Struening EL, A study of the residents of the New York City shelter system, New State Psychiatric Institute, 1986, unpublished).

Patient acceptability

The rationale or rationalization given for housing the chronically mentally ill in public shelters stems from the commonly held belief that such individuals would refuse to live in more highly structured residential settings. Rather than succumb to the restrictiveness and demands of such high-quality, but more structured accommodations, the argument is laid out that most would prefer to remain on the streets. A variant of this position holds that the severely ill homeless are simply unable, rather than unwilling, to accommodate to the demands of such structure. Stark (67) disagrees. Rather, she suggests that such patients have developed

> 'a set of behavior modes that 'work' and have certain rewards, in particular, a form of survival that is based on controlling, through structured behavior, the seemingly chaotic environment in which they find themselves . . .' (67, p. 95)

The question of whether mentally ill homeless individuals would accept residential services has been hotly contested. Lipton and his colleagues provide one of the only longitudinal, controlled outcome studies in the literature (59). Fifty-two patients presenting to the Psychiatric Emergency Services of Bellevue Hospital who were homeless, chronically mentally ill, and in need of hospitalization were randomly assigned to two study groups. The control subjects received routine discharge dispositions, while experimental subjects were offered a room in a supportive living program for the homeless mentally ill located in a renovated single-room occupancy hotel. Virtually none of the subjects refused the placement, and 69% of them were still living there 12 months after admission, more than double the percentage of control subjects who were permanently housed. In addition, the experimental group demonstrated statistically significant differences from the controls in the proportion of nights spent in a hospital, the number of nights spent undomiciled, and the ratings of adequacy of and commitment to their living arrangements. This, despite the fact that on follow-up the two groups did not significantly differ in their degree of psychopathology on a number of rating scales. Lipton concludes that this seriously questions that point of view which contends that homelessness is intricately related to the patient's psychopathology; and rather, it reflects a lack of available and acceptable housing alternatives.

Long-term supportive housing

The facility to which Lipton sent his experimental group, one of the St. Francis Residences, has served as a prototype for a number of similar programs around the country. Located in converted single-room occupancy hotels, the residences provide permanent humane and dignified housing for chronically homeless individuals with severe mental illness. Since the buildings are owned by the Franciscan order, room rent can be held below market value. In addition, the program provides low-cost meals and clothing. Clients maintain individual rooms, knowing that they can safely accrue personal possessions. Staff are available to talk with the clients; formal medical, psychiatric and social work care is provided through cooperative arrangements with Bellevue Hospital (68).

Individuals living there are regarded as tenants, thereby avoiding the stigmatization of being labeled mentally ill. Although psychiatric services are available, and approximately 40% of the St. Francis tenants receive psychotropic medication, participation in ongoing treatment is not a condition for continued stay. Rather, the program is designed with the recognition that with the slow development of trust and connection to staff who demonstrate their respect for, and connection to the tenants, staff recommendations will increasingly be seen as well-motivated and worthwhile. By providing services, but not requiring participation in them, patients are able to vary their level of involvement without feeling pressured, or concerned about being penalized for non-participation.

Such an approach, based on the notion of availability without intrusiveness, has proved to be both acceptable to and effective with homeless schizophrenics. Variations on the model have involved altering the size and physical structure of the program, referral sources, and the nature and extensiveness of program activities. Although the provision of permanent housing is clearly a critical feature, other residential services have applied the same treatment philosophy within transitional living situations. What appears essential if the program is to be successful is that staff treat residents with respect, maintain their dignity, and offer support when required. They must be willing to accept the fact that the patient's engaging in treatment must be a goal, not a prerequisite.

The most successful of such services tend to provide a broad array of treatment modalities and means of assistance, including, but not limited to, food, clothing, vocational rehabilitation, medical and psychiatric care, work programs, access to entitlement programs, psychoeducation and social activities. In those communities where such comprehensive residential programs exist, there is rarely an empty room. The number of homeless schizophrenics nationally exceeds the capacity of such programs many hundred-fold. Until an adequate number of residential beds can be made available, other models of providing comprehensive services to the population must be implemented.

Other program components

The array of services necessary for the adequate treatment of homeless schizophrenics differs little from those needed for any other schizophrenic population. Rather than attempt to address all program modalities here, the reader is referred to the appropriate chapters in this volume. What is essential is that such services be sensitive to the cultural needs of the homeless, a principle of program planning which is hardly limited in its application to services designed for this particular subculture (70). Thus, groups at a day treatment program must focus on the realistic needs and problems of the homeless population. An outpatient clinic cannot schedule treatment sessions that conflict with meal time at the local soup kitchen if they intend to have the services be accessible to homeless patients (41). Vocational rehabilitation programs must include not only training for jobs, but also help with obtaining suitable clothing to attend job interviews.

Ideal services for this population would involve an integration of medical, psychiatric and social services approaches. In 18 American cities, small pilot projects combining medical, mental health and social work staff were initiated in 1984. Funded by a large grant from the Robert Wood Johnson Foundation, these services use a variety of treatment approaches, depending on the needs and services available in their home cities. At some sites, care is provided by mobile vans; at others, by multidisciplinary outreach teams to the shelters. Some cities have large and sophisticated clinics, others provide services in whatever corner of a shelter they and the patient can achieve some privacy. Many of the projects provide case management; several include psychiatrists as part of the ongoing treatment team. All have come to recognize that chronic mental illness is among the most frequent and devastating clinical conditions they are asked to treat (39).

THE HOMELESS SCHIZOPHRENIC AND THE TREATMENT SYSTEM

Systemic contributions

The current prevalence of homeless schizophrenics must be seen as a function of the confluence of deinstitutionalization, a lack of available housing, decreased federal entitlement programs and fundamental flaws in the community-based mental health system. Although one can address particular service modalities and how implementing them might improve care for this population, the core issue does not lie only in the absence of specific settings or programs. Rather, it reflects a failure in the design and implementation of adequate and effective alternatives to the comprehensive care provided in the state hospital (5, 13). Certainly, deinstitutionalization has resulted in many patients living successfully with families or in other supportive settings. However, as Lipton et al. note,

> 'for many of the chronic mentally ill discharged into the community, the alternative care system we created – or failed to create – has led to destitution, recidivism, criminalization and homelessness'. (59, p. 40)

In addition to its individual service components, an effective treatment system must be guided by certain overarching principles (69). Bachrach (70) has offered a conceptual analysis of those factors influencing continuity of care for chronic mental patients. Goldfinger and Chafetz (40) have provided a series of dimensions specifically applicable to the chronically mentally ill homeless. They propose seven qualities which must apply in any system designed to meet their needs.

Capable

Services must have available to them adequate staff, physical plant and resources. Without a community-based system capable of meeting their needs, this population will continue to over-utilize the expensive services of acute care settings (62).

Comprehensive

Comprehensive care 'has unique connotations for the homeless mentally ill, who generally have nothing and need everything'. (5, p. 40) Since the services required by this population are not limited to psychiatric needs, alliances must be forged between the mental health and social service system. Integrated approaches in such areas as money management, medical care, and supervised low-cost housing must be developed.

Continuous

Even if services were comprehensive, the homeless mentally ill frequently suffer from discontinuities within the treatment system. Discontinuities of information are frequent, with shelter and mental health program staffs rarely communicating.

Discontinuities of treatment philosophy take a particular toll in this sensitive population. In order to receive ongoing services in a variety of settings, the patient may be forced to adapt to differing views of what is and is not acceptable at each site. Discontinuities of person are often a neglected problem. Schizophrenic individuals, with tenuous therapeutic alliances, are often asked to change their primary care givers with each change of clinical status and treatment site. Ongoing primary contact with a clinical case manager may be the only way to provide for continuity of information, approach and primary relationship.

Accessible

Services must be available where homeless schizophrenic patients live, open when they can come, and welcoming. Staff must be sensitive to the cultural expectations of those they are to serve. With populations such as homeless schizophrenics, we may only be able to make our services accessible by providing them where such individuals congregate. For no other clinical group is the need for outreach services so clear.

Individualized

No single kind of service or style of intervention will be appropriate for all homeless schizophrenics. We cannot refuse to treat those who do not fit our mold, but must change our treatment approaches. Thus, for example, discharge plans must be reexamined in order to recognize those which, implicitly if not explicitly, assume that a patient will be discharged 'home' to a regular apartment or stable dwelling. Thus, for example, a wheelchair-bound patient may be ready for discharge home from an inpatient psychiatric service when his acute psychotic symptoms disappear. However, asking a recently stabilized homeless schizophrenic to manage the stress of living on the streets or in shelters in a wheelchair is a misapplication of discharge criteria designed for a different population. We must adjust our expectations, taking into account the massive impact of being undomiciled on daily activities.

Flexible

Flexibility is the system equivalent of individualization. Just as the treatment plan must change as the patient changes, our services must change in order to accommodate to this population. Perhaps the inflexibility which most directly affects members of the homeless schizophrenic group is unrealistic expectations about length of stay in residential services. With no long-term resources available to them, lengths of stay for this group must be made more flexible. It is clinically useless and ethically intolerable to treat somebody intensively for 30 days and then discharge them to nowhere.

Willing and tolerant

Lacking adequate resources, many agencies deliberately exclude homeless schizophrenics from treatment, preferentially serving less demanding and needy individuals. With greater resources, more experience and a better understanding of the population, an increased number of providers may be willing to accept the responsibility of work with these patients.

Meaningful

Perhaps most importantly, services need to begin to offer interventions which are considered meaningful by those they serve. Rather than imposing on them what clinicians feel is necessary, services must begin to address those problems that homeless schizophrenic clients themselves define as most important. Since patients do not come asking for treatment, but asking for help, we must begin to offer those concrete services which they find helpful (47). Through comprehensive outreach services and client-focused clinical case management activities, we can begin to reintegrate this most disaffiliated and disenfranchised population.

Providing asylum

One of the key functions of the state hospital in times past was the provision of asylum. Bachrach (71) has pointed out that we frequently engage in a strange linguistic flaw when discussing these asylums, mistaking the container for the thing contained. With the loss of state hospitals as facilities, we have also lost many of the functions of asylum that these facilities provided. Asylum, in the sense of a safe haven and refuge, falls at the intersection of the provision of shelter and of mental health care. As we evaluate a service for the homeless schizophrenic, we must ask ourselves not only if it provides adequate treatment and adequate domicile, but whether it includes that intangible, but essential, function of asylum (72).

CONCLUSIONS

Providing for adequate psychosocial treatment of homeless people with schizophrenia will require a collaborative effort between multiple agencies and individuals. Given the diversity of the needs of this group, it is only by establishing partnerships between social service, mental health and medical providers that effective treatment plans and community placements can be achieved. One cannot begin to address the needs of this population until adequate food, clothing and shelter have been provided. When, and only when, these basics have been made available, attempts at addressing their psychiatric problems can begin.

In most respects, the psychosocial treatment of homeless schizophrenics involves the same programmatic considerations as those for other domiciled individuals – a full range of acute, subacute and residential facilities, day treatment and vocational activities and the provision of ongoing clinical and medication services. As with other disenfranchised, resistant or non-engaged populations, however, the availability of an array of passive services is not enough. Active outreach and other strategies to 'seduce' them into participating in treatment must be developed and the experiences which have resulted in their disillusionment with existing mental health services must be addressed.

The social costs of neglecting this population are enormous. The resources used in providing only intermittent, fragmented acute care services are staggering (62). The existence of this population, and the severity of their needs will not disappear without active and concerted efforts at designing and implementing appropriate interventions. As clinicians, and as citizens, it is our professional and ethical responsibility to do so.

REFERENCES

1. Solenberger AW (1911) One Thousand Homeless Men, The Russell Sage Foundation. William F. Fell, Philadelphia.
2. Baker AT (1918) Vagrancy. *Ment. Hyg., II*, 595.
3. Hopper K, Hamberg J (1984) The Making of America's Homeless: From Skid Row to New Poor. *Community Service Society of New York*, New York.
4. Baxter E, Hopper K (1981) Private Lives/Public Spaces. *Community Service Society of New York*, New York.
5. Bachrach, LL (1984) The homeless mentally ill and mental health services: an analytic review of the literature. In: Lamb HR (Ed), The Homeless Mentally Ill, pp. 11 – 54. *American Psychiatric Association*, Washington, DC.
6. Fischer RJ, Breakey WR (1986) Homelessness and mental health: an overview. *Int. J. Ment. Health, 14*, 4, 6.
7. Lipton FR, Sabatini A, Katz SE (1983) Down and out in the city: the homeless mentally ill. *Hosp. Community Psychiatry, 34*, 818.
8. Arce AA, Tadlock M, Vergare MJ, Shapiro SH (1983) A psychiatric profile of street people admitted to an emergency shelter. *Hosp. Community Psychiatry, 34*, 812.
9. Fischer RJ, Shapiro S, Breakey WR, Anthony JC, Kramer M (1986) Mental health and social characteristics of the homeless: a survey of mission users. *Am. J. Public Health, 76*, 519.
10. Crystal S, Ladner S, Towber R (1986) Multiple impairment patterns in the mentally ill homeless. *Int. J. Ment. Health 14/4*, 61.
11. Jones RE (1983) Street people and psychiatry: an introduction. *Hosp. Community Psychiatry, 34*, 807.
12. Bassuk EL (1984) The homelessness problem. *Sci. Am., 251*, 40.
13. Lamb HR (1984) Deinstitutionalization and the homeless mentally ill. *Hosp. Community Psychiatry, 35*, 899.
14. Ropers RH (1986) The Rise of the New Urban Homeless. Public Affairs Report, 26/5 – 6, 1. Institute of Governmental Studies, University of California, Berkeley.
15. Hope M, Young J (1984) From back wards to back alleys: deinstitutionalization and the homeless. *Urban Soc. Change Rev., 17/2*, 7.
16. Talbott JA (1982) The Chronic Mentally Ill: Treatment Programs and Systems. *Human Sciences Press*, New York.
17. Appleby L, Desai PN (1985) Documenting the relationship between homelessness and psychiatric hospitalization. *Hosp. Community Psychiatry, 36*, 732.
18. Wing JK (1978) Who becomes chronic. *Psychiatr. Q., 50*, 178.
19. Roth D, Bean J, Lust N, Saveanu T (1985) Homelessness in Ohio: A Study of People in Need. Ohio Department of Mental Health, Columbus.

20. Rossi PH, Fisher GA, Willis G (1986) The Condition of The Homeless in Chicago. *Social and Demographic Research Institute*, Amherst, MA.
21. Pepper B, Kirshner MC, Ryglewicz H (1981) The young adult chronic patient: overview of a population. *Hosp. Community Psychiatry, 32*, 463.
22. Schwartz SR, Goldfinger SM (1981) The new chronic patient: clinical characteristics of an emerging subgroup. *Hosp. Community Psychiatry, 32*, 470.
23. Hopper K, Baxter E, Cox S (1982) Not making it crazy: the young homeless patients in New York City. In: Pepper B, Ryglewicz H (Eds.), *The Young Adult Chronic Patient*, pp. 33 – 42. Jossey-Bass, San Francisco.
24. Hopper K (1985) Whose lives are these, anyway. *Urban Soc. Change Rev., 17/2*, 12.
25. Segal SP, Baumohl J, Johnson E (1977) Falling through the cracks: mental disorder and social margin in a young vagrant population. *Soc. Probl., 24*, 387.
26. Kaufman CA (1984) Implications of biological psychiatry for the severely mentally ill: a highly vulnerable population. In: Lamb HR (Ed.), The Homeless Mentally Ill, pp. 201 – 242. *American Psychiatric Association,* Washington, DC.
27. Lamb HR and Talbott JA (1986) The homeless mentally ill: the perspective of the American Psychiatric Association. *J. Am. Med. Assoc., 256*, 499.
28. The Department of Housing and Urban Development (1984) A Report to the Secretary on the Homeless and Emergency Shelters, Washington, DC.
29. Larew BI (1980) Strange strangers: serving transients. *Soc. Casework, 63*, 107.
30. United States General Accounting Office (1985) Homelessness: A Complex Problem and the Federal Response. Washington, DC.
31. Bachrach LL (1987) Issues in identifying and treating the homeless mentally ill. In: Bachrach LL (Ed), Leona Bachrach Speaks: *Selected Speeches and Lectures*, pp. 43 – 62. Jossey-Bass, San Francisco.
32. Bachrach LL (1984) Interpreting research on the homeless mentally ill: some caveats. *Hosp. Community Psychiatry, 35*, 914.
33. Chafetz L, Goldfinger SM (1984) Residential instability in a psychiatric emergency setting. *Psychiatr. Q., 56*, 20.
34. Roth D, Bean J (1986) New perspectives on homelessness: findings from a statewide epidemiological study. *Hosp. Community Psychiatry, 37*, 712.
35. United States Department of Health and Human Services (1983) Alcohol, Drug Abuse and Mental Health Problems of The Homeless. Rockville, MD.
36. Arce AA, Vergare MJ (1984) Identifying and characterizing the mentally ill among the homeless. In: Lamb, HR (Ed), The Homeless Mentally Ill, pp. 75 – 90. *American Psychiatric Association*, Washington, DC.
37. Robertson MJ (1988) Mental disorder, homelessness and access to services: a review of the empirical literature. In: Jahiel R (Ed), *Homelessness And Its Prevention.* Johns Hopkins Press, Baltimore, in press.
38. Wright JD, Weber E (1988) Homelessness and Health. McGraw-Hill, Washington, DC.
39. American Psychiatric Association (1982) Diagnostic and Statistical Manual of Mental Disorders, 3rd Ed. *American Psychiatric Association*, Washington, DC.
40. Goldfinger SM, Chafetz L (1984) Developing a better service delivery system for the homeless mentally ill. In: Lamb HR (Ed.), The Homeless Mentally Ill, pp. 91 – 108. *American Psychiatric Association,* Washington DC.
41. Segal SP, Baumohl J (1980) Engaging the disengaged: proposals on madness and vagrancy. *Soc. Work, 25*, 358.
42. Fischer PJ (1988) Criminal activity among the homeless: a study of arrests in Baltimore. *Hosp. Community Psychiatry, 39,* 46.
43. Lamb HR, Grant RW (1982) The mentally ill in an urban county jail. *Arch. Gen.*

Psychiatry, 39, 17.

44. Schwartz SR, Goldfinger SM, Ratener M, Cutler DL (1983) The young adult chronic patient and the care system: fragmentation prototypes. In: Cutler DL (Ed.), *Effective Aftercare for the 1980s*. Jossey-Bass, San Francisco.
45. Lipton FR, Sabatini A (1984) Constructing support services for homeless chronic patients. In: Lamb HR (Ed.), The Homeless Mentally Ill, *American Psychiatric Association*, Washington DC.
46. Cournos, F (1989) Involuntary Medication and the Case of Joyce Brown. *Hosp. Community Psychiatry, 40*, 136.
47. Goldfinger SM, Hopkin JT, Surber RW (1984) Treatment resisters or system resisters? Towards a better service delivery system for acute care recidivists. In: Pepper B, Ryglewicz H (Eds.), *Advances in Treating the Young Adult Chronic Patient.* Jossey-Bass, San Francisco.
48. Susser E (1988) Working with people who are mentally ill and homeless: the role of a psychiatrist. In: Jahiel R (Ed), *Homelessness And Its Prevention*. Johns Hopkins University Press, Baltimore. In press.
49. Clark ME, Rafferty M (1985) The Sickness That Won't Heal. *Health PAC Bull. 16/4*, 20.
50. Ball FIJ, Havassy BE (1984) A survey of the problems and needs of homeless consumers of acute psychiatric services. *Hosp. Community Psychiatry, 35*, 917.
51. Sullivan JP (1981) Case management. In Talbott JA (Ed), *The Chronic Mental Patient*, pp. 119 – 131. Human Sciences Press, New York.
52. Intagliata J (1982) Improving the quality of community care for the mentally disabled: the role of case management. *Schizophrenia Bull., 8*, 655.
53. Turner J, Shifren I (1979) Community support systems: how comprehensive? In: Stein L (Ed), *Community Support Systems for the Long-Term Patient,* Jossey-Bass, San Francisco.
54. Lamb HR (1980) Therapist-case managers: more than brokers of services. *Hosp. Community Psychiatry, 31*, 763.
55. Deitchman WS (1980) How many case managers does it take to screw in a lightbulb? *Hosp. Community Psychiatry, 31*, 788.
56. Harris M, Bergman HC (1987) Case management with the chronically mentally ill: a clinical perspective. *Am. J. Orthopsychiatry, 57*, 296.
57. Frances A, Goldfinger SM (1986) 'Treating' a homeless mentally ill patient who cannot be managed in the shelter system. *Hosp. Community Psychiatry, 37*, 577.
58. Brigg, D (1979) The trainee and the borderline client: counter-transference pitfalls. *Clin. Soc. Work J., 7,* 133.
59. Lipton FR, Nutt S, Sabatini A (1988) Housing the homeless mentally ill: a longitudinal study of a treatment approach. *Hosp. Community Psychiatry, 39*, 40.
60. Robertson MJ, Cousineau MR (1986) Health status and access to health services among the urban homeless. *Am. J. Public Health, 76*, 561.
61. Brickner PW, Scharer LK, Conanan B, Elvy A, Savarese M (1985) *Health Care of Homeless People.* Springer Publishing, New York.
62. Kelly JT, Goldfinger SM (1988) Hospitalization of the homeless: an analysis. In: Jahiel R (Ed) *Homelessness and Its Prevention.* Johns Hopkins University Press, Baltimore. In press.
63. Schatzberg AF and Cole, JO (1986) Manual of Clinical Psychopharmacology. *American Psychiatric Press*, Washington.
64. Diamond RJ (1984) Increasing Medication Compliance in Young Adult Chronic Psychiatric Patients. In: Pepper B, Ryglewicz H (Eds) *Advances in Treating the Young Adult Chronic Patient*, pp. 59 – 69. Jossey-Bass, San Francisco.

65. Talbott JA, Lamb HR (1984) Summary and Recommendations. In: Lamb HR (Ed) The Homeless Mentally Ill, pp. 1 – 10. *American Psychiatric Association*, Washington, DC.
66. O'Connor J (1986) Project to help homeless make transition to community. *Psychiatr. News, March 21*, 1986, 3.
67. Stark LR (1986) Strangers in a strange land: the chronically mentally ill homeless. *Int. J. Ment. Health, 14/4*, 95.
68. Levine, IS (1984) Service programs for the homeless mentally ill. In: Lamb HR (Ed) The Homeless Mentally Ill. *American Psychiatric Association*, Washington, DC.
69. Minkoff K (1987) Beyond deinstititionalization: a new ideology for the postinstitutional era. *Hosp. Community Psychiatry, 38*, 945.
70. Bachrach LL (1981) Continuity of care for chronic mental patients: a conceptual analysis. *Am. J. Psychiatry, 138*, 1449.
71. Bachrach LL (1985) Slogans and Euphemisms: The Functions of Semantics in Mental Health and Mental Retardation Care. *Hogg Foundation for Mental Health*, Austin, TX.
72. Bachrach LL (1984) Asylum and chronically ill psychiatric patients. *Am. J. Psychiatry, 141*, 975.

CHAPTER 18

Support and advocacy groups for the mentally ill

PHYLLIS VINE AND C. CHRISTIAN BEELS

HISTORY

Self-help movements and associations for mutual assistance and benevolence began with people belonging to the same religion, occupation or profession. Ranging from the Huguenots in Catholic France to those who failed to qualify for relief under the Poor Laws of Elizabethan England, people have traditionally bonded together to provide for essential social services and needs that were otherwise unavailable. Later, mutual aid societies were founded to respond to the disruptions caused by the industrial revolution, and still others were outgrowths of the guild system. By the 18th century, C.P. Thompson notes they appeared to be:

> 'locally organized and directed, self-governing and multifunctional. They combined the functions of providing loans for the needy and insurance for the sick with the assumption of burial tasks. They also served as vehicles for convivial club nights, picnics, outings, and feasts. Thus, the 'friendless' embodied kinship values in a quasi-primary group' (1).

By the 19th century in American society, labor unions as well as immigrant societies provided for the self-help and mutual aid which was missing from the larger culture. Anticipating the problems of widows or the costs of dying and funerals, and caring for the unique needs of ethnic minorities, these groups served functional and social purposes to insure that their own sub-group did not suffer.

Self-help societies organized around people who are consumers of health care and medical services constitute a new development in the theme of mutual assistance. With the exception of Alcoholics Anonymous, which began in 1935, and Recovery, Inc., founded in 1937, it was not until the 1940s that more groups began to function, and not until the 1950s that they begin to grow vigorously. By 1949 only 14 self-help groups (not including Alcoholics Anonymous) had formed. One decade later, in 1959, 421 could be counted. By 1972, over 2000 had been identified and, according to Gartner and Riessman, 'Over the past decade self-help groups have become an important way of helping people cope with various life crises'. At the beginning of the 80s it was estimated that more than 15 million people were involved in a self-help or mutual support group. By 1990, according to the Department of Health and Human Services 'the number of persons reached by mutual support or self-help groups should double' (2).

Handbook of Schizophrenia, Volume 4: Psychosocial Treatment of Schizophrenia.
M.I. Herz, S.J. Keith and J.P. Docherty, editors.

Groups which were founded by families or significant others are also relative newcomers. Toughlove, Families Anonymous and the National Alliance for the Mentally Ill are all products of the 1970s. According to Thomas Powell, part of their growth can be explained by a

> 'more conservative social climate of the eighties [which] has buttressed the growth of significant-other self-help organizations and more conservative views about the possibility of people changing have made it easier for caregiving families to come out' (3).

At least two things contributed to the rise of the family and patient self-help movements for the mentally ill. One was the gap between the initial optimism and the resulting frustration in the treatments for these diseases and the second stemmed from the failure of outpatient community services to meet the needs of the long-term patient.

A CLASSIFICATION OF SELF-HELP GROUPS IN THE MENTALLY ILL POPULATION

In the mental health field, consumer organizations fall into three quite different types, each with its own membership, purpose and philosophy. As a consumer of mental health services, the experience with treatment depends on whether one is: (1) an involuntary patient who has had a bad experience with psychiatric services and needs a group which helps to make a response to that experience; (2) a patient who has, through membership in the self-help group, had a good experience with that role and with the patient label; or (3) a family member whose relative had not been helped sufficiently by the delivery system, whether public or private.

Patient organizations are independent organizations founded by patients themselves. They are mainly made up of people who take a critical attitude towards standard psychiatric treatment, based on their negative personal experience. Many of them find medication and confinement of any kind objectionable, and some see both as the main purpose of organized psychiatry, which they therefore regard as an oppressive power elite. Almost all of them would say that involuntary treatment is without any merit even in the presence of self-injury or suicide. These organizations range from the Network Against Psychiatric Assault and others with similar titles to the National Alliance of Mental Patients (NAMP), whose principal goal is to advocate and work for the patient's right to exercise choice in the selection of treatment, including the possible choice of no treatment at all. Members frequently attend professional meetings either to picket or present. The NAMP is the largest and probably best organized of these.

Self-help treatment organizations are generally similar to the original prototype, Alcoholics Anonymous. Of interest in the treatment of schizophrenia are a handful of organizations which, like AA, had an inspirational founder, a specific treatment method, and which exist to promote and spread that method. The oldest, and probably largest, is Recovery, Inc. Self-help groups differ from patient organizations in that they have no political agenda and, on the whole, have an accepting view of their social and moral situation as former mental patients, which they have been able to modify by using the treatment.

Relative organizations are the largest, the best organized and the most powerful of the three. They are made up mostly of parents of patients with schizophrenia who have responded to the failure and insufficiency of treatment programs, especially outpatient programs, for patients with serious chronic illness. Very political, they are seeking to improve services within organized psychiatry by lobbying and education. While they are eclectic in their ideologies, they tend to be pro- rather than anti-psychiatry.

PATIENT ORGANIZATIONS

As we said above, there are a number of patient organizations, but we will describe the largest and best organized of these, the National Alliance of Mental Patients.

National Alliance of Mental Patients

This national organization has a thousand dues-paying members and twice as many on its mailing list (personal communication). It has strong organizations in urban centers such as Cambridge, Massachusetts, Berkely, California, and Baltimore, Maryland. A number of articulate leaders write books and monographs, and appear on talk shows to spread their message. Other strategies of this group are filing amicus briefs in legal proceedings, lobbying, and sitting on the boards of mental health centers.

One of the best ways to appreciate the character of the NAMP is to read the book which is generally at the head of its reading list, Judi Chamberlins's *On Our Own* (4). It includes a theoretical chapter which is a summary of anti-psychiatry writings; a very moving account of Chamberlin's badly mismanaged hospital treatment of her illness when she was a young woman, and of the beginning of her recovery in a patient-run program; a description of a patient-run residential alternative, Stone House, which had been started in Massachusetts at that time, and which was clearly a place where she would prefer to have been treated; and, finally, some very sobering chapters on the difficulties of organizing, funding, and holding together groups of former patients. Chamberlin describes the problems of finding money, space and time for people who are under great stress, poor, stigmatized and against the establishment.

In spite of these difficulties, there are some real accomplishments, including patient-run services in Cambridge, Cleveland and Ontario. The Cambridge service operates on a charter and partial funding from the Massachusetts Department of Mental Health. NAMP takes the position that mental illnesses are not diseases and therefore should not be treated with drugs and confinement. Obviously, the only way they can implement the leading goal of the organization is for the consumers themselves to design and control the alternatives to medical treatments. They also oppose diagnosis, saying that it only leads to stigma, discrimination and the collection of professional fees. Unfortunately, opposition to diagnosis will make it difficult to assess the really interesting question of how effective this type of non-medical management is and with what kinds of patients.

SELF-HELP TREATMENT ORGANIZATIONS

We are especially interested in two of these: Recovery, Inc., which is very old, large, and well established, and GROW, which is new and, we believe, an important innovation in the community treatment of severe mental illness.

Recovery, Inc.

A good introduction to this organization of 16,000 members with over a thousand regular weekly meeting groups can be found in the following paragraphs from one of their brochures.

> 'The late Dr. Abraham A. Low, psychiatrist, developed the Recovery techniques to help prevent relapses in former mental patients and chronicity in nervous patients. The Recovery method was initiated by Dr. Low in 1939, as a research project at the Pscychiatric Institute of the University of Illinois Medical School. In 1941, the organization became independent and was incorporated as a non-profit corporation under the laws of the State of Illinois with headquarters in Chicago. Although the Recovery method was developed by a professional, the organization now functions as a completely lay group. Its objectives are to preserve intact the Recovery method and to make it available to all who may have need of it' (5).

The method is basically educational and cognitive. Each session opens with the reading of a chapter from Low's book, *Mental Health through Will Training* (6), or a tape recording of one of his lectures. Under the guidance of the leader, group members describe applications of the method to their daily lives. Later, they break up into more conversational small groups, where people did not speak in the larger group can get encouragement and support. Tactics for managing symtoms include 'spotting' irrational fears or symptomatic experiences such as hallucinations or depressive thoughts, identifying them as neither dangerous nor life-threatening, and choosing a strategy for bearing the discomfort, such as thinking about or doing something constructive. 'Endorsing' one's self, either when alone or at the meeting, is a form of self-reinforcement for successful use of these strategies. Readers acquainted with the 'new' cognitive therapies and psychoeducational approaches to serious mental illnessess will recognize an anticipation of some of these techniques by over 40 years.

Recovery, Inc., charges annual dues and takes up a collection at each meeting. This provides the income for the support of its two main strategies, publicity and training. Publicity, in newspapers and professional publications, promotes referral, of which 37% comes from mental health professionals, particularly psychiatrists. The second component, training, promotes leadership for the local groups. There is a nation-wide training hierarchy, with local, state and national meetings. All group leaders are former members who decide to take the next step, and they qualify for greater responsibility through training conferences. The national leadership is elected from the members nationwide, and the headquarters is located in Chicago, in a building whose mortgage the organization has paid. Recovery, Inc., employs two members as permanent staff.

The organization's attitude towards professionals is respectful, patients' therapists and others interested are welcome to attend meetings, and members are encouraged to follow professional direction as to medication and other therapy. To avoid the suggestion of sponsorship, groups do not meet in hospitals and clinics and the organization does not take money from outside sources.

Unlike some patient organizations, Recovery, Inc. is hospitable to unobtrusive forms of classification and research, and there have been a few studies of their effectiveness with severe illness. Galanter (7) surveyed a random sample of leaders and members, comparing their present state with their state prior to joining. It is not possible to say how many members of Recovery, Inc., would have been diagnosed as schizophrenic, but Galanter finds that half of each group (leaders and members) had been hospitalized before joining and that 39% had taken major tranquilizers.

Although the retrospective questionnaire method necessarily leaves many questions unanswered, Galanter reports that all measures of anxiety were markedly improved after an average of 1.5 years' participation for members, or 13.9 years for group leaders, and that rates of working for pay went from 40% to 60%, and that there was a marked decrease in the use of both psychotherapy and medication.

GROW

GROW is an organization founded in Australia by a Jesuit priest named Cornelius Keogh, who had what he refers to as a mental breakdown when he was a younger man. In 1985 there were 500 GROW groups in different parts of the world, 400 of them in Australia, and 40 in central Illinois, where Father Keogh was invited in 1978 by O. Hobart Mowrer, a professor of psychology at the University of Illinois. This rapid expansion is one of the reasons for our interest in GROW, and also because it combines some features of other organizations which make it uniquely applicable to long-term seriously handicapped individuals; it is a truly independent self-help organization, but it also makes use of salaried field workers who relate its work to other resources inside and outside the official mental health system.

Like Recovery, Inc., the essential part of the GROW organization is the weekly meeting, and again like Recovery, Inc., there is a text for the meeting which in GROW is called the Blue Book. This contains the format for the meeting, which Rappaport et al. describe as follows:

> 'The meetings open and close with group recitations of prayers and pledges, and a period of objective discussion and learning of GROW literature is sandwiched

between two periods of group interaction... The GROW training manual outlines five ingredients of a good meeting:

1. An encounter of persons through personal testimonies, i.e., descriptions of a member's decline to maladjustment and growth to maturity.
2. Friendly help and support through current problem solving.
3. Adult education through reading and discussion of GROW literature.
4. Mutual activation through the recommendation of pratical tasks to be carried out in day-to-day living between meetings.
5. Personal development through reports on and assessment of members' progress.' (8).

More important than this objective description is the loving and caring atmosphere which pervades the meeting. Clearly, in their belief that 'you've got to love people back to health', the organization adds a secular form of Christian *caritas* to the Alcoholics Anonymous format and the cognitive and educational techniques described above.

Salaried field workers called program coordinators structure the meeting. They visit and monitor the weekly meetings, select and train their member-leaders, locate resources (publicity, funding, clinical and social services, volunteer help from members and others) and help to start new groups. They are an important link between the members of the organization and their resources, and their initiative is the essential ingredient which makes up for the difficulty which long-term mental patients, especially those with schizophrenia, have in staying organized.

There is a continuum of leadership in these organizations between the program coordinators and the volunteer member leadership. The program coordinators in GROW are different from Recovery, Inc., group leaders in that they need not be, in fact almost always are not, former members. They are recruited by the central organization and paid from donations, grants, and public mental health and social service contracts. The Illinois organization, still under the direction of Father Keogh, employed 11 such workers for its 40 groups in 1985.

Rappaport et al. (8) first became involved with GROW when the organization requested an evalution. Recognizing the difficulty of assessing the impact of self-help activities and meetings on individuals, they agreed to a collaborative approach which included observing meetings from different groups in Illinois, keeping logs to document the amount of time GROW spends with each person and whether the contact was useful, attending the bi-weekly staff meetings, and keeping track of how GROW mobilizes resources as the empirical basis for their work. The eventual findings will do much to help explain how such organizations provide ongoing support and an alternative to hospitalization. What is important to note here is that GROW regards professional evaluation as an important tactic for improvement and promotion of growth.

Self help groups and diagnosis

We know of only two self-help organizations specifically organized for people suffering from schizophrenia: Schizophrenia Anonymous and The Schizophrenia Fellowship. Note that they have been organized *for* rather than *by* schizophrenic patients. We have no example of what an organization made up primarily of schizophrenic patients would look like.

Schizophrenia Anonymous was a short-lived effort in New York City in the late 1960s which attempted to apply AA principles to schizophrenia and was also heavily influenced by orthomolecular megavitamin philosophy. The other organization, The Schizophrenia Fellowship, started in Great Britain has spread to other commonwealth nations. It grew out of a partnership between British National Health and consumer organizations. It maintains a fairly direct connection with the psychiatric profession and the National Health, to which it is clearly an adjunct. Acitivities of the Schizophrenia Fellowship include issuing publications describing patients' life experenciences with illness and treatment, and sponsoring meetings, but it has no treatment method and no political agenda.

A reading of the extant autobiographical accounts from the leaders of patient organizations will often suggest to the reader interested in diagnosis that they suffered from misdiagnosed or mistreated affective disorders. Indeed, there may be some awareness of this among the groups' leadership, since although they do not believe in diagnosis there is an item in one of their questionnaires which asks, 'Have you ever been misdiagnosed?' It certainly agrees with clinical experience with patient self-government that leadership is provided by non-schizophrenic patients, while many patients with schizophrenic diagnoses benefit from membership.

On the other hand, there is a whole group of affective patients who believe they have received correct diagnoses, and have made that a positive basis for their self-help organization. The National Association for Depressive and Manic Depressive Disorders had been loosely organized since 1978, and formed a national organization in 1986. With headquarters in Chicago, it reaches about 25,000 people in almost 90 chapters throughout the United States and Canada (personal communication). They have a vigorous political agenda and have been lobbying for better treatment facilities and programs. This organization, unlike the National Alliance of Mental Patients, believes in diagnosis and medication. Like other groups they are angry about the way they have been treated, but they have decided to remain within and reform psychiatry rather than go outside it.

RELATIVE ORGANIZATIONS

Deinstitutionalization

The growth of relative organizations cannot be isolated from deinstitutionalization. Due to the transfer of thousands of patients from hospitals to the community after the 1960s, parents, siblings, children, and in some instances, spouses, were asked to play a role over the long term and accept responsibilities which were new to them. After the 1963 Mental Health Act, a new generation of seriously mentally ill was being treated almost exclusively as outpatients. This was accentuated during the 1970s when new requirements mandating treatment or discharge were ordered by the courts and legislatures.

The ideology of deinstitutionalization promised that seriously and chronically ill patients would receive medicine and follow-up care in the newly created Community Mental Health Centers. For many or even most, these services did not arrive. Funding shortages, the transfer of disability benefits from the federal government to the states, and the lack of coherent programs to treat the mentally ill in the community, all complicated the process of deinstitutionalization by slowing the actual delivery of programs to those who were most in need.

Tensions between families and professionals

The emergence of the family and consumer movement in the 1970s was coincidental with and contributed to heightened tensions between mental health professionals and families of the mentally ill. Since the 19th century, there had been writers in psychiatry who viewed the families as toxic and pathogenic factors in the etiology of mental illness. Some of these, in the 1950s and 60s, took the form of overtly perjorative explanations of the onset of illness such as the 'schizophrenogenic' mother or family, or the 'double-bind' hypothesis of schizophrenia which located the etiology in family communications.

The families, for their part, were no more charitable toward the psychiatric profession. Frustrated by the numerous and varied modalities for therapy, critical of the numbers of foreign medical graduates who staffed the state hospitals leading to misunderstandings arising from the subtlety of language, and hurt by the disdain with which they were regarded, the families were harsh critics of the profession.

Stigma and isolation

In addition to the lack of services, families also felt the powerful stigma which surrounds mental illness. As late as 1978 the *Task Panel Reports Submitted to the President's Commission on Mental Health* identified stigma as the 'primary barrier in every phase of the provision of mental health services in this country (9). Recognizing the impact of this impediment, efforts to combat stigma have been an ongoing part of the educational agenda of self-help and advocacy groups on behalf of the mentally ill, and will be discussed below. Some of the early leaders realized that the first step in combating stigma is to come out of the closet and take a positive approach to their problem.

Part of the success of self-help movements stems from the ways in which they help members transcend an isolation imposed by the illness. Gartner and Riessman note:

> 'In self-help the participant is not an isolated individual, but part of a group that provides support, reinforcement, a safe haven, feedback, sanctions, and norms . . . Many of the groups also provide an ideology – a perspective on one's problems, others' attitudes, and the ways one may respond.' (10).

Thus, in the 1970s, whether in or out of the closet, families formed groups to redefine deviance and use it not to exclude, but as a badge of admission. According to Steinman and Traunstein (10), this is how the families of the mentally retarded, as well as alcoholics, began to form associations. They designed 'mechanisms for the 'stigmatized' to serve one another as an alternative to being labeled or neglected by professionals and bureaucracies' (11). At first, they only talked and shared their burdens. In the words of one parent, 'the first months of those early meetings, all we could do was discuss our problems. And, cry a little bit.' (12).

Growth of the movement

The families of the mentally ill appear to be relative latecomers to the self-help movement compared to other groups (such as parents of the mentally retarded, the visually disabled, or families with cancer). Relatives and friends of the mentally ill have, however, grown quickly and strongly since 1979, when about 80 organizations sent 300 delegates to Madison, Wisconsin to form the National Alliance for the Mentally Ill (13, 14). The grassroots organizations, which numbered more than 825 in 1987, are the basis for the family consumer movement which makes up the National Alliance for the Mentally ill in all 50 states.

The National Alliance for the Mentally ill has not required members to adhere to scientific or political positions which could polarize their efforts or the movement. While a fervent commitment to biological research prevails (and is one of the few isues on which there is general agreement) there are also a few enthusiasts for orthomolecular cures, and while the organization has tried to remain independent of professional domination, some professionals are consulted, invited to meetings and called upon as resources and technical advisers.

In this movement, it was mostly parents who started self-help groups, although other relatives have become visible and active as well, primarily in middle-class suburbs. A recent article reviewing the demographic patterns among NAMI families estimates that 70% have patient relatives who are male and single, with median age 33. Slightly more than one-third (38%) of the patients live at home at any given point in time. Among family members specifying relationship to the patient, 85% were parents who were most probably in their 50s or 60s. This differs somewhat from earlier studies which indicated a larger proportion of slightly older, female patients (15,16).

It is probably no accident that the initial groups formed in the middle-class suburbs and not in the urban centers or the distant rural communities. In the suburbs, there were people with education and resources who had become aware of the promise of deinstutionalization and were intolerant of failure to deliver announced and promised services. They had not been part of the inner-city, university-sponsored training centers or model programs, and they had been frustrated in their efforts to identify new resources. They were different in important ways, from the economically disenfranchised inner-city resident who had greater experience with public systems, however much those systems failed to meet their needs. They were also unlike their rural cousins whose informal networks of caretaking supplied help and assistance as part of the recurring demands of community. Thus, in places like Seattle, Washington; Bethesda, Maryland, Evanston, Illinois, and Madison, Wisconsin, middle- and working-class households, professionals, white- and blue-collar workers, as well as mothers who had never held a job, began to share their frustrations and pains and draw strength from one another.

HOW THE NATIONAL ALLIANCE FOR THE MENTALLY ILL WORKS

The local level

The local affiliates, which were started at the grassroots, respond most immediately to the needs for mutual support, local networking, identifying local resources and supplying information to members. Newsletters and meetings are common vehicles for disseminating information, and in some of the larger cities more than one group exists or more than one meeting is scheduled per month to meet the members' needs. The regularly scheduled meetings frequently invite outside expert speakers to address scientific, policy or legislative issues. Other meeting times are set aside for members with more personal and immediate needs to talk about their own situation. Spearheading local advocacy, most organizations have a newsletter, with information relevant to commitment, hospitalization, insurance, Social Security, vocational rehabilitation, new medication, or changes in state and federal law. If local broadcast personalities make stigmatizing remarks, or if a newly released movie denigrates the mentally ill, newsletters note this and list the names and addresses to whom complaints should be mailed.

Sometimes the local groups are structured geographically – all those who live near a city, for example. In other instances they are formed by families whose relatives are in the same hospital. Thus, it is likely that where a state or county hospital exists, a family group does, too.

The state level

Since most mental health services for this population are organized and funded by states, the state organizations, which generally provide an umbrella for the local NAMI affiliates, have become strategic parts of the organization. They are also the most recent structural component. While some of them were formed as early as 1980 or 1981, most have evolved in the past five years and have grown rapidly since. AMI of Massachusetts, for example, began with three local affiliates in 1982, and by 1987 it had 42. In Pennsylvania a similar story can be told. From 15 local affiliates in 1983, 36 existed by 1987 (personal communication). These groups play a significant role in setting policy and coordinating activities at the state and local level.

Such growth reflects deliberate efforts to expand the organizations at the state and grassroots levels as families recognize that a new power has come from their numbers. A survey we undertook in the summer of 1987 to assess the goals and accomplishments of the 42 formally constituted state organizations, contained an open-ended question asking 'please discuss your state AMI's most important goals for the next 3 years'. Of the 26 responses, 22 identified increasing the membership. Their abilities to affect policy and legislation, the impact they have on eradicating the stigma, as well as fund-raising activities and media coverage are perceived to be related to increasing the size of the membership and transforming a self-help group into advocacy.

As a result there are changes in state-wide legislative efforts throughout the nation. Indiana, for example, is among a handful of states which have successfully forced a revision of confidentiality criteria. After hearing about changes in confidentially laws in other states, members of the Indiana alliance returned home with inspiration and a model from one of the annual conventions of the National Alliance for the Mentally Ill. According to Evelyn Taylor, President of the Indiana AMI, the change in confidentiality criteria was important to families who were acting as caregivers in so many instances.

> 'We wanted this change for a couple of reasons. One was because families are the primary caregivers in so many instances and they were left without the tools to do the job because they didn't know what was wrong, what was going to be done. They were considered as part of the 'treated' instead of as part of the treatment team . . . Also, we wanted to relieve the medical profession of being afraid of lawsuits and things of that nature. We felt that many of the doctors, and the other mental health professionals who were dealing with this population of people, would like to share this information but because of the laws they couldn't. They were hampered because they could not share' (personal communication).

The Indiana law (Public Law 188-1985), was enacted on 1 September 1985 and itemized those people who could receive information after a written request. They include the spouse, parent (if the patient does not have a spouse), adult child (if neither a spouse nor a parent exists), or a sibling in the absence of all of the above. Information which can be released includes summary of the patient's or client's diagnosis, types of medication that have been prescribed, and a summary of the prognosis. Although allowing the release of information without the patient's prior consent could be a potential source of tension between the family and patient advocacy groups, there was no opposition to the bill, and it passed the legislature without public challenge and with only one dissenting vote (96-1 in the House and 46-0 in the Senate) (17).

Political activities and lobbying consume long hours of time and energy. As Peggy Straw, President of AMI New Hampshire, noted:

> 'We have testified on bills, served on Community Mental Health Center Boards, Department of Mental Health task forces and advisory councils to Department of Mental Health and Vocational rehabilitation. We served on the 1990 state plan task force, we have coalesced with the New Hampshire Association of Mental Hospitals and the American Psychiatric Association. We have appeared on television, on the radio, and in news articles.'

In 1986 the Texas Alliance for the Mentally Ill monitored 39 bills through the legislative session and, after testimony and a letter-writing campaign, saw $40 million added to funding Community Services. In Tennessee, the state-wide AMI (which was founded in October 1985) was included in planning and implementing a federal grant for the mentally ill and their families. Elsewhere, sponsoring educational conferences for the members, legislative lobbying days and annual conventions, as well as jointly sponsoring conferences with other organizations, have been part of the activities occupying the attention of the state groups.

State AMIs have advocated the creation of new services and the increased funding of old ones by active lobbying. This has, in turn, led to the creation of new services such as mobile crisis units or expanded case management services. According to Powell, because members are mobilized to seek new services, they simultaneously stimulate their creation (3). Another evidence of success at the state level is the number of professional organizations which have been seeking collaboration with the various AMIs. 'They want to be visible with us,' noted the president of the Connecticut Alliance fo the Mentally Ill, a comment echoed by many. Equally important, several of the states identified, through the survey, the emergence of a good 'working relationship' with State Offices of Mental Health.

State AMIs have also spearheaded efforts to enumerate and identify membership needs and utilization patterns through large-scale surveys. To make available these kinds of information to decision makers, a consumer survey of mental health services in Minnesota was conducted in 1984 and prepared by the Mental Health Advocates Coalition of Minnesota in 1985. Findings recorded that fewer than half of the respondents (48%) felt they had 'adequate access to mental health services' while almost as many (42%) felt they did not have access. Outpatient care and housing or residential treatment opportunities, as well as social workers who met their needs, were identified as particularly unavailable. While disparities existed between counties, they existed within them, too, creating 'a multi-class system of mental health services in Minnesota' (18).

Such surveys are becoming increasingly important to various state-wide family advocacy movements, as they represent an attempt to document areas of unmet for policy makers, legislators and politicians. Groups in New York, Tennessee, Massachusetts and California have shown the value of documenting family and patient needs as part of the ability to plan for appropriate services. In California, for example, a survey was conducted in 1985 among parents to assess the housing needs of their mentally ill children. The survey indicated that parents felt there was a lack of suitable housing, partly due to the burden introduced when adult children return and remain at home, and partly due to the demographic realities of aging parents who fear for the welfare of their children when they are no longer able to care for them (19).

NATIONAL ALLIANCE FOR THE MENTALLY ILL (NAMI)

At the national level, NAMI serves as an umbrella to the local affiliates while it outlines an agenda for influencing federal spending, new legislation and directing governmental policy. It also strives to educate professionals and the society to the needs of the mentally ill.

Officers of NAMI are family members whose affiliation began at the grassroots, either state or local. A paid staff, headed by an Executive Secretary, has replaced the strictly volunteer personnel which started NAMI. The difficulty of volunteer workers, most of them with mentally ill relatives, to continue to staff the increasingly successful organization necessitated the shift to paid professionals. This has been seen at the state level as well. Despite the many meetings and much of the organization which still occurs in private homes and around dining-room tables, the need to employ professionals for daily management was mentioned frequently by those presidents of state AMIs who answered the authors' survey.

Among the issues of importance to NAMI are: those which concern allocations of federal resources for research and treating mental illness; definitions of disabilities use by entitlement programs such as Supplemental Security Income or Community Support Services; criteria for receiving federal assistance in housing, health or medical benefits; access to treatment for mental illness and increasing services to meet needs; budgetary allocations for research within the National Institute of Mental Health; fiscal definitions of 'catastrophic' in hearings about catastrophic health insurance; and the mounting of various campaigns to eradicate stigma.

Some of the legislative concerns are defined by the political winds to which NAMI must respond. In recent years this has meant that budget cuts by the Reagan Administration have required intensive lobbying to restore monies to needed programs. Between 1972 and 1983, Congress, for example, 'failed to keep pace with inflation with the NIMH research budgets'. Thus, the \$158.3 million budgeted for NIMH in 1983 had the spending power of \$70.3 million in 1972 dollars. By 1986 the actual dollars climbed to \$214 million, but the Gramm-Rudman Anti-Deficit Act threatens annual reductions until 1991. One way which the National Alliance has used to measure the funds available is to compare them to defense dollars: 'One B-1 bomber costs as much as the entire NIMH research budget for 1986,' noted a newsletter (20).

NAMI and the professionals: mutual education

One of the most interesting and complex parts of this story is the NAMI effort to educate the professionals who control many aspects of the care of their relatives. In the beginning, with the publication of books such as Claire Claiborne Park and Leon N. Shapiros *You are Not Alone* (21) and Phyllis Vine's *Families in Pain* (12) relatives of patients would tackle the particular professionals they had to deal with one at a time. Armed with the factual information they got from reading, and encouraged by chapters in these books such as 'How to talk to psychiatrists', they would try to persuade their relatives' doctors and social workers to pay attention to their needs. This approach had individual instances of success, but more often it failed in the presence of professional defensiveness, mystification and bureaucracy, which kept the parents out of a mutually educational dialogue. Professionals would invoke 'confidentiality' when they did not want to face the difficult task of advising family members how to cope with the patient.

Professional insensitivity was often fortified by the 'family therapy-family dynamics' tradition, which since the early 1960s had portrayed family communication patterns as part of the etiology of schizophrenia. The implication was that if the family had helped to cause the illness, the correct professional approach was either to keep them away or somehow to fix them with family therapy so that they would not be so toxic to the patient.

While textbooks and diagnostic categories continued to cite family culpability, other mental health professionals were beginning to rethink this association. They argued that the professional blame on the family interfered with successful treatment, produced iatrogenic effects, and generally failed to serve the patient. There were occasional articles questioning family role in causing the illness and suggesting an underlying biochemical basis for mental illness, but the distance between the new research and clinical practice was still great.

Also during the 1970s, another group of professionals was trying to change the approach to families of the schizophrenic patient by devising new programs of treatment. These new treatments still came under the heading of 'family therapy', something the leaders of NAMI felt they had had quite enough of. But this new family therapy was trying to do be something different. As described in detail in other chapters of this volume, the innovations of Anderson and Hogarty, Falloon and Liberman, Goldstein, Leff, and McFarlane, were all being developed and publicized. They had in common a respectful, joining approach to families, a method of treatment which did not regard them as causes of the disorder, or necessarily noxious to the patient, but on the contrary, as the most important part of the outpatient treatment team. It was an explicit part of these therapies that families had strengths which could make the crucial difference in a patient's survival, and that the way to help bring out these strengths was by education, support and positive behavioral strategies which families experienced as helpful and respectful. Most of these innovators were brought together at a 1980 conference at the College of Physicians and Surgeons, Columbia University, along with some of the strategic family therapists such as Cloe Madanes. The final keynote speaker at the conference was Agnes Hatfield, then president of NAMI. On this and other occasions like it around the country, the public-academic dialogue between the professionals and NAMI began.

An important ingredient in the exchange has been the development of a professional group within NAMI which addresses researchers and academics in the mental health professions on an equal footing. Hatfield is herself Professor of Education at the University of Maryland, and other members of the NAMI committees who have worked on the conferences and publications have been clinical and research psychologists, social workers and nurses. They have their own treatment and research agendas and have had a keen sense of the power relations in places like NIMH.

Research

Without giving an account of the whole research controversy, it is important to mention here that NAMI wants to educate professionals about the relevance of research. Starting with the position that the social science writings of the 1960s blamed family communication patterns for the pathogenesis of schizophrenia, NAMI has raised doubt about the value of all social-environmental research in this area. This applies, as well, to those family-environmental factors which affect the course rather than the origins of the illness. Hatfield (21) has objected to the concept of expressed emotion and its development in the literature of relapse, because she feels it blames the families for the problem. This represents a major difference between some family advocates and some family researchers and therapists. The professionals find that the expressed emotion line of research has inspired a way of working with families which they find more sympathetic and positive.

Partly in response to research of this kind, and partly because they believe that scarce research money should be spent on biological and genetic investigations, NAMI representatives have joined the biological scientists in national councils on research priorities to shift money away from social and towards biological research on schizophrenia.

Education

The educational goal has been furthered by two important publications. One is *Families of the Mentally Ill: Coping and Adaption* (22) edited by Agnes Hatifeld and Dr. Harriet Lefley, Chairperson of the NAMI Curriculum and Traning Committee and Associate Professor in the Department of Psychiatry, University of Miami. Explicitly aimed at professionals, the editors claim that if they are to be successful

> 'they must know mental illness from the perspective of the family . . . and walk in the shoes of the family for a while' (22, viii).

Therefore, they have attempted to provide a new conceptual framework for understanding families by detailing the components of stress and crisis, and outlining steps which move relatives closer to adapting. The goal is to replace current theories of families with those which stress coping mechanisms as vehicles for empowerment.

The other book (23) is the proceedings of a conference held in February, 1986, and co-sponsored by NAMI and NIMH. Members of the NAMI Curriculum and Training Committee presented chapters setting out their views of the history and nature of the family's experience with mental health treatment, ethical and legal considerations of the relations between professionals and families, research directions for a new conceptualization of families, a curriculum guide for professional training, and experiences in collaborative teaching. Each of the eight papers was paired with a response and commentary by professionals outside NAMI. This publication will represent the beginning of a discussion between providers and consumers about how future providers should be taught to deal with future consumers. It makes the point that the two groups need to speak the same language. Once that common ground had been established, it is the providers' responsibility to understand and empathize with the experience of the consumers of services. Only when they are trained to do that will they be effective.

NAMI's impact

If publications like these, and training programs based on them, become a part of the professional curriculum, NAMI will have gained one of its most important objectives. In the meantime, there are a number of other accomplishments through which NAMI's impact may be seen. Organized discussion of policy among groups such as the American Psychiatric Association, Departments of Psychiatry, or State

Offices of Mental Health rarely occur without reference to NAMI (and their state organs). These professional groups have made special efforts to meet with NAMI groups, to understand their goals and to establish liasons. In many localities, for example, the local district branch of the APA has formed an ad-hoc committee to work with members of state and city AMI members. Other activities, such as the conferences jointly sponsored by AMI groups in Texas and the School of Social Work at the University of Texas, or the one on the Homeless Mentally Ill in conjunction with the New Mexico State Psychiatric Association, illustrate the pattern that is being repeated throughout the nation. The creation of the National Association for Research on Schizophrenia and Depression, a direct outgrowth of a spirit of cooperation between NAMI and other mental health organizations, is beginning to inform research agendas for foundations and academicians. The last two plenary sessions at meetings of the American Family Therapy Association were devoted to relations with NAMI and families of the mentally ill.

The efforts to work with NAMI occurs at all levels of government. In Connecticut, CAMI members actively particpate on all 22 Mental Health Catchment Area Councils and all five regional mental health boards, and two members sit on the State Board of Mental Health. In North Carolina the legislature's Joint Appropriations Committee on Human Resources invited an AMI member to speak at its prelegislative meeting. At the national level, NAMI has been engaged in a constant dialogue with the leadership of NIMH and was an active member of the Ad Hoc Advisory Board in the preparation of a National Plan of Research on Schizophrenia (24).

THE FAMILY BURDEN

The social and personal costs associated with caregiving are among the pressing concerns of the parents as well as of other spokespersons for the family movement (15). While the burden of caring for a mentally ill relative is thought to be high, surprisingly little research has studied this important area. The recent efforts to discuss this burden theoretically may offer insights while we wait for empirical findings and case studies.

Social stress

The literature on social, family or individual 'stressors' has shown that we can describe what is upsetting about the most stressful life events. Several factors which contribute to high stress could well describe the family burden on a family with a mentally ill relative who may or may not live at home: the inability to control an outcome through one's personal behavior, an isolation imposed by stigma, changes which are unpredictable, and outcomes which are undesirable (25). Concretely, this may include negotiations with the local mental health system or health professionals; interruptions in household or occupational activities; undesirable encounters with agencies (eg., police); unanticipated financial costs; and a host of emotions including guilt, shame, anger and frustration, resentment or embarassment. A 1982 study of relatives of 125 deinstitutionalized patients from three state hospitals near Cleveland, Ohio, reported a 'universality of emotional burden across families of different composition, different social class and race'. Seventy-two percent expressed feeling of 'overload' in their caregiving roles, and 42% expressed those of being trapped (26). Elsewhere there are indications that the stress increases over time and that each year it is greater than in previous years. Given the increasing numbers of mentally ill people for whom treatment is life-long rather than of short or predictable duration, being a caretaking family may, by definition, mean being a family at risk for stress and its sequelae (25).

Among the mitigating factors which have been reported to cushion the stress of family burden are social networks through which relatives interpret their circumstance and derive support for it. According to Potasznik and Nelson,

> 'Parents who report a high degree of satisfaction with the support they receive from their networks will perceive the patient as less of a burden than parents who report lower degrees of support satisfaction.' (27, p. 592).

It is in this way that the self-help and advocacy groups can be identified concretely as one of the mechanisms contributing to the reduction of stress. 'Finding people who truly understand their situation was associated with feelings of relief and a reduced sense of isolation', they noted (27).

To the extent that mental illness burdens a family and disables a patient, how has the the movement for self-help and advocacy affected the participants? According to one advocate, Peggy Straw, President of the New Hampshire Alliance and one of the founding members of NAMI, advocacy itself is part of the coping process (personal communication). It may be due to the sense of empowerment as well as reducing feelings of victimization or it may result from redirecting energy into the goal of advocating for something of lasting importance. For whatever reason, fighting for services and laws has been an especially attractive option for thousands of relatives who have swelled the membership of the National Alliance for the Mentally Ill in such a short time.

CONCLUSION

As they become stronger and recognized as spokespersons on behalf of the mentally ill, differences between patient self-help and family advocacy groups are likely to emerge. Among the questions over which they might disagree are how should monies be spent and policies enacted; how resources are allocated – whether money is directed to the local self-help groups or pumped into official public services; what role professionals should play, and under what auspices; and, what research will receive endorsement and who should be doing it?

The movements themselves might struggle over how to remain independent from the professionals and the bureaucrats at the same time as some of them they are being courted by policy makers. Another area where the groups are likely to encounter difficulty drawing a clear and easy line is over that of providing services. It is apparent that they may hold different opinions about this, depending on their goals. For patient groups like GROW, which is committed to non-professional help and has a major investment in developing its patient-membership for positions of leadership, direct funding may be a particularly attractive alternative to increased financing of services at the state level (8).

Direct funding of this nature presents less of a problem for patient groups than for family groups, which have tried to avoid becoming service providers even when they have done so reluctantly. They argue that the social contract requires that the needs of the seriously and persistently mentally ill, just like those of other people afflicted with disabling conditions, be met with qualified professionals and publicly supported services. To funnel monies to these organizations rather than supply services to the mentally ill assigns to families a caretaking responsibility which exists nowhere else in the health care system.

It is still somewhat early to determine whether the dialogue between the academic leadership of the profession and the political leadership of the self-help and consumer movements has had any impact on helping patients live independently while managing symptoms. It is clear, however, that, the agendas they have presented, the power they have accumulated, and the respect they have earned have changed the professional scope of accountability and responsibility for the seriously and persistently mentally ill.

ACKNOWLEDGEMENTS

We would like to thank the various state leaders in the National Alliance for the Mentally Ill for responding to our survey. We are also grateful to others who answered our queries: The Manic and Depressive Support Group, Peggy Straw, Evelyn Taylor, Rae Unzicker and Beverly Young.

REFERENCES

1. Thompson EP (1963) *The Making of the English Working Class,* p. 421. Vintage, New York.
2. Gartner JG, Riessman F (1982) Self help and mental health. *Hosp. Community Psychiatry, 33,* 631.
3. Powell T (1987) *Self-Help Organizations and Professional Practice,* p. 217. National Association of Social Workers, Silver Spring, MD.
4. Chamberlin J (1979) *On Our Own.* McGraw Hill, New York.
5. Recovery, Inc. (1980) *Directory of Group Meeting Information.* Recovery Inc., Chicago.
6. Low AA (1974) *Mental Health through Will Training,* Willett, Boston.
7. Galanter M, (1988) Zealous self-help groups as an adjunct to treatment: a study of 'Recovery'. *Am. J. Psychiatry, 145,* 1248.
8. Rappaport J, et al. (1985) Collaborative research with a mutual help organization. *Soc. Policy, 15,* 12.
9. President's Commission on Mental Health (1978) *Task Panel Reports, Vol. 2,* p. 345. United States Government Printing Office, Washington, DC.
10. Gartner JG, Riessman F (1982) Self-help and mental health. *Hosp. Community Psychiatry, 33,* 631.

11. Steinman R, Traunstein D (1976) Redefining deviance: the self-help challenge to the human services. *J. Appl. Behav. Sci., 12,* 350.
12. Vine P (1982) *Families in Pain,* p. 222. Pantheon, New York.
13. Snowdon J (1980) Self-help groups and schizophrenia. *Aust. N.Z. J. Psychiatry, 14,* 265.
14. Hatfield A (1981) Families as advocates for the mentally ill: a growing movement. *Hosp. Community Psychiatry, 32,* 641.
15. Lefley H (1987) Aging parents as caregivers of mentally ill adult children: an emerging social problem. *Hosp. Community Psychiatry, 38,* 1063.
16. Potasznik H, Nelson G (1984) Stress and social support: the burden experienced by the family of mentally ill person. *Am. J. Community Psychol. 12,* 589.
17. Fort Wayne News-Sentinel, May 14, 1985.
18. Mental Health Advocates Coalition of Minnesota (1985) Consumer Survey of Mental Health Services in Minnesota.
19. Housing Committee, California Alliance for the Mentally Ill (1986) Patient housing options as viewed by parents of the mentally ill. *Hosp. Community Psychiatry, 37,* 1239.
20. NAMI News, February 1986, 7. NAMI, Arlington, VA.
21. Claiborne Park C, Shapiro LN (1976) *You Are Not Alone.* Little Brown, Boston.
22. Hatfield A (1987) Expressed emotion theory: why families object. *Hosp. Community Psychiatry,* 38.
23. Hatfield A, Leffley H (1987) *Families of the Mentally Ill: Coping and Adaptation.,* Guilford Press, New York.
24. Leffley H, Johnson D (Eds), (1990) *Families as Allies in the Treatment of the Mentally Ill: New Direction for Mental Health Professionals.* American Psychiatric Press, Washington, DC.
25. National Advisory Mental Health Council (1988) A National Plan for Schizophrenia Research Report of the US Department of Health and Human Services. *DHHS Publication No. (ADM)* 88 – 1571. DHHS, Washington, DC.
26. Vine, P (1985) Social Stress, Chronic Illness and the Family. M.P.H. Thesis, Columbia University School of Public Health.
27. Thompson EG, Doll W (1982) The burden of families coping with the mentally ill: an invisible crisis. *Fam. Rel., 31,* 386.
28. Potasznik H, Nelson G (1984) Stress and social support: the burden experienced by the family of a mentally ill person. *Am. J. Community Psychol., 12,* 589.

Conclusions

It is evident that a wide variety of psychosocial treatment interventions are effective for schizophrenic patients. However, since patients often display dysfunctions in a variety of spheres, it is necessary to view treatment from a systems framework. A well-designed treatment program should be multi-faceted, flexible and appropriate for every phase of the illness. What is needed is collaboration, cooperation, coordination and integration of treatment services both within the mental health service delivery system and between that system and other community agencies and programs such as social services, vocational services, housing and medical care. A basic principle for a large majority of schizophrenic patients is that some form of treatment and support must continue over the long-term course of the illness. Evidence has shown that once treatment and support are terminated, many patients regress, becoming less functional and more symptomatic. The aim of treatment should be to help prevent relapse, decrease symptomatology, increase coping skills and optimize functioning, as well as to reduce the burden on families and communities.

There is a need to develop more valid and reliable assessment instruments. Most clinical research outcome data has focused on psychopathology and social and vocational role functioning. Other important measures should be quality of life, patient and family satisfaction, family burden, and economic costs and benefits. Several of these areas of assessment need refinement of measuring instruments, especially role functioning in various spheres, such as quality of self-care, vocational, social, and the like.

A major problem is inadequate dissemination of new knowledge. Many mental health service personnel are not aware of the latest research findings in psychosocial treatment. Professional organizations and governmental health agencies such as the National Institute of Mental Health and state Departments of Mental Health should explore new and better modes of dissemination of new knowledge. But even awareness is not adequate: there is a necessity to develop training manuals and training programs to facilitate the learning of new psychosocial treatment methods by those who deliver mental health services.

Many clinical studies of schizophrenic patients have assumed the homogeneity of this population, yet there is a strong likelihood that schizophrenia consists of a group of disorders with different etiologies, courses and outcomes. Patients who are diagnosed as schizophrenic may be categorized by a variety of psychosocial and biological parameters. The latter may include Magnetic Resonance Imaging and biochemical data, for example. Outcome may be affected by gender, ethnic background and age and co-morbid psychiatric and substance abuse disorders. Personality characteristics such as coping skills, assets, motivation and a variety of other personality factors need to be taken into account. Other psychosocial methods of categorizing patients have been according to family characteristics, i.e., high and low Expressed Emotion, and social networks. It is known that social supports and social networks can be very important in influencing course and outcome. Future research studies should focus on the unique treatment and service needs of specifically defined subpopulations of schizophrenic patients and probably should include interaction of pharmacological and psychosocial treatments.

In conclusion, there appears to be a renewed interest and enthusiasm for expanding research efforts in psychosocial treatment. There needs to be, however, a major new initiative by funding agencies to increase research funding in this area. Psychosocial treatments can have an immediate and critical impact in improving patient care and well-being.

Subject index